Brazilian Species of *Hyla*

# Brazilian Species of *Hyla*

*Text by* B E R T H A   L U T Z

*Photographs by* G U A L T E R   A.   L U T Z

Foreword by W. Frank Blair

UNIVERSITY OF TEXAS PRESS, AUSTIN & LONDON

Library of Congress Cataloging in Publication Data

Lutz, Bertha, 1894–
  Brazilian species of Hyla.

  Includes bibliographical references.
  1. Hyla. 2. Frogs—Brazil. I. Lutz, Gualter
Adolpho, illus. II. Title.
QL668.E2L88      597'.8      70-39502
ISBN 0-292-70704-5

Composition and presswork by The R. L. Bryan Company,
                         Columbia, South Carolina
Binding by Universal Bookbindery, Inc., San Antonio, Texas

Publication of this book was assisted by a grant
from the National Science Foundation

*To the memory of*
ADOLPHO LUTZ
GUALTER A. LUTZ
JOAQUIM VENANCIO

# CONTENTS

# FOREWORD

This book is the outcome of an interesting family effort by three members of a remarkable Brazilian family. This effort had its beginnings with Dr. Adolpho Lutz, a legendary figure in Brazilian and South American medicine, public health, and natural history. Toward the end of a career so distinguished that the Brazilian nation in 1955 celebrated the first centennial of his birth, Lutz's interest in trematode parasites led him to an interest in the vast diversity of Neotropical frogs. He described numerous new anuran species and published monographs of the genera *Leptodactylus, Bufo,* and *Cyclorhamphus,* and of the subfamily Elosiinae. He died without being able to give similar attention to the huge family Hylidae, but the work was carried forward by his daughter, Dr. Bertha Lutz, and his son, Dr. Gualter A. Lutz.

Both son and daughter inherited their father's propensity for involvement in a diversity of activities. After receiving her degree from the Sorbonne, Bertha Lutz became secretary, then naturalist and zoologist, at the National Museum, which is a part of the Federal University of Rio de Janeiro. In this latter capacity, and through extensive field work and collecting, she became the authority on Brazilian frogs. At the same time, she was a leader in the woman suffrage movement, was elected to the Brazilian Congress, and was a Brazilian delegate to the 1945 San Francisco Conference that founded the United Nations. The late Gualter Lutz graduated as a doctor of medicine from the University of Brazil and had a long career as professor of forensic medicine at the National School of Medicine of the University of Brazil. Starting photography as a hobby, he became increasingly interested in photographing frogs in color.

This book represents a combination of the ecological and natural history information about Brazilian *Hyla* accumulated through the long and active career of Bertha Lutz and the results of Gualter Lutz's avocational career in photographing these same animals. As such, it provides an extremely valuable base on which ultimately to build a complete story of the evolutionary history and present diversity of a huge and fascinating group of Neotropical anurans. Hopefully it will also stir in the tropical American countries an increased appreciation of their vast heritage of beautiful and fascinating tropical animal species and will lead to increased efforts to assure the preservation of this heritage.

W. FRANK BLAIR

# PREFACE

This book should have been written by my father, Dr. Adolpho Lutz, who began our work on amphibians. By vocation Lutz was a naturalist, by profession a physician. The conjunction of his two main interests led him to become the earliest pioneer in medical zoology, parasitology, and tropical medicine in Brazil. After a long period of active work that revolutionized public health methods, Lutz devoted himself entirely to pure research. He opened up a number of new fields through a series of monographs that have become classics. To the Brazilian amphibians he came late in life, via their trematode parasites. Besides describing a good number of new frogs, he monographed the genera *Leptodactylus, Bufo,* and *Cyclorhamphus* and the Elosiinae. Unfortunately time was not granted him to monograph the Hylidae, nor was he able to carry out his great project of publishing a color atlas of the Amphibia Anura of Brazil, a modern version of the beautiful books of some of the older naturalists.

The continuation of the herpetological work thus devolved on me. In fact, it soon became a family enterprise, since the color photographs used in this book are the work of my late brother, Professor Gualter Adolpho Lutz. On retiring from the National School of Medicine of the Federal University in Rio de Janeiro, he devoted much of his leisure to photographing animals, especially amphibians. He gave careful attention to the problems of photographing these small, easily disturbed animals. He acquired, adapted, or built suitable equipment, and he carefully calculated means of magnification, distances, and angles of illumination. He worked steadily until satisfied or waited patiently for the frog to feel sufficiently reassured to pose for its portrait.

One other person must be mentioned: Joaquim Venancio, a modest worker at the Instituto Oswaldo Cruz. When Joaquim first came to our laboratory, Lutz was just beginning to turn his attention from helminthology to herpetology. Venancio remained with us for over thirty years, until shortly before his death. Though illiterate and for many years not interested in book learning, he acquired a scientific outlook and a fine knowledge of systematics; these he allied to a natural flair for animal ecology that, though highly individual, may have been partly due to his African origin. Were it not for the lack of educational opportunities in youth he might have become an independent research worker. He was a gentleman, a friend, and an excellent collaborator.

It is a profound and lasting sorrow to me that none of them should have lived to see the publication of this book which embodies so much of their work.

This publication is just one installment of the herpetological work planned by Lutz. I am anxious to go on to the publication of the other Hylid genera and to the projected atlas of Brazilian frogs. Toward it there are Lutz' notes and the series of watercolors that were painted for him, a large number of beautiful color photographs of frogs generously taken for me by Gualter A. Lutz, a modest amount of facts gathered by me during several decades of work in the field and in the laboratory, plus the frogs collected by J. Venancio, myself, and others and kept under observation. The difficulties cannot be minimized, but one may hope to overcome them in part at least. The frog fauna of Brazil is not only rich in species but diversified in its ways of living. It provides interesting examples of survival by adaptation and of adequate use of the environment.

# ACKNOWLEDGMENTS

I gratefully acknowledge the stimulus and support given my work by the Conselho Nacional de Pesquisas (National Research Council of Brazil), its former president, Professor A. Moreira Couceiro, and the scientific director, Dr. M. da Frota Moreira; the generous efforts of Dr. W. Frank Blair, professor of zoology at the University of Texas at Austin, to get this work published; the encouragement received from Miss Heloisa Alberto Torres and from Dr. J. Lacerda de Araujo Feio, directors of the Museu Nacional, Rio de Janeiro.

Thanks are due to a number of other persons and institutions. Some of the contacts go back to the time when A. Lutz began to work on frogs, or even before. Lutz met Boulenger in Europe and had pleasant relations with him. Later he received help with literature and exchange specimens from Lorenz Müller, Professor Mertens, and some other European herpetologists, and from Drs. Helen T. Gaige, Noble, and Barbour in America.

As the work progressed, a number of people interested in natural history made contributions to the Lutz Collection; among them were D. Bento Pickel, director of the Benedictine Agricultural Station at Tapera, Pernambuco; Dr. Rocha, founder and owner of the Museu Rocha in Fortaleza, Ceará; Dr. Nelson Davis of the Rockefeller Foundation, while stationed in Bahia; Commander Braz Dias de Aguiar, of the Brazilian Frontier Commission with Venezuela; Dr. Afranio do Amaral, director of the Instituto Butantan and Dr. A. Carini of the Laboratorio Paulista de Biologia; Drs. Octavio Magalhães, Marques Lisboa, Oswaldo de Mello, and Aroeira Neves, in Belo Horizonte; Professor Rudolph Gliesch in Porto Alegre; Drs. Lauro Travassos and Cezar Pinto, of the Instituto Oswaldo Cruz; young Oswaldo Lamartine, from Rio Grande do Norte also gave Lutz some frogs. Drs. Salvador Mazza in Argentina, Foerster in Uruguay, Wolff-huegel in Chile, G. Schouten in Paraguay, and Stahel and Geyskes in Surinam also sent him some specimens. Miranda Ribeiro, Melin, and Doris M. Cochran named frogs after him.

I have also received specimens and help with bibliography from the same and other scientists, and contributions to the Lutz Collection from many persons. They include the following members of the staff of the National Museum: Roger Arlé, who also painted some excellent watercolors for me; Johann Becker, Roppa, and other assistants working on the radioactive area of Poços de Caldas, Minas Gerais; Antenor Leitão de Carvalho, fellow herpetologist; the former directors, J. C. M. Carvalho and Newton D. dos Santos; the present director, Dr. J. L. de Araujo Feio and his son; my former assistants Gertrud Rita Kloss and Maria de Lourdes Mercier; Drs. Victor Stawiarski and Helmut Sick, the ornithologist; Mario Rosa, former preparator, and others, including the paleontologist Dr. C. de Paula Couto and Paulo Miranda Ribeiro. Fine specimens were received from Dr. Hoge of Butantan and his young son, Affonse Richard; also from other boys such as the young Curtises. Other naturalists also contributed valuable material, for instance the Swiss anthropologist F. Casper and the zoo collectors Oswald and Kaethe Schmidt; Dr. Fittkau, while working at the Amazonas Research Institute in Manaus, and Dr. Paul Ledoux while at the Agricultural Research Institute in Belem do Pará; Dr. Lobato Paraense, of Belo Horizonte, the Amazonian explorer Nunes Pereira and his colleague Nelson Cerqueira; Manfred Rauschert has sent fine frogs from Northern Pará and the Indian Village maintained by him near the Guianas with patronage from the army.

W. C. A. Bokermann has lent some types and

cotypes and sent specimens at first to me, later to the Museu Nacional. A number of botanists have sent me valuable frogs. Chief among them are the late Dr. Walter Egler, director of the Museu Goeldi in Belem do Pará; Dr. Geraldo Kuhlmann, late director of the Botanical Gardens in Rio; and the retired botanist A. C. Brade. The late Dr. F. C. Hoehne, director of the first Botanical Station founded in Brazil, at Alto da Serra in the coastal mountains of São Paulo, made Dr. Lutz and his assistants welcome there; Dr. F. Segadas Viana of the National Museum and his group, José Vidal and Dalibor Hansch, retired members of our staff, collected some specimens. Dr. Henrique P. Velloso, of the Instituto Oswaldo Cruz, and Mulford and Racine Foster obtained good frogs while collecting bromeliads; Professor Normelia Vasconcellos of Belem helped the author collect at Santa Isabel and offers to continue to do so.

Some medical men have also helped; Professor Riet Correa, of Rio Grande do Sul; Professor Mario Pinto de Morais, director of the School of Medicine in Manaus, and his wife, who very kindly housed me; Dr. N. Gofferjé of Paraná and Santa Catarina; Dr. Aristoteris Leão, now in Goiás, Dr. Aristoteles de Araujo e Silva, and others have given me specimens.

Personal friends have contributed in diverse ways. Mrs. Marian Cutler collected frogs while her husband hunted for wild cereals. The Meekers added the search for frogs to their other field work. Mrs. Margaret Bensusan, writer and journalist, sent a few specimens. Mrs. Vera Schilling, Miss Maria Koltzau, and Mrs. Amanda Finch entertained me while collecting; Mrs. Finch even lent her cook, Maria Amelia Teixeira, who was much interested and helped obtain *Liolaemus lutzae* and *Hyla humilis*. Praeses Schluenzen and the mayor of São Bento do Sul in Santa Catarina also dispensed hospitality and transportation. Helmut Hamacher collected for me at one time.

The administrator of the Agricultural Station at Agua Limpa, Sr. Helio Raposo, and the administrator at the substation of Pomba, Mr. Ezechias Herringer, first received me and helped me to collect and later sent more specimens. One of the most interesting hosts was General Osiris Denys, then a major, in charge of the military post at Benfica. He accorded me the privileges of an army captain, lent me two soldiers to help with the field work, and finally drove my car back through the worst flood seen in southern Minas Gerais for many years. General Americo Marinho Lutz offered facilities while director of the Northwestern Railway. Other members of the family provided hospitality on the Serra da Bocaina.

Deep thanks go out to Dr. Wanderbilt Duarte de Barros and his family for hospitality and every kind of help while he was administrator of the National Park of Itatiaia, and to Mr. Gil Sobral Pinto for similar help at the Organ Mountains National Park. I was also well received at Iguassu. Elio Gouvea and J. Coutinho gave much help at Itatiaia—especially the former, who was a very good field man in his youth. Some of the national parks still help on occasion.

I am much indebted to the National Service of Rural Endemics, especially to the former director-general, Dr. Mario Pinotti, Dr. Gildo Aguirre, and their collaborators in Bahia and to the men in charge of the work in the state of Santa Catarina in 1949–1950, and in Alagoas in 1962.

Recently facilities for collecting have been received from Dr. F. C. Iglesias, director of the Department of Natural Resources of the state of Guanabara, the Instituto de Pesquisas da Amazonia in Manaus, and Dr. Murça Pires, of the INPA in Belem.

The excellent Argentinian National Park Service has shown me much courtesy in Buenos Aires, Iguazu, and at Finca El Rey in the province of Salta.

Mention must be made of my younger colleagues. Many years ago when collecting we tried to make Dr. Lutz comfortable and then went after the specimens. At present some of the nice herpetologists of the younger generation are beginning to do the same for me. Dr. Luiz Dino Vizotto from São José do Rio Preto, and Dr. Eugenio Izecksohn of the Rural University of the state of Rio de Janeiro have given me much help. Miss Anna Carmen da Silva Fernandes is a very active and bright assistant. Some of the younger Texas men were also helpful, both at Austin and in Colombia. I would like to mention W. F. Martin, Brownell, J. Bogart, and Sheldon Guttman.

When I took over the care of my father's herpetological collection at the Instituto Oswaldo Cruz, I found that it had been badly neglected and harmed while Lutz's first successor occupied his laboratory. I am much indebted to the then director of the Institute, the late Dr. Henrique Aragão, and to his succesor, Dr. Francisco Laranja, for their interest and help in furnishing vials, chemicals, and assistants. Miss Heloisa Alberto Torres, director of the National Museum, also encouraged and fostered my self-imposed task in a number of ways. Very much later it became expedient to send the Lutz Vertebrate Collection to the National Museum. I then became indebted to Dr. Genard Nobrega, director of the Hospital for Tropical Diseases of the Institute, and Dr. Newton Dias dos Santos, then director of the National Museum, for their good offices; also to Dr. J. Teixeira de Freitas for the work done by him in the preparation of the transfer.

Other Brazilian and foreign institutions have also been of assistance. Dr. Paulo E. Vanzolini, director of the Department of Zoology of the state of São Paulo, and his predecessors have made it possible for me to examine and study many specimens belonging to the very excellent collection of that institution.

In 1952 I was granted a fellowship of the British Council for Cultural Relations Abroad for six weeks study at the British Museum (Natural History). This enabled me to examine many of the Guenther and Boulenger types of Brazilian species and to peruse the interesting notes pasted by Boulenger into his working copy of the second edition of the catalogue of batrachians at the British Museum. The museum ought to republish this classic, complete with the Boulenger notes. During my stay in London I received hospitality and much courtesy from Dr. and Mrs. Malcolm Smith, Mr. Battersby, and Miss Ethel Trewawas of the museum; Mr. Jack Lester, Lord Chaplin, and others at the zoo, also received me and made me a correspondent member of the Zoological Society of London.

I visited a number of important collections on the Continent. I saw the Goeldi and Baumann types in Bern with the latter, some of those of Tschudi at Neuchatel with Aellen, the Fuhrmann frogs in Geneva, and older types at Basel with Forcart. I also visited the zoo at Zurich with Hediger. In Sweden I saw the Andersson types at Stockholm, thanks to Professor Renndahl, and those of Melin at Goeteborg, thanks to Professor Nyebelin. In Munich I visited my father's friend Lorenz Müller and Hellmich, his assistant, and learned the sad fate of the Spix types of Hylids. I also saw types at the Senckenberg Museum in Frankfurt and Mertens' interesting private vivarium. The Steindachner types available were shown to me in Vienna by

Eiselt. The Dutch collections were seen with Mrs. Brongersma and Dr. P. van Bree; those in Brussels were shown by Frechkopp and Laurent. I saw the Reinhardt and Lütken types in Copenhagen. In Paris I was shown many of the Duméril and Bibron and some of the Daudin types by Guibé. I was not able to travel to Madrid to see those of Espada.

In Paris I also gained theoretically by talks with my former professor, Maurice Caulléry, and with young Lamotte, and at Münster with Professor Bernhard Rensch.

I arrived too early in the herpetological field for the wonderful opportunities to study in the United States now being offered to my younger colleagues. Nevertheless, I have had the privilege of repeated examination of the leading North American collections of Neotropical amphibians. At the American Museum of Natural History I was made welcome first by Noble and later by Bogert and Zweifel and their assistants; in Cambridge first by Loveridge and later by Miss Elizabeth Deichman and E. Williams. At the Philadelphia Academy of Science I was very kindly received by Drs. Rehn, Fowler, and others, benefiting greatly by the stimulating company of Emmet and Merle Dunn. In Washington, work was done during happy days spent with my old and valued friend Doris M. Cochran. Shorter visits to Chicago, Pittsburgh, California, and Colorado also led to pleasant contacts with Inger, Graham Netting, the Goins, and others.

I have seen Venezuelan, Colombian, and Peruvian collections of frogs. I have received duplicates from Gustavo Orcès in Ecuador and Hernando Macedo and Nelly Espinoza in Lima. I collected in Paraguay and must acknowledge material sent later by Phillips from Primavera in the northern part of that country.

In Uruguay I had the expert guidance of Professor Raul Vaz Ferreira in the field. Dr. Klappenbach also gave me some tree frogs. I have collected more extensively in Argentina, mostly with Dr. Avelino Barrio. I also examined the large collection in Tucumán and the small but excellent one put together by Cei in Mendoza, besides a collection from the Hylaea lent by the field museum awaiting naming by me and Cei. D. Sylvana Cei was the kindest of hostesses. Don Bernardo Houssay, the president of the Argentinian Council for Scientific and Technological Research, an old friend of my father, encouraged this work. Diverse forms of help and stimulus were also provided by Dr. Marcos Freiberg, president of the Latin American Association of Herpetologists and my colleagues, Celia Limeses de Ikonicoff, Marina Tio, and Martha Miranda in Buenos Aires, Martinez Aschenbach in Santa Fé, V. Roig and Dr. Raquel Cohen in Mendoza, A. Saez and Nadir Brum de Zorilla in Montevideo, and of late by Drs. Pedro Ruiz C., Julia Sanchez de Hernandes, Jorge Hernández Camacho in Bogotá. Dr. Alonso Gamero showed me much courtesy, and Drs. Haydee Solano de Chacin and James Roze showed me some interesting specimens in Caracas. Drs. Roze and Racenis took me on an excursion to the llanos. I express my appreciation to all of them.

I also extend thanks to all those who provided help with the manuscript: Dr. Charles Bogert kindly read much of it; Mrs. Adda Abendroth not only copied but also made suggestions on the final draft. Mr. Roger Arlé, Mrs. Gloria Sidwell, and the late Paul Sandig painted watercolors of great use in the earlier phase of the work, which would have made classic illustrations for the text before color photography permitted more life-like illustrations. I also thank those who did ancillary work, such as the typist Nelson Henrique dos Santos, the preparator Esmeraldino de Souza, the laboratory helpers Jorge and Tadeu, and the field workers A. Barcellos and his sister, Maria José, who look after the living animals when I am away and who have a very good understanding of the needs of living creatures —even frogs.

The research that went into this volume was carried out largely under a grant from the Conselho Nacional de Pesquisas (National Research Council). Grants from the Conselho de Pesquisas da Universidade Federal do Rio de Janeiro helped to finance some of the ancillary work. I am very grateful to the past and present authorities of the two councils and appreciate the help of the successive directors of the Museu Nacional.

# ABBREVIATIONS

ALC     Adolpho Lutz Collection, Museu Nacional, Rio de Janeiro

AMNH    American Museum of Natural History, New York City

DZSP    Departamento de Zoologia, São Paulo

FMNH    Field Museum of Natural History, Chicago

IBM     Instituto de Biología, Facultad de Ciencias Médicas, Cuyo University, Mendoza, Argentina

LIH     Laboratorio de Investigaciones Herpetológicas, University of Buenos Aires

MACN    Museo Argentino de Ciencias Naturales, Buenos Aires

MCZ     Museum of Comparative Zoology, Harvard University

MNR     Museu Nacional, Rio de Janeiro

MZUM    Museum of Zoology, University of Michigan, Ann Arbor

NMS     Natur-Museum Senckenberg, Frankfurt am Main

USNM    United States National Museum, Washington, D. C.

WCAB    Werner C. A. Bokermann, private collection, São Paulo

ZMB     Zoologisches Museum, Berlin

Brazilian Species of *Hyla*

# Introduction

*Hyla,* the type genus of the true tree frogs, or Hylidae, is very widespread, although a hiatus in its range occurs in the Indonesian, Malayan, Polynesian, Ethiopian, and Madagascan regions. However, there is a much larger number of species of *Hyla* in the Neotropical region than elsewhere, especially in Brazil and the cisandean-cisplatine area of South America. Most of the other genera of the family are also Neotropical. Under these circumstances it seems logical to ascribe a Neotropical origin to these genera, even if one does not postulate a Neotropical origin for *Hyla,* a hypothesis put before the Third South American Congress of Zoology in Santiago (1965) by Goin.

The main osteological character that differentiates the family from the other Arcifera Procela is the claw-shaped terminal phalanx allied to an intercalary cartilage between it and the penultimate phalanx. This is an important character, since, together with the well-developed disks of the digits, it subserves one of the main modes of locomotion of *Hyla,* climbing by adhesion and friction. The sacral diapophyses are dilated in the species really belonging to the type genus that have been examined. The pollex rudiment is long and sharp in large species. The males of some of them use it as a weapon. *Hyla alvarengai* seems almost pentadactylous. Odontoids on the vomers are lacking only in a few very minute forms. A number of species have green bones due to biliverdin, as discovered by Barrio (1962). In some of these species the inside of the mouth and the lower ventral aspect of the disks are glaucous green. In some other families green bones also occur. The pupil is horizontal, rarely very slightly rhomboid. A large median vocal sac is the rule, but paired lateral vocal sacs occur in a group of large species evolving toward another genus.

The life history conforms to what is considered typical for the whole order of Anura in the textbooks, though there are many exceptions to it in the tropical belt. The eggs are very small and very numerous, with a pigmented animal pole and a cream-colored vegetal one. Shortly before spawning, the masses of eggs greatly distend the abdomen of the female or even the whole trunk. With few exceptions they are laid on the water where the spawn of large species forms an extensive veil. *Hyla faber* builds a nest with clay walls within the pond in which to start its progeny. The embryos hatch at a very rudimentary stage. The larvae are aquatic; in the tropical belt they grow fast and metamorphose after a relatively short time. The adults are generally scansorial.

I estimate that there are 100–200 Neotropical species. About 120 forms, belonging to at least 80 species, some of them with geographic races, live in Brazil.

These species vary greatly in size and build, from minute forms less than 20 mm long, like *Hyla sanborni,* to others like *Hyla boans* that are six times larger. Some species are narrow and torpedo shaped, such as *Hyla squalirostris,* which is small, or the members of the group of *Hyla daudini,* which are large, streamlined, long-legged frogs. Some forms are robust, for instance *Hyla minuta* at one end of the scale and the altitudinal form of *Hyla circumdata* at the other end.

Morphological features show lesser differences, which is not surprising, since they have a limited gamut of variability. The patches of vomerine teeth, for example, are generally present, occasionally absent, and sometimes only palpable or barely visible. They may be implanted at different levels of the space between the choanae and occupy most or very little of this space or reach beyond it. They may be separate or contiguous, round, straight, curved, or angular; together they may form an arch or a chevron. This about exhausts their possibilities. The same applies to the tongue. It may be wide or narrow, circular, oval, elongate, or heart-shaped. It may be entire, slightly emarginate, or deeply notched; the extent of free hind border also varies. Moreover, the tongue, being a soft organ, can be influenced by processes of fixation, and is often not quite uniform in all the specimens from the same preserved sample. Some of the morphological features are group characters rather than specific ones. And yet until quite recently all descriptions of new species have been based on them. The characteristics of the living animal are much more significant, and natural systematics must take them into account. They are not only more reliable, but they also may furnish some evidence for the processes of speciation and be indicative of evolutionary trends.

One of the most significant characters of the living frog is its voice. The specific call of the male is recognized by the female of the same species and leads her to him. This fact has long been known and considered as established by those of us who are field naturalists. Recently it has been subjected to experimental proof by the Blairs, Bogert, Barrio, and others. Sexual selection by the appraising female is thus seen to be a functional isolation mechanism correcting the blind impulse of the male in the breeding season.

Some species of *Hyla* are easily disturbed while calling and stop until all sound and movement die away; others go on blithely singing even when approach is heralded by snapping twigs and the flashlight. They remain where they are, whereas others flee and resume calling farther away. Most of the species call only at the mating period, near the appropriate spawning site. A few call the whole year round. This is the case of *Hyla albofrenata,* a montane southeastern Brazilian species that hides in epiphytic bromeliads and has a beautiful voice. It calls from aloft, descending only as the nuptial period approaches. The weak voice of *Hyla catharinae trapicheiroi* is also heard for many months near the ground. Some voices are weak, as in this form and in most members of the *Hyla catharinae* group. Others are very loud; *Hyla hebes* sounds like a short-circuited automobile horn. Some call singly, others sing in chorus, which is started by one, goes on for a time, dies away, and begins again. *Hyla faber* drums that way. Where the wet season is clearly separated from the dry one, a great many species of *Hyla* and other frogs wander to the nearest pool at the onset of the rains. A deafening and often dissonant chorus ensues.

The flash colors and the pattern connected with them in some species are highly distinctive. They are usually not displayed when the frog is quiescent but come into play when it moves and sometimes also when it relaxes on the surface of the water while calling for a mate. The role of these colors as a sexual attraction is not as evident as that of the voice. The flash colors generally occupy the upper anterior and posterior parts of the thigh, the hind parts of the flanks concealed in repose, and other upper or inner limb surfaces, like the inside of the tibia, tarsus, and the dorsal aspect of the inner digits. These colors may be dull, as in *Hyla senicula,* but more often they are bright. They are also very diverse, ranging from yellow, orange, scarlet, deep red, and rose color, to blue, lavender, purple, and slate color.

The webs may also be aposematic and vivid, such as the orange webs of *Hyla albomarginata.* Sometimes the concealed pattern is distinctly mimetic. The flash color of *Hyla anceps,* for instance, is near flame-scarlet and the hindlimbs are crossed by wide black bands perpendicular to the long axis. This frog likes to press its upright body to a cattail, or bulrush, with each hindfoot grasping the stalk nearest to its side. In this stance it conveys the image of a small coral snake.

In the Neotropical region there are more green species of *Hyla* than elsewhere. They blend admirably with the foliage. Many other species have a brownish, grayish, or olivaceous cryptic dorsal surface. They may be either plain or ornamented with spots, stripes, marks, or blotches, and match the branches, boles, and trunks of trees. In some species the dorsal surface is smooth, in others rough or granular. Several present a complete, generally white, glandular outline that fits the contours of the reposing frog very accurately but is distributed along the edges of different parts, such as the edges of the mouth, the forearm, the tibia, tarsus, and outer digits, the area of the side of the body left uncovered in repose, and the anal region. A few have tubercles or a flap of skin at the knee (*H. langsdorffii, H. geographica*).

Often there is a pattern that is very repetitive in allied forms, among them in the *Hyla rubra–Hyla x-signata* complex. The pattern on the body sometimes extends to the dorsal aspect of the permanently visible areas of the limbs, thus becoming coincident and disruptive. An interesting feature of the pattern of many Neotropical species of *Hyla* is its quite variable intensity. I have a live *Hyla crepitans* from Venezuela that is generally pale, almost cream colored, but it sometimes develops a very marked mid-dorsal pattern, especially on dull days. When the frog grows light the pattern evanesces; the eyes remain a pale green.

The iris should be closely examined in every living species of frog. Sometimes a lighter or a deeper shade of the same color, a dull brown or a distinct coppery glint, permit separating closely allied forms in the field, for instance *Hyla cuspidata, Hyla aurata,* and even *H. rubra altera* mihi. The dorsal pattern of the diverse forms of *(Hyla) Phrynohyas venulosa* are very similar and very repetitive, so much so that those of one form reappear in others. The color and the pattern of the iris differ and furnish a key for separating them. The southeastern Brazilian green species can be separated immediately by a glance at their eyes.

I have taken over the use of the iris for taxonomic purposes from the pioneer use of the color and the pattern in the eyes of Tabanidae by A. Lutz and have found it extremely useful. In some species the nictitating membrane also helps. Cope created a separate genus for those like *Hyla boans* and *Hyla geographica*, which have golden arabesques on the transparent part of the lower lid. They are allied and belong to the same natural group.

The tympanum is less important, but in the cycle of *Hyla pulchella (raddiana)* or *Hyla rubra–Hyla x-signata* the color is constant throughout the group and contrasts with the surrounding color at the sides of the head. In *(Hyla) hebes* the pale brown middle part of the tympanum is surrounded by green.

The ventral aspect is generally light and mostly immaculate, though there are exceptions. The surface is apt to be granular, especially on the belly and midventral aspect of the thigh. The vocal sac of males of small species is often some shade of yellow, and in larger ones it may be either black or infuscate. Some species have very vivid colors on the ventral aspect of the thigh and sometimes on the abdomen, *Hyla bipunctata* among them. The most beautiful ventral coloring is that of *Hyla marmorata,* whose forearms and legs are black and which has black spots on a background passing from white to yellow on the body besides orange-colored webs.

I have succeeded in keeping several Brazilian and cisandean species of *Hyla* alive for relatively long periods. Some have been with me for over four years. In cool weather they are apt to remain sluggish, except for some of the Argentinian forms. They sometimes rest for several days in the same position and in the same place, be it a leaf, a bromeliad, a branch, or a log. The long quiescent periods do not prevent them from giving great leaps when stimulated or taken out of their living quarters. When rain threatens some utter rain calls.

Some learn very quickly to feed in daytime; they wait for live insects to be introduced and some catch grasshoppers or flies as soon as they are put in. A small batch of *Hyla duartei caldarum* are alert all day and make lunges at the flies put in for their neighbors. One recently metamorphosed *Hyla p. pulchella* brought from Santa Luzia near Montevideo proved to be such a quick catcher and voracious feeder that other frogs put in with it were in danger of starvation. It grew very fast, attaining almost adult size in a few months. Its early cream color became green. Both colors are seen in natural populations and undergo a certain amount of individual variation.

Reproductive behavior and breeding habits are much more stereotyped in *Hyla* than in more specialized genera of the family. Almost all Brazilian species breed in standing water and some of the very small ones like *Hyla perpusilla* spawn in the small reservoirs of the leaf cups of the bromeliads in which they live. Similar habits are adopted by small coelonotous Brazilian genera, but the eggs of the latter remain on the back of the mother until submetamorphosis. The prolonged embryonic period gives them an advantage over *Hyla*, which hatch in a very rudimentary stage without sense organs. The tadpoles of *Hyla claresignata*, one of our most striking large southeastern montane species, live in swift, sometimes torrential streams. They cling to the vertical rocks by the mouth and have the highest tooth formula seen on the beaks of the running-water species observed by Orton. A more rudimentary version of this behavior is displayed by the tadpoles of a member of the group of *Hyla catharinae*, probably *Hyla flavoguttata*. They live in small, shallow but swift brooks; their tooth formula is not high, and they cling in a horizontal position to stones, pieces of driftwood, and other substrata, even to the rubber boots of wading naturalists.

Two very small southeastern forms, *Hyla decipiens* and *Hyla berthalutzae* hang their spawn from the tip of herbaceous vegetation overhanging the water of the marshes where they breed. The embryos fall directly into the proper environment, but not at an advanced stage like those of *Centrolenella*, *Phyllomedusa*, or *Pithecopus*, which all spawn on leaves, the first on the open underside, the others rolling the leaf into a funnel while spawning. These minor changes in reproductive behavior of the two little species of *Hyla* mentioned above are very simple, but they serve as indicators of the trend found in more advanced stages among the specialized genera and subfamilies.

There are also a few other indicators of a more structural kind. The horizontal pupil of *Hyla* cannot go over gradually into the vertical pupil of the Phyllomedusinae; nevertheless, some species of the type genus have slightly or definitive rhomboid pupils. These occur in the casque-headed forms Triprioninae in which increased ossification, especially of the skull, is also a trend, which in some genera goes to the extreme of forming a complete helmet or spiked skullcap. A modest beginning is evident in some large species whose frontoparietals have elevated carinae; thus *Hyla langsdorffii*. Double vocal sacs are present in the group of *Hyla venulosa*, now put into *Phrynohyas* by Duellman and more accurately called *Acrodytes* by Cope. The quantitative rather than qualitative nature of several of these changes sometimes leads to uncertainty over the actual dividing line between certain Hylid genera.

One word must be added as to the order in which the species recognized in this book are presented. To a certain extent they place themselves. Close study of the genus *Hyla* makes it abundantly clear that the Neotropical species tend to form a certain number of groups. Each of these groups offers a number of characters that set it apart from the others, but which are common to its own components. Morphologically they are often so similar that the description of the oldest-known one by a competent herpetologist fits most of the others, not perfectly, of course, but like a ready-made garment in need of minor adjustments. It is just this morphological similarity that makes it imperative to study each living form and its behavior in its proper environment.

I have tried to put each form into the right group and yet bring out its own diagnostic characters. It is not always easy when dealing with very similar forms, especially vicariants. In addition to the other difficulties there is the fact that some species are fully known even as to habits, life history, range, and ecology, whereas knowledge of others is reduced to the morphological description of one museum specimen. I have tried my best to deal with these problems effectively. Mistakes must have crept in nevertheless. However, this is the first attempt to monograph the Neotropical species of *Hyla* that occur in Brazil and to cover them as accurately as possible. The comprised area amounts to almost half a continent, where the gaps in herpetological work are larger than the areas whose frog fauna has been closely observed. Moreover, the work had to be undertaken without the benefit of modern biochemical or genetic methods.

The ecology and range of the different species are given for the following divisions of the eastern subregion of South America (B. Lutz, 1972): 1. Hylaea or Amazonian equatorial forest belt with discrete nuclei of savannas. 2. Continental province, which occupies the central depression and includes parts of Argentina, Brazil, Paraguay, and eastern Bolivia, forming an arc over the highlands of Goias and Minas Gerias, extending to the northeastern states of Brazil; it is subdivided into Chaquean, Planaltine, and Northeastern subprovinces. 3. Southern Cisplatine and Platine province, which occupies the *campos* of Rio Grande do Sul, Uruguay, and adjacent eastern parts of Argentina. 4. Atlantic province along the Brazilian coast, which comprises the following life zones: maritime scrub formation (*restinga*); lowlands; montane rain forest, moors, and meadows above the timber line.

# I. Large Species

# 1. Species with Long, Sharp Pollex Rudiment

*Hyla faber* Wied, 1824

WIED-NEUWIED, MAXIMILIAN A. 1821. *Reise nach Brasilien in den Jahren 1815 bis 1817*, 1:173.
————. 1824. *Abbildungen zur Naturgeschichte Brasiliens*, pls. 89–90.
————. 1825. *Beiträge zur Naturgeschichte von Brasilien*, 1:519–524.

This species is one of the few tree frogs with a common name in Brazil, where it is called *ferreiro* ("smith"). It was first mentioned, figured, and described by Prince Maximilian zu Wied-Neuwied, who traveled in Brazil, mostly in Espirito Santo and Bahia, during the years 1815–1817. In the account of his journeys he mentions taking up night quarters at the Fazenda do Agá, between the rivers Itapemirim and Iriritiba, near 21° of south latitude. There was a small swamp near the dwellings and at dusk he was very much astonished by the voice of an unknown frog. It sounded like a smith working on tin or copper with a hammer, though the sound was deeper and fuller. Later he describes the catching of the "smith frog" at St. Agnes (Santa Inês) near the Rio de Contas. Having sent out some of his collectors on a bright night, they caught several specimens by the light of ignited pieces of wood. In his *Beiträge*, he describes the frog that is also figured in his atlas (1824).

The habit of building miniature private pools for spawning was not discovered at the time, but was observed much later by Goeldi on his estate, Colonia Alpina, at Teresópolis and described (1895) with slight inaccuracies.

My own experiences with *Hyla faber* began by coming straight onto their spawning sites in an artificial pond built by market gardners in Santa Alexandrina, a suburb of Rio de Janeiro. Having thrust my head through the bottom of the hedge bordering it to see the frogs I had to withdraw hastily because of threats of shooting from the distant house of the owners, who, in spite of our flashlights, took us for thieves. Friendly relations were, however, soon established and the first specimens of A. Lutz and later those of Doris M. Cochran came from that garden. My observations on nest building were mostly carried out at the Açude da Solidão on the edge of the Tijuca forest, and also in Rio in 1951, with the help of the late J. Venancio and my brother, G. A. Lutz, who took the photographs; we resumed the work in 1959 and published the results in *Natural History* (January 1961: 73–77).

DIAGNOSTIC CHARACTERS. Size very large. Head massive, wider than the body at the corner of the mouth, constricted behind. Dorsal surface brown, varying from pale chamois to ruddy or olivaceous brown; dark vertical stripes, often bifurcated, on the flanks and parts of the thigh hidden in repose. Belly orange or flesh-colored. Voice like the sound of a hammer beating against an anvil. Rudiment of pollex used as a weapon by the male, which builds nests on the margins or in shallows of ponds with a clay bottom.

TYPES AND TYPE LOCALITY. The types were collected at the Fazenda Santa Inês, near the Rio de Contas, state of Bahia. I do not know where the types are, but the species cannot be confounded once it is heard.

DESCRIPTION. Size very large, average 90–95 mm, snout to vent, occasionally 85–100 mm, or more. Habit robust. Head massive, obtusely triangular, wider than the shoulders at the corners of the mouth, constricted behind it. Legs long, the tibiotarsal articulation reaching beyond the tip of the snout when the hindlimb is adpressed. Snout oval, canthus rostralis blunt but distinct; loreal region concave, flaring. Eye large, prominent. Tympanum large, vertical, almost equal to the diameter of the eye. Interorbital space wider than the upper eyelid and much wider than the internarial space. Vomerine teeth mostly in heavy and narrowly separated, chevron-shaped patches, between the choanae, reaching beyond their posterior edge. Tongue large, rounded, slightly free, entirely, or slightly emarginate in preserved specimens. Hands and feet large, digits flat, with rounded disks. Hands about half-webbed, webs on feet longer. A distinct rudiment of the pollex, claw-shaped in males. A pronounced oval inner metatarsal tubercle. Skin of dorsal surface smooth, sometimes showing irregular lines as if scratched (see Wied). Skin of belly and lower aspect of thigh distinctly granular, of throat slightly so. A white glandular ridge on the forearm and tarsus, from the outer digit to the elbow and knee. A similar ridge over the anus. A marked supratympanic fold.

SECONDARY SEX CHARACTERS. Rudiment of pollex robust, bony, claw-shaped and protrusible in male. Vocal sac large, median. Gula dark, blackish, or gray. Pollex rudiment of female cartilaginous (fide A. L. Carvalho). Gula paler. Difference of size not very marked.

COLOR AND PATTERN. As already mentioned by Wied, the dorsal coloring is brown, but ranges from very pale to quite dark; sometimes it is slightly reddish or olivaceous. This is not a sexual character as he surmised, but varies in the same

individual. Dark specimens caught at night become quite pale in daytime and, conversely, pale specimens resting in a light place get darker at night, or even in daylight, if handled. The specimens figured by Wied and painted in watercolor for A. Lutz are both light and devoid of much pattern, though they show the dark vertebral line that generally occupies a slight median depression. It may be longer or shorter than the body, entire or interrupted, straight or deflected. Many individuals show irregular, insular, anastomosed, occasionally fenestrated spots and blotches on the dorsal surface, mostly larger at the level of the shoulders, becoming horizontal and narrowing caudad. In the pale phase the spots become quite indistinct. Shiny black spots, mostly small, and white spots of guanine also occur. Oblique bars on the permanently visible surfaces of the hindlimbs variable, wide or narrow, or alternatively narrow and wide, long or short, pointed or squarish. Grayish, vertical bars on the sides of the body and upper parts of the thigh concealed in repose, on the latter sometimes with a violet tinge. A yellow-orange suffusion on the belly and sometimes on all the parts of the limbs concealed in repose; at others, the latter with a violet or vinaceous tint. Iris with a metallic sheen of similar or paler color than the dorsal surface and with dark centripetal angular lines, strongest at the periphery and an accumulation of pigment at the edges of the equator forming a pseudocolobom. Edge of lower jaw white.

Juvenile specimens more delicately colored than the adults, paler above, the concealed aspects more pink. Individual differences of pattern already present.

SIZE. Wied indicates a length of 3 inches and 4 lines, roughly corresponding to 85–88 mm. The female specimen on his plate is, however, 93 mm long. Doris M. Cochran, in *Frogs of Southeastern Brazil* (1955), gives a length of 87 mm. Most of our specimens are larger, 90–96 mm or more, occasionally 100 mm or more. This character does not depend on sex or geography, although most of the southern specimens in our collection, both males and females, are robust.

VOICE. The main characteristics of the voice have been given by Wied and are the origin of the popular name. The males sing in chorus. First one begins, then another; more join in and soon most of the males present seem to be calling. After a time the chorus dies down, then starts again. The calls of each individual are quite even and maintained at the same pitch. Sometimes a beat is missed; longer pauses also occur and there may be an acceleration for a few notes. I have timed the drumming; it varies a great deal, from 100–105 calls per minute to 82–85 and 60–65, sometimes only some 40–45 beats; the pauses are not regular, nor do they last the same time. This makes it difficult to time the call. The dissonances heard are due to differences of pitch between individuals. Sometimes muted notes or an appoggiatura are produced.

CLAY NESTS. The nests are clay pans with raised walls, built at the edges or in shallows of pools. Perfect nests are rounded, about 30 cm in diameter and 7–9 cm deep, with a rampart rising 5–7 cm above the water. It is the male who builds them. He gets into the water, sits in a shallow place, and circles around in it, thus forming the cavity, and gradually deepening it. The walls are built by pushing up the clay and patting it onto the edges with the hands. Occasionally the frog goes under, brings material up on the snout and pushes it onto the wall.

REPRODUCTIVE BEHAVIOR. When the nest is finished, sometimes even before, the male stops working and starts singing, inside the nest, on the rampart, or even outside, but near it. Females ready to spawn are attracted by his drumming. They approach cautiously, halting now and then, in a peculiar position, sitting on the hindlimbs and resting on the hands with the arms outstretched. After a time, one gets into the nest, swims up behind the male and eventually lays a hand on his back. At first he goes on calling then suddenly he turns and seizes the female.

We witnessed fights between males several times. They may break out in the nest or outside it. The fighters encircle each other's head and neck with the arms and place their hands in positions enabling them to drive the sharp curved pollices in. Meanwhile, they may wrestle with their long legs, trying to push each other under and to keep their own nostrils above water. Sometimes they thrash around, at other times they lie still, the legs drawn up under the greatly inflated body. If one is stronger or more agile he gets on top and tries to drown the other.

While fighting, the frogs may fall out of the nest,

and continue the battle on shore, or in the pond, or break off. A pair of fighters can be lifted up together, moved, and examined. One sees that the skin round the rudimentary pollex is pushed down and the curved point bared. The fighters may have both pollices dug into the foe. If one gently lifts a pollex out it is promptly pushed in again. After some handling they break apart and hop away.

In one set of fighters, a male singing the night before at the nest nearby was recognized. It seems likely that this species has developed a rudimentary sense of territory limited to the spawning site. The males may also simply fight for possession of the available nests. These seem to be used several times over, since one sometimes finds eggs or embryos, small larvae, and large tadpoles in the same nest.

EGGS. Unlaid eggs are very numerous and very small, about 1.5 mm diameter. The animal pole is black and the vegetal one cream.

The spawn forms a rounded sheet on top of the water inside the nest, not quite reaching the edges and it shows a certain pattern in the distribution of the eggs. It is exposed to some hazards; it may dry out if the water level decreases rapidly and the water evaporates; or again, it may be floated off by flooding. Twice, rounded sheets of spawn were observed floating on the surface of the general pool after heavy rain; one had two damsel flies entangled in it. The eggs continued to develop in a basin in which we placed them.

EMBRYOS. The embryos are black. Before hatching they assume an upright position inside the egg membranes. At hatching there is a cement organ and soon after they develop gills.

LARVA. Spiraculum sinistral, anus dextral, as usual in Hylid tadpoles. Body oval, somewhat flattened above, longer ventrally, with bulging gut. Tail robust; muscular part wide, crests moderate, the upper slightly wider than the lower, but not quite reaching the back. Tail tapering somewhat, slightly raised toward the tip, generally pointed, blunt in some specimens. Border of mouth surrounded by dense rows of papillae, except in the median upper part. Beaks strong, very black, with serrated edges; the upper short and wide, the lower long and narrow. Teeth in $\frac{2}{3}$ rows, plus one series of short fragments of weak teeth beneath the lowest row. First row above entire, longer than the second, which is divided, like the two inner lower ones.

(See formula on following page.)

Formula:  $\dfrac{\begin{array}{c}1\\1-1\\1-1\\1-1\\1\end{array}}{}$

Last row shorter. Lower lip forming a pair of submedian vertical folds with a vertical recess in the middle, followed by another pair of folds, one at each of the corners. Nostrils oblique, kidney-shaped, with a valve on the inner edge. Eyes oblique also, much larger and more widely spaced than the nostrils, covered by transparent skin; eyelids formed at submetamorphosis. Spiraculum nearer to the eye, but more distant from the mouth than from the anus, visible from above, hyaline, turned slightly upward. Anus reaching the edge of the lower crest. Body dark. Tail with dark blotches or large round dots. At metamorphosis the edges of the crests darken.

DIMENSIONS. Largest tadpoles: length of body 30–37 mm, width about 17 mm. Length of tail 55–74 mm, height approximately 17 mm, before metamorphosis begins. Mouth on average 4 mm, internarial space 4 mm, interocular space 10 mm. Spiraculum and anus, each, about 4 mm long. Distance from spiraculum to eye two-thirds to three-fourths its distance from the anus.

ECOLOGICAL NOTES. *Hyla faber* is a robust species whose presence may well depend on appropriate biotopes for the larvae, such as standing sheets of water with clay bottoms and shallow margins or islands.

VAGILITY. Individuals moving steadily in one direction were seen twice; the first one was climbing the road from Lagoa Santa toward Belo Horizonte and the second hopping along the mountain road to Petrópolis, halfway up from the lowlands.

KNOWN RANGE. The geographical distribution of South American frogs cannot be stated with precision, as only relatively few, often discrete, localities and regions have been collected in. Prince Maximilian first heard *Hyla faber* in the state of Espirito Santo, slightly below 21° South. He then collected it near the Rio de Contas in the state of Bahia. The most northern point from which I have seen this species is Palmeira dos Indios, in the state of Alagoas, at approximately 9° 30′ South. Our most southern specimens were taken at Caracol, near Canelas, approximately 29° 20′ S. 50° 53′ W. Gr., in Rio Grande do Sul. In the state of Paraná it has been obtained at Curitiba, near the coast, in the south between Palma and Bituruna, and in the Na-

tional Park at Iguaçu on the southwestern border of the state with Paraguay and Argentina. It also occurs in the Argentinian territory of Misiones (26°–28° S. 56°–58° W. Gr.). In Minas Gerais it ranges west at least to Lagoa Santa outside Belo Horizonte and has been taken at Governador Valadares. The highest altitude at which we have collected it is about 800 m. Higher up, sheets of standing water with clay bottoms become scarce. The known range thus comprises some 19° in a north-south direction, about the same east-west, and 2,400 feet above sea level.

AFFINITIES. *Hyla faber* forms part of a group of large species of Neotropical tree frogs with rounded snout, long legs, and a sharp pollex rudiment that can be used as a weapon. The skin is smooth, the dorsal surface brown, varying from light to dark; a pattern of vertical gray-black stripes is generally present on the flanks.

In Brazil this group also comprises *Hyla crepitans* Wied and *Hyla circumdata* Cope.

The nearest species to *Hyla faber* may well be *Hyla rosenbergi* described by Boulenger from northwestern Ecuador. According to Breder (1941) and Dunn this species also builds clay nests for spawning. The habit and size are similar, the dorsal color, vertebral stripe, and pattern on the flanks also. However, the skin of *Hyla rosenbergi* is pustular and, according to some authors, there is an elongate gland on the flanks of the male. The head seems less massive, the snout longer than in *Hyla faber*, and the webs fuller. *H. rosenbergi* seems to be characteristic of northwestern South America and Panama.

*Hyla faber* differs considerably from *Hyla boans*, which is larger and has a pattern of golden arabesques on the transparent part of the lower eyelid, an appendix on the heel, and a different geographic distribution.

## *Hyla crepitans* Wied, 1824

WIED-NEUWIED, MAXIMILIAN A. 1824. *Abbildungen zur Naturgeschichte Brasiliens*, pl. 47, fig. 1.
———. 1825. *Beiträge zur Naturgeschichte von Brasilien*, 1:525–529.

HISTORY. *Hyla crepitans* was described from Brazil by Prince Maximilian zu Wied-Neuwied but has a very wide known distribution, ranging through parts of this country and of northern South

America to Panama. The first specimen was caught jumping from a tree, at Tamburil, in the Brazilian state of Bahia, but more were taken later by Wied in woods between Giboia and Conquista, also in Bahia.

TYPE. The American Museum of Natural History has one of the specimens collected by Wied, labeled "Maximilian." It is slightly smaller than the size he indicated. After over 140 years it has become somewhat macerated and rather fragile, but it has the right morphology; there are vestiges left of the pattern on the flanks, the upper parts of the thighs, and the gula.

DIAGNOSTIC CHARACTERS. Living or well-preserved specimens can be determined by the ensemble of size, build, and color, especially of the parts concealed in repose and by the typical aspect of the granular, triangular area on the midventral aspect of the thigh. This is a fairly large, somewhat scraggy species with long legs. Color, brownish, grayish, occasionally greenish white above, with or without darker blotches on the back; smooth concealed parts orange. Granular area of thigh limited by two rows of larger or more conspicuous granules coming from the anus and opening up into a large V.

Poor or faded preserved specimens may be confounded with similar species, such as *Hyla circumdata* Cope and *Hyla pardalis* Spix, but can be separated by the geographic distribution. Smaller than *Hyla faber;* voice quite different.

DESCRIPTION. Size fairly large: males from 50–63 mm, mostly 55 or 56 mm, females with eggs from 59–75, most of them 70 mm or more, from snout to vent. Build not very robust with long legs. Head oval, slightly wider than long, rather straight behind the eyes; snout short, especially in the Bahia specimens; canthus rostralis blunt, truncate between the nostrils; loreal region slightly concave below the canthus. Eye large, prominent, its longest diameter equal to the distance from its anterior corner to the nostrils, whence the snout slants toward the mouth. Tympanum one-half to two-thirds the diameter of the eye. Interorbital space very slightly wider than the upper eyelid or of the same width. Tongue rounded, fairly large and thick, entire, or slightly emarginate behind, barely free. Vomerine teeth in two short arches between and behind the choanae, more or less parallel to their inner rim. Legs long, but variable in length, especially the tibia; tibiotarsal articulation generally reaching either to the nostril or between it and the eye when adpressed. Hands, feet, disks, average. A rudiment of the pollex. An elongate inner metatarsal tubercle. Webs on hand short; on feet to the last articulation of the toes except on fourth toe, which shows a fringe beginning on the penultimate one. Dorsal skin smooth, delicate; belly granular; a well-defined triangular granular area on the midventral part of the thigh, limited by larger tubercles coming from the anus and widening into a V-shaped figure. Gula granite-like, similar to the granular part of the thigh.

COLOR AND PATTERN. The dorsal coloring and pattern described by Wied are accurate. The ground tone above is a grayish or brownish white, sometimes with a greenish tint, especially towards the sides. Beneath it is orange rather than the color pictured by Wied. A large dark blotch often occupies much of the dorsal area between the shoulders and the sacrum. It is variable and generally irregular in shape, sometimes fenestrated, at others somewhat squarish or composed of two bilateral, elongate, more or less confluent portions; irregular narrower prongs may be sent out toward the eyelids. The main blotch is often followed by irregular horizontal spots or bars, continued by coincident bars across the permanently visible parts of the limbs, especially the thigh and leg. On the flanks the dorsal pattern is prolonged into narrow, vertical, often double stripes; similar stripes or dark spots on the upper parts of the thigh concealed in repose. In dark specimens the dorsal pattern is conspicuous, whereas in light phases it is often rather faint. Beneath immaculate; white on the granular gula and midventral portion of the thigh, save for strings of melanophores between the granulations ( ♂ ) or a brownish edge to the mouth. Belly, concealed upper portions of thighs, ventral and inner parts of the limbs orange.

VOICE. Short quacks. The specific name given by Wied and his simile of snapping twigs describes the call accurately. The males sing in chorus, as observed by him and also by us.

SECONDARY SEX CHARACTERS. Quite a difference of size occurs between the smallest males (50 mm) and the largest females (75 mm). Some males, probably the nuptial ones, exhibit a large vocal sac, generally much pleated, occasionally forming a square bib under the mouth. The pollex rudiment of the male is elongate, curved outward, and contains a thin sharp spur; the gula has dark pigment between the granules. The pollex rudiment of the female is knob-like and the throat lighter.

EGGS. The ovarian eggs are very numerous and small, with dark animal and cream-colored vegetal pole.

BEHAVIOR AND ECOLOGY. In the capital of the state of Bahia, we caught *Hyla crepitans* singing in low bushes above artificial trenches of water in gardens and nurseries. At Cachoeira, in the same state, they perched on shrubs at the edges of flooded paths in the kitchen-garden of the Fazenda Santa Maria. Near San Mateos, on the border of the state of Guarico in Venezuela, they were calling on the vegetation of a bank above a sheet of water that partially flooded the highway. Wied mentions collecting his species in a wood, but the parts of Brazil in which *H. crepitans* occurs have been greatly devastated since his time, and the species seems adapted to more or less open terrain or at least tolerant of it.

KNOWN RANGE. The specimens collected and seen in Brazilian collections range from northeastern Minas Gerais, through the state of Bahia, into Alagoas, Pernambuco, and Paraiba. A. Lutz found it common at Natal, the capital of the state of Rio Grande do Norte and observed large tadpoles of this species in the Rio Baldo. In 1925, he collected specimens in Trinidad, B.W.I., and in Venezuela (Maracay, Caracas) and I also collected it at Trinidad and in the Venezuelan state of Guarico in 1954. I collected some at Girardot, Colombia. Other specimens from Colombia and Panama were seen in American museums and a few were exchanged with us.

AFFINITIES. *Hyla doumercii* and *H. levaillantii* Duméril & Bibron from Surinam are generally considered synonymous with *H. crepitans*. The type of *H. doumercii* seen in Paris (766 Muséum d'Histoire Naturelle) is similar. The holotype of *H. levaillantii* has a slightly longer web on the hands. *Hyla indris*, which was published by Cope *sine descriptio*, except for a mention of shorter legs, is also generally considered synonymous. As seen above, the length of the leg varies. *H. indris* comes from Surinam; some of our Venezuelan specimens are very long-legged.

Dr. Doris Cochran considers *H. crepitans* and *Hyla circumdata* synonymous. *H. crepitans* differs from *H. circumdata* by the more scraggy build, longer legs, more delicate skin, typical aspect of the granular surfaces of thighs, not to mention the quite different color of the concealed parts and details of the pattern as well as the voice and the distribution, *Hyla crepitans* is a lowland species, not montane. Both Wied and A. Lutz point out a greater similarity with *Hyla pardalis* Spix, but they rightly consider the two species distinct. *H. crepitans* diverges from *H. pardalis* by its shorter webs, color, and distribution; the green bones and mouth and the glandular wavy outline of the latter bring it closer to *Hyla langsdorffii*.

## *Hyla circumdata* (Cope), 1867

> COPE, E. D. 1867. On the families of raniform Anura. *J. Ac. Nat. Sc. Phila.*, ser. 2, 6:189–296 (*nulla descriptio*).
> ———. 1870–1871. Eighth contribution to the herpetology of tropical America. *Pr. Am. Phil. Soc.* 11:555.
> BOULENGER, G. A. 1882. *Catalogue of the batrachia salientia in the British Museum*, p. 351.

DIAGNOSTIC CHARACTERS. The slender dark circles on the upper parts of the thigh concealed in repose from which the trivial name is derived; the thumb spur of the male, which really "is more striking than in any other of the genus," as stated by Cope. According to A. Lutz: "This *Hyla* has a very variable dorsal coloration and may even be quite light, like whitish bark, reminding one of *Hyla corticalis*, which is synonymous with *Hyla pardalis*. In life the hindlimbs show an intense blue-violet color on the inner aspects of the thigh and the inner and lower aspect of the leg. The pupil is transversally elliptic. The males have a very marked rudiment of the pollex ending in a spur; the female also has the rudiment but not the spur. This species always lives near running water."

TERRA TYPICA: "Brazil," fide Cope.

DESCRIPTION. Size rather large (55–70 mm). Build robust. Legs fairly long, the tibia not much longer than the femur; the tibiotarsal articulation generally reaching between the eye and the tip of the snout when adpressed. Head oval, slightly broader than long but not wider than the body. Snout rounded, a little longer than the eye, with blunt canthus rostralis and concave, slightly oblique, loreal region. Eye large, very prominent, its longest diameter about equal to the distance from its anterior corner to the nostril. Tympanum large, often two-thirds or more of the diameter of the eye. Tongue large, rounded, very wide and flat in many specimens, smaller and more compact in others, with longitudinal grooves, slightly emarginate and scarcely free behind. Vomerine teeth either forming a chevron, an arch, or two almost straight groups between the choanae, parallel to and beyond their inner border. Web on the hand reaching beyond the antepenultimate articulation of the third finger. On the foot, the web reaches the disk of the toes except on the fourth, where it is wide to the penultimate articulation and forms a fringe beyond it. Wide part of the webs between the digits very variable in width and shape. Rudiment of pollex very pronounced, ending in a sharp, curved point in the male. Palm of hand full of tubercles, an elongate one parallel to the rudimentary pollex; in large specimens a horizontal series under the outer fingers. Inner metatarsal tubercle large, oval; outer very indistinct. Skin of dorsal aspect smooth but thick, of sides sometimes very loose; large, rounded, even granules on the belly and the mid-lower aspect of the thighs, beginning at the edges of the anus and forming an elongate triangle which interrupts the pattern of circles. A series of glandules from the elbow to the fourth finger; a light bilateral ridge over the anus; a strong supratympanic fold. Sometimes a glandular tubercle or minute flap on elbow and knee.

COLOR. As pointed out by Lutz, the dorsal coloring is variable, a fact conveyed by watercolors and photographs of different individuals in the Lutz Collection. Living specimens are brown, varying from light tan to dark chocolate brown. The iris is a metallic, not quite golden yellow and has a very characteristic shape, owing to the slight notches above and below and the narrowing at the horizontal edges. Upper parts of the thigh concealed in repose lilac or blue violet; the circles darker. Granular part of the ventral surface yellow almost maize-colored. Preserved specimens mostly remain brown for a long time; those from the Upper Itatiaia and a few other very large specimens acquire a purplish tone; they may also have a very light reddish tint on the belly and ventral aspect of the thighs.

PATTERN. The circles from which the specific name is derived constitute the most characteristic part of the pattern. Their form and number is slightly variable (8–12). They occur on the concealed upper aspects of the thighs and sometimes extend to the flanks and the inside of the tibia and more often to the inner dorsal aspect of the tarsus and foot; in some specimens the circles are visible from the sides and below but in others they are limited to the dorsal surface. A vertebral line, often short, may occur on the back. Irregular spots, or blotches, mostly disposed more or less horizontally, cover a portion of the dorsal surface of many individuals and may overlap onto the sides. In dark phases they are very indistinct. A certain percentage of specimens display opaque, guanine-like, mostly white, occasionally reddish spots or dashes, generally above the anus, and at the corners of the elbow and knees. They may also be single, eccentric, and irregular, or, very seldom, substituted by a sprinkling of white dots. A few examples show irregular groups of black spots, like agglomerations of melanophores, on the back.

SIZE. The smallest male, with a vocal sac, comes from the Serra de Cubatão near São Paulo; it is only 38 mm long and has no sharp spur. The largest, from the National Park at Serra dos Orgãos is 70 mm. Average male specimens range from 60 to 66 mm long. Our smallest female in a breeding condition is 55 mm, the largest 71, and most of the others are 60, 63, or 66 mm long. A series of small nuptial males like the one mentioned above were obtained by Mr. Werner Bokermann at the Biological Station at Alto da Serra outside São Paulo; he described them as *Hyla astartea*.

SECONDARY SEX CHARACTERS. *Hyla circumdata* is a tree frog with exceptionally marked sexual differences. Not only do the males have the spur, the vocal sac, and a dark border to the throat, but nuptial excrescences appear on the inside of the pollex and of the first finger; the forearms become huge, like those of the large species of *Leptodactylus*. The nuptial pads are not easy to see because the pollex rudiment and first finger are held parallel to each other facing inward.

VOICE. The voice is loud and rough. It sounds like guffaws (J. Venancio) or like stertorous breathing (Gualter A. Lutz).

JUVENILES. Metamorphosis occurs between 18–22 mm of length. The juveniles are rather deceptive. The pale buff dorsal surface is evenly sprinkled with sparse black dots. The rudimentary pollex and palmar tubercles are characteristic and unexpected in such small individuals. At first, the light surface of the thighs is rosy to cherry red instead of violet and devoid of circles. The young are often found on bushes or on tall herbs, such as *Hedychium coronarium*, near running water.

BEHAVIOR. As soon as one seizes a male *Hyla circumdata* it digs in its spurs. It would be interesting to know if the males fight like those of *H. faber* since, relatively speaking, *circumdata* is better equipped. Mr. Bokermann saw this species swarming at the Biological Station outside São Paulo, the swarm being entirely composed of males. The undersized nuptial males in his collection were taken while they were sleeping in bromeliads. *Hyla circumdata* rests in different sites; sometimes it calls from epiphytic bromeliads on quite high trees; at the Granja Comari in Teresópolis a pair was taken out of a bromeliad growing on a large branch of a tree that had been blown down by a storm and was standing upright in the water of a flooded brook. At Marumby, near Curitiba, a specimen was found asleep on a rock under a curtain of vegetation. Lutz's observation that *H. circumdata* always lives near running water is very pertinent and confirmed by all our finding places. On the Sumaré ridge above Rio de Janeiro, they come to the wet cliffs from which water perennially drips. An incipient rampart seen there in an artificial trough below the cliff and another observed by Elio Gouvea elsewhere suggest the possibility that nesting pans are built by this species also. Metamorphosing tadpoles were obtained at the Sumaré; others come from a very shallow, swift and cold brook, Córrego Frio, in the Serra dos Orgãos National Park at 2,700–2,900 feet altitude. Nearby, a set of males was caught singing on stones at the edges of the bed of a mountain stream. The other specimens were caught on bushes above or near streams and brooks.

EGGS. The eggs are small. Like those of other Brazilian species of *Hyla*, they have a black animal and cream-colored vegetal pole.

ECOLOGY. *Hyla circumdata* is a montane species peculiar to the forested coastal ranges of eastern to southern Brazil. It is possible that life near running waters in montane forest is due to temperature preferences of the adults or more likely to adaptation of the larvae to cold water.

VARIATION. As shown above, *Hyla circumdata* is variable as to size, color, pattern, and details of morphology. Our largest sample from one place comes from Boracea, the Biological Station of the Department of Zoology of the state of São Paulo between the capital and the sea; a good many dark individuals seem to occur there.

On the Mantiqueira Range the usual form of *Hyla circumdata* has been collected from 1,300 m to well over 2,000 m at Mauá.

HIGH ALTITUDE FORM. Another form occurs on the Upper Itatiaia Mountains, which at first seems so different that one might be tempted to consider it a separate species. The first of these specimens was taken at Macieiras, in rain forest, near a brook flowing into a pool. The others were obtained at Brejo da Lapa at over 2,000 m altitude where the forest thins out into elfinwood. In only one of the specimens are the circles present, even so, paradoxically, light on dark, on the permanently visible surface of the thigh and faintly darker on the concealed part behind it. In the others all the concealed surfaces of the hindlimb are such a deep dark violet-black that every vestige of pattern has been wiped out. The dark color extends to the dorsal inner aspect of the tarsus and foot concealed while at rest. In life the dorsal coloring is medium brown, without any spots or blotches except for the clumps of melanophores seen on one or two of them; the pollex, the tubercles on the palms, and the general morphology are the same. The teeth incline to be shorter and the webs to become more robust, forming wider fringes on the toes. The head also seems shorter. In most of them the legs reach beyond the eye but one or two have very short hindlimbs. The build is extremely robust, though the size is the same as that of large individuals of the common form. Our largest specimen is a female 71 mm long. This length is almost attained by a male of 70 mm with the usual coloring from Teresópolis, but in this lot also there is a trend toward the violet to slate color of preserved specimens from the Upper Itatiaia. If this should be race it might well be called *alticola*.

KNOWN RANGE. *Hyla circumdata* has been collected from Espirito Santo (Santa Tereza) to northern Rio Grande do Sul (Gramado), mostly on the different parts of the Maritime Range that go by local names in the states of Rio de Janeiro, Guanabara, São Paulo, Paraná, and Santa Catarina. On the parallel Serra da Mantiqueira, it has so far been collected only at and not far from Itatiaia, at Mauá, Piquete, and Eugenio Lefèvre (Campos do Jordão). The lowest point at which it has been obtained is the Tijuca forest outside Rio, at about 350–400 m.

AFFINITIES. Cope considers *Hyla circumdata* a good species of the genus *Hypsiboas*, which he characterizes by the multijointed pollex rudiment and the absence of pattern in the lower eyelid. In very large specimens, there may, however, be a slight sprinkling at the corner of the transparent part of the eyelid. Boulenger (1882) accepts the species, which was a *nomen nudum* at first. Dr. Cochran unexpectedly puts *Hyla circumdata* to the synonymy of *H. crepitans* Wied. I cannot agree. The morphological resemblances she points out are present to a certain extent but, as Boulenger puts it, *Hyla circumdata* is stouter and has a different coloration. I would add that the gula is smoother, the shape is less scraggy, and the legs are shorter. Besides these and other differences, *Hyla crepitans* is found in warm lowlands from Minas Gerais and Bahia to Panama, Venezuela, and Trinidad, whereas *H. circumdata* is a southeastern Brazilian montane rain forest form. They may be evolved from a common origin, like other Neotropical frogs, but they have drifted widely apart and have become adapted to quite different habitats and ways of life. From the evolutionary viewpoint, voice, flash color of concealed surfaces, and ecological adaptation are evidently more significant than morphological details.

## *Hyla langei* Bokermann, 1965

BOKERMANN, W. C. A. 1965. *Hyla langei*: A new frog from Paraná, southern Brazil. *J. Ohio Herp. Soc.* 5(2):49–51, figs. 1–5.

This is one more of the fairly large, very stout, thick-skinned tree frogs with a long, curved pollex rudiment.

DIFFERENTIAL DIAGNOSTIC CHARACTERS. Very similar to *Hyla circumdata* Cope, especially to its robust altitudinal form from the Serra da Mantiqueira. Differs by the indistinct tympanum, different dorsal pattern, fuller webs, shorter head, and the smaller and straighter patches of vomerine teeth.

TYPE AND TYPE LOCALITY. Holotype male WCAB collection n. 30.428. An additional specimen from Marumbi, on the Serra do Mar between Curitiba and Paranaguá, state of Paraná.

DESCRIPTION. Size rather large; two males 61 and 66 mm snout to vent. Build very robust. Head massive, shorter than wide. Hindlimb not very long, the tibiotarsal articulation reaching the eye when adpressed. Snout short, rounded in front, sloping to the mouth opening in profile. Nostrils subcanthal, not terminal but near the tip of the snout. Eye large, its horizontal diameter longer than the distance to the nostril, very slightly longer than the distance to the end of the snout. Tympanum not evident in either the type or the additional specimen. Interorbital space very slightly wider than the internarial space. Tongue rounded, barely emarginate, hardly free behind. Vomerine teeth in small transverse patches beyond the choanae. Forelimb short, very robust, with palpable edge of humerus and very thick forearm ( ♂ ). Hand robust with rather long fingers; a short web between the outer three and a robust prepollex on the edge of the first finger. Femur and tibia almost equal in length. Foot, long, stout. Disks of toes smaller than those of the hand. Toes very fully webbed. Web wide to the disk on the outer side of the first, second, and third, and on fifth, slightly fringed on their inner side, wide to the penultimate articulation and straight across on both sides of the fourth toe. Skin of dorsal aspect and sides very thick, granular beneath, except on the three distal segments of the hindlimb. Many tubercles and ridges on hand and foot.

SECONDARY SEX CHARACTERS. Those indicated above for the male. Female not seen.

VARIATION AND MEASUREMENTS. Very little difference between the holotype and the additional specimen. The former 66 mm, the latter 61 mm snout to vent. Femur of both: 35 mm, tibia 34 mm, tarsus of type 18 mm; of other 19 mm; foot 30 mm in both. Head length to width, type 21:23; other specimen 22:23 mm.

COLOR AND PATTERN. Not seen alive. Preserved type chocolate brown. Additional specimen with obscure dark blotches and ill-defined lighter areas, transversally disposed between the shoulders and the groin. Indistinct dark bars with light irregular intervals on the permanently visible dorsal parts of the limbs; best defined on the femur; quite vestigial on the forelimb.

Unfortunately no information available about the habits, but apparently a more southern form of the montane *Hyla circumdata* complex, this one from the montane rain forest zone with streams that lie between the capital of Paraná and the escarpment of the Maritime Range. It may be a full species or not.

## *Hyla martinsi* Bokermann, 1964

BOKERMANN, W. C. A. 1964. Dos nuevas especies de *Hyla* de Minas Gerais y notas sobre *Hyla alvarengai* Bok. *Neotropica* 10(32):67–76. *Hyla martinsi*: 67–71, figs. 1–9.

This *Hyla* is very near to *Hyla circumdata* Cope. It may have attained full specific status as it lives in a somewhat isolated part of the mountains of Minas Gerais with a rather differentiated environment that has only quite lately been studied for herpetological purposes.

DIFFERENTIAL DIAGNOSTIC CHARACTERS. The shorter webs; the green bones; the apparently more developed ossification of the humerus and perhaps of the pollex rudiment. The chestnut-colored iris; the spotting on the dorsal aspect of the body. Smaller tympanum, shorter webs.

TYPES AND TYPE LOCALITY. Holotype WCAB n. 14759 and paratype 14758, both males; female allotype 14761; n. 14760 was dissected. Type locality: Serra do Caraça, approximately 100 km southeast of Belo Horizonte, Minas Gerais; obtained near the Convent at about 1300 m altitude; leg. Bokermann et al., February 14, 1964. Paratype WCAB 12695 from the Serra do Cipó, collected earlier, is juvenile. It is just like *Hyla circumdata* and may not be conspecific with the types.

DESCRIPTION. Size large, build robust, both average for the *Hyla circumdata* group. Head large, body tapering only slightly beyond the sacrum. Hindlimb too stiff to adpress. Head massive, about as long as wide. Snout fairly short, rounded in front, not sloping back toward the mouth opening in profile. Canthus rostralis blunt, truncate between the nostrils. Loreal region concave, rather vertical. Nostrils subcanthal, almost terminal. Eye large, prominent, its horizontal diameter longer than the distance to the nostril and to the tip of snout. Tympanum very distinct, less than half the diameter of the eye. Tongue rounded, entire, slightly free behind. Vomerine teeth forming an obtuse angle between and behind the choanae, more or less parallel to their inner rim. Forelimb short, robust, especially in the male (see below). Disks large,

fingers wide, slightly fringed; a basal web between the outer ones. A decided rudiment of pollex ( ♂ ). Hindlimb average; tibia slightly shorter than femur. Toes about half-webbed. A distinct inner and a smaller outer metatarsal tubercle. Skin of dorsal aspect smooth. Skin of chest, belly, and midventral aspect of thigh minutely granular. A marked supratympanic fold.

MEASUREMENTS (mm). Snout to vent/hindlimb: Holotype 64/112, male paratype 59/102; female allotype 56/91. Tympanum 4, 3, eye 8, 7.2, eye nostril 7, 5.5, interorbital space 5, internarial space 5.

SECONDARY SEX CHARACTERS. The male holotype and the paratype are larger than the female allotype. Bokermann figures a very large pollex rudiment with a small spur and a femur with a large crest and two very much developed apophyses (WCAB n. 14760). The thick forelimb of the male paratype indicates the presence of these characters, but they are evidently less developed than in the holotype, which was not seen. This is evidently a group character, though it may show quantitative differences in the diverse forms belonging to the group.

COLOR AND PATTERN. Unfortunately there are no detailed indications as to the color of the living individual. Bokermann merely states that the iris is a uniform light chestnut (brown ?), that the dorsal aspect is chestnut (brown ?) with numerous lighter spots varying from brown to straw color. The circles on the limbs are mentioned but without any indication of the flash color, which is regrettable as this is a very important point. Ventral aspect pale straw.

The color of the iris is different from the light distinctly yellow iris of typical *Hyla circumdata*.

The circles on the thighs are very like those of *Hyla circumdata*. In the female those on the thigh, tibia, and permanently visible aspect of the leg and tarsus to foot are evident. On the arms they are less neat. In the male paratype they are more numerous and very distinct on the thigh, less so on the tibia and the forelimb; more evident on the outer parts of the tarsus.

LIFE HISTORY. Unknown; probably very interesting considering the habitat.

HABITS AND ECOLOGY. The author of the species states that the female was caught while moving around between stones on the edge of a brook. The males were localized by their call in a torrential mountain stream. They were not shy and were easily caught, but defended themselves with the prepollices and by pressure from the arms. This again is very similar to the habits of *Hyla circumdata*.

VOICE. Bokermann describes the call as isolated, raucous and like that of *Stombus* or *Odontophrynus*, which are lesser Ceratophrydids. In this it may differ from *Hyla circumdata*, which gives loud guffaws.

RANGE. So far known only from the type locality and a somewhat dubious juvenile from another Serra, also in Minas Gerais.

## *Hyla (Plectrohyla?) alvarengai* Bokermann, 1956

> BOKERMANN, W. C. A. 1956. Sôbre uma nova espécie de *Hyla* do estado de Minas Gerais, Brasil. *Papeis avulsos do Departamento de Zoologia de São Paulo* 12(18):357–362. 6 text figs, 1 photo.
> ――――. 1964. Dos nuevas especies de *Hyla* de Minas Gerais y notas sobre *Hyla alvarengai* Bok. *Neotropica* 10(32):75–76, fig. 16.

It is very interesting that so large and well-characterized a frog should have remained unknown to science until quite recently. The specimen on which the description is based was collected in 1921, but remained in the Zoological Collection of the state of São Paulo for thirty-five years before it was described. We ourselves have also had five specimens for several years. They were given to us by Professor Amilcar Martins, of the Faculty of Medicine of Minas Gerais, former director of the Instituto Oswaldo Cruz. Description was refrained from because of their imperfect condition in the hope that better specimens would eventually be collected. Our younger colleague, Mr. Werner Bokermann, forestalled this event by describing the oldest specimen. It is only to be regretted that since this most unusual frog was first collected by the prominent botanist F. C. Hoehne, who was an excellent field naturalist, the species should not have been dedicated to him, and another opportunity awaited to manifest deserved appreciation for the help received by the young naturalist from Commander Alvarenga of the Brazilian Air Force; he is also a very good collector but did not find this particular tree frog. A more characteristic name such as *pollicata* or *pentadactyla* would have been most appropriate.

DIAGNOSTIC CHARACTERS. This frog is aberrant from the usual generic characters of *Hyla*. Rudiment of pollex, or first metacarpal, of the male so conspicuous as to be practically equivalent to the absent first digit; stout at the base, curved, pointed at the tip; devoid of an intercalary cartilage. Head very short and high; snout short, bulldog-like, truncate between the nostrils. Eyes oblique. Tongue extensively free behind. Sacral diapophyses relatively narrow.

TYPE AND TYPE LOCALITY. The holotype, DZSP, n. 1680, presumably male, was collected January 1921, by F. C. Hoehne at Santa Barbara, not far from Belo Horizonte, Minas Gerais. The specimens from the Amilcar Martins Collection were obtained in the Serra do Cipó, near Alto do Palácio, between Belo Horizonte and Ferros, in *cerrado* (arborescent scrub formation), at approximately 1350 m altitude.

DESCRIPTION. Size very large: 76–80 mm from snout to vent. Build heavy, extremely robust. Body massive. Hindlimb long, the adpressed tibiotarsal articulation reaching from near the nostril to beyond the tip of the snout. Head very short, wide and high; one-fifth to one-third wider than long. Snout very short, truncate between the nostrils, sloping very slightly backward to the opening of the mouth. Canthus rostralis very short, truncate at the nostrils, which mark the upper extremity of the snout. Loreal region very high, slightly grooved between nostril and eye. Mouth opening rounded, shallow; jaws well marked, oblique. Interorbital space equal to or slightly wider than the internarial space. Eyes large, double their distance from the nostrils, directed obliquely forward. Tympanum very distinct, its horizontal diameter equal to half the diameter of the eye. Tongue short, fleshy, very wide, extensively free behind. Vomerine teeth in two short, horizontal patches, or in somewhat narrower, slightly arched ones, between and slightly beyond the choanae. Forearms robust. Pollex rudiment of male as impressive as in *Leptodactylus pentadactylus*. Fingers robust, with short, wide disks, about one-half the diameter of the tympanum. Pollex rudiment containing a large metacarpal, ending in a sharp point but devoid of intercalary cartilage. A short web between the lateral fingers. Toes webbed to the disks on the outer side of the second, third, and on the fifth, but web reduced to a fringe on the inner side of the second and third, and reaching only to the penultimate articulation on the fourth toe. Inner metatarsal tubercle large, elongate. A ridge of pustules from the outer digit along the forearm and the tarsus, respectively, to elbow and knee. A pronounced peritympanic ridge. Disseminated pustules, thicker and more plentiful on the head, less numerous on the back and the dorsal aspect of the limbs; in the last two often light in color and occupying the center of the spots. Belly and midventral aspect of the thigh slightly granular. A fold under the gula in the better preserved specimens. Inside of limbs and their dorsal concealed surfaces perfectly smooth.

VARIATION. The series is too short for an accurate study of variability. The main difference lies in the fact that some specimens have very robust vomerine teeth in two very short, almost straight patches, and others in more elongate, oblique, thinner ones. Pollex slightly smaller in a good smaller specimen ( ♀ ?) 69 mm long; button-like in juveniles, 44 and 38 mm snout to vent.

COLOR AND PATTERN. Unfortunately not seen alive as yet. In his second publication, Bokermann mentions that the iris is yellow with intense black vermiculation. Bones not green. Dead specimens are dark brown, with a blotchy marbling in a darker tone than the background on the dorsal surface and a light glandule in the center of the blotches, which are slightly stellate. Dark color somewhat extensive to the sides. Dark crossbars on the permanently visible dorsal surface of limbs more regular in some than in others, extending to the fourth finger, the fifth toe and a longitudinal section of the fourth toe, which are visible in repose. Concealed surfaces of limbs more purplish. Underside immaculate, except for a heavy stippling on the very short and wide gula similar to the stellate spots of the dorsal aspect; the rest more olivaceous than the back; subarticular tubercles and webs somewhat gray.

SECONDARY SEX CHARACTERS. Prepollex of male curved very robust. Forearms robust.

This is apparently a very sluggish frog, which is not surprising considering its build. Its appearance is very similar to stones covered with lichens (fide Bokermann).

KNOWN DISTRIBUTION. So far only the type locality Santa Barbara and Serra do Cipó between Belo Horizonte and Ferros in the highlands of Minas Gerais. Cerrado country between 19–20° S. and 43–44° W. Gr., well over 1000 m above sea level.

AFFINITIES. Devoid of affinities with the very large Brazilian species of *Hyla*; perhaps somewhat akin to the Mexican and Central American forms of *Plectrohyla* Brocchi.

## *Hyla pseudopseudis pseudopseudis* Miranda Ribeiro, 1937

MIRANDA RIBEIRO, A. 1937. Alguns batrachios novos das collecções do Museu Nacional. *O Campo*, pp. 66–69, 5 figs. *H. pseudopseudis*: 68.

This is one of the relatively few species described from the state of Goiás. It is very unlike the usual Neotropical kinds of *Hyla*, except for an evidently closely related form.

DIAGNOSTIC CHARACTERS. The robust, relatively short build, the long legs, oblique eyes and small disks; the general resemblance in habit to more aquatic genera; the shagreened skin of the dorsal surface and the blotches disseminated on it without forming a pattern. Male with a sharp prepollex.

TYPES AND TYPE LOCALITY. Miranda Ribeiro had three specimens, two adult females, and a third specimen, probably also female, opened in front so as to examine the sternum. They were bought from J. Blaser, who got them at Veadeiros, state of Goiás; MNR nos. 579, type and paratype; 579A, the opened specimen.

DESCRIPTION. Female type and paratype 46 mm in the original description, now both 44 mm snout to vent. Body short, elongate, ellipsoid in shape, with rounded snout and postsacral region. Hindlimb, thin, long, the tibiotarsal articulation reaching the nostril (holotype) or not quite reaching it (paratype) when adpressed. Femur and tibia almost equal in length. Head massive as long as wide. Snout oval from above, truncate between the nostrils, sloping only very slightly to the mouth opening in profile. Canthus rostralis blunt and curved. Loreal region slightly concave between the nostril and the eye. Nostril subcanthal, rather small, round, not terminal. Eye oblique, in alignment with the canthus, probably prominent in life; its horizontal diameter longer than the distance from its anterior corner to the nostril, slightly shorter than the distance to the tip of the snout. Tympanum very distinct, approximately one-half the diameter of the eye. Interorbital space slightly wider than the internarial space. Patches of vomerine teeth slightly oblique, parallel to and behind the inner edge of the choanae. Tongue large, oval, slightly emarginate, and only slightly free behind. A rudiment of web between the lateral fingers. Disks moderate, smaller than the tympanum. An elongate callosity (rudiment of pollex) outside the first; a bifid tubercle under the third and fourth fingers, a number of palmar tubercles. Toes about two-thirds webbed, the web forming a fringe on the inner side of the first toe and the inner distal parts of the second, third, and both sides of the fourth, on the latter from the antepenultimate tubercle; wide to below the disk on the outer side of the second and third and on the fifth. An elongate inner and a small round outer metatarsal tubercle. Disks small. Skin of dorsal surface distinctly shagreened. Throat, chest, belly, and midventral aspect of thigh granular; otherwise limbs smooth. A glandular ridge on the forearm from the fourth finger to the elbow; similar ridges on the tarsus. A distinct supratympanic ridge; perianal region glandular. No distinct fold of skin appears at the base of the throat in the types.

MEASUREMENTS (mm). Female type and paratype both 44 snout to vent. Hindlimb 82 and 79, femur 24, tibia 25 and 24, tarsus 15 and 14, foot 18 and 16. Head length to width 17:17 and 16:16. Tympanum 3, eye 6, eye-nostril 4, interorbital space 5, internarial space 4.

SECONDARY SEX CHARACTERS. The type and paratype have an elongate callosity but no sharp prick in the region of the prepollex. The paratype is very much distended by eggs and slightly constricted in front. The underside is devoid of pigment in both.

Three males (MNR 30001) were collected in the same state but in the county of Amaro Leite by A. L. Carvalho. Two are adult and respectively 50 and 49 mm from snout to vent; one has greatly enlarged forearms. The gula of the larger is dark and that of the second shows faded round spots of pigment in the center and on the edges. The third is smaller, 45 mm long and seems subadult. There are some spots on its gula, but the forearms are not enlarged nor are the prepollices sharp. The patches of vomerine teeth seem slightly shorter than in the female types.

COLOR AND PATTERN. Unfortunately none of the specimens were seen alive by the original author or by me. They are now brown above, an immaculate light buff beneath. The preserved female types are lighter than the males.

There are blotches, not a regular pattern, on the dorsal aspect. The female types show only large relatively plain, more or less blunt, dark blotches on the head and body and short, blunt, very well-delimited squarish bars on the permanently visible dorsal aspect of the limbs; the dorsal stripes of the thigh concealed in repose are plain, quite dark in one, less dark in the other.

In the males from Amaro Leite the blotches are somewhat stellate with irregular prolongations reminiscent of nerve cells or amoebae with pseudopodia. The prolongations may meet and coalesce and are present on the limbs as well as on the head and trunk. In one they are limited to the parts visible in repose; in the second they invade the concealed parts slightly, and in the third and smallest one more extensively so. This is probably not a variation due to sex, as in a very closely related form from Minas Gerais the pattern is also stellate. Dead specimens olivaceous mottled in black, "like *Pseudis mantidactyla*. The outer aspect of this animal suggested the name under which I described it," says Miranda Ribeiro.

No other data are available on *H. p. pseudopseudis*, but it probably has similar habits to those of *H. p. saxicola*.

Mr. Antenor Leitão de Carvalho collected a large male *Hyla* 64 mm long, with very accentuated secondary sex characters on the Chapada dos Veadeiros near the type locality of *Hyla p. pseudopseudis*. He put it to that species to which it shows marked morphological similarity. In size it is, however, much larger. The forearms are extremely robust, and the prepollex is large, curved, and sharp. The throat is slightly dark. The glandular ridge on the forearm is also very marked and in part composed of double rows of glandules. The ridges on the tarsus are also very marked. The tympanum is rather small. This specimen is rather melanistic. The blotches on the body are somewhat obscured, but there is a very definite complex of irregular and ornate blotches and tapestry-like bars on the dorsal aspect of the limbs. It is evidently an unusually large male, perhaps belonging to a divergent population or race of *H. pseudopseudis*.

MEASUREMENTS (mm). Snout to vent 64. Hindlimb 107: femur 30, tibia 30, tarsus 20, foot 27. Head length 25, width 24. Tympanum 4, eye 8, eye-nostril 5, eye-snout 10. Interorbital space 8, internarial space 6.

## *Hyla pseudopseudis saxicola* Bokermann, 1964

BOKERMANN, W. C. A. 1964. Dos nuevas especies de *Hyla* de Minas Gerais y notas sobre *Hyla alvarengai* Bok. *Neotropica* 10(32):67–76. *Hyla saxicola:* 71–75, figs. 10–15.

Bokermann described a tree frog under the name *Hyla saxicola,* which he concedes to be very similar to *Hyla pseudopseudis* Miranda Ribeiro. In fact, it is so similar that it seems better to consider it as a subspecies of Miranda Ribeiro's form. The slight differences and the gaps in the known distribution prevent me from synonymising it outright.

TYPES AND TYPE LOCALITY. The type locality of *H. saxicola* is the Serra do Cipó, in the county of Jaboticatubas, state of Minas Gerais. The male holotype WCAB 14734; female allotype 14745, two female paratypes 14743–44 and nine male paratypes 14735–42 and 14945 were collected by Bokermann, A. Machado, and J. Evangelista.

DIFFERENCES. The specimens sent to the National Museum by Bokermann are, as usual, chosen among his lesser paratypes (WCAB 14737 and 14743). He mentions differences of pattern, especially on the dorsal aspect of the limbs, a smaller tympanum and a more rounded head. The only really evident distinction resides in the size of the tympanum. The pattern on the limbs of *H. pseudopseudis* seems variable even in Goiás. Bokermann's figure 13 of his holotype is extremely like the co-types of Miranda Ribeiro. The paratypes sent to Rio are like his figure 14. These specimens are gray instead of brown. The dark spots on the dorsal surface of the head and trunk are so much narrowed and anastomosed that they form a more or less dendritic network. The larger paratype 14737, shows light and dark bars on the thighs like those of the types of *H. pseudopseudis* and dark concealed portions also like theirs. In the smaller one the spots on the dorsal aspect of the limbs are stellate, occupying alternate areas on the two edges like in the males from Goiás. The white streak over the anus is present but they do not have the white spot on the tibiotarsal articulation mentioned for the holotype. The gula of the larger specimens is fuscous. The prepollex is palpable in both specimens but not well-developed in either of them. They are probably subadult. Bokermann mentions the prepollex of his large specimens and gives a drawing of

the hand that also fits *H. p. pseudopseudis.* He also mentions that the bones are green. This is an important point that needs to be checked in *H. p. pseudopseudis* and eventually in the other members of the group of saxicolous sharp-darted *Plectrohyla*-like forms.

MEASUREMENTS (mm). The size is similar or slightly smaller, Holotype: male 43; paratype male 14742: 45; allotype: female 40; paratype female 14744: 43 snout to vent.

HABITS. The most interesting part of Bokermann's description is his note on the biotope and behavior of *H. saxicola.* All his males were caught at night, sitting on stones in the bed of small mountain streams where the spray hit them. He mentions the procryptic coloration that blended with the background. He also mentions the extremely distended vocal sac, visible from a distance. The singers were isolated and the call very loud. At the slightest disturbance they leapt into the water and hid under stones. This behavior is a hylid counterpart of the behavior of the diurnal leptodactyloid genus *Elosia,* which also has a penetrating voice and does not sing in chorus. Nor should it be expected to do so considering the noise of the rushing water. Bokermann recorded the voice, which needs to be compared with that of *H. p. pseudopseudis,* alas not available as yet.

A few topotypes, most of them in a rather poor condition are present in the Lutz Collection, to which they were presented by Prof. Amilcar Martins. The best one agrees with Bokermann's description and with that of Miranda Ribeiro for the nominate form.

It is 48 mm long and the hindlimb 80 mm. It does not have distinct sex characters. There is also a rather large female specimen (55 mm long). It is very much like the types of *Hyla p. saxicola* but paler and larger. This specimen is somewhat soft and macerated and may have faded though that is not sure. The head is rather flat; the patches of vomerine teeth and the tongue are like those of *H. p. saxicola.* The hindlimb is, however, very short; the tibiotarsal articulation does not reach beyond the eye, though the specimen is very soft. The pattern is similar and quite stellate but the spots are completely separated from each other and stand out from a very pale background. The pattern over most of the permanently visible parts of the dorsal aspect of the limbs is similar to that of the male *H. p. pseudopseudis* and of the *H. p. saxicola* paratypes; on the thigh it is substituted by perpendicular, rather irregular bars that cut across both visible and concealed parts. On the flanks there are similar bars.

My one visit to the type locality of *saxicola* and *Hyla alvarengai* was undertaken with Dr. Amilcar Martins, who later conducted Bokermann's tour. It was made under extremely unfavorable conditions in very cold weather during several days streaming rain. Only a few individuals were seen, hiding deep in the crevices of the stone walls that are a feature of the landscape. The preserved specimens given me were also rather poor for description. The terrain is rocky and quite open; there is very little vegetation and that rather thin and sparse scrub. The water table overflows part of the ground. The tree frogs there have evidently become adapted to alternating between stone crevices on land and sitting on stones in the beds of the little streams. *Hyla pseudopseudis* from Goiás may be as saxicolous as the ones from Minas Gerais. In this, as in the well-developed pollex rudiment, *Hyla alvarangai, pseudopseudis, martinisi,* and *saxicola* show affinity with *Hyla circumdata* Cope, especially with the large dark specimens. *Hyla circumdata* is also somewhat saxicolous. It likes the vicinity of running water and of stony brooks.

# 2. Species with Undulated Glandular Outline

## Hyla pardalis Spix, 1824

SPIX, J. B. von. 1824. *Animalia nova sive species novae testudinum et ranarum quas in itinere per Brasiliam, annis 1817–20, collegit et descripsit.* Atlas, pp. 34–35, tab. VIII, fig. 3.

BURMEISTER, C. H. C. 1856. *Erläuterungen zur Fauna Brasiliens. Hyla corticalis*: 95, pl. 30, figs. 7–12. *Hyla (Centrotelma) lundii*: 101, pl. 31, fig. 8.

REINHARDT, J., and LÜTKEN, C. F. 1862. Bidrag til Kundskab om Brasiliens Padder og Krybdyr. *Vid. Medd. Naturh. Foren.* (Copenhagen) 3 (10–15). *Hyla pustulosa*: 192.

DISCOVERY. *Hyla paradalis* was described by Spix from the state of Rio de Janeiro without mention of a type locality. A good Latin diagnosis and a fairly good figure were published by him (1824), but they did not prevent redescription of the frog. The first time it was described by Burmeister from Nova Friburgo, in the same state, under the name of *Hyla corticalis*, which would have been a very good name. The second time the same author redescribed it as *Hyla lundii* on a preserved specimen from Lagoa Santa, near Belo Horizonte in the state of Minas Gerais. Reinhardt and Lütken (1862) redescribed it a third time, from the same place, under the name of *Hyla pustulosa*. Their type was not full grown. Later Lütken himself put a label of *Hyla pardalis* to their type specimen. A. Lutz soon reached the conclusion that all these names were conspecific, and this view was adopted by Dr. Doris M. Cochran (1955).

TYPE. When the Second World War broke out, the Spix types of frogs were in the Zoological Collection of the state of Bavaria, in Munich. Lorenz Müller, the curator, suggested putting them into a safe vault, but the authorities refused on the plea that bombardment of Germany by the allies was not possible; consequently, he put them into the deepest cellar of a private house. Unfortunately, the place was hit and most of the Hylid types were buried under the rubble of the upper cellar, which fell in on the lower one, though the *Bufo*, which were on the sides of the upper one, were spared. *Hyla pardalis* is, however, a good species with distinctive characters.

DIAGNOSTIC CHARACTERS. Living or well-preserved specimens have an undulating or scalloped glandular outline, which follows the contours of the body in repose. The dorsal color is similar to tree bark or to lichen. The flanks and webs are rosy and the lower aspect of the hands and feet and the long bones sea-green. The build is plump. Dead specimens can be differentiated from the other tree frogs of the same size, with oval head, rounded snout, stiletto-like rudiment of the pollex ( ♂ ), vertical stripes on the flanks and full webs by the glandular scalloped outline of the body in repose.

DESCRIPTION. Size: adult females, with eggs, 58–75 mm, mostly 70 mm; nuptial males 48–63, often 60 mm from snout to vent. Build robust, form flat; axillary region as wide as the greatest width of the head. Leg rather long, the adpressed tibiotarsal articulation generally reaching beyond the eye, almost to the nostril. Head slightly broader than long, rather straight behind the eye. Snout oval, with blunt canthus rostralis, slightly curved toward the nostrils, whence the snout slopes down to the mouth; loreal region slightly concave in front of the eyes. Interorbital space depressed, a little wider than the upper eyelid or of the same width. Eye large, prominent, longer than the distance from its anterior corner to the nostril. Tympanum oval, more than half the width of the eye. Tongue oval, rounded, entire or slightly emarginate, hardly free behind. Vomerine teeth in two arches, behind the choanae, more or less parallel to their inner rim. Hands, feet and disks large. Webs quite full on hand and foot, except between the first and second fingers and for a fringe on the last articulation of the third finger and fourth toe; outline of webs rather straight. A distinct rudiment of the pollex. An elongate, conspicuous, inner metatarsal tubercle. Dorsal skin glandular; a glandular outline limiting the body in repose, composed of the outer border of the tarsus, from a short tubercle on the heel to the fifth toe, where it is smooth; a similar border on the forearm, with a small tubercle at the elbow; a glandular fold above and beyond the tympanum, with small pustules; a bilateral glandular border below the anus; in some specimens, a few glandules on the sides of the body, which is left exposed between the adpressed forearm and tarsus when the frog is at rest. Ventral aspect of thigh and belly granular.

VARIATION. The length of the legs varies greatly; when adpressed, the tibiotarsal articulation may reach any point from the anterior corner of the eye to beyond the snout, though it mostly reaches beyond the eye and near the nostril; this individual difference seems independent of size or sex.

SECONDARY SEX CHARACTERS. Male: rudiment of the pollex generally curved outwards ending in a visible or palpable dart; vocal sac large, much folded, sometimes forming a square bib under the mouth; gula dark; forearms robust. Female: gula smooth, light, or slightly pigmented near the border of the mouth. Tongue large, more rounded, thicker, and longitudinally grooved; vomerine teeth more robust. Tympanum large. The last three differences seem correlated with the larger size.

SIZE. Twenty-seven females were measured. The two smallest are 61 and 63 mm long, the two largest 75 mm, the rest range from 65–71 mm, with a third of them 70 mm from snout to vent. Out of eighty males, fifty are 60 mm long, sixteen range from 54–59 mm, and ten from 61–65 mm; the three largest reach 66, 67, and 69 mm; one very small male is only 48 mm long from snout to vent. The hindlimb is variable in length; in some individuals it is proportionate to the body, in others not.

COLOR. *Hyla pardalis* ranges from very pale to quite dark. Pale individuals may be gray or drab, dark ones a deep or a dusky brown. Occasionally the dorsal color shows a greenish tint. The color of the permanently visible dorsal aspect of the limbs may be somewhat paler than the back. The upper parts of the thigh, concealed in repose, its ventral aspect and the inner parts of limbs, also concealed, are more or less pink; the color is deeper, sometimes almost coral, on the upper parts of the thigh, paler on the ventral and inner surfaces and especially so on the webs of hand and foot. The long bones and the phalanges of the digits are green and may appear bluish by translucency. The hypochondria may have a light glaucous blue tint. Four large females from different places have light rounded areas devoid of pigment on the dorsal surface. In one of them they were a rosy orange in life.

PATTERN. The wavy, glandular border of the body in repose, the coloring and pattern and the granular aspect of the dorsal surface produce a disruptive effect, making *Hyla pardalis* rather similar to a patch of lichen or to tree bark, as expressed in the name *Hyla corticalis* proposed by Burmeister. While describing the back, Spix says: "irregulariter fusco-marmoratum, granulis nonnullis obsitum." Some individuals are marbled above, in others there are so many irregular lines on the dorsal aspect that it looks as if the whole back had been scribbled on.

Some individuals are quite plain and show only very indistinct marks. Besides the marbling and scribbling, many others have a large dark patch over most of the dorsal surface or a large spot on the middle of the back. At its most handsome, the central patch is elongate and narrow in front, wide and hollowed out to each side behind. Burmeister calls this the lily form, presumably from the heraldic fleur-de-lis. It is the pattern shown in his figure of the type of *Hyla lundii*. The spot may also be more uniform in width but extremely irregular in outline and shape, and it may form prongs between the eyes and over the sacral region. Additional dark patches may be present on the head. Now and then the spot is fenestrated in the middle, but this is less common than in *Hyla crepitans*.

The dorsal, permanently visible, parts of the limbs may also be marbled or show crossbars above, which reach the tip of the outer digits but do not cover the inner ones and are generally alternatively wide and narrow. The flanks and the concealed upper parts of the thighs have a pattern of irregular, often double, gray stripes. In a number of individuals they are lacking in the posterior upper portion of the thigh. In very good specimens two rather angular parallel stippled stripes are visible to each side of the anus, in front of the glandular outline.

VOICE AND HABITS. *Hyla pardalis* calls in single, low, gruff notes: *wank*. The males may be far apart or closer together; they often sit low, near the ground, in marshy fields and meadows or at the edges of shallow ditches with semi-aquatic vegetation and a generally sluggish current. They also climb. Our largest female was caught sitting on one of the posts of the gate to my brother's house in Teresópolis. Burmeister mentions that his attention was called to the type of *Hyla corticalis* by a little boy; he himself had some difficulty in spotting it. The frog was sitting high up on a tree and it blended with the color of the bark.

*Hyla pardalis* males fight among themselves in the same manner as those of *Hyla faber*. I suspected this, but it was first seen by my brother, Prof. Gualter A. Lutz, who called my attention to a pair thus engaged, in the same ditch in which the nests had been discovered some months earlier.

NESTS. *Hyla pardalis* builds clay nests, similar to, though smaller and slightly less perfect than those of *Hyla faber*. These nests were discovered by us during the first days of January 1960, at Teresópolis in the Organ Mountains of the state of Rio de Janeiro. First a male was seen calling in a depression on the bank of a shallow ditch, on January 1, 1960. Next morning a small oval cavity with a slightly pushed-up wall containing water was found in the same place. The male returned to this cavity, worked on it, and sang there. On January 5 a clutch of eggs was found floating in it. Subsequently many other nests were found and a couple were observed mating so that there is no longer any doubt as to the habit. The most perfect nest was 18 x 24 cm outside, 14 x 18 cm inside, and the cavity was 2 cm deep; it also had a rampart of 2 cm. The nests are slightly funnel-shaped, and the wall is rather roughly finished. The particular ditch, one of hundreds of similar ones, carrying off the water that seeps out of gardens, is subject to great changes of regime during violent storms and deluges of rain, in summer, or, alternatively, to drying, during periods of intense heat and drought. During the rest of the year they also have to endure periodic weeding, opening up and being used as a dumping ground. The shallow nests seem more often in danger of drying than those of *Hyla faber*. They are also apt to be covered or even to have their contents washed away. Nevertheless, the established population continues to live and to breed there. Young metamorphosing specimens were obtained in the deeper and quieter reaches overgrown by *Jussiaea* and other aquatic plants (B. Lutz, 1960).

JUVENILES. The juveniles of *Hyla pardalis* are very deceptive, as they have a quite different livery from that of the adults. When they have left the water they are a very light gray, slightly greenish, near putty color. A number of large dark brownish red or maroon dots soon develop all over the dorsal surface and have an oily look. The concealed aspect of the limbs and webs are a burnt orange. Such specimens were often seen by Prof. A. Lutz and me, first in the Serra da Bocaina, then in Petrópolis. Lutz had a watercolor painted and for reference called them *Hyla rubropunctata*, but he refrained from publishing as he strongly suspected that they were the young of a larger species. A visit to Copenhagen in 1952 showed me that *H. punctatissima* Reinhardt and Lütken is the same; the types still showed the faded oily dots.

The young from Teresópolis were kept alive long enough to show that they were the juveniles of *Hyla pardalis*, so that *H. punctatissima* becomes synonymous with it. After some weeks a dark shadow began to appear on the dorsal surface; at first it was evanescent but later it no longer disappeared and assumed the characters of the rather elusive dark blotches on the dorsal surface of adult *Hyla pardalis*. In the beginning the red-brown spots concurred with the obscure blotches, but gradually the juvenile characters were overlapped and obliterated by the adult livery. Even in these, the skin looks rather oily. Meanwhile, the visible ventral aspect of the limbs becomes a dull yellow-orange up to the scalloped glandular edges, whereas the concealed inner aspect of the limbs and the upper hind part of the thighs and hypochondria become a dull green.

KNOWN DISTRIBUTION. The specimens of *H. pardalis* seen by us come from the states of São Paulo, Rio de Janeiro, Espirito Santo, Minas Gerais, and Goiás. They suggest that this species likes open country of a certain altitude. The known distribution places it on the Brazilian Plateau. In some of the places in the state of Rio it approaches the escarpment. It is one of the species that do not occur in the former Federal District, now called state of Guanabara.

AFFINITIES. Morphologically, *Hyla pardalis* comes near to *Hyla crepitans* and shares the characters of the group of species to which they belong. It differs from the others by the full webbing of the lateral fingers, wavy glandular outline, coloring, and distribution. It may serve as a transition to *Hyla langsdorffii*, which is also similar to bark or lichen but is very large and has shorter webs on the fingers and a very distinctive complex anal pattern. *H. pardalis* could perhaps be included in the group of tree frogs for which Tschudi proposed the name *Lophopus*, but the species of that group are smaller, have a quite short snout and an axillary web or patagium connecting the trunk with the arm.

## *Hyla langsdorffii* Duméril & Bibron, 1841

DUMÉRIL, A. M. C., and BIBRON, G. 1841. *Erpétologie générale ou histoire naturelle des reptiles*, 8:557–558.

This very large and showy tree frog was discovered by N. Langsdorff, who was the Russian consul in Brazil and keenly interested in natural history, and who traveled up the Paraguay River and the Amazonas. The type locality of *H. langsdorffii* must, however, not have been far distant from his country place at the foot of the Serra da Estrela, on the way to Petrópolis, in the state of Rio de Janeiro.

Günther (1868) and Boulenger (1882) mention *H. langsdorffii* in their editions of the catalogue of the frogs in the British Museum, but Boulenger rightly puts the Günther specimen to the synonymy of *Hyla maxima*, which is very different and has quite another distribution.

DIAGNOSTIC CHARACTERS. A unique pattern around and below the anus. It consists of an irregular, somewhat angular, transversal dark spot, followed by a pair of small lateral areas containing a dark network surrounding minute white spots; they are separated by a longitudinal groove and end in a pair of thick, white, glandular subanal flaps. Similar white, glandular ridges are present on the forearm and tarsus, from the elbow and heel to the tip of the outer digits and at the corners of the upper jaw behind the mouth. They complete the scalloped outline of the bark-like upper surface that remains visible in repose. Dorsal aspect beset with scattered, minute conical tubercles.

DESCRIPTION. Size very large. Male 67–77 mm or more, largest female seen 99 mm from snout to vent. Build elongate, relatively slender, tapering at and beyond the sacrum. Leg long, the tibiotarsal articulation reaching either the tip of the snout or near it when adpressed. Head flat; snout forming an obtuse angle, rounded at the tip, truncate between the nostrils; tympanic area and posterior edges of head straight, vertical. Outline from beneath elongate, distinctly truncate. Canthus rostralis thick, blunt, curved above the back of the nostrils. Crown concave, limited by the canthi and the two prominent ridges formed by the border of the frontparietals, which unite on the occiput. Loreal region concave, the upper jaw flaring under it. Nostrils subcanthal, oblique, with slightly raised rim. Eye prominent, its longest diameter equal to the distance from its posterior rim to the nostril. Tympanum large, round, from one-half to two-thirds the diameter of the eye. Interorbital space much wider than the internarial space. Tongue large, flat, thin, hardly free behind, with concave posterior rim; in some specimens longitudinally grooved. Vomerine teeth forming two short, heavy, more or less widely separated arches, between the choanae, reaching their posterior rim. Two roughly triangular grooves on the palate, to the sides of the parasphenoid. Hands and feet big with very large disks. A marked elongate tubercle or pollex rudiment at the base of the first finger; last subarticular tubercle on the fourth finger double or enlarged; a large, pointed, elongate, inner and a small, rounded, outer metatarsal tubercle. Web of hand short between the first and second fingers, reaching the last articulation on the second and fourth, the penultimate on the third, but continuing as a fringe to the base of the disk. Web on the foot reaching the disk on all the toes except the fourth, on which the last part is narrowed to a fringe. Webs deeply emarginate on both hands and feet. Skin of the dorsal surface beset with scattered conic tubercles, especially on the edges of the canthi, the upper jaw, and the sides of the head beyond the mouth opening. Outer edge of forearm and tarsus limited by a glandular white ridge from the elbow and heel to the tip of the outer digit; a glandular ridge above and behind the tympanum; large glandular flaps below the anus; taken altogether they form a scalloped outline of the body in repose. Most of the concealed upper parts of the sides, of the flanks and thighs and lower surface of the other limb segments smooth. Posterior part of the abdomen and ventral aspect of the thigh granular as if paved; some of the glandules larger, standing out from the rest; chest less granular; gula with scatttered tubercles. A few conspicuous tubercles on the heel; in one large female also at the shoulder and on the elbow.

COLOR AND PATTERN. Permanently visible upper parts like tree bark covered with lichens or moss and outlined by a glandular border that follows the contours of the frog. Iris pale gold with very narrow black lines, mostly centripetal. Tympanum a warm shade of brown, conspicuous. Dorsal aspect olivaceous brown, or greenish gray with an ill-defined pattern in darker shades. In some individuals a very roughly W-shaped interocular spot, which may be somewhat prolonged backward and is generally irregular and fenestrated. It may be followed by a similar spot between the shoulders or toward the sacrum. A transverse, also irregular and fenestrated spot before the anus is more constant. Other individuals do not show separate interocular and sacral spots but a large irregular fenestrated reticulum that covers most of the back. The light conic tubercles or glandules are caught in the spots or meshes and stand out from the dark pigment. A series of crossbars, similar in color to the dark parts of the back are present on all the limb segments visible in repose. Their width and shape varies,

sometimes becoming anteriorly concave. Glandular outline of the dorsal aspect brilliant white and scalloped, comprising the sides of the head, the outer edge of the forearm and fourth finger and of the tarsus and fifth toe; especially conspicuous in the perianal region, because of the large white flaps and the black reticulation on the lateral areas in front of them; some larger glandules on the heel; in one very large specimen also on the elbow and the shoulders. Belly and ventral aspect of thigh ochraceous to tawny orange, very glandular as if paved, some glandules larger and lighter standing out from the rest. Chest less glandular, gula with scattered glandules, both off-white or a very pale gray-blue. Concealed aspects of the limbs, upper parts of thigh, inside and ventral aspect of the other limb segments, most of the sides of the body and the flanks blue-gray, the color most intense on the fleshy ventral aspect of the disks. Long bones, articulations and phalanges somewhat glaucous through translucency. Inside of mouth pale sea-green.

VOICE. Joaquim Venancio kept a male alive for some time in a vivarium. He compares the call to the beating together of the palms of interlaced hands or to the distant rattle of a machine gun. Vocal sacs lateral, double, white, much pleated.

BEHAVIOR. *Hyla langsdorffii* is not common in collections and seems to be seldom obtained. I have seen altogether sixteen specimens, several of them alive. It is probably very retiring and may spend much time aloft. Vizotto caught one in a bromeliad at Itanhaen on the coast of São Paulo; another was caught by Aristoteles de Araujo e Silva on a banana plant at Guaratiba in the state of Guanabara. A third, from the Brazilian National Park at Iguassú, was detected in my presence while it was calling in a tree. I have kept the female from Itanhaen alive for three years. She is very quiet and does not move about much in the vivarium.

KNOWN RANGE. All our specimens, except the one from Iguassú, were taken on the coastal lowlands mostly in the states of Rio de Janeiro, Guanabara, and São Paulo, one of them in southern Bahia. It is probable that a sketch of a frog from Itapeva made in colored pencils by Professor Rudolf Gliesch of Porto Alegre belongs to the same species; this would extend the range to the coast of northern Rio Grande do Sul. The one exception to the Atlantic distribution is the Iguassú specimen, as the park is located on the frontier of Brazil with Paraguay and Argentina.

AFFINITIES. The nearest Brazilian species may be *Hyla pardalis* Spix, which has a partly overlapping geographical range but is much smaller and montane. It has the scalloped outline but lacks the anal pattern and the concealed surface may be suffused with a pink tint.

Two other South American tree frogs seem similar to it: *Hyla tuberculosa* Boulenger from Ecuador and *Hyla wavrini* Parker from Venezuela. The similarity between them raises interesting evolutionary problems. Similar forms seem to occur in Central America.

One more point deserves to be mentioned: the presence of frontoparietal carinae. This led Cope to put *Hyla langsdorffii* to the genus *Osteocephalus*. They are also present in other large South American species of Hyla without concrescent skin and bone on the head, like *Hyla l. leprieuri*, *Hyla l. brittoi*, and *Hyla taurina*, which have also been placed in *Osteocephalus*; they may all belong to that genus.

# 3. Species with Pattern on the Transparent Part of the Lower Eyelid

*Hyla boans* (Linnaeus), 1758

> LINNAEUS, C. 1758. *Systema Naturae.* 10th edition, 1:213.
>
> LAURENTI, J. N. 1768. *Specimen medicum, exhibens synopsin reptilium emendatum cum experimentis circa venena et antidota Reptilium Austriacorum.* 214 pp., 5 pls.
>
> ANDERSSON, L. G. 1900. Catalogue of Linnean type-specimens. *Bib. Svenska Vet-Akad. Handl.* 26(1):1–20.

*Hyla boans* has been known for a long time, which is not surprising considering its great size. Boulenger considers *Rana virginiana exquisitissima* Seba, 1734, as identical with *Hyla maxima*; the valid trivial name was until recently that given by Laurenti, although he also placed it in the wrong genus, *Rana*. Now it seems that Linnaeus had already named it *R. boans*. Schneider (1799) mentions it under the name of *Calamita maxima*. Daudin (1803) rightly places it in the genus *Hyla* because of the large disks, but unfortunately he calls it *Hyla palmata*. This name is erroneously applied in part to *Hyla faber* by Duméril and Bibron (1843). Cope (1867) proposes a new generic name, *Cinclidium* for this *Hyla* because of the pattern of golden arabesques on the transparent part of the lower eyelid. This is a good character that is also found in the smaller species *Hyla geo-graphica* Spix. B. Lutz (1963) revives it as a character of the group.

DIAGNOSTIC CHARACTERS. The network of golden arabesques on the transparent part of the lower eyelid plus the great size and the range. Very full webs on hands and feet: "pedibus anterioris posterioribusque palmatis," fide Lacepède. (*Synopsis methodica quadrupedum oviparorum*).

DESCRIPTION. Size very large, 80–120 mm snout to vent. Build robust. Legs long, the adpressed tibiotarsal articulation reaching the nostril. Head massive, wider than the body, a little broader than long, widest at the tympanum, slightly constricted behind. Body elongate, tapering slightly. Snout obtusely triangular. Loreal region oblique, concave in front of the eye. A lozenge-shaped depression on the vertex, limited anteriorly by the angular canthi rostralis, posteriorly by the less sharp edge of the frontoparietals. Eye large, prominent. Tympanum very conspicuous, almost as wide as the eye. Interorbital space much wider than the upper eyelid and the internarial space. Tongue large, round, entire, almost connate. Patches of vomerine teeth angular, forming an open M-like figure, between and beyond the choanae. Lateral fingers completely webbed, except for the fringed last articulation of the third. Toes entirely webbed. A very distinct pollex rudiment. An elongate inner metatarsal tubercle. Skin of dorsal aspect finely shagreened, sides somewhat granular; belly and midventral aspect of thigh more coarsely so, the granulations smaller toward the chest. Margin of lower jaw, forearm and tarsus, and perianal region glandular; a short triangular appendage on the heel.

VARIATION. The specimens from Jacaréacanga on the Tapajós River collected by Dr. Helmut Sick and those from the lower Tapajós are relatively small. Some individuals have an oval tongue narrower than usual. This is the case in a small series from Jacaré, on the River Xingú, and of some but not all the specimens from the lower Kuluene. Those from Jacaré also have a narrow head. The skin is rougher in all the southern specimens.

SECONDARY SEX CHARACTERS. Differences between the sexes are not very marked. The tip of the pollex rudiment of the male is less evident than that of some other large species, like H. faber and Hyla circumdata. The forearm, though robust, is not disproportionate, but the gula is dark in the male. The difference of size in favor of females is less accentuated than in some other smaller species of Hyla.

COLOR. Dorsal aspect variable in tone, from a very light tan, sometimes with a rosy tinge, to dark, reddish, or olivaceous brown. Ventral aspect immaculate.

PATTERN. Some specimens are entirely devoid of pattern on the dorsal aspect. This is especially so in the light phase or when the background is so dark as to obliterate all marks. A number of individuals show a vertebral stripe which ends somewhere between the axilla and the sacrum. It is generally simple and straight, but occasionally it becomes irregular and angular; in one specimen seen it was very wide. The stripe is generally darker than the back; however, in five individuals from Trinidad, B.W.I., it was not only lighter but had a still lighter margin.

Other specimens display a pattern of spots on the back which vary greatly in shape, size and the area covered by them. Often, they are horizontally disposed, forming a series beginning on the head or in the interocular region and covering most of the back. They are generally more symmetric and more orderly than the similar spots occasionally seen in Hyla faber. Still other individuals show different, very dark, and vertically disposed spots. These are also variable and may be very large

forming showy blotches. In one specimen the pattern is so long and sinuous that it resembles a fragment of intestine with several loops. The spots of Hyla boans generally have rather irregular and slightly ragged outlines. Small, dark, brilliant spots, composed of agglomerations of melanophores, are occasionally seen on very light specimens. On the other hand, very dark examples may display light areas distributed over the back and the sides of the head, even to the edge of the mouth.

The differences between the pattern on the permanently visible dorsal aspects of the limbs and those concealed in repose are less marked than usual. The bars on the permanently visible parts of the limbs are rather indistinct and not always evident. When present, they have the same irregular and ragged outline as the spots on the back. They are alternatively wide and narrow, dark and light and generally extend all the way to the base of the disk of the outer digit. A few specimens from the lower Kuluene, toward the southern end of the range, show peculiar light plaques of a greenish color, similar to lichens, on the permanently visible parts of the limbs. Similar, but rosy, plaques occupy the elbow, heel, its appendage, and the anal region of some specimens from Benjamin Constant on the upper Amazonas.

The flanks generally show the grayish, vertical, or oblique, often geminated, stripes seen in the species of this group. They may be visible from beneath.

ECOLOGY. The habits of Hyla boans are not very well known. It has mostly been collected by traveling naturalists. The Surinam specimens obtained by Geyskes and sent to us by Stahel were mostly found on trees. Mine, from Trinidad, B.W.I., were calling aloft on very tall bamboos growing by the Arima River, which is shallow and swift. Many of the other specimens were taken near rivers. In northern Pará, Rauschert found and photographed a very light specimen, which was fast asleep in daytime on a very dark rock.

DISTRIBUTION. Hyla boans seems to occupy the whole Amazonian Hylaea and to extend beyond the northern limits of South America. Besides Brazil and the Guianas it has been collected in Trinidad, B.W.I., Colombia, Peru, and Ecuador. In Brazil it was taken in the territory of Amapá by R. A. Hoge and by J. C. Carvalho and in northern Pará on the Maicurú, Eirunepé, and Cuminá rivers, and on the Trombetas, a northern tributary of the Amazonas, by M. Rauschert. It was brought from Uaupés (0°–2° N. 68°–70° W. Gr.), upper Rio Negro, by J. C. Carvalho and from Benjamin Constant on the Solimões, near the Brazilian frontier, by Miss Rita Kloss. This *Hyla* reaches the southern affluents of the Amazonas. Dr. H. Sick brought specimens from the Tapajós River; it occurs on the Xingú and as far south as the Kuluene River, 41 km from its confluence with the Xingú. In Peru it was obtained at Pebas, near Iquitos (2°–4° S. 72° W. Gr.), and in Ecuador at Chicharrota on the Bobonaza River (0°–2° S. 76°–78° W.). The American Museum of Natural History has specimens from the Atrato River in Colombia (6°–8° N. 76°–78° W. Gr.), almost at the northwestern corner of the continent. *Hyla boans* is not limited to the river valleys. The Geyskes specimens were taken on the Tumuc-Humac Range near the frontier of Brazil and Surinam. The National Museum in Rio has specimens from the Chapada dos Parecis in Rondonia Territory, not far from Bolivia. In South America it thus ranges from 10° or 11° N. to 16° S. and from 52°–78° W. Gr.

NOTE. Duellman pointed out some time ago that Andersson found a tree frog of this species in the Royal Museum of Sweden that had been examined by Linnaeus and published by him in the tenth edition of *Systema Naturae* as *Rana boans*. This ensures ten years priority over Laurenti for Linnaeus' name. It is to be regretted that a change has to be made. The name *Hyla maxima* has been long established and is really more appropriate than *Hyla boans*.

## *Hyla geographica* Spix, 1824

> SPIX, J. B. VON. 1824. *Animalia nova sive species novae testudinum et ranarum*, pp. 39–40, pl. XI, fig. 1 e 2.

Spix was the first to describe this species, which was subsequently redescribed several times, for the simple reason that the adult livery is very different from that of recently metamorphosed juveniles. In fact, he gave two descriptions, one as *Hyla geographica*, from the forest near the River Teffé, a southern tributary of the Amazonas, the other as *Hyla geographica* var. sive *semilineata* from the province of Rio de Janeiro. The distance between the two localities is very great, but no

clear-cut differences are apparent between the two forms. Reinhardt and Lütken (1862) redescribed the species as *Hyla spectrum,* presumably from Minas Gerais. What they had was a very small, recently metamorphosed specimen, only 23 mm long. The name given was probably due to the large head, attenuated body and very thin limbs. Some authors consider *Hylella punctatissima* Reinhardt and Lütken also synonymous, but the type, seen by me in Copenhagen, is more like another small form, which is the juvenile of a different species. In 1867, Cope redescribed *H. geographica* as *Centrotelma cryptomelan,* later amended to *cryptomelas* by Boulenger. The Cope types were evidently melanistic; his specimen *a* retained the dark color of the flanks and concealed parts of juveniles; specimen *b* had the blackish, granitelike, marbling seen in a certain percentage of specimens, irrespective of locality and the others were intermediate. Similar forms still occur in Bahia and two of our specimens from Pombas, Minas Gerais, have also retained the dark color on the flanks and the concealed upper surfaces of the thighs. Peters, (1870), described *Hyla geographica* once more, also from a juvenile, albeit a slightly larger specimen (28 mm) than *Hyla spectrum,* this time from Santa Catarina. He even made it the type of a new genus, *Cophomantis,* whose differential characters, separating it from *Hyla,* were the absence of maxillary teeth, tympana and Eustachian tubes. At the beginning of the description of the type species, *C. punctillata,* Peters states that it is blue-gray with dark dots above, dirty yellow beneath, and blackish brown on the concealed upper surfaces; this is exactly the color of juvenile *H. geographica,* and the size agrees too. At the end of the description he confesses to having hesitated long before setting up this species as representative of a new genus because the lack of maxillary teeth and the transverse depression above the anus were suggestive of a juvenile *Hyla.* Later (1872) he withdrew his genus and suggested the same treatment for *Hyllela* Reinhardt and Lütken, because he found isolated teeth in the soft maxilla. A. Lutz mentions in his notes that the vomerine teeth may be present in very small specimens, but covered by the skin; this is evident in a good series of metamorphosing larvae and juveniles from the state of Rio, in the Lutz Collection. In the same publication, a comment on the Spix species of frogs,

Peters (1872) puts *H. geographica* to the synonymy of *Hyla maxima,* whose range is overlapped by that of *geographica,* but which is a very large and robust species peculiar to the tropical basins of South America and which does not extend as far south as *H. geographica.* This opinion may have led Boulenger to set up his *Hyla appendiculata* from Ecuador and Bahia. Our largest female *Hyla geographica* is not over 63 mm long whereas those of *Hyla boans* range to 120 mm, while the smallest adult male is 65 mm from snout to vent. Parker suggests that there are two races of *H. geographica,* a northern and a southern form. Comparison of our specimens from Trinidad, Guaporé, Bahia, and southern Brazil hardly supports this hypothesis. Only very large series and the filling of the wide gaps in the known distribution would enable one to definitively support or disclaim this separation. Under the circumstances, it seems more prudent to lump the specimens together under the specific name. Dr. Doris M. Cochran mistakes *H. punctatissima* Reinhardt and Lütken for *geographica,* and *spectrum* for *Hyla albopunctata.*

DIAGNOSTIC CHARACTERS. A pattern of golden arabesques and dots on the transparent part of the lower eyelid together with the small size and streamlined build, the thin limbs and cutaneous triangular appendage on the heel. Upper surface light tan to dark brown. Iris golden to bronze. Flanks and concealed parts of thigh with dark vertical stripes or marbling on light ground. Concealed surfaces of limbs and belly orange, gula and chest white to cream.

TYPES. The types presumably perished with most of the other Spix Hylid types of the Zoological Collection in Munich during the Second World War. The type of *Hyla spectrum* is in Copenhagen and that of *Hyla appendiculata* at the British Museum of Natural History.

DESCRIPTION. Size medium: males with nuptial characters from 40–46 mm, mostly between the two extremes. Females with eggs up to 63 mm. Build slender or slightly robust, body streamlined, widest at the tympanum, tapering toward the groin. Legs fairly long, but variable in length, the adpressed tibiotarsal articulation reaching from the front of the eye to the tip of the snout or even beyond, often to the nostril. Limbs slender, especially the upper arm and the femur. Head massive, broader than long; crown with a diamond-shaped

depression on top, limited by the sharp canthus rostralis and the less marked frontoparietals. Snout triangular between the canthi, truncate above the nostrils, which are lateral, rounded, and small; loreal region concave, sloping obliquely toward the mouth; interorbital space much wider than the upper eyelid and the internarial space. Eye large and very prominent, its longest diameter slightly exceeding the distance from its anterior corner to the nostril. Tympanum one-half to two-thirds the diameter of the eye. Tongue more or less cordiform, slightly emarginate and slightly free behind. Vomerine teeth in two long M- or bridge-shaped series behind the choanae, parallel to their inner rim. Palms full of tubercles, soles less so; webs granular; an elongate inner metatarsal tubercle; a moon-shaped callosity below the first finger; pollex rudiment generally not perceptible. Web inserted below the disk on the outer side of the second and on the fourth, reaching the penultimate subarticular tubercle on the third. Toes more fully webbed, reaching near to the disk on the outer side of the second and third, on the fifth, and to the penultimate subarticular tubercle of the fourth, thence fringed. Skin minutely shagreened above, granular on flanks, midventral aspect of thigh and belly, the granulations flattening out on the chest; perianal region glandular; a supratympanic fold deflected to the edge of the mouth; a slight edge to the jaws, the forearm and the tarsus, sometimes forming a minute tubercle or appendage on the elbow and generally a triangular or conical appendage on the heel.

VARIATIONS. Except for the large size of the type of *Hyla appendiculata* Boulenger and of a few specimens from the southern part of the upper Amazonas, or Solimões, the variations seem rather individual than regional. Our Santa Catarina sample, which is small, has mostly shorter legs. There are two melanistic individuals, like those of Cope, from eastern Minas Gerais, but the British Guiana specimens also have very dark flanks. The eyes of the Trinidad specimens do not differ from those from the vicinity of Rio de Janeiro, and the main variations of the pattern on the flanks and the flecks on the ventral surface recur in quite different regions.

COLOR AND PATTERN. Above, from cream or light tan to reddish or dark brown. As A. Lutz aptly puts it: "The groundcolor varies through the tints of coffee with milk." The color changes considerably, sometimes even during short periods of observation. The dorsal surface may show a vertebral stripe or dark markings or may be more or less intensely dotted with black, especially in the light phase. The marks on the back are sometimes similar to those of the Spix figures or intermediate between them; more often they are less distinct, like those seen in the watercolors of a light and a dark phase painted for A. Lutz. Sometimes they are reminiscent of faintly outlined maps. Bars, variable in width and distinctness may be present on the constantly visible upper surface of the limbs; sometimes they are very faint, especially in light phases. Perianal glandules white, pinkish, or slightly violet. Tympanum the color of the skin, occasionally iridescent. Appendage on heel white, cream, or brown edged; sometimes similar opaque spots on the back, mostly whitish or cream, but occasionally of a greenish tint. Iris golden to bronze with venation of the same color standing out as if embossed from beneath. Pupil horizontal, opening irregular, very noticeably rhomboid. Arabesques on the transparent part of the lower lid golden or lemon yellow; a characteristic greenish pattern on the lower nontransparent part. Flanks light, either with dark gray to black, vertical, irregular, rather broken stripes, or more or less marbled by melanophores disposed round the white granulations of the skin, or intermediate between these aspects; in a very few melanistic individuals, black as in juveniles. (*H. cryptomelas* pattern). These stripes extend to the grayish concealed part of the thighs and are sometimes visible from beneath; others more indistinct and masked by the ground color. Some individuals have flecks all over the belly, on the sides, or in the middle, as if in continuation of the pattern on the flanks. Lower aspect of the limbs, hands and feet and abdomen intensely suffused with orange (yellow orange or a duller buff). Underside of disks gray; armpits violet; chest and gula white or cream, with a slight pigmentation at the edge of the mandible. Bones of jaw and marrow of the long bones green.

SECONDARY SEX CHARACTERS. Not very marked except as to size. Males are roughly three-quarters the size of the females. Vocal sac small, consisting of a few subgular folds. Nuptial pad on the first finger not often present; it is deciduous and has to be looked for.

VOICE. Rather feeble. Often the males produce a chorus of clucking or whimpering noises similar to those constantly made by litters of young nursing puppies, but occasionally the call rises to *crr-aaw* or *ccrick-ccrick, tac-tac, ta*.

HABITS. Spix says of the type of his *H. g. semilineata* from the province of Rio de Janeiro that it was found "in arboribus." Ours have mostly been collected very near the ground, on, or even under, grass and other lowly vegetation. In daytime this species is very sluggish. When resting the conic heel appendages stand out, in two points, sometimes with the tip of the coccyx forming a third cone between them. The iris is also very effectively masked. If handled they often remain quiescent, as if pretending to be dead, lying on their backs, though they may also pass water or take a sudden leap. When touched a strong musty smell of crushed plants is given out.

KNOWN RANGE. Knowledge of the exact range of *Hyla geographica* is very much hampered by the fact that large sections of Brazil and of South America have hardly been collected in, especially for frogs. In the northeastern part of the Amazonian Hylaea, the species has been collected at Belém do Pará, in the Guianas, and in Trinidad, B.W.I. (8–10° N). We have some from the Guianas that do not differ markedly from our Brazilian ones. To the west the type of *Hyla geographica* was collected near the River Teffé and we have specimens from the Tapajós, Rio Branco, a tributary of the Guaporé, and from Santa Cruz de la Sierra, Bolivia. The only doubtful point might be the conspecificity of *Hyla appendiculata*, but both Boulenger and Cope lumped their Ecuadorian specimens with those from Bahia in Brazil. There is a hiatus between Belém and Alagoas in the collections, but from southern Bahia down the species has been obtained in Espirito Santo, southeastern Minas Gerais, the states of Rio de Janeiro, Guanabara, São Paulo, Paraná, and Santa Catarina, mostly not very far from the coast, often on hills and at lower elevations but not on the high peaks.

AFFINITIES. The nearest species is undoubtedly *Hyla boans*, which compared to *Hyla geographica* is a giant form, almost twice the size. They overlap in part of the range, such as the Amazonas Valley and in Trinidad, where *Hyla boans* was found calling aloft on high bamboos by the River Arima and *geographica* was collected in the herbaceous vegetation of the marsh alongside the Churchill-Roosevelt Road near Port of Spain.

*Hyla picturata* Boulenger 1899, known only from Ecuador, also seems near, but it lacks the pattern on the lower eyelid and the appendage on the heel. The type resembles only the most ornate individuals of *Hyla geographica*, like one we have from Caravelas in southern Bahia, and another from Utinga in Belém do Pará.

## Hyla secedens B. Lutz, 1963

LUTZ, B. 1963. New species of *Hyla* from southeastern Brazil. *Copeia* 3:561–562, 1 fig.

A series of thirteen tree frogs from Barro Branco, in the state of Rio de Janeiro, rather similar to but not identical with *Hyla geographica* and also slightly reminiscent of *H. bischoffi multilineata* were bought from a commercial collector and described under the name of *Hyla secedens*.

DIAGNOSTIC CHARACTERS. *Hyla secedens* is characterized by the following combination of characters: relatively long head and elongate snout; slender build; orange background and very regular black vertical stripes on the upper posterior aspect of the thighs and hind part of the flanks concealed in repose; a few open lines and a slight accumulation of golden dots on the edge of the transparent part of the lower eyelid; a pointed narrow triangular flap on the heel; rudiment of pollex provided with a sharp prick ( ♂ ).

TYPES AND TYPE LOCALITY. Holotype: MNR 3591. Barro Branco, in the state of Rio de Janeiro, rising from the coastal lowlands to the Serra da Estrela, near the bay of Guanabara and on the way to Petrópolis; collected by A. Passarelli, November 1962 (approximately 22° 23′ S. 43° 15′ W. Gr.). MNR type: 3591 ( ♂ ). Paratypes: 3592–3595 ( ♂ ).

DESCRIPTION. Size medium. Type 56 mm snout to vent; paratypes 55–57 mm, apparently all males. Build slender. Head large, long, widest at the tympanum; body elongate, narrower than head at the shoulders, still narrower between the sacrum and the groin. Legs thin, not very long, the adpressed tibiotarsal articulation reaching to the front of the eye. Snout elongate, slightly raised between the nostrils, rounded in front from above, declivous to the edge of the mouth in profile; canthus rostralis forming a long curve to the nostril, which is lateral, small and open upward; loreal region oblique, slightly concave. Interorbital space much wider than the internarial space. Eye large, prominent, its longest diameter equal to the distance from its anterior corner to the nostril. Tympanum half the diameter of the eye. Tongue oval, slightly emarginate, not free behind. Vomerine teeth in two long series, forming an inverted V behind the choanae, more or less parallel to their inner rim. Web rudimentary between the first and second fingers, reaching the first subarticular tubercle between the second and third, slightly above it between the third and fourth, continuing as fringes on the lateral fingers, especially on the third. Web on toes broader, inserted below the disk on the outer side of the first, second, third, and on the fifth toe and at the level of the second tubercle on the fourth; narrowed to a fringe on the inner side of the second and third and on both sides of the fourth toe. A thick rudiment of pollex ending in a sharp point. An elongate inner metatarsal tubercle. Palm well padded; vestiges of dark pigment on the nuptial pads. Skin very finely shagreened above. A fold over the tympanum reaching the axilla. Perianal region, midventral aspect of thigh and belly granular, the granulations flattening out on the chest; gula almost smooth. A row of minute tubercles on the lower edge of the forearm, from the base of the fourth finger to the elbow where they are slightly larger and may end in a small fold. A similar rim without tubercles on the tibia, ending in a relatively long, glandular, and narrow triangular appendage on the heel (types); tympanic area granular.

MEASUREMENTS (mm). Types: male 55–57 snout to vent. Two new subadult (?) frogs from the Organ Mountains National Park 45 and 50 snout to vent.

COLOR AND PATTERN (types). In life dorsal color very pale, the color of wash leather or very light buff. A dark vertebral stripe from the snout to the anus in all the specimens. In two of them additional very faint stripes on the permanently visible dorsal surface of the limbs. A number of minute, opaque drops, mostly white, scattered on the dorsal aspect (guanine?), pinkish in specimen no. 3592, which is slightly darker and rubbed. Iris golden with a few dark veins; a few golden lines and dots and a small deposit of golden pigment at the fore and hind corners on the transparent part of the under eyelid. Surfaces of limbs concealed in repose, orange. A pattern of narrow vertical stripes on the upper posterior area of the thigh, not visible from beneath; similar, generally fainter, stripes on the hind part of the flank.

ADDITIONAL SPECIMENS. *Hyla secedens* was not seen alive again for many years, though a specimen seen in the collection of Professor P. Sawaya in São Paulo seemed to be conspecific with it. In March 1968 two more were caught on a very rainy night by our helper A. Barcellos in the Organ Mountains National Park. They are slightly smaller than the types and may be subadult, though the smaller one has a sharp pollex rudiment, and both have some fuscous dots on the throat.

The larger one shows that the pale dorsal color can go over into a not very dark shade of brown. It has several spots of guanine. When it becomes paler a row of horizontal irregular grayish bands down the back coincident and slanting onto the visible surface of the leg becomes apparent. The smaller one has remained cream-colored for several weeks. Its dorsal pattern is quite shadowy. Both have the dark vertebral line, but in the larger one it is incomplete and in the smaller one it is visible only anteriorly. This one has spattered drops of fuscous pigment on the head and a large blotch of similar drops on the forepart of the back. The iris is pale gold with a few dark veins and blends with the sides of the head. The lower eyelid is like that of the types. The color and pattern on the upper surfaces of the thigh and of the flanks concealed in repose also agree. On the flanks the flash color inclines to be more yellowish. Both color and pattern reappear on the outer edge of the foot. The inner concealed aspects of the limbs are carneous and slightly olivaceous, the long bones not readily visible. The hind part of the abdomen, the ventral aspect of the thighs and limbs visible in repose, the hands, feet digits, and webs are orange; so is the upper aspect of the inner digits. The light borders of the permanently visible dorsal aspects of the reposing frog are outlined in dark pigment, especially at the edge of the mouth, forearm and tarsus; a dark subanal patch is very marked. These two individuals lack appendages on the heels like those of the types.

AFFINITIES. Morphologically, the forms nearest to *Hyla secedens* seem to be *Hyla geographica* and *Hyla bischoffi multilineata*, especially the former. However, *H. secedens* differs from both and from the other regional species of Hyla of the same size by the diagnostic characters mentioned above. It lacks the arabesques on the transparent part of the lower eyelid of *Hyla geographica* but has a reduced pattern on it. It also differs by the longer and narrower head and snout, more slender build, shorter web on the hand and the pointed tip of the pollex rudiment. The males seem larger than those of *Hyla geographica*, which occurs near Barro Branco. *Hyla secedens* resembles *H. bischoffi*, especially *H. bischoffi multilineata*, in the texture of the skin, and vertical stripes on the thighs. It is, however, sharply separated from it by the shape of the vomerine teeth and the color of the concealed surfaces of the limbs. The dorsal pattern is not longitudinal and composed of multiple lines, but horizontal and composed of rather faint and evanescent bands.

## *Hyla calcarata* Troschel, 1848

TROSCHEL. 1848. *Reisen in Britisch-Guiana in den Jahren 1840–44*, 3:660.

GÜNTHER, A. 1858. *Catalogue of the batrachia salientia in the British Museum. Hyla fasciata:* 100, pl. VII, fig. D.

DIAGNOSTIC CHARACTERS. Build similar to that of *Hyla geographica*, but concealed aspect of the limbs bluish, not orange, and no golden arabesques on the transparent part of the lower eyelid. Appendix on heel spur-like, very distinct in carefully preserved specimens. Perpendicular bars on the sides of the body and thighs well defined, straight, or tending to form blotches. Amazonian Hylaea.

TYPES AND TYPE LOCALITIES: Troschel described the species in Schomburgk (1848), who traveled in British Guiana. Günther's specimen belongs to the Frazer Collection and is stated to be from the Andes(!) of Ecuador. His type was seen in the British Museum and appears to be synonymous with Troschel's species.

DESCRIPTION. Specimens from Serra do Navio in the Brazilian Territory of Amapá; four others seen, all females. Size not very large, 45–53 mm snout to vent. Build similar to that of *H. geographica*, with large oval head, wider than the body and with very thin, long legs; tibiotarsal articulation reaching beyond the tip of the snout when adpressed. Head oval with rather long snout, thick, rounded, curved canthus rostralis, truncate at the level of the lateral nostrils; loreal region grooved, oblique. Tympanum small but quite distinct, between one-third and one-half the horizontal diameter of the eye. Interorbital space very slightly wider than the upper eyelid. Eye prominent, almost equal to the distance from its anterior corner to the tip of the snout. Tongue flat, rounded oval, entire, hardly free. Vomerine teeth in the two bridge-like series typical for the *H. geographica* group. Disks large, rounded. A rudiment of web between the lateral fingers, especially between the second and third. No prominent rudiment of the pollex (females). Web on foot scooped out, reaching below the disk on the inner side of the second, third, and fifth, to the last subarticular tubercle on the outside of the second and third, and on both sides of the fourth. Inner metatarsal tubercle very small. Tibia longer than femur. Foot not much longer than tarsus. A very distinct, spur-like, appendage on the heel. Skin of dorsal surface finely shagreened. Ventral surface granular on the belly and the midventral aspect of the thigh. An indistinct supratympanic ridge to the shoulder. Narrow but very distinct edges on the outer side of forearm and tarsus to the outer digits.

COLOR AND PATTERN. Unfortunately not seen alive. The recent and extremely well-preserved specimen from the Serra do Navio collected by J. C. Melo de Carvalho is reddish brown on the dorsal surface with a dark vertebral stripe from the snout almost to the groin and a very obscure horizontal pattern of irregular darker areas on the body and alternative wide and narrow bars on the permanently visible part of the limbs. Sides of the body, upper hind surface of the thighs and other areas of the limbs concealed in repose grayish blue or violet, with dark, almost black, perpendicular bars. They are very conspicuous and clear-cut on the sides of the body and the thighs, far less distinct on the inside of the leg and the inner dorsal aspect of the tarsus and foot. Concealed surfaces abruptly separated longitudinally from those visible in repose, including on the foot. Edges of tarsus, forearm, and outer digits light; anal region, inner ventral aspect of the thigh and inner aspect of the forearm and tarsus dark, blue-gray; palm, sole, and webs slate-colored or deep violet, almost black. Ventral aspect immaculate except for the edges of the dorsal pattern; minute dots on the lower part and on the

transparent section of the lower eyelid. Vestiges of gold color on the iris.

MEASUREMENTS (mm). Snout to vent 53.1 Hind-limb 97.2: femur 28.1, tibia 31.1, tarsus 18, foot 20. Head length/width 19.1:17.1, interorbital space/upper eyelid 6:5. Tympanum 2.5, eye 7, eye-nostril 6, eye-tip of snout 7. Left heel spur 3 mm, right spur 2 mm long.

Other specimens: northern Pará: Maicurú River, one female 53.1; another female (sources of the river) 45.1. Amazonas: Benjamin Constant one female 52 mm.

VARIATION. The three specimens from the Maicurú River, northern part of the state of Pará, do not differ much from our best specimen, that of the Serra do Navio, Amapá. They are less reddish. The larger one has an obscurely stippled irregular horizontal pattern on the back composed of minute dark dots. The bars on the concealed parts are wide. The tongue is slightly wider. In the smaller one the concealed pattern is irregular and formed of blotches with a characteristic leopard-like aspect; the vertebral stripe is barely visible, and there is no distinct pattern on the back. The specimen from the vicinity of the sources of the Maicurú River has a stippled horizontal dorsal pattern, stippling on the tympanum and gula, and distinct stippling on the lower part of the lower eyelid. The specimen from Benjamin Constant, state of Amazonas, diverges a little more. The sides of the head behind the mouth-opening are less curved than in the others. The tongue is long, narrow and somewhat free behind. The leg is shorter, especially the femur. It is also devoid of a vertebral stripe. The concealed pattern is of the blotched type.

SECONDARY SEX CHARACTERS. All our five specimens are females. Those over 50 mm snout to vent contain large eggs with a dark and a light pole. The smallest one, 45 mm, contains minute cream-colored eggs. Male unknown to us.

ECOLOGY. The only information available is the fact that the specimen from Benjamin Constant was found asleep between the outer leaves of a bromeliad by Miss Gertrude Rita Kloss.

KNOWN RANGE. Shomburgk's specimens were from British Guiana. Ours are from the two extremes of the Amazonian Hylaea, four from the east approximately 0° 7' 2" S. and 51° 17' 4" W. Gr. Climate: *Am* (tropical) Köppen from Serra do

Navio, in Amapá Territory (Maicurú River) and northern part of the state of Pará; the other was gotten at Benjamin Constant, not far from the frontier of Brazil with Peru and Colombia, 4° 2′ 42″ S. and 69° 54′ 13″ W. Gr. 65 m above sea level. Climate: *Af* Köppen.

Günther believes that his type was collected in the Andes, which seems rather doubtful in view of the other finding places.

SYNONYMS. *Hyla fasciata* Günther. The pattern figured by him is the same as that of our Amapá specimen, though the habit seems slightly different.

AFFINITIES. This species seems close to *Hyla geographica*. However, it diverges from *Hyla geographica* and *Hyla boans* by the bluish color of the concealed surfaces and by the lack of distinct golden arabesques on the transparent part of the lower eyelid.

Three from the east: Amapá Territory and northern Pará, Rio Maicurú. One from the western frontier of Brazil with Peru and Colombia.

# 4. Long-Headed, Streamlined Species

## Hyla daudini B. Lutz
(nomen novum for *Hyla boans* Daudin, 1802)

DAUDIN, F. M. 1802. *Histoire naturelle des rainettes, grenouilles et crapauds,* p. 31, pl. 11.
———. 1803. *Histoire naturelle générale et particulière des reptiles,* pp. 64–67.
LATREILLE, P. A., and SONINI, C. S. *Histoire
naturelle des reptiles,* 2:184–186, fig. 3, p. 176.
DUMÉRIL, A. M. C., and BIBRON, G. 1841.
*Erpétologie générale ou histoire naturelle des
reptiles,* 8:604–607.
DUELLMAN, W. E. 1970. *The hylid frogs of
Middle America* 1:261.

Because it now seems that the name *Hyla boans*
is preoccupied by Linné, I propose the name *Hyla
daudini* instead, since it was described by Daudin.

DIAGNOSTIC CHARACTERS. Those of the group of
large species of *Hyla* with long head and pointed
snout, elongate build, and very long hindlimbs.
Differs from *Hyla albopunctata* and *Hyla raniceps*
by the absence of pattern on the thighs and flanks,
from *Hyla lanciformis* by the absence of light insular spots on the gula and chest, the smoother
skin of the dorsal surface, and the less lanceolate
build; perhaps also by a lesser size.

TERRA TYPICA. According to Daudin, the species
hails from Surinam. The types are presumably at
the Muséum in Paris, but I did not see them there.

DESCRIPTION. Size large. Our largest specimen,
from Jorge Pataló, northern part of the state of
Pará, is 63.1 mm. The smallest adult, from Livramento, Bragança Railway, also in the state of Pará,
is 40 mm snout to vent. Build slender but robust.
Head slightly longer than wide, body narrowed
from the shoulder to the groin. Hindlimb very
long, double or almost double the length of the
body; tibiotarsal articulation reaching far beyond
the snout when the hindlimb is adpressed. Snout
narrow, rounded only in front, with sharp canthus
rostralis and almost vertical, slightly concave
loreal region. Nostrils approximately one-third of
the distance from tip of snout to the eye and two-
thirds from anterior corner of orbit. Eye large,
prominent, its horizontal diameter equal or almost
equal to the distance from its anterior corner to
the nostrils and approximately two-thirds of the
distance to the tip of the snout. Tympanum one-
half to three-sevenths the diameter of the eye. Proportion of interorbital space to upper eyelid variable. Tongue oval, slightly free, distinctly notched
behind. Vomerine teeth forming parentheses or
M-shaped group, the hind borders of which generally touch the palatines, as stated by Duméril
and Bibron. Lateral fingers fringed with a very
short web at the base. Toes two-thirds or more
webbed, the web longer on the outer side of the
second and third than on the inner, leaving two or
three joints free on the fourth toe (Duméril and
Bibron). A rudiment of pollex; a small inner metatarsal tubercle; a number of palmar tubercles, two
of them large: one under the first, the other under
the third and fourth fingers; the latter wide. A dis-

tinct fold across the chest. A straight glandular fold from the eye to beyond the shoulder, above the tympanum. A distinct, short supra-anal ridge. Very slight ridges on the forearm, tibia, and tarsus, reaching the outer digit of hand and foot.

VARIATION. The available series is small, comprising one specimen from Paramaribo, two from Goiás and several others from the state of Pará. In regard to proportions the Surinam specimen agrees better with the excellent description given by Duméril and Bibron than those from Brazil. In some of these the head is wider, justifying Daudin's statement, "capite oreque latis." Tongue rounded to oval in most of them. Proportion of tympanum to eye 3:7 in one from the Maicurú River and one from the Cururú River, both in the state of Pará; 1:2 in another, from the region of the right-hand source of the Maicurú River, whose legs are also shorter, the adpressed tibiotarsal articulation not reaching far beyond the snout. One of the two small specimens from Amaro Leite, in the state of Goiás, has still shorter legs, the tibiotarsal reaching only to the nostril.

SECONDARY SEX CHARACTERS. None of our specimens show very marked sex characters. The three largest, presumably females, have a very distinct fold across the chest and an elongate callosity outside the first finger, in place of the knob-like rudiment with a sharp point of the males. Vocal sac modest ( ♂ ). A larger number of not full-grown specimens in the Museu Nacional are devoid of sex characters.

COLOR AND PATTERN. Two individuals sent from Belem do Pará by Dr. Walter Egler some years ago were seen alive and photographed in color by Prof. Gualter A. Lutz. In one the dorsal aspect was pale buff, almost cream, with the sides of the head, tympanum and iris deeper in color. Ventral aspect pale, immaculate. Concealed aspect of the thighs a brownish vinaceous color varying in intensity. The other was darker and somewhat tawny: the concealed upper aspects of the thigh a dark luminous brown, the tibia a dull seal-brown and the edges of the limbs dark brown. The iris is paler than in *Hyla albopunctata* and in *Hyla lanciformis* and slightly roseate. The glandular ridges, folds, and the pollex rudiments very marked.

In November 1968 Dr. Normelia Vasconcellos and I had the opportunity to obtain three living specimens on the property of Miss Maria Koltzau, at Santa Isabel, near Belem do Pará. These specimens were also photographed by G. A. Lutz. They are 45, 47, and 55 mm long and seem adult but were not calling. The two smaller ones are probably males, as they prick with the prepollex. They vary in color from pale tan, almost cream, to a medium or a slightly darker and more reddish brown. They undergo moderate changes of color even during short periods of observation. In the darker phases the pattern of horizontal bars on the back and the limbs may become discernible but it is seldom distinct. The upper half of the iris is luminous and more golden than the lower half, which inclines to be grayish. The canthus and the subcanthal area are darker than the rest. The hypochondria may show a slightly violaceous tinge that may extend toward the anterior upper part of the thigh. The color of this and of the other concealed parts varies from slightly violaceous or fawn to a fairly dark brown-gray, with the lighter tints on the thighs and the darker ones on the outer strip of the tarsus and the webs. The gula is smooth and tan or pale brown; the belly white, slightly yellowish or, in the presumably male specimens, with a pale orange-yellow suffusion. The midventral part of the thigh shows a glandular formation like that of *Hyla lanciformis* but much less marked. A few white glandules form a double row on the ventral subanal region. The supra-anal white ridge is very evident. None of the specimens seen alive shows the spectacular white blotches on the anterior part of the ventral aspect, the brilliant edge of the upper jaw and the white disks of the three outer fingers which are characteristic for *Hyla lanciformis*. The ventral outline of the mouth is ogival, but the snout seems shorter and the build less lanceolate than in *Hyla lanciformis*, which attains a larger size. Neither of the Hylean species shows any pattern on the concealed surfaces of the limbs.

Daudin gives the dorsal color of preserved specimens as grayish white. Duméril and Bibron state more accurately that they may be whitish, reddish brown, violaceous, or light chestnut brown, with a dark vertebral stripe from the tip of the snout to the lumbar region and narrow stripes of the same color across the dorsal surface of body and limbs. This is exactly the pattern of our specimen from the right source of the Maicurú River and of one of the two from Goiás, except that the transversal bands are neither uniform nor very narrow. The vertebral line may be lacking. The dark area over the sides of the head, on the tarsus and underside of forearm and tibia is present in all specimens seen by us though deepest in the darker ones.

AFFINITIES. There seems to be a close affinity between the different forms of this group, especially between *Hyla daudini* and *Hyla albopunctata* Spix.

KNOWN DISTRIBUTION. The confusion of different forms in much of the literature and in some collections and the relatively small number available to us for detailed examination make it difficult to trace the exact limits of the range. *Hyla daudini* occurs in the Guianas and in the state of Pará, which seems to indicate occupation of the eastern part of the Amazonian Hylaea. There are, however, two small, very southern specimens from Amaro Leite in the state of Goiás. *Hyla albopunctata* occupies a large territory on the Central Brazilian Plateau, approaching the maritime escarpment in nonforested terrain.

## Hyla albopunctata Spix, 1824

SPIX, J. B. VON. 1824. *Animalia nova sive species novae testudinum et ranarum quas in itinere per Brasiliam*, p. 33, pl. 6, fig. 5.

REINHARDT, J., and LÜTKEN, C. F. 1862. Bidrag til Kundskab om Brasiliens Padder og Krybdyr. *Vid. Medd. Naturh. Foren.* (Copenhagen) 3 (10–15):189.

DIAGNOSTIC CHARACTERS. Those of the group of large species of *Hyla* with slender habit, long head, narrow snout, and very long legs; pattern of the upper hind surface of the thighs and of flanks concealed in repose, composed of yellow spots on a blue background. Occupying much, if not the whole central plateau, of Brazil, as well as adjacent territory in Argentina, approaching the maritime escarpment in open ground. Very near *Hyla daudini* (ex-*boans*), of which it may be a subspecies.

TYPES AND TYPE LOCALITY. Spix's diagnosis and description leave much to be desired, nor does he indicate a type locality: "Exigua, supra rosea, subtus albicans, maxillis et tarso albomarginatis, femoribus postice albo-punctatis.

"DESCRIPTO. Corpus minutus, gracilis, supra rosaceus, subtus albicans, maxilla, tarsusque postice albomarginatis, stria ab oculos ad nare nigra, fem-

ora nigra (?) hypochondriaque pone albopunctata. Longitudo corporis 1" 2'."

Spix's name has been retained for the following reasons: A few preserved specimens have a pinkish tinge on the dorsal surface; the edge of the maxilla and tarsus are white, though this also occurs in other forms; the ornamental yellow spots fade to white after death; and the ground color of the concealed aspect of the thigh may be dark in very much pigmented specimens. Peters (1872), whose comments on Spix's Brazilian species of frogs are not always accurate, states positively that the type though small was sufficiently well preserved for identification with a cotype of *Hyla oxyrhina* Reinhardt & Lütken (1862). Dr. Cochran, who saw the type before its loss, also considers the names synonymous. Were it not for the sometimes illogical and altogether too drastic rules of zoological nomenclature, it would be preferable to use the name proposed by Reinhardt and Lütken, whose description, based on eleven specimens, is good, whose cotypes are available, and who state a type locality, "Lagoa Santa, Minas Gerais," where the form still is one of the most common tree frogs.

DESCRIPTION. Size large. Largest cotype of *oxyrhina* 75 mm. Thirty females seen, from 55–66 mm snout to vent, males 40–60 mm. Habit slender. Body rectilinear, progressively narrowed from the shoulder blades to the supra-anal ridge. Leg very long, the adpressed tibiotarsal articulation of most specimens reaching far beyond the snout. Tibia generally longer than the femur. Head very long, about one-third the total length of the body, less wide than long. Snout narrow, rounded only in front; upper jaw projecting considerably beyond the lower jaw, which has the shape of a long isosceles triangle (A. Lutz). Canthus rostralis sharp, loreal region high, very slightly concave below the eye. Nostrils lateral, one-third nearer the tip of the snout than the anterior corner of the eye. Interorbital space as wide or very slightly wider than the upper eyelid. Eye very prominent, its horizontal diameter two-thirds to four-fifths the distance to the tip of the snout. Tympanum rounded, about one-half the diameter of the eye. Tongue elliptic, slightly notched, free only at the hind edge. Vomerine teeth in separate "cuneiform" groups (fide Reinhardt and Lütken), angular, occasionally more arched, parallel to the inner border of the choanae. Lateral fingers with a rudiment of web at the base; toes one-half webbed, with or without a narrow distal fringe. Rudiment of pollex present, button-shaped, containing a claw-like narrow point ( ♂ ) or forming a callus outside the first finger ( ♀ ). An inner metatarsal tubercle. Palmar and subarticular tubercles present, moderate. Dorsal surface smooth (finely granular according to Reinhardt and Lütken), ventral aspect granular behind the fold across the chest. A narrow, straight, glandular fold from the hind corner of the eye over the tympanum reaching beyond the shoulder. A very narrow outer ridge on the forearm, tibia, tarsus, and foot, reaching the outer digit of hand and foot. A light edge to both jaws. A fold across the chest, a discoidal fold distinctly visible in some specimens.

SECONDARY SEX CHARACTERS. A sharp, claw-like, prickle in the pollex rudiment of the male, very thin, seldom visible, not always palpable. Vocal sac large when distended. Adult female larger. Fold across the chest more distinct. A number of specimens in the collection of the MNR which are as large as breeding males but which lack distinct sex characters are probably juvenile females.

VARIATION. Besides marked individual variation there seems to occur geographic variation in regard to habit and size. Our specimens from several places near the maritime escarpment, or not far from the eastern ranges, are larger and robust (Piraquera, near Curitiba, state of Paraná; São Paulo, Ipiranga, and Alto da Serra; Piquete, on the Mantiqueira range; Teresópolis, state of Rio de Janeiro; Belo Horizonte and Itamonte in Minas Gerais), females over 60 mm; males over 50 mm from snout to vent. Those from Lagoa Santa and places not far from the type locality of *oxyrhina* have long, narrow snouts, justifying the name given by Reinhardt and Lütken. The adult specimens from Goias (Brasília, São João da Aliança, Rio São Miguel and Jataí) and those from Mato Grosso (Campo Grande, São Vicente, and Ponte de Itaquira) are relatively small and slender, adult males from 38–49 mm, females less than 60 mm snout to vent.

INDIVIDUAL VARIATION. Length of hindlimb very variable, double the length of the body, more or less. Head from 1–4 mm longer than wide. Tympanum one-half, two-fifths, very rarely two-thirds the diameter of the eye; eye two-thirds, four-fifths, seven-eights, or eight-elevenths, of the distance from its anterior corner to the tip of the snout.

Tongue occasionally wider or flatter. Vomerine teeth arched instead of angular in some individuals.

COLOR AND PATTERN. The most diagnostic colors and pattern are those of the upper posterior part of the thigh and of the flanks concealed in repose, consisting of bright yellow spots on a blue background. The spots may vary in size, number, and shape, from rounded, to figures of eight or drops with irregular outlines. In good specimens the background varies from campanula blue or slate color to lighter tones of the dorsal coloration, being blue in good, live, fairly light specimens. Dorsal color very variable even in the same individual, ranging from lemon or chrome yellow to reddish brown and chestnut; intermediate tones of buff or leather common. The color covers the whole dorsal surface of the head and body and the parts of the limbs visible in repose. Sides of the head darker than the back; a light edge to the upper jaw, lemon yellow in light specimens, cream-colored or yellowish in brown ones; a similar light margin on the lower jaw, forearm, tarsus, hand, and foot; a more marked, though short, supra-anal ridge. Iris copper-colored or brassy, the inner zone nearer to gold. Tympanum covered with dark dots. One or two, similar, dark-dotted bands on the forearm, one on the inside of the tibia and another covering the lower aspect of tarsus and foot; similar but lighter dots on the gula. Ventral aspect immaculate except for the dark dotted bands on the limbs and diffuse brown dots on the throat; granulation of thigh whitish.

DORSAL PATTERN. In many specimens no dorsal pattern at all. In others a pattern of elongate bars or spots across the body and similar, horizontal or oblique ones on the permanently visible parts of the limbs. Spots or bars slightly darker than the background, often with lighter edges, variable in outline and width. As pointed out in A. Lutz's notes they are generally not marked and may be quite faint. There are, however, some brightly marked individuals in which this pattern is very much more distinct; similar to a graceful marbling according to Reinhardt and Lütken, more like a tapestry with a design of arabesques to me. Figure 9, page 80 in Dr. Cochran's book (1955) serves to illustrate this phase.

VARIATIONS IN COLOR OF LIVING SPECIMENS. Living specimens change color or tone often and easily, though the very light ones do not get very dark nor the very dark ones as light as the former.

A group of *Hyla albopunctata* received by A. Lutz from Passa Quatro and kept alive by him arrived brown, except for one that was yellow. By next day they were all yellow; further changes followed. Two specimens, caught at night hopping across the road near Itamonte, Minas Gerais, December 1960, were also kept for some time; one was light, the other dark. The light one was almost constantly lemon yellow, sometimes almost chrome, rarely slightly buff. The other was generally a light reddish brown. During the following weeks they also showed frequent changes, though the yellow one was always lighter and more yellow than the brownish one.

Just after death the concealed pattern of the light one was deep chrome yellow on lavender; in the darker one a pale purple on pale brownish purple ground. Lower limb surfaces brownish drab.

Well-preserved dead specimens show different sets of tones, most of them based on yellow and orange, some with a little red in them, and all admixed with neutral gray and black. After death, light-colored specimens may become somewhat ochraceous, more rarely pinkish as stated in Spix's description, and occasionally a grayish tone of buff. The darker ones exhibit a greater gamut of reddish brown tones, from rather light to quite dark chestnut, even chocolate, or purplish olivaceous tints.

VOICE. The call of *Hyla albopunctata* consists of two short, separate croaks, sometimes followed by a third one at a lower pitch.

BEHAVIOR. This form seems to like somewhat open terrain. At night, it often calls on low vegetation, less frequently on bushes, at the edge of standing water, even artificial ponds surrounded by gardens or lawns.

KNOWN RANGE. To judge by the places where it has been collected, *Hyla albopunctata* must occupy a very large area on the Central Brazilian Plateau. It approaches the Maritime Escarpment, not in forest, but in more or less open ground. In the state of Minas Gerais it is present in a number of places; also in the parts of the state of São Paulo where frogs have been collected. It reaches the state of Paraná. In Goiás it was collected at São João da Aliança and on the Rio São Miguel by Mr. A. L. de Carvalho; it has also been caught in the Zoological Gardens of Brasilia. At Amaro Leite (a forested area), however, the specimens are devoid of pattern and seem to be *Hyla daudini*. Male specimens were collected by us in Jaraguá

near Campo Grande, which is relatively high and at Itaqui and São Vicente, also in Mato Grosso by Mr. Henrique Veloso. In the Pantanal and Gran Chaco only *Hyla raniceps* seems to occur.

*Hyla albopunctata* has also been found in Argentina. Dr. J. M. Cei, of Cuyo University, showed me three robust specimens, two of them from Misiones, which abuts on the Brazilian state of Santa Catarina, the herpetofauna of the western part of which is poorly known. Another hailed from Playadito in the province of Corrientes. The larger of the Misiones specimens, a male 54 mm snout to vent, has a vocal sac and a small but sharp prickle at the end of the pollex rudiment; the tibiotarsal articulation reaches well beyond the tip of the snout, and the dorsal color is somewhat vinaceous. The smaller specimen, 51 mm snout to vent, is slightly more roseate. In both specimens and in the one from Playadito, IBM n. 0671, light spots are numerous, spread over the border of the lower aspect of the thigh, and are visible from beneath. The specimens collected by Dr. Cei and his assistants were sitting on relatively low vegetation near water, as they do in Brazil.

RELATIONSHIP. Very close to the other forms of the group, specially to *Hyla daudini*, from which it differs by the distribution, and the pattern on the concealed aspect of the upper parts of the thigh and the flanks. They may be geographic races and are apparently vicariants.

## SPECIMENS INTERMEDIATE BETWEEN *H. DAUDINI* and *H. ALBOPUNCTATA*

Some specimens in the collections of the Museu Nacional in Rio and of the Department of Zoology of the state of São Paulo seem somewhat intermediate between typical *Hyla daudini* and *H. albopunctata*, though perhaps closer to *H. daudini*. They were collected between the southern limit of the Amazonian Hylaea and the northern edge of the Central Plateau, in a region where *mesetas* occur and where *cerrado* (scrub) is interspersed with, or close to, equatorial rain forest.

DIFFERENTIAL CHARACTERS. Morphologically similar and within the proportions of *Hyla daudini* and *Hyla albopunctata*. Differing from either by the upper posterior aspect of the thighs, with light, not very distinct, short streaks or spots, apparently derived from and in continuation of the light margins of the perpendicular bars present on the anterior, permanently visible dorsal aspect of the thigh. In some specimens spots small, rounded, detached; intensity variable, quite distinct in some specimens, so faint as to have to be looked for in others. Specimens perhaps smaller in size.

DESCRIPTION (MNR n. 3171). A very homogenous series of good specimens, one female and twenty-six males collected by Antenor Leitão de Carvalho, 30 km upstream from the village of the Tapirapé Indians on the Tapirapés River, northern Mato Grosso.

Female distended by eggs, 50 mm snout to vent. Pattern on upper posterior aspect of thigh imprecise, just continuing the light edges of the bars on the anterior part of the thigh; the same in two males. Streaks and spots more distinct in nine males; pattern dissolved into small rounded separate spots in fifteen males. Bars on the permanently visible upper aspect of the limbs present in all the males, unequally distinct, in some fading toward the extremities. No horizontal pattern on the back of the female. Dorsal pattern faint in nine males, distinct in seventeen. Some very brilliant black marks, composed of open melanophores, on the dorsal surface of the female and five males, similar but less marked in five other males; brownish indistinct spots in six, no spots in ten males. Dorsal coloring rather uniform, centering on russet-tawny, vinaceous-cinnamon, and orange-cinnamon (Ridgway, 1912). Size of males 47.1–51.4 mm, mean and median 49–50 mm snout to vent.

Series 21838–21843 DZSP. Serra do Cachimbo, eastern Pará, leg. P. E. Vanzolini. Three loaned for closer study: 21843, female with eggs, 52 mm snout to vent; white spots and streaks on upper posterior concealed aspect of thigh present, distinct, more numerous on right thigh, only a few on the left one; 21838, male 47.5 mm, lighter also with distinct light spots apparently continuing the light edges of the bars across the permanently visible anterior part; 21840 male 45.9 mm, speckled pattern of minute dots. On DZSP 21839 the dots are larger, nearer to the typical thigh pattern of *Hyla albopunctata*. Specimens rather small. Feet only half-webbed. Leg relatively short, the tibiotarsal articulation reaching just beyond the snout when adpressed; 21838 and 21840 somewhat rosy; 21840 darker with dorsal horizontal pattern present.

## *Hyla raniceps* (Cope) 1862

COPE, E. D. 1862. Catalogue of the reptiles obtained during the explorations of the Paraná, Paraguay, Bermejo and Uruguay rivers by Cap. Thos. J. Paige, U.S.N. *Pr. Ac. Nat. Sc. Phila.* 14. *Hypsiboas raniceps*: 353–354.

BOULENGER, G. A. 1889. On a collection of batrachians made by Prof. Charles Spegazzini at Colonia Resistencia, South Chaco, Argentine Republic. *An. Mus. Genova*, ser. 2, 7(27). *Hyla spegazzinii*: 247, pl. 2.

PROCTER, JOAN B. 1921. On a small collection of reptiles and batrachians made by Mr. Goodfellow in E. Bolivia (1918–1919). *An. Mag. Nat. Hist.* 9(7):181–192. *Hyla goodfellowi*: 191–192.

This very widespread species has been described several times: first by Cope (1862) from the Rio Bermejo, which serves as a border between the Argentinian provinces of Formosa and Chaco, on material gathered by the expedition of Captain Thomas Paige. It was redescribed by Boulenger (1889) from Resistencia, the capital of Formosa, on specimens collected by Prof. Charles Spegazzini. In 1921 it was redescribed from eastern Bolivia by Miss Joan Procter, who called it *Hyla goodfellowi*. *Hyla steinbachi* Boulenger is probably another name for it.

DIAGNOSTIC CHARACTERS. The elongate shape, long head, snout, and legs of this group of large species of *Hyla*. The stouter build, broader, subacuminate snout, and the different pattern of the concealed parts separate it effectively from the other members of the group. In life, dorsal surface from light cream to dark or reddish brown, with or without a dorsal pattern; characteristic broad, purplish-black, or dark slate-colored, perpendicular stripes on the thighs and sides of the body concealed in repose, on a bluish violet background. Very wide range along the waterways of the Continental and Hylean areas of Brazil, extending to Argentina, Paraguay, and eastern Bolivia.

TYPES AND TYPE LOCALITIES. This species was described first by Cope from the Bermejo River on the border of the Argentinian province of Chaco, then by Boulenger from Resistencia, the capital of the province of Formosa. I saw types of Cope's large series (nos. 5408–5436) in the USNM and of Boulenger in the British Museum.

DESCRIPTION. Size large, though variable; males from 44 to 64 mm, exceptionally 67 mm or more from snout to vent; females from 50–77, one 81 mm long. Build robust and elongate, but less slender than *Hyla albopunctata* or *Hyla daudini*. Hindlimb long, the tibiotarsal articulation reaching beyond the snout when the leg is adpressed. Head slightly longer than wide, with elongate, subacuminate snout, rounded canthus rostralis, and oblique, almost vertical loreal region. Nostrils lateral, small, twice as far from the eye as from the tip of the snout. Eye not very prominent, equal to or slightly longer than the distance from its anterior corner to the nostril. Tympanum more than one-half, often four-sevenths the horizontal diameter of the eye. Upper eyelid unusually wide, equal to, or slightly wider than the interorbital space. Tongue oval, wide, very slightly free and notched behind. Vomerine teeth in two angular groups; the inner limb very short (Cope). Lateral fingers webbed at the base. Pollex rudiment knoblike as usual ( ♂ ), or forming a ridge outside the first finger ( ♀ ). Only the two last phalanges of the fourth toe free, sometime fringed. A distinct inner metatarsal tubercle; outer one round, small, often imperceptible in adults. Palm full of tubercles. Skin thick above, granular beneath, more coarsely so on the belly and midventral aspect of the thigh. A sharp, supratympanic ridge, deflected and ending somewhat behind the eardrum. Narrow ridges on forearm and tarsus; a supra-anal ridge; no appendage on the heel. Pectoral and discoidal folds very distinct.

VARIATION. Morphological details less variable than usual in Brazilian species of *Hyla*; variation mostly affecting color, pattern, and size, and apparently individual rather than geographical, except perhaps for the small size of breeding individuals from the island of Marajó and the predominance of light specimens in southern Mato Grosso and of dark specimens from the Kuluene and Madeira rivers in the collection of the MNR.

SECONDARY SEX CHARACTERS. A very large vocal sac and sharp pollex rudiments in a series of fine nuptial males from Miranda, southern Mato Grosso; one large female from Porto Espiridião, in the same state, with such a large egg mass on the right side that it reaches the shoulder and makes her seem hunchbacked. Otherwise, sex characters not very pronounced. Large males attain the size of average females. Vocal sac often puckered together and pollex rudiment not palpable. As mentioned above, specimens from 44 to 47 mm snout to vent without sex characters are probably juvenile females.

COLOR. Dorsal ground color the usual gamut of tones seen in brown tree frogs, from almost cream or pale buff, to quite dark, somewhat violaceous,

reddish or dull orange-green tones. Concealed posterior dorsal surface of thigh and other concealed parts of limbs bluish violet; in one specimen from southern Mato Grosso they have a rosy tinge. Bars on the concealed surfaces very dark: slate blue, madder blue or madder violet. Iris too dark for gold but the upper half more vivid, the inner rim light and provided with two minute central knobs, one above, the other beneath. Free rim of transparent part of lower eyelid and lateral edges somewhat golden. Underside pale, the gula and the ventral aspect of the thighs stippled brownish. Vocal sac a dull, dirty yellow. Webs gray.

PATTERN. On the thighs very characteristic, composed of vertical, rather stout bars, inclined to form spots or irregular chevrons (specimens from an island in the Paraná River, state of Goiás). In some specimens the bars continue onto the inner aspect of the tibia and the back of the tarsus and foot. Similar bars on the sides of the body, sometimes beginning at the shoulder; unequally developed, in some individuals more distinct posteriorly, in others altogether rather faint. The bars on the thighs, the very dark supratympanic ridge, the light edge to the lower jaw and the external ridges on forearm, tarsus, elbow, and knee are constant. In dark specimens the latter are underscored by dark areas.

Dorsal pattern often very obscure, especially in light cream or buff specimens; where perceptible, it is tapestry-like, composed of intricate figures often with a lighter grayish rim (a female from São Felix on the Araguaya River). In other dark or well-pigmented individuals, the dorsal pattern consists of very irregular, more or less horizontal bars (specimen from Barra do Corda, state of Maranhão), or of three vertical rows of elongated spots (a female from Igarapé de Tapirebá, island of Marajó); or it forms blotches (specimen from Rio das Mortes); or the pattern is composed of both horizontal and vertical elements inclined to anastomose into a bold version of the faint tapestry-like pattern of light specimens (frogs from the Araguaya River, from Barreiras in Bahia and from Porto Espiridião, Mato Grosso; or it forms stellate figures (specimens from Mucuripe, Ceará). In two or three specimens the central row is darker and more conspicuous than the lateral rows.

A small percentage of specimens has a vertebral stripe (such as those from Aquidauana and Miranda in southern Mato Grosso and elsewhere). Vertebral stripe seldom very dark, generally not covering the whole midline of the back. In two or three individuals black, very distinct, accompanied to each side by a row of a few very large dots, or short dashes, reminiscent of the juvenile livery (specimen from Porto Velho).

The dorsal pattern and especially the bars on the concealed parts of limbs of the heavily pigmented specimens (Uberlandia, Minas Gerais; northwestern Amazonas) are occasionally as marked on the permanently visible anterior part of the thigh as on the posterior portion, thus becoming rather zebra-like. In some, but not all, such specimens and in a few others bars on limbs visible from beneath.

Gula also spotted in brown in dark specimens, both males and females, in extreme cases accompanied by scattered brown flecks on the chest (specimens from the Kuluene River and from Uberlandia, Minas Gerais).

Dead specimens retain the dorsal color and the dark pigments fairly well, but the dorsal pattern fades from light specimens and is masked by the dark colors of melanistic ones. The bars and even the ground color of the upper concealed part of the thigh are occasionally rather well preserved, especially if not exposed to light being covered by the legs. In a certain percentage of specimens the ground color of the thigh is a dull reddish orange instead of violet, a fact also noticed by Lorenz Müller, who calls the tint "krapproth," which is the red color of madder, *Rubia tinctoria*, and a few other allied Rubiaceae. This is neither a geographic nor an individual variation, but is probably due to chemical change. Our six very large females from Crato show both tones in a faded condition on the same thigh. This phenomenon may have certain analogy with the pigments derived from madder, such as the dark reddish brown powdered dye and the brilliant purplish-red given to cleared skeletons by dissolved alizarine derived from *Rubia*.

JUVENILE LIVERY. *Hyla raniceps* is one more large Neotropical frog with a misleading juvenile livery. According to Dr. Doris Cochran and Helen Gaige, from preserved specimens, and Mr. Leitão de Carvalho, from larvae, metamorphosing, young, and juveniles collected by him on the São Francisco River and in Ceará, the juveniles are light green (emerald green and pale Paris green fide Cochran, except for the white knees and anus and for the

sepia, russet, or bronze-colored pattern). The latter consists of a dark frenal line, a spot on each upper eyelid, an irregular interocular bar, prolonged and narrowed backward, and often broken up into segments.

This livery is very similar to that portrayed by Prince Wied for his *H. infulata*, which is considered synonymous with *Hyla albomarginata*. However, Wied mentions that in his species some parts are yellow.

VOICE. A rasping croak.

BEHAVIOR AND ECOLOGY. *Hyla raniceps* seems more aquatic than *Hyla albopunctata*. The specimens from Puerto 14 de Mayo, Bahia Negra, northern Chaco, Argentina, in the IBM bear a note by Spegazzini mentioning that they lived in the lagoon. In southern Mato Grosso we usually found them sitting or calling either in the water or on the vegetation growing in ponds and lagoons. A number of specimens in the collections examined by us were caught on the banks of large rivers, a not very usual site for tree frogs in Brazil. Käthe and Oswald Schmidt from Biel, Switzerland, found a female inside their canoe at São Felix and caught two males on the banks of the river while navigating the Araguaya.

In dry places or seasons *H. raniceps* shows great ingenuity in finding suitable resting places. At Guaicurús, in southern Mato Grosso, I spied a specimen asleep between the outer leaves of a large cabbage, growing in full sunlight, at a temperature of 40° C. Two others were taken sitting just inside the upper end of the canvas hose attached to the reservoir on a high tower made of lattice work and used to water the locomotives of the Northwestern Railway. Lorenz Müller, who collected this species in Mexiana on his trip to northern Brazil, and who gives an excellent summary of it, under the name *H. spegazzinii* in his publication on the frogs of the Gran Chaco, calls it a camp frog. I would add that it is a lowland species spreading along waterways and not inhabiting the highlands between them. On the other hand, it was caught calling on a tree in a lowlying place not far from a lagoon at Maceió in the state of Alagoas on the northeastern coast.

KNOWN RANGE. *Hyla raniceps* occupies a very vast area of Brazil and of cisandine and cisplatine South America. It is characteristic of the central depression known as the Gran Chaco, called "Pantanal" in Brazil. It reappears in the semiarid northeast, whose anuran fauna is mostly either the same or only subspecifically different from that of the Central Depression. In the Chaco it seems to follow the basin of the Paraguay River and its tributaries, Pilcomayo (Tacaaglé, L. Müller), on the border of Argentina and Paraguay, and the Bermejo between the Argentinian provinces of Formosa and Chaco. The DZSP has one specimen from the Cachoeira do Marimbondo, on the Rio Grande, a tributary of the Paraná that serves as part boundary between the states of São Paulo and Minas Gerais. Those from Uberlandia, Minas Gerais, are not far from the other branch, the Parnaiba River. *Hyla raniceps* has however also entered the basins of the other great river systems, the São Francisco, the Tocantins, and even the Amazonas, the headwaters of whose southern tributaries occasionally form temporary connections with the headwaters of the Paraguay-Paraná system.

I did not collect it in western Paraná, but it is very common all over southern Mato Grosso (Pantanal), from Miranda to Porto Esperança and beyond, also at São Luiz Cáceres, Corumbá, and Porto Espiridião at the confluence of the rivers Jaurú and Aguapehy. The specimens from the Kuluene River, at the headwaters of the Xingú and those from the Rio das Mortes, which flows toward Goiás and into the Araguaya, are succeeded by others found on the Araguaya itself. In Goiás it has been caught near the Cana Brava and the Paranã rivers, headwaters of the Tocantins, that flows north, outside the Amazonian system. *H. raniceps*, however, occurs also on the Rio Madeira and has been collected at Porto Velho in the territory of Rondonia, formerly Guaporé, near northern Bolivia, and further north at Borba in the state of Amazonas. It has also been taken in the eastern part of the Amazonian Hylaea at Belem do Pará and on the islands of Marajó and Mexiana in the estuary of the Amazonas and at Mazagão in the territory of Amapá. The specimens from Marajó and Amapá seen by us are very small. In the northeast there seems to be a continuous distribution. In this region *H. raniceps* ranges from Alagoas (Maceió), over Pernambuco (Tapera, Afogados, Jequiá), and Paraíba (Coremas), and to Rio Grande do Norte (Natal, juveniles), to Mucuripe and Crato in Ceará (six enormous females, one 81 mm snout to vent). There are also isolated specimens from the state of Maranhão, which generally speaking forms a zone of transition between the northeast and the Amazonian Hylaea. One of them is from the middle course of the Pindaré River, and the other from Barra do Corda, which flows into the Mearim. These specimens may or may not be connected with unknown populations from the lower Tocantins basin. As to the São Francisco basin, there are good collections from five points: Pirapora, Minas Gerais, on the upper course, and Bom Jesus da Lapa, Bahia, in the middle course; the others are from Barreiras, São José, and Jupaguá between Barreiras in Bahia and Barra, on the Rio Grande, one of the largest western affluents of the São Francisco. The only other specimens from Minas Gerais seen are those from Uberlandia mentioned above.

*Hyla raniceps* probably occupies most of Paraguay, as it has been collected in many different places, such as Puerto Sastre, Puerto Casado, Primavera, Nueva Germania, Ipuan, Asuncion, and Trinidad. It occurs in eastern Bolivia. (Esperanza is the type locality of the synonymous *Hyla goodfellowi* and Sara province of *Hyla steinbachi*.) It reaches Santa Cruz de la Sierra, which does not lie at a great height. The type locality given by Cope, Rio Vermejo, and that of Boulenger, Resistencia, are in Argentina. It has also been collected at Ingeniero Juarez, Gran Guardia, Formosa in the Central Chaco, at Copiazzuti in Salta and Ituzaingó, and in northern Corrientes near Paraguay (J. M. Cei).

This distribution would seem to indicate that *Hyla raniceps*, a very robust form, spreads out from the Continental Depression along the large waterways. It certainly occupies the valleys, but has not been collected either on the slopes, or on the watersheds of the central plateau. Except for Barreiras and perhaps for the specimen from the Cachoeira do Marimbondo in São Paulo, provided it was got above the falls, none of the finding places are over 500 m altitude, and many of them, especially those in the Chaco, are below 200 m. Those in the Amazonian Hylaea may be only a few tens of meters above sea level. The extremes of latitude and longitude seem to be approximately as follows: 28° S. in the Chaquean region of Argentina, 63–64° W. Gr. in Bolivia, 4° 48′ S. at Borba, in the western section of the Amazonian Hylaea, just a few minutes north of the equator in the island of Mexiana, 34° W. Gr. at Pernambuco and between 34° to 48° W. Gr. on the great rivers of Brazil.

SYNONYMS. *Hyla goodfellowi* Procter (1921) from Esperanza, eastern Bolivia, seems synonymous with *Hyla raniceps*. This may also apply to *Hyla steinbachi* Boulenger (1905), though the latter differs by the presence of a small appendix on the heel. The cotypes of *Hyla megapodia* Miranda Ribeiro (1926–1927) from São Luiz de Caceres, Mato Grosso and the figure published by him in 1926 do not support Dr. Cochran's view that this is also *H. raniceps*. There must be some mistake because the type in the MNR, and the author's figure shows that *megapodia* is very evidently a member of the *Hyla rubra–x-signata* complex.

AFFINITIES. The closest affinities of *H. raniceps* seem to be with the other large elongate forms of *Hyla* with long head, snout and legs, *i. e. Hyla daudini*, *Hyla albopunctata*, and *Hyla lanciformis*. *H. boans* and *H. raniceps* are sometimes confounded in collections and in the literature, such as the figure of a perfectly typical specimen of *Hyla raniceps* published by Miranda Ribeiro (1926, Pl. VII, fig. 3), under the name of ex-*Hyla boans*. As pointed out by Boulenger, the latter has a more pointed snout, is more slender and devoid of pattern on the concealed aspect of the limbs. *Hyla raniceps* differs from this and the two other members of the group not only by its concealed pattern but also by its stouter build and its ecological preferences. It has a large and partly overlapping range.

There is a superficial resemblance between *Hyla crepitans* Wied and very large and stout specimens of *Hyla raniceps*, which have a wider head than usual, or those with short patches of teeth and/or a reddish ground color on the thighs. A trained eye and careful consideration of habits and ecology are useful in separating them. The only similarity with *Hyla circumdata* lies in the similar ground color and dark bars on the thighs, but these are narrow and almost circular in *Hyla circumdata*, which is a short-headed, broad-snouted, montane rain-forest species, from southeastern Brazil.

## *Hyla lanciformis* Cope, 1870

> COPE, E. D. 1870. Eighth contribution to the herpetology of tropical America. *Pr. Am. Phil. Soc.* 11:553–559.

> MIRANDA RIBEIRO, A. 1926. Notas para servirem ao estudo dos gymnobatrachios (Anura) brasileiros. *Arch. Mus. Nac. Rio de Janeiro* 27. *Hyla hypocellata*: 70–71.

DIAGNOSTIC CHARACTERS. Very large size, lanceolate build, long narrow head and snout, very long hindlimb. Color: different tones of brown; sometimes very dark. A very marked light edge to the upper jaw. Light, dark-edged insular spots, often elongate, on the gula and fore part of the chest. Skin of dorsal surface minutely shagreened.

TYPE AND TERRA TYPICA. The author has seen neither the type nor the original description. Ecuador is given as the type locality in Nieden. The type is probably a female to judge by its large size, 87 mm.

DESCRIPTION. Size very large. Females: 78–87 mm, snout-vent. Males 54–67. Build slender, lanceolate, with long oval, pointed head and snout and very long hindlimbs, sometimes almost double the length of the body; tibiotarsal articulation reaching well beyond the snout when the leg is adpressed. Head 2–4 mm longer than wide. Snout long, narrowed in front; canthus rostralis sharp, loreal region concave, not very declivous. Nostrils not quite terminal but about one-third from the tip of the snout and two-thirds from the eye. Eye large, prominent, its horizontal diameter roughly two-thirds the distance from its anterior corner to the tip of the snout. Tympanum one-half to two-fifths the diameter of the eye. Interorbital space as wide as the upper eyelid, according to the literature, slightly wider in most of our specimens. Tongue long, elliptic, much narrowed in front, in accordance with the shape of the snout; indistinctly emarginate and slightly free behind. Vomerine teeth forming a more or less M-shaped group between the choanae. Lateral fingers with a rudiment of web at the base. A knob-shaped pollex rudiment, with a minute needle-like point ( ♂ ) or forming a callosity ( ♀ ). Feet about three-fourths webbed. Skin minutely granular or shagreened above; belly and midventral aspect of thigh more coarsely granular. A fold of skin across the chest. A straight, narrow, glandular fold from the posterior corner of the eye, over the tympanum to above the shoulder; slight glandular ridges to the forearm, tibia, and tarsus; a short supra-anal ridge.

VARIATION. The usual variation in length of hindlimb, the tibiotarsal articulation reaching the tip of the snout but not beyond it in the two smaller and more northern specimens, from Uaupés. In female n. 3003, from Benjamin Constant, femur unusually short. Width of head also slightly variable, unusually wide in specimen n. 4939 A. Lutz Collection from Bolivia. Groups of vomerine teeth closer together and more arched in this specimen. The proportion of interorbital space to upper eyelid, described as equal, is also variable, which is only to be expected since the upper eyelid is a soft part; equal only in the two Uaupés specimens mentioned above; interorbital space wider in the larger females. Proportion of tympanum to eye generally nearer two-fifths or one-half than two-thirds.

SECONDARY SEX CHARACTERS. The males seen are considerably smaller than the females. In the male Brazilian ones the vocal sac is gathered together and not striking as in the Bolivian one. Pollex rudiment button-shaped, ending in a very thin point. In the three females reduced to a blunt ridge outside the first finger. Some of the species and group characters, such as the long head and narrow snout, the dark sides of the head, and the very long hindlimbs, more marked in these larger specimens, which may have one longitudinal row of larger granules on the midventral aspect of the thigh.

MEASUREMENTS (mm). Three females are respectively 78, 80, and 82.7 mm long. Five former males range from 54 to 68 snout to vent length. New males from Manaus range 50–55 mm snout to vent.

COLOR AND PATTERN. The dorsal aspect of living specimens ranges from a pale to a rather dark brown. One of them being kept alive varied somewhat but was generally a slightly grayish drab on the back. The dark sides of the head and the white edge of the jaw are very marked. The three inner fingers have white disks. A dark vertebral stripe and a series of horizontal bars down the back are present, but the latter vary in intensity. They coincide with similar horizontal bars on the permanently visible upper parts of the limbs. Iris dull gold with thin, dendritic, dark lines, of which a curved one near the periphery is more distinct than the rest. Concealed upper aspect of the limbs slightly vinaceous, devoid of pattern. Gula light tan, smooth. Chest, belly and midventral portion of the thighs white, very granular; a V-shaped row of larger granules on the thighs. Very con-

spicuous light blotches with a darker outline on the throat, the fore part of the chest and the root of the arms provide one of the diagnostic characters.

Dead specimens also range from pale to dark brown with the dorsal pattern and vertebral stripe present or not. The blotches on the underside are very evident. Sides of the head very dark contrasting greatly with the white upper jaw.

HABITS. At Benjamin Constant *Hyla lanciformis* was collected on a thorny tree by Miss Gertrude Rita Kloss. In November 1968 I had the good fortune to obtain five males that were calling on bushes at the edge of a ditch on a road leading into Manaus. Many others were present despite the heavy traffic, but proved inaccessible because of the depth of the water between them and us.

KNOWN DISTRIBUTION. Cope described the species from Ecuador. In his catalogue (1882) Boulenger mentions a specimen from Canellos in Ecuador. The American Museum of Natural History has a series from Peru. A very faded and not very characteristic specimen, but which has vestiges of the gular spots and pattern, from Ivon in Bolivia in the A. Lutz Collection was obtained by exchange from MZUM. The other specimens used in this description are from the Amazonian Hylaea in Brazil: four of them from Benjamin Constant (4° 21' 42" S. 96° 54' 32" W. Gr.), one from Itacoai near by, 30 km from the Javarí River, and two from Uaupés on the upper Rio Negro, five from Manaus, one from Fortaleza on the Acre River (n. 4476), and others from the middle course of the Purús River. The DZSP has three specimens from Rio Acre (nos. 6515–6517) in the territory of the same name.

CLIMATE. *Af* Koeppen; vegetation; equatorial forest.

AFFINITIES. A close general resemblance obtains between the large, narrow, long-headed, long-legged forms of this group. The main difference seems to lie in the very lanceolate build, large size, and extremely long legs of *H. lanciformis*, especially between the largest specimens of *lanciformis* and average *daudini*. The insular spots on the gula and chest and the very marked light border of the upper jaw are also very characteristic. Neither of the two has a pattern on the concealed aspect of the limbs, like those of *Hyla albopunctata* Spix and *Hyla raniceps* Cope (*spegazzinii* Blgr.).

# 5. Montane Southeastern Forms

## Hyla claresignata Lutz & B. Lutz, 1939

LUTZ, A., and LUTZ, B. 1939. New Hylidae from Brazil. *An. Ac. Brasil. Sc.* 11(1):67–89, 6 figs. *Hyla claresignata*: 67–69.

LUTZ, B., and ORTON, G. 1946. *Hyla claresignata* Lutz & B. Lutz, 1939. Aspects of the life-history and description of the rhyacophilous tadpole. Bol. Mus. Nac. Rio de Janeiro, n. ser., *Zoologia* 70. 20 pp., 15 figs.

DIAGNOSTIC CHARACTERS. The size, allied to the color, pattern, distribution, and ecology. Tympanum very small; tongue short and wide; legs and webs long; hands and feet very large. Maize color or light buff above; unusual, dark, white-edged insular marks, especially on the flanks and sides of the body. Larva rhyacophilous, adapted to life in torrential waters, with disruptive coloration, clinging mouth, and very high tooth formula. Adult bromelicolous, montane. Endemic in the Serra do Mar (Maritime Range), southeastern Brazil.

TYPES. Holotype: female, which was caught by J. Venancio while it was jumping from a bromeliad in the garden of Mr. Arnaldo Guinle at the entrance of the Granja Guarany, Teresópolis, state of Rio de Janeiro, November 9, 1929; now, n. 1971 of the A. Lutz Collection at the MNR. Allotypes: two young males from the Segredinho stream in the Serra da Bocaina, also caught by J. Venancio, January 1930. One of them was asleep in a bromeliad; the other was fished out of the water while Venancio was looking for tadpoles; nos. 2088, 2089 A. Lutz Collection, MNR.

TERRA TYPICA. Organ Mountains: 22° 26′ 12″ lat. S. 42° 58′ 42″ long. W. Gr.; altitude 900 m. Rain forest vegetation. Climate subtropical with cool summer (Köppen: *Cfb*). Serra da Bocaina 22° 32′ 30″ lat. S. 44° 35′ 30″ long. W. Gr.; altitude about 1,200 m at the collecting place; vegetation and climate the same. Köppen: *Cfb*.

DESCRIPTION. Size: type, female, 61 mm; allotypes and other males 36–42 mm, average 40 mm snout to vent. Build robust. Type very robust with long legs and massive head. Body slightly narrowed in the postaxillary region. Tibiotarsal articulation reaching beyond the snout when the leg is adpressed. Snout rounded, short, with distinct canthus rostralis and gradually sloping loreal region. Eye large, very prominent, almost as long as the distance from its anterior corner to the tip of the snout. Interorbital space slightly wider than the upper eyelid, double the distance between the nostrils. Tympanum small, less than one-third the diameter of the eye, but very distinct, partly covered above by a short, heavy ridge. Vomerine teeth in two separate, oblique groups, behind the large choanae, parallel to the posterior half of their inner border. Tongue very broad and short, entire, hardly free behind. Lateral fingers about one-third webbed; the fourth longer than the second, just reaching the base of the disk of the third; subarticular tubercles well developed; an angular pollex rudiment. Toes webbed almost to their tips; on the third and fifth the webs attached to the base of the disks. An inner metatarsal tubercle. Narrow metatarsal ridges; no dermal appendage on the heel. Skin smooth above, granular beneath, on throat minutely so.

VARIATION. The small series of fourteen specimens shows only the usual variation in the length of the hindlimb, slightly fuller or less full webs, entire or emarginate tongue, more or less separated groups of vomerine teeth.

MEASUREMENTS (mm). Holotype female: snout to vent 61. Hindlimb 112: femur 31, tibia 33, tarsus and foot 48. Head length:width 20:23. Eye 8, tympanum 2.5, eye-nostril 6, eye to tip of snout 9; interorbital space 6.5; upper eyelid 6.

Male paratypes 37, 41; largest male 42. Hindlimb 60–66 mm.

COLOR AND PATTERN (recorded in watercolor made from living type). Ground color pale yellow above; sides, concealed upper parts of thigh, hands, feet, and webs deeper chrome yellow; paler beneath. Gula and concealed ventral aspect of thigh pale, vinaceous. Tympanum also lighter. A series of very characteristic, irregular, roughly triangular, black or clove brown, insular spots outlined in white along the dorsolateral region of the body, upper parts of thigh, knee, and anal region give the species its name. Numerous gray dots all over the dorsal surface. Perianal surface and edges of knees black.

COLOR VARIATION. Two other watercolors (of the two male allotypes) record different color phases. One is pale yellow with gray spots on elbow, heel, sides of body, and three, small, roughly triangular spots, pointed forward, on the thigh; a gray shadow on the upper eyelids and loreal region and indistinct gray bars on the leg. The other is dark brown. It shows unexpected bars on the permanently visible dorsal aspect of thigh and leg. In the specimens observed by us from metamorphosis, the ground color varied in tone from cream to brown. The distinctness of the pattern and the density of the isolated gray dots also seem individually variable. Ventral aspect immaculate.

In alcohol very light, uniform, drab buff with faint vestiges of the spots.

SECONDARY SEX CHARACTERS. Adult males with a thin, sharp, needle-like prick inside the pollex rudiment, which can be felt at the side of the first finger and is visible in one specimen. Vocal sac large, median. Leg apparently shorter than in female type, which is one-third again as large as most males.

VOICE. Not recorded.

ECOLOGY. The adults live in bromeliads, epiphytic on trees, growing above or near the beds of swift or torrential brooks and streams. The apparent rarity of the species is perhaps due to the difficulty of collecting it. Except for the type, which was full of eggs and was probably climbing down to spawn, and one paratype fished out of the river, we have never seen adults outside their habitat; all the others were found asleep in bromeliads. In this they differ from some other more abundant species like *Hyla circumdata*, which often sit on shrubs or on stones in brooks. The bromeliad-bearing trees may be very slender, tall, and inaccessible.

The montane character of the species is probably tied to the ecological specialization of the larval stage. The adults do not show perceptible traces of specialization, and bromeliads occur also in the lowlands.

LARVAL HABITAT. Pools and basins in swift mountain streams and brooks, with stones or boulders in the beds, surrounded by very agitated water and subjected to sudden onrushes or floods, especially after rainstorms.

BEHAVIOR OF LARVA. The tadpole was first seen in the Bonito stream at the Serra da Bocaina after a flood, having evidently been swept down from one of the swift mountain brooks flowing into it. For several years others were occasionally seen, but they were only identified after a population was found in the Beija-Flor stream in the Serra dos Orgãos National Park at Teresópolis, which included a number of larvae approaching metamorphosis. In every instance the tadpoles were found attached to the rocks in the bed, sometimes horizontally, but generally vertically, hanging down immobile well below the surface, often quite near the bottom. When disturbed they swam just far enough to reach a similar spot and fasten themselves on again. They do not come up to the surface periodically, as most unspecialized tadpoles do, but occasionally they move along the rock surface in a jerky manner clinging by the mouth and beaks. The mouth is greatly enlarged and quite ventral. The posterior part of the body and the tail hang free.

LARVA (Dr. Grace Orton, 1946): "In common with many other tadpoles living in swift streams, or in pools in streams subject to periodic flooding, the larva of *Hyla claresignata* is highly modified for adhering to the substratum.

"DESCRIPTION. Head large, broad, somewhat depressed; snout very long and wide, rather truncate anteriorly. Eyes rather small, dorsal, moderately close together, appearing to be nearly halfway back on body, because of the great prolongation of the snout. Nostrils small, distinctly closer together than eyes, very much closer to eye than to either tip of snout or lateral base of lip; inner edge of nostril projecting as a distinct papilla. Spiracle sinistral, with a projecting tube, situated far back on side, much closer to ventral base of tail than to either tip of snout or eye; more nearly equidistant between eye and ventral base of tail in large, submetamorphic specimens; unusually posterior relative to tip of snout, due principally to enlargement and elongation of head region. Anus dextral, opening just above edge of ventral fin. Rectus muscles of abdomen moderately well developed but not unusually so. Tail of moderate length; musculature rather thick at base, strongly tapering distally; caudal fins moderately well developed, the dorsal originating on base of tail or slightly farther forward.

"MOUTHPARTS. Lips very greatly enlarged, flattened, sucker-like, nearly as wide as snout; entirely bordered with a single row of small, narrow, pointed papillae; surface with an overlapping fold ventrolaterally. Tooth formula 7/11 to 9/14, usually about 8/12; innermost row on each lip divided medially; intermediate rows continuous; outermost one or more rows occasionally interrupted, forming a series of short segments. Labial teeth of moderate size, extremely numerous, closely crowded, and in a single series per row; teeth becoming smaller and less heavily pigmented in outer rows. A small area of submarginal papillae on lip surface between ends of upper and lower tooth rows, some of these papillae bearing short, inconspicuous lines of minute, pale brown teeth. Gape of mouth moderately wide in lateral direction but with narrow black edges; marginal serrations obscure; margin of upper beak shallowly convex; horny part of

upper beak prolonged laterally, fading out as a brownish streak on surface jaw.

"MEASUREMENTS of a large tadpole (in mm); total length, 60; head and body length, 25; length of hindlimb, 31; width of lips, 9; length of lips, 6.

"COMPARISONS. The larva of *Hyla claresignata* has the highest tooth formula known in the Hylidae, and it is among the most specialized of known stream-inhabiting tadpoles. In number of tooth rows, it is most nearly approached by the Hispaniolan *Hyla heilprini*, with a tooth formula of 6/9, and the Panamanian *Hyla colymba*, with a formula 6/8 to 7/8. Neither of these forms, nor any other described hylid tadpole known to us, has the excessively hypertrophied snout of *claresignata*. The enlargement and flattening of the snout in *H. claresignata* parallels the specialized condition of such well-known and unrelated larva as *Bufo penangensis*, of southeastern Asia, and *Heleophryne purcelli*, of South Africa."

METAMORPHOSIS. At metamorphosis, the arms are already quite long, while the larval mouth and tail persist. In this species the process involves considerable change; as pointed out by Dr. Orton, there is a great deal of larval jaw tissue to absorb. The adult has a very different contour of the head with a short snout and a very wide mouth. Average size at metamorphosis: head to body 23–25 mm, tail 35–40 mm, hindlimb 38–40 mm.

JUVENILES. The juveniles seem very hardy compared to the specialized larvae. Seven of them brought alive to Rio adapted themselves. Five of them lived ten months and two for a year. The first five, apparently all males, grew almost to full size for their sex. The other two, probably females, without a sharp pollex rudiment, which lived two months longer, were not more than two-thirds the size of the female holotype.

The diagnostic characters of the species appear soon after metamorphosis. The pattern develops slowly. It began to show at nine weeks. At seven months the pattern was present in all seven but very unequal in intensity, most of them showing the dark dashes on the legs seen in the male paratypes. At twelve months, the two survivors showed the specific characters very clearly and had acquired the adult color on hands, feet, and gula.

BEHAVIOR. Some of the juveniles were stronger and more active than the others from the beginning. One learned to catch flies in the vivarium in daytime several days before the others. The smell of crushed plants was first noticed in seven-weeks-old specimens while measuring them. It seems probable that when young *Hyla claresignata* leave the water definitively they climb into the epiphytic bromeliads of the trees growing nearby.

GROWTH (in captivity). At seven weeks: snout to vent 25–27 mm; hindlimb 38–42 mm. At ten months (5): snout to vent 37 mm (2), 38 mm (3). Hindlimb 54 mm (1), 58 mm (2), 60 mm (1), 62 mm (1). At twelve months (2): snout to vent 40 and 41 mm. Hindlimb 63 and 66 mm.

RELATIONSHIPS. *Hyla claresignata* does not show any marked affinities with other species. *H. clepsydra* Lutz, which is also montane, bromelicolous, and very rare, also has a very small tympanum. However, the coloring is different, and according to Dr. Cochran it has two lateral vocal sacs. They seem to occur together in the Serra da Bocaina.

DISTRIBUTION. Except for the paratypes from the Serra da Bocaina, all our adult specimens are from the Serra dos Orgãos near Teresópolis. They were obtained at different sites and at altitudes ranging from some 600 to over 1,100 m above sea level. We have tadpoles from the Rio Beija Flor (tadpole types), the Rio Paquequer at 1,100 to 900 m, from the Rio Garrafão and another parallel stream at Fagundes, near Barreiras, all in the same range. Tadpoles were also obtained in the Serra da Boa Vista at Theodoro de Oliveira outside Nova Friburgo (22° 17′ lat. S. 42° 32′ W. Gr.; altitude 1,000 m). During a short excursion to Marumbi, outside Curitiba, in the more southern state of Paraná, very similar tadpoles were collected below a waterfall. One of them, with long legs, may be slightly larger than usual: head to body 26 mm, tail 34 mm, hindlimb 31 mm. The distribution of pigment differs somewhat: there is a row of large, round dots on the upper crest instead of the vertical bar across the tail seen in the typical form. Unfortunately, despite very strenuous efforts, no adults were raised from them.

## *Hyla clepsydra* Lutz, 1925

LUTZ, A. 1925. Batraciens du Brésil (II). *C. R. Soc. Biol. Paris* 93(22):211–214.

LUTZ, A. 1926. Nota previa sobre especies novas de batrachios brasileiros. *Publ. Inst. O. Cruz*, 9 pp. English translation: 10–16.

COCHRAN, D. M. 1955. Frogs of Southeastern Brazil. *U.S.N.M. Bull.* 206:87–89, pl. 7, fig. B.

DIAGNOSTIC CHARACTERS. Small disks, especially that of the first finger; very small tympanum; almost smooth midventral aspect of the thigh; distinctive color, pattern, and habitat. Above cream to buff, the type with a large, conspicuous, dark, hourglass-shaped mark covering much of the dorsal surface, from which the specific name is derived; clear-cut separation of permanently visible dorsal parts of the limbs from those concealed in repose; the former cream, with crossbars, inclined to be semi-annular on the tibia and the forearm, the latter flesh-colored, immaculate. Bromelicolous, montane; known only from the type locality and in the male.

TYPE AND TYPE LOCALITY. Holotype male, almost adult, collected by Joaquim Venancio in a bromeliad at the Fazenda do Bonito, in the Serra da Bocaina, state of São Paulo, Brazil, January 31, 1925, no. 976 of the A. Lutz Collection at the MNR. I collected one additional specimen, also in a bromeliad, at the same place, April 1951.

Type locality: 22° 22′ 30″ S. 44° 35′ 30″ W. Gr.; local altitude 1,100–1,500 m. Rain-forest vegetation. Climate subtropical with cool summers (Köppen *Cfb*).

DESCRIPTION (Note: Unfortunately the type is in a poor condition and damaged by mold. However, it was carefully described by Dr. Doris M. Cochran in her book *Frogs of Southeastern Brazil*, pp. 87–89). I am indebted to her for most of the description but have added the variation of characters observed in the additional specimen.

Size: Holotype 39 mm from snout to vent. Build robust in life. In the preserved specimen body narrower than head. Hindlimb relatively short, the heel reaching only to the anterior corner of the eye when the leg is adpressed. To quote Dr. Cochran: "Snout moderately short, rounded at the tip when viewed from above, truncate in profile, the upper jaw projecting only slightly beyond the lower; nostrils lateral. Canthus rostralis distinct but rounded; loreal region concave and sloping. Eye large, prominent, its diameter slightly less than the distance from end of snout; interorbital diameter about 1 1/4 times the width of upper eyelid. Tympanum very small but distinct, about 1/3 the diameter of the eye. Vomerine teeth in two exceedingly heavy, long, transverse, well-separated series behind the posterior level of the choanae; tongue slightly less than two-thirds as wide as the mouth-opening, widely oval, almost entirely attached behind and with hardly a trace of an indentation. Fingers webbed at the base, fourth much longer than second, reaching to disk of third, which practically covers the tympanic area; a pollex with a very sharp, needle-like spur projecting from the side of the first finger; toes one-half webbed, the third apparently shorter than the fifth; disks very small, that of the fourth toe apparently covering only one-half the tympanic area; a very prominent inner but no outer metatarsal tubercle; no tarsal ridge, no dermal appendage on heel. Skin of upper parts smooth; a heavy ridge encircling tympanum and ending on shoulder; skin of throat and chest smooth, of belly and postanal region coarsely granular, of lower femur almost smooth; no apparent skin fold across the chest. A pair of lateral external vocal sacs."

VARIATION (MNR no. 4090). Slightly smaller, 38 mm. Hindlimb longer, the heel reaching beyond the nostril when the leg is adpressed. Interorbital space 5/3 the width of the upper eyelid. Diameter of eye longer than the distance from its anterior corner to the nostril. Tympanum very small, less than one-third the diameter of the eye. Disk of the first finger very small. Webs slightly longer than described above; last two articulations of the fourth toe fringed. Groups of vomerine teeth robust but not very widely separated nor exceedingly heavy or long. Specimen probably less adult.

MEASUREMENTS (mm). Type: head and body 39 mm, femur 17; tibia 22. Head, length:width 14:14. Additional specimen: snout-vent:hindlimb 38:68, femur 20, tibia 20, tarsus and foot 28. Head, length to width 13:14. Interorbital space: upper eyelid 5:3, tympanum between 1–2, eye 5, eye:nostril 5:4.

SECONDARY SEX CHARACTERS. Male with a thin sharp spur in the pollex rudiment. According to Dr. Cochran, the forearm is greatly developed and the arm weak in the type, making it difficult to straighten and measure the forelimb. These characters are not marked in the additional specimen. In Lutz's manuscript notes there is a query regarding the possibility of *Hyla clepsydra* being a *Nototrema*. It may well be, in view of some of the characters, but an adult female is needed to make sure.

COLOR AND PATTERN. According to A. Lutz, 1925: "Upper side light beige, ventral white. Snout with a brown angular spot on top. Another, very large, brown spot, in the shape of an hourglass, has its anterior margin on and between the eyelids; the posterior one in the lumbar region ends in two lateral oblique extensions connected by a transverse anastomosis. Limbs with brown crossbands inclined to be semiannular on tibia and forearm (according to the MSS). Posterior aspect of thigh immaculate, light pink."

Dr. Cochran calls attention to a dark bar on the loreal region, the narrowing of the hourglass-shaped mark before the shoulders, its black border and the heavier crossbars on the forearm and tibia. She does not mention the fenestration between the two posterior prongs of the *clepsydra*. All these characters are visible on the excellent watercolor painted by P. Sandig for A. Lutz.

I am struck by the separation of the permanently visible upper surfaces from those concealed in repose, by the slightly fenestrated sacral part of the *clepsydra*, and by the very characteristic appearance of the crossbars on the thigh and tibia.

In the additional specimen, the hourglass shaped spot is substituted by an indistinct, evanescent, dark blotch, occupying much of the back, plus a few black spots on the flanks. When it was photographed, the light dorsal surface did not show the blotch; only dark disseminated dots and the spots on the flanks were in evidence. The whole of the permanently visible dorsal aspect was between cream and a light slightly roseate tan and the concealed parts a deep flesh-color. "Iris tawny olive, the pupil black and somewhat elliptic" (fide Cochran).

The faded and mutilated type has lost its coloring and is drab all over. The light tints of the additional specimens have also faded; the dark marks are ill-defined and indistinct; the crossbars persist, especially the typical ones on the thigh and a few dark spots on the flanks.

HABITAT. This is an extremely rare frog, of which only two certain specimens have been seen, both in the type locality and in bromeliads. The type was collected in one and the additional specimen was taken from another by felling a very tall, thin, dead tree that had bromeliads near its tip.

AFFINITIES. *Hyla clepsydra* does not show any marked affinity with other species, but it is similar to *Hyla claresignata* in having a very small tympanum and in being bromelicolous and montane. The tongue is narrower, the webs are longer, and the coloring and pattern diverse. The two forms are apparently sympatric in the Bocaina part of the Maritime Range.

# II. Medium-Sized to Small Species

# 6. Green Species

The species of *Hyla* belonging to this group which occur in Brazil are characterized by their light green color and medium size. They vary in habit, morphological detail, and distribution. Their differential characters are less evident in museum specimens than in the living animals. The call and the color of the iris are diagnostic.

## ATLANTIC PROVINCE

One of the species of this group, *Hyla albomarginata* Spix, has a long north-south distribution along the coast. The others, *Hyla albofrenata, H. albosignata,* and *H. musica,* are southeastern and montane. They succeed each other altitudinally with slight overlaps at the altitudinal limits of their range.

## *Hyla albomarginata* Spix, 1824

SPIX, J. B. von. 1824. *Animalia nova sive species novae testudinum et ranarum quas in itinere per Brasiliam, annis 1817–20, collegit et descripsit.* Atlas, p. 33, pl. 8, fig. 1.

LUTZ, B. 1948. Anfíbios anuros da Coleção Adolpho Lutz. II Espécies verdes do gênero *Hyla* do Leste Meridional do Brasil. *Mem. Inst. O. Cruz,* 46(3):555–559, table I, figs. 2, 5, 9. English summary: 572.

This is a very handsome and abundant species that has been known for a long time. It was described over 140 years ago.

DIAGNOSTIC CHARACTERS. A light glandular dorsolateral margin from behind the eye to the middle of the body. In life, iris silvery; color very light green; webs, flanks, and parts of the thigh concealed in repose bright orange. Lowland form with a long north-south distribution along the coast.

TYPES AND TYPE LOCALITY. Spix says, "Habitat in Provincia Bahiae." The types were either destroyed or buried under the rubble of a cellar during the bombardment of Munich in the Second World War. This species is, however, common and easily recognized.

DESCRIPTION. Size relatively large for the group. Males 39–55 mm, females 50–62 mm. Build robust, elongate. Hindlimb long, thin. Head large. Snout oval and slightly acuminate, or shorter and more truncate, from above, slightly curved in profile, the upper jaw not projecting much above the lower one. Canthus rostralis blunt, loreal region slightly concave, oblique. Interorbital space one and a half to twice the width of the upper eyelid. Eye prominent, rather lateral, its diameter equal to or slightly greater than the distance from its anterior corner to the nostril. Tympanum one-half or less of the diameter of the eye. Tongue wide, rounded or heart-shaped, notched or entire, hardly free behind. Vomerine teeth in two robust groups, parallel to the inner rim of the choanae, forming a chevron directed forward. Lateral fingers half-webbed; an elongate tubercle (pollex rudiment) on the outer edge of inner finger; palms well padded. Foot about four-fifths webbed; a blunt inner metatarsal tubercle; soles also padded. Leg generally long, the tibiotarsal articulation reaching the tip of the snout or beyond it, or at least almost to the nostril when the leg is adpressed. Dorsal skin almost smooth, often with a few spots of guanine; skin of gula and chest fairly smooth, belly and midventral aspect of thigh granular. A glandular, dorsolateral margin, a supra-anal border, a similar or less-distinct glandular edge on the forearm, tarsus, and foot to the outer digit, forming a slight fold at the elbow and a small appendage on the heel; the margins on the limbs are more visible from beneath.

MEASUREMENTS.    Out of twenty-three females measured, one is exceptionally large: 69 mm snout to vent. The others vary from 51–62 mm; average 57. Hindlimb 85–118, average 105 mm. Head length to width 16:20 or 16:21.

Males quite variable. Of fifty-five measured, fourteen are 50 mm from snout to vent, seven are 48, eight are 45, and five are 40, the others in between. Hindlimb 67–92 mm.

VARIATION.    The size is variable because sexually mature specimens go on growing. Nevertheless, our samples from the Tijuca Mountains in Rio and Joinville in Santa Catarina are mostly large. Those from Santa Tereza in Espírito Santo, which were probably collected at different periods, vary greatly in size. The ones from the coastal lowlands in the states of Rio and Guanabara are smaller than those from the slopes. The length of the hindlimb and the femur to tibia ratio are individually variable. In most specimens the head is slightly wider than long, but in some width and length are the same. Some specimens from Caxias, state of Rio de Janeiro, are very much webbed. The tongue varies as usual and the shape and degree of separation of the vomerine teeth also vary.

SECONDARY SEX CHARACTERS.    Males with large vocal sac, sometimes very tightly folded, covered by a citrine membrane; rudiment of pollex button-shaped, mostly blunt, sharp in our large males from Brusque (Santa Catarina) and some of those from Rio; forearm somewhat thickened. Female very robust, eggs generally visible by translucency; rudi-

ment of pollex forming just a thickened edge to the first finger.

COLOR.    Whole of dorsal aspect visible in repose a very delicate light green. As mentioned by A. Lutz: "The basic green color extends to the bones, muscles, and even to some of the internal organs. This color may fade to yellow in life or after death. The chromatophores composed of isolated cells are not always visible in the living animal. On the ventral aspect the color becomes blue-green or blue; the glandular dorsolateral and supra-anal margins are yellowish rather than white. Iris metallic, silvery, differentiating it immediately from that of the other green species of *Hyla* even during development. In sleep pupil reduced to a horizontal slit in the silvery surface. Another distinctive character is the brilliant orange color of the flanks and the concealed parts of the thighs and webs. These two characters make it impossible to confound the species with any other one."

The glandular, lemon yellow or cream margins on the sides of the body and the anus are best seen from above, but those on the edges of the forearm and tarsus, including the appendage on the heel are equally visible from beneath. Gula bluish green ( ♀ ). Chest and belly opaque, the white peritoneum showing through the skin with a distinct orange tint. Midventral aspect of thigh also somewhat opaque. A deeper blue-green tone over the large articulations and on the forearm; other limb segments a slightly more yellowish green. Inside of mouth also green, the tongue paler than the lining.

One frog from Manguinhos (Guanabara), out of a great many from different locations examined alive, displayed pairs of faint horizontal white lines across the dorsal surface. Some individuals show spots of guanine, generally white; in one from Barro Branco (state of Rio de Janeiro), the spots were rose-colored. Scattered, sometimes very numerous, chromatophores may also be present and give the dorsal surface a dark tint. The sclerotic often shows as a blue circle round the iris. The upper surfaces of the thighs concealed in repose, the inner digits and disks, also tucked away, are bright orange like the webs.

After death the specimens fade, first to yellow then to either white, ivory, or light gray. The turning of the green color to yellow in life seems to be a sign of ill health often preceding death. The dark chromatophores may also persist.

VOICE.    *Hyla albomarginata* calls in a chorus

very similar to the quacking of ducks. Lutz describes the voice as "staccato" quacks, somewhat reminiscent of the song of the bellbird, *Chiasmorhynchus nudicollis,* or of the sound produced by striking a glass with the knuckles.

BEHAVIOR. *Hyla albomarginata* gathers near the sheets of standing water in which it breeds and is mostly seen in the herbaceous vegetation around ponds. As soon as summer begins, the weather grows warm, or rain threatens, it raises its voice.

ECOLOGY. This is a lowland species, though it may rise a few hundred meters above sea level where there is standing water available for the larvae. At the edge of the Tijuca forest, outsidè Rio de Janeiro, it lives at 380 m altitude. There it comes in contact with *Hyla albofrenata* at the Açude da Solidão, an artificial open pool at the edge of the woods, but it does not enter the forest nor does *Hyla albofrenata* emerge from it. *Hyla albomarginata* is known to occur at similar altitudes in a few other places. In residential suburbs of Rio de Janeiro and more frequently in those of Salvador, the capital of the state of Bahia, its terra typica, *Hyla albomarginata* can be heard quacking in gardens or market gardens provided with artificial ponds.

KNOWN DISTRIBUTION. The ALC and that of the MNR have series of specimens from a number of points between Brusque and Joinville in the state of Santa Catarina, and Natal, the capital of the state of Rio Grande do Norte, mostly along the coastal plain, though they may reach 400 m elevation. *Hyla albomarginata* has been collected from approximately 27°–5° S. and 48°–35° W. Gr., following the contours of the Brazilian coast. The climates involved are *As, Aw, Am, Af* Köppen, with high temperature and not very marked dry season.

SYNONYMS. *Hyla infulata* Wied is a synonym of *Hyla albomarginata. Hyla massarti* de Witte is also synonymous with it.

RELATIONSHIPS. Some authors put part of the green kinds of *Hyla* found in the northern part of this continent, or even in Central America, into the species of Spix. The only specimen thus labeled in our collection, an exchange with E. R. Dunn, comes from Panama. The webs are very wide on all the digits, and it is much smaller than the Brazilian form. Dr. Dunn had a watercolor of such a frog from Panama, but the webs are nearer to scarlet than to orange and the proportions slightly different. The Costa Rican specimens of the British

Museum seem to lack the dorsolateral margins. I do not believe that they are identical, but they may be allopatric vicariants. The Dunn picture is probably *Hyla rufitela* Fouquette.

## *Hyla albofrenata* Lutz, 1924

LUTZ, A. 1924. Sur les rainettes des environs de Rio de Janeiro. *C. R. Soc. Biol. Paris* 90(2):241.
———. 1926. New Species of Brazilian Batrachians. Preliminary Note. *Mem. Inst. O. Cruz,* March 1926, p. 14.
LUTZ, B. 1948. Anfíbios anuros da Coleção Adolpho Lutz. II Espécies verdes do gênero *Hyla* do Leste Meridional do Brasil. *Mem. Inst. O. Cruz,* 46(3):551–577. *H. albofrenata*: 559–562, table I, figs. 1, 6, 10.

*H. albofrenata* is one of the three green species of *Hyla* of the *H. albomarginata* group living in the southeastern coastal montane forest of Brazil and also the only one that occurs in the vicinity of the city of Rio de Janeiro.

DIAGNOSTIC CHARACTERS. A. Lutz (1926): "Smaller than *Hyla albomarginata* Spix (*infulata* Burm.) and lacking the orange-colored spots found on that species while alive. A white stripe on the sharp-edged canthus rostralis. Iris distinctly copper-colored. The call is quite different from that of *Hyla albomarginata* and sounds like drops of water falling into an empty bottle. The tadpoles in metamorphosis are frequently found in water, but the adults hide in the dense foliage and especially in the epiphytic Bromeliaceae. They are not rare, as their call is heard at night in all the woods near Rio." One might add that no vivid flash colors are present on the concealed surfaces; Iris hazel, pale plum or copper. Ventral outline of head and mouth ogival, very characteristic. Calls the whole year round.

TYPES AND TYPE LOCALITY. Montane forest surroundings of Rio de Janeiro. Syntypes: USNM 963401, Paineiras on Corcovado mountain and USNM 96339–45 (cotypes of Cochran) plus other cotypes mentioned by her (1955). A. Lutz Collection 577 and 577a, Tijuca, Rio at MNR; leg. A. Lutz et al. November 1923.

DESCRIPTION. Size: males 37–40 mm, largest female seen 45 mm snout to vent. Build less robust than that of the other species of the group. Body narrower than the head, except in the postaxillary region, tapering beyond the sacrum. Leg fairly short, the tibiotarsal articulation reaching the eye when adpressed. Snout pointed, triangular from above, rounded in profile. Ventral outline of head very characteristic, ogival, the snout projecting slightly, the jaws curved, the gular region drawn inward. Canthus rostralis straight, sharp. Loreal region concave, rather vertical. Nostril small, lateral, not terminal. Eye prominent in life, its horizontal diameter about equal to its distance from the nostril. Tympanum two-fifths or one-half the diameter of eye. Interorbital space much wider than internarial space. Vomerine teeth in two short, separate, robust, slightly arched groups between and mostly behind the choanae. Tongue large, rounded, slightly emarginate and barely free behind. Fingers short with round disks; a basal web between the first and second; lateral fingers half-webbed, fringed to the base of the disks. A large elongate callosity at the edge of the inner finger, which is held as if opposable. Palms well padded. Toes short, especially the inner ones, which have a short web between them. Others about three-fourths webbed, the webs continuing as a fringe to the disks; wide part of webs hollowed. A conspicuous, oval, inner metatarsal tubercle. Skin smooth above, granular on the abdomen and midventral aspect of thigh, minutely so on the chest and gula. A white glandular canthal line ending on the opaque upper eyelids. A very slight ridge over the tympanum. A slightly glandular ridge on the outer side of the forearm ending in a pustule on the elbow; a similar one over the foot and tarsus, forming a pointed tubercle on the heel; a slight elevated perianal ridge. Living or well-preserved specimens with the glandular ridges well developed may present a few postanal glandules but not rows of "milium" like those of *Hyla albosignata*.

MEASUREMENTS. Well-grown males generally 39–40 mm long, exceptionally large ones 41, smallest, from Barro Branco, 37 mm. Largest female seen 45 mm. Juveniles 23–24 mm long common. Metamorphosis at 17–18 mm head and body length.

VARIATION. The adpressed tibiotarsal articulation reaches slightly beyond the eye in a few specimens from the type locality and a larger percentage of those from the northern block of the Serra do Mar, namely Teresópolis. In these and those from Itatiaia the canthal ridge is prolonged over the tympanum and on the sides till near the elbow. One specimen from Barro Branco has a very

pointed head and a small triangular flap on the knee.

SECONDARY SEX CHARACTERS. Not pronounced. Forearm of breeding males much enlarged. Vocal sac large.

COLOR. *H. albofrenata* is green and devoid of pattern except for the white glandular ridges and glandules. Dorsal aspect a delicate light green slightly more yellowish than that of *Hyla albomarginata*. No flash colors on the surfaces concealed in repose. Gula deep blue green. Bones green, large articulations malachite green. Color over peritoneum lemon yellow; liver black, sometimes visible by translucency. Mouth cavity also blue green. Iris of adults hazel, pale prune purple or coppery, with a network of slightly darker lines. Pupil quadrilateral but with slightly rounded outline and minute median lobes. Sometimes minute dark chromatophores over the dorsal surface or a few brilliant light spots of guanine.

In alcohol these frogs become first yellow, then ivory. In some the chromatophores become a slightly reddish brown.

VOICE. As mentioned by Lutz, the call sounds like drops of water falling into an empty bottle. It is composed of isolated, sometime double, liquid, well-separated notes. *Hyla albofrenata* calls the year round, aloft, in the bromeliads or on the trees. Its voice is one of the most beautiful sounds heard at night in the mountain forests.

BEHAVIOR. The adults are tree frogs protected by their color and their biotope in bromeliads on high trees occasionally in tufty *Dracaena* or in cracks in the rocks. We once found two partly grown ones buried in the mud of an artificial trench that caught permanently dripping water from a cliff. They descend only at the breeding period, when they sit up to two meters above the beds of rivulets or brooks. They are then quite oblivious to noise or light.

ECOLOGY. *Hyla albofrenata* belongs to the fauna of the rain forest on the coastal mountains, between approximately 400 and 800–900 m altitude. It reaches the edge of the forest, but does not occupy open, treeless terrain. Its lower limit coincides with the upper limit for *Hyla albomarginata* and the upper practically with the lower limit for *Hyla albosignata*. At the Açude da Solidão, an artificial pond at the edge of the Tijuca Mountains in Rio, the metamorphosing young of the first two emerge from the same waters, but the adults remain in their own habitats, *H. albomarginata* in the clearings and *Hyla albofrenata* on the trees in the woods.

DISTRIBUTION. The known range of *Hyla albofrenata* is restricted. Besides the type locality at Rio de Janeiro, state of Guanabara, it has been collected in the adjacent state of Rio de Janeiro, on the northern block of the Serra do Mar; at Barro Branco, Petrópolis and especially at Teresópolis; also on a forested island close to the coast. It has been found further south on the Serra da Bocaina in the state of São Paulo and on the Serra da Mantiqueira, at Itatiaia and Passa Quatro in the states of Rio de Janeiro and Minas Gerais. The known range does not go beyond 22° and 23° 30′ south latitude.

## *Hyla albosignata* Lutz & B. Lutz, 1938

LUTZ, A., and LUTZ, B. 1938. *Hyla albosignata* n. sp. Two new Hylae. *An. Acad. Bras. Sci.* 10(2):185–189.

LUTZ, B. 1948. Anfíbios anuros da Coleção A. Lutz. II Espécies verdes do gênero *Hyla* do Leste Meridional do Brasil. *Mem. Inst. O. Cruz,* 46(3):562–565, table 569. English summary 574–575, figs. 3, 7, 11.

DIAGNOSTIC CHARACTERS. In life, the unusual color of the iris, composed of two zones, the inner one gray, the outer eosin-colored, more rosy in sleep, coppery when the animal awakes; scarlet in the population from Teresópolis. An agglomeration of minute light glandules, like "milium," disposed in several rows below the anus, visible also in well-preserved specimens. Color green. Voice like the sound of whistling over the neck of an empty bottle. Montane southeastern rain forest form.

TYPE LOCALITY AND TYPES. Holotype n. 722 of the A. Lutz Collection, now at the MNR, from Alto da Serra de Cubatão near São Paulo. Paratypes n. 1325 from Independencia, Petrópolis and four from São Bento, state of Santa Catarina, n. 1978–1981, one paratype from Alto da Serra, n. 96781 at the USNM in Washington, D. C.

DESCRIPTION. Size: 32–52 mm from snout to vent. Build rather heavy, large specimens somewhat ovoid; greatest width of body just behind the axilla, slightly narrowed at the neck and behind the sacrum. Hindlimb individually variable, the ad-

pressed tibiotarsal articulation generally reaching the eye. Head rectilinear behind the eye, length and width equal or subequal. Snout moderately elongate, oval or bluntly acuminate from above, rounded at the edges in profile, the upper jaw standing out very slightly beyond the lower one. Canthus rostralis short, blunt, slightly curved; loreal region sloping slightly outward, with a slight ridge just above the mouth. Eye prominent, its horizontal diameter equal to or slightly longer than the distance from its anterior corner to the nostril. Tympanum very distinct in dead specimens, two-fifths, one-half, or three-fifths the diameter of the eye. Interorbital space much wider than the internarial space. Vomerine teeth in two robust, triangular or arched patches behind the choanae, converging slightly forward but separate. Tongue rounded to cordiform, emarginate, very slightly free behind. Lateral fingers about one-third webbed but with a narrow strip almost to the base of the disk on the second and fourth and to the last tubercle on the third. An elongate callosity outside the first finger ( ♂ ) but no sharp pollex rudiment. Palm well padded. Toes more than half-webbed with narrow fringes almost to the disk of the second, third, and fifth, and to the last tubercle on the fourth. A distinct inner metatarsal tubercle. No white frenal or dorsolateral lines. A supratympanic fold to the axilla. Very distinct glandular ridges on the outside of the forearm and tarsus to the outer digit, very marked around the elbow, forming a triangular flap on the heel. An undulated, often bilobed, glandular ridge above the anus. Below it, an agglomeration of glandules similar to those called milium in dermatology; they are disposed in several horizontal rows that widen as they recede; the proximal row is sometimes bisected by a vertical, median, postanal groove. They are best seen from behind or from beneath as they extend onto the midventral part of the thigh. It is from these glandules that the specific name is derived. In living and well-preserved specimens minute glandules on the palm, sole, forearm, and tarsus. Dorsal skin fairly smooth, throat minutely granular, anterior part of the sides, belly, and ventral aspect of femur more coarsely granular.

VARIATION. Our specimens vary greatly in size. The smallest breeding male (32 mm snout to vent) was taken in the black water of a marsh at the bottom of devastated forest in Agua Limpa, Juiz de Fora, Minas Gerais, with the vocal sac fully distended. Three specimens from Mauá in the region of the Itatiaia, on the border of the same state, are also relatively small: 40, 40, and 42 mm long. Seven from São Bento, Santa Catarina, range from 34 to 47.5 mm (both paratypes). The series of twenty-three from Teresópolis taken in the Organ Mountain forest vary from 42 to 52 mm, with a predominance of large specimens with very marked specific characters. The length of the hindlimb is variable, as usual, the adpressed tibiotarsal articulation reaching some point from the posterior corner of the eye, or even behind it, to between the eye and nostril (one specimen). Snout either rounded or slightly acuminate. Tongue generally rounded or cordiform; in a number of specimens longer and narrower; entire in some of them. Tympanum unusually small in two specimens, one from Santa Catarina and one from Teresópolis. Webbing fuller in those from Teresópolis and Mauá. Extension of milium also variable but seen at its best in well-grown specimens.

SECONDARY SEX CHARACTERS. Not very marked. Males without extensible, claw-like pollex rudiment; forearms moderately enlarged. Sex uncertain unless the vocal sac is distended or eggs are evident. Paratype 1980, a female with eggs, is 45 mm from snout to vent, has thin arms and a small callus on hand; the adpressed tibiotarsal articulation reaches the eye.

COLOR. Intensely green all over except for the parts of the limbs concealed in repose, the gula, the opaque peritoneum, the ridges and glandules. Dorsal aspect of head and body rather dark; permanently visible strips of the forearm, tibia, and tarsus grayish blue-green; tympanum also. Hand and foot, upper arm and thigh citron yellow, the latter sometimes more olive; glandular ridges yellowish mostly underscored with black or dark clove brown chromatophores. Appendage on heel yellowish or green. Sides of body emerald in front, yellowish over the belly, the abdominal organs visible by translucency, lemon chrome over the peritoneum. Ventral surfaces of body laved with dark green, especially the suboral region, chest, and thigh. Large articulations blue-green or bottle green. Hands, feet, forearm, tarsus, milium, and other glandules citron or lemon yellow. Edge of lower jaw light. Iris with gray inner zone and orange or eosin-pink outer one, more rosy in sleep,

more coppery when the frog is awake. In the Serra dos Orgãos population deeper in tone, approaching scarlet. Sometimes white spots, probably guanine, or numerous melanophores on the dorsal surface, less visible in life than in preserved specimens.

After death the specimens fade, becoming clay-colored, buff, wood brown, or ivory with light glandules, ridges, outline of the lower jaw, and upper eyelids. The supra-anal ridge stands out longest.

VOICE. The voice of *Hyla albosignata*, which led to its discovery, has the sound of a wind instrument. The call, *hoouh hoouh,* can be imitated by blowing lightly over the neck of an empty vial. The notes are isolated, flute-like, liquid, and have an eerie quality when heard at night in the heart of the forest. *Hyla albosignata* sings only in summertime.

BEHAVIOR. As a rule, *Hyla albosignata* sings aloft on tall shrubs, small trees, or vines above human height, sometimes two or three meters from the ground. Its coloring is protective and it is very difficult to see. It is, however, rather impervious to noise and light and goes on calling while one cuts one's way toward it. The slight movements of the vocal sac are visible from a certain distance. It comes down to breed. A number of males were caught on reeds at the edge of the Lagoa dos Penitentes in the Granja Comari at Teresópolis. One male was caught in Nova Friburgo on the ground, hiding under roots of grasses, so that it had to be dug out. The call was different, more like the croak of a *Paludicola.* The vocal sac was hugely distended, and the whole body much inflated at the sides by the enormously increased volume of the lungs. It was in a state of great excitement that lasted for some time. Our smallest male, caught in the thick dark water of a marsh, was calling in the usual manner.

DEVELOPMENT. The tadpoles develop in running water; three juveniles with mouth slits forming were caught in the Serra da Bocaina and others at Teresópolis.

ECOLOGY. This frog is a montane rain forest species. In the well-forested Organ Mountains very fine specimens were caught in the woods. Our three from the ecotone at Mauá are smaller and the one from the marsh in the ruined forest at Agua Limpa is almost a dwarf (32 mm). It seems possible that size is tied to the conditions offered by the environment.

KNOWN DISTRIBUTION. The known range of *Hyla albosignata* is much larger than that of *H. albofrenata* and *H. musica*. The extremes of latitude are 26° 14′ 55″ S. at São Bento do Sul, in Santa Catarina and 21° 35′ 0″ S. at Agua Limpa near Juiz de Fora. It probably occupies much of the still-forested part of the Maritime Range, but it does not occur in the mountains outside the city of Rio de Janeiro, which are lower and isolated from the main serra. Most of the collecting places are at least 800 m above sea level, though Agua Limpa is only 400 m and may represent an unfavorable extreme. In the Serra da Bocaina and in the Organ Mountains it occurs at 1,150 m altitude, slightly higher than *H. albofrenata*, which reaches 1,000 m in Teresópolis, where *H. musica* occurs at 1,200 m. *Hyla albosignata* also occurs in the Serra da Mantiqueira; it seems abundant at Mauá in the vicinity of the National Park of Itatiaia but was also heard near 2,000 m altitude toward the upper limit of the rain forest, at the edges of the National Park.

## *Hyla musica* B. Lutz, 1948

> LUTZ, B. 1948. Anfíbios anuros da Coleção Adolpho Lutz. II Espécies verdes do gênero *Hyla* do Leste Meridional do Brasil. *Mem. Inst. O. Cruz*, 46(3):565–567, tab. 1, figs. 4, 8, 12. English summary 576–577.

DIAGNOSTIC CHARACTERS. Nuptial excrescences on the first finger of the hand (males). Skin thin, slimy, with an irritating secretion that affects the mucosae even without contact. Distinct white granular margins and some pustules but no "milium," melanophores or appendices. Dorsal aspect luminous green, becoming lighter and yellowish toward the edges and on the limbs, hands, feet, ventral aspect of the forearm, tarsus, palm, and sole. Iris light, pale pinkish. Montane rain forest form known only from the Serra dos Orgãos.

TYPES AND TYPE LOCALITY. Seven male syntypes caught by Elio Gouvea at km 4.5 of the trail to the Campo das Antas, in the Serra dos Orgãos National Park at Teresópolis, state of Rio de Janeiro, altitude 1,200 m, latitude 22° 26′ 12″ S. long. 42° 54′ 55″ W. Gr. Nos. 3213–3219 in the collection of the Museu Nacional at Rio de Janeiro. Climate *Cfb* (Köppen), subtropical with cool summers; rain forest vegetation.

DESCRIPTION. Size 44–50 mm from snout to vent.

Body robust but not heavy, slightly flattened and tapering somewhat at the groin. Head slightly shorter than wide, or length and breadth subequal. Hindlimb variable in length, the tibiotarsal articulation reaching in front of the eye but not to the nostril when adpressed. Tibia and femur almost equal in length. Forearm thick ( ♂ ). Snout short, rounded to oval from above, projecting slightly over the lower jaw in profile; ventral outline of the head and mouth wide and fairly short. Canthus rostralis distinct, curved, truncate in front; loreal region steep, concave. Eye fairly prominent, slightly shorter than the distance from its anterior corner to the tip of the snout. Tympanum small, two-fifths the diameter of the eye. Nostrils very small, lateral, inserted obliquely below the anterior corner of the canthus. Interorbital space double or almost double the width of the upper eyelid, much wider than the internarial space. Vomerine teeth in two short, separate, slightly curved groups behind the choanae. Tongue flat, disk-shaped, hardly free or emarginate behind. A callosity below the first finger. Vestiges of nuptial excrescences outside it, more distinct in glandular males with thick forearms. Fingers about two-thirds webbed, but with fringes almost to the disks. Foot about two-thirds webbed. Metatarsal tubercle squarish, distinct. A white glandular margin on the edge of the lower jaw, a very distinct glandular ridge on the forearm and hand, tarsus, and foot, outlining the contour of the joints in glandular specimens but not produced into appendages. A short supra-anal ridge and a few scattered, round pustules near the anus and on the midline of the ventral aspect of the thigh, but no serried rows of milium-like glands as in *H. albosignata*. Skin delicate, very minutely granular on the abdomen and the posteroventral aspect of the thigh.

MEASUREMENTS. Syntypes: snout to vent 50, 49, 47, 45, and 44 mm.

VARIATION. Slight individual variation in the proportions of the head, length of the hindlimb, and extent of webbing. The series of types and additional specimens is too small to furnish significant data on the extent of variability.

COLOR. Simpler and more unifrom than in the other southeastern species of the group. Whole dorsal aspect a deep saturated green, lighter on the forehead, upper eyelids, and tympanum, admixed with yellow toward the periphery; near apple green at the sides, pale yellow-green on the hands and feet and on the disks. Concealed aspects of the thigh beneath very deep in the middle, more yellow to the sides; throat and belly a very light green yellow, almost a greenish cream at the edges of the mouth. Chest over the scapulary belt and large articulations deep bluish green. Iris much lighter than that of the other regional forest species, toward the periphery pale salmon or a very pale pink.

VOICE. The call consists of short staccato notes, similar to those of *H. albofrenata* but higher and at a faster tempo. In chorus it sounds very musical, something like the orchestral glockenspiel or old-fashioned miniature chimes struck by small hammers. All the males in the vicinity may call together and at the same pitch, but occasionally some go slightly off tune, producing a peculiar and arresting dissonance.

BEHAVIOR. In summer *Hyla musica* calls sitting on small trees, like *Hyla albosignata*, but seems to perch even higher. Sometimes the forepart and the vocal sac stand out beyond the small branches or large leaves on which it is sitting. When the frog is grasped, the slimy secretion is released; it affects the eyes and nostrils, and is somewhat reminiscent of massed garlic plants in bloom.

ECOLOGY. Our population lives in a magnificent stretch of forest in the Organ Mountains National Park. The types come from a colony found on a steep slope between the trail and a small foaming stream. The arboreal canopy is formed of large trees, some supported by light buttresses or anchored to boulders by serial root systems. The frogs were sitting on smaller trees about 3 m above the ground. A tall *Begonia* with white flowers and large, entire, slightly asymmetric leaves (*B. ruegeli*?) dominates the shrub canopy. Another set belonged to a colony singing on large gnarled trees directly over the bed of a torrential stream, not very far from the first.

LIFE HISTORY. Unknown.

KNOWN DISTRIBUTION. Only the type locality, in the Organ Mountains.

RELATIONSHIPS. Until other colonies are found, the taxonomic position of this form may be somewhat uncertain, as it is very similar to *Hyla albosignata* in behavior but resembles *Hyla albofrenata* in voice; the build is nearer to that of *Hyla albomarginata*, but this has a quite different coloring and distribution. None of the others have an irritant secretion or nuptial excrescences.

## AMAZONIAN HYLAEA

LUTZ, B. 1949. Anfíbios anuros da Coleção Adolpho Lutz. IV Formas aliadas às Hylas verdes da região Leste Meridional. English translation: IV species allied to the green Hylas from southeastern Brazil. *Mem. Inst. O. Cruz* 47(3–4): 319–335, 1 pl., 1 map.

The group of green Hylas from southeastern Brazil seems to be represented by allied species in other well-defined cisandean regions. This applies to the Amazonian Hylaea and the Gran Chaco, both taken in a very wide sense.

For the Amazonian Hylaea, there are a number of names and descriptions in the literature, namely *Hyla punctata* Schneider, 1799; *Hyla variolosa, H. papillaris,* and *H. cinerascens* Spix, 1824; *Hyla rhodoporus* Guenther, 1868; *H. granosa* Boulenger, 1882; *H. gracilis* Melin (1941); and *H. ornatissima* Noble, 1923.

So far only two names seem to have been used for those from the Chaco and adjacent territory: *Hyla punctata* and *H. granosa.* The former is included in the Paraguayan fauna by Boettger (1885) and in that of northern Argentina by Boulenger (1889). Following them, it was placed on a checklist of the frogs of Paraguay by Bertoni (1913) and on that of the Argentinian ones by Berg (1896), though the latter specifies that he did not see the species himself. Peracca (1904) records it from Mato Grosso, whence Lutz received it too. Boulenger also lists his *H. granosa* from Asunción (1894). They are probably both the same as the form I described as *H. punctata rubrolineata.*

The northern forms share a peculiar property, absent from those of southeastern Brazil, and apparently also from those of the central region, namely the presence of pink pigment on the dorsal surface. Rose-colored upper eyelids are mentioned in all the descriptions; the dots on the upper eyelids are, however, stated to be subfulvous in *H. cinerascens* by Spix. *H. ornatissima* has dark areas on the upper eyelids, but they also are outlined in pink. The rose color extends onto the rest of the dorsal surface in most of these forms. Spix mentions that his *H. variolosa* (which is generally considered as synonymous with *Hyla punctata*) is "supra rosea." A small frog in our collection that seems to be *H. granosa* has a very faint pink tinge all over the dorsal surface including the upper eyelids. Noble mentions that *H. ornatissima* has the dorsal surface finely sprinkled with small pink spots and that the gaudy brown dorsal pattern is broadly edged with pink. The specific name of *H. rhodoporus* is derived from the minute rose-colored dots found on the dorsal pores; according to Guenther, they are confluent on the upper eyelids and, to judge by the watercolor that accompanies the description, they are present on the tympanum also. *Hyla cinerascens* is stated to be bluish or grayish rose and to have numerous rose-white dots on the dorsal surface. It may be identical with *Hyla rhodoporus*.

The present taxonomic status of the northern forms is rather complex. *Hyla punctata* Schneider 1799 has evident priority over the other names. *Hyla variolosa*, *H. papillaris* Spix, and *Hyla rhodoporus* Guenther are considered as synonymous with it, fide Peters (1872). I do not like to give a definite opinion on this point, since I am sure one cannot judge the species without examining the living frogs. So far I have seen only a few specimens of *Hyla punctata* alive. The types of *Hyla variolosa*, *cinerascens*, and *papillaris* have been destroyed. Peters (1872) states that the type of *papillaris* was 30 mm long and had 5 mm of tail rudiment. This makes it almost too large to belong to the group. *Hyla rhodoporus* has a larger tympanum, shorter webs, deeper dorsal coloring, and no dorsolateral lines. Melin says that *Hyla granosa gracilis* is greenish yellow above with fine brown dots. He mentions a dark iris, a claw-shaped pollex rudiment (in one specimen) an indistinct tympanum, one-half the diameter of the eye, and shorter webs than those of the Boulenger form.

The fact that there are so many names and so strong a tendency to reduce them shows the inherent difficulties. Comparison of the specific characters provided by the authors brings out only a few marked differences. In an earlier paper on these forms (1949) I attempted to make a key for them. Here, I limit myself to the descriptions and notes that follow.

## *Hyla punctata punctata* (Schneider), 1799

SCHNEIDER, J. G. 1799. *Historiae amphibiorum naturalis literariae . . . Jena* 1:170.
SPIX, J. B. VON. 1824. *Animalia nova sive species novae testudinum et ranarum quas in itinere per Brasiliam. Hyla variolosa*: 37, tab. IX, fig. 4.

HISTORY. This species was one of the earliest to be described and may have been redescribed since. It seems practically certain that *Hyla variolosa* Spix is synonymous with it. Other names for green species of *Hyla* from the Amazonian Hylaea may also be synonymous with it, but at present this point remains obscure.

ORIGINAL DESCRIPTION. "Colorem griseum albidum distingunt puncta nivea sine ordine sparsa, inter oculos et per totum dorsum; taenia etiam nivea, dorsus utrique cingit, ab oculis ducta supra aures usque ad femora."

DIAGNOSTIC CHARACTERS. Short snout and angular canthus rostralis; dorsolateral stripes and large dots on the dorsal surface.

TYPE AND TYPE LOCALITY. The Schneider publication is not available in Brazil. The description is copied from Guenther, and I do not know whether Schneider indicated a type locality or how many specimens he had. The present description is based on a series of eleven specimens collected by Mr. V. Quesnel and me in the ditch and adjacent marshy ground below the Churchill-Roosevelt Highway, nine miles from Port of Spain, Trinidad, B.W.I., on July 4, 1955.

DESCRIPTION. Size: males 33–38 mm snout to vent. Build not very robust. Head and body flat. Hindlimb fairly long, the tibiotarsal articulation reaching the nostril or between it and the eye when the leg is adpressed. Head very slightly wider than long. Snout very short, round in front, with fairly distinct canthus rostralis and oblique, barely concave, loreal region. Eye large, prominent, its horizontal diameter slightly longer than the distance from its anterior corner to the nostril. Tympanum small, about two-fifths the diameter of the eye. Interorbital space wider than the upper eyelid and the internarial space. Tongue thin, disk-like, slightly wider behind than in front, connate, but its posterior border reflected over it in some dead specimens. Vomerine teeth in two short, slightly separated and arched groups between and slightly beyond the choanae. Lateral fingers with a rudiment of web at the base. Feet from two-thirds to three-fourths webbed, the web continued by a fringe especially noticeable on the fourth toe. Rudiment of pollex in the form of an elongate callosity outside the first finger. Disk of the third finger slightly smaller than the tympanum. Skin smooth or very slightly shagreened above, beneath granular on the belly and more minutely so on the postero-ventral aspect of the thigh. Dorsolateral fold or stripe and upper eyelids slightly thickened, opaque. In most dead specimens a few white spots on the dorsal surface.

VARIATION. There is some variation as to the length of the web, especially on the feet, in this series of eleven specimens. The distinctness of the dorsolateral stripes or folds and of the spots and the number of the latter also vary.

SECONDARY SEX CHARACTERS. Eight of the eleven specimens are males in a nuptial condition with a large medium vocal sac (especially MNR 3353), slightly thickened forearms, and a distinct callosity under the first finger. Female not seen unless specimen 3349 (36 mm long) is of that sex; it has no male characters nor is it distended by eggs. Two other nonbreeding small specimens seem to be males.

COLOR. Green, the color deeper on the dorsal aspect. Dorsolateral white margins present, underscored in very dark red, distinct anteriorly, more attenuated caudad, preceded by a similar narrower margin on the canthus rostralis between nostril and eye. Iris very pale, almost white.

AFFINITIES AND DISTRIBUTION. This short-headed form is very like Spix's figure of his *Hyla variolosa*, but the snout is less truncate. Our specimens from the lower Amazons belong to this nominate race. Those from the western part are larger and have a longer snout, which is less rounded and more oval in outline. They are described under the subspecific name of *H. p. rubrolineata* (see below).

## *Hyla punctata rubrolineata* B. Lutz, 1951

> LUTZ, B. 1951. Anfíbios anuros da Coleção Adolpho Lutz. IV Species allied to the green Hylas from southeastern Brazil. Addendum to Part II. *Mem. Inst. O. Cruz* 47(3–4): 319–336. Pls. 324–326, pl. I, figs. 2, 2a, 2b, 2c.

*Hyla punctata* has been listed several times from the Chaquean subprovince of the Continental province of South America. The first specimens I saw from this region seemed slightly different from the classic description of *Hyla punctata* Schneider; this led me to describe a subspecies under the name *H. p. rubrolineata* and to define it by the differential characters given below. Subsequently, I had the opportunity to see specimens from the western

part of the Amazonian Hylaea and to collect a few typical *Hyla punctata* with Mr. V. Quesnel on the island of Trinidad, B.W.I. The snouts of those from Trinidad and the eastern Hylaea seem shorter and the vomerine teeth slightly longer. The morphological details and proportions of the western Hylaean specimens are nearer to those of the types of *H. p. rubrolineata* from Bolivia. However, comparison of a good series of photographs of a living specimen of *H. p. rubrolineata* from Forte do Principe da Beira on the Guaporé River and two of a frog from Trinidad show only slight differences in the dorsal pattern. The dorsolateral line is generally present but not very distinct.

DIAGNOSTIC CHARACTERS. Snout slightly longer than that of the eastern Hylaean specimens, oval, subacuminate; canthus rostralis rather indistinct; vomerine teeth short. Dorsolateral stripes and small carmine or purple vinaceous spots disseminated on the back, some with small lemon yellow enclosures. Pattern imprecise and evanescent.

TYPES AND TYPE LOCALITY. Two syntypes from Buena Vista, department of Santa Cruz, Bolivia, collected by J. Steinbach and exchanged with Dr. Helen T. Gaige of the MZUM, now nos. 4698 and 4699 of the A. Lutz Collection, MNR.

DESCRIPTION. Size relatively small; syntypes 35 and 30 mm snout to vent. Body oval, very flat in repose. Tibiotarsal articulation reaching between the eye and the tip of the snout when adpressed. Head flat, slightly broader than long, with rather indistinct canthus rostralis and steep loreal region, flaring at the upper jaw. Eye prominent, almost equal to the distance from its anterior corner to the tip of the snout. Tympanum small, half the diameter of the eye. Interorbital space double the width of the upper eyelid. Tongue entire, disk-like, thin, and adherent. Vomerine teeth in two short, slightly separated groups between and beyond the choanae. Lateral fingers slightly webbed but widely fringed. A large, elongate callosity at the base of the first finger. Hands well padded. Outer edge of toes webbed to the last articulation, except the first and the fourth; fringes to the base of the disk on the inner side of the second and third and on both sides of the fourth. Skin smooth or very slightly shagreened above with disseminated minute opaque white dots. Sides of body and belly minutely granular; ventral aspect of thigh less minutely so. A dorsolateral glandular line from the thick, opaque upper eyelids to the sacrum. Vestiges of a light frenal line on the smaller syntype.

VARIATION. A specimen from Forte do Principe da Beira on the Guaporé River in the territory of Rondonia is also small and seems to be an immature female. The head is shorter; the groups of vomerine teeth are small and the palms of the hands smooth. A female with eggs from Borba, state of Amazonas, is also small, 36 mm snout to vent. The other specimens from the western part of the Hylaea are more robust and have longer and more oblique groups of vomerine teeth. The interorbital space seems narrower in proportion to the upper eyelids.

SECONDARY SEX CHARACTERS. The other eight females from the western Hylaea are larger (37–40 mm snout to vent). The body is hard, and the skin is distended by the masses of eggs. The adpressed leg does not reach so far because of the enlarged abdomen. Nuptial males have a subgular vocal sac and relatively thick forearms.

COLOR AND PATTERN. Only living specimens seen, from Forte do Principe da Beira, Guaporé River, territory of Rondonia, leg. W. Bokermann, June 1962. Rather uniform and monotonous light green, somewhat yellowish on the dorsal surface of the body, a purer green on the permanently visible parts of the thigh and limbs; webs and tips of fingers paler; ventral surface more bluish. Iris very pale, greenish, almost white, differing from the iris of the southern species of the Atlantic province, including that of *Hyla albomarginata*, which has gray or silvery eyes, is larger and has orange-colored webs. Pattern inconstant, evanescent; composed of a purple-vinaceous dorsal stripe on each side from the upper eyelid to the sacrum, not always visible or distinct; small, rounded spots of the same color disseminated on the back and a very similar, indistinct row on the permanently visible surfaces of the limbs; some of the dorsal spots with a lemon-yellow part. Ventral aspect bluish green, especially the gula and the limbs; peritoneum opaque, bluish white, outline of body yellowish green.

An apparently unfinished watercolor of a recently dead specimen from Maracajú in southern Mato Grosso shows a more uniform and darker green on the back, the stripes more symmetrical, much more definite and longer, extending to the nostrils; spots also more definite, fewer, and larger.

Some months after death, the specimen from Forte do Principe da Beira, which had been kept in a dark phial, showed more vivid dorsolateral stripes and spots than in life; they are rose colored. The upper eyelids are now also rose colored, and there is a suffusion of minute pink dots on the back. It recalls Günther's picture of the type of *Hyla rhodoporus*, but the latter never showed dorsolateral stripes. Most of the specimens now range from ivory to buff. Only three large females from the western Hylaea show vestiges of the dorsolateral stripes and spots, faded to white. Their pattern is similar to that of Spix's illustration of *H. variolosa*, but the latter has a quite short and truncate snout.

GEOGRAPHIC DISTRIBUTION. It is possible that *Hyla punctata* occupies the whole territory between the Amazon Basin and that of the Paraguay River, but there is no information as to this point nor as to forms of transition between the specimens from Guiana and Trinidad and those from western Hylaea, Rondonia, Bolivia, and southern Mato Grosso. The species has been recorded from Argentina (Resistencia) and Paraguay. In Brazil *H. p. rubrolineata* seems to range from southern Mato Grosso (Maracaju) north, perhaps as far as Borba and Benjamin Constant (Amazonas).

AFFINITIES. It is possible that *rubrolineata* may not deserve subspecific recognition. There are few specimens of either form available, and the gaps in distribution are enormous. There is also some uncertainty as to the synonymy between *H. p. rubrolineata* and forms such as *H. variolosa* Spix (types destroyed), *rhodoporus* Günther, and *granosa gracilis* Melin.

## *Hyla rhodoporus* Günther, 1868

> GÜNTHER, A. 1868. *Pr. Zool. Soc. London*, pt. 2: 488–489, pl. 37, fig. 4.

ORIGINAL DESCRIPTION (transcribed; no specimens were seen). "This species belongs to the group in which the vomerine teeth are placed in two curved series forming together an arch with the convexity towards the front; however, the series are less distinctly curved than in the other species, this species being less developed in size than its natural allies. It is very closely allied to *H. albomarginata* or *H. infulata*. The snout is much depressed, with the canthus rostralis very obtuse and the loreal region concave. Eye of moderate size, shorter than the snout. Choanae wide. Tongue scarcely notched behind; tympanum two-thirds the size of the eye. Fingers very slightly webbed; toes two-thirds webbed. The length of the body equals the distance between the vent and the heel and is thrice the length of the foot. Skin smooth, with numerous minute pores on the upper parts. Light olive colored, each pore with a minute rose-colored dot; the dots confluent into spots on the eyelids; no band along the canthus rostralis or on the legs, the exposed parts of which are colored like the back. Uniform whitish below.

One specimen was found by Mr. Bartlett on the upper Amazon; it is 38 mm long, the length of the hindlimb being 60 mm. Another example, from Surinam, appears to belong to the same species."

## Hyla granosa Boulenger, 1882

BOULENGER, G. A. 1882. *Catalogue of the batrachia salientia in the collection of the British Museum. H. granosa*: 358, pl. 24, figs. 2–3.

Boulenger, in his catalogue of the frogs in the British Museum (1882), described a new species of tree frog under the name *Hyla granosa.*

He based the description on two females, one from British Guiana, the other from Brazil, and on two males, one from Brazil, the other from Ecuador. The colorless condition of his preserved specimens and their rose-colored upper eyelids bring these specimens into the group of green species from the Amazonian Hylaea. I transcribe the original description, since I have only one specimen that seems to belong to this species.

ORIGINAL DESCRIPTION. "Tongue subcircular, entirely adherent. Vomerine teeth between the large choanae, in two oblique series, forming together a chevron, the point of which is turned forwards. Head moderate, broader than long; snout rounded, once and a half as long as the diameter of the eye; canthus rostralis rather indistinct; loreal region oblique, slightly concave; eye very prominent; upper eyelid narrow; interorbital space much broader than the latter; tympanum distinct, half or not quite half the diameter of the eye. Three outer fingers half-webbed or nearly so; a rudiment of pollex, slight in females, claw-like in males; toes three-fourths webbed; disks as large as, or nearly as large as, the tympanum; subarticular tubercles little developed. The hindlimb being carried forward

along the body, the tibiotarsal articulation reaches the tip of the snout. Upper surface, belly and lower surface of the thighs granulate. Colourless; males with a few scattered white dots on the head and back; females with a cross-streak between the eyes, a streak from the nostril and a few spots on the back, forearms, and tibiae purple; upper eyelid rose as in *H. punctata*. Male with external gular vocal sac. From snout to vent 40 mm.

Guianas; N. Brazil; Ecuador.
  (a)  ♀ Demerara Falls
  (b–d)  ♂ Santarém. H. A. Wickenham Esq. (C.)
  (e–f)  ♀ Interior of Brazil
  (g)  ♂ Canelos, Ecuador, Mr. Buckley (C.)"

One small tree frog that I caught at Utinga, Belém, agrees rather well with the plain males indicated by Boulenger and shown in figure 3 b of one of his cotypes. It has the vomerine teeth in a very open chevron. The tongue is disk-like, thin, and very broad at the back. The short and rounded snout has a very curved canthus rostralis. In life it was a uniform green and had a light, hazel iris. The preserved specimen is ivory with a very faint rosy tinge on the dorsal surface and the upper eyelids. The skin is porous rather than granular. Mr. Venancio suggested that its delicate appearance indicated a forest dweller. This hypothesis is borne out by the absence of flash colors and the finding place, an open aqueduct at the edge of the woods.

As sexual color dimorphism is rare in the genus *Hyla,* and the differences between the green species of this particular group are difficult to evaluate in preserved specimens, it seems possible that Boulenger, who gives *granosa* a very wide distribution, may have had more than one form under the same name. The ornamented females might be akin to *Hyla ornatissima* Noble.

Both were described from British Guiana, but the Brazilian specimens of *H. ornatissima* seen by me were as ornate as Noble's type. Should *H. ornatissima* be conspecific with Boulenger's *granosa* females, this name would either have priority over that of Noble or, alternatively, cover only the plain male syntypes. If the latter are different from any of the older described species and the name *granosa* is preoccupied by the female types, I would suggest calling the plain form *Hyla inornata.* I would further suggest that Venancio's hypothesis that this is a forest form be submitted to the test of ecological observation. All the green forms from the Amazonian Hylaea need to be caught and kept alive for a while.

## Hyla granosa gracilis Melin, 1941

MELIN, D. 1941. Contributions to the knowledge of the amphibia of South America. *Meddelanden från Göteborgs Musei Zoologiska Avdelning* 88:21, fig. 8.

ORIGINAL DESCRIPTION (transcribed; no specimens available). "Body wedge-shaped, depressed, with large head and long, narrow hindlimbs. Tongue subcircular, in the hinder part slightly nicked. Vomerine teeth between the hinder parts of the fairly large, triangularly rounded choanae, forming two slightly convex broadly separated, anteriorly converging rows. Head flattened, subcircular, about as broad as long; snout a little longer than the diameter of the eye; tip of the nose marked, truncate, not very prominent; rostral edge indistinctly marked; loreal region oblique, concave; nostril small, near the tip of the nose, a little farther from the eye than the diameter of the latter; eyes prominent, but seen from above not reaching the margins of the head; pupil horizontal; interorbital space more than twice as broad as the upper eyelid; tympanum somewhat diffuse, rounded, dorsally a little incurved, about half the diameter of the eye; lower jaw terminally with a slight knob. Lateral fingers at most one-third webbed, toes somewhat more than half; disks moderate, of the fingers partly as large as the tympanum, of the toes smaller; subarticular tubercles small; first finger thickened at the base, nearly as long as the second; rudiment of pollex projecting at an obtuse angle, in one specimen with a spine-like process; no metatarsal tubercles or tarsal fold. The hindlimb being carried forward along the body, the tibiotarsal articulation reaches the tip of the snout; tibiae about as long as the thighs (heels not crossing). Upper surface and region around the seat marked with fine warts; sides and lower surfaces, excepting head but including basal part of the thighs, areolate-warty; sides with slight longitudinal folds; transversal fold of the chest laterally distinct; limbs smooth. According to my field notes, colour greenish yellow, above with a brown, fine, and fairly thin dotting, in one specimen faintly marked; iris dark, in the central area with metallic lustre.

Males with external gular vocal sacs. Length about 36 mm, thighs 19 mm.

"Two males, Rio Uaupés (north of Ipanoré), Brazil, collected 17.5.1924. This species was very common at a little *igarapé* (river branch) of the western shore of the river, where it occurred among high grasses and small bushes of Melastomae together with *H. tintinnabulum* and *lutzi*. Judging from its dull and coarse, bell-like sound, the species in question may also occur in the trees, both at the above locality and at Taracuá. The intense music making, together with the fine sound of *tintinnabulum* imitating rapid firing (at a greater distance a kind of grinding), was not disturbed by light. When captured, the frogs proved more or less sluggish, and it could clearly be seen that the vocal sacs were strongly distended.

"Systematically seen, the above form resembles a good deal *H. granosa* Boulenger (1882 b, p. 358, Pl. 24, fig. 2). According to the description of this species the first finger has 'a rudiment of pollex, slight in females, claw-like in males.' Now, as my own specimens have a very stout rudiment of pollex, projecting at an obtuse angle (first finger, contrary to the figure of Boulenger, being very thick at the base), and in one specimen provided with a spine- (not claw-) like process, I am not quite certain that the two types are identical. In any case the form described above has a different appearance from that shown by Boulenger. Irrespective of its different color and smaller size, it seems indeed to be much slenderer. The trunk is more wedge-shaped and provided with narrower limbs. The head is not as long as the trunk itself but much shorter. The snout is not pointed but strongly subcircular. In addition to this the tympanum is not very distinct, the web smaller, and the first toe considerably longer than is pointed out by the figure in question. Because of these differing characteristics the form described above may at least form a subspecies of *granosa*."

## Hyla leptoscelis Boulenger, 1918

BOULENGER, G. A. 1918. Descriptions of new South-American Batrachians. *An. Mag. Nat. Hist.*, ser. 9, 2(11):427–433. *H. leptoscelis*: 432.

The type of this species and only specimen known hails from Lago do Icahy, São Paulo de

Olivença, on the Solimões River, rather near the border of Brazil and Colombia. The place names are misspelled, being probably transcribed from a manuscript label. The type was examined by me in 1952. It is in a poor condition, gray in color, with vestiges of the dorsal markings described by Boulenger, and conveys the impression of a juvenile, probably of a green species of *Hyla* with long, thin legs. As it cannot be definitely identified, the original description is transcribed.

"Tongue circular, entire and slightly free behind. Vomerine teeth on a level with the posterior borders of the very large choanae, in slightly curved oblique series forming a chevron pointing forward. Head as long as broad, very strongly depressed; snout rounded, not projecting, as long as the eye; canthus rostralis obtuse; loreal region very oblique, feebly concave; nostril near the tip of the snout; interorbital space a little broader than the upper eyelid; tympanum distinct, half the diameter of the eye. Fingers moderate with moderately large disks, outer with a slight rudiment of web; no projecting rudiment of the pollex. Hindlimb extremely slender, tibiotarsal articulation reaching a little beyond the tip of the snout. Tibia eight times as long as broad, two-thirds the length of the head and body. Toes two-thirds webbed; a feeble tarsal fold. Skin smooth, granular on the belly and under the thighs; heels with a pointed dermal appendage which is half as long as the eye. Yellowish above with purplish brown markings; a large spot on the snout; two V-shaped bands between the eyes, two cross-bars on the back, a V-shaped band on the sacral region, and angular cross-bars on the limbs. From snout to vent 26 mm."

## *Hyla ornatissima* Noble, 1923

> NOBLE, G. K. 1923. New batrachians from the tropical research station, British Guiana. *Contr. Zoologica*, 3(14): 289–299. *H. ornatissima*: 291–293.

The type specimen of this very beautiful frog was collected by Beebe near the tropical research station called Kartabo and located at the confluence of the Cuyuni and Mazaruni rivers (see map published by Noble). *Hyla ornatissima* is rare in collections though perhaps not in nature. Of late, Mr. Bokermann was presented with three specimens from the Rio Amapari, near the Serra do Navio,

Amapá Territory, and kindly lent them to me for examination and use.

DIAGNOSTIC CHARACTERS. The striking shape and apparently pink to wine-red coloration of the dorsal pattern consisting of an interocular portion, like a pair of spectacles; a sacral, diamond-shaped or roughly oval spot, prolonged backward and forward by a median prong; two comma-shaped stripes on the straight terminal part of the canthi, enveloping the nostrils; small, similar, rounded spots, sparsely disseminated on the dorsal surface of the body and forming a row on the permanently visible dorsal area of the limbs. Size 28–41 mm. Head as wide as long, snout short. Leg long, the adpressed tibiotarsal articulation reaching the tip of the snout or beyond it.

TYPE AND TYPE LOCALITY. AMNH. A-13.941 adult female from Meamu, Mazaruni River, British Guiana, leg. W. Beebe, June 10, 1920. Seen and figured by me (1951).

DESCRIPTION. Female type 40 mm; n.5693 of the Bokermann Collection 41 mm snout to vent, abdomen bulging with eggs; two males 28 and 31 mm snout to vent. Head very slightly wider than long or length and width equal. Snout short, rounded in front; canthus rostralis first angular then straight; loreal region sloping to the edge of the mouth. Interorbital space slightly wider than the internarial space. Eye prominent. Tympanum distinct, round, small, less than half the diameter of the eye. Tongue round, entire, not free behind. Groups of vomerine teeth arched, almost contiguous, behind the choanae, the outer corner of their anterior margin on a level with the posterior border of the inner nares. Leg long, the tibiotarsal articulation reaching beyond the tip of the snout (measured, too brittle to adpress). According to Noble, hand two-thirds webbed; foot almost entirely webbed; penultimate phalanx of the fourth toe fringed. A small callosity at the edge of the inner finger; a similar, elongate, inner metatarsal tubercle. Disks very large though smaller than the tympanum. Skin smooth above, thin, the blood vessels visible by translucency; over the spots opaque. Beneath, still more translucent except over the peritoneum which hides the inner organs.

VARIATION (smaller specimens, probably males, too brittle for handling). Tongue oval in 5694; narrower, more elongate in 5692. Vomerine teeth slightly more separate, the right patch smaller than the left in both specimens. Forearm fairly thick. A callus outside the first finger with a sharp tip.

COLOR. Unfortunately not seen alive. Dorsal background now buff to straw-colored. Iris showing vestiges of a golden color with venation and a horizontal pupil, slightly irregular and lozenge-shaped. Dorsal pattern very spectacular, resembling a pair of spectacles over the eyes and interocular region, plus a short dash over each nostril and a diamond-shaped or oval spot on the sacrum, prolonged backward and forward by a long median prong. Dashes, edges of spectacles, sacral spot, and prong darkest, wine-colored or maroon. Central part of sacral and interocular ornaments much paler, almost buff. A pinkish, opaque halo round the large spots. A few isolated dark spots and some pink ones on the dorsal surface; a linear row of well-defined round dots on the permanently visible dorsal surface of the limbs. Beneath uniform buff.

ECOLOGY, LIFE HISTORY, AND DISTRIBUTION. Unknown as yet.

AFFINITIES. *Hyla ornatissima* is probably one of the light-green tree frogs like *Hyla punctata*. The head is like that of the green species. It might have affinities with the *Hyla geographica* group, but the absence of an appendix on the heel and especially the absence of reticulation on the transparent part of the upper eyelid speak against approximation to the *H. geographica* group.

It is also possible that *Hyla ornatissima* may be synonymous in part of *Hyla granosa* Boulenger. The female specimen figured in the Boulenger catalogue has a rather similar but considerably reduced pattern; also, *H. granosa* may include more than one species, as sexual dichroism is rare in *Hyla*. However, the three additional specimens of *H. ornatissima* have practically the same pattern as the type specimen.

# 7. The Cycle of *Hyla pulchella*

*Hyla pulchella* Duméril & Bibron, 1841

RADDI. 1823. Di alcune specie nuove di rettili e piante brasiliane. *Mem. Mat. Fis. Soc. Ital. Sc. Modena* 19:67. *Hyla lateralis* nec Daudin 1803: 67.

FITZINGER. 1826. *Neue Classification der Reptilien. Hyla raddiana*: 63.

DUMÉRIL, A. M. C., and BIBRON, G. 1841. *Erpétologie générale* 8. *Hyla leucomelas*: 576, *Hyla pulchella*: 588–589.

BELL, T. 1843. *The zoology of the voyage of H. M. S. Beagle. Hyla agrestis*: 46–47, pl 19, fig. 2.

BURMEISTER, H. 1856. *Erläuterungen z. Fauna Brasiliens*, p. 106, pl. 31, figs. 2, 2 a–e.

————. 1861. *Reise durch die La Plata Staaten der Argentinischen Republik. H. leucotaenia*: 531–532.

STEINDACHNER, H. 1864. Batrachologische Mitteilungen. *Verhd. Zool. Bot. Ges. Wien* 14:241, pl. 9, figs. 2–2c.

KOSLOWSKY, J. 1895. Batracios y reptiles de la Rioja y Catamarca. *Rev. Mus. de La Plata* 6:357.

MÜLLER, L. 1924–1925. *Über neue oder seltene mittel- und südamerikanische Amphibien und Reptilien. Hyla raddiana andina* nov. subsp.: 77–78.

FERNANDEZ, K. M. 1927. Sobre la biología y reproducción de algunos batracios argentinos. *Bol. Ac. Sc. Córdoba* 29(2):271–328. *Hyla raddiana*: 313–319.

BARRIO, A. 1965. Las subespecies de *Hyla pulchella* Duméril y Bibron. *Physis* 25(69):115–128, 2 pls.

BOKERMANN, W. C. A. 1965. Nota sobre los anfíbios brasileños citados y descriptos por Raddi. *Neotropica* 11(34):32. *H. pulchella*: 11.

For a very long time this species was called *Hyla raddiana* Fitzinger. It seems now that the name will have to be changed to *Hyla pulchella* Duméril and Bibron. Bokermann (1961) finds that Raddi did not travel beyond Rio de Janeiro, where the species does not occur.

*Hyla pulchella* is very pleiomorphic and comprises a number of vicariant forms that are generally looked upon as geographic races. The nominate form also has a series of synonyms. Duméril and Bibron described it as *H. pulchella* and as *Hyla leucomelas* (1841). *Hyla vauterii* Bibron, in the same volume, is considered as synonymous by some authors, but this seems doubtful to me. In *Zoology of the Voyage of the Beagle*, Bell (1943) described the species once more as *Hyla agrestis*. *Hyla leucotaenia* Burmeister (1861) seems to be correctly interpreted by most authors as the juvenile of *Hyla pulchella*. Hensel (1867) called it *Hyla bracteator*. Another form was described as

*Hyla riojana* by Koslowsky (1895). Lorenz Müller (1924–1925) created a subspecies, *H. p. andina*, for the robust form found in the Andes. Barrio (1965) described *H. p. cordobae*.

In Argentina four races at least are recognized: *Hyla p. pulchella, andina, riojana,* and *cordobae*. The race *pulchella* from the eastern plains (Platine province) also occurs in Uruguay and on the plains of the Brazilian state of Rio Grande do Sul. Besides these there also occurs a robust form on the Brazilian Plateau. More delicate specimens occur elsewhere.

DIAGNOSTIC CHARACTERS. The characters common to all these are vomerine teeth in two short, robust patches at the level of the posterior border of the choanae, sometimes slightly more in front or reaching further back. Head short, high, length and width subequal. Build elongate. In life, color of the permanently visible dorsal surfaces cream, greenish cream, buff, deeper green, or bronze. Iris from gold to bronze. A broad light edge to the upper jaw; generally, similar dorsolateral margins and edges to the permanently visible limb segments. Dark spots or stripes on the flanks and on the upper posterior part of the thigh concealed in repose on violaceous ground, sometimes with a slightly reddish undertone. Preserved specimens buff, gray or slate-colored, with a purplish or brownish tint.

TYPES AND TYPE LOCALITIES. The types of Duméril and Bibron were sent from Montevideo, Uruguay, by Gaudichaud and D'Orbigny. They are in the Musée d'Histoire Naturelle in Paris. Brumeister described his as *Hyla leucotaenia* from Paraná, capital of the province of Entre Rios in Argentina. Lorenz Müller's types of *Hyla p. andina* were collected by Weiser at Caspinchango and Valle de Calchaqui at 2,500 and 2,000 m altitude, in the Argentinian province of Catamarca. They have presumably perished with the other Hylid types of the Munich collection, but Dr. Kati M. Fernandez had some topotypes. *H. riojana* hails from the Argentinian Province La Rioja (Aguadita). *H. cordobae* is found in the sierras of Cordoba and in San Luis.

COMPOSITE DESCRIPTION. Size generally between 40 and 50 mm snout to vent, subject to geographic variation. Build delicate to robust, according to size. Head high, short, length and width subequal. Body elongate, rectilinear until the sacrum, narrowing toward the groin. Leg fairly long, the tibiotarsal articulation reaching between the eye

and the nostril when the hindlimb is adpressed. Snout short, sloping downward beyond the nostrils, rounded and slightly convex in profile. Canthus rostralis distinct, loreal region vertical, grooved between the eye and the nostril. Interorbital space wider than the internarial space. Eye fairly prominent, its horizontal diameter longer than the distance from its anterior corner to the nostril. Tympanum less than half the diameter of the eye. Tongue large, almost heart-shaped, emarginate, somewhat free behind. Vomerine teeth in two short, robust patches, generally at the level of the posterior border of the choanae, sometimes reaching beyond them. Fingers very slightly webbed at the base. Toes two-thirds to three-fourths webbed. An inner metatarsal tubercle. A supratympanic fold. Folds under the gula. Skin smooth above or delicately shagreened; granular beneath, the granulations coarser on the gula and ventral surface of the body, especially in large montane specimens.

SECONDARY SEX CHARACTERS. A sharp pollex rudiment ( ♂ ). Vocal sac very much puckered together in the middle, forming large oblique folds to the sides, diverging backward. Sexual characters more marked in large andine specimens or those from montane parts of southeastern Brazil: gula dark, forearms thick, pollex rudiment sharp, more palpable than in the more slender specimens from the southern plains.

One female, only 36 mm long, from the outskirts of Porto Alegre, contains eggs. Other Brazilian females with eggs 44–56 mm. Largest female 62 mm snout to vent (Andean subspecies).

VARIATION. Geographic differences in build and size may be summed up thus:

1. Relatively small size, delicate build, dainty color, and less precise concealed pattern in the frogs from the southern plains: *Hyla p. pulchella* (*Hyla agrestis, Hyla vauteri* (?), *Hyla leucotaenia, H. bracteator*).

2. Large size, stout build, short head, strong pollex rudiment, different color and pattern, gray, like granite, with brick-red, bronze, or golden spots on the back and close marbling on the concealed surfaces in the Andean frogs: *Hyla p. andina*.

3. Large size, stout build, short head and a very beautiful coloring of bronze-gold spots on a plain green ground, all over the permanently visible dorsal surfaces of body and limbs in our specimen of *Hyla p. riojana*.

4. Slightly smaller; head wide. Pattern composed of a fine network enclosing larger spots: *Hyla p. cordobae*.

5. Large size, robust, elongate build, bronze dorsal coloring with very prominent light cream margins on jaw, sides of body and margins of limbs; specimens from the plateau in the state of São Paulo. Less robust specimens, more like *H. p. pulchella* occur elsewhere.

JUVENILES. Everywhere the juveniles seem to be pale above, with distinct straight, light edges. The ornamental spots on the concealed surfaces remain absent for some time after metamorphosis. The larger ones incline to favor the shape of concealed pattern more characteristic for the area they hail from.

PRESERVED SPECIMENS. Also vary in color. The light cream and tan ones remain light; the green frogs tend to show a bluish gray color, the darker ones are either gray or brown, according to the background color of the living frog. Here again there are some geographical differences, but they are not absolute; the majority of those from one locality become the same color.

CHANGES OF COLOR AND LIVERY. Dr. Kati M. Fernandez observed a number of individuals from different parts of the Argentinian range for long periods. She discovered individual, seasonal, and altitudinal differences. Her lowland frogs underwent seasonal changes of coloring, but they also showed certain permanent individual differences. Surprising changes of color and details of the livery occur even during quite short periods. Prof. Gualter A. Lutz had good proof of this while photographing two females from Punta Lara in the province of Buenos Aires, in Rio. Dr. Fernandez also found that the frogs from the Sierra de Cordoba, which live 2,000 m or more above sea level, became like those of the plains when kept in captivity in the lowlands for two years.

Dr. Fernandez correlates the changes of color with temperature and season but stresses that the gamut of change is also individual and gives examples of this. She points out that during the summer the frogs are apt to be green, with individual differences, growing darker in winter. These differences, already quite noticeable in the specimens from the Argentinian plains, are more marked in those from the mountains. The frogs from the Sierra de Cordoba, while living in or at cold, deep,

running water are granite-gray with bright brick-red spots. Her captive specimens did not change much while kept in the mountains, nor did they become green with beautiful golden spots. Three of them, taken down to sea level at La Plata, became dark green in winter and a brilliant light green in summer. During two years in captivity they never displayed their mountain dress again, not even in spring while living in the water and making attempts to mate. They became like those from the eastern plains. The Hylas collected by Weiser in Tilcara and in Caspinchango (type locality of *H. p. andina*) on rocks at the edge of water, all showed different tints of green or blue-gray. However, those collected in a warm spring at Amaiche, temperature 18° to 20° C, were different, with vivid dark spots on a cinnamon background.

It is not easy to decide whether all the differences seen are sufficient to warrant taxonomic recognition, especially as small specimens and juveniles differ less from each other than large adults. Nor can one overlook the rapid changes of color and pattern in individual frogs and especially the changes undergone by those brought to the Argentinian plains from the Andes. It may, however, be permissible to say that a cooler climate seems to favor increase of size, more robust form and deeper coloration. The circumstances also bring up the point as to how far the botanists' concept of ecophenotypes may apply to the animal kingdom.

VOICE. Berg (1896) states that the males sing after sunset and reproduces the call as a semimetallic and rather loud *clic, clic, clic*. According to Dr. Fernandez, the most common call is rather varied, somewhat bird-like and produced at regular, rather long, intervals. There is generally an appoggiatura, slightly lower than the principal note. If several males are present and can hear each other, it is very rare for one to start vocalizing without the others joining in. The pitch may vary from individual to individual, but the pauses are quite regular; this results in a series of different notes that follow each other in the same order. In other words, the third *Hyla* to begin calling remains the third, during the repetition of the series of twenty or more calls. The chorus seems pleasing to them. The sounds are limpid, sonorous, and musical. The chorus is rhythmical and does not last more than a few minutes.

I have heard the call of Uruguayan specimens of

*Hyla pulchella pulchella*, from Santa Lucia, singing in my vivarium. I have also heard the call in two national parks in Argentina. The latter did not seem very different. It consisted of very beautiful bell-like notes. The form from Salta was determined as *H. p. andina* by Barrio, who was present on the occasion. The singers were rather small.

The topotype of *H. prasina* was calling *carará, carará* in a rough and loud voice when it was caught by us. As the call seems of paramount importance as a specific character and as this call differs greatly from that of *Hyla pulchella*, I now consider *Hyla prasina* as a full species.

BEHAVIOR AND ECOLOGY. Bell quotes Darwin as stating that this species was found in large numbers in the open grass plains and likewise in the swamps about Maldonado. He adds that they never climbed trees, as these are entirely wanting at the places frequented by them(!) About *Hyla vauterii*, Bell quotes Darwin as saying that he took it at Maldonado under a stone and at Rio de Janeiro on palms. This speaks against it being *pulchella*, as the latter does not occur in Rio, nor does the description really tally.

Burmeister (1861) mentions finding *leucotaenia* on bushes on the edges of lagoons and says that it is similar to *leucophyllata* but more slender, with a more pointed head and a rounded, projecting snout. This fits juvenile specimens of *H. pulchella* perfectly.

According to Fernandez, the mountain form lives at or in cold, deep running water but was also found near a warm spring.

LIFE HISTORY NOTES. According to Dr. Kati M. Fernandez, she never found the eggs, but they were taken in the Sierra de Cordoba by Dr. Max Biraben, who turned them over to her. (This must have been one of the highland forms.) There was a group of fifteen eggs clinging to a submerged stalk. The youngest eggs were 1.5 mm in diameter and contained embryos with a blastopore. They had little pigment, but the vegetal pole was light and the animal pole dark, which seems to be the rule in *Hyla*. Twenty-three days later the first larvae hatched but clung to the outer envolucre by the cement organs. (This is very slow development compared to that of species of *Hyla* observed in Rio de Janeiro.) They were 4 mm long, 3 for the body and 1 for the tail, and had unbranched gills. The gills began to ramify the next day, while the

tail grew longer. Four days later one of the branchiae was already covered, and the tail had grown to 4–4.5 mm, the upper crest reaching the middle of the body, which was then 2.7 mm long.

LARVAE. The larvae collected in clear water in the Sierra de Cordoba were bright-colored and had much pigment on the tail, contrasting with those from the yellowish water of the marshes round La Plata.

*Hyla pulchella pulchella* is very abundant in the suburbs of La Plata, and the tadpoles can be found in very large numbers in the marshes outside the city. Ten to twenty were taken at a time for Dr. Fernandez by putting a net into the muddy water. They were either clay-colored or very light greenish with an almost olive tail. Six specimens were reared to adult size by her from these tadpoles. At the last stage the larvae are good swimmers and adapted to deep water. They are not unlike the larvae of *Pseudis mantidactyla*, fide Fernandez.

DESCRIPTION OF LARVA (Platine form). Spiraculum sinistral, anus dextral. Tooth formula 2/3. Spiraculum at two-thirds the distance from the front, directed backward. Interorbital space double the internarial, slightly inferior to the mouth opening, which in large tadpoles is 4–5 mm wide. Border of papillae simple, except on the ventro-lateral edges of the lower part, which are prolonged downward; papillae absent only from the median upper part. Beaks dark, not very wide. Labial teeth variable, generally $\frac{1-1}{3}$. At metamorphosis the inner row of the lower lip divided in two. Mouth opening ventral. Eyes lateral. Body wide at the insertion of the tail, tapering forward but rounded in outline. Width of body slightly superior to its height, about 1/3 of its length. Tail wide except toward the pointed tip; muscular part very wide; crests wider after it narrows, the upper one extending onto the back.

Largest tadpole seen by Fernandez 71 mm, of which 22 mm for head and body. Metamorphic ones 17–21 mm head and body length. Interorbital space narrowing from 5–6 mm in large tadpoles to 3 mm in metamorphic specimens.

JUVENILES. The tadpoles obtained in La Plata in October metamorphosed in November. They left the water and immediately hid themselves, often bunched together tightly, on the ground, under the vegetation. A few days later they climbed up the walls of the vivarium and onto the plants in it. They behaved like the adults, prefering high places and having almost entirely terrestrial habits.

Submetamorphic and metamorphic specimens from Rio Grande do Sul, Brazil, leg. R. Gliesch, near Porto Alegre, now in the A. Lutz Collection, include large tadpoles with tails: 21–24 mm head and body, tails from 18 (broken off) to 2 mm. Two others with a stump of tail: 22.1 and 22.3 mm head and body length.

Juvenile specimens from São Paulo show two different sizes, some being 21 or 21.5 to 23.1 mm snout to vent, the others much larger, 25.2 to 28 mm. All of them have the *leucotaenia* pattern of light margins, and most of them have a dark vertebral line, often accompanied by dots to its sides; one with irregular longitudinal dorsal pattern. As yet, no pattern on the concealed surfaces.

GEOGRAPHIC DISTRIBUTION. *Hyla pulchella* is a tree frog from the more temperate zone of South America on the eastern side of the Andes. It ranges from Argentina into Bolivia and through Uruguay into Brazil. The extreme points known seem to be Bahía Blanca in Argentina, Lindoia in the state of São Paulo, and Poços de Caldas in Minas Gerais in Brazil.

In Argentina, *Hyla pulchella* has an extraordinary range of altitude, from the seaboard to the Andes, along the sierras of Cordoba, Mendoza, Jujuy, Catamarca, and Tucuman. The Brazilian specimens available mostly hail from the plains of Rio Grande do Sul and the plateau in the state of São Paulo plus one population living at a high altitude in Poços de Caldas, Minas Gerais.

FROGS FROM THE SOUTHERN PLAINS. Living specimens from the southern plains (platine and cisplatine provinces) are green, greenish yellow, cream, or buff above, sometimes with a pale greenish suffusion on a cream or light buff background, occasionally a grayish tan. Dorsolateral light edges sometimes reduced to a light border of the dorsal mantle, sometimes forming very characteristic, straight or undulating margins, mostly extending from the hind corner of the eye to the groin, often brilliant white or with a rosy, mother-of-pearl, silver, or slightly golden tint. Similar dark margins on the sides of the head and at the edge of the upper jaw, reaching slightly beyond the tympanum or almost to the elbow, on the upper outer edge

of the tibia and of the forearm, on the latter obliquely from the elbow to the wrist; a short supra-anal border. Sometimes a light edge along the canthus. All the margins have a contrasting dark border under them except the maxillary one, where the dark area is above the light margin and spreads over the sides of the head. Dorsal surface mostly devoid of pattern; occasionally with dark, angular, or sinuous, rather indistinct flecks or streaks, or amoeboid spots, generally disposed more or less longitudinally. In a few individuals irregular, indistinct longitudinal darker areas discernible on the back; much more rarely light dots, streaks, or spots instead. Light spots below the dorsolateral edge of a very few mantled specimens.

Iris more or less golden, especially the upper half, the lower inclining to the darker color of the sides of the head. Tympanum light brown, almost always contrasting with the color of the background.

Surfaces concealed in repose, i. e. flanks near the groin and upper posterior area of the thigh, with a pattern composed of dark spots on the flanks; pattern larger and bolder, on the thighs, forming either stripes, bars, or blotches. In a number of individuals the pattern extends to the inner aspect of the tibia, to the dorsal aspect of the inner half of the tarsus and foot, and even to the webs between the inner toes, which are of the same color as the other concealed surfaces. Background of spots pale violaceous or a reddish tint on the thighs, nearer bluish white on the flanks. Uruguayan specimens are similar.

A series of *H. p. pulchella* from the plains of Rio Grande do Sul, the most southern state of Brazil, photographed in color by Prof. Gualter A. Lutz, were also green, cream, buff, or light cinnamon, occasionally grayish, with a slight, more or less obscure dorsal pattern visible in the darker ones. The pattern on the concealed parts was composed of small dots and rounded or blunt-edged spots on the flanks and slightly larger ones on the thighs. The light margins are straight in some phases, very slightly wavy in others, mostly the deeper-colored ones. They are very similar to those from the eastern plains of Argentina seen by us. Duméril and Bibron's name *Hyla pulchella* seems admirably suited to them, the more so as most of those from the Rio Grande do Sul are small, with a predominance of light tints. Ventral surface of thighs a paler tint than the concealed dorsal aspect. Vocal sac yellow.

FROGS FROM THE SOUTHEASTERN BRAZILIAN PLATEAU. In Brazil *Hyla pulchella* occurs on the plateau beyond the southeastern mountain slopes. One series of specimens from near the capital of São Paulo, in a devastated area near the escarpment, comprised well-grown individuals, some cream colored, with brown sides to the head and others with a peculiar, rather deep, bilious, greenish yellow color, and very neat undulated margins. Both have a rather light iris and distinct brown tympanum.

The frogs of another series, from Poranga in the southern part of the state of São Paulo, and others from São André do Campos, are robust in build and rather dark. Fine specimens of this form have a bronzed, permanently visible dorsal aspect, with wide, plain, very distinct and deep cream-colored margins to the upper jaw, sides of the head and body and outer edge of the permanently visible segments of the limbs. A greenish color shows through in some parts, especially on the upper eyelids and slightly less so on the sides of the head. The iris is a lighter or darker bronze. The tympanum is lighter than the background and stands out. The concealed surfaces are violet, with or without an underlying reddish tint, and bear large dark blotches. Belly white, immaculate as usual. Gula of male a deep bronze.

A population of *Hyla pulchella* was unexpectedly found in Poços de Caldas in the mountains of Minas Gerais (21° 50′ 20″ S. 46° 33′ 55″ W. Gr.; altitude approximately 1,100 m above sea level. A visiting naturalist thought that the call, which he recorded, was similar to that of *Hyla pulchella* from his country. Barrio considered the call recorded as identical with that of *Hyla pulchella pulchella*.

RACES FROM WESTERN ARGENTINA. The western Argentinian races are robust and ornate. *Hyla p. riojana* is a very beautiful frog. The living one, given to me by A. Barrio, was a soft green, rather like pale moss, liberally sprinkled with somewhat large, amoeboid, bronze or dark golden spots over the whole dorsal surface of the body; an inner and outer row of elongate or squarish, similar spots covered most of the permanently visible upper

aspects of the limbs. Concealed surfaces a soft green with blotches and spots. No dorsal bands present. Pollex rudiment well developed and sharp. Size 47–50 mm up. Call generally composed of three to four notes. For sonagram, see Barrio (1965).

*Hyla p. andina* seems to become very large and robust: 47–60 mm (Barrio). Fernandez mentions the granite gray color and brick-red spots of live frogs from the Sierra de Cordoba. Robust specimens of *H. p. andina* in the A. Lutz Collection, collected by Förster, have become dark gray with numerous darker spots. However, the examples of *Hyla p. andina* (fide Barrio) we saw and collected in the Finca El Rey National Park in Salta, at approximately 900 m altitude, are neither large nor robust. One of them inclined to a somewhat metallic and golden, very light green color. The others were generally cream colored to pale tan or chamois, sometimes light buff, generally without any pattern and not unlike the forms from the plains. When the specimens were handled, faint ochraceous or salmon spots became visible. Iris bronze colored or tawny. Tympanum standing out from the background. Perpendicular brown spots on the concealed anterior and posterior edge of flank and thigh; smaller ones at the edge of the arm; all have a metallic glint. Bones green, blue-gray through translucency. Edge of upper jaw sometimes golden. Barrio mentions the following characters: dorsolateral bands present; pollex rudiment large; call similar to that of *H. p. riojana*. Catamarca, Jujuy, Salta, Bolivia (very large and robust specimens).

*Hyla p. cordobae* Barrio, 1965, slightly smaller, 39–50 mm. Head wide. From cinnamon brown to green, some specimens with a golden sheen. When gray or brown a fine reticulum of dots with large isolated spots between the network. No dorsolateral bands. Pollex rudiment smaller than in the other two. For sonagrams, see Barrio (1965).

AFFINITIES. A few other forms from southeastern and southern Brazil and from Misiones in Argentina belong to the same group as *Hyla pulchella*, and some of them may belong to the same species. They are discussed below and comprise *Hyla joaquini* mihi, *Hyla semiguttata* Lutz, *Hyla cymbalum* Bokermann, and Barrio's proposed new form *Hyla parapulchella*.

## Hyla pulchella joaquini B. Lutz, 1968

LUTZ, B. 1968. New Brazilian Forms of *Hyla*. Texas Memorial Museum. The Pearce-Sellards series (10):1–19. *H. raddiana joaquini*: 13–15, fig. 7.

This very beautiful tree frog was collected in the highest and most southern part of the state of Santa Catarina at almost 1,400 m altitude. It is dedicated to the cofinder, whose name coincides with that of the type locality.

DIAGNOSTIC CHARACTERS. In some ways similar to *Hyla p. pulchella*, especially to the specimens with a dorsal mantle ending in light dorsolateral margins. It differs, however, by the absence of pattern on the concealed surfaces of thighs and flanks and the more ornate back; also by the very short snout, truncate between the subterminal nostrils, and by the better-developed pollex rudiment.

TYPE AND TYPE LOCALITY. The holotype and a smaller paratype, both males, were caught December 30, 1949, by Joaquim Venancio and me at São Joaquim on the Serra Geral in Santa Catarina, 28° 17′ 19″ S. 49° 55′ 56″ W. Gr.; approximately 1,360 m of altitude. Alpine meadow formation, one of the coldest places in Brazil. Now MNR nos. 4033 (holotype) and 4034 (paratype).

DESCRIPTION. Type male: size 51.5 mm. Paratype 40.1 mm snout to vent. Build robust. Body elongate, narrowed only between the sacrum and the groin. Leg fairly long, the adpressed tibiotarsal articulation reaching in front of the eye. Head almost square. Snout short, truncate between the almost terminal nostrils, abbreviated and very slightly convex in profile. Canthus rostralis short, distinct. Loreal region, high, vertical, grooved between the eye and the nostril. Head slightly concave between the eyes. Interorbital space not much wider than the upper eyelid. Eye large, its horizontal diameter not quite double the distance between its anterior corner and the nostril. Tympanum less than half the diameter of the eye. Vomerine teeth in two short, robust, well-separated groups at the level of the posterior edge of the choanae. Tongue short, very wide, entire, slightly free behind. A short web between the three lateral fingers, to the first subarticular tubercle, thence narrowed to a fringe. A very distinct pollex rudiment ending in a sharp spine. Web between first and second toes oblique to the level of the first subarticular tubercle; on the outer three longer, wide to the second subarticular tubercle. A very modest inner but no outer metatarsal tubercle. Skin smooth above, very slightly granular on the chest, gula, and midventral aspect of the thigh, with small but very distinct and regular granulation on the abdomen.

SECONDARY SEX CHARACTERS. The type and paratype are both males, with distinct, very sharp-pointed pollex rudiments and very thick forearms. Vocal sac not very conspicuous. Females not seen as yet.

MEASUREMENTS (mm). Holotype: SV: HL 51.1:99. Femur 29, tibia 28, tarsus 17, foot 24. Head length to width 15.1:15.2. IS:Ue 5:4. Tympanum 3. Eye 7, eye-nostril 4. Paratype: 40.1 SV. Femur 20, tibia 20, tarsus 13, foot 17.

COLOR AND PATTERN. In life, head and body covered by a beautiful green color like a mantle, with luminous, white, dorsolateral margins from the back of the eye to the sacrum. Similar slightly more sinuous, white margins, outlined in dark, on the sides of the head. A bronze suffusion on the forepart of the head and of the upper eyelids. A similar, slightly browner, longitudinal area on the median hind part of the back. A longitudinal series of insular, olive-green spots, very small in front, growing larger and becoming elongate caudad on each side of the body just inside the light margin, the last one forming an inlet the color of the sides, so that the margin ends as a prong. Forelimb and tibia similar in color to the body, but lighter. Thighs quite different, with three brilliant white spots on the left one and some large scallops on the right one, limited in front by the vinaceous color of the anterior part of the thigh and behind by the olive-green tone of the upper hind part concealed in repose. Tarsus and foot less distinctly ornamented, with longitudinal light scalloped areas inclosing dark spots. Sides of body dark olive-green. Ventral aspect light, immaculate.

Color variable. In one phase inclined to deep yellow green on the front of the body and much lighter tones on the forelimb; the upper arm and digits more yellow. Hind part of body distinctly blue-green. In another, more uniform phase without a yellowish or bluish tinge, just plain green. Spots and inclosures olive green; scallops and spots on thigh white, slightly mother-of-pearl; anterior part of thigh a deep or light purplish to vinaceous color; feet pale.

BEHAVIOR. The type was found sitting on a stone in a clear stream. The paratype was taken from a tree in the vicinity.

AFFINITIES. The mantle has a general resemblance to the dorsal aspect of certain specimens of *Hyla pulchella*, of which it may be an altitudinal form. However, *H. joaquini* lacks the pattern of spots or stripes found on the concealed areas of flanks and thighs of *Hyla pulchella* and has an unusually short and truncate snout.

## *Hyla semiguttata* Lutz, 1925

LUTZ, A. 1925. Batraciens du Brésil. *C. R. Soc. Biol. Paris* 93(22):211–214. *H. semiguttata*: 211.

———. 1926. New Species of Brasilian batrachians. Preliminary note. *Publ. Inst. O Cruz. H. semiguttata*: 10.

CEI, J. M., and ROIG, V. G. 1961. Batracios recolectados por la expedición biologica Erspamer en Corrientes y selva oriental de Misiones. *Notas Biol. Facult. Ciencias Exactas, Fisicas y Naturales, Corrientes Zool.* 1. *H. semiguttata*: 10.

In 1925 Lutz described a new species of *Hyla* on the basis of a specimen received from the mountains of northern Santa Catarina. He called it *Hyla semiguttata* on account of the three longitudinal bands on the back partly fragmented into large drops. The type was a female, probably adult, but without eggs; being unique, it could not be dissected. For many years no additional material was forthcoming, except for one specimen collected by Prof. R. Gliesch at Canelas in northern Rio Grande do Sul. Watercolor sketches were made of both specimens after death. In 1949, during an excursion to the south, Joaquim Venancio and I received and found a few specimens of this frog at Caracol in Rio Grande do Sul, not far from the finding place of the Gliesch specimen; also at Estrada do Saraiva quite close to and slightly below the type locality, São Bento do Sul. Much later, Cei and Roig (1961) collected typical *Hyla semiguttata* in the Argentinian province of Misiones, which is entered by a spur of the Brazilian Serra Geral. Cochran (1955) erroneously put *H. semiguttata* into the synonymy of *Hyla polytaenia* Cope. She may have been misled by the lack of more abundant material and by the fact that in very large specimens of *Hyla polytaenia*, mostly from the Serra da Mantiqueira, the pattern is apt to be simplified to the three main stripes. Nevertheless, the disparity in size is considerable. Also, as Lutz saw from the first, the affinities of *H. semiguttata* are not with *H. polytaenia* but with *Hyla pulchella*.

DIAGNOSTIC CHARACTERS. Size medium. Build fairly robust, similar to that of *Hyla pulchella*. Limbs rather thin, legs long. Dorsal surface dark greenish brown in life, brown after death; three longitudinal dark bands on the dorsal surface, partly fragmented into large drops; more or less abundant white dots or a black-and-white reticulation on the flanks; a light dorsolateral border in continuation of the light edge of the upper jaw; often a similar, lower, lateral light edge. Bones green. Male with a spur.

TYPE AND TYPE LOCALITY. Type female, n. 68 of the ALC at the MNR, collected in São Bento do Sul on the Maritime Range in northern Santa Catarina, at approximately 800 m altitude.

DESCRIPTION. Size 39–42 mm; type 41 mm snout to vent. Build fairly robust. Hindlimb long, the tibiotarsal articulation reaching beyond the snout when adpressed. Head rather high, very little wider than long. Snout short, rounded in front. Canthus rostralis truncate in front of the nostrils; loreal region nearly vertical, slightly concave. Eye longer than the distance from its anterior corner to the nostril. Tympanum about one-half the diameter of the eye. Interorbital space wider than internarial space. Minute tubercles on the palm; subarticular tubercles normal; disks average to small. Lateral fingers about one-third webbed. Toes about one-half webbed, fringed. Skin almost smooth above, granular in the usual places beneath.

VARIATION. Specimens as yet too few and gaps in the known distribution too large to permit breaking up into races. Slight differences in webbing. Differences in length of hindlimb; in the three specimens from Misiones it is shorter. This factor is too variable in *Hyla* to be worth taxonomical recognition.

MEASUREMENTS. Females: type 41 mm; two from Caracol, Rio Grande do Sul, 39 and 41.5 mm snout to vent. Males from San Pedro, Misiones, Argentina, largest 41.6 mm, others 39–41.5.

SECONDARY SEX CHARACTERS. The females seen belong to the southern Brazilian populations. They are relatively small, not larger than the southern males present; they are not distended by eggs and may not be full-grown. The specimens seen from Argentinian collections are all males. The Argentinian ones have a sharp pointed pollex rudiment.

COLOR AND PATTERN. Lutz describes the color and pattern of the recently dead specimen received by him as follows: "Tympanum rather large, brown. Back light brown with darker, median and lateral, longitudinal bands, sometimes dissolving into oval or round spots. On each eyelid and leg is a similar spot. The back is white-edged behind and laterally. Limbs light brown with somewhat reddish brown longitudinal stripes. Underside cream-colored, granulated, and dotted with gray on the body, the posterior side of the thighs and at the end of the limbs."

Our notes on one of the living frogs from Caracol record metallic tones of greenish brown on the dorsal aspect; back greenish olivaceous, anteriorly more brownish, posteriorly more greenish; longitudinal brown dorsal bands darker. Edges of the upper jaw and dorsolateral edges light; beneath it, flanks dark with minute light spots; sometimes a lower light edge visible. A darkish stripe on the outside of the tibia and over the foot. A distinct light edge over the anus. Underside cream; gula olive yellow ( ♀ ); webs gray. Long bones green, by translucency with a light glaucous tint. Another living specimen was dark brown with a very distinct pale gold stripe on the upper jaw and on the dorsolateral edges, a lower one on the sides of the body and light dots on the flanks. Upper half of iris lighter than the lower, which blends with the sides of the head.

Cei and Roig say of their Misiones specimens that they were olivaceous in life and that the bands on the back break up into drops, in accordance with Lutz's description of *Hyla semiguttata*. They also mention the light irregular line along the sides from the canthus to the groin, followed by a dark smoky area on the sides on which white, rounded, or elongate spots of different shapes and sizes stand out.

The details of the pattern are also slightly variable. The Lutz type has a large dark dot on each upper eyelid not seen in the other specimens. In one of the Canelas frogs the dorsal bands are entirely fragmented into less-rounded drops; in another the median band is dissolved into scattered drops. In one of those from Estrada Saraiva, the median band is absent and the lateral ones meet on a point on the head. The number of drops on the permanently visible part of the limbs varies from none to several.

VOICE. No sonagrams are available, only subjective impressions of the call. To J. Venancio and me it sounded similar to the call of *Hyla albopunctata* when heard at Caracol in northern Rio Grande do Sul.

ECOLOGY. The specimens collected by Venancio and me in Caracol were sitting and calling on the low vegetation of a trench sending water into the Caracol River over a bed of rock. This habit is not unlike that of the Argentinian *H. pulchella* heard by me and confirms the affinity.

I have the impression that this is a frog that prefers the ecotone of forested or formerly forested terrain. It is evidently montane and pertains to the fauna of the southern and perhaps southeastern coastal mountains.

KNOWN DISTRIBUTION. The finding places are very disjointed. The type locality is near the southern end of the Serra do Mar. São Bento is a small town on the edge of the rain forest, approximately 800 m altitude. Estrada Saraiva lies below it on the way down to the valley. The specimens from Rio Grande do Sul are from the northern part of the state where the coastal mountains, or Serra Geral, are separated from the main Maritime Range, though they probably belong to it. San Pedro, Misiones, is near the Brazilian border, where a spur of the same Serra Geral enters Argentina via southwestern Santa Catarina. Other frogs from the Serra do Mar have been collected there. The gap between the Santa Catarina and the Rio Grande do Sul specimens is occupied by lower terrain.

AFFINITIES. A note by Lutz on the watercolor of the first Canelas specimen queries, "aberrant variety of *Hyla raddiana?*" Either *Hyla semiguttata* has attained the status of a full species or the isolating mechanism must be a narrow ecological or altitudinal factor. It is also possible, but not very probable, that it is a recurrent color phase.

## *Hyla cymbalum* Bokermann, 1963

BOKERMANN, W. C. A. 1963. Una nueva especie de *Hyla* del sudeste Brasileño. *Neotropica* 9 (28):27–30, figs. 1–3.

In 1962 Bokermann described a *Hyla* under the name *Hyla cymbalum.* It is certainly a member of the *Hyla pulchella* group and conspecific either with it or with *Hyla semiguttata.*

The morphological characters of *Hyla cymbalum* and *Hyla semiguttata* are very similar. There are slight differences in webbing and in the length of the hindlimb, but this character is individually variable in many Brazilian species of *Hyla.* The main difference is the larger size of *Hyla cymbalum,* especially the holotype, which is 49 mm long; one paratype is 45 and another specimen (14074) is 44 mm from snout to vent.

SECONDARY SEX CHARACTERS. Only males are known. Bokermann states that the forearms are thickened and mentions a sharp prepollex as a specific character. However, it occurs in the whole *pulchella* complex. The specimen lent to me (14074) has a more or less marked prepollex, fuscous black vocal sac, and a dark, granular gula; the granulations extend to the root of the arms on the chest. The prepollex is palpable.

COLOR AND PATTERN. The type of *H. cymbalum* was dark green in life and became olivaceous brown after preservation. It is a very large, not very typical, and evidently a rather melanistic specimen. The description does not mention any dark bars on the sides of the dorsal surface. A very distinct black and white reticulation is present on the flanks and on the posterior upper concealed aspect of the thighs. In *H. semiguttata* this is unequally developed; it is very little marked in the type of *H. semiguttata,* better developed in the other specimens, and extremely distinct on the frog of this species collected by Gliesch in Canelas, Rio Grande do Sul.

Bokermann also overlooked the different colors of the two halves of the iris; the upper half is lighter than the lower one, which blends with the sides of the head. This is precisely the greatest point of similarity between *Hyla semiguttata* and *H. cymbalum.*

VOICE. Bokermann considers the call quite different from that of *Hyla pulchella.* He finds it metallic, compares it to that of *Hyla polytaenia,* and uses the word *cymbalum* for the trivial name. Barrio, who heard and compared the sonagrams, finds the calls quite similar. I have heard *Hyla pulchella pulchella* repeatedly and also heard *Hyla p. andina*

at Finca El Rey in Salta, Argentina. They both sound very bird-like to me. *Hyla polytaenia* trills and chirrups at an unusually high pitch. None of these calls are in the least like cymbals.

HABITS. Bokermann collected the types on shrubs in a little wood by the side of a brook on an island in the type locality. He mentions that their habits, including those in captivity, were similar to those of *Hyla pulchella.*

TYPE LOCALITY. The place, Campo Grande, is near one of three former villages, Santo André, São Bernardo, and São Caetano, which have developed into small industrial towns, quite near the escarpment of the Serra do Mar and not far from the city of São Paulo. Large typical *Hyla pulchella* have been collected at Santo André.

STATUS. The likeness in the color of the iris, the similarity in color and pattern, and the difference in size between *Hyla cymbalum* and *Hyla semiguttata,* plus the *pulchella*-like call, are rather perplexing. *Hyla cymbalum* probably is either conspecific with *Hyla pulchella* or *Hyla semiguttata* or constitutes a race of one or the other.

## *Hyla prasina* Burmeister, 1856

BURMEISTER, C. H. C. 1856. *Erläuterungen zur Fauna Brasiliens,* p. 106, pl. 31, fig. 2.

*Hyla prasina* was described by Burmeister in 1856. It is very closely allied to *Hyla pulchella* as already mentioned by him and is mostly considered synonymous with it. I held it so at first but have now decided to separate them because of the different calls.

DIAGNOSTIC CHARACTERS. The call was heard in Nova Friburgo, the type locality, before tape recorders were introduced. It differs from the melodious call of *Hyla pulchella* and is rough, sounding somewhat like *carará, carará.* The build is narrower and more elongate. The tan or brown color phase seems absent; the pattern on the upper part of the thigh concealed in repose is composed of vertical purplish stripes on a violet background.

TYPES AND TYPE LOCALITY. No type was designated, but several specimens were obtained by Burmeister, mostly early in the morning, sitting on leaves at the edge of the rain forest of Nova Friburgo, in the northern block of the Serra do Mar. We have one topotype.

DESCRIPTION (topotype). Size large; male 55 mm from snout to vent. Build narrow but robust. Head large, slightly wider than long. Body elongate; postaxillary region as wide as the head, narrowed beyond the sacrum. Hindlimb rather long, the tibiotarsal articulation reaching between the eye and the nostril when adpressed. Snout short, bluntly rounded in front from above, slanting forward in profile, the upper jaw projecting slightly over the lower one. Canthus rostralis curved, fairly distinct: loreal region sloping to the mouth; a diagonal furrow from the eye to the nostril. Nostrils raised, superior rather than lateral, much nearer to the end of the snout than to the eye. Eye prominent, its diameter equal to the distance from its anterior corner to the nostril. Tympanum distinct, about one-half the diameter of the eye. Interorbital space wider than the internarial space. Tongue very broad, cordiform, slightly indented and very slightly free behind. Vomerine teeth in small, round, distinct, well-separated patches between the choanae. Fingers webbed at the base; a minute but sharp spine on the first. Toes half-webbed; a small inner, no outer metatarsal tubercle; an inner and an outer tarsal ridge. Skin of upper parts smooth; a slight glandular ridge over the eye and tympanum and down the sides of the body to the groin; a transverse glandular ridge in front of the anus; a very faint glandular line outside the forearm and the tibia. Skin of throat coarsely granular. A heavy vocal sac across the throat forming large skinfolds.

MEASUREMENTS (mm). Male topotype: snout to vent 55; head length 10, width 17–18, femur 27, tibia 28, tarsus and foot 32.

COLOR AND PATTERN. According to Burmeister and his colored figure, *Hyla prasina* is light green with the dorsal surface brilliant as if enameled. The dorsolateral margins are silvery or mother-of-pearl; they are scalloped and have a dark edge under them; sometimes light dots are visible beneath them; similar margins are present on the forearm from the elbow to the wrist and on the leg from the knee to the ankle. Ventral aspect white, the flesh shining through a light violet background. Blue-violet perpendicular bars on a light violet background on the concealed upper aspect of the thighs, flanks, and a small inner portion of the legs.

Our topotype was also bright green above and looked as if enameled. The dorsolateral margins were golden at night and sometimes mother-of-pearl or pale rose in daytime, always metallic but never silvery. The scallops of the dorsolateral margins did not stand out in relief. They began at the tympanum and stopped short of the groin. Abdomen and ventral aspect of the limbs white with a fine violet mesh. Flanks and upper concealed aspect of the thighs violet with darker, purplish, perpendicular bars. Outside of thigh pale orange with light brown spots. Iris golden. Tympanum light brown. After some time in captivity this frog became gray while still alive.

Some similar tree frogs collected by us in the coastal mountains of northern Santa Catarina were also green in life. The concealed surfaces of the flanks and thighs were violet with darker blue-violet or purplish, very definite stripes. One of these frogs showed an interrupted white vertebral stripe beginning behind the shoulder; there were also a few white dots in linear series on each side of the back. The iris was darker than in the topotype of *H. prasina* and that of *Hyla pulchella* from the southern plains. The light brown tympanum stood out. They probably belong to *Hyla prasina*, though this was described from the northern block of the Serra do Mar in the state of Rio de Janeiro, where it now seems very rare. The southern frogs are more elongate, narrower and less robust than our topotype. The head seems proportionately longer.

VOICE. When caught our topotype was calling loudly and harshly, *carará, carará*. The specimens from Santa Catarina were obtained in the forest and their call was not recorded.

HABITS. The topotype was caught at night in marshy ground, sitting on a tall bush growing on a bank above the artificial pond of a brick factory. When illuminated by the flashlight it launched itself at J. Venancio, who caught it. This was fortunate as it had been quite out of reach.

AFFINITIES. *Hyla prasina* has some affinity with *Hyla joaquini* mihi, which has a scalloped mantle but is devoid of pattern on the flanks and thighs. The mantle is sometimes slightly olivaceous. The snout is truncate and very short.

## *Hyla marginata* Boulenger, 1887

BOULENGER, G. A. 1887. Descriptions of new or

little-known South American frogs of the genera *Paludicola* and *Hyla. An. Mag. Nat. Hist.* 20, ser. 5:295–300. *H. marginata*: 298.

Although I saw the type in London I have been unable to identify this species with any of the specimens seen before or since. It cannot be near to *Hyla rubicundula* Reinhardt and Lütken, which is very small and akin to *Hyla nana*. Nor does it seem to be near *Hyla polytaenia*, which is sometimes mistaken for *Hyla rubicundula*. Its affinities seem rather with the *Hyla pulchella* group. In some ways it approaches our *Hyla joaquini*, though not in color or livery. Consequently it is best to transcribe the original description and leave it at that.

"Tongue broader than long, entire, posterior fourth free. Vomerine teeth in two transverse oval groups, close together, on a line with the posterior border of the choanae which are of moderate size and much larger than the eustachian tubes. Head moderate, broader than long; snout rounded, shorter than the diameter of the orbit; canthus rostralis angular; loreal region not very oblique, concave; nostril nearer the end of the snout than the eye; interorbital space broader than the upper eyelid; tympanum distinct, half the diameter of the eye. Fingers one-third webbed; a distinct rudiment of pollex; toes about three-fifths webbed; disks a little smaller than the tympanum; subarticular tubercles moderate; no tarsal fold. The tibiotarsal articulation reaches halfway between the eye and the end of the snout. Skin smooth; belly with large granules; throat indistinctly granulate. Upper surfaces of head and tibia and back finely powdered with brown on a colorless ground; a few small dark brown spots on the head and back, one on each upper eyelid; a dark brown line from the end of the snout along the canthus rostralis and superciliary edge, above the tympanum, and along each side of the body as far as the sacral region, also along the outer side of the forearm and tibia; a transverse dark brown streak, edged above with white, above the vent and at the heel; a white line round the upper lip; lower surfaces colorless. From snout to vent 50 mm. Mundo Novo, Rio Grande do Sul: a single female specimen, collected by Hr. Bischoff."

# 8. Species with Glandular Outline and Lichenous Dorsum

## *Hyla marmorata* (Laurenti), 1768

LAURENTI. 1768. *Synopsis Reptilium*, p. 29.

DUMÉRIL, A. M. C., and BIBRON, G. 1841. *Erpétologie générale* 8:571–573.

COPE, E. D. 1848. Reptilia and batrachia obtained by the Orton Expedition. *Pr. Ac. Nat. Sc. Phil.*: 111

This species has been known for a long time. It was mentioned, described, and figured by several of the older authors, such as Seba, Laurenti, and Daudin. The best description seems to be that given by Duméril and Bibron (1841). There are no synonyms, which is not surprising as this is a very characteristic species with a spectacular aspect.

DIAGNOSTIC CHARACTERS. The conspicuous black spots and marks on the vivid yellow and orange background of the ventral surface; the *Rhacophorus*-like webs, digits, and disks, the patagium (humero-thoracic fold) and the loose upper eyelids; the wavy outline of the body and the barklike aspect of the dorsal surface. At home in the equatorial rain-forest belt.

TYPE AND TERRA TYPICA. I do not know where Laurenti's specimens are. Daudin states that the specimen figured by Seba was on exhibition at the Muséum in Paris. Terra typica is Surinam.

DESCRIPTION (specimen belonging to the Museu Goeldi at Belém do Pará). Female: 46 mm from snout to vent, hindlimb 85 mm. (Indications in literature are 35–52 mm head and body length.) Body an elongate oval in this gravid female. Hindlimb rather thin, too stiff to be juxtaposed to the body but evidently of average length. Head short, thick, very slightly wider than long, somewhat inclined downward in front. Muzzle very short, rounded; canthus rostralis blunt; loreal region vertical. Nostrils overhanging the tip of the snout due to the depression of the head. Eye about as long as the snout. Tympanum one-half the diameter of the eye. Interorbital space slightly wider than the upper eyelid. Tongue large, thick, rounded, slightly emarginate, very little free behind. Vomerine teeth forming a short, heavy, barely interrupted transverse row between the choanae. Digits flattened, very wide, with very large disks, as mentioned by Duméril and Bibron. Dilated part of web reaching the base of the disk on all digits, except on the inner side of the first finger, forming a wide fringe on the inner side of the second and on the upper half of both sides of the last articulation of the third. Free outline of web very straight. Subarticular tubercles small. An elongate tubercle outside the lower half of the first finger; an oval inner metatarsal tubercle. Skin very loose, especially on the upper eyelids (as in *Rhacophorus*, according to Duméril and Bibron); in this specimen also on the sides at the sacrum. Outline of frog in repose wavy, due to the scalloped glandular outline of the forearm, tibia, and tarsus, the pustular edges of the sides and the lower edge of the tympanum. Scattered pustules on the dorsal surface, especially on the head; perianal region granular, belly and midventral aspect of thigh coarsely granular, the granules in serrated formation on the belly. A triangular fold of skin (patagium) from the arm to the trunk, continuing as a pectoral fold.

MEASUREMENTS (mm). Two females with eggs from the Javari River. Snout to vent 46 (2). Hindlimb 85, 70. Cucui juvenile (?) 37.

SECONDARY SEX CHARACTERS. Eggs of slightly different sizes present in both females, half black, half yellow. A very distinct subgular fold.

COLOR AND PATTERN. The reposing frog must be very inconspicuous in a forest environment, as its dorsal surface is similar to tree bark, either simple or ornamented by lichens. In life, coloring rather luminous in blended tones of dark and tawny brown. Iris also with similar blended tones, forming a mosaic, and with broad pseudocolobom. Ventral aspect very beautiful. Background of head, body, and thighs suffused with orange from the periphery toward the middle, where it becomes pale yellow. Fairly large, black spots disseminated all over these surfaces, more concentrated on the belly. Granular, stippled in gray, granite-like at the edges of the mouth and parts of the sides uncovered by the limbs when at rest; the margins of the segments of the limbs that limit the body in repose are similar, i. e., forearm, hand, tarsus, and foot to the outer digits; very marked, granite-like granulations on the anal region and midventral strip of thigh. Ventral aspect of forearm, tibia, tarsus, hand, and foot deep black. Webs bright orange (living frog from Príncipe da Beira, Rondonia, southwestern part of the Brazilian Hylaea). Another photographed in Peru by Blair is quite similar; above blending with the tree bark.

The color and pattern of the permanently visible surfaces seem to keep fairly well in preserved specimens of this group. The female of the Museu Goeldi from the Javari River shows black dots on the gula going over into fragmented angular spots on the belly, which grow larger caudad. Dorsal surface ornamented by gray, irregular, somewhat ang-ular streaks with a wide, dark, almost black border on a reddish brown background. Blotch-like spots or crossbars on the concealed parts of the thigh and ventral aspect of the tibia. Hands and feet black. A bluish tint on the groin.

The Museu Nacional female also has a reddish brown background over most of the back, ornamented with a continuous, labyrinthine band winding about between the eyes and the sacrum, outlined in dark gray; black in life. The pattern continues disruptively onto the visible parts of the sides and limbs. Concealed aspect of thigh and ventral light areas faded to white. Gula gray, like powdered granite, with some glandules. Patagium and pectoral fold light. Chest and belly marbled in black, like in the other specimen, but the spots more rounded and more uniform in size. Hand, foot, tarsus, tibia, and forearm black; a grayish edge on the forearm. Distal parts of the web now white.

KNOWN DISTRIBUTION. *Hyla marmorata* is widespread and may well occupy the whole equatorial rain-forest belt. The first specimens seen by the older authors were taken in the Guianas, whose anuran fauna became known earlier than that of Brazil, Peru, and Ecuador. Surinam is mentioned several times by them. The British Museum has specimens from the Mazaruni River, Bartica, and the upper Cuyuni, 6–8° N. 58–60° W. Gr. in British Guiana, and from the Huallaga River in Ecuador. Those seen by Cope were obtained on the Pastaza River in Peru on the headwaters of the Amazonas, where it is still called Marañon, and on the Rio Napo, its tributary. Our two specimens were both taken near the borders of Brazil, one at Cucui on the upper Rio Negro, near Venezuela (0° 8' 93" S. 67° 5' 8" W. Gr.) and the other in the west on the Javari River, at a place called Esteiras do Ecuador, near the border of Peru and Colombia, 4° 21' 42" S. 69° 54' 13" W. Gr. It reaches the southwestern part of the Hylaea as well.

RELATIONSHIPS. Castelnaud, Duméril and Bibron, and Burmeister confounded this species and a similar one, which is less spectacular and occupies a very large territory further south. Thus Rio de Janeiro is mentioned, quite erroneously, as a finding place of *Hyla marmorata* by them. Cope rightly recognized the differences and proposed the name *Hyla senicula* for the southern form, described and figured as *Hyla marmorata* by Burmeister. The differences are very evident, both as to ventral color and as to pattern; the *Rhacophorus*-like characters of *Hyla marmorata* are lacking in *Hyla senicula*. Dr. Cochran treats *senicula* as a subspecies of *Hyla marmorata,* evidently on the basis of morphology alone. I am not in agreement with her, for reasons which will become apparent in the text on *Hyla senicula* below. There is, however, a general relationship between this species and the others pertaining to the group.

## *Hyla senicula senicula* Cope, 1868

BURMEISTER, C. H. C. 1856. *Erläuterungen zur Fauna Brasiliens,* p. 93, pl. 31, figs. 1 a–f.

COPE, E. D. 1868. An examination of the reptilia and batrachia obtained by the Orton Expedition to Ecuador and the upper Amazonas, with notes on other species. *Ac. Nat. Sc. Phil.,* 20:96–140. *H. senicula:* 111.

————. 1887. Synopsis of the batrachia and reptilia obtained by H. H. Smith in the province of Matto Grosso, Brazil. *Pr. Am. Phil. Soc.* 24: 44–60. *Hyla melanargyrea:* 45.

In his *Erläuterungen zur Fauna Brasiliens,* Burmeister applies Daudin's name *Hyla marmorata* to a tree frog of the same group collected by him in Rio de Janeiro. Cope (1868), while studying a collection from Ecuador and the upper Amazonas, saw that Burmeister's frog could not belong to *Hyla marmorata.* This is a larger species and has a spectacular pattern of black, orange, and yellow on the concealed surfaces. Consequently, Cope proposed the name *Hyla senicula* for the species found in Rio de Janeiro. Four years later Peters (1872), on examining the Spix Collection, also realized Burmeister's mistake and offered the name *Hyla vermiculata* (p. 211), amended by him to *Hyla vermicularis* on p. 680 of the same volume. The frogs collected by H. H. Smith in Mato Grosso, which were studied much later by Cope (1887), included one very similar to *Hyla senicula.* This was called *Hyla melanargyrea* by Cope. The main differences between the two forms seem to be the more definite dorsal pattern and the black color of the concealed parts of the thigh, plus the vivid white spots on the permanently visible dorsal aspect of *H. melanargyrea.*

DIAGNOSTIC CHARACTERS. Both the Cope names are very well found. *Hyla senicula* has the short head, bulldog-like snout, short, robust body, pata-

gium from axilla to arm, and scalloped glandular outline of the body in repose peculiar to the group. Its own dorsal coloring is, as A. Lutz puts it, generally gray and like tree bark. This coloration, plus the glandular skin and the irregular insular spots, which look as if they were outlined by a black thread, convey an impression of senescence. Some specimens from Rio are olivaceous brown and rather dark.

TYPE LOCALITY. Burmeister found his frog in Laranjeiras, a residential part of Rio de Janeiro, below the Corcovado Mountain. It is a lowland form and is replaced in the mountains of the state of Rio de Janeiro by *Hyla microps,* a different and smaller species.

DESCRIPTION. Size moderate, males 29–36 mm, females 36–43 mm snout to vent. Build robust. Head and body short. Hindlimb also short, the tibiotarsal articulation reaching the eye when the leg is adpressed. Head as wide as long. Snout very short, rounded from above, not projecting beyond the mouth in profile, bulldog-like. Canthus rostralis short, blunt; loreal region slightly concave, vertical. Nostrils small, slightly tumefied. Eye very prominent in life, as long as the distance to the tip of the snout. Interorbital space slightly wider than the internarial space. Tympanum distinct but small, at most one-half the diameter of eye. Vomerine teeth in two short groups between the choanae. Tongue wide, rounded to cordiform, distinctly notched, somewhat free behind. Hands and feet large. Fingers webbed to the disk on the outer side of the second, and on the fourth, to the penultimate subarticular tubercle, or below disk, on inner side of the second and on both sides of the third finger. Disks large, that of the third finger covering the tympanum. A callosity on the outer sides of the first. Feet robust. Toes fully webbed: wide part of web reaching the disk on outer side of the first, second, third, and on the fifth, below it on their inner side and on both sides of the fourth toe; a fringe outside the first toe, beginning at the inner metatarsal tubercle; in some specimens a minute outer metatarsal tubercle. Skin pustular with disseminated warts, especially on the head, upper eyelids, and back. Margins of jaw, anal region, and outer edge of limbs (forearm, hand, tarsus, and foot) glandular, scalloped, forming a wavy outline of the frog in repose. A distinct ridge around the tympanum. Very distinct folds across the chest. A patagium (axillary fold), from the root of the arm to the axilla. Beneath very granular, especially the edge of the gula, belly, midventral part of thigh, and the outer edges of limbs.

The size (37 mm) indicated by Boulenger, agrees with average females. Ours range from 36 to 43 mm snout to vent. Males smaller, 30–36 mm, 30–31 as a rule.

SECONDARY SEX CHARACTERS. Very marked in the male. Vocal sac huge, ballooning out below the throat to the axillae. Sides of gula or whole throat fuscous. Females distinctly larger, throat granular, marbled.

VARIATION. Morphological characters very uniform in the specimens seen from the lowlands of the states of Guanabara and Rio de Janeiro. Tongue well-notched and somewhat free in all of them. Proportions very similar. In a very few, leg slightly longer, the tibiotarsal articulation reaching the anterior corner of the eye. One of the samples from Barro Branco, state of Rio de Janeiro, comprises eight very large specimens, the females 42 and 43 mm long.

COLOR. As conveyed by the name, coloration discreet. Permanently visible dorsal aspect like tree bark, as stated by A. Lutz. Often various tones of gray, sometimes brownish. Some specimens from the lowlands of Rio de Janeiro and Guanabara olive brown, mostly dark, sometimes slightly tawny. Burmeister attributes this color to ambient humidity (!).

PATTERN. In Guanabara, Rio de Janeiro, and Espírito Santo specimens essentially composed of an interocular and a sacral spot, both extremely irregular in shape. Spots mostly outlined in fuscous black as if by a single or double thread, delimiting areas on the back of similar color or somewhat darker than the rest. This may have inspired Peters' name vermicularis. Sacral spot sometimes fragmented and/or supplemented by other small spots between it and the interocular one, which is bipartite and often prolonged backward, sometimes into strange shapes. In some specimens dark areas below the canthus. Edges of mouth blotched or marbled in dark and whitish. Disseminated glandules and glandular patches light, furthering the similarity to mottled tree bark. Iris grayish at the periphery, more olivaceous or slightly tawny toward the free inner rim, with short centripetal lines or with the aspect of a dark-edged mosaic. A few

specimens from the Baixada Fluminense have the central area of the back darker than the rest but also very irregular and individually variable.

On the permanently visible dorsal aspect of the thighs either whitish gray spots on darker ground or alternating whitish areas and dark stripes, as on the rest of the permanently visible dorsal aspect of the limbs. Anterior and posterior, dorsal, concealed parts of thigh, smooth, devoid of pattern, generally dark. Glandular edges whitish, scalloped in all the specimens. Ventral aspect light; gula either fuscous at the sides or entirely black above the light sac in males; marbled, granite-like in female specimens.

VOICE. Heard outside Rio de Janeiro; rather rough and loud for the size of the frog. Burmeister likens the call, heard singly and in chorus, to a crackling noise.

HABITS. Burmeister noted the presence of a number of individuals on an avocado tree (Persea gratissima) in the garden of his friend Mr. Lallemant, a hundred years ago. Alas, H. senicula is now heard only farther away. We have caught it singing on the ground in marshy patches at Taquara, near the International Radio Station, and at Pavuna sitting at the edges of pools.

RANGE. I have seen specimens of this form, which agree with Burmeister's description, from the states of Guanabara, Rio de Janeiro, and Espírito Santo, but it may occur in other adjacent areas.

The specimens from the interior of Goias, Bahia, and the northwest in the A. Lutz Collection and that of the MNR differ somewhat in livery and are described below as H. s. melanargyrea.

## Hyla senicula melanargyrea Cope, 1887

> COPE, E. D. 1887. Synopsis of the batrachia and reptilia obtained by H. H. Smith in the province of Matto Grosso, Brazil. Pr. Am. Phil. Soc. 24:44–60. H. melanargyrea: 45.

There are very few specimens of Hyla melanargyrea available for study in the collections seen by me. I saw the type many years ago in Philadelphia and found it very similar to Hyla s. senicula. The main differences seem to reside in the diagnostic characters used in the Cope name. Of late, owing to the kindness of Dr. Eugenio Izecksohn of the Rural Federal University of the state of Rio de Janeiro, I have been able to examine four specimens from Mato Grosso that exhibit these characters. The specimens hail from Sitio Castiçais, Rio Jaurú, municipality of Cáceres, leg. L. F. Veit, January 1964. In November 1968 I unexpectedly came upon *H. s. melanargyrea* at Belém do Pará.

DIAGNOSTIC CHARACTERS. The deep purple-black color of the dorsal and inner parts of the thighs, hind part of the flanks, inner aspect of the segments of the limbs concealed in repose, and patagium; the oval or rounded, silvery, or light, drop-like, spots on the thighs, and the very regular alternatively dark and light crossbars on the other permanently visible segments. Build apparently more slender and elongate than that of typical *H. s. senicula*, though size not very different.

TYPES AND TYPE LOCALITY. Mato Grosso, Brazil; part of the H. H. Smith Collections. Cope mentions that after a short sojourn in Cuiabá, Smith resided in the village of Chapada, thirty miles to the northeast. He adds that "the species embraced in the following list were obtained at or near this town." "Three specimens."

DIFFERENTIAL DESCRIPTION (Mato Grosso specimens). Size moderate, males 30–34 mm, female 37 mm snout to vent. Build slender, elongate. Hindlimb short, too stiff to adpress. Head short, length and width subequal. Snout short, bulldog-like, rounded, projecting only very slightly above the mouth. Tongue variable, from entire to emarginate. Other morphological characters the same as those of *Hyla s. senicula*. Skin apparently more warty, the pustules more prominent. Glandular margins outlining the frog in repose very distinct, white, wide, with granite-like aspect; on perianal region very marked.

MEASUREMENTS (mm). Female (E. Izecksohn Collection n. 1763): snout-vent to hindlimb 37:62; femur 18, tibia 18, tarsus 11, foot 15. Head length: width 11:11. Tympanum 2, eye 4, eye-nostril 4, eye-snout 4. Three males (1764, 1765, 1766): snout-vent to hindlimb 30:48.5; 33:50; 34:49; femur 13, tibia 15, tarsus 9, foot 12, 12, 13. Belém specimens slightly larger; 3 females, 39, 40, 41 mm; 1 male 37; 1 more specimen 35 mm long.

COLOR. Dorsal aspect various tones of more or less olivaceous brown, the spots dark, the intervals between them somewhat rufous. Spots outlined in black as if sutured. Interocular spot fenestrated in most of them. Bars on the limbs not always distinct. Edges of the limbs and body which outline the frog in repose white, glandular, scalloped. Iris

brownish with a pattern of numerous crisscross, rufous-brown lines, except at the inner edge which is golden. Concealed aspects, i. e. sides of the body, patagia, inside of the arms, anterior and inner part of the forearms, anterior and posterior upper aspect of the thigh, inner aspect of the tibiae and tarsi, purple-black. A row of metallic drab spots, round or irregular, sometimes forming figures of eight, on the dorsal aspect of the thigh. Ventral aspect immaculate. Gula pale but with abundant dark dotting, especially at the edges of the mouth, even in females; glandular white dots on the violaceous belly and midventral portion of the thigh. Feet and webs black, hands slightly more gray. Occasionally the dorsal aspect becomes ash-gray, as in the Bolivian specimen mentioned below.

Preserved specimens not very different from living ones; grayish brown above, concealed aspects of limbs purple-black. Ventral aspect immaculate; gula of female fuscous at edges; sacs of males much folded, more or less extensively infuscate. Belly slightly fuscous in the middle. Patagia, inner aspect of limbs, hands, and feet black.

PATTERN. Dorsal pattern composed of interocular and sacral spots plus a few insular spots between them. Spots sutured in black, variable in shape. Interocular spot produced behind in some. Sacral spot spreading onto the sides of the body between lighter areas; both more symmetrical than in *Hyla s. senicula*. Dark bars on limbs alternatively wide and linear on lighter ground; very regular, occupying all the permanently visible dorsal parts including the outer digits; substituted by purple-black on the inner toes, which are concealed in repose. Irregular light areas between the eye and the edge of the upper jaw. Drop-like silver spots on dark background, on the upper concealed aspects of the thigh very distinct.

RELATIONSHIPS. *H. s. melanargyrea* is treated here provisorily as a subspecific vicariant for *Hyla s. senicula*, in the Continental province. It seems very widespread and somewhat variable, as shown by the specimens and populations discussed below.

NOTES. A male specimen from Anápolis, Goiás, in the central area of Continental province (MNR 2390) is only 35 mm long but conforms to the general description of *H. melanargyrea* as to morphology, webbing, etc., all of which are really not very different from those of *H. senicula*. In color it is brown, not gray. The pattern comes near to that described by Cope on account of the more regular, albeit very ornate design on the dorsal aspect and the oval, silvery white dots on the dark background of the thighs. The interocular spot is very complex; the sacral one large, saddle-shaped, and visible from the sides; there are two small spots between them, one to each side, also large dark irregular spots round the nostrils.

A female specimen (MNR 2361) from Aldeia dos Tapirapés, at the northern tip of Mato Grosso, though somewhat intermediate also seems near to the *Hyla s. melanargyrea* livery. It is 36 mm long and robust. The dorsal pattern is very ornate but roughly symmetrical, with very large, complex, interocular spot, large, irregular, saddle-shaped sacral spot visible on the sides, and two oblique spots between them. The thigh pattern is composed of oval white spots on a dark background, and the concealed upper parts of the thigh are also dark. The dorsal surface ranges from tan to brown.

Our only specimen from the range of *Hyla s. melanargyrea* outside Brazil is a large male, 37 mm long (ALC 4000), from Buena Vista, Bolivia, obtained by exchange with the MZUM through the kindness of Mrs. Gaige. This specimen is pale gray. It has a quite regular, bluntly triangular spot between the eyes and other dark insular spots with slightly less dark outlines on the back. The dark bars on the permanently visible dorsal aspect of the thighs are visible on the concealed surface, which is less dark than one would expect from the name and description.

NORTHEASTERN POPULATIONS. A number of specimens of *Hyla s. melanargyrea* from the Northeastern States are much smaller than those from Belém do Pará and slightly smaller than those from Mato Grosso; also less robust than *H. s. senicula* from the states of Rio de Janeiro and Guanabara. The males with inflated vocal sac range from 29–31 mm snout to vent length. A female without eggs is only 28 mm long. The hindlimb is shorter; it reaches to just behind the eye in the male specimens, to the hind corner of the eye in the female and in the juveniles. The morpohological characters agree with those of the larger forms from elsewhere. Some specimens are fully webbed; in others the webs do not quite attain the base of the disks.

The dorsal pattern is regular like in *H. s. melanargyrea* with the separate elements plainer. The interocular spot inclines to be drawn back into an elongate triangle, and the sacral spot is wide enough to be visible on the sides. In some individuals the spots are blunt and quite regular; in others they are angular and very irregular in outline. They may be supplemented by additional small spots. The pattern on the permanently visible dorsal aspect of the thighs is composed of isolated, oval, white drops on a dark ground; there are regular stripes on the other permanently visible dorsal aspect of the limbs.

A male specimen from Japaguá in the interior of the state of Bahia is of the same size and habit, but it is brown. The dorsal pattern is obscure and very much fragmented, and there are more glandules on the body than in the others. I have this form from the coastal lowlands of the states of Ceará (Mucuripe, Fortaleza); Rio Grande do Norte (São Paulo do Potengi) and Pernambuco; a female also from Bahia but inland, in the basin of the Rio São Francisco. All these places are in the semiarid *caatinga* sector of the Continental province.

By the pattern on the thigh and the occupation of the lowlands of one of the subareas of the Continental province, these specimens seem nearer to *Hyla s. melanargyrea* than to *H. s. senicula*. It seems probable that the northeastern populations are stunted because of the probably adverse conditions in the drought region where they live. Antenor Leitão de Carvalho suggests that they constitute a geographical race. This hypothesis will eventually have to be submitted to a genetic test. If they prove to be different they might well be called *H. s. attenuata*. For the time being, I consider them as *Hyla senicula melanargyrea*.

## *Hyla senicula acreana* Bokermann, 1964

BOKERMANN, W. C. A. 1964. Notes on tree-frogs of the *Hyla marmorata* group with description of a new species. *Senckenbergiana Biologica* 43(3–5): 345, figs. 1–2, 5–6.

Bokermann has described two more forms of the *Hyla senicula* group; *H. acreana* from the northwestern territory of Acre, and *Hyla novaisi* from the Maracás Plateau of the *cerrado* section of the state of Bahia. The first is provisorily treated here as a subspecies of *H. senicula*.

The only specimen seen of *Hyla s. acreana* is paratype n. 1362 sent by Bokermann to the National Museum in Rio under the terms of the fellowship granted him by the Conselho Nacional de Pesquisas, the National Research Council of Brazil.

TYPES AND TYPE LOCALITY. Type and paratypes from Tarauacá, territory of Acre, Brazil, at approximately 8° S. and over 70° W. Gr.; collected further north than the specimens seen of *H. senicula melanargyrea*, on a level with the headwaters of the Amazonas in Peru.

DISTINCTIVE CHARACTERS. Paratype n. 1362, 35 mm long, is of average size, build, and habit for *Hyla senicula senicula* and slightly smaller than our Bolivian specimen of *H. s. melanargyrea*. The hindlimb is relatively short, the adpressed tibiotarsal articulation failing to reach the eye. Tongue almost entire.

Dorsal aspect brown, slightly chestnut toward the middle. In livery it diverges from the others by the pale ventral aspect of the hindlimb, indicated as yellow in life, a brighter color than that usually seen in *H. senicula* "sensu lato." Ventral aspect of the forelimb, hands, and feet very dark, almost black, as in *H. s. melanargyrea*. Webs with an unusual light edge narrower than in *Hyla marmorata*. Thigh with regular dark crossbars between lighter areas, occupying the whole dorsal aspect, much less contrast on the dorsal aspect of tibia; dark bars slightly widened at the tips, which are visible as dark spots when viewed from beneath.

Interocular spot with dark outline, roughly Y-shaped, compatible with all forms of *H. senicula*. Sacral spot saddle-shaped but fenestrated, with narrow central parts, prongs forward, and wide branches behind. The latter dilated into a large black blotch on each side of the body and preceded by a squarish black spot separated from them by a light interval. Patagium and root of arm dark, forming a black spot as indicated for *melanargyrea* by Cope. Gula granular, pigmented folds of vocal sac, also pigmented quite dark at the sides. Chest light, belly more pigmented, with dense dark dots; both granular. Very granular midventral and subanal regions. The body outlined by a light glandular border as in all the other forms of the group.

It is difficult to make a definite statement on the taxonomic status of *Hyla acreana* on the basis of one individual, neither the largest, nor probably the most typical, of a very short series from one solitary finding place. It may be an aberrant population, or perhaps one more subspecies of *Hyla*

*senicula* "sensu lato." It is also barely possible that it is a hybrid. The similarity between paratype n. 1362, *Hyla senicula melanargyrea*, and even *Hyla senicula senicula* is too great to make it likely that *Hyla acreana* may be an aberrant population of *Hyla marmorata*.

## Hyla senicula novaisi Bokermann, 1968

BOKERMANN, W. C. A. 1968. Three new *Hyla* from the plateau of Maracás, Central Bahia, Brazil. *J. Herp.* 1(1).

This is one more form that agrees so well with the structural and morphological characters of *Hyla senicula* that it seems best to regard it as a geographical race of the Cope species.

Only one specimen is available for examination, paratype 31756, now MNR 4049; the description was also not at hand until now.

DIAGNOSTIC CHARACTERS (based on paratype 31756). Adult female; size small, only 32 mm snout to vent. Dorsal aspect rather silvery; the usual spots present, bilaterally symmetrical and ornate; background tapestry-like. Webs very slightly shorter than in nominate form.

TYPES AND TYPE LOCALITY. Fazenda de São Onofre, 10 km east of Maracás, itself reported as 80 km northeast of Juquié and at an altitude of 1,300 m. This seems excessive for the state of Bahia, though evidently located at a high elevation above the lowland scrub section of the state. Types collected by W. Bokermann and F. M. Oliveira, November 1967.

NOTES (paratype). Build robust. Size small, comparable only to that of northeastern populations of *H. melanargyrea*, which are small, slender, elongate, have a quite different pattern, and live on the coast. Webs very slightly shorter than in nominate form; other characters the same, slightly attenuated.

MEASUREMENTS (mm). Snout to vent 32. Hindlimb 51; femur 15, tibia 15, tarsus 10, foot 11 (short). Head length to width 10:10.

COLOR AND PATTERN. Dorsal surface somewhat silvery and tapestry-like. Pattern unusually symmetrical; the spots ornate and sutured in black as in the other races. Interocular spot much prolonged behind, bipartite. Sacral spot regular, i. e., hat-shaped or produced forward in the middle, like a cottage loaf. Rest of the dorsal surface tapestry-like; permanently visible aspect of fore and hindlimb, except thigh, similar. Very regular dark bars on light ground on the upper parts of the thigh, not reaching the posterior aspect, which is concealed in repose. This, the inner upper parts of the tarsus and foot and ventral aspects, also concealed when at rest; light ventral aspect also light, immaculate, except for some dotting on the gula. White glandular edges very distinct from beneath.

RANGE OF THE SPECIES. It now becomes evident that *Hyla senicula* occupies a much larger area of South America than surmised. It also becomes evident that the small samples available from widely separated parts of the range differ more from the nominate form and from each other in size and in dorsal pattern than in structure and morphology. Consequently, it seems better to regard these samples as pertaining to different geographic races until the gaps in distribution and in knowledge are filled.

The specimens seen suggest that *Hyla s. senicula* occupies the coastal lowlands of the mesic part of the Atlantic area of Brazil; that *H. s. melanargyrea* lives in the central *cerrado* section of the Continental province and extends in attenuate form to the xeric northeastern subarea of the same province; *Hyla senicula novaisi* seems to be isolated on a high, discrete part of the central plateau; *H. acreana* comes from the southwestern Hylaea.

Cochran (1955) identifies *Hyla dasynota* (or *-us*) Günther with *H. senicula*. I might agree were it not for Günther's statement that "the skin from the frontoparietals along the spine to the sacrum [is] immovable and rough with bony deposits." This makes it a "species inquirenda"; Miranda Ribeiro even proposes a special generic name, *Guentheria*, for it.

## Hyla nahdereri B. Lutz & Bokermann, 1963

LUTZ, B. and BOKERMANN, W. C. A. 1963. A new tree-frog from Santa Catarina, Brazil. *Copeia* 3:558–561, photos.

In 1963 Bokermann and I described a new species with the morphological characters of the *H. marmorata–H. senicula* group from northern Santa Catarina. It is larger than *H. senicula*, the webs are shorter, the skin more pustular, the dorsal pattern and the flash colors are different. It is more southern and montane.

DIAGNOSTIC CHARACTERS. Size large for the group:

males 37–45 mm, two females 46 and 49 mm snout to vent. Dorsal color tones of gray or brown, somewhat purplish or ruddy. Dorsal pattern composed of irregular, insular, angular, elongate, occasionally oblique, sometimes confluent spots on a lighter background; minute glandules disseminated at their angles and on the rest of the dorsal surface of the body and limbs, especially on the head, eyelids, and edges that outline the frog in repose. A marked thoracic fold, a small patagium (humerothoracic fold). Webs shorter than in the other members of the group.

TYPES AND TYPE LOCALITY. Three male syntypes, nos. 3294, 3295, and 3296 in the amphibian collection of the MNR, collected December 1949 by Nahderer at Estrada Saraiva, outside and slightly below São Bento do Sul, a small town in northern Santa Catarina, Brazil (26° 14′ 55″ S. 40° 22′ 50″ W. Gr.; 800 m altitude). Original vegetation montane rain forest, now partly destroyed by man. Climate Koeppen *Cfb*. Female allotype MNR n. 3509 from Rio Vermelho, also outside São Bento do Sul, collected October 1958. Five paratypes from the same place collected by Nahderer, three older specimens nos. 4–6 in the A. Lutz Collection, and a series of good specimens belonging to Bokermann.

DESCRIPTION. Three male syntypes: size relatively large, 42, 41, and 40 mm snout to vent; hindlimb 70, 70, 66 mm. Build robust. Hindlimb short, the tibiotarsal articulation reaching the eye when the leg is adpressed. Head often depressed in dead specimens; short, very slightly wider than long; occipital outline distinct; narrowed behind. Snout very short, truncate between the nostrils, rounded in front, falling almost vertically in profile; canthus rostralis blunt, loreal region high, slightly concave. Eye very prominent, slightly longer than the distance to the nostril, which is equal to the internarial space. Interorbital space narrow, about equal to the upper eyelid. Tympanum very distinct, two-fifths or one-third the diameter of the eye. Tongue oval, distinctly notched, free behind. Vomerine teeth in two short, robust, transverse groups between the choanae. Hand less than one-half webbed. A narrow fringe of web on the inner side of the first toe; web inserted just below the disk on the other toes but reduced to a fringe on the last phalanx on the outer side of the second and third and on both sides of the fourth toe. A large narrow callosity at the base of the first finger; an elongate inner metatarsal tubercle; minute tubercles on palm and sole; subarticular tubercles moderate. Skin of dorsal aspect punctuated by glandules, sometimes produced into minute lappets of skin scattered on the dorsal surface, especially marked at the edges of the forearm, tarsus and foot, elbow and heel, sides of the body, and supratympanic and perianal region. Skin of chest, belly, and midventral aspect of thigh minutely but compactly granular. A supratympanic fold. A small patagium or humerothoracic fold. A very marked thoracic fold.

SECONDARY SEX CHARACTERS. Male: an enormous, pendulous, subgular vocal sac (specimen n. 5189, Bokermann Collection) reaching below the shoulder; upper part black or sooty. An elongate callosity almost involving the first finger. As large as or even larger than *H. senicula* females.

ALLOTYPE. Female, n. 3509 MNR, from Rio Vermelho, October 1958. Size large: 49 mm snout to vent. Build extremely robust; abdomen dilated by egg masses 24 mm wide, 9 mm wider than the head. Tongue very large, grooved longitudinally, distinctly notched. Groups of vomerine teeth very robust. Callosity on first finger smaller than in the male. Gula marbled in gray. Some spots below the free dark rim of the transparent section of lower eyelid. Supratympanic ridge very marked. Outer metatarsal tubercle minute but present, round. Some of these characters may be a function of the large size. Female, WCAB n. 510, from São Bento do Sul is smaller, 46 mm snout to vent. Light gray; gula the same as in allotype.

VARIATION. Not more than the usual variation in Brazilian species of *Hyla*.

COLOR AND PATTERN. Unfortunately not seen alive, but reddish vestiges on concealed dorsal surface of the thigh. Permanently visible dorsal surface of the very well-preserved types and most paratypes in two tones of dark, rather purplish or brownish gray, sometimes plain gray. Pattern composed of dark, very irregular, insular, angular, spots within a lighter mantle. It might be interpreted vice versa were it not for the only slightly spotted smallest syntype and some plain gray paratypes. Pattern disruptive and coincident, i. e. continuous over the permanently visible dorsal surface of head, trunk, and limbs, to the outer digits; spots nearest to the dorsolateral area deflected onto the side of the

trunk where the color becomes olivaceous gray with lighter areas between the dark spots, sometimes containing a dark streak. Light areas on the sides of the head also; one minute, vertical area at the hind edge of the eye is diagnostic; a horizontal one, very variable in size and shape beneath the orbit, sometimes continued toward the shoulder under the tympanum. On the limbs, dark and light spots disposed alternatively in rounded blotches or cross-bars, which are coincident with the spots on the body, especially the anterior prolongations of the dark concealed posterior upper part of the thigh. Edges of mouth and outline of the frog in repose lighter on account of the light lappets or glandules. Ventral aspect immaculate, except for the perfectly visible edges of the dorsal and lateral pattern; a discreet mosaic of scattered dark points around the light granulations of the chest and the anterior part of the abdomen. Throat of males black or very dark, including the upper part of the large, pendulous, median vocal sac. In females, gula marbled in light and dark gray. A dark rim to the free edge of the transparent part of eyelid. Sides of body grayish olive. Ventral aspect pale. In males, gula and upper part of vocal sac black, fuscous or clove-brown. In female, the gula is olive gray, almost white.

LIFE HISTORY. Unknown.

NAME. This species is dedicated to the collector Nahderer, who assembled not only the type but the whole series, except for the three older specimens in the A. Lutz Collection and the Bokermann specimens.

## *Hyla microps* Peters, 1872

PETERS, W. H. C. 1872. Ueber eine Sammlung von Batrachiern aus New-Freiburg in Brasilien. *Mbr. Ak. Wiss. Berlin*: 680–684.

COCHRAN, D. M. 1955. Frogs of southeastern Brazil. *Bull. Nat. Mus.* 206:177–180.

BOULENGER, G. A. 1920. Descriptions of two new frogs from Brazil. *An. Mag. Nat. Hist.* 5(8): 122–124 (*Hyla hilli*).

MERTENS, R. 1950. Froschlurche aus Rio de Janeiro und seine Umgebung. *Wochenschr. Aquar. Terrk.* 44:173–178 (*Hyla giesleri*).

DIAGNOSTIC CHARACTERS. Those of the group of *Hyla senicula* but size small. Snout short, vertical, patagium present; flash color vivid orange. Dorsal surface reddish brown to chocolate color; pattern similar to tree bark; outline of body in repose glandular, composed of white pustules. Maritime Range, southeastern Brazil.

TYPE AND TYPE LOCALITY. The type, n. 7472 ZMB, is a female from Nova Friburgo in the mountains of the state of Rio de Janeiro. I did not see it, but it was correctly identified and redescribed by Dr. Doris M. Cochran (1955). It seems to have a narrower head and longer teeth than most other specimens. Boulenger (1920) and Mertens (1950), perhaps misled by these differences and the correct but not very characteristic original description, redescribed the species, the former as *Hyla hilli* from Teresópolis, the latter as *Hyla giesleri* from Barro Branco. *Hyla microps* occurs in Teresópolis and is apparently common in Barro Branco, a place name that covers different parts of a slope. Boulenger's type, also a female, is a somewhat aberrant and an unusually large specimen.

DESCRIPTION. Size small; males 23–26 mm from snout to vent, mostly 25, extremes 20–26; females 30–33. Body elongate. Hindlimb short, the tibiotarsal articulation reaching the eye when the leg is adpressed, occasionally failing to do so. Head short and wide, slightly constricted at the neck. Snout very short, bulldog-like, forming an open triangle, truncate in front. Canthus rostralis defined by the concavity of the vertical loreal region. Interorbital space slightly wider than the internarial space. Nostrils anterolateral, practically terminal, slightly tumefied. Eye large, very prominent, its horizontal diameter about 1.5 times the distance from its anterior corner to the nostril, generally longer than the distance to the tip of the snout. Tympanum very small, one-third the diameter of the eye. Tongue oval, distinctly notched, somewhat free behind. Vomerine teeth in two transverse, slightly V-shaped groups, between the posterior borders of the choanae, which are small. Hand one-half webbed. Toes three-fourths to almost completely webbed. An elongate callosity at the base of the inner edge of the first finger; an elongate inner and a small outer metatarsal tubercle. Skin of the dorsal surface beset with some minute tubercles, mostly on the head, especially on the upper eyelids, and around the eardrum. Body in repose outlined by white glandules that form a border on the outer edge of the forearm, hand, tibia, tarsus, and foot; a few scattered pustules on the sides of the body; very glandular perianal region, midventral aspect of the thighs, and outer edge of the elbows and heels where there is sometimes a row of very minute tubercles. Skin of ventral aspect granular beyond the shoulder girdle; the pustules very thick in the median inner part of the thigh, in continuation of the perianal glandules.

MEASUREMENTS (mm). Two series of males, one from Barro Branco (thirty specimens), the other from the Serra da Bocaina (nine specimens), give approximately the same measurements. Snout to vent ranging from 23–26 mm, mostly 25. Hindlimb from 36 to 41, very variable, mostly 39 mm in Barro Branco (nine), slightly shorter, 36 (three), 37 (three) in those from the Serra da Bocaina; three of the latter with tibia and femur of equal length. Specimens up to 21–22 mm without adult sex characters. Females generally 30–33 mm. Eggs very small.

VARIATION. The most noticeable variation is the presence of a vertical raised pustule on the upper eyelid in the Barro Branco specimens, which looks almost like a minute, blunt horn. The usual variation occurs in the length of the hindlimb, which is relatively short. In some specimens it falls just short of the eye, in a very few it almost attains the anterior corner, but mostly it reaches the posterior corner or, at best, the posterior half of the orbit. The Serra da Bocaina specimens are slightly shorter-legged. The teeth may be more separate or more contiguous, the tongue wider or narrower and more or less deeply notched. Variations of color are given below.

SECONDARY SEX CHARACTERS. Even fewer female specimens of this species than usual seem to have been collected, and it is peculiar that females should have twice become types. The main differences seem to lie in the larger size and the marked fold across the chest, which is masked by the vocal sac in the male. The latter may be very much expanded or folded, giving the erroneous impression of bilateral symmetry. The forearms are relatively thick in the small males.

COLOR AND PATTERN (Serra da Bocaina specimen). This is a very beautiful little tree frog. Dorsal surfaces a warm reddish brown, correctly described as chocolate color by Peters for some; in others more chestnut colored. Dorsal pattern not always very distinct; it blends with the background and is composed of an interocular spot and two dorsolateral spots or areas. Interocular spot sinuous, following the outline of the eyes in front, sometimes bipronged or roughly W-shaped. Dorsolateral spots generally deflected onto the sides of the trunk, where they stand out more boldly, being offset by alternating light areas, which begin on the head under the eyes. Indistinct crossbars on the narrow, permanently visible strip of the thigh, the tibia and the outer part of the tarsus, hand, and foot. The edges of the dorsal pattern very distinct from the side; crossbars on limbs forming bold spots and blotches at the edges of the lower surface (Bocaina specimens), sometimes so large as to be almost confluent and to suggest the black crossbars of *H. anceps*. Dorsal surface of the thighs concealed in repose wide, immaculate, bright orange in life, well separated from the dorsal pattern by a wide black band; a similar curved band forms a complete or incomplete circle that separates the body from the thigh. Patagium either black or surrounded by a broad black band. The webs of the inner digits, concealed in repose, are orange; the others and the palms and soles are dark. Ventral aspect of tibia pale lavender. Belly pale green-yellow. Gula of male suffused with clove brown above the sac; scattered dark chromatophores on the belly mostly to the sides, and on the ventral surface of the limbs, inside the glandular edge, which is white or ash gray. A well-marked glandular area round and below the anus, with a black edge, forms part of the outline of the resting frog. Iris blended to background, grayish in the center, more brownish at the periphery.

The specimens from Barro Branco are slightly different. The color is nearer to a roseate gray. The permanently visible dorsal surface is very neatly separated from the surfaces concealed in repose. The pattern is not prolonged laterally and does not spill over onto the lower surface. Together with the horn-like pustule on the upper eyelid it becomes very characteristic, either as pertaining to a population or as a regional variant.

Dr. Doris Cochran took excellent photographs of the type specimen in Berlin. The dorsal pattern is unusually distinct. It comprises a roughly W-shaped interocular spot extending onto the eyelids, followed by two pairs of large marks, the first axillary and postaxillary, elongate and angular, the second one short, over the sacrum, leaving the middle of the back free except for smaller dark spots; both are deflected onto the upper part of the dorsolateral region, standing out boldly from the light area that covers the sides of the head and trunk; there are a few smaller scattered black spots under them. Pattern of the dorsal strip of the thigh visible in repose and of the rest of the limbs also very distinct; all the edges of all marks visible from beneath. Outline of clear spaces concealed in repose and of the curves abutting on them in strict agreement with those of all the other specimens.

An enormous female specimen (38 mm), collected at Angra dos Reis by Dr. L. Travassos in 1934 and unfortunately gutted for helminthological purposes, was recorded in a watercolor sketch of the ventral aspect for Dr. A. Lutz. The figure shows a white gula and chest with scattered dark dots, grayish belly, and shadowy edges of the dorsolateral pattern. The whole ventral surface of the hindlimbs (except for the glandular edge), the median hind part of the abdomen, a spot on the patagium, and the upper arm and webs of both hands and feet are bright orange; there are a few very dark marks on the edges of the forearm and elbow and a linear series of dark dashes inside the white glandular border of the tibia, tarsus, and foot from the knee downward.

The bright colors faded in the preserved specimen, the dorsal aspect became a warm dark brown; no white areas or spots on the sides of the head and very little contrast between the lighter and darker areas are visible on the sides of the trunk. A small tubercle on the upper eyelid. This specimen is so large that it first suggests *H. senicula*, but the raised blunt tubercle on each upper eyelid, the details, flash color of the sketch, and the pattern undoubtedly belong to *Hyla microps*. Vomerine teeth unusually long and slightly oblique, their outer edges reaching well beyond the choanae, thus in better agreement with those of the type than with the other specimens.

VOICE. The call of *H. microps* sounds like the chirping of a cricket or the sound produced by winding a rather small alarm clock.

HABITS AND ECOLOGY. As mentioned in Adolpho Lutz's notes: "*Hyla microps* only calls after nightfall. It sits on herbaceous vegetation above the clear water of mountain marshes which are sometimes quite shallow and have a slight flow."

AFFINITIES. The nearest species seems to be *H. parviceps*, which is even smaller in size, from the Hylaean rain forest.

# Hyla parviceps Boulenger, 1882

BOULENGER, G. A. 1882. *Catalogue of the batrachia salientia in the British Museum*, p. 393, pl. 25, fig. 3.

MELIN, D. 1941. Contributions to the knowledge of the amphibia of South America. *Medd. f. Goeteborgs Musei. Zool. Avd.* 88:23–24, fig. 9.

BOKERMANN, W. C. A. 1963. Duas espécies novas de *Hyla* de Rondonia, Brasil. *Rev. Brasil. Biol.* 23(3):247–250. *H. rondoniae*: 247–249, figs. 1–3.

This is a small, poorly known, and apparently rare member of the *Hyla marmorata* complex.

DIAGNOSTIC CHARACTERS. Those of this short-headed group of species with a marked patagium under the arms and a sinuous glandular outline. Size small, head very short, snout truncate. Flash colors bright; overlap of the dorsal dark blotches onto the sides of the body. Vomerine teeth just behind the choanae.

TYPE AND TYPE LOCALITY. British Museum of Natural History n. 80.12.5.124, Sarayacú, Ecuador, collected by Buckley. I saw the type in London in 1952.

Melin (1941) redescribed the species from Tara-cuá on the Rio Uaupés, just south of equator in the northwestern part of the Brazilian Hylaea. The holotype of Bokermann's species *H. rondoniae* is probably the second specimen of *Hyla parviceps* collected in Brazil. The slight difference in the length of the head and the webs on the hand mentioned by him seem too meager to justify creating a new species for a frog of which only four specimens are mentioned in the literature. I have seen all of these specimens.

DESCRIPTION (adapted from Boulenger and in part from the other two authors). Size small: type female 26 mm, Melin's specimen 21, Bokermann's specimen male 22 mm snout to vent. Head short, body slender. Hindlimb thin, short, the adpressed tibiotarsal articulation reaching the front of the eye. Head wedge-like, with "bulldog face" (Melin). Snout very short, wide, high, truncate, barely projecting in profile; canthus rostralis distinct, loreal region almost vertical. Interorbital space wider than the upper eyelid (Boulenger), less broad (Melin). Eye large, prominent, longer than the distance from its anterior corner to the tip of the snout. Tympanum distinct, one-third the diameter of the eye. Tongue circular (Boulenger), angularly

elliptical (Melin), free and slightly notched behind; vomerine teeth in two short, transverse groups just behind the choanae. Lateral fingers about one-third webbed; no projecting pollex rudiment. Disks as large as the tympanum. Toes almost completely webbed. Skin smooth above; belly, hind part of chest, and median ventral area of thigh granular.

COLOR AND PATTERN (specimen seen alive by Melin): "Upper surfaces mottled with white on a dark brown ground; irregular, band-like, black spots behind the eyes and on the shoulders (latter [chevron] shaped); iris mottled brown and silver gray; upper jaw with white spots; sides of trunk blackish brown with two oblique transversal bands at the sacral region and the groin, reaching a little way up the back (posterior band dissolved into spots); on each side of the former band, large, partly triangular, white spots; thighs blackish brown with two white cross-bands on the anterior half and their inner side medially white; tibiae and tarsi above with a broad and a narrow, respectively, diffuse black-edged cross-band; inner side of tibiae blackish brown; a long, orange-colored spot at the base; a similar spot at the base of inner side of the forelimb; feet and hands blackish with white disks; first finger and seat whitish; lower surface white with blackish brown belly; throat and front of chest mottled and marbled with brown respectively." A younger specimen mentioned by Melin had the spots of the limbs partly orange-colored.

Boulenger gives the following color notes: "Olive brown above, turning to reddish on the back, with darker markings, viz. a broad streak along the canthus rostralis, a vase-shaped marking on the back of the head and nape (the anterior border between the eyes), and two oblique streaks on sacral region; limbs and sides blackish, with large white spots; a large white space on throat and front part of belly white, the remaining parts blackish."

The large white spots on the concealed limb surfaces mentioned in both descriptions were probably orange-red in life, as described by Melin.

Bokermann's description of the dorsal color and pattern are not in disagreement with those of Boulenger, and the interocular and dorsal markings are quite similar if allowance is made for the differences in presentation of their figures and for the respective size of their specimens. The white mark under the eye of the Bokermann specimen is asymmetrical and in agreement with the white marginal glandules of the group. The large white spots mentioned by both authors were probably at least partly colored in orange-red, as in Melin's additional juvenile specimen. As he remarks, these colors fade after death.

HABITS. Melin's (younger ?) specimen, which was found on a leaf of a bush, "where it entirely escaped discovery by squatting," differs little from the description by Boulenger, fide Melin.

AFFINITIES. This form is very near to *Hyla microps* Peters.

DISTRIBUTION. Each of the three authors mentioned here obtained their specimens from a different place. The localities are rather far apart, and it is possible that later the species may have to be split up. However, the Amazonian Hylaea is rather uniform except for a few elevations and some areas of scrub with a poorly known frog fauna. The climate of the forested parts ranges from *Af* to *Am* Köppen, both equatorial with great, or with very great, precipitation. Many Neotropical species of *Hyla*, even very small ones, have very extensive ranges.

## *Hyla inframaculata* Boulenger, 1882

> BOULENGER, G. A. 1882. *Catalogue of the batrachia salientia in the collection of the British Museum. Hyla inframaculata*, pp. 354–355, pl. XXIII, fig. 3.

The frog from Santarém, state of Pará, described under the name *Hyla inframaculata* by Boulenger, seems to belong to the group of *Hyla marmorata* and has a bold pattern of spots. No similar specimens have been seen since. Consequently, it seems best to limit myself to transcribing the original description, and to refer the reader to the figure that accompanies it.

"Tongue circular, entire, adherent. Vomerine teeth on a level with the hinder edge of the rather large choanae, in two slightly curved series, forming together an arch, the convexity of which is turned forwards. Head moderate, depressed, a little broader than long; snout rounded, as long as the diameter of the orbit; canthus rostralis very indistinct; loreal region slightly concave; interorbital space as broad as the upper eyelid; tympanum very distinct; two thirds the diameter of the eye. Three outer fingers nearly two thirds webbed; no prominent rudiment of pollex; toes entirely webbed; disks of fingers half the diameter of the tympanum; of toes a little smaller; subarticular tubercles moderate. The hind limb being carried forwards along the body, the tibio-tarsal articulation reaches nearly the tip of the snout. Head and back covered with small, irregular tubercles; beneath granulate. Grey above, indistinctly marbled with darker; sides of body and thighs, and lower surfaces of hind limbs black- and white-marbled; lower surfaces of head and body whitish, brown-spotted. From snout to vent 44 millim. Amazonas".

TYPE AND TYPE LOCALITY. A female from Santarém collected by H. A. Wickham. Now BM 75.10.22.6.

REMARKS. I have not seen *Hyla inframaculata* alive, nor have I found it in the collections I have examined. However, in 1952 I had the opportunity to see the type.

Although it is not unlike some of the members of the group of *Hyla catharinae*, I concluded that it belongs to the group of *Hyla marmorata*. It does not have such a conspicuous glandular outline as the latter, but the dark drops on the gula, chest, and edges of the belly are still very evident and the black and light marbling on the thighs and lower aspect of the hindlimbs very showy. The extent of the webbing also brings it into the group. Santarém is in the state of Pará, i. e., in the Amazonian Hylaea.

# 9. Species with Patagium and Vivid Flash Colors

The species of this group are morphologically rather similar to those of the preceding group, with wide short head, high rounded snout, and rather full webs. Most, if not all, have a small patagium, but they all lack the wavy glandular outline of the *Hyla marmorata* complex. Not only are the flash colors vivid but the dorsal aspect is often striking. These species constitute a small complex of very elegant little tree frogs.

*Hyla anceps* Lutz is the largest species of the group: males up to 37 mm, females up to 42 mm snout to vent length. Head more triangular than usual; canthus rostralis also sharper than in the others. Dorsal aspect brown, sides darker. Concealed aspect of the limbs, patagium, and webs aposematic; the legs brilliant coral red, with black bands like those of a coral snake. Known range small: coastal lowlands of the states of Guanabara and Rio de Janeiro.

*Hyla leucophyllata* Beireis, slightly smaller; largest female seen 38 mm long. Range very great in the Atlantic province and the Amazonian Hylaea. Dorsal pattern geographically variable. A large brown spot, mostly quadrangular, occupies much of the back and is surrounded by a white mantle.

In the southern Atlantic form (*H. elegans* Wied), the mantle is continuous on the head, body, and the permanently visible dorsal aspect of the limbs; ventral aspect lemon yellow on body, nearer to orange on the limbs. In the Guiana form (*H. frontalis* Daudin), the shape of the central brown spot is slightly more variable. Sacral part of mantle forming a large leaf-shaped or rounded spot; similar round spots on the dorsal aspect of the limbs; concealed aspects of one living frog scarlet to red. Intermediate forms seen in Brazilian Atlantic area. Races or allied species occur in the Hylaea and Central America, for example *H. l. sarayacuensis* (*bifurca*) and *ebraccata*.

ALLIED HYLAEAN FORMS. *Hyla zernyi* Ahl: holotype and only specimen known 21 mm, probably not adult. Type locality Santarém, Pará, within the range of the Beireis species. *Hyla mimetica* Melin: adult type 35, paratypes 24 mm. Type locality Roque, Peru. *Hyla luteo-ocellata* Roux: very small; lectotype 21 mm, adult female? *Hyla reticulata* Espada: type 33 mm. Morphology similar, coloring diverse. One small specimen seen from Peru; has been found also in Brazil.

## *Hyla anceps* Lutz, 1929

LUTZ, A. 1929. Une nouvelle espèce de *Hyla*. *C. R. Soc. Biol. Paris* (Soc. Brés. Biol.) 101:943.
LUTZ, B. 1949. Anfíbios anuros da Coleção Adolpho Lutz do Instituto Oswaldo Cruz. I Anuros

da Coleção Adolpho Lutz da região sudeste do Brasil. *Mem. Inst. O. Cruz* 46(1):295–313, 3 pls.

It is astonishing that this very showy species, with a loud and characteristic call, should have remained undiscovered until A. Lutz began to study the frog fauna around the former capital of Brazil.

DIAGNOSTIC CHARACTERS. The double mimicry, of which Lutz says: "Seen from above, or from the side, in repose, with the limbs folded, it greatly resembles *Paludicola olfersi*, from which it can, however, be distinguished by the well-developed disks. The lower aspect presents a very unusual, coral-red color which spreads over the trunk and extends to the webs but is especially conspicuous on the arms and legs. The latter show perpendicular black spots suggesting in a striking manner, a small, partly concealed coral snake, though there are also two black bars across the upper surface of the thighs. This is not a simple coincidence but a case of intimidating mimicry." Lowland species from the marshlands of the states of Guanabara and Rio de Janeiro. Climate *Aw* Köppen, i. e. two seasons, summer and winter, the former rainy the latter dry. Marsh vegetation, in many places with *Typha latifolia* as dominant.

TYPES AND TYPE LOCALITY. Eight syntypes caught by J. Venancio, January 1929, at Estrella, now called Imbarié, a district of the county of Duque de Caxias, state of Rio de Janeiro in the coastal lowlands known as Baixada Fluminense, approximately 22° 47′ 10″ S. 43° 18′ 30″ W. Gr., only a few meters above sea level; now at MNR, nos. 1776 and 1777 of the A. Lutz Collection; the others in the National Museum at Washington, D. C.

DESCRIPTION. Size: males 35–37 mm, extremes 31–40 mm. Females 39–42 mm. Build robust. Body short, leg average, adpressed tibiotarsal articulation reaching between the eye and the nostril. Snout moderate, forming an obtuse triangle when seen from above, rounded in profile, the upper jaw projecting somewhat beyond the lower one; canthus rostralis angular; loreal region slightly concave. Nostrils not terminal, placed about two-thirds the distance from the eye to the tip of the snout. Eye average, slightly shorter than the distance from its anterior corner to the tip of the snout. Tympanum small, one-half, two-fifths, or even less of the diameter of the eye. Interorbital space wider than the upper eyelid which is about the same as the

internarial space. Tongue wide, rounded, emarginate, slightly free behind. Vomerine teeth in two short, slightly separated, heavy, transverse patches between the choanae, at the level of the hind margin. Fingers half-webbed, but with fringes to the base of the disks and a seam outside the first; an elongate tubercle under the first finger, a double or two single tubercles under the third and fourth; numerous small tubercles clustered in the palm and disposed in series along the digits; subarticular tubercles well developed; disks smaller than the tympanum. Toes about three-quarters webbed; a narrow seam outside the first; an elongate inner and an indistinct, round, outer metatarsal tubercle. A linear series of small plantar tubercles. Skin granular on the abdomen and the midventral aspect of the thighs; smooth above except for the glandular borders of the spots, which show a few pustules, especially on the forearm and tarsus; a pair of tubercles on the heel, one at the elbow and, in some individuals, an additional pair at the knee. A pectoral fold continued into a small patagium, or axillary fold. Pupil horizontal, slightly rhomboid.

VARIATION. Within the limited area in which *H. anceps* has been collected, only slight individual variation is seen, especially as to the length of the hindlimb, the shape of the head, the development of pustules, the presence or absence of tubercles at the knee; there are also small differences as to the width of the tongue and the depth of its notch, the diameter of the eye and of the tympanum, which may be due to the conditions of preservation. A small percentage of specimens has the teeth contiguous.

SECONDARY SEX CHARACTERS. The male has a very large, hyaline, subgular vocal sac, either inflated and balloon-like or much folded; the pollex forms an elongate hard tubercle outside the first finger but not a sharp prickle. The female seems to be only slightly larger. Eggs may be palpable. Both have a dark gula and relatively well-developed forearms.

MEASUREMENTS (mm). Female allotype and two others 42, 40, 39. Hindlimb: 73, 71, 67. Twenty-one males: 34–37, extremes 31–40, majority 37. Hindlimb 58–64.

COLOR AND PATTERN. Procryptic on the permanently visible surfaces with a coincident disruptive design; pseudaposematic (Cott 1941) on those concealed in repose, enhanced by a striking pattern. Procryptic coloration brown, extensive to the dorsal aspect of the head and body, forearms, and tibiae, outside of the hands and feet. Disruptive pattern darker in shade, composed of insular and irregular parallel, horizontal spots on the head and body, including a constant, forward-pointing, post-scapular chevron and roughly coincident, alternatively wide and narrow bars on the visible surface of the limbs, all of them with lighter, raised, glandular margins. Sides of the head to a point beyond the axilla very dark brown almost black, masking the tympanum and the lower half of the iris. Pseudaposematic coloration especially vivid, scarlet on the patagia, webs, and concealed parts of the limbs, including the back of the inner digits; less vivid orange on the abdomen. Pattern lucent black, composed of large, incomplete rings, open below, on the concealed aspects of the limbs and two wide bars on the upper inner side of the feet. A brownish-gray network on the abdomen, which is suffused with orange. Inguinal region and dorsal aspect of the thigh pale buff to clay, admixed with greenish gray. Iris brown, the upper half lighter, with a few centripetal veins. Disks, throat, and chest, especially the wrinkled folds of the vocal sac, brown but paler tinted than the dorsum. Hues of brown individually variable. Aposematic surfaces remarkably constant. In preserved specimens the dark colors fade and the red surfaces become white, but the black pattern persists.

VOICE. The call is loud, high in pitch and rapid in rhythm. It consists of a gasping intake of breath, followed after an interval by a series of accelerated and wild quacks: *hii, cá-cá-cá*. Sometimes only the first tone is emitted. The call is so distinctive that the lack of earlier discovery must be attributed to the inaccessible habitat and to its habit of fleeing deeper into the marsh.

MIMICRY. *Hyla anceps* is a good example of Batesian mimicry. The resemblance of the hindlimbs to a small partly concealed coral snake, pointed out by A. Lutz, is enhanced by the behavior of the frog. When in movement, *H. anceps* spreads the legs wide, grasping a rush or stem in each foot, thus displaying the pseudaposematic surface and pattern. If it stands still the body is pressed against an intermediate support. The vivid inner digits, patagia, and sides of the ventral surface add to the color effect. These positions are often assumed in vivaria. During repose only the procryptic surfaces, broken by the disruptive pattern, are seen. It often sits in water with only the tip of the snout showing. Calling males view with each other and are bold. If pursued, they may dive, but more often they flee along the vegetation, deeper into the marsh. As soon as disturbance ceases they resume calling. When grasped a strong odor of crushed plants and a thin viscous secretion, tasteless and nonirritant to the conjunctiva, is released. The frog wriggles; if it falls on the ground it feigns death, generally on its back in a curved position. The females are very elusive.

EGGS. The clutches are unknown. Ovarian eggs are half-dark half-cream, about 1 mm in diameter. There are several hundred of them.

LARVA. A very characteristic tadpole. Body broad and high in front, compressed at the sides, attenuated caudad. Tail an elongate oval anteriorly, but tapering greatly posteriorly and ending in a flail. A light horizontal bar across the tip of the snout; color above reddish, mostly burgundy to gray-green, underside bluish, dark. Proximal part of tail either uniformly dotted in dark or with large dark blotches, especially in large tadpoles. Pigmentation ceases abruptly in the tapering part, which is hyaline and invisible in water. This larva can easily be distinguished from the other regional tadpoles with mucronate tails, which also like relatively deep, lentic water. Those of Phyllomedusinae have a ventral though sinistral spiraculum; those of *Hyla leucophyllata* are smaller, narrower, and have a quite different shape and coloring.

DESCRIPTION. Spiraculum sinistral, inserted low at the side, hyaline, tubular, nearer to the anus than to the tip of snout. Anus dextral, not reaching the margin of the lower crest. Mouth small, narrower than the space between the nostrils. Tooth formula 2/3; inner upper row reduced to lateral fringes. Lips surrounded by papillae except for the upper median part, papillae double in the median lower one. Tail twice the length of the body and of its own height. Fins extending slightly onto the body.

MEASUREMENTS (mm). Larva minima: Body to tail 11:15, maior: 35 mm. Total length: body 14, tail 21. width of body 7, height of tail 10. Larva with short jointed hindlimbs: total length 44. Head and body to tail 14:29; narrow part of tail 12. Width of mouth 2.8; internasal space 4, eye to tip of snout 3, eye diameter 3, insertion of spiracle 9 mm from the tip of the snout, 5 mm from the anus.

BEHAVIOR. Except for the flail, which is kept in constant vibration, the tadpoles remain immobile for long periods, resting on the ground, floating obliquely with the head down, or hanging vertically from the surface film, a position more common in full-grown specimens.

METAMORPHOSIS. Occurs at about 15–16 mm, occasionally at 14 mm of head and body length; the tail is 26–28 mm long at the begining and the hindlimb 26–28 mm at the end of the process.

JUVENILES. Specimens are lighter than the adults. At metamorphosis the back is suffused with a metallic green to gold sheen. The red surfaces of the adult are chrome yellow to brownish or reddish orange. The ventral network is absent. The disruptive pattern appears after about two weeks. Of two young captive specimens one was agile, the other sluggish.

GEOGRAPHIC DISTRIBUTION. This is a lowland species. It inhabits the marsh that occupies large stretches of the coastal plain (Baixada Fluminense) between the sea and the Maritime Range, at 22–23° S. and 43–44° W. Gr. It has been collected at a number of points around the bay of Rio de Janeiro and 47 km inland on the road to São Paulo. The real range probably coincides with the extent of the marsh.

RELATIONSHIPS. True affinities are remarkably absent. The simultaneous presence of procryptic and aposematic surfaces and of contrasting colors and pattern occurs in a number of Neotropical Hylidae, such as *Opisthodelphys oviferum* and *Opisthodelphys fissipes* Boulenger, whose generic characters, colors, and geographic distribution differ. This applies even more to the superficial similarity of the African frog *Rhacophorus fasciatus*. Patagia are seen in the other species loosely grouped with *Hyla anceps* by me. These similarities, especially the general resemblance to two species of *Paludicola*, *Physalaemus olfersi* and *bresslaui*, are probably due to convergent evolution and serve to illustrate the limited scope of phenotypic variation in frogs.

## *Hyla leucophyllata* Beireis, 1783

BEIREIS, G. C. 1783. Beschreibung eines bisher unbekannten amerikanischen Frosches. *Schrift. Ges. Naturf. Freunde, Berlin* 4:178–182, pl. 11, fig. 4.

DAUDIN, F. M. 1802. *Histoire naturelle des rainettes, grenouilles, et crapauds*: 24, pl. 7, figs. 1–2, 1803:45.

WIED-NEUWIED, PRINZ MAXIMILIAN ZU. 1824. *Abbildungen z. Naturg. Brasiliens*, pl. 85, fig. 1. Verz. der Amphibien welche im zweiten Bande der Naturg. Brasiliens.

————. 1825. *Beitraege zur Naturgeschichte von Brasilien* 1:529.

GUENTHER, A. C. L. 1868. First account of species of tailless batrachians added to the collection of the British Museum. *Proc. Zool. Soc. London*, 1868, p. 489, pl. 38, fig. 4.

SHREVE, B. 1935. On a new teiid and amphibia from Panama, Ecuador and Paraguay. *Occ. Papers of the Boston Soc. of Nat. Hist.* 8:209–218, 215–216.

ANDERSSON, L. G. 1945. Batrachians from East Ecuador. *Ark. f. Zoologi* 37(2):79–81, fig. 25.

COPE, E. C. 1874. Description of some species obtained by Dr. John F. Bransford, assistant surgeon U.S. Navy, while attached to the Nicaraguan Survey Expedition in 1873. *Pr. Acd. Nat. Sc. Philadelphia*, 1874, p. 69.

DUELLMAN, W. E. 1970. The hylid frogs of Middle America. *Monogr. Mus. Nat. Hist. Kansas Univ. 1.*

*Hyla leucophyllata* occupies a vast territory along the Atlantic area, from São Paulo and Itanhaen on the coast (24° 11′ 1″ S. 46° 17′ 19″ W. Gr.) at least, to the Guianas. It also seems to spread in a western direction all along the Amazonian Hylaea. There are at least two well-defined forms in Brazil: one from the northern part of the range (*Hyla frontalis* Daudin), which occurs from Pernambuco north and for which the figure of Beireis is not perfectly typical; and a southern form (*Hyla elegans* Wied), which has been found in the states of São Paulo, Rio de Janeiro, Guanabara, Bahia, and southeastern Minas Gerais. Forms with intermediate patterns have been collected in the States of Espírito Santo and Pernambuco. Two specimens from the state of Amazonas are different, but a third one is typical of the northern form. Besides these there are descriptions of Ecuadorian tree frogs based on one or two specimens, which are either synonymous or subspecifically distinct.

DIAGNOSTIC CHARACTERS: The pattern, color, and size: 20–36 mm snout to vent. A large, elongate, roughly quadrangular, dark spot, occupying most of the back behind the eyes and in front of the sacrum; a short, wide, triangular light area over the whole head; behind it either a narrower, longer triangle from the sacral to the anal region (southern livery) or a leaf-like, oval or round light spot (northern livery). Central spot brown; light mantle surrounding it, opalescent white, golden, pinkish, or darkened by brown chromatophores overlying the white color. A light strip covering the whole dorsal permanently visible strip of the tibia (southern livery) or a series of two or three rounded or oval light spots on it (northern livery). Pattern more rarely intermediate. Permanently concealed segments of the limbs from ochraceous yellow to orange, vermilion or almost scarlet. Ventral aspect lemon yellow. Head short, wide; snout blunt in front. Vomerine teeth short, rounded, separate, often weak, sometimes absent. Skin smooth. Web on foot long.

TYPES AND TYPE LOCALITIES. This very handsome species was first described in 1783 by Beireis, who states that the type was in his collection at Helmstadt. His description and figure apply more or less to the form from the Guianas.

*H. leucophyllata* was redescribed several times. Daudin (1802), who figures the Guiana form, called it *frontalis*. His type is presumably at the Muséum in Paris. Prince Maximilian zu Wied-Neuwied described the southern form from Ponte do Gentio on the Alcobaça River, southern Bahia, as *H. elegans* (1824). His figure depicts the southern form. The AMNH has a specimen labelled Maximilian 219, which is probably the type. It is a robust female, opened to show the sternum; the white lateral edges are unusually narrow. Snout to vent 32 mm. Hindlimb 57; head length to width 10 to 11. Specimen 298 has an arm detached and a few fingers gone, but is recognizable.

SOUTHERN FORM
(*Hyla elegans* Wied, 1824)

DESCRIPTION. Size fairly small. Males 20–27 mm, mostly 23, 24, or 25. Females 29–36 mm. Build robust. Body slightly elongate. Leg short, the tibiotarsal articulation generally reaching some point of the eye when adpressed. Head short, slightly narrowed behind the eye. Snout short, bluntly triangular; canthus rostralis also blunt; loreal region vertical, slightly concave; upper jaw sloping slightly back to the mouth. Nostrils small, circular, terminal. Internasal space about equal to the distance from the anterior corner of the eye to the nostril, slightly less than the interorbital space.

Eye large but not prominent. Tympanum small, approximately one-third the diameter of the eye, circular, not very distinct. Tongue fleshy, not very wide, hardly free, distinctly notched behind. Vomerine teeth in two small, rounded, well-separated patches between the choanae, sometimes weak or absent. Hands one-third to one-half webbed. An elongate tubercle at the base of the first finger, but no sharp-pointed pollex rudiment. Feet four-fifths webbed, the web narrowed on the inner side of the last phalanx of the second, third, and on both sides of the fourth. A small but distinct inner metatarsal tubercle. A very slight ridge above the tympanum and a distinct edge on the inside of the tarsus but no appendages. A small patagium and a distinct fold across to chest. Skin smooth above; belly and midventral aspect of the thigh granular.

INDIVIDUAL VARIATION. The usual variation in size and relative length of the hindlimb; the adpressed tibiotarsal articulation reaching from the hind corner to the anterior corner of the eye, occasionally just in front of it. Tongue more constant than usual but in some specimens slightly more oval and in others more rounded. Vomerine teeth weak, sometimes one or both groups absent, or rather indistinct. Web on hand variable in length; extent of the apical fringe of the toes also variable.

SECONDARY SEX CHARACTERS. Females relatively large and very robust; belly sometimes one and a half times as wide as the head, when distended by eggs. Fold across the chest very distinct.

Males small, vocal sac median, fairly large; forearms not very thick. According to Duméril and Bibron, there are two large oval rugose plaques on the hind part of the chest of breeding males (Guiana form). Similar, slightly more granular areas, indistinctly outlined but not rugose, were seen by me in some southern specimens; one of them is, however, a large female with eggs. Smallest male 20 mm, largest 30. Average 23–25, occasionally 26 (Itatiaia) 27 (Rio); hindlimb average 40–45 mm. (Over seventy measured.)

PATTERN. The characteristic dorsal pattern is composed of a dark central spot and surrounding light area. The spot is elongate and occupies most of the middle of the back, from the interocular region to the sacrum. It is not quite quadrangular; one side may be slightly longer than the other; the corners are generally rounded and the parts between them somewhat concave. The light mantle is continuous, occupying the sides of the back, between a short, wide, triangle covering the whole top of the head and a longer, narrower triangle over the whole postsacral and anal region. A similar strip on the upper part of the tibia; sometimes minute light spots on the elbows. Tibial light strip either quite regular or the hind inner part narrower and slightly concave.

COLOR. Central spot on the back brown, somewhat reddish, walnut or chocolate-coloured, occasionally lighter, almost tawny, or dark enough to be between olive brown and clove color. Surrounding mantle brilliant opalescent white in a certain percentage of individuals, occasionally with a metallic sheen; almost golden in some (Itatiaia at 800 m); in others flesh colored, pinkish cream, or a light vinaceous brown when the light surface is overlaid with dark chromatophores. Iris brassy or coppery with a golden edge to the pupil. Light strip on the tibia the color of the mantle; light dots on the elbow sometimes the same, at others lemon yellow. Sides of the head and body darker than the central spot. Ventral aspect mostly lemon yellow, sometimes paler on the belly and gula than on the hands and feet. Vocal sac of male lemon yellow. Segments of the limbs concealed in repose, i. e. thigh and tarsus, from brilliant Saturn red or vermilion to orange or ochraceous yellow. Webs and toes from lemon yellow to almost scarlet.

In dead specimens the central spot remains perfectly visible; the light mantle is sometimes dead white, even slightly silvery, or again the dark chromatophores on it become very distinct.

VOICE. The call is something like the song of a cricket: *tick, tick, tick,* or *crick, crick,* often repeated and quite loud.

When handled *Hyla leucophyllata* gives out a strong smell of nasturtium leaves.

BEHAVIOR. They seem to prefer sitting above not very shallow water, generally not very close together though there may be quite a number round one pond.

ECOLOGY. The species seems very tolerant in regard to climate, hence the very large territory occupied by the different races. At the latitude of the states of Guanabara, Rio de Janeiro, and southwestern Minas Gerais it occurs both in the low-

lands and on the slopes of mountains. At Itatiaia we have gathered it 800 m above sea level, near the remnants of artificial ponds.

LIFE HISTORY NOTES

The females become very much dilated by the egg masses. The eggs have a light and a dark pole like those of the other Brazilian kinds of *Hyla*.

LARVA. The tadpole is streamlined and rather similar to a *Phyllomedusa* larva. From above, body elongate oval, slightly compressed at the sides; somewhat torpedo-like in profile. Tail the shape of a blade or a narrow oar, the upper crest fairly rectilinear, the lower slightly less so, both wide in comparison with the muscular part, which is narrow and grows still more attenuated caudad; both crests reaching well onto the body in front and narrowed in a sharp curve near the tip, which ends in a flail. Length of body approximately two-fifths the length of the tail, width approximately one-half the length. Height of tail one-fourth to one-fifth of the total length, four-fifths of it wide, one-fifth a thin flail. Mouth terminal, perpendicular to the body, very small, narrower than the internasal space, with round lips, relatively strong beaks and teeth. Eye small, quite lateral, shorter than the distance from its anterior corner to the mouth. Spiraculum rather ventral, turned slightly upward, nearest to the eye, very slightly nearer to the anus than to the tip of the snout.

COLOR. Body yellowish or greenish olive above and on the sides, with a light margin round the dorsal surface and a lateral line below the dark sides. Ventral aspect immaculate, brilliant white. Eye small, iris with a few spots. Tail mottled in dark and light; in young specimens the light, distal part red or reddish; blotches darker and larger towards the tip, more cloudy or forming a vague reticulum toward the body; flail hyaline; musculature transversed longitudinally by a light stripe.

Smallest tadpole measured: length of body 6 mm, width 3 mm, tail 11 mm, height 3 mm. Tadpole with very small limbs: length of body 10, width 5; tail 25, 3 mm of which is the flail. Tadpoles with limbs 15 mm long (femur 4, tibia 5, tarsus and feet 6): length of body 10.5–11 mm, width 5–6, length of tail 27 mm (flail 5–6); height approximately 6 mm, mouth less than 2 mm; eye 1.5–2 mm; eye-snout 3 mm.

The tadpoles vibrate the tail while swimming. They do not always remain horizontal but move up and down; occasionally they stand on their heads, lie on the bottom, or hang down from the surface by their mouths.

METAMORPHOSIS. Metamorphosis occurred at an approximate length of 13 mm; tail 22 mm in one, 9 mm in the other. The metamorphosing young have the same livery as the adult.

## GEOGRAPHIC VARIATION IN LIVERY

SOUTHERN FORM. Out of the great many specimens from the contiguous areas of the states of Rio de Janeiro and Guanabara, only one has a rounded light spot like the northern form, instead of the usual postsacral triangle of the southern one. Three, from Barro Branco, have the lateral parts of the light mantle discontinuous from the posterior part, i. e. one side curved and rounded at the end, the other side prolonged into an irregular, excentric, somewhat blunt area. A single specimen, also from Barro Branco, has a minute excentric leaflet instead of a triangle on the hind part of the back. The percentage of brilliant white mantled specimens is very variable in the different samples seen.

INTERMEDIATES. Thirty-six preserved specimens from the state of Espírito Santo, belonging to the Museu Nacional, show aberrations of pattern and color. The dorsal pattern is quite regular, like in the more southern specimens, with a roughly quadrangular spot in twenty-nine of them. It is irregular in three from the Biological Station at Santa Teresa, and completely irregular in four from Rio Perdido. The three from Santa Teresa have a prong on one side of the mantle; on the other side there is a small excentric triangle, which corresponds to the posterior part of the normal southern dress; it does not, however, cover the proper area and has an outline similar to a map of South America in two and of its inverted image in the other. Two of the four irregular forms from Rio Perdido have a pair of short anterior prongs and a pair of longer, asymmetric, posterior ones; there are small fenestrations in one of them; in the other the spot is fragmented into a horizontal anterior and a vertical posterior part. The pattern of the other two is completely irregular. In these four the median spot is reddish brown and the rest of

the dorsal surface tan. One large female, no. 1374, from Santa Teresa, has the central spot gray and the outer mantle a darker brown. The light area on the tibia is entire and typical in fourteen specimens; it is composed of three spots in nineteen; in the former the outline is partly concave and narrowed on the inner side; in the latter the spots are irregular in shape; in the other three the tibial pattern is intermediate with three spots on one tibia and two spots on the other i. e. a long spot like in the southern specimens, preceded by a minute round spot on the knee.

## NORTHERN FORM

In the northern form the posterior triangle is substituted by a large light spot, which occupies most of the sacral and postsacral area, though it does not do so in the figure of the type given by Beireis. This spot, from which the specific name is evidently derived, may be round, oval, or look like a perfectly symmetrical leaflet of a composed leaf. The sides of the mantle are discontinuous in the posterior part, each of which ends in a blunt, wide, and somewhat divergent tip. The light stripe on the tibia is generally substituted by two or three rounded spots, but it may also be continuous and concave on the hind half of the inner side. The details of the pattern vary. In Beireis's figure the sacral spot is wide and rounded at the apex, and has a short narrow base produced into a minute stem. The light strip on the tibia is continuous and concave on the hind inner half; there is a ring-like spot on each wrist not seen by us in any specimen. A frog from Cachoeira do Castanhal in the state of Pará has a perfectly round postsacral spot and three spots on the tibia. Another specimen from Itacoai, state of Amazonas, has the usual dorsal, northern pattern, with a large oval postsacral spot and two, not three, light round spots on the tibia. Two others from the state of Amazonas, one from Itacoai, the other without specified locality, show only a dark reddish brown, median quadrangle surrounded by the light tan, quite uniform dorsal surface of the body and limbs.

In another example, this one from Tapera, state of Pernambuco, the postsacral spot is leaf-like but dentate and sessile in front, not so narrow behind as in the Beireis figure. The lateral parts of the light mantle form two bands, each ending in a blunt tip in front of the leaflet. There is a light spot on each knee followed by two others on the tibia; also a minute light dot on each elbow. This specimen, sent by Dom Bento Pickel, O.S.B., was painted in water colors for A. Lutz. The light mantle and spots are a pinkish cream; the central spot is light chestnut and continuous with the parts of the back not occupied by the mantle and with the dark sides of the head and body. The dorsal surface of the limbs is buff, slightly vinaceous, and luminous on the segments concealed in repose. It is possible that this specimen was painted soon after death.

COLOR. I have seen only one live specimen of the northern form, a very beautiful frog from Principe da Beira, Rondonia, in the southwestern Hylaea.

The light parts of the pattern consist of a cap over the head and the outer parts of the upper eyelids, continued by a sinuous band on each side, enclosing an ill-defined darker central area and ending before a large oval postsacral spot. One large spot on each leg reaching the tibiotarsal joint; a little similar pigment on the knee. Light areas and spots pale gold; central area light chestnut. Iris tawny. Gular region ochraceous yellow. Belly and glandules on midventral strip of thigh white and outer ventral edges of limbs light in a pale phase. All the rest of the body and limbs red, almost scarlet. In a dark phase glandules and belly slightly lighter than the rest but whole frog deep red.

SIZE. The Hylaean form seems to exhibit wide extremes of size. Twenty-two females were measured by us. The largest, 38 mm snout to vent, hindlimb 65, came from Cachoeira do Castanhal, state of Pará; the smallest, with eggs, only 25 mm snout to vent, hindlimb 44, state of Amazonas. Our other females range from 28–35 mm snout to vent length.

SYNONYMS AND AFFINITIES. There are large gaps in the known distribution of the diverse forms of *Hyla leucophyllata* "sensu lato." One of them is between Bahia and Pernambuco, another from there to Pará and the Guianas. The specimens from the Amazonian Hylaea are widely scattered. Consequently it is difficult to adjudge taxonomic status to certain forms described as a species on the basis of one or two specimens. *Hyla triangulum* Gün-

ther, "probably from Brazil," is generally considered synonymous with *leucophyllata*, though the spot is triangular and not quadrilateral and limited to the interocular and postocular region. The absence of a type locality does not help matters. The adjudication is probably right.

Cochran (1955) considers *Hyla leucophyllata sarayacuensis* Shreve, 1935, as synonymous because of a similar, melanistic, individual from Rio de Janeiro. It seems, however, to have longer legs, a slightly larger tympanum, and still weaker vomerine teeth. The light mantle is much reduced. It may be considered a subspecies. *Hyla bifurca* Anderson, 1945, from the Rio Pastaza in Ecuador, which shares these characters and is also very dark, should be synonymous with it. It was put into *Hyllela* by Anderson because of the absent vomerine teeth.

*Hyla ebraccata* Cope, 1874, from Nicaragua, presents an interesting problem. Cope realizes the similarity with *Hyla leucophyllata* and suggests that *ebraccata* may be a color variety of it, but adds, "It is a very distinct one and probably geographically circumscribed, and hence until intermediate forms are discovered may be considered as a species." The leg seems even longer than in the Ecuadorian form. The central dark spot forms the base of a large triangle between the eyes and is produced backward, forming a similar large spot on the back. The lateral dark areas seem purplish; there are silver spots on the arms, a large yellow spot below the eye and light dots on the dark band on the sides of the body. In some specimens seen by me in American collections, the light dots occur also on the dark dorsal area. Günther shows a light specimen with dark dorsolateral lines in Biologia. Central Americana. Pl. LXXII, figs. C and D. *Hyla ebraccata* is certainly a closely allied form. Duellman (1970) discusses *ebraccata* from Central America and gives a series of drawings of variations in the dorsal pattern (fig. 92) and a watercolor (Pl. 49, fig. 8).

## RELATED FORMS

### *Hyla zernyi* Ahl, 1953

AHL, E. 1933. Ueber einige neue Froesche aus Brasilien. *Zool. Anz.* 104:25–30. *H. zernyi*: 27–28.

DIAGNOSTIC CHARACTERS. Besides those of the group of *Hyla leucophyllata,* with short head, vertical loreal region, "bulldog face," and short limbs, the distinctive color and pattern. According to Ahl, dorsal aspect silvery with a dark brown pattern, composed of a vertical stripe between the interocular region and the sacral one, limited in front by a curved stripe perpendicular to the eyes. Size 21 mm.

TYPE AND TYPE LOCALITY. Holotype and only known specimen collected at Tapeirinha near Santarém, state of Pará, by Zerny, for whom it was named. Seen by me in the National History Museum at Vienna in 1952. It was placed in overstrong alcohol, but is nevertheless in good condition.

DESCRIPTION. Size very small, 21 mm, probably not adult. Hindlimb rather short, the adpressed tibiotarsal articulation reaching the anterior corner of the eye. Head large, wider than the body, with rounded snout, truncate in profile, distinct curved canthus rostralis and oblique, concave loreal region. Interorbital space one and a half times the width of the internarial space. Eye very large and prominent. Tympanum round, approximately half the diameter of the eye. Tongue rounded, entire, not free. Vomerine teeth in two groups at the level of the hind edge of the choanae. Forearm robust, fingers also robust with spatulate disks. A rudiment of web between the lateral fingers; third finger longer than the snout; an indistinct rudiment of the pollex. Feet three-fourths webbed, the last articulation fringed. A small oval inner metatarsal tubercle. Skin of dorsal aspect smooth but a few minute pustules on the upper eyelids, the back, and sides of the body; ventral aspect granular.

COLOR AND PATTERN. Very beautiful even in alcohol. Dorsal aspect silvery except for the pattern in the middle which is dark brown and consists of a horizontal stripe, concave in front between and in part on the upper eyelids and a perpendicular stripe down the middle of the back, narrowed behind and reaching the sacrum. Head marbled alternatively in short silver and dark perpendicular bars; a white bar over the tip of the snout. Sides of body surrounded by a dark outline, dorsal permanently visible aspect of the limbs and edge of mouth silvery, including the permanently visible upper parts of the hands and feet. Upper concealed aspect of thighs marbled in yellowish brown and dark brown. Margin of lower jaw dotted in dark.

AFFINITIES. Ahl suggests that his species is close to *Hyla auraria* Peters, which I have not seen and cannot visualize from the description. To describe the terra typica as "South America" is not of much help.

*Hyla zernyi* seems very close to *Hyla leucophyllata,* but neither the morphological details nor the pattern agree. It seems more ornate and the range of the northern form of *Hyla leucophyllata* must cover the type locality of *H. zernyi.* It is probably also akin to the other short-headed species with a patagium belonging to this group. Until further specimens come to light I must abide by the description above, which was derived from the original, and from examination of the type.

## *Hyla mimetica* Melin, 1941

MELIN, D. 1941. Contributions to the knowledge of the Amphibia of South America. *Medd. f. Goeteborgs Musei Zool. Avd.* 88:24–26, fig. 10.

Although this frog has been described from Peru, it is included here because the author (Melin) considers it closely related to if not identical with *Hyla zernyi.* From *Hyla leucophyllata* he separates it by the vomerine teeth and the longer hindlimbs.

DIAGNOSTIC CHARACTERS. Those of the group of *Hyla leucophyllata* with short, "bulldog face" (fide Melin) and patagium. Dorsal pattern composed of two thick dark bands, entire, or broken, one to each side of the midline of the back, dark, on silvery white ground; similar spots on other parts of the body visible in repose. Leg long. Tympanum relatively large.

TYPES AND TYPE LOCALITY. Two syntypes, collected by Douglas Melin, 11.5.1925, at Roque, eastern Peru, a little village near La Campana mountain, 35 km southeast of Moyabamba and not far from Yurimaguas (approximately 6° S. and 76° W. Gr.). Types in the Goeteborg Museum, seen by me in 1952.

DESCRIPTION. (adapted from Melin). Size 35 and 24 mm. Build robust. Leg long, the adpressed heel reaching or nearly reaching the tip of the snout. Head large, length and width equal; snout very short, as long as the eye, truncate, projecting only slightly in profile. Eye large, prominent. Interorbital space wider than the upper eyelid. Tympanum nearly one-half the diameter of the eye. A callus-like pollex rudiment. Fingers webbed at the base. Toes almost entirely webbed. Upper surface fairly smooth, slightly warty, belly and thigh granular.

COLOR AND PATTERN (fide Melin). "Above whitish-gray (silver-gleaming) with a dark, wedge-shaped, spot-like, design on each side of the vertebral line, from the eyes to the sacral region and then continuing as round spots; iris dark, with sparse, silver-white radiating lines; upper jaw partly whitish with narrow dark transversal bands. A blackish band from the tip of the snout, through the eye, to the base of the forelimb. Tympanum brownish light-edged. Upper jaw partly whitish with narrow dark stripes. Iris dark with radiating silvery white lines. Dark reticulation and black spots on the sides of the body. Dark, irregular, fairly broad crossbands on the dorsal aspect of the limbs. Hindlimbs light, beneath, with fine dark mottling; forearm and tarsus darkish with light spots; a single white spot at the base of the arms, on the heels, and on the outer side of hands; and feet." Ventral aspect of body whitish mottled in brown, especially on the head and chest.

"The smaller specimen with a whiter ground and more distinct spots, the black ones on the upper surface, ring-shaped; some white spots on the lower jaw." Iris with linear dark spots. "Forearm, tarsus and seat white, spotted brownish beneath."

ECOLOGY. The types were collected by Melin in a *chacara* on plants, partly under bark of a very similar color. (In Brazil a *chacara* is either a market garden, a garden selling vegetables, ornamental plants, and flowers, or a very small private property outside town.)

## *Hyla bokermanni* Goin, 1959

GOIN, C. J. 1959. Description of a new frog of the genus *Hyla* from northwestern Brazil. *An. Mag. Nat. Hist.* 2(24):721–724, fig. 1.

This is one more Hylaean species described on a solitary specimen, moreover one whose adult status is queried by its own author, probably in view of its exiguous size.

DIAGNOSTIC CHARACTERS. (Deduced from the description and figure; holotype not seen.) The small size, short, wide head, small tympanum, relatively short hindlimb, distinct vomerine teeth and details of pattern.

TYPE AND TYPE LOCALITY. WCAB 2881 adult (?) female, leg. Bokermann at Tarauacá, Acre territory, Brazil, December 4, 1956.

DESCRIPTION (also based on Goin). Size very small. Type: adult (?) female 17.8 mm snout to vent. Head as wide as long. Postaxillary region of the body wider than the head. Hindlimb short, the adpressed tibiotarsal articulation reaching the middle of the eye when adpressed. Snout short, wide, bluntly triangular from above, projecting beyond the mouth opening in profile. Canthus rostralis slightly defined; loreal region concave, nearly vertical. Nostril much nearer the tip of the snout than the eye. Diameter of the eye slightly longer than its distance from the nostril. Tympanum small, about one-fourth of the ocular diameter. Interorbital space very much wider than the internarial space. Vomerine teeth in short, approximate groups at the level of the hind border of the choanae. Tongue almost cordiform, slightly notched, posterior border free. Fingers slightly webbed at the base. Toes slightly more than one-half webbed. Skin of upper parts of throat, chest, belly, and ventral aspect of the thigh smooth. No patagium, glandular ridges, or folds.

MEASUREMENTS (mm). Holotype: head and body 17.8, head length 5.1, head width also 5.1. Femur 8.2, tibia 8.5, foot 11.7.

COLOR AND PATTERN (in alcohol, fide Goin). "Dorsal ground color dark chocolate brown; tip of snout and canthal region slightly darker than the rest of the head; a small white dot below each nostril, a more conspicuous white mark from the eye downward and backward to the edge of the jaw. A very distinct white stripe from behind each eye to the groin, widening behind and meeting the pale color of the ventral aspect which extends up into each groin region, forming a pale area posterior to the end of the dorsolateral stripe. The anterior face of each thigh is marked by a very distinct, oval white blotch surrounded by dark pigment. The dorsal surfaces of the thighs are marked by a couple of pale brown ovate blotches surrounded by a dark brown ground color. The tip of each heel is pale but not white. Otherwise the dorsal surfaces of the limbs are dark brown. Beneath there are dark blotches under the chin and the throat, and a fairly heavy concentration of pigment on the under surfaces of the thighs. Otherwise ventral surface pale with only scattered melanophores on the belly."

REMARKS. After excluding this species from the genus *Phyllobates* because of the absence of dorsal scutes on the disks and the presence of an intercalary cartilage in the digits, Goin goes on to compare it to *Hyla parviceps* Boulenger and *Hyla microps* Peters. To me it seems more akin in habit, structure of the skin, and color and pattern to the frogs from the Amazonian Hylaea grouped by me with *Hyla leucophyllata. Hyla bokermanni* differs from *Hyla bifurca* Andersson by the lack of a white mantle on the head, the normal vomerine teeth and the short hindlimbs. It seems closer to *Hyla zernyi* Ahl from the eastern Hylaea by the color, and the pattern on the sides of the head and on the dorsal aspect of the thigh. The dorsal pattern differs. It seems still closer to *Hyla luteo-ocellata* Roux, from Venezuela, in size, habit, morphological details, and in the presence of a light ocellus surrounded by dark color on the thigh. The light dorsolateral bands, the pattern on the sides of the head and on the dorsal aspect of the thigh are also similar. It differs mainly by the hidden tympanum of *H. luteo-ocellata* and the vestiges of yellow color noticed by Roux in the ocelli of his type. It is very likely that they are conspecific. However, until many more of these small Hylaean tree frogs are forthcoming the status of the species based on one solitary specimen cannot be considered as definitely established.

## Hyla luteo-ocellata Roux, 1927

ROUX, J. 1927. Contribution à l'erpétologie du Venézuela. *Vrhdl. Naturf. Ges. Basel* 38:252–261. *H. luteo-ocellata*: 260–261.

DIAGNOSTIC CHARACTERS. The short head, bulldog face, hidden tympanum, patagium, and rather short hindlimb. Large ocelli, white or silvery in death, presumably yellow in life, under the eyes,

on the flanks, thighs, and ventral aspect of the tibiae near the knees.

TYPE AND TYPE LOCALITY. Lectotype 3900 and paratype 3901 in the herpetological collection of the Naturhistorisches Museum in Basel, Switzerland. Collected by Drs. Kugler and Vonderschmidt at Mene, State of Falcon, N. W. Venezuela, between 10–12° N. and 70–72° W. Gr.; seen by the author June 1952. Lectotype stated to be a female by Dr. L. Forcart.

DESCRIPTION (adapted from the original). Size very small, only 21 mm. Hindlimb rather short, the tibiotarsal articulation reaching the eye when the leg is adpressed; 32 mm long; ratio to body approximately 3:2. Head slightly wider than long, with a rounded snout barely longer than the horizontal diameter of the eye. Loreal region high, hardly inclined; canthus rostralis moderately distinct. Eye large, prominent. Tympanum invisible. Interorbital space double the width of the upper eyelid. Fingers webbed at the base. Toes two-thirds webbed, last two joints of fourth toe free. Disks rather wide. Skin smooth above and beneath in front of the pectoral fold. Abdomen reticulate in front; hind part of abdomen and ventral aspect of thigh granular.

COLOR (in alcohol). Dorsal aspect gray-brown; on the sides of the body lighter, putty colored; minute black dots disseminated irregularly and wide apart on the head and back. A more or less distinct brown band between the eyes. A light, narrow stripe beginning on the tip of the snout, following the canthus rostralis, and continuing behind the eye and bordering the light dorsolateral zone; a wide, dark brown band covering the canthus rostralis crossing the eye and continuing onto the sides of the body, passing above the forelimb. A white spot over the whole hind part of the flanks; a white oval spot under each eye surrounded by brown, continuing onto the lower jaw. Ventral aspect whitish; a few brownish spots on the gula. A very special pattern on the hindlimb: underside of the thigh occupied by a large, elongate, oval white spot encircled in black, the circle broader in front; upper surface light brown with two more or less rounded white spots. (Roux states that when the specimen was received these spots showed vestiges of a beautiful yellow tone; they were presumably bright yellow in life.) Tibia grayish above, with a light, elongate spot on its lower surface near the knee. Tarsi and feet peppered (*mouchetés*) in white and gray. (Description from the type and the original description.) This species is described here because it may occur in Brazil.

## *Hyla reticulata* Espada, 1871

ESPADA, DON M. J. DE LA. 1871. Faunae neotropicalis species quaedam nondum cognitae. *J. Ac. Sc. Lisboa* 3:57–65. *H. reticulata*: 61–62.
————. 1875. Vertebrados del viaje al Pacifico . . . batracios. *H. reticulata*: pl. 3, figs. 7, 7a.

*Hyla reticulata* was not described from Brazil but from Ecuador.

ORIGINAL DESCRIPTION (translated). "Head high, rounded in front, with horizontal crown, declivous in front; snout perpendicular, canthus rostralis barely distinct; eyes very large, prominent; tympanum hardly standing out from the skin; tongue subcordiform, longitudinally furrowed, free at the edges of the sides as well as behind; hands half-webbed, feet webbed to the base of the penultimate phalanx. Skin smooth all over, except the abdomen and ventral aspect on the thighs. Above euphorbiaceous green with large, round, droplike, orange-colored spots on the dorsal surface; snout, loreal region, and limbs beautifully reticulate."

HABITAT. Ecuador, on the banks of the Napo River near Mazan, collected in the mouth of August at slightly over 3° lat. S. approximately 73° long. W. Gr. by Don Marcos Jimenez de la Espada.

RANGE. The Museu Nacional in Rio de Janeiro has one specimen from Pebas, near Iquitos, Peru (between 71–72° long. W. Gr. and slightly above 3° south latitude).

This Hylaean species was first included because of its great beauty and the hope that it might be found in Brazil. This wish has now come true. The MNR has another specimen collected by Parko in 1944 at Vila da Cachoeira do Samuel, in the region of the Javarí River, state of Amazonas. Although somewhat soft and faded, it is described here.

DISTINCTIVE CHARACTERS. Build short, stout, hands and feet extensively webbed, vomerine teeth very near the front edge of the choanae; a light reticulum around somewhat polyhedric darker spots on the permanently visible surfaces. In life reticulum green, spots orange.

DESCRIPTION. Adult male size 32 mm from snout to vent. Build robust. Head wide, postaxillary region of the body as wide as the head. Tibiotarsal articulation reaching in front of the eye when the leg is adpressed. Snout short, flat from above, rounded in front, declivous to the mouth opening in profile. Canthus rostralis hardly perceptible. Loreal region perpendicular. Nostrils small, lateral, marking the beginning of the frontal declivity of the snout. Eye probably prominent in life; its horizontal diameter longer than the distance from its anterior corner to the nostril. Tympanum small, slightly less than one-half the diameter of the eye, not very distinct but largely visible under the supratympanic ridge. Interorbital space distinctly wider than the internarial space. Tongue large, rounded, hardly emarginate, free at the lateral edges and behind. Vomerine teeth in two short, well-separated groups between the choanae, very near their anterior border. Hand one-half webbed, with wide fingers and disks, that of the first one slightly narrower than the others. Feet very extensively webbed. A fringe of web on the inner side of the first toe; web wide to below the disk on its outer side, on the second, on the outer side of the third and on the fifth, wide to the penultimate tubercle on the inner side of the third and on both sides of the fourth, but continued as a wide fringe. A callosity outside the first finger; another one at the edge of the first toe (male character?). Skin smooth; very loose beneath. A huge subgular vocal sac continuous with the patagia and with a large fold on each side of the chest. Skin of belly and midventral strip of the thigh granular as if paved.

COLOR AND PATTERN. Unfortunately somewhat faded. A pale putty-colored reticulum surrounding somewhat polyhedric light brown spots on the dorsal surface of the head and body, forming a network around smaller spots on the loreal region and sides; less evident on the permanently visible upper parts of the limbs, especially of the hind ones. Otherwise pale, immaculate.

The specimen portrayed by Espada (1875, Pl. 3, fig. 7) is similar to ours in habit; it has a high head, short body, and extensive webs. The reticulation is very evident on the sides of the head and on the forearm, tarsus, and foot; on the head and back the spots are, however, isolated and on the tibia they are disposed toward the edges leaving the middle part of the leg free.

Dr. James Bogart of the University of Texas collected three specimens at Iparia, Peru. He kindly sent me fine black-and-white photographs of two of them. One of them is like the figure published by Espada and described in the last paragraph. The other is like the Brazilian specimen in the MNR as to livery, but is better preserved.

# 10. Elongate Species with Red Flash Colors

*Hyla polytaenia polytaenia* Cope, 1870

> COPE, E. D. 1870. Seventh contribution to the herpetology of South America. *Pr. Am. Phil. Soc.* 11:164–165.

DIAGNOSTIC CHARACTERS. A number of longitudinal brown stripes on a lighter, buff background over the whole dorsal surface; similar stripes on the sides of the body and on the edges of the permanently visible dorsal parts of the limbs; concealed surface of the limbs rufous, devoid of pattern, even on the upper aspect of the thighs. Well-preserved specimens retain the dorsal color and the pattern, though the stripes may become more olivaceous. The color of the concealed surfaces of the limbs fades. Size moderate, 28–42 mm. Montane. Somewhat variable, individually and geographically.

Cope does not indicate a type locality, and by way of a terra typica mentions only "from Brazil." Two specimens were collected by G. Sceva, a member of the Thayer (Agassiz) Expedition, which covered much ground. The types belonging to the MCZ n. 906 seen by me do not correspond exactly to Cope's data.

DESCRIPTION. Size fairly small. Build elongate. Limbs slender; hindlimb variable in length. Adpressed tibiotarsal articulation generally reaching in front of the eye. Head robust, muzzle short, rounded; canthus rostralis blunt; loreal region concave, rather vertical. Interorbital space slightly wider than the internarial space. Eye large, prominent, longer than the distance to the nostril. Tympanum about one-half the diameter of the eye. Tongue wide, subcircular, notched, slightly free behind. Vomerine teeth in two short, separate, rounded groups at the level of the hind edge of the choanae. Hands webbed at the base; feet more or less one-half webbed. Palms and soles full of tubercles; a knob-like rudiment of the pollex; an elongate inner metatarsal tubercle. Skin smooth above, granular on the chest, belly and midventral part of the thigh. A supratympanic and supra-anal fold, a slight ridge on the tarsus, often ending in a small tubercle on the heel. Male 23–33 mm, female 37–42 mm snout to vent.

VARIATION. Morphologically *H. polytaenia* is no more variable than other Brazilian species of *Hyla* except as to size.

The chief individual variation regards the length of the hindlimb, the adpressed tibiotarsal articulation reaching anywhere from the posterior corner of the eye to between eye and nostril. Variations of pattern are discussed below.

SECONDARY SEX CHARACTERS. The pollex rudiment has a sharp point, which can be felt in some but not in all males; it is covered by a small knob, hardly noticeable in the female. A few males have thick forearms, mostly with tubercles on the lower outer edges. The median vocal sac may be very much distended. Females much larger than the males.

COLOR. In life dorsal ground color buff or cream, sometimes slightly more pinkish, especially toward the extremities of the limbs including the outer digits and the disks. Longitudinal stripes darker. Iris similar in tone to the dorsal surface, especially the upper part, the lower half and the tympanum colored in accordance with the wide lateral dark stripe; inner zone golden with embossed veins of the same color or slightly deeper in tone; minute, central knobs above and below; dark pigment of varying intensity at the sides, especially the hind edge producing a pseudocolobom; sclerotic iridescent, deep golden, with green and bluish lights and dark spots striking upward from the outer rim of the iris; pupil oval, regular. Concealed aspect of the limbs more or less rufous, translucent, devoid of pattern. Lower aspect cream to white. Some populations more reddish or more melanistic with the background darker and the stripes very deep, almost black. Long bones and jaw green.

PATTERN. The typical pattern consists of a number of longitudinal brown stripes on a lighter pale buff background on the whole dorsal surface, one or two stripes on the sides of the body and similar dark edges to the permanently visible dorsal aspect of the limbs. Pale ornamental grayish lines and spots with lighter borders on the gula, following the contour of the lower jaw.

Well-preserved specimens retain the dorsal color and pattern, but the concealed surfaces of the limbs fade.

VARIATION OF PATTERN. Variation of pattern is not uncommon. It includes fragmentation of the stripes into elongate segments or into drops, or even dots, when the stripes are narrow. Occasionally a stripe forms a curve or a half-loop. A recently metamorphosed juvenile (Bocaina) and a large female (Nova Friburgo) show slight anastomoses between the stripes. In a few specimens the stripes are narrow, almost linear. Out of several hundred, I have seen four specimens without any dorsal pattern.

The dark stripes are apparently not all equiva-

lent; the central one and two of the lateral ones are constant and may be regarded as primary; this also applies to the main stripe on the sides. The other pairs may be absent, linear, or substituted by large dots, often present only in the hind part of the back. This is the main simplification observed. In large female specimens from the Maritime Range, the pattern is generally simplified, to the three main stripes, which stand out boldly while the others are either indistinct or reduced to a few large drops mostly on the postsacral region.

Cochran (1955) considers simplification of pattern due to size and perhaps also to sex. She goes so far as to say that in every frog over 40 mm in total length seen by her, the body pattern clearly consists of three dorsal and two lateral stripes with very little trace of the others. As all the frogs above 40 mm are females, she believes that simplification may also be the result of sex. Up to a certain extent this is true, but there is also a geographic factor involved.

The specimens seen by Cochran came from the Serra do Mar or from the outskirts of São Paulo. In these places the species has been collected at altitudes of approximately 800 to 900 m, exceptionally at 1,000 (Teresópolis) and 1,200 m (Serra da Bocaina), always in the proximity of natural or artificial pools and ponds. The upper altitudinal limiting factor is probably the presence of standing water and the lower perhaps the temperature requirements of developing eggs and larvae.

*Hyla polytaenia*, however, also occurs on the Serra da Mantiqueira, opposite the Serra da Bocaina, but inland, across the valley of the Paraiba River. It has been collected at Campos do Jordão (1,585–2,030 m) by the Department of Zoology of the state of São Paulo, and on the Itatiaia Mountains by me and others.

The specimens from the lower part of the Itatiaia (800 m at the headquarters of the National Park) and those from Campos do Jordão (DZSP) are of the usual size, but show a trend toward variation and simplification of pattern in males as well as females, with or without secondary stripes and the main ones variable. The upper Itatiaia boasts of a few pools of very clear standing water near the sources of mountain brooks at altitudes of 2,000–2,200 m and slightly higher. Females from these pools have a length of 50 mm and become very robust. Occasionally small ones with eggs are also present. Comparison of a small one and two large ones shows a more complete though partly fragmented pattern in the little one and simplification in the two larger ones.

VOICE. The call of *Hyla polytaenia* is a very high-pitched chirruping sound, ending on a long trill: *tsssiiip, tsssiiip, tsssiiip, tsssirrrp*. It is one of the most common and cheerful Hylid calls in the mountain resorts of the state of Rio de Janeiro above the eastern seaboard. At night it resounds in gardens, hedges, and roadsides, at the edges of ponds and marshes, and is as charming as the appearance of the songster, one of the prettiest of the lesser species of Brazilian tree frogs.

BEHAVIOR. In captivity the nightly concert and mating go blithely on, even in small jars or during transportation in all sorts of vehicles; this might cause embarassing situations were it not for the rather bird-like quality of the song.

EGGS. The eggs (small and numerous) are laid in gelatinuous masses, which float on the water of mountain pools, some of them derived from running water. Egg membranes slightly polyhedric in shape, about 5 mm in diameter after swelling. One female laid 150 eggs in captivity.

EMBRYOS. Visible on the third day, about 3 mm long and touching the egg membranes. The eye protuberances and two others, probably cement organs, very prominent. A few lay outside the membrane but inside the gelatinous capsule. On the fifth day they hatched, with some mortality. Body, gills, and tail muscle sooty with lighter crests. By the seventh day body oval, upper crest reaching the back, lower one rectilinear. On the eighth day still mostly quiescent, resting on the bottom of the aquarium, but darting around quickly when touched. Eyes and nostrils visible, pigment beginning to differentiate toward the future larval pattern. Gills, especially the right ones, beginning to involve. On the eleventh day eyes rotating, iris gold with dark pigment.

LARVA. Generic characters of *Hyla*, anus dextral, spiraculum sinistral. Tooth formula $\frac{2}{3}$. Spiraculum nearer to the anus than to the mouth. Body oval, olive above, mottled and blotched beneath with dark blue and gold forepart; tail with alternate light and dark olive bars above; lower crest rectilinear, tip blunt, upper crest continuing onto the back. In aquaria the tadpoles like to hang down from the roots of *Eichhornia* or *Myriophyl-*

*lum.* One tadpole with long legs and the arms visible inside the branchial chamber had part of its tail bitten off. After that it could only lie on its back or cling inverted to the vegetation provided for it.

METAMORPHOSIS. At metamorphosis the tadpoles are from 13–18 mm long, more often 15, 16, or even 18, with from 44 to 32 mm of tail before it shrinks. By the time the limbs are out, the long bones and the whole skeleton are green. In metamorphic specimens, the eyes are more coppery and the back darker than in adults, save the middorsal area; a longitudinal accumulation of dark pigment at the edge of the limbs is present. Reddish concealed surfaces of adults, yellowish in juveniles.

ECOLOGY. Adult *Hyla polytaenia* seem hardy, but the species does not occur much below 800 m above sea level. The range is probably limited by appropriate spawning sites at the right altitude. The larvae or the eggs are probably more stenicolous than the adults. The species does not occur in the vicinity of the city of Rio de Janeiro, where only the rocky slopes of the highest peaks reach 800 m. In the Serra da Bocaina and outside Teresópolis we have collected it respectively at 1,500 and 1,300 m above sea level, in the first place in a little pool formed by a small brook and in the latter in an artificial pond.

KNOWN DISTRIBUTION. *Hyla polytaenia polytaenia* occurs and is common in what the geologists call the northern block of the Maritime Range, comprising the serras near Petrópolis, Teresópolis, and Nova Friburgo. It has been found on both sides of the valley of the Paraiba River, in the Serra da Bocaina, on the Serra da Mantiqueira, and near the city of São Paulo. It also extends into Minas Gerais. It has been obtained at Poços de Caldas. We have specimens collected at Agua Limpa near Juiz de Fora, and at Embaubas outside Belo Horizonte; the latter are small.

Two series of small tree frogs evidently very closely allied to *Hyla p. polytaenia* but from quite distant finding places show simplification of pattern independent of size or sex. One series from the highlands of eastern Goiás are of average size but have longer legs. Vestigial or absent secondary stripes characterize this series, whose dark pigment has a powdery appearance.

A more interesting change is present in a sample

from the Serra do Cipó, 134 km northeast of Belo Horizonte. In these specimens reduction of the pattern to three very definite stripes is accompanied by change in the color of the background and by a different design on the gula.

Although they cannot at present be submitted to genetic testing, I treat them as a subspecies because all the specimens obtained differ from the typical form, the finding place is peripheral, and the population seems reproductively isolated from the typical form found below the serra.

## Hyla polytaenia cipoensis B. Lutz, 1968

> Lutz, B. 1968. Geographic variation in Brazilian species of *Hyla*. Texas Memorial Museum. The Pearce-Sellards Series 12:9–11, fig. 5.

DIAGNOSTIC CHARACTERS. Morphologically like *Hyla p. polytaenia* but differing greatly in color, dorsal pattern, and pattern on the gula. Lateral pattern more similar. Size and build more moderate.

TYPES AND TYPE LOCALITY. Three male syntypes, MNR 4039, collected December 1947 by B. Lutz, two females, allotype 4040, paratype 4041, and paratypes 3224–28 and 4042, collected in the same year by Prof. Amilcar Vianna Martins, all near Alto do Palácio in the Serra do Cipó municipality of Jaboticatubas, between Lagoa Santa and Ferros, Minas Gerais, at approximately 1,300 m altitude. Types in collections of the MNR, paratypes in the A. Lutz Collection also at the MNR.

DESCRIPTION. Male syntypes: 29, 27, and 26 mm from snout to vent. Hindlimbs 48, 47, 46 mm, the adpressed tibiotarsal articulation reaching in front of the eye. Head as long as wide, except for the largest one, in which it is barely wider. Snout short, loreal region concave, high; canthus rostralis distinct; interorbital region wider than the upper eyelid. Eye longer than the distance from its anterior corner to the nostril. Tympanum less than half the diameter of the eye. Tongue variable, entire in two, slightly emarginate in the third, very slightly free. Vomerine teeth in small, rounded separate groups. A short web on the lateral fingers. Toes about half-webbed; palms and soles full of tubercles; pollex rudiment present, knob-like; an oval, inner, metatarsal tubercle. Skin of abdomen and midventral part of the thigh very granular.

Female allotype much larger, 37 mm long but the hindlimb relatively shorter, the tibiotarsal artic-

ulation reaching only to the eye (64 mm). Build more robust. Pollex rudiment not noticeable.

Paratypes: 36 (female); 33, 28 (males); 23 and 24 mm (juveniles) from snout to vent.

PATTERN AND COLOR. Dorsal pattern reduced to three main dark stripes, one vertebral, two lateral, the first ending on the head before the tip of the snout, the others on the inner hind edge of the upper eyelids. No vestige of the other stripes from which the name of *H. p. polytaenia* was derived. Dark stripes well delimited from the rest of the dorsal surface, which grows lighter at the edge of contact. Permanently visible dorsal portion of the limbs similar in color to the dorsal surface, light-edged. Main dark lateral stripe passing under the canthus rostralis, starting before the tip of the snout (as in *H. p. polytaenia*), enclosing the eye and the tympanum and ending before the groin.

Dorsolateral edge light; beneath the brown stripe a light area of the same length, brilliant white; edge of maxilla also white except in front where the color is that of the dorsal background. A brilliant white stripe on each side of the gula. In life dorsal aspect completely different in color from the browns and buffs of the nominate form. Two color phases: dark and light. The dark phase is more common; the background is a dull green, lighter on the parts of the limbs and outer digits visible in repose; stripes purplish brown. Light phase: background clear, pale, lemon yellow, stripes grayish lavender. Iris similar to the tones of the dark lateral stripes but more metallic and luminous.

Good dead specimens show vestiges of pigment, especially of the green one, which acquires a bluish tint. In the allotypes, which were preserved in a different fluid, the pigment is gone; the specimens are brown all over, the stripes deeper in tone.

VARIATION. Length of hindlimb variable (as in *H. p. polytaenia* and in most Brazilian species of *Hyla*), but on the whole short. Head wider than long in the medium syntype. Shape of the tongue also variable; though this is probably an artefact. Additional short, light and dark lateral areas in the large female paratype.

SECONDARY SEX CHARACTERS. Not marked in our series. Vocal sac of male not large; claw-shaped point of the pollex rudiment not palpable; only the medium syntype has thickened forearms.

The short stay of two days and nights, in the

type locality mostly under torrential rain, did not yield much information on habits and voice of this frog.

ECOLOGY. The Serra do Cipó constitutes a most interesting environment. The vegetation is of the type called *cerrado* in Brazil (scrub with tortuous bushes and many open spaces). A brook runs between banks below Alto do Palácio, but the water table seems to flow on the surface of the higher ground. Low herbaceous vegetation grows in marshy places that squelch under foot. Rocks are plentiful and are used for erecting stone walls.

DISTRIBUTION. Not known. The typical form, *Hyla p. polytaenia*, occurs at Embaúbas, outside Belo Horizonte, 134 km from the Serra do Cipó, and some 500 m lower.

## *Hyla polytaenia goiana* B. Lutz, 1968

> LUTZ, B. 1968. Geographic variation in Brazilian species of *Hyla*. Texas Memorial Museum. The Pearce-Sellards Series 12:11–13, fig. 6.

This is the outmost population of *Hyla polytaenia* yet known. While immediately reminiscent of the species, it diverges not only by the distance of its finding place from the rest of the known range but also by the dull color and powdery aspect of spots and pigment, in contrast with the usually brilliant aspect of *H. polytaenia*, and, finally, by the longer legs.

Unlike most forms described here, I have not seen the specimens from the highlands of Goiás alive. I give them subspecific rank on account of the characters mentioned above, albeit with some doubts about the validity of this race.

TYPES AND TYPE LOCALITY. São João da Aliança, highlands of Goiás, leg. A. L. Carvalho, May 1956. Type: MNR n. 3235 male. Paratypes: male 3233, 3234, 3236, and 3237, from Jatobasinho Camp.

A series of nine males belonging to the Museu Nacional in Rio de Janeiro, collected by Mr. Antenor Leitão de Carvalho in the county of São João da Aliança above 1,000 m altitude, diverge from the typical form of *Hyla polytaenia*. Five, from Jatobasinho Camp, are pale and seem faded; four, obtained in another camp called Jatobá, are very dark.

DESCRIPTION. Size and habit similar to those of the typical form; 30 to 31 mm from snout to vent; one 29, another 33, both from Jatobá Camp. Build similar, head apparently narrower, length and width

subequal. Hindlimb relatively long, the adpressed tibiotarsal articulation reaching almost to the nostril or even beyond the snout in all but one shorter-legged specimen. Vomerine teeth forming a straight row; vocal sac puckered in the middle, in some specimens with two lateral, oblique, folds. Forearm thick in the nuptial condition; rudiment of pollex present in all, but no sharp point perceptible.

COLOR AND PATTERN. Preserved specimens brown, some pale, others very dark. Dorsal pattern simplified; one entirely devoid of pattern, the others with the three main stripes only, very uniform in width, not fragmented or forming drops, the two lateral rather near the central stripe. Vestiges of secondary stripes fragmented into drops present only in the largest specimen. Dark borders of limbs noticeable on forearm and tarsus, like in the nominate form; a light upper border over the anal and the tarsal folds. In large specimen only, some vestiges of rounded spots made up of minute dots, occupying the permanently visible dorsal strip of the femur and corresponding area of the tibia. In all nine specimens spots and pigment with a powdery aspect.

## *Hyla bischoffi bischoffi* Boulenger, 1887

> BOULENGER, G. A. 1887. Descriptions of new or little-known South American frogs of the genera *Paludicola* and *Hyla*. An. Mag. Nat. Hist. 20: 295–300. *H. bischoffi*: 298–299.

This is one of several species described by Boulenger from Rio Grande do Sul, where collecting was sporadic during the eighteenth and the first decades of the nineteenth century. It may sometimes have been confounded with *Hyla pulchella* (*raddiana*) in collections; in life the flash colors of the concealed surfaces are quite different. Forty years ago Lutz and Venancio found a northern subspecies near São Paulo. The relationship between the two only became known after Dr. Cochran had the opportunity to see Boulenger's types in the British Museum.

DIAGNOSTIC CHARACTERS. In life *Hyla bischoffi* is very easily recognized by the rosy red color of the concealed surfaces of the limbs, especially the thighs, whose upper surface is ornamented with deep ultramarine, vertical, inverted Y-shaped, or horseshoe-shaped marks. In death it may be confused with *Hyla pulchella* and one or two other southern forms of similar size, but can be told apart by the large head and oblique loreal region; also by the more or less montane distribution.

TYPES AND TYPE LOCALITY. The types were collected at Mundo Novo in the state of Rio Grande do Sul by Bischoff, for whom the species was named. They were seen by me in 1952 at the British Museum of Natural History, where they also have a few specimens from Santa Catarina. There is a good series of some eighty specimens in the A. Lutz Collection and the collection of the Museu Nacional; two of them were obtained by Joaquim Venancio and the author at São Francisco de Paula in northern Rio Grande do Sul, and one in Brusque, Santa Catarina; the others by them, F. Rank, and Nahderer in or near São Bento do Sul and at Rio Vermelho in northern Santa Catarina, at approximately 800 m altitude.

DESCRIPTION. Size slightly smaller than that of the more northern subspecies, *H. b. multilineata*. Female type: 55 mm, others from 53–56 mm; one exceptionally large, 60 mm from snout to vent. Males from 35 to 43 mm. Build fairly robust. Head large, slightly broader than long, depressed in some preserved specimens. Legs fairly long but variable in length, the adpressed tibiotarsal articulation reaching some point between the eye and the nostril. Tibia 1 or 2 mm longer than the femur; foot 3 or 4 mm longer than the tarsus. Snout oval, rounded in front, about as long as the eye, whose horizontal diameter is slightly greater than the distance from its anterior corner to the nostril; canthus rostralis angular; loreal region concave, very oblique; interorbital space very little wider than the upper eyelid. Tympanum about one-half the diameter of the eye. Tongue oval to rounded, slightly emarginate and free behind. Vomerine teeth in two strong, short, rounded groups, often reaching slightly beyond the hind edge of the choanae. A distinct pollex rudiment. Hand about one-fourth webbed, palm full of tubercles. Foot more or less one-half webbed, with a distinct inner metatarsal tubercle. Skin smooth above, granular beneath, especially on the belly and the midventral portion of the thighs. A light glandular edge to the sides and the back, the forearm and the tarsus, sometimes forming a triangular outline or a minute tubercle on the heel, but not a real appendix like that of *H. b. multilineata*.

VARIATION. In a few individuals the head is as long as broad, or the interorbital space equal to the upper eyelid, or the tibia is not longer than the femur. The tongue may be more rounded or narrower and more or less emarginate, but this may be an artificial condition due to the preservative. The vomerine teeth range from well-separated to contiguous and may or may not extend beyond the hind margin of the choanae.

SECONDARY SEX CHARACTERS. The males are much smaller than the females. The vocal sac is generally though not always evident, even if they were calling when caught; it may be much folded or extend below the throat. The spike in the pollex rudiment is not always very sharp. Only a few have thick forearms.

The length of fifty-three males, carefully measured, ranged from 34–42 mm, but forty-eight of them were within 35–40 mm. The other five were 34, 34.5, and 42 mm long. The hindlimb is variable, though roughly proportionate to the length of the body.

The females are large; they have a smooth gula and blunt pollex rudiments. They may be distended with eggs.

Out of seven adult females, only one is 60 mm from snout to vent and has hindlimbs 94 mm long. Three others are 56 mm for head and body and respectively 95, 97, and 103 for the hindlimb. Two more are 55 mm, like the cotypes, and their hindlimbs 98 and 103 mm long. The smallest is only 53 mm and has a hindlimb of 90 mm.

Some specimens below 34 and two 48 to 49 mm long did not show secondary characters. The two large ones are probably immature females.

COLOR AND PATTERN. In life, dorsal aspect buff, sometimes olivaceous, at other times very light, with a faint roseate tinge and metallic sheen, especially toward the back and on the limbs; the hands and feet are often quite pale. The head is more olivaceous and its sides, over the loreal region and somewhat beyond, may be grayish or olive; this is also seen in *H. b. multilineata*. There is a light margin to the jaws, the body, and the limbs, underscored by a dark border. Upper half of iris similar in tone to the head, lower half more like the darker shades of the loreal region, with an accumulation of pigment at the lateral edges of the pupil; tympanum not contrasting with the background. Concealed surfaces of the dorsal and inner aspect of the limbs a distinctly roseate red, the color especially deep on the concealed upper parts of the thigh which show bold, inverted Y, or almost horse-shoe-shaped marks, which are a deep blue, often with a mauve or pinkish halo. Gula cream; jaw and long bones green. In dead specimens the blue marks become black thus increasing the likeness to *H. b. multilineata*, in which they are black in life also.

Some specimens are entirely devoid of dorsal pattern; in others it may be reduced to confetti-like dots inclined to be greenish olive. In many others, however, there is a longitudinal accumulation of pigment to both sides of the midline. It may be quite faint and shadowy or more distinct. Occasionally it is composed of narrow elongate spots but more often of blotches with rounded scalloped outline, though they may be quite irregular, forming prongs or prolongations, becoming fenestrate or even confluent into an irregular spindle over the middle. Dead specimens are more grayish than those of *H. b. multilineata*, which are generally the color of wash-leather. They can be distinguished from the more northern form not only by the smaller size and more southern distribution but also by the absence of the multiple longitudinal lines that are characteristic of *H. b. multilineata*.

VOICE. Very similar to the grunts (*quô, quô*) of *Pithecopus burmeisteri*.

HABITS. Very little is known about the habits of this form. The specimen collected by us in Brusque and the two from São Francisco de Paula were in forest, the former not very high and very much disturbed, the latter in a well-preserved private estate. Our large series from northern Santa Catarina, including those of F. Rank, were collected at night on the vegetation above an open trench that is part of the waterworks at Rio Vermelho near São Bento do Sul. Those of Nahderer, from Estrada Saraiva, were collected in similar formation in terrain that dips somewhat but is quite near to São Bento.

EGGS. Like those of the other kinds of *Hyla*, with a dark and a light pole.

JUVENILES. Our two metamorphosing young are 21 and 22 mm long and have only 7.5 and 5 mm of tail left. The mouth opening is that of the adult. The limbs are out. There is no pattern, only a sprinkling of dots.

KNOWN DISTRIBUTION. The nominal form, *Hyla bischoffi bischoffi*, has so far been collected only in Rio Grande do Sul and Santa Catarina in more or less wooded country, not flat, and not very far from the coast. In Paraná we found the more northern subspecies *H. b. multilineata* described from São Paulo by A. Lutz and B. Lutz, 1939. One of the northern Paraná specimens has the *H. b. multilineata* pattern somewhat fenestrated and more irregular, forming more whorls than usual. At Bituruna, in southern Paraná, the livery is that of *H. b. bischoffi*.

AFFINITIES. The affinities of *H. b. bischoffi* are with the other species of the group, more especially *H. b. multilineata*, the more northern and slightly larger subspecies, whose description follows. Though smaller than *H. b. multilineata*, *H. b. bischoffi* is much larger than *H. polytaenia* Cope. The color of the red concealed surfaces is intermediate between that of the other two.

## *Hyla bischoffi multilineata* Lutz & B. Lutz, 1939

LUTZ, A., and LUTZ, B. 1939. New Hylidae from Brazil. *An. Ac. Bras. Sc.* 9(1):72–74, 85–86, pl. II, figs. 3–3a.

COCHRAN, D. M. 1955. Frogs of southeastern Brazil. *U.S.N.M. Bull.* 206:84–86, fig. 10.

HISTORY. *Hyla multilineata* was described as a full species by A. and B. Lutz. However, when Dr. Cochran saw the Boulenger types in London, she realized that our species was very close to his *H. bischoffi*. A. Lutz never saw the latter alive, nor did Dr. Cochran see living specimens of either. In the summer of 1949–1950 I collected *H. b. bischoffi* in Santa Catarina and realized both similarities and differences. *H. b. bischoffi* lacks the lines of *multilineata* and the ornamental bars on the thighs are ultramarine blue instead of black. I now also regard the two forms as subspecies.

DIAGNOSTIC CHARACTERS. *Hyla b. multilineata* is characterized by the multiple, narrow, longitudinal lines all down the dorsal surface and the unusually bright, rose-red color of the concealed surfaces of the hindlimbs, especially the thighs and adjacent parts of the flanks, which are ornamented with black bars and markings. It is a montane rain forest form with a very limited known range on the Serra do Mar in the states of São Paulo and Paraná.

TYPES AND TYPE LOCALITY. The type ( ♀ ) n. 726 and allotype ( ♂ ) n. 727 with paratypes nos. 728–733 were collected in January 1924 at Alto da Serra de Cubatão, near the city of São Paulo, by A. Lutz and J. Venancio and are in the A. Lutz Collection at the MNR.

DESCRIPTION. Size rather large: females 62–69 mm, males 40–45 mm from snout to vent. Build elongate. Head massive, slightly broader than long, bent downward in some preserved specimens. Body less wide than the head at the axilla, narrowing posteriorly. Length of leg variable, the tibiotarsal articulation reaching somewhere between the front of the eye and the nostril. Snout oval, rounded in front, high in profile; upper jaw prominent, one or one and a half times as long as the eye; canthus rostralis sharp, curved; loreal region concave; interorbital space slightly wider than the upper eyelid. Eye large, prominent. Tympanum distinct, its diameter one-half to two-thirds that of the eye. Nostrils lateral. Tongue rounded, longer than broad, entire, slightly free behind. Vomerine teeth in two heavy groups between and/or behind the choanae. Fingers webbed at the base; subarticular tubercles well-developed; disks large, that of the third finger nearly covering the tympanum. Toes one-half to two-thirds webbed, web longer on the outer toes. A rudiment of the pollex ( ♂ ). A pronounced, inner metatarsal tubercle. A distinct dermal appendage on the heel. Skin smooth above, granular beneath, finely so on chest and belly; granulations coarser on thigh and anal region. A supratympanic fold continuing beyond the axilla.

VARIATION. Some variation is seen in the tongue and the vomerine teeth. The tongue may be narrower, entire, wavy in outline, or slightly notched. In the female type it is entire; in two female paratypes it is wavy in outline, notched in a third. In the male allotype it is notched and almost heart-shaped; it is narrow in two male paratypes and slightly notched in three. The vomerine teeth are close together in most of them, contiguous in one. The eye is relatively larger and the tympanum relatively smaller in the male allotype.

SECONDARY SEX CHARACTERS. The angular pollex rudiment ends as a spike in the male, the vocal sac forms folds over the chest. The female is considerably larger than the male.

MEASUREMENTS. Female type: snout to vent 69 mm. Hindlimb 113, femur, 30, tibia 33, tarsus and foot 50.

Allotype male: snout to vent 45 mm. Hindlimb 77, femur 21, tibia 23, tarsus and foot 33.

COLOR AND PATTERN. In life, ground color variable, from light buff to wash-leather, with very numerous, narrow, parallel, longitudinal (mostly narrow) lines down the whole dorsal surface and similar, often indistinct, lines on the limbs. A dark canthal stripe, interrupted by the eye and ear, continues behind them along the side; a longitudinal dark stripe on the outside of leg and forearm, a dark cross-stripe over the anus; dark folds over the heel and elbow sometimes appearing dull gray-green; the canthal and anal stripes greenish; occasionally a yellowish tinge on the occiput and a pea-green one in the sacral region; the narrow dorsal lines sometimes evanescent in the sacral region (allotype), anastomosed or curved outward in whorls (type). In dark specimens a few wider stripes are also present, especially on the anterior part of the sides. At night the frogs become paler, the lines contrasting less. Concealed parts of groin, thighs and legs, feet, webs, and a small fold at the elbow, a vivid rosy-red with conspicuous black vertical bars, mostly bifurcated posteriorly on the concealed upper surface of thighs, and black markings on the sides of the body near the groin. Throat cream with a few very indistinct ornamental flecks on the sides; belly yellowish, lower aspect of thighs not visible in repose, white, all of them immaculate, except for the edge of the dorsal markings, visible from beneath; webs paler toward the ends of digits. Long bones and lower jaw green, visible by translucency.

VOICE. According to A. Lutz the call is a short croak sometimes followed by a few staccato notes.

HABITS. *Hyla b. multilineata* is nocturnal in its habits. When kept alive it sleeps deeply all day. It may be considered as a montane subspecies breeding in still or slack waters in the rain-forest zone.

REPRODUCTION. After a night excursion in February 1923, during which a number of adult specimens were caught, mating was observed. The male shuts his hands into fists and digs the sharp spike of the pollex rudiment perpendicularly into the breast of the female.

EGGS. Small dark eggs with a light vegetal pole were laid. The metamorphosis of the young was also observed. Four-legged, tailed specimens are about 16–18 mm in head and body length. They have blunt snouts and rosy thighs; the green color of the long bones is already visible by translucency.

KNOWN RANGE. *H. b. multilineata* occurs north of *H. b. bischoffi*. The type locality is outside the capital of the state of São Paulo and it has been collected in the adjacent state of Paraná between Curitiba and the coast, in a place quite similar to Alto da Serra de Cubatão. Both places are in the Maritime Range. *H. b. bischoffii* seems slightly smaller to judge by our specimens.

AFFINITIES. *Hyla polytaenia* Cope is the species that resembles *H. multilineata* most, but it is not the same. It is very much smaller, the largest females only just attaining the size of adult *H. b. bischoffi* males. The call is quite different. The dorsal stripes differ; there are no bars or any kind of markings on the concealed parts of the body and thighs, whose ground color is a different, duller, tone of red. *Hyla squalirostris* differs still further in size, pattern, call, and morphology. *Hyla guentheri*, which belongs to the same group, is smaller, and the areas concealed in repose are orange and brown, not rosy.

## *Hyla guentheri* Boulenger, 1886

> GÜNTHER, A. 1868. First account of the species of tailless batrachians added to the collection of the British Museum. *Proc. zool. soc. London*, 1868, pp. 489–490, pl. 40, fig. 4. (*Hyla leucotaenia*).
>
> BOULENGER, G. A. 1886. A synopsis of the reptiles and batrachians of the province of Rio Grande do Sul, Brazil. *An. Nat. Hist.* 18 (ser. 5):423–445. *H. guentheri*: 445.

*Hyla guentheri* was named by Boulenger from a specimen wrongly determined as *Hyla leucotaenia* Burmeister by Günther. He also included *Hyla bracteator* nec Hensel, listed in the catalogue (1882). Burmeister's name is a synonym of *Hyla pulchella* covering the juvenile form. Since then *Hyla guentheri* has been mentioned only a few times, mostly by Argentinian authors. We found it unexpectedly during a night journey from Blumenau to Joinville very near the latter town. Its bird-like call and its livery seemed new to us, but a dim memory of Günther's figure led to comparison and determining it as this species. There do not seem to be any genuine synonyms.

DIAGNOSTIC CHARACTERS. Size intermediate between that of *Hyla polytaenia* and of *Hyla bisch-*

*offi*. In life orange ocelli on the brown-orange background of the upper posterior part of the thigh concealed in repose; ocelli opaque white on paler orange yellowish background after death. Tympanum small. Males with the vocal sac unusually large and the forearms unusually thick for their size.

TYPES AND TYPE LOCALITY. *Hyla guentheri* was renamed by Boulenger on a specimen from Rio Grande do Sul, erroneously determined as *Hyla leucotaenia* by Günther. The type, British Museum 62.5.8.9., was seen by me in 1952. The label does not mention whether the state or the town of Rio Grande do Sul is meant by the terra typica.

DESCRIPTION. Size moderate, males 33 to 40 mm, mostly 37; two females 44 and 47 mm from snout to vent. Moderately slender, snout rather obtuse, with angular canthus rostralis and with the loreal region subvertical. Hindlimb slightly variable but relatively short, the adpressed tibiotarsal articulation reaching the eye or just in front of it. Interorbital space not much wider than the upper eyelid. Eye in life prominent, longer than the distance from its anterior corner to the nostril; tympanum half or less than half the horizontal diameter of the eye. Tongue wide, slightly free, entire or emarginate. Vomerine teeth in small rounded groups at the level of the posterior edge of the choanae, which are narrow and small. Outer fingers webbed at the base; toes about half-webbed, the fourth very long; palms and soles tubercular; an oval, inner, metatarsal tubercle; a pronounced rudiment of the pollex (males). Dorsal surface smooth, chest, belly and midventral aspect of the thigh granular.

MEASUREMENTS. Two females 47 and 44 mm from snout to vent, hindlimb 74 and 69; males (thirty-four specimens) 33–40 mm (one-fifth of them 37 mm); hindlimb 56–67.

VARIATIONS. We have specimens from two populations only, of which thirty-one were collected by Mr. J. Venancio and me. The other five were sent to the Museu Nacional. This fact may account for their seeming less variable than other species. Variations in the shape of tongue may be artificial; variations in length of the hindlimb seem to occur in most Brazilian species of *Hyla*. Only two specimens have longer hindlimbs, one from each locality; the tibiotarsal articulation reaches almost to the nostril in the one from the larger series. The five sent to the Museum are smaller and four paler but otherwise similar. Variations of color and pattern are discussed below.

SECONDARY SEX CHARACTERS. Vocal sac enormous, balloon-like in the males of our larger series, the forearms very thick for their size.

COLOR AND PATTERN. The most distinctive color and pattern are those of the upper posterior aspect of the thigh, concealed in repose; the brown-orange background is ornamented with orange or golden ocelli, generally round, sometimes irregular in shape, or appearing confluent, even in figures of eight; ocelli numerous in twenty out of thirty, mostly pigmented ones; less numerous in eight, absent from two. In eighteen specimens similar, lesser, ocelli on the flanks, near the groin; absent from twelve.

Dorsal aspect, including the permanently visible strips of the limbs and outer digits, mostly pale, the color of very light wash-leather, a delicate light buff or a warmer brown; sometimes with a pale golden sheen or a rosy, flesh-colored tone; occasionally slightly more olivaceous on the limbs. Pigment composed of reddish brown chromatophores disposed either in dense dark bands in the more open longitudinal series of confetti-like dots or even as isolated dots. A dense lateral band on each side of the head, below the canthus rostralis, covering the tympanum and eye and continuing onto the sides, enhancing the light dorsal edge and reaching the elbow, beyond it, or near to the sacrum, gradually fading out or going over into more open series of dots; a similar light streak over the anus and on the outer edges of the limbs, especially on the forearm and tibia, outlined above in light; open series of chromatophores on the jaws; isolated dots on the fingers, palms, soles, edge of the gula, and midventral aspect of the thigh. Width and intensity of the bands individually variable, generally more accentuated in darker specimens. Dorsal surface of pale individuals often immaculate; others showing shadowy spots similar to those of *Hyla b. bischoffi*; one-fifth of the darker specimens with longitudinal series of thick blotches composed of confetti-like chromatophores on the dorsal surface; in two specimens lines similar to the pattern of *H. multilineata* but wider.

Iris with two minute median notches on the inner rim; upper half golden, lower half the color of the lateral pigmented band; transparent part of the lower lid with a light metallic free rim and a few dots and spots on the slightly maculate lower part; cornea dull purplish mauve, somewhat lighter than in *Hyla bischoffi*.

Gula off-white or pastel tones of violet, with small chromatophores forming a stippled outline near the edge of the mandible. Webs and disks grayish, the webs more delicate than those of *H. bischoffi*. Granulations of ventral surface and granular part of the forearms (males) opaque white, tesselated, with a shell-like glint. Folds of the lower part of the vocal sac tinted with orange. Bones not green as in most of the species of the group. The articulations have a greenish gold glint.

In some well-preserved ten-year-old specimens, the golden color of the upper half of the iris and the spots on the transparent part of the lower lid persist. The shadowy spots of the lighter specimens are now olivaceous gray; the bolder blotches and the dorsal surface of the darker specimens have the pinkish vinaceous tones described by Ridgway. The orange-brown surfaces of the concealed aspect of the thigh have faded to pale orange-yellow, or pale yellow-orange, whereas the ocelli have acquired an opaque white color; the confetti-like chromatophores are light reddish brown.

VOICE. Our specimens were found by their call, which recalls the song of the thrush but has a preliminary appoggiatura.

ECOLOGY. The specimens were collected at night on the reeds of a marsh.

KNOWN DISTRIBUTION. *Hyla guentheri* is known from the type locality of the state or town of Rio Grande do Sul, southern Brazil. Our series was taken 15 km south of Joinville on the road from Blumenau, state of Santa Catarina; the five in the Museum, labeled Rio Piraí, are presumably from the same state, as there is a Piraí River not very far from Joinville.

AFFINITIES. *Hyla guentheri* seems to fit best into the group of *Hyla polytaenia*. Morphologically they are rather similar, but *Hyla guentheri* seems to occupy a slightly more distant position than the others in regard to the shape of the vomerine teeth, the head, and the length of the snout. The presence of a vivid color and pattern on the concealed areas of the thigh also agrees. However, it lacks the green skeleton of most of the group. The finding places are at lesser elevations than usual in the *Hyla polytaenia* group.

## *Hyla squalirostris* Lutz, 1925

Lutz, A. 1925. Batraciens du Brésil (II). *C. R. Soc. Biol. Paris* 93(22):212.

————. 1925. New species of brasilian batrachians. Preliminary Note. *H. squalirostris*: 14. (Translation) *Publ. Inst. O. Cruz* 10(3).

Lutz, B. 1952. Anfíbios anuros da Coleção Adolpho Lutz. VIII *H. squalirostris* Lutz 1925. *Mem. Inst. O. Cruz* 50:614–624. English summary: 621–624, 2 pls.

Schmidt, K. P. 1944. New frogs from Misiones and Uruguay. *Zool. Ser. Field Mus. Nat. Hist.* 29(9):153–160. *H. evelynae*: 156–158, fig. 21.

Gallardo, J. M. 1961. *Hyla strigilata* Spix e *Hyla squalirostris* Lutz en la República Argentina. Comunicaciones del Museo Argentino de Ciencias Naturales. *C. Zool.* 3(5):145–158.

*Hyla squalirostris* was discovered through its call, heard late at night, generally between 10 P. M. and 3 A. M., in a marshy pasture in front of the house at the Fazenda do Bonito, Serra da Bocaina, on the border of the state of São Paulo with the state of Rio de Janeiro. It was described by A. Lutz, who called it *Hyla squalirostris* because of the long, shark-like snout, overhanging the mouth. In Brazil the species is montane except in the south. I found it twice again in the Serra da Bocaina and a third time it was found by me and J. Venancio in a quite juvenile specimen near Osório on the plains in Rio Grande do Sul. It has also been collected in the mountains at Poços de Caldas, Minas Gerais, by J. Becker and at Bituruna, Paraná, by V. Staviarsky. In 1961, Cei showed me some specimens obtained by him in the Argentinian province of Corrientes, which he rightly surmised to be *Hyla squalirostris*. He had already collected some earlier ones on islands in the delta of the Paraná. The same year Gallardo examined a series of specimens belonging to the MACN and hailing from the province of Buenos Aires. On the strength of the Schmidt type and of his own specimens, Gallardo put *Hyla evelynae* into the synonymy of *Hyla squalirostris*; Cei and I agree.

DIAGNOSTIC CHARACTERS. In his description, A. Lutz (1925) already calls attention to the large head and projecting snout, which overhangs the opening of the mouth; the small size and slender body and limbs; the translucent skin with the tissues shining through, especially on the limbs with a rosy tinge; the double black longitudinal bands behind the eyes divided by a white interval; the limbs without crossbars but slightly dotted in black; the lemon-yellow vocal sac and other characters.

TYPES AND TYPE LOCALITY. Male syntypes from the Serra da Bocaina, state of São Paulo, collected January 16–31, 1925, by A. Lutz, B. Lutz, and J. Venancio, now nos. 954 and 955 of the ALC in the MNR, also n. 96719 USNM (syntype described by D. M. Cochran 1955) collected on the same occasion.

Type locality: Serra da Bocaina, a branch of the Serra do Mar, 22° 32′ 30″ S. 44° 35′ 39″ W. Gr.; altitude 1,100 m. Climate subtropical with cool summers, Köppen *Cfb*. Open marsh.

DESCRIPTION. Size small, 24–29 mm. Build slender, elongate. Head large, longer than wide and wider than the body, contained less than three times in the total length. Body and limbs very slender. Body narrower than the head in the postaxillary region, still narrower between the sacrum and the groin. Hindlimb fairly long, the tibiotarsal articulation reaching in front of the eye when the leg is adpressed; tibia longer than femur. Snout very elongate, acuminate from above, angular in profile, shark-like, projecting and sloping backward to the opening of the mouth. Eye moderate, its horizontal diameter equal to less than half the distance from its anterior corner to the tip of the snout. Tympanum distinct, approximately half the diameter of the eye. Interorbital space more than double the width of the upper eyelid. Nostril subterminal. Canthus rostralis long, well-defined toward the nostrils; loreal region concave, sloping downward. Tongue wide and long, oval, very slightly free and emarginate behind. Vomerine teeth in two short groups between and slightly behind the posterior edge of the choanae. Outer toes not quite half-webbed. A distinct inner and a very minute outer metatarsal tubercle. Skin smooth, above and beneath, except on the belly and midventral part of the thigh. A slight ridge on the inside of the tarsus. A supratympanic ridge. Vocal sac very large, with longitudinal folds.

MEASUREMENTS (mm). Male syntype n. 954: snout to vent 27. Hindlimb 43: femur 11, tibia 14, tarsus and foot 18. Syntype n. 955: snout to vent 27. Specimens obtained later at Lageado in the same Serra: 28, 27, 25 mm long.

COLOR AND PATTERN. Dorsal ground color brownish, with flesh-colored suffusion on the translucent surfaces, especially on the limbs. Darkest on head growing gradually lighter on the back. A narrow, black vertebral line; a black canthal line, bordered in white. Behind each eye, two black, longitudinal stripes, enclosing a slightly wider, white or faintly flesh-colored interval. Limbs also brownish above, flesh-colored on the surfaces concealed in repose. No pattern on the limbs, except a longitudinal, dorsal assemblage of darker dots on the leg extending slightly onto the thigh. Femoral blood vessels visible by translucency. Beneath immaculate, flesh-colored on chest and limbs, greenish yellow on gula and belly. Vocal sac lemon-colored. Belly pale greenish yellow. The specimens from Lageado, at a higher altitude on the Serra da Bocaina, are darker with a chestnut-colored dorsal aspect, including the forearm and tarsus. Some of the Argentinian ones are very pale.

VOICE. As A. Lutz puts it, the call is like the sound produced by winding a watch: *crr crr crr,* with the *rr* trilled. In the valley of the Bonito (at 1,100 m) it sang only very late at night. At Lageado (between 1,500 and 1,800 m) it began to call earlier, already at nightfall.

BEHAVIOR AND ECOLOGY. The first specimens from Bonito were caught climbing *Juncus* reeds growing in shallow marsh or singing near the apex. At Lageado, they sang on the low vegetation of an open trench. Our Uruguayan and Argentinian specimens were also caught climbing up reeds in ditches and pools in wet plains.

JUVENILES. Metamorphic specimens were obtained in soaked marshy terrain in April 1951 at Ponte Alta, Serra da Bocaina, between Bonito and Lageado, but nearer to the latter and at a higher altitude than the Bonito Valley. The largest were 12 to 13 mm long (head and body). The younger ones, with tails 6 mm long and hindlimbs from 3 to 3.5 mm in length, did not have over 11 mm of head and body length. No adults were found on the occasion.

KNOWN RANGE. In Brazil the species is montane at the latitude of the states of São Paulo, Rio de Janeiro, and Paraná (Serra do Mar), and was once collected in Minas Gerais on the parallel Serra da Mantiqueira. In Rio Grande do Sul it occurs on the plains.

In Argentina *H. squalirostris* seems more common than in Brazil. It has been collected often in the province of Buenos Aires at San Isidro and Libres del Sur, on islands in the delta of the Paraná River; in the province of Corrientes, at Bañado de Ayuí, Ituzaingó, and Iberá. In Uruguay it was obtained by Schmidt (*H. evelynae*) at San Carlos and in the department of Treinta y Tres and quite recently by Prof. R. Vaz Ferreira, at Santa Lucia near Montevideo.

This form covers approximately 22° to 27° S., along the seaboard in the platine-cisplantine and Atlantic provinces. This kind of distribution is not unique, it occurs in other cisplatine and southern frogs. The same phenomenon occurs among plants. Thus the epiphytic fern *Hymenophyllum magellanicum,* from the straits of Magalhães, near the tip of the continent, is found growing on the ground at the top of the Organ Mountains in the Brazilian state of Rio de Janeiro at 2,200 m altitude and only 22° 26' 12" southern latitude. In these cases the determining factors must be the compensation of higher latitude by altitude, plus adaptation to or tolerance of low temperatures.

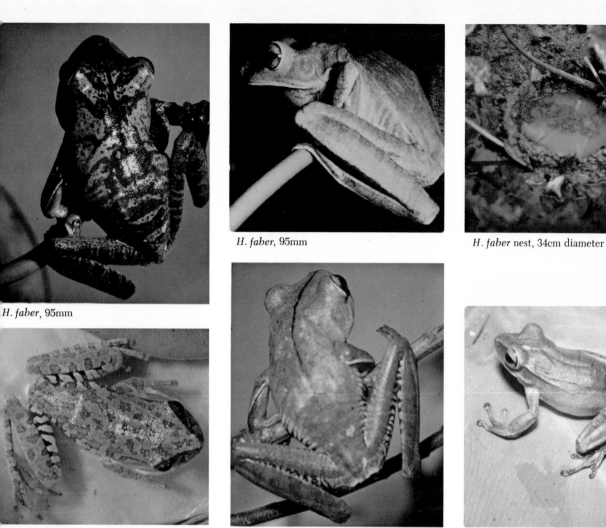

*H. faber*, 95mm

*H. faber*, 95mm

*H. faber* nest, 34cm diameter

*H. pseudopseudis saxicola*, 43mm

*H. secedens*, 55mm

*H. daudini*, 45mm

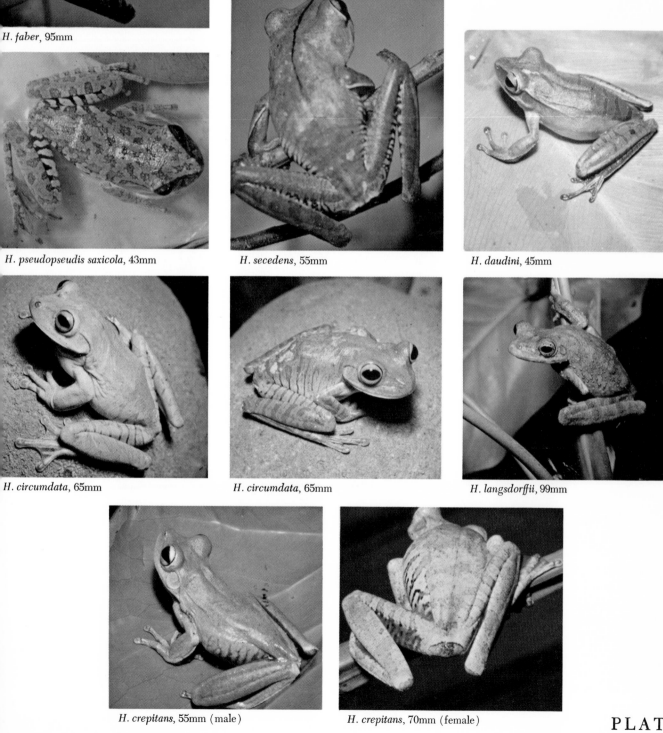

*H. circumdata*, 65mm

*H. circumdata*, 65mm

*H. langsdorffii*, 99mm

*H. crepitans*, 55mm (male)

*H. crepitans*, 70mm (female)

PLATE I

*H. albosignata*, 50mm

*H. albosignata*, (swimming)

*H. lanciformis*, 55mm

*H. pardalis*, 60mm

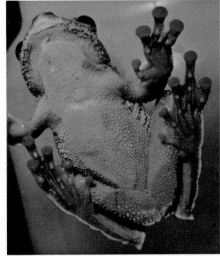

*H. pardalis*, 50mm

*H. pardalis*, 18mm (juvenile)

*H. albomarginata*, 45mm

*H. albopunctata*, 60mm

*H. raniceps*, 60mm

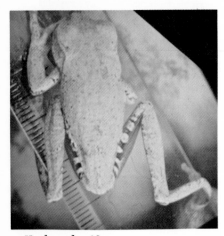

*H. clepsydra*, 38mm

*H. albofrenata*, 37, 40mm

*H. pulchella riojana*, 47mm

# PLATE II

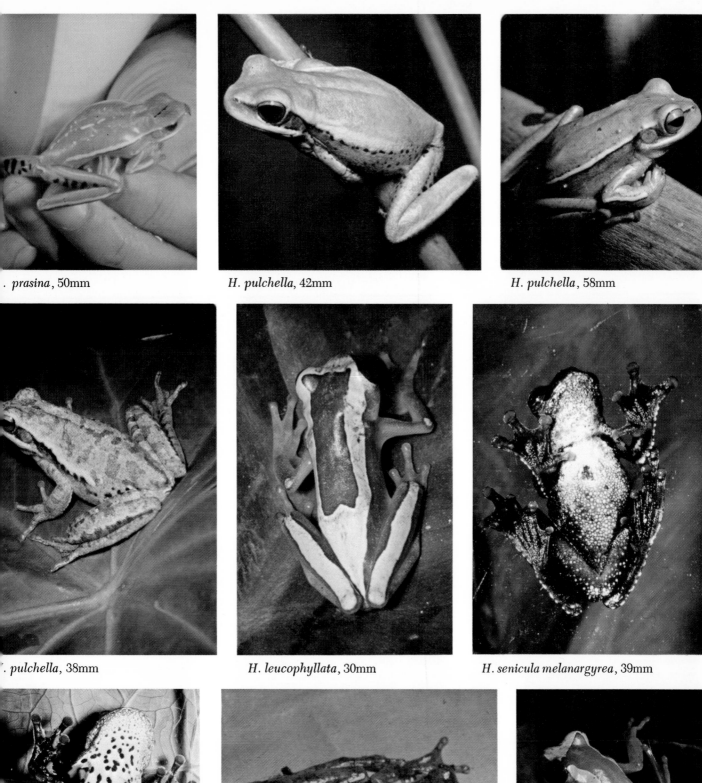

. *prasina*, 50mm      *H. pulchella*, 42mm      *H. pulchella*, 58mm

. *pulchella*, 38mm      *H. leucophyllata*, 30mm      *H. senicula melanargyrea*, 39mm

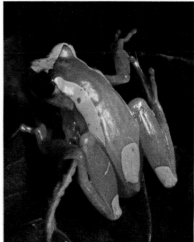

. *marmorata*, 46mm      *H. senicula senicula*, 33mm      *H. leucophyllata*, 35mm

PLATE III

*H. rubra altera*, 25mm         *H. duartei caldarum*, 25mm         *H. x-signata similis*, 35mm

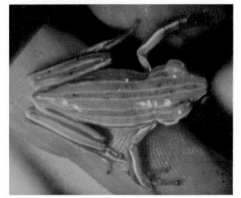

*H. polytaenia polytaenia*, 40mm    *H. polytaenia cipoensis*, 26mm    *H. bischoffi multilineata*, 65mm

*H. anceps*, 34mm                *H. squalirostris*, 24, 29mm        *H. fuscovaria*, 34mm (juvenile)

PLATE IV        *H. x-signata nasica*, 34mm              *H. craspedospila*, 29mm

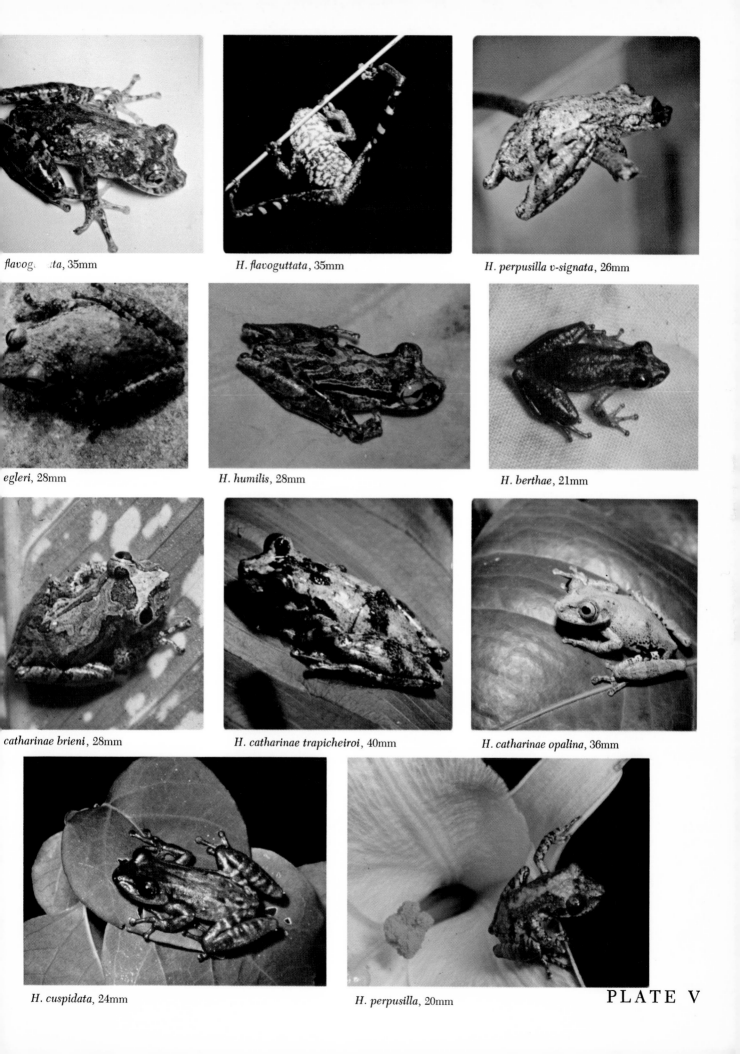

*flavog. ...ta*, 35mm

*H. flavoguttata*, 35mm

*H. perpusilla v-signata*, 26mm

*egleri*, 28mm

*H. humilis*, 28mm

*H. berthae*, 21mm

*catharinae brieni*, 28mm

*H. catharinae trapicheiroi*, 40mm

*H. catharinae opalina*, 36mm

*H. cuspidata*, 24mm

*H. perpusilla*, 20mm

PLATE V

*H. misera misera*, 19mm

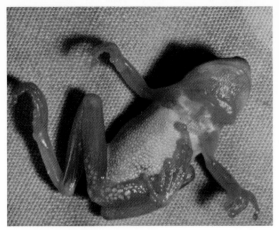

*H. elongata*, 19mm

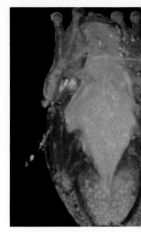

*H. bipunctata*, 25mm

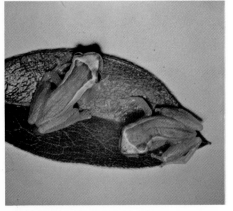

*H. decipiens decipiens*, 18, 20mm

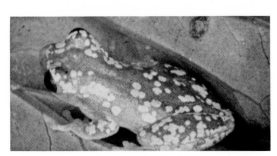

*H. decipiens branneri*, 17mm

*H. bipunctata*, 25mm

*H. misera meridiana*, 22mm

*H. berthalutzae*, 24mm

*H. minuta*, 22mm

*H. nana*, 20mm

*H. sanborni*, 18mm

*H. sanborni*, 18mm

PLATE VI

*...ynohyas venulosa*, 71mm

*Phrynohyas mesophaea*, 72mm

*Phrynohyas venulosa imitatrix*, 61mm

*...truncata*, 41mm

*H. langsdorffii*, 99mm

*Phrynohyas venulosa hebes*, 75mm

*...anceps*, 34mm

*H. pardalis* nest, 18x24cm

PLATE VII

# III. The *Hyla rubra-Hyla x-signata* Complex

*Hyla rubra* can no longer be looked upon as a simple species nor *Hyla x-signata* Spix as a mere synonym of it. They comprise a large number of different forms that occupy large areas of South America.

The frogs of this group are characterized by the stout build, short hindlimbs, muscular legs, well-developed and rounded though short disks, not very full webs, short patches of vomerine teeth between small choanae, and a more or less sub-circular tongue; also by the dull brown, olivaceous, or drab color and modest dorsal pattern and the rather unobtrusive flash colors of the concealed surfaces. They are very pleiomorphic, but it is not known what degree of panmixis prevails among them. Nevertheless, a certain number of different forms may be recognized and told apart by persons familiar with the group.

There is a certain correlation between the degree of differentiation of the forms and their environment. They are all very adaptable and seem to be satisfied with minimum requirements for reproduc-tion and spawning. For instance, they enter human habitations freely, in quest of cool, dark, and humid environments; they have been found in Indian huts at Cape Orange, on the frontier of Brazil and Dutch Guiana, in the machine houses of the water-works at Juiz de Fora. Minas Gerais, and also in the stables at the Instituto Oswaldo Cruz in Rio de Janeiro; there they hunt freely at night on the mesh-enclosed windows of the laboratories. One specimen was caught in a shoe. When tree frogs are caught in a house and brought to me they are almost always members of this group.

At the present time it seems easiest to subdivide the group into several sections. One of them includes the large species that do not seem very closely related to each other. The next one constitutes the *Hyla x-signata* sector with its variants. A third one takes in *Hyla rubra* proper and its races. After that there come several small, and one very small species that are somewhat divergent from the ones mentioned above, and finally two closely allied forms that diverge further from them.

# 11. The *Hyla x-signata* Group

## LARGE SPECIES

Four species of this group are much larger than the others, attaining between 40 and 50 mm or even more of snout-to-vent-length. They are *Hyla fuscovaria (megapodia, trachythorax); Hyla acuminata (phrynoderma); Hyla longilinea;* and *Hyla hayii.* The fundamental pattern is that of *H. x-signata.*

*Hyla fuscovaria* has a very large range over much of Brazil and cisandean South America. It is stout, long-legged, and often has the dorsal pattern fragmented into spots or forming a reticulum with or without white dots. The nuptial plaques on the breast of the male are deciduous and seem to occur in a number of species of the complex.

*Hyla acuminata* is a form of the Chaquean subprovince, stout in build, with acuminate snout, very wide and short disks, and a rather rough skin.

*Hyla hayii* is endemic to the coastal mountains of Brazil and is known from the state of Rio de Janeiro to northern Santa Catarina. It is sometimes stout but not elongate, often olivaceous and devoid of pattern, except for the flash color on the concealed surfaces, especially in the northern part of the range. In the south the pattern becomes more evident. *Hyla hayii* decreases greatly in size toward the southern end of its distribution.

*Hyla longilinea,* known only from the holotype and one juvenile, was obtained in the mountains of Minas Gerais. It is streamlined and has long, very thin legs and a much rougher skin than *Hyla acuminata.*

## Hyla fuscovaria Lutz, 1925

*(Hyla megapodia* Miranda Ribeiro 1926, 1937)
*(Hyla trachythorax* L. Müller and Hellmich, 1936)

LUTZ, A. 1925. Batraciens du Brésil (II) *C. R. Soc. Biol. Paris* 93(22):211–224. *H. fuscovaria:* 212.

———. 1926. Nota previa sobre espécies novas de batrachios brasileiros. New species of Brazilian batrachians. Preliminary Note. Portuguese: 3–9. English: 10–16. *H. fuscovaria:* 7–8, 12–13. *Publ. Inst. O. Cruz* March 10, 1926.

COCHRAN, D. M. 1955. Frogs of southeastern Brazil. *U.S.N.M. Bull.* 206. *H. fuscovaria:* 137–139, pl. 12, figs. A–B.

MIRANDA RIBEIRO, A 1926. Notas para servirem ao estudo dos gymnobatrachios (anura) brasileiros. Arch. Mus. Nac. Rio 27, *H. megapodia* Mir. Rib. Pl. V, fig. 5, no mention in the text.

———. 1937. Alguns batrachios novos das coleções do Museu Nacional. O campo, maio 1937. *Hyla megapodia:* 67–68.

MÜLLER, L., and HELLMICH, W. 1936. *Wissenschaftliche Erbgebnisse der Deutschen Gran-Chaco Expeditionen.* Amphibien und Reptilien, 1 Teil. *Hyla trachythorax:* 77–80, fig. 27.

*Hyla fuscovaria* is one of the large members of

the *Hyla x-signata* sector of the *Hyla rubra–Hyla x-signata* complex. It was described in 1925 by A. Lutz, from Agua Limpa outside Juiz de Fora, Minas Gerais, in what I call the Atlantic area or province of Brazil. Cochran (1955) redescribed it from one of the Lutz cotypes. She reproduced Lutz's *lapsus calami* in saying Agua Branca, instead of Agua Limpa, and in her list of specimens she adds erroneously that the type locality is near Ouro Preto. She also compared it with *Hyla nasica* Cope and stated that she found very little difference between *Hyla fuscovaria* and specimens of *Hyla nasica* from Misiones, Argentina. She did not realize that two species were being confounded under Cope's name. *Hyla nasica* is a small tree frog. Its size was accurately given in the original description, but this did not prevent subsequent confusion with a larger sympatric species. In 1936, L. Müller and Hellmich, working on the material collected by the German Gran Chaco Expedition, separated the larger species and called it *Hyla trachythorax*. Miranda Ribeiro had already offered the specific name *H. megapodia* (1926) under a picture of it, but had completely omitted mention of it in the text. He published the description in 1937. The specimens of this large species are so similar to Lutz's *fuscovaria* (1925) that I consider them as conspecific with it.

Lutz, who had not seen either *Hyla x-signata* or *nasica* in 1925, compared his type to *Hyla rubra* from the Guianas and derived the name *fuscovaria* from the more intricate, reticulated, dorsal pattern of many specimens of *fuscovaria*. Miranda Ribeiro derived his name from the relatively long legs. L. Müller and Hellmich called it *Hyla trachythorax* because of the nuptial plaques seen by them on the chest of breeding males; they considered this character unique but I have seen it also in males of other species of the *H. x-signata* sector of the complex.

TYPES AND TYPE LOCALITIES. The A. Lutz types are from Agua Limpa, near Juiz de Fora, Minas Gerais, leg. J. Venancio, 1920. Type ALC n. 76 at MNR; paratypes USNM 96988, 96992-4 (1921).

Miranda Ribeiro (1937) gives the following indications: Hab. Mato Grosso: Cáceres (Rio Paraguay) and Porto Esperidião (Rio Jaurú), where he collected three specimens for the Museu Nacional. At present there are only two cotypes in the MNR., n. 223, both from São Luis de Cáceres. Cochran

(1935) mentions a paratype from Porto Espiridião in the USNM and adds that it is undoubtedly a specimen of *Hyla raniceps* Cope, which the two in Rio certainly are not. The two Müller and Hellmich cotypes 156 (1 ♂, 1 ♀) are from San Luiz, in what they call Apa-Bergland, Paraguay, and were destroyed during the Second World War.

DIAGNOSTIC CHARACTERS. The large size and long legs; the reticulated or fragmented dorsal pattern plus the bars and scrolls surrounding the flash color on the concealed upper parts of the limbs. Differs from the other large species of the sector; from *Hyla acuminata*, by the completely different dorsal pattern, less rough skin, more marked canthus rostralis and better defined snout; from *H. hayii* by the build and the shorter head and leg and the ocelli of the latter. Known range much greater. From the other species of the complex it differs by size, length of hindlimb, and/or distribution.

DESCRIPTION. Size large for the group. Male type 41 mm, cotype USNM 96988, 42.5 mm, three female topotypes MNR 48, 45, and 43 mm snout to vent. Build robust. Head plane, elongate. Trunk straight, postscapular region almost as wide as the head, tapering beyond the sacrum. Hindlimb long, the adpressed tibiotarsal reaching to the nostril (male cotype) or almost to the nostril (female topotypes). Snout ogival, roundly acuminate from above, projecting over the mouth in profile. Canthus rostralis distinct, blunt; loreal region concave, sloping outward. Nostrils slightly tumefied, not terminal, much farther from the eye than from the tip of snout. Eye prominent in life, its horizontal diameter equal to the distance from its anterior corner to the nostril. Tympanum very distinct, one-half to two-thirds the diameter of the eye. Interorbital space wider than the internarial space. Tongue very wide, almost subcircular, free behind and emarginate. Vomerine teeth in two small groups between the choanae. Fingers with a rudiment of web at the base, more distinct between the first and second. Disks short, very wide in front. A callosity at the base of the first finger, a bifid tubercle below the third and fourth fingers. Feet almost two-thirds webbed; web fringe-like on the inner side of the first, second, and third toes, reaching the base of last joint or slightly beyond it on the outer side of the second, third, and on the fifth, fringe-like on the two joints below the disk on both sides of the fourth toe. An elongate inner and a minute, round outer metatarsal tubercle. Skin somewhat pustular above, minutely granular on gula, slightly more coarsely so on the chest, belly, and midventral aspect of the thigh. A thin ridge on the inner side of the tarsus. A supratympanic ridge. A fold across the chest; in ♀ topotypes a pair of small axillary folds.

SECONDARY SEX CHARACTERS. Full-grown females of *Hyla fuscovaria* generally larger than males; difference in size less marked in some of the large male specimens from the Chaquean Subarea. Nuptial plaques on the chest of males, described by L. Müller and Hellmich (*trachythorax*), were seen by us in specimens from the Paraiba River Valley, also in nine specimens from Rio Grande do Sul, one of them from Porto Alegre, near the coast, the other eight from Santo Augusto, in the western Brazilian Missions. The plaques are not very frequent, generally vestigial, and almost certainly deciduous. Very robust males are deceptively like females in shape. Pigmentation on the edge of the gula variable, more intense in males but traces of it in some females also. Vocal sac also variable. In the off-season, sexual characters not distinct.

VARIATION. The Lutz form from the Atlantic province is used for description here and the small differences between it and the specimens from the other areas are pointed out. Races of this frog, which has a very wide range, may have evolved in the geographically differentiated areas, but subspecific differences are unclear and all the known populations live in similar environments. At present it seems best to lump them together under the species name.

A. *Geographic*: The specimens from the Chaquean subarea (*megapodia, trachythorax*) seen are also large and robust and do not seem very different. The canthus rostralis may be better defined, the skin rougher, the webs on the feet very slightly longer, but all these characters vary individually as well as geographically.

The examples seen from the northern part of the Atlantic area, at the edges of the Hylaea, are large and not very different from the others.

In the *cerrado* country on the plateau, in the states of Minas Gerais and São Paulo, the frogs of this species are slender and have a narrow head and long snout.

This explains the difference in size noted by Cochran between her largest specimens from Misi-

ones (49 mm) and her largest female from Lassance (44 mm snout to vent) on the Rio das Velhas, in the basin of the Rio São Francisco, state of Minas Gerais.

Juveniles are generally slender and similar in build to the frogs from the *cerrado* and plateau. Their legs are mostly proportionately longer but not invariably so, nor over the whole range.

B. *Individual variation*. Not marked. Length of hindlimb slightly variable, the adpressed tibiotarsal articulation reaching some point from in front of the eye to the tip of the snout, generally near the nostril.

COLOR. In the original description and his manuscript notes Lutz states: "Ground color of the back 'café au lait' with numerous dots and a network of dark blotches containing lighter points. Limbs with brown cross-bars on the thighs. A narrow strip at the edge of the belly and on the flanks, the anterior margin of the tarsi and the posterior and interior margin of the legs lemon-colored. The rest of the ventral aspect cream, somewhat pink and mottled with brown, principally on the margin of the jaw." He adds that one male kept alive for some time showed no variation in color and marking. Lutz also mentions that the lemon color may fade during life, that the dark subcanthal stripe, passing over the eye and above the tympanum, is not constant, the tympanum is light brown and the iris golden or bronze yellow. Kaethe and Oswaldo Schmidt put a note to one of their specimens from Goiás stating that the iris was grayish; this probably applies to the lower half, which tends to approach the color of the sides of the head though slightly metallic and rosy.

Cochran (1955) analyzes the tones of a watercolor painted for Lutz by Sandig, according to the first edition of Ridgway. According to the new edition, I would say the dorsal background is drab to light drab, Saccardo's umber or sepia, overlaid by a sepia or clove brown pattern; the rest of the coloring as indicated by Lutz.

Two living males from the Chaquean subarea, caught at Santo Pipó, Misiones, Argentina, October 7, 1965, do not differ essentially in color from the Minas Gerais specimens described by Lutz and Cochran. Dorsal aspect of body and limbs from pale drab or drab to dark almost sepia, with the pattern darker. Tympanum distinctly brown, standing out well from the background. Iris bronze to gold, especially the upper half, the lower inclined to approach the color of the sides of head and slightly rosy; a dark horizontal pseudocolobom across the middle of the eye, a perpendicular notch in the middle of the free rim of the lower half and a slight reticulation on the iris. Flash color lemon-yellow to pale lemon-yellow, forming a minute spot at the axilla and an edge to the flanks and belly, occupying the upper concealed parts of the flanks and thighs, and the inner ventral aspect of the tibia, extending slightly onto the edges of the hind-limb; dark spots on the flanks and thighs. Gula of these two males more pigmented than stated by the authors, in tones similar to those of the dorsal background, the pigment extending slightly onto the anterior part of the chest where the plaques develop; rest of belly whitish; ventral aspect of thighs with a pale brownish, grayish, or purplish suffusion; hands and feet gray, webs mottled.

Dead specimens are either brown or gray, varying greatly in tone and intensity, from quite light, with very marked pattern, to melanistic with the pattern obliterated though sometimes discernible by changing the incidence of light. In melanistic specimens flash colors reduced to minute and not very light dots.

PATTERN. The pattern described by Lutz for *fuscovaria* is much more complex than the usual double, inverted parentheses of the *x-signata* sector of the group. It is composed of a dark network on a lighter background, occupying the dorsal aspect, completed by scattered white dots. The reticulation may be due to fragmentation of the original pattern and coalescence of the fragments.

This pattern is not universal, and many specimens exhibit simplified versions of it. Sometimes the network is incomplete and vestiges of bilateral symmetry are apparent. The original parentheses may be discernible within the reticulation, as in a number of specimens from Santo Augusto in western Rio Grande do Sul. Fragmented parentheses plus ornamental spots also occur. Sometimes both pairs of parentheses remain visible, with or without additional white dots or dark spots. The two elements of each parentheses may also fuse together. In our two living males from Santo Pipó, the anterior pair has coalesced into a large W-shaped scapular spot with the two elements entirely joined in the larger, incompletely so in the smaller example. The posterior pair forms an arched sacral

spot, composed of the two elements that do not join at the top. The large male is dark and shows the white dots described by Lutz; the smaller one is lighter and has a few larger dark marks on the back.

Fragmentation of the posterior pair only is very common, the anterior pair being then followed by a series of fragments. The elements of the anterior pair may remain simple or change their shape. Sometimes they develop an interior prong. When they approach each other and coalesce they may acquire a different shape from the W described above. Sometimes they form a thin, rough chevron reminiscent of the sternal bone of a bird, but irregular and prolonged in front. Occasionally, though not often, the two pairs of parentheses become confluent and produce a central figure wider, thicker, and more irregular than a conventional W.

In juvenile specimens, as mentioned by Lutz, the pattern is generally simple. Both pairs of parentheses are mostly present and have the usual shape. This pattern is also common in the slender and relatively small specimens from the plateau.

The interocular spot is generally narrow and sometimes fragmented into two parts. It may be roughly rectilinear, concave anteriorly, or prolonged backwards forming a V. In this case it may fuse with a chevron-shaped anterior pair (L. Müller and Hellmich figure). Sometimes it's much longer and wider and occupies much more room. This the case of two solitary, aberrant specimens of *Hyla* from the state of Bahia, which otherwise seem nearer to *H. fuscovaria* (*megapodia*) than to any other known form.

The gaps in the known distribution and the differences in number between samples from different places hardly permit definite conclusions as to the geographic distribution of the diverse patterns, the more so as they recur irrespective of finding place. One may venture the following tentative suggestions: reticulate patterns seem more frequent in the Atlantic province than in the Continental province or near the Hylaea. The pattern of fragmented parentheses, figured by Miranda Ribeiro, is common in adults from the Chaquean subarea but was also seen in samples from Paraiba River Valley and from São Bernardo do Campo, between São Paulo and the maritime escarpment. The pattern of narrow stripes with coalesced interocular and anterior pairs of parentheses (Müller and Hellmich) is rare.

The simple pattern with all the elements present is characteristic of juveniles and seems common in the slender, narrow and relatively small specimens from *cerrado* sections of the highlands. Aberrant patterns occur in several places near the eastern limit of the range where the territory of another form is approached.

VOICE. The usual rasping croak of the large forms of the group.

HABITS AND ECOLOGY. This species seems limited to open, nonforested terrain. The adults show the usual tolerance of the whole group for all sorts of diverse environments; thus their peculiar habit of entering human dwellings. One specimen was caught in a shoe in his bedroom by Dr. R. Shannon at Maracajú, Mato Grosso. Kaethe and Oswald Schmidt found theirs in the bathhouse of the Indian post at Aragarças in Goiás. We got some from the wet galleries of the powerhouse at the Açude João Penido, near Juiz de Fora, Minas Gerais. However, they also perched on wet outcrops of rock in the military station at Benfica, near Juiz de Fora, and were found on banana trees, Indian corn, and other vegetation in fields or near streams at Pomba, Minas Gerais. The specimens from the Brazilian National Park at Iguaçu Falls were sitting on the edges of the pond in the horse corral. At Santo Pipó, Misiones, Argentina, they were in an artificial tank. In the northern block of the Serra do Mar, very melanistic specimens with aberrant pattern were got twice inside an ornamental fountain at the head of an artificial lake at Cumary Grange, Teresópolis. In the surrounding forest only *Hyla hayii* was obtained.

KNOWN RANGE. Taken in its widest sense (that is with *megapodia* and *trachythorax* as synonyms), the known range of *H. fuscovaria* is very great. In Brazil it probably covers the whole of the state of Rio Grande do Sul and the nonforested parts of Paraná, since it was obtained on the western frontier and also near the coast in both states. There is however a gap for Santa Catarina in the collections examined. In São Paulo it has been taken near the coast where the rain forest is gone, on all the outskirts of the capital, and in western and northwestern parts of the state. It occupies the Paraiba River Valley, both in São Paulo and the state of Rio de Janeiro. The population at Teresópolis seems isolated. In Minas Gerais this frog has been obtained in a devastated part of the Atlantic province near

Juiz de Fora and at Pomba; also the highlands of Belo Horizonte at the edge of the scrub (alt. 800 ms s/m) and along the semiarid basin, on the São Francisco River system. It reaches the states of Goiás and Bahia. It is common in the Chaquean subarea where in Brazil it extends to Mato Grosso, at least as far north as Porto Espiridião on the Jaurú River and Chavantina. A number of large specimens were got in Goiás, in Aragarças, Santa Maria do Araguaya, Cana Brava, and elsewhere. It also ranges through northern Argentina (Misiones, Tucuman, Jujuy) and Paraguay, to the lower eastern slopes of Bolivia. The degree of genetic divergence between specimens from nonforested sections of the Atlantic province, the Chaquean subprovince and the *cerrado* country on the plateau is unknown. We have seen specimens that agree with it from the state of Pará, north of the Amazonas.

## *Hyla eurydice* Bokermann, 1968

> BOKERMANN, W. C. A. 1968. Three new *Hyla* from the plateau of Maracás, Central Bahia, Brazil. *J. Herp.* 1(1).

*Hyla eurydice* Bokermann, 1968 is certainly a form closely akin to *Hyla fuscovaria* Lutz. It lives in a very differentiated environment, in the scrub section of the Northeastern subarea of the Continental province, at a very high elevation for the region (1,300 m). It may have gone some or all the way toward speciation, but this cannot be ascertained now; morphologically, structurally, and in habit it agrees with *H. fuscovaria* "sensu lato" except for a few details.

Paratype n. 31806, now MNR n. 4050, the only one seen, is a male of average size. The hindlimb is relatively short, but this is an extremely variable feature in Brazilian forms of *Hyla*. The pattern on the dorsal surface is only slightly fragmented and not reticulate, a condition that also occurs elsewhere in the very extensive range of *Hyla fuscovaria* and is occasionally seen as an individual variation in series of specimens from one locality. The fundamental pattern is present, with elongate blunt interocular spot, two pairs of inverted dorsolateral parentheses, and a few additional large dots, but there is no sacral spot; quite regular bars on the permanently visible dorsal aspect of the limbs and minute light dotting on the posterior aspect of the thigh concealed in repose. Tympanum light brown as usual in the group.

MEASUREMENTS (mm). Snout to vent 42. Hindlimb 74: femur 21, tibia 23, tarsus 13, foot 17. Head length to width 14:14, eye 5, eye to nostril <5, tympanum 2.5; interorbital space 4, internarial space >3.

## *Hyla acuminata* Cope, 1862

(*Hyla phrynoderma* Boulenger, 1889)

COPE, E. D. 1862. Catalogue of the reptiles obtained during the explorations of the Parana, Paraguay, Vermejo and Uruguay Rivers by Capt. Thos. J. Page, U.S.N. I, The Paraguay Collection. *J. Ac. Sc. Phila.* 14:346–355. *Hyla acuminata*: 354.

BOULENGER, G. A. 1889. On a collection of batrachians made by Professor Charles Spegazzini at Colonia Resistencia, South Chaco, Argentine Republic. *An. Mus. Stor. Nat. Genova* (27): 246–249, pl. 2. *Hyla phrynoderma*: 248, figs. 3, 3a.

MÜLLER, L., and HELLMICH, W. 1936. Wissenschaftliche Ergebnisse der Deutschen Gran-Chaco Expeditionen. Amphibien u. Reptilien. I Teil: 120 pp., 35 figs., 8 pls., 1 map. *H. phrynoderma*: 70–73, fig. 25.

*Hyla acuminata* was described by Cope in one of the earliest papers on the fauna of the Chaco. The description is quite conventional, and none of the diagnostic characters stand out. It was redescribed as *Hyla phrynoderma* by Boulenger, in connection with another early collection in the Chaco, that of Professor Spegazzini from the La Plata Museum. The description and figure are diagnostic. This is one of the largest forms of the *Hyla rubra–Hyla x-signata* complex, and, once seen, it is recognized immediately.

DIAGNOSTIC CHARACTERS. *Hyla acuminata* is characterized by the large size, robust build, rough skin, and short, very wide disks. The dark dorsal pattern is also characteristic. The interocular spot is triangular, prolonged backward and blunt. The often saddle-shaped sacral spot is somewhat variable. Both it and the relatively narrow and short dorsolateral curved stripes are occasionally quite shadowy so that only a darker outline or black glandular segments of them stand out from the background.

TYPES AND TYPE LOCALITY. Cope indicates the

route followed by the expedition in Paraguay, Argentina, and Brazil but does not specify a type locality. The whole terrain is within the range of the species. Cochran (1961) indicates two cotypes, USNM n. 5843 and 102.700, from Paraguay, leg. Thos. J. Page. Boulenger specifies Resistencia, southern Chaco, Argentina, as type locality; the type specimens are BM 2.12.78 and 2.12.79 leg. Charles Spegazzini.

DESCRIPTION. Size large for the group. Largest specimen seen 45 mm snout to vent. Build very robust. Body somewhat oval, narrowed and slightly acuminate in front, narrowed also beyond the sacrum. Hindlimb moderately long, tibiotarsal articulation reaching between the eye and nostril when the leg is adpressed. Head flat, as long as wide, or slightly longer. Snout ogival; canthus rostralis not marked; loreal region slightly grooved behind the nostrils. Eye fairly large and prominent, its horizontal diameter equal to or slightly shorter than the distance to the nostril. Tympanum large, distinct, three-fourths or three-fifths the diameter of the eye. Nostrils much nearer the tip of the snout than the eye. Interorbital space wider than the internarial space. Tongue large, circular, notched and slightly free behind. Vomerine teeth in two short, stout, contiguous groups between the choanae, which are small. Fingers unwebbed. Disks very short, wide in front, narrowed at the base. An elongate tubercle at the base of the first finger, a double tubercle at the base of the third and fourth fingers. Toes very fully webbed: a fringe on both sides of the first, in some specimens a short fringe outside the fifth toe; webs reaching the base of the disks on the outer side of the second and third and on the inner side of the fifth toe, to the distal subarticular tubercle on the inner side of the second and third and on both sides of the fourth toe; continuing as a fringe to the base of the disks on all three. A moderately distinct, elongate, inner, and a very small, rounded, outer metatarsal tubercle. No tarsal folds or appendages on the heel. Skin of dorsal surface very rough, beset with sharp, minute glandules. Ventral aspect granular, paved. A very strong fold of skin from eye to shoulder, partly screening the tympanum. A fold of skin across the throat, a deeper one, below it, partly covering a pair of short folds from the axillae to the chest.

SECONDARY SEX CHARACTERS. Generally not marked.

Females with eggs may have dots of dark pigment on the throat. The vocal sac of preserved males does not often stand out, though there may be small slightly blacker semicircular folds on the sides of the gula. One male from Porto Esperança, Southern Mato Grosso, has black pigment on the upper part of the gula and large unpigmented folds below.

MEASUREMENTS. Females with eggs seen by us range from 40–44 mm snout to vent, males from 39–43, with one 45 mm long. Unsexed specimens from 35–45 mm, two smaller juveniles, from Ciervo Petizo, Formosa, Argentina, 27 and 28 mm long.

COLOR. The majority of well-preserved Argentinian specimens, seen by us, are gray above with the pattern also gray but much darker than the background. Beneath either off-white and immaculate or, more often, with a dense sprinkling of minute brown dots on the throat and fore part of the chest; this may be present in both females and males.

Some dead specimens are brown, as seen in Paraguayan samples of the German authors. Two Argentinian ones from Formosa (Monte Lindo) IBM 0209, one of them a female, are deep brown instead of gray. Our specimens from southern Mato Grosso are mostly brownish.

PATTERN. Essentially that of the *H. x-signata* sector of the group. Interocular spot large, forming a blunt triangle with the base between the eyes and the narrow part behind them, regular except for an expansion over each eyelid. Sacral spot also large, saddle-shaped (Boulenger), trapezoid (Müller and Hellmich), occasionally prolonged anteriorly into an irregular chevron or developing two horns directed forward, more rarely two short horns at the back; in some specimens with a rather geometrical aspect; sometimes only the glandular border really distinct. Dorsolateral stripes (anterior parentheses) generally well marked, short, curved, or forming a point directed inward, sometimes reduced to a dark glandular cordon or segments of it. Coarse oblique bars across the permanently visible dorsal surfaces of the limbs, alternating with finer and longer lines. Hind part of thigh and other surfaces concealed in repose, more or less marbled on dark reddish brown or brown-orange. The inner aspects of the limbs concealed in repose may show part of this pattern when viewed from beneath. Oblique alternative light and dark areas from the eye and canthus to the edge of the upper jaw. Tympanum rather light brown, contrasting with the other colors of the dorsal surfaces. A dark pseudocolobom across the iris.

HABITS. Specimens collected by me and others at the edge of the Chaco, at Ipuã, near Nueva Italia, Paraguay, were sitting on the wet ground of the great marsh.

AFFINITIES. This species has the morphological characters of the *Hyla rubra–H. x-signata* complex, but it is one of the most differentiated as well as one of the large forms of the group. It is sympatric with the much smaller *Hyla nasica* and also with the equally large but quite different *Hyla fuscovaria* in part of the much wider range of the latter.

DISTRIBUTION. *H. acuminata* belongs to the fauna of Continental Depression, which I call the Chaquean subprovince of the Continental province of South America. It has not been found in the highlands nor in the northeastern subprovince of the same province.

I have seen specimens from Chaco, Formosa, Misiones, Corrientes, and Santa Fé in Argentina, Asuncion, and Ipuã, near Nueva Italia, in Paraguay, Miranda, Salobra, Porto Esperança and São Luiz de Caceres in southern Mato Grosso, Brazil.

## *Hyla hayii* Barbour, 1909

> BARBOUR, T. 1909. Some new South American cold-blooded vertebrates. *Pr. New Engl. Zool. Club* 4:47–52, pls. 4–5 *Hyla hayii*: 51, pl. 5, lower figure.
>
> BARBOUR, T. and LOVERIDGE, A. 1929. Typical reptiles and amphibians in the Museum of Comparative Zoology. *Bull. Mus. Comp. Zool.* 69: 205–360. *Hyla hayii*: 278.

Typical *Hyla hayii* are large but seem nearer to the *Hyla rubra* than to the *Hyla x-signata* sector of the complex. Although described early in the century it has only been collected more abundantly since work in the montane rain forest of the Brazilian coastal serras was intensified by A. Lutz and B. Lutz.

DIAGNOSTIC CHARACTERS. The size plus the broad, heavy build, the plain, olivaceous-green or brown color of the dorsal aspect, often devoid of pattern, and the apparently thick, glandular, skin; the distinctive yellow ocelli on the concealed parts of the flanks and limbs, especially the upper posterior part of the thigh; the range, along the rain forest zone of the coastal mountains, and the habitat, in bromeliads. Differs from the other large species of the group by the absent or vestigial dorsal pattern, the ocellar pattern of the concealed parts and the distribution. Specimens from the more southern part of the range mostly with some pattern on the dorsal aspect; smaller in size. (See Southern Form.)

TYPE AND TYPE LOCALITY. Petrópolis, state of Rio de Janeiro.

DESCRIPTION. Based on female allotype ALC 3941. Quitandinha, Petrópolis: size, 43 mm snout to vent. Build robust. Body heavy, as wide as the head in postaxillary region, narrowed beyond the sacrum. Hindlimb fairly long, the tibiotarsal articulation reaching almost to the nostril when the leg is adpressed. Head large, slightly longer than wide. Snout rounded from above, pointed in front; rounded and slanting back to the mouth opening in profile. Canthus rostralis inevident. Loreal region almost flat, oblique. Nostrils slightly raised, superolateral, opening above, placed at approximately two-thirds of the distance from the eye to the tip of the snout. Eye large, prominent, its horizontal diameter slightly longer than the distance to the nostril and equal to about two-thirds the distance from the tip of the snout. Tympanum rounded, distinct, two-fifths the diameter of the eye. Interorbital space wider than the internarial space. Tongue very wide, almost circular, notched and free behind. Vomerine teeth in two short, transverse groups, close together, between the choanae. Fingers webbed at the base. Disks short, very wide. A large tubercle under the first finger, a similar, bifid, one under the third and fourth fingers. A glandular ridge on the outside of the hand to the first subarticular tubercle of the fourth finger. Toes four-fifths webbed. A narrow fringe on the inner side of the first, to the subarticular tubercle; on inner side web wide to first subarticular tubercle of the second toe, to second tubercle of the third; to penultimate, on both sides of the fourth; wide to below the disk on the outer side of the second and third and on the fifth toe. A glandular ridge on the outside of the foot, continuing as a fringe to the fifth toe. An elongate inner, a smaller outer metatarsal tubercle; rows of minute palmar and plantar tubercles. A faint glandular ridge on the inner side of the tarsus; a short supratympanic ridge; a mass of glandules behind the tympanum and the upper corner of the mouth. Skin of dorsal aspect beset with glandules. A fold across the chest, covering a pair of short axillary folds. Skin of gula minutely granular, of belly and midventral aspect of thigh more coarsely so.

VARIATION. Extremes of size are rather far apart, but most specimens fall within average limits. Build generally heavy and robust; the author has seen few slender adults. Hindlimb variable in length; the adpressed tibiotarsal articulation reaching between the nostril and eye in most specimens, to the former in a few, only to the latter in a larger number, especially females. Head mostly 1 or 2 mm longer than wide but some individuals short-headed; snout often rounded in outline instead of forming a point in front. In some specimens canthi rostrales evident though blunt. Teeth seldom slightly separate, sometimes practically contiguous, often near the posterior edge of the choanae. Tongue sometimes narrower, more elongate, entire or hardly emarginate. Glandular outer ridges of hand and foot, especially the latter, not equally well developed in all individuals. Size of tympanum slightly variable; in some individuals the supratympanic ridge covers its upper part.

SECONDARY SEX CHARACTERS. Females much larger than males; hindlimb generally relatively shorter, the tibiotarsal articulation reaching only to eye or just in front of it. Concealed pattern often very extensive and very marked; gula frequently dotted in dark. Males smaller, extremes of size less wide apart. Outer edge of the first finger thickened into a light pad at the nuptial period, forearms sometimes thick.

MEASUREMENTS. Females 43–49 mm snout to vent; an exceptionally large one, from Teresópolis, 53 mm snout to vent. Other large specimens: Estação Biológica at Alto da Serra, São Paulo, 1 female, USNM 97780, 49 mm fide Cochran; from Boracéa, outside São Paulo MNR 2886, 48 mm; another from Parati, southern part of the state of Rio de Janeiro MNR 1463, 47 mm long. Males average 39 or 40 mm to 42 mm snout to vent length. Size at metamorphosis 14 mm, or slightly more, head and body length.

COLOR AND PATTERN. In life distinctly olivaceous above, mostly olive green, sometimes olive yellow or brown. Tympanum a more vivid brown, edge of upper lip light, minutely dotted in dark. Iris buff with golden sheen, dark equatorial pseudocolobom, black reticulation toward the periphery and small median notch on the free edge of the lower rim.

Dorsal color generally uniform. Bright, rounded, lemon-yellow ocelli on the hind part of the flank and dorsal aspect of the limbs concealed in repose, especially the posterior part of the thigh; sometimes a similar ocellus at the edge of the upper arm. In very ornate specimens the concealed pattern sometimes visible from beneath and continued onto the inner ventral aspect of leg, occasionally onto the dorsal aspect of the tarsus and of the inner toes, all of them concealed in repose. Sides, at edges of pattern, tinged with lemon yellow. Ventral aspect immaculate. Gula of male yellow. In females white, dotted with brown, the dots sometimes extensive to the chest or sides of the body and ventral aspect of the thigh. Belly opaque, white. Lower aspect of the limbs somewhat violaceous. Webs mottled. Ventral edge of thigh similar to the edge of the upper lip. Ocelli on thigh, either rounded and disposed in one row, seldom in two, or horizontally elongate, as if confluent, with a wavy outline derived from the darker background. On flank mostly one elongate oblique ocellus, sometimes others continuing onto the ocelli or light areas of anterior upper aspect of thigh.

Examples from the northern block of the Serra do Mar, including the type locality, are generally devoid of pattern on the permanently visible dorsal aspect, though an obscure mark on the shoulders is mentioned in the original description, and a few specimens show shadowy vestiges of pattern on the back, often just darker areas. In life the pattern seems to be evanescent, and its presence or absence in dead specimens is dependent on the condition of the chromatophores at the time of fixation. A number of specimens from further south are also devoid of dorsal pattern. This is the case of the large female from Parati mentioned above and of some other large females from the biological stations at Boracéa and Alto da Serra, outside the city of São Paulo; also of two small females, one from the Serra da Bocaina and another from Rio Vermelho, in northern Santa Catarina which though only 40 mm long are the largest specimens seen from their finding places. All these females have the flash pattern of ocelli on the thigh very marked and continued onto the ventral aspect of the leg. There is, however, a trend toward greater fre-

quency and distinctness of dorsal pattern in the southern part of the range. (See Geographic Variation.)

VOICE. A rasping croak like in other species of the group: *kraw, kraw* fide Cochran.

ECOLOGY. *Hyla hayii* is a species from the eastern coastal mountains. Adults have been found asleep in bromeliads in daytime and sitting on their outer edges, or near pools and still reaches of rivers at night. They probably live in the bromeliads near the edge of the forest and breed in lentic waters. Juveniles have been caught climbing up the vegetation not far from water at night, for instance on *Hedychium coronarium* outside the Organ Mountains National Park.

KNOWN RANGE. The collections examined by the author comprise specimens from both ends of the Serra do Mar and from places between them, in the states of Rio de Janeiro, São Paulo, Paraná, and in northern Santa Catarina; also one solitary specimen, whose origin may be open to doubt, labeled Sernambetiba, in the state of Guanabara. Under the circumstances, it seems justifiable to extend the range of *Hyla hayii* "sensu lato" to the whole of the Serra do Mar and possibly to the Mantiqueira as there are a few specimens from the Itatiaia National Park on that Serra, across the valley of the Paraíba River, from the Serra da Bocaina, which is part of the Serra do Mar.

GEOGRAPHIC VARIATION. The main trends of geographic variation are toward decrease of size and the presence of a distinct pattern on the dorsal aspect.

### SOUTHERN PART OF RANGE

SIZE. The differences of size are very great. The largest females from the samples of small individuals (40 mm) are smaller than the largest males of those from the other localities (42 mm). A cline toward reduction of size is, however, not apparent. The only samples composed of small individuals seen are one from the Serra da Bocaina in the northern part of the state of São Paulo and all those from the most southern part of the range, i. e., northern Santa Catarina. South of the Bocaina there occur populations comprising very large individuals; at both the biological stations outside the city of São Paulo and those from the Itatiaia and Bituruna, Paraná, they are of normal size.

PATTERN. The larger samples from the parts of

the range of *Hyla hayii* south of the northern block comprise many individuals with a dorsal pattern, but they also comprise some without any pattern on the back, possibly with a tendency to absence of dorsal pattern and presence of good concealed pattern in the larger individuals, most of them females. Samples of three populations are discussed below:

## ALTO DA SERRA, SÃO PAULO

The frequency and distinctness of the *H. rubra–H. x-signata* pattern, or elements of it, on the back is not allied to decrease of size in the samples from the Biological Station at Alto da Serra de Cubatão. The variations of pattern and of certain morphological details are fully discussed by Cochran (1955). The main patterns are obscure reticulation on the back, and slightly curved dorsolateral stripes, generally with a distinct triangular interocular spot that may be prolonged backward and joined to a large W-shaped scapular mark instead of the stripes. These patterns reappear in the Serra da Bocaina and Rio Vermelho and in other specimens from Alto da Serra. This sample also comprises some melanistic specimens, with very dark brown dorsal aspect and the ocelli on the concealed surfaces very much reduced. Our smaller sample from the Biological Station at Boracea, also outside the city of São Paulo, does not show dorsal marks like those from Alto da Serra.

Melanistic individuals occur elsewhere also; one from the Ilha Grande, state of Rio, is almost devoid of ocelli; however, another very dark example from the Itatiaia has quite small but very bright ocelli. Some individuals are devoid of ocelli without being very dark. (Specimen from Angra dos Reis, MNR). A living frog from Bituruna, Paraná, kept alive in the vivarium for many months, shows only minute light intervals on a blended green-brown background on the thigh and nothing on the flank. There is a very distinct dark subcanthal stripe, a triangular interocular spot, a pair of rather indistinct dorsolateral curved stripes and an obscure sacral spot, plus indistinct spots on the permanently visible dorsal surfaces of the limbs varying in sharpness. It is probably quite typical for the southern livery.

## SERRA DA BOCAINA

Our specimens are small. Three females measure 42, 40, and 37 mm snout to vent, and the males are 35 or 36 mm long. The hindlimb is mostly short, but this may be partly a function of size. In one of the larger females the adpressed tibiotarsal articulation reaches between the eye and the nostril but in the others only to the eye. Canthus rostralis blunt but more marked than in the northern specimens. Glandular outer edge of hand and foot and corner of mouth less evident. Tongue either entire or with a very shallow notch; vomerine teeth sometimes slightly apart. Interocular spot, vestiges of curved dorsolateral stripes in most specimens but not in the largest female; generally also oblique spots or bars on the permanently visible aspect of the limbs. Pattern on the concealed dorsal aspect of the thigh not ocellar, but more elaborate, with the light intervals separated by incomplete, perpendicular dark stripes, coming from two horizontal dark areas, below and above. Flash color of the flank less spot-like, more general, but interrupted by dark arabesques.

Unless the specimens collected are smaller than the usual run of Bocaina adults, the Serra da Bocaina population seems to be differentiating away from the nominate form by size and the other characters mentioned above.

## NORTHERN SANTA CATARINA

The specimens from northern Santa Catarina seen are composed of small and mostly slender individuals, many of them with some pattern on the permanently visible dorsal aspect. Our largest sample comprises forty-five specimens, thirty-six males, one female with eggs plus eight smaller specimens without sex characters, probably immature females. They come from Rio Vermelho, outside São Bento do Sul. They are mostly so different from the large northern specimens that one is tempted to regard them and those from the Bocaina as a separate polytopic subspecies. One must however consider the following facts: (a) similarity in build and concealed pattern between the largest southern adult female (40 mm long), a completely typical one from Parati state of Rio de Janeiro, which is 47 mm snout to vent, and other large females from the northern block; (b) similarity in dorsal pattern between small Santa Catarina specimens and large individuals from the biological station at Alto da Serra, São Paulo, including one female 48 mm long; (c) small size of the specimens from the Serra da Bocaina, north of places where large specimens occur; (d) the presence of melanistic specimens in populations both of large and small-sized individuals south of the northern block of the Serra do Mar.

DIFFERENTIAL CHARACTERS. The Santa Catarina specimens differ from the typical ones in the following characters: size considerably smaller, build slender, much less robust. Largest female 40 mm. Males 33–35 mm on an average, extremes 30 and 38 mm snout to vent. Dorsal pattern more evident.

The following unpublished note by A. Lutz mentions seeing many specimens of the *Hyla rubra* group from São Bento do Sul and probably refers to living examples of this form: "Color very variable, dorsal aspect smooth, rarely glandular. Size up to 40 mm. When the background is not very dark, a dark canthal stripe, a sinuous line from eye to shoulder, passing above the tympanum, an interocular spot, two elongate longitudinal ones from the scapular region backwards and a chevron-shaped one pointing forward on the lumbar region, insular, citrine spots separated by a blackish background on the concealed parts of flanks, anterior part of thigh and tibia and dorsal posterior aspect of thigh. Anterior border of gular region with or without dark dots. External vocal sac large, [tongue] slightly emarginate on posterior border. Gular region finely, belly coarsely granular; a semilunar fold from axilla. Fingers not, but toes extensively webbed. Bars on dorsal aspect of limbs inconstant. A frequent species over an extensive range especially in the South."

COLOR AND PATTERN. Dorsal color of preserved southern specimens: light gray, gray-brown, light brown and dark brown. Some dorsal pattern present in most specimens. Most common pattern: a more or less distinct, triangular, pointed or blunt, interocular spot and a pair of curved dorso-lateral stripes. In three specimens interocular spot more or less fused with a large W-shaped spot (as in some of the Alto da Serra specimens). One male with inverted Y-shaped sacral spot. Another with white dots; two stippled in dark. Concealed part of flank with dark arabesques on light area. One male with only dark dots on the flanks. Large female without any pattern on the back. The usual round ocelli of *H. hayii* present only in this specimen, which has two rows on the posterior concealed part of the thigh, and one row on the anterior part of the thigh; pattern continued onto the ventral aspect of the leg. In the other specimens, the dark background predominates over the light ocelli, which

are small, minute, or absent, and round, elongate, or almost angular. In one male, a deep yellow color on ocelli is still present after fifteen years.

The other samples from northern Santa Catarina comprise fewer specimens. They are in general agreement with the large series from Rio Vermelho and with Lutz's note, but some individuals are slightly larger and more robust like those from the Serra da Bocaina and have a slightly rougher, more glandular skin.

These southern specimens thus have some but not all characters in common with those seen from the Serra da Bocaina, which are also small, though slightly more robust and with a divergent concealed pattern.

## *Hyla longilinea* B. Lutz, 1968

LUTZ, B. 1968. New Brazilian Forms of Hyla. Texas Memorial Museum. The Pearce-Sellards Series 10:18. *Hyla longilinea*: 5–8, fig. 3.

A unique specimen of a relatively large *Hyla* of streamlined, *Eleutherodactylus*-like, build was obtained during field work by the Institute of Biophysics of the Federal University of Rio de Janeiro, the National Museum, and the U. S. Atomic Energy Commission in the naturally radioactive area round Poços de Caldas.

DIAGNOSTIC CHARACTERS. Relatively large size, long-lined build, with elongate head and snout and long hindlimbs; permanently visible parts of the dorsal aspect very pustular. Morphological details rather similar to those of *Hyla acuminata* Cope (*phrynoderma* Blgr.) of the *Hyla rubra–H. x-signata* complex. Differs by the larger size, long-lined build, thinner and longer hindlimbs, longer, less acuminate snout and apparently still rougher dorsal surface. Differs from *Hyla fuscovaria* by the different habit, texture of the skin and pattern.

TYPE AND TYPE LOCALITY. Holotype ♀, now MNR n. 4060, collected by Heber Nobrega da Cunha, December 17, 1963, in daytime, at the Water Reservoir of Morro de São Domingos, Poços de Caldas, Minas Gerais. 21° 50′ 20″ S. 46° 33′ 53″ W., 1,200–1,300 m altitude.

DESCRIPTION. Female, 48 mm long, somewhat bent. Build long-lined, somewhat spindle-shaped, attenuated in front from the tympanic region to the tip of the snout, tapering more sharply behind, from sacrum to anal region. Hindlimb relatively long, the adpressed tibiotarsal articulation reaching the nostril. Head massive, longer than wide, with a slight depression between the eyes. Body robust, almost as wide as the head at the shoulders. Snout very long, oval in outline from above, sloping slightly to the mouth opening in profile. Canthus rostralis fairly distinct; loreal region grooved behind the nostril. Nostril subcanthal, small, not terminal but much further from the eye than from the tip of the snout. Eye moderate in preserved type; very slightly longer in diameter than the distance to the nostril, shorter than the distance to the tip of the snout. Tympanum slightly oblique, its transverse diameter about one-third the diameter of the eye. Interorbital space wider than internarial space. Tongue very large, fleshy, rounded but distinctly notched and somewhat free behind. Vomerine teeth in two small groups between the choanae, as usual in the *Hyla rubra–H. x-signata* complex. A bare trace of web between the fingers. A callosity at the edge of the first, a flat, bifid tubercle under the third and fourth fingers. Disks wide, short, rounded in front, constricted behind; that of the first finger relatively smaller than the others. Toes rather fully webbed; a narrow fringe on the inner side of the first and on the outer side of the fifth; web wide to below the disk on the outer side of the second, third and on the fifth, to the penultimate articulation on the inner side of the second and third and on both sides of the fourth toe. Disks slightly smaller than those of the fingers. A small inner and a minute outer metatarsal tubercle. Faint ridges on tarsus and forearm; glandules, but no real appendix, on heel. Skin of dorsal surface rough on all the parts of the body and limbs visible in repose except on the thigh, seeming rougher to the touch than that of *Hyla acuminata*. A very marked supratympanic ridge from eye to shoulder; glandular ridges in lieu of the apparently much fragmented dorsolateral stripes and sacral spot. Disseminated pustules all over the head, upper eyelid, back, sides of the body, and limb segments visible in repose. No distinct fold across the chest. Skin of gula, chest, belly, and midventral strip of the thigh granular, as if paved.

MEASUREMENTS (mm). Holotype ♀: 48 from snout to vent. Hindlimb 84: femur 23, tibia 25, tarsus 16, foot 20. Head length to width: 19:17. Eye-snout 8, eye 6, eye-nostril 5, tympanum 2, interorbital space approximately 5, internarial space 4.

COLOR AND PATTERN. Dorsal surface medium brown, pattern and pustules very much darker. Interocular spot prolonged backward, bluntly triangular, bifid, with a faint light halo in front and a central pustule in the middle of the anterior border. The usual curved, inverted (left to right) parentheses-like, dorsolateral stripes and the sacral spot much fragmented, the segments disposed over the back with a certain bilateral symmetry, very glandular, beset with large-based pustules. Subcanthal stripe and supratympanic ridge similar; faint, alternatively light and dark oblique areas from the eye to the edge of the mouth. Tympanum rather light brown, as usual in the whole group. Thigh smooth, without dark bars (present in *acuminata*) but with a very minute marbling in non-contrasted tones of brown, the lighter spots slightly larger and more horizontally disposed in the posterior portion, concealed in repose. Edges of pattern on limbs not very marked when viewed from beneath.

Unfortunately no ecological or other notes were sent with the specimen, which was not seen alive.

AFFINITIES. This solitary specimen is very streamlined in appearance. The name was suggested by Prof. G. A. Lutz by derivation from the terminology of the Italian typologists, who divide humans into a long-lined and a short-lined type. This is exactly the impression gained when the new form is compared to the females of *Hyla acuminata*, which seem nearest to it in skin surface and pattern. Despite the acuminate snout, these are shorter (40–44 mm) and more squat, with the plump legs so often seen in the *H. rubra–H. x-signata* complex; the tibiotarsal articulation fails to reach the nostril and often it does not go much beyond the anterior corner of the eye. The difference in build of *H. longilinea* is impressive. In size it contrasts with all but the largest specimens of *Hyla fuscovaria*, which is smoother, more rounded in outline, and less flattened. In Brazilian forms of *Hyla* the morphological details seem to be group characters rather than specific ones; in this particular the shape and position of the vomerine teeth, the shape of the tongue, and the shape of the disks agree with those of the group.

The finding place is very different from the range of *Hyla acuminata*, which belongs to the fauna of the Chaco, i. e. the Continental Depression. *H. longilinea* was taken in the southeastern orographic system, albeit somewhat far from the coast. *H. fuscovaria* has a very extensive range that in part covers the coastal mountains. The type locality of *Hyla longilinea* is at a much greater altitude, in a location where the forest has been preserved. A second, juvenile, specimen was found much later than the holotype.

## RACES OF *HYLA X-SIGNATA* SPIX

The forms described next differ from the large species by their modest size and build and their short hindlimbs. A slight constriction behind the head is often evident.

These forms are very closely allied to *Hyla x-signata* Spix. Most of their morphological characters are very similar, but some slight differences obtain as to pattern and in one case at least as to call. Each occupies a particular area, though the limits with the adjacent areas are not accurately known. Pending further investigation, the Spix form is taken as the nominate subspecies and the others as geographical races of it. The apparent differences are as follows:

*Hyla x-signata x-signata* Spix
  Northeastern subprovince of the Continental province
  Size moderate (30 mm); build exiguous, average, or robust
  Dorsal pattern very distinct double parentheses
  Flash color evident, horizontal spots in a dark net
  Call like winding of a stout watch

*Hyla x-signata nasica* Cope
  Chaquean subprovince of the Continental province
  Size average; build average; constriction at the neck often marked
  Dorsal pattern less well defined, second parentheses sometimes absent
  Flash colors modest
  Call like the tapping out of Morse code

*Hyla x-signata similis* Cochran
  Coastal lowlands of the states of Guanabara and Rio de Janeiro
  Size average; build not subexiguous, more or less robust
  Trend toward fragmentation of dorsal pattern anastomosis and coalescence into a network with white dots, halos, or areas

Flash color in small spots on concealed surfaces, tapestry-like
  Call: *crack crack*

*Hyla eringiophila*
  Eastern lowlands of Platine province: Argentina, Uruguay, and southern Brazil
  Size slightly larger (36 mm); build robust
  Dorsal pattern often bold, but variable; some individuals melanistic or like *similis* or *nasica*
  Flash color orange (f. Gallardo)
  Call: *trac trac* (f. Gallardo)

*Hyla camposseabrai* Bokermann
  Plateau of Maracás, Bahia 1,300 m elevation
  Size very exiguous; build *Engystoma*-like
  Melanistic (only specimen seen)
  Light marbling on concealed surfaces, very marked
  Call unknown

## *Hyla x-signata x-signata* Spix, 1824

> SPIX, J. B. VON. 1824. *Animalia nova, sive species novae testudinum et ranarum, quas in itinere per Brasiliam, annis 1817–20 . . . collegit et descripsit.* Atlas 22 pls. *Hyla x-signata*: tab. XI, fig. 3.
>
> PETERS, C. W. H. 1872. Ueber die von Spix in Brasilien gesammelte Batrachier des Koenigl. Naturalien-Kabinets zu Muenchen. *Mtsb. d. Akad. Wiss. Berlin*: 166–227.

*Hyla x-signata x-signata*, from which the specific name is derived, is the earliest described form of the group with inverted parentheses-shaped dorsal pattern. Nevertheless, the description does not tally entirely with the diagnostic characters and can be applied almost as well to some of the other forms of the same group.

DESCRIPTION (translation of original). "Body subexiguous, above pale brownish, subgranular, beneath immaculate, yellowish-greenish. Head flat, subacute, above with a fuscous band between the eyes, on the sides black-striped between the eyes and the nostrils which are approximate, behind the tympanum fuscous spots. Upper jaw with two fuscous stripes; back marked by two X-shaped spots, anterior and posterior; hypochondriae substriped in fuscous, fore and hind feet [limbs] fuscomaculate above; digits raniform, subfringed, posterior ones subpalmate. Length of body 1 1/2′.

"Habitat in the Province of Bahia."

This description does not fit all individuals. Small and slender ones may be called subexiguous, but some well-grown specimens are very robust. The digits are not raniform, but rather inclined to be short and they are provided with short but very wide disks. A short basal membrance occurs on the lateral fingers of many specimens, and the feet are more than one-half webbed. The length of the body is accurate for the average, as this form falls in the 30 mm class, mostly toward its middle.

DIAGNOSTIC CHARACTERS. The size plus the distinct, X-shaped dorsal pattern composed of two pairs of inverted parentheses-like marks and the distribution. Morphological characters those of the group.

*H. x-signata* differs from *Hyla fuscovaria (trachythorax)* by the smaller size, much shorter legs, and less fragmented pattern. Distribution partly sympatric, largely allopatric. Juveniles very similar, but the legs of juvenile *x-signata* are generally shorter than those of the other species. It differs from *Hyla x-signata nasica* by the shorter, wider, triangular and truncate snout, the better defined pattern, the slightly shorter web and the more uniform relative length of the hindlimb; it grows larger; some specimens approach *Hyla x-signata similis* from southeastern Brazil in pattern. Geographic limits of each subspecies not very clear.

TYPES AND TYPE LOCALITY. Spix limits himself to the laconic: "Habitat in Provincia Bahiae," which is a very large state. The types at Munich, which I did not see, were destroyed during the Second World War.

DESCRIPTION. Size relatively small to medium for the group. Adults from 29–39 mm snout to vent, occasionally less, seldom more. Average 35 mm. Build slender or robust. Head plane, body not very elongate, separated from the head by a slight constriction. Hindlimb short, tibiotarsal articulation reaching the eye when adpressed. Thighs and legs often plump. Snout forming a blunt, fairly wide, triangle between the eyes and nostrils, projecting slightly over the mouth in profile. Nostrils subterminal. Horizontal diameter of the eye equal to its distance from the nostril. Tympanum half the diameter of the eye. Interorbital space approximately one-third wider than the internarial space. Tongue large, rounded, almost entire, somewhat free behind. Vomerine teeth in two short patches between the choanae. A rudiment of web between the lat-

eral fingers. A tubercle under the first, a larger, double, tubercle under the third and fourth fingers. Subarticular tubercles well-developed, palms padded. Disks short, very wide in front. An elongate, inner, a very small, or absent, outer metatarsal tubercle. A fringe of web on the proximal side of the first toe. Wide part of web relatively straight, the last joint, or more than the last joint, fringed on the inner side of the second and third and on both sides of the fourth; on the fifth toe the web reaches below the disk. Dorsal surface subgranular, with minute scattered pustules; beneath granular, more coarsely so on belly and midventral aspect of the thigh. A supratympanic fold and a pectoral fold partly covering a pair of short folds from the axillae.

SECONDARY SEX CHARACTERS. A surprisingly large number of specimens, some of them well-grown without evident secondary sex characters, which seem to be apparent only at the nuptial period. One solitary male from Joazeiro, Bahia, and three out of a series of twenty-eight from Mucuripe, Ceará, show vestiges of nuptial plaques on the chest. Vocal sacs from large to medium or quite discreet. Females with eggs hard and stout, in some the abdomen one-third wider than the head. Average size of males and females similar; 35 mm in a large series of twenty-two females and thirty-one males from Mucuripe, Ceará. One or two females 41 mm snout to vent; largest males 37–39 mm long.

COLOR AND PATTERN (based on two living specimens from Maceió, Alagoas). One yellowish gray above, the other olive gray; pattern much darker than the background. Iris golden with some dendritic black marks and a horizontal pseudocolobom between the subcanthal and supratympanic stripe. Tympanum light brown. Aspects of thigh and flank concealed in repose with bright yellow flash-colored spots.

Pattern composed of two pairs of thick parentheses-like spots on the back, a dark subcanthal stripe prolonged above the tympanum; bars, or bar-like, spots on the permanently visible dorsal aspects of the limbs and a dark more or less open reticulum surrounding the flash-colored spots on the parts concealed in repose. Webs mottled in diverse tones of gray. Interocular band narrow, slightly prolonged backward in the middle. Yellowish gray individual with a somewhat angular anterior pair of parentheses curved inward and up-ward in the middle, outward behind; posterior pair short, oblique outwards; bars on legs forming elon-gate irregular spots; flash color on thigh disposed horizontally and separated into spots by dark reti-culum, which is very open on the flanks. Gray individual with short angular anterior parentheses; the posterior ones angular outward in front but prolonged slightly inward into a narrower more vertical hind part; a few additional dark dots. Bars on limbs complete, flash color deeper and more continuous than in the other individual.

Although the pattern is more distinct and con-stant than in *Hyla x-signata nasica,* some variation occurs. The interocular spot may be prolonged backward, becoming bluntly triangular. The an-terior pair of parentheses may have a thin anterior part and a pronged thicker posterior portion. The posterior pair may be absent or slightly frag-mented. There may be additional ornamental marks on the back or a certain degree of anastomosis and confluence, approaching the network of *H. x-s. similis.* A white halo or lighter area may surround the parentheses, or there may be a sprinkling of discrete white dots on the back.

The spots on the concealed dorsal aspect of the thighs are also slightly variable. Horizontally elon-gated ones are as often present as round ones and the size of the spots also varies. In some preserved specimens the flash color becomes a brilliant opaque white. The dark reticulum may be more or less open and formed of curved lines, or it may be confluent into a thick horizontal part behind, giv-ing rise to vertical bars, coincident with those on the permanently visible parts. On the flanks they are generally open and in some cases much re-duced, like in *Hyla x-s. nasica,* the light area thus becoming more or less continuous. The two stripes from eye to maxilla mentioned by Spix are present in only two specimens, one from Januaria, Minas, and one from Maranguape, Ceará. Some have an indistinct mottling on light ground instead of it, for instance seven males from Mucuripe, Ceará.

VOICE. Somewhat similar to the winding of a largish clock.

HABITS. *H. x-s. x-signata,* like the other forms of the *H. rubra–Hyla x-signata* complex, belongs to the large majority of tree-frogs breeding in stand-ing water. It has been caught calling on vegetation above ponds (Maceió) and small pools (Paulo Afonso) by the author. It has also been collected under rotten pieces of wood in the *caatinga* forma-tion by A. L. Carvalho and Bailey (São Francisco Valley) and in a roadside ditch and under torn bark of maniçoba, (Maranguape, Ceará) by Marian Cutler.

VARIATION. The usual trivial variation occurs, such as the degree of approximation between the patches of vomerine teeth and the notching of the tongue, but not to a very marked degree. The length of the hindlimb varies as in other kinds of *Hyla* but less so than usual. In most specimens the adpressed tibiotarsal articulation reaches the eye; it seldom fails to do so and reaches slightly in front of the anterior corner in a few full-grown indi-viduals. Still fewer have longer legs, with the tibio-tarsal articulation reaching between eye and nos-tril. Some specimens from Ceará and our three most northern ones from Maranhão are long-legged. In small specimens the snout and hindlimb seem pro-portionally longer than in adults, but the hindlimb does not reach the snout as in many specimens of *Hyla* (*megapodia*) of similar or even larger size.

The numerous specimens observed vary greatly as to build, so much so that at first one is inclined to believe that two different forms are present. There are two main builds, slender "subexiguous" specimens, agreeing with the definition of Spix, and large, robust individuals very unlike them. Further examination shows that robust large individuals have been collected together with small slender ones, or in the same locality, and that some of the samples and many of the specimens from the north-eastern states of Pernambuco, Ceará, Paraiba, and Rio Grande do Norte are intermediate.

The subexiguous specimens are mostly small; some are medium, though a very few large indi-viduals are also slender. The subexiguous speci-mens often have the dorsal pattern similar to that described by Spix, i. e. two pairs of inverted, pa-rentheses-like (X-shaped) spots on the back, a nar-row interocular band, a stripe from nostril to eye and over the tympanum and bars on the legs. The two dark stripes from the eyes to the maxilla men-tioned by Spix are generally not evident, but some specimens have a mottling instead of it. Preserved specimens of this build, especially small ones, are often pale, with the dorsal pattern obsolescent and that of the concealed aspect of the thighs still more difficult to perceive. Juveniles are often pustular with minute warts scattered on dorsal surface, especially on the head. Our smallest subexiguous specimens are 22, 23, 24, or 25 mm long. The largest, relatively slender one, found together with other very robust ones, is 38 mm from snout to vent (Januaria, Minas Gerais).

The robust specimens are mostly large (35 to 40 mm snout to vent). They have a wide, short, triangular snout, a slight constriction behind the head, and a stout body. The hindlimbs are also relatively robust with plump thighs and legs. The pattern is often very pronounced, with thick parentheses on a grayish or yellowish gray ground, very distinctive flash-colored spots, often elongated horizontally, on the concealed aspect of the thigh and bars or spots on the permanently visible ones.

Between these two extremes there are many specimens which are neither exiguous nor stout. Our largest samples from Mucuripe, Ceará (MNR 1678), composed of nineteen females and twenty-eight males, indicates an average size of 35 mm for both sexes without either a subexiguous or a very robust build. Most of the other specimens from Ceará, Rio Grande do Norte, and Pernambuco are medium also.

DISTRIBUTION. The known distribution indicates that *Hyla x-s. x-signata* belongs to the fauna of the northeastern Brazilian subarea of what I call the Continental province of South America, and taken here to include the medium and lower basin of the Rio São Francisco. The very few specimens from its upper course with a slightly less arid climate (Pirapora, Minas Gerais), though carefully compared with this subspecies, seem to belong to *H. x-s. nasica*, like those from Belo Horizonte. The gaps in the areas do not permit a closer approximation than this.

The range of the nominate subspecies may lie approximately between 16° and 5° S. and 36–46 W. Gr., within medium annual temperatures of 24–26° C, an annual thermic amplitude of 3–5° C, rainfall from 200 to below 1,000 mm in the subarid climate, with *caatinga* vegetation, which is classified as *Bsh* by Brazilian geographers, following Köppen. The subspecies may occur near maritime scrub vegetation, and at the periphery of its range it approaches subareas with tropical climate classified as *Aw* and with *cerrado* vegetation. This is characterized by greater rainfall and a more regular rainy season.

We have specimens from the following states and localities:

Minas Gerais: Januaria, on the Rio São Francisco.

Bahia: Bom Jesus da Lapa, Rio São Francisco, Joazeiro, Rio São Francisco, Barreiras on the Rio Grande, tributary of the São Francisco.

Pernambuco: Petrolina, Rio São Francisco, opposite Joazeiro; Recife and suburbs, Dois Irmãos, Jequiá, Ipiranga, Alagoas de Baixo and Afogados; Tapera, Bonito.

Alagoas: Maceió, Paulo Afonso, on the Rio São Francisco.

Paraíba: Soledade, Juazeirinho, Acauã, Praia Timbaú, João Pessoa.

Rio Grande do Norte: Natal, São Paulo do Potengi.

Ceará: Mucuripe, Iguatu, Maranguape, Fortaleza, Chapada de Araripe. The last place is high and the solitary specimen is small and atypical.

Maranhão: São João dos Patos.

Pará: Belém. A few specimens from the capital are almost too much like typical *Hyla x-signata* to be excluded from it, though this would carry the range of the species into the Amazonian Hylaea.

A live Venezuelan tree-frog kindly given me by Dr. J. Rivero is very similar to the Brazilian specimens of *Hyla x-signata*. Its dorsal color varies from light brown or gray brown to a dark olivaceous tone. The interocular spot and the two pairs of parentheses are present; the latter are thick and rather chunky like the blotches on the permanently visible dorsal aspect of the limbs. In a deep olivaceous phase they become indistinct or a deeper olivaceous green. In the usual lighter phase they and the blotches may show an outline of light dots. A line on the middle of the back and other small spots and lines also become visible in this phase. The flash color varies from greenish to lemon yellow; a dark horizontal reticulation on the concealed upper aspect of the thigh is very like that seen in specimens from our northeastern state of Alagoas. The upper half of the iris is golden, the lower has a greenish glint; the pseudocolobom is average, the peripheral dark reticulation and a dark dot of pigment in the middle of the lower free rim are very distinct. The gula is pale, but there is a little olivaceous pigment at its edges and on those of the ventral aspect of the limbs. This frog must belong either to the nominate race of *H. x-signata* or at least to a more northern form of the species.

## *Hyla x-signata nasica* Cope, 1862

Cope, E. D. 1862. Catalogue of the reptiles obtained during the explorations of the Parana, Paraguay, Vermejo and Uruguay Rivers by Capt. Thos. J. Page, U.S.N. I, The Paraguay Collection. *J. Ac. Sc. Phila.* 14:346–359. *H. nasica*: 354.

*Hyla nasica* was described by Cope with other frogs from the Paraná Basin collected by the Thomas J. Page Expedition. Until L. Müller and W. Hellmich (1936) separated the much larger *fuscovaria* from *H. nasica*, under the name of *trachythorax*, all the Chaquean members of the *H. rubra–Hyla x-signata* complex, except perhaps the unmistakable *H. acuminata* (*H. phrynoderma*), were lumped together under the name *H. nasica*. The latter is, however, much smaller than the other two and so similar to *Hyla x-signata* that at present it may best be regarded as a geographic race of the Spix species. *H. nasica* occupies the Chaquean subarea of the Continental province of South America.

Diagnostic characters. Most morphological characters are specific rather than subspecific. Size small; a slight constriction at the neck. Leg short, tibiotarsal articulation reaching the eye, sometimes failing to reach it when adpressed. Pattern less well-defined than in the other races. Color yellowish gray or brown; dark specimens sometimes slightly rufous. Voice, like the tapping out of Morse code.

Types and type locality. Cope merely mentions n. 5835 of the Page expedition and does not indicate a definite finding place. Cochran (1961) cites two cotypes, nos. 5835 and 32371 and adds "Paraguay, T. J. Page"; the types are now in USNM, where the author saw and compared them with specimens from southern Mato Grosso.

Description. Size relatively small, though medium for the *H. rubra–H. x-signata* complex, average 27–34, rarely more, sometimes less. Habit slender. A slight constriction between head and body. Hindlimb short; tibiotarsal articulation generally reaching the eye when the leg is adpressed. Length and width of head subequal. Snout triangular, roundly pointed in front, projecting slightly over the mouth in profile. Canthus rostralis rather indistinct, loreal region oblique. Nostrils superolateral. Diameter of the eye the same as the distance

from it to the nostril. Interorbital space slightly wider than internarial space. Tympanum half the diameter of the eye. Tongue oval, emarginate, free behind. Vomerine teeth in two short, contiguous groups between the choanae. Disks short, very wide in front. Fingers unwebbed or a rudiment of web at the base. Toes about two-thirds webbed. A tubercle under the first finger, a larger, bifid one under the third and fourth fingers. A moderate oval, inner and a very minute, outer metatarsal tubercle. Very small warts disseminated on the dorsal surface. Gula areolate. Belly and midventral aspect of the thigh granular. A very distinct fold of skin from eye to shoulder, passing over the upper edge of the tympanum. A distinct pectoral fold covering a shorter fold from each arm to the chest.

Variation. The usual variation in size, length of hindlimb and other proportions or morphological details seen in Neotropical forms of *Hyla*; web reaching the base of the disks on the outer side of the third and fifth toes in some specimens.

Secondary sex characters. Nuptial plaques, such as described by L. Müller and Hellmich for *Hyla* (*trachythorax*) and considered by them as unique, are visible in a certain proportion of *H. nasica* males (eighteen out of sixty-two males from Miranda, Mato Grosso, and two from S. Salvador Choya, Santiago del Estero, Argentina). The plaques are evidently deciduous and when present mostly vestigial in both species. Size of the two sexes not very different; males from 25–35 mm, average 28–35 mm, rarely more; one 36 mm from Santiago del Estero, one 36 mm and six males 37 mm long from Tucuman, Argentina. Females 27 to 35; one 37 mm snout to vent from Ponta Porã, southern Mato Grosso, one 36, one 39 mm from Tucuman, Argentina.

Color. Specimens from Ipuã, and Nueva Italia, Paraguay olivaceous grays and buffs above, the pattern darker. Beneath white, inclined to a slightly mauvish tint, especially on the limbs. Iris blending with dorsal surface, somewhat golden, with dendritic black marks especially on the upper half, the lower more like the loreal region in tone; a dark pseudocolobom across the eye between the dark subcanthal and supratympanic stripes. Gula of male yellow to cadmium; concealed aspects of thigh close to body and suprascapular region citron to lemon yellow, posterior upper aspect of thigh more vivid, nearer to orange.

Dead specimens appear grayish yellow or brownish, the latter sometimes slightly ruddy.

PATTERN. The fundamental pattern is that of *H. x-signata* and composed of two pairs of inverted parentheses on the back, an interocular spot, and a dark subcanthal stripe continuing onto the shoulder, over the tympanum. The parentheses may be quite simple, like in Spix's figure of *H. x-signata*, or, in a few specimens only, slightly irregular, sinuous, and more ornate in outline.

VARIATION. This pattern is however variable and not always distinct, either altogether, or caudad from the anterior parentheses. When both pairs are present the posterior one begins slightly to the inside of the anterior one but opens out obliquely. Often it is indistinct or reduced to indefinite spots or marks. There may also be additional ornamentation on the midback. Some dark specimens show a few white dots or ocelli, usually without forming a real network like that of *Hyla x-signata similis* Cochran, and much less ornate than in *Hyla x-signata eringiophila* Gallardo.

The interocular spot may be slightly triangular and prolonged backward or narrow, almost horizontal or slightly concave in front. Sometimes it is bipartite. The subcanthal stripe is plain when visible.

GEOGRAPHIC VARIATION. Our samples that come nearest to the descriptions of Cope and of L. Müller and Hellmich as to size, habit, and pattern are those from Paraguay and southern Mato Grosso. Those from the Chaco province of Argentina are very like them. Some of the specimens from more eastern Santa Fé are of the same size, but tend to be more ornate and may come near to the livery of *H. x-s. similis* Cochran or of *H. eringiophila* Gallardo. The specimens from the provinces of Santiago del Estero and Tucumán are larger, though too small for adult *fuscovaria* (*trachythorax*) and not like them in livery or habit. Those seen from Santiago del Estero range from 35 to 37 mm, and the leg is slightly longer, the adpressed tibiotarsal articulation reaching in front of the eye. The disks are very wide. Two from San Salvador Choya, incline to a dark network pattern like *H. x-s. similis;* in the other specimens, from Tala Pozo, the dorsal pattern is indistinct; they are dark and the skin seems thicker.

VOICE. The call, heard by us in southern Mato Grosso, is very distinct. It resembles the tapping out of signals in Morse code and differs from the rough, rasping croak of the large forms of the group, like *Hyla fuscovaria*.

HABITS. Like the other Chaquean frogs *Hyla x-s. nasica* is adapted to finding moist resting places during the dry season and to start breeding at the onset of the rains. At Miranda, in southern Mato Grosso, we found a large assembly of all sorts of frogs gathering at the local pond after the first rainfall. *Hyla x-s. nasica* was peering out of holes in the fence posts and vocalizing; it also occupied all other suitable spots available, including the heads and backs of larger frogs also engaged in nuptial song. At Colastiné Sur, outside the capital of Santa Fé, Argentina, Dr. G. Martinez Aschenbach, director of the Museo Florentino Ameghino, took several specimens for me out of the reservoirs above the water closets in the simple bathrooms of the Fishing Club. Phillips collected two in a dairy (Primavera, Paraguay) and A. L. Carvalho found his under dead branches and in hollows elsewhere.

DISTRIBUTION. *Hyla x-s. nasica* may be considered as the Chaquean form of *Hyla x-signata* Spix. It occurs in Paraguay and some northern provinces of Argentina, such as Santa Fé, Chaco, Tucuman, and Santiago del Estero, and in the central and southwestern section of Brazil (Mato Grosso and Paraná). Some specimens have been taken outside the continental depression of this area, in the relatively high *cerrado* sections of the states of São Paulo (Pirassununga, Campinas) and Minas Gerais (Belo Horizonte), at the edge of the scrub, and in Lagoa Santa nearby, also at Lassance and Pirapora, in the São Francisco River basin.

The specimens from Lassance, on the Rio das Velhas, and from Barreiras on the Rio Grande, Bahia, seem closer to the description of *Hyla x-signata* by Spix, but they differ considerably from the robust samples of the latter with the typical pattern from the northeastern localities near the coast. It is possible that transition is gradual, or that the semiarid conditions of the inland northeastern section do not allow more than a subexiguous build.

As mentioned above, some of the specimens from Tucumán and Santiago del Estero are very large and robust. The exact status of these forms may have to be changed when the present gaps are filled.

## *Hyla x-signata similis* Cochran, 1952

Cochran, D. M. 1952. Two new Brazilian frogs, *Hyla werneri* n. nov., *Hyla similis* n. sp. *J. Wash. Acad. Sc.* 42(2):50–53.

———. 1955. Frogs of southeastern Brazil. *U.S.N.M. Bull.* 206. *H. similis*: 148–150, text-fig. 17, pl. 13, figs. A–D.

Lutz, in some manuscript notes written on the mounts of the watercolors of his *Hyla fuscovaria* from Minas Gerais and of similar specimens from the coastal lowlands of Rio de Janeiro, remarked on the smaller size of the latter but did not provide a new name for them. He did not have either *Hyla x-signata* from the northeast or *H. nasica* from the Chaco for comparison with them. Cochran (1955) described the Rio de Janeiro frogs as a new species, *Hyla similis*. She remarked on their similarity to *Hyla fuscovaria* and mentioned the need of good specimens of *Hyla x-signata* for comparison. She does not mention *Hyla nasica* Cope.

Although I have more complete material than either A. Lutz or Cochran, the taxonomic status of *H. similis* does not seem quite definitive to me. It is treated here as a geographic race of *H. x-signata*, in the same manner as the genuine *H. nasica* Cope, because it is nearer to them in size and in proportions. The pattern is more similar to that of certain *H. fuscovaria* specimens but it differs from the latter on three important points: smaller size, relatively shorter snout and shorter hindlimb. The pattern on the dorsal aspect of the thighs concealed in repose is also different, being dull and minute in many specimens, tapestry-like in others. It differs from *Hyla x-s. x-signata* by the generally more complex and often less clear-cut dorsal pattern and also by the concealed pattern. Its build is probably more uniform, since *H. x-s. x-signata* varies from subexiguous to robust. The head is less widely triangular. From *H. nasica* it also differs by the concealed pattern and the details of the dorsal pattern, often indefinite in *x-s. nasica,* with the posterior pair of parentheses indistinct. Besides these differences, the three forms occupy different areas. *H. x-signata* belongs to the northeastern and *H. nasica* to the Chaquean fauna of the Continental province, whereas *H. similis* has a short known range along the Atlantic Coast (states of Guanabara and Rio de Janeiro).

Diagnostic characters. The distribution on the coastal lowlands of the states of Guanabara (former Federal District) and Rio de Janeiro; the trend toward anastomosis and coalescence of the dorsal spots into a network with white dots, intervals, or halos; the dull flash color composed of minute light alveoli, or of a tapestry-like pattern of light intervals and darker bars or spots. Hindlimb short.

Type and type locality. Type, adult male USNM 97317, from Manguinhos, near the city of Rio de Janeiro, leg. J. Venancio, February 25, 1935, on the grounds of the Instituto Oswaldo Cruz.

Description. Size relatively small, average 35 or 36 mm, but with extremes from 27–40 mm. Build generally plump. Body more or less oval, narrowed behind the head, often raised over the sacrum. Hindlimb short, the tibiotarsal articulation reaching the eye when the leg is adpressed. Head plane, length and width subequal. Snout bluntly rounded from above, projecting well over the mouth in profile, with straight canthi rostrales and very oblique, slightly concave, loreal region. In some specimens snout slightly acuminate. Nostril canthal, subterminal, slightly tumefied. Eye fairly large, its horizontal diameter equal to its distance from the nostril and to about four-fifths the distance from the end of the snout. Tympanum very distinct, at least one-half the diameter of eye. Interorbital space slightly wider than the internarial space. Vomerine teeth in two short, more or less robust, almost contiguous groups between the choanae. Tongue large, oval, slightly emarginate behind. Fingers unwebbed or barely webbed at the base. A tubercle under the first, a double tubercle under the third and fourth fingers. Feet one-half webbed or more. Web reduced to a fringe about the level of the first subarticular tubercle on the inner side of second and third, reaching the penultimate tubercle or somewhat below the disk on their outer side and on fifth, leaving from one to one and a half phalanges free on both sides of fourth toe. An oval inner and a minute outer metatarsal tubercle. Dorsal aspect beset with glandules, especially the median anterior part of the body. Ventral aspect granular. A ridge from eye to shoulder, over the upper part of the tympanum; a fold of skin below the gula and a slight pectoral fold.

Secondary sex characters. The females measured range from 27 to 38 mm. The smallest is from São João da Barra and belongs to a sample of four small specimens, but one from Atafona in the same region is 37 mm long. The largest, 38 mm, is from the type locality. Most of the others are from 36 to 33 mm long. The males show even wider extremes, 27–41 mm snout to vent length. The smallest is from Atafona, where the large female mentioned above comes from, and the two largest, 41 mm snout to vent, are from the state of Guanabara, one from the type locality, the other from a sample of thirty males and six females collected in Jacarepaguá by A. L. Carvalho. The majority of the males are smaller, nine of them only 35 mm long. One must not forget that size may depend on age and that specimens taken at the same time may belong to the same clutch originally.

VARIATION. Size fluctuates greatly, but the majority of specimens fall within medium snout to vent lengths. The length of the hindlimb is less variable than usual in Brazilian species of *Hyla*. The adpressed tibiotarsal articulation does not reach beyond the eye in any of our specimens, and mostly only to its hind half, or near to the hind corner. It fails to reach the eye in only three small northern specimens, not going beyond the tympanum in one of them. The specimens from the localities between Manguinhos and the northern block of the Serra do Mar seem to be slightly larger and to have a more elongate, slightly more acuminate snout and the plainer pattern. The least typical ones are those from Barro Branco, some of which are found on the way up the mountains.

COLOR. Lutz defines the dorsal coloring as a dark tree-bark gray. Cochran describes her living specimens as either drab, clay color, or malachite to sage green. Those seen by me are gray, drab, or olivaceous, but not really green. The pattern is dark; Cochran defines it as approximately sepia; other similar tones also occur. Iris pale gold at the free inner rim, transversed by a dark equatorial pseudo-colobom and with a slight notch in the median lower part; outer part with a dark reticulation growing dense toward the periphery. Tympanum light brown, contrasting greatly with the sides of the head. Ventral aspect light, whitish or grayish in the middle, immaculate; dots of pigment on the gula in both sexes, especially males from some localities. Gula of male citrine. Flash color of the alveoli in the dark reticulum on the dorsal part of the thigh concealed in repose not very bright, brownish yellow (Lutz), honey yellow, or orange

ochraceous (Cochran). Webs mottled in the grays of the dorsal surface.

PATTERN. Fundamentally the pattern is that of the *x-signata* sector of the group. There is, however, the definite trend, mentioned above, toward fragmentation of the elements, especially the posterior pair of parentheses, anastomosis and coalescence of the dark parts, and the presence of white dots or areas between them or of a halo at their edges. Dark bars present on the permanently visible dorsal parts of the limbs and flash-colored ocelli on those concealed in repose.

The component parts of the dorsal pattern lend themselves greatly to variation since so many different combinations are possible. Nevertheless, there are two main forms: (a) one in which all the elements have coalesced into a network occupying most of the back, interspersed with the white dots or areas mentioned above; in some specimens anterior pair of parentheses more or less distinct; (b) another in which the interocular spot and the anterior pair are preserved and the posterior pair is broken up into large, very irregular, often rather indistinct fragments; the second pair is also preserved in specimens from the more northern parts of the Baixada Fluminense between Manguinhos and the northern block of the Maritime Range.

VARIATION OF EACH ELEMENT. Dark subcanthal stripe not always visible. Mottling on the sides of head variable, from distinct to practically absent. Interocular spot also variable, from a narrow band, either horizontal or slightly crescent-shaped, entire or bipartite, to a blunt triangle, prolonged backward and regular or irregular in outline. Anterior pair of parentheses, when visible, often with white dots at the periphery, generally short, wide, curved, convex, or produced into a point toward the middle of the back; sometimes coalesced into a single, large, W-shaped spot. Posterior pair either merged into the general reticulation, fragmented into large blotches, separate and thin, or coalesced into an extremely variable, often quite irregular, median sacral spot. Large oval diagonal spots, with a dark outline, on the dorsal aspect of the tibia, sometimes similar, lesser ones, on the femur; similar bars, alternating with lines, on the dorsal aspect of fore-arm and tarsus. Pattern of the dorsal surface of femur concealed in repose either composed of minute light alveoli, on a rather indistinct background, or of slightly larger ocelli, in an irregular reticulum;

in some specimens the whole dorsal aspect of the thigh rather tapestry-like, similar to patterns seen on the sides of some Crotalid serpents. A few specimens without any pattern on the thighs. Often isolated dots of black pigment on the flanks, like those seen in *Hyla nasica* or slightly larger.

GEOGRAPHIC VARIATION. The differences of pattern are not based on sex or population, since the proportion of each kind varies in different samples from the same place and the variations recur in different localities. For instance, the specimens from the northern part of the known range seem to show a trend toward an irregular median spot, but Cochran portrays this feature in her type from the southern part of the range. On the whole, the specimens from the seaboard, even those from the northern part of the state of Rio de Janeiro, seem more like those from the type locality than the specimens from slightly inland parts of the plains, between Manguinhos and the northern block of the Maritime Range. The most aberrant are those from Barro Branco, part of which is already on the slope. In these, the pattern inclines to plain parentheses, either one or two pairs.

VOICE. A relatively high-pitched croak: *crack, crack, crack.*

HABITS. *H. x-signata similis* is abundant on the grounds of the Instituto Oswaldo Cruz, at Manguinhos, Rio. In summer *similis* can generally be obtained from under large flowerpots with an outlet for water at the bottom. The are also found in the stables and even in the laboratories. Old-fashioned earthen water pitchers are in use in some laboratories, and *H. x-s. similis* may shelter in them. They also get into the faucets and into the pipes below the sinks and occasionally sing there. At night they hunt on the outside of the glass panes or wire screens of the very large windows. Many must live in the trees at the sides of the building. Miss Cochran and J. Venancio were privileged to see them swarming by the hundreds in one of these trees. Lutz and Venancio also found them inside decapitated bamboo and elsewhere in the bases of live or dead banana leaves.

ECOLOGY. *Hyla x-signata similis* is a lowland coastal form from the Baixada Fluminense in the states of Guanabara and Rio de Janeiro.

The finding places are either quite near the sea or not far from the coast, mostly below 200 m altitude, with a climate of the type *Aw* (Köppen), precipitation of 1,000 to 1,250 mm per year, a mean temperature of 20–22° C and fluctuations within 5–7° C of amplitude. Vegetation either maritime scrub formation, marsh, or open plain.

DISTRIBUTION. Cochran mentions only Manguinhos and nearby Bonsucesso, since her Amorim is a former name for Manguinhos. However, the Museu Nacional and the Lutz Collection now have specimens from points farther out along the northern suburbs, including Cordovil, São João do Meio, Caxias, Estrela, and Barro Branco; also from Jacarepaguá and the suburbs along the Central Railway, especially the Rural University, 47 km along the road to São Paulo. Other series of samples come from the northern part of the state of Rio de Janeiro, such as the coastal lowlands at Pontal de Cabo Frio, São Pedro da Aldeia, São João da Barra, Campos, and Atafona. The lower part of the Paraiba River seems to mark a minor barrier for some kinds of anurans. This may be the case of *H. x-s. similis.* However, the area just north of the Paraiba River has not been collected in, and we have one specimen that is very like *H. x-signata x-signata* from the state of Alagoas, north of Bahia, the terra typica of the latter. Known Range short, 24° to 21° S., 41–44 W. Gr.

## *Hyla x-signata camposseabrai* Bokermann, 1968

> BOKERMANN, W. C. A. 1968. Three new *Hyla* from the plateau of Maracás, Central Bahia, Brazil. *J. Herp* 1(1).

It is regrettable that the peculiar fashion of shunting several names into generic appelations for fossils, introduced by Ameghino, should be carried over into the choice of very long specific names for very minute frogs. Bokermann's *Hyla camposseabrai* is an illustration of this, which I hope will prove to be as ephemeral as most other extravagant fashions.

DIAGNOSTIC CHARACTERS. The very reduced size and exiguous build, both very marked, even for a dwarf form of the "subexiguous" *Hyla x-signata* Spix. Dorsal surface melanistic, pattern obscure. Sides of body, flanks and concealed upper aspects of thigh marbled in light and dark. Disks large.

TYPES AND TYPE LOCALITY. This species was listed by Bokermann in his book on Brazilian frog types (1966) before the description became available, hence the number of types is not specified. Paratype n. 31766 ♂, the only one seen, is now MNR n. 4048. Type locality Fazenda São Onofre, Cana Brava, Maracás Plateau, in the State of Bahia, stated to be 1,300 m above sea level.

DESCRIPTION. Size small. Adult male with large vocal sac only 30 mm long. Body very elongate, slightly ovoid, *Engystoma*-like. Hindlimb very short, the adpressed tibiotarsal articulation barely reaching the tympanum. Snout oval from above, sloping back to the mouth opening in profile. Canthus rostralis not marked; loreal region fairly high. Nostrils very small. Eye slightly longer than the distance to the nostril. Tympanum very small, not very distinct. Interorbital space slightly wider than the internarial space. Tongue large, oval, slightly emarginate. Vomerine teeth in two small groups, as usual in the whole *H. rubra–H. x-signata* complex. Disks relatively large, short, rounded in front, also a group character. A minute callosity under the first finger. Disks of feet large too. Web forming a fringe on the inner side of the first and second, narrow on the inner side of the third toe, reaching beyond the subarticular tubercle on the outer side of the first and second, below the disk on the outer side of the third and fifth to the penultimate tubercle on both sides of the fourth toe. A small inner metatarsal tubercle. Skin minutely shagreened above; skin of gula and vocal sac, body and midventral aspect of thighs granular. A narrow supratympanic ridge; folds over chest, if present, masked by the vocal sac.

MEASUREMENTS (mm). Paratype n. 31766: snout to vent 30. Hindlimb: 43; femur 12, tibia 12, tarsus 8, foot 11.

SECONDARY SEX CHARACTERS. Vocal sac pigmented and granular, very large for the size but giving the impression of being artificially distended. Vestiges of pigment in the usual location of the nuptial plaques of the males of the *Hyla rubra–Hyla x-signata* complex. Female not seen.

COLOR (dead specimen). Dorsal aspect dark gray, forming a mantle to the sides of the body. Dorsal pattern quite obscure. Slight oblique bands or minute marbling between the eye and the upper jaw. Flanks minutely marbled in light and dark; light areas disposed perpendicularly, like crossbars, on the anterior part of the thigh concealed in repose. Dark crossbars on the dorsal segments of fore

and hindlimb visible in repose. Gula and sac pigmented gray. Otherwise, ventral aspect immaculate.

AFFINITIES. This form seems obviously derived from the "subexiguous" type of *H. x-signata* described by Spix. It is so much reduced in size and probably so well isolated that one might almost consider it as a full species.

## *Hyla x-signata eringiophila* Gallardo, 1961

> GALLARDO, J. M. 1961. *Hyla strigilata* Spix e *Hyla squalirostris* A. Lutz en la República Argentina y algunas observaciones sobre otros anfíbios del grupo de *Hyla rubra* Daudin. *Com. Mus. Arg. C. Nat. C. Zool.* 3(5):145–158, 1 pl. *H. s. eringiophila*:147–153, figs. 1, 2.

*Hyla eringiophila* is a southeastern form. It was described by Gallardo in 1961, from the province of Buenos Aires, as a subspecies of *Hyla strigilata* Spix. *Hyla strigilata* is the prototype of the *Hyla catharinae* complex and was described from the state of Bahia. The types were destroyed during the Second World War, but the terra typica makes it almost certain that it is none of the forms of the *Hyla catharinae* group from the mountainous southeastern region of Brazil with which Cochran and Gallardo associate Spix's name.

*Hyla eringiophila* seems to have more affinity with the *Hyla rubra–Hyla x-signata* complex, especially with *H. x-s. nasica*, which occupies more or less adjacent territory and is also in the 30 mm class, albeit a little smaller. *Hyla phrynoderma*, also compared to *H. eringiophila* by Gallardo, belongs to the *rubra–x-signata* complex, but it is one of the large forms, above 40 mm in snout to vent length.

DIAGNOSTIC CHARACTERS. The bold, often wide, dorsal pattern; the distinct bars or elongate spots on the permanently visible dorsal aspect of the limbs; the rough pustular skin of the dorsal surface, especially the upper eyelids, vertex, and anterior part of the trunk; the elongate snout, projecting well over the mouth in profile; the tumefied nostrils; the wide subcircular tongue. Differs from *Hyla nasica* by the bolder pattern, somewhat larger size and other diagnostic characters; also by the more eastern distribution: province of Buenos Aires, Uruguay, and Rio Grande do Sul, Brazil.

TYPES AND TYPE LOCALITY. Holotype male, allotype female, leg. Gallardo at Bella Vista, province of Buenos Aires, Argentina 27.1.1959; four para-types, one female, three males, 28.1.1959, same collector, same place: now series MACN 2413. Types not shown to the author.

DESCRIPTION. Size of adults 32–38 mm snout to vent. Build fairly robust. Hindlimb moderately long, the tibiotarsal articulation reaching in front of the eye when adpressed. Head as long as wide or slightly longer, plane. Snout elongate, roundly curved from above, truncate and projecting well over the mouth in profile. Canthus rostralis not marked. Loreal region sloping, slightly concave. Nostrils superolateral, not terminal, tumefied. Eye prominent in life, its horizontal diameter almost equal to its distance from the nostril. Tympanum over one-half the diameter of eye. Tongue subcircular, slightly emarginate, free behind. Vomerine teeth in two short groups between the choanae. Fingers free or nearly so. Disks short, very wide in front. A callosity under the first finger, a larger double tubercle under the third and fourth fingers. Toes appearing half-webbed, web fringe-like on the inner side of the first, second, and third; wide part leaving half to one phalanx free on their outer side and on fifth, two phalanges, or slightly less, on both sides of fourth toe. An oval inner and a minute outer metatarsal tubercle. Dorsal surface warty, especially the upper eyelids, the vertex of head and the anterior part of the trunk. Beneath granular, gula minutely so. A supratympanic ridge, a postaxillary, transverse, pectoral fold.

SECONDARY SEX CHARACTERS. Males slightly smaller than females; maximum seen 36 mm. Vocal sac subgular, very large. Forearms somewhat thickened in some. Females up to 37 or 38 mm snout to vent length.

COLOR. Unfortunately not seen alive by this author. According to Gallardo, dorsal surface light brown; a juvenile specimen from Nuñez, province of Buenos Aires, that he saw alive was golden brown. The flash color is described as *anaranjado;* I take it to mean inclined to orange. Preserved specimens: Gallardo describes the male type and one male paratype as light gray; the female allotype, a female, and two male paratypes as darker gray than the type; juveniles from Nuñez are described as dark. The preserved specimens observed by me are either gray or brown, some of the Brazilian ones very dark, one of them quite melanistic.

PATTERN. The dorsal pattern consists of the typical *x-signata* elements, which are also seen in the *H. catharinae* group. The interocular spot is generally somewhat prolonged backward and individually very variable in shape. The inverted, parentheses-like spots are often thick and chunky. Both pairs, or only the anterior, may be present and entire, with the posterior one fragmented. Additional ornamental spots also occur. Some specimens show the white dots recurrent in the whole *x-signata* group; the dots tend to be localized along the edges of the parentheses. In one specimen from Rio Grande do Sul (MNR 3827) they are few, but a continuous light halo surrounds the parentheses and dark spots. When the white dots are numerous, especially when the dark spots are very much fragmented, the pattern approaches the network of *Hyla x-signata similis* from the coastal lowlands of the states of Guanabara and Rio de Janeiro. The dark stripes from eye to maxilla, mentioned by Spix for the nominate form, in which I have seldom found them, are common in *eringiophila,* and the lower part of the maxilla is often pale. Upper arm also pale. Permanently visible dorsal surface of limbs with parallel vertical bars or elongate spots alternating with narrow lines in some specimens. The light fields on the concealed upper surfaces are limited by dark bars. Ventral aspect light, immaculate, or with a fine sprinkling of pale brown chromatophores at certain spots, such as the edge of the gula. Edges of dorsal pattern often visible on the leg from beneath.

VARIATION. Thirteen specimens were seen. One male from Maldonado, Uruguay (FMNH 9655) and three males from Montevideo (FMNH 10298, 10225, 10232) are very like the description and the figures of Gallardo, not very dark brown, very variegated, with a distinct pattern of two pairs of parentheses and additional ornamental spots on the back. The other (FMNH 10228) is very like *H. nasica.* Two females from Montevideo (IBM 00881) are darker but also have a bold pattern. Four males from Santo Augusto, western Rio Grande do Sul, comprise two pale gray (MNR 3827, 3827a) and two very dark brown males (MNR 3825, 3829). One of the gray ones has large chunky parentheses; in the other there are white dots at their periphery. The dark ones hardly show any pattern, nor does a female from the same state (MNR 2089), without locality, which is also brown. The Brazilian specimens have a rather pointed snout, a more elliptic tongue and a slightly longer web on the feet. Two specimens, without distinct sex characters, from km 31.200 Desvio Hudson, Buenos Aires, are gray, with simple dark pattern and peripheral white dots. The skin is smooth, the snout very short. A sample from San Gregorio, in the northwestern department of Artigas, Uruguay (IBM 0836), comprises five small specimens, one female, 32 mm, one male 29 mm long, and three juveniles, 27, 25 and 24 mm snout to vent. The snout and hindlimb are rather short, the adpressed tibiotarsal articulation reaching the eye. The female has a pattern of confluent dark spots forming a reticulum with light intervals, very like that of *H. x-signata similis* from Rio. Two have a similar but more attenuated network, leaving the anterior pair of parentheses clear. The pattern of one juvenile (25 mm) is simple and slightly indistinct, as in many specimens of *nasica*. The other one has the two pairs of parentheses, one of them fairly wide. The female is smooth; the others are fairly warty, especially the smallest one. They seem too near *nasica* to be included here.

VOICE. Not heard by the author. Gallardo states that he heard the male type calling in a temporary marsh, one meter above the water, sitting on a fallen branch of an elm tree; its call was a repeated *trac, trac,* and sometimes seeming like the quack of a duck. Other individuals of the same species responded to this song; it began at dusk and continued during the night. The call described is not very different from that of subspecies of *H. x-signata*, such as *H. similis*, whereas the members of the *Hyla catharinae* are characterized by very weak calls more like *tche, tche.*

HABITS. Gallardo mentions that the subspecific name is derived from the habit of several frogs of the genus *Hyla* that live between the leaves of diverse kinds of *Eryngium*. (The widespread genus *Eryngium* is very different from most of the other genera of Umbelliferae and somewhat like a bromeliad. There is generally a rosette of stiff, often prickly, leaves at the base of the stem, which is longer than the central flower stalk of most bromeliads. The rosette may form a cup and hold water.) In southern Brazil (1959) I found *Hyla pulchella* in the rosette of *Eryngium eburneum* in daytime, in places where no bromeliads were present. In December 1964, Barrio and I, acting on informa-

tion from an observant inhabitant of the island of Talavera, in the Delta of the Paraná, found that a very tall *Eryngium* is the habitat of an interesting, slightly casque-headed hylid, *Trachycephalus siemersi.*

TAXONOMIC POSITION. Three of the thirteen specimens seen, two from 31.200 km, Desvio Hudson, outside Buenos Aires, leg. et ded. Barrio, and FMNH 10228, from Maldonado, Uruguay, are very similar to *Hyla nasica,* especially the two former. The other, mostly larger, specimens agree well with the description and with Gallardo's figures, if allowance is made for the excessive magnification of the latter. It is not likely that *H. eringiophila* should have affinities with the members of the *Hyla catharinae* group from southeastern Brazil, which are mostly montane. *Hyla strigilata,* the prototype, is almost a "species inquirenda"; the types are no longer extant, the terra typica has a different fauna from the Brazilian southeastern serras, and Peters (1872), who examined the type, mentions vestiges of *blue* color on the thighs. Since neither the types nor any of the other specimens in the MACN were shown to me by the author of *eringiophila,* I cannot settle this point.

KNOWN RANGE. Gallardo indicates parts of the province of Buenos Aires as the known range. I have seen quite typical specimens from Maldonado and Montevideo in Uruguay, and from Santo Augusto in western Rio Grande do Sul. Barrio informs me that he has collected it in other parts of Rio Grande do Sul; 5 specimens from San Gregorio, Dept. of Artigas, NW Uruguay, are like typical juvenile specimens of *x-s. nasica.* It is difficult to separate the two forms without the adults and the uncollected terrain between the known range of each makes it impossible to know whether distribution is discrete or whether a gradual transition obtains. The specimens from the Sierra de la Ventura may be diverse.

## ALLIED FORMS

Two small species described from Brazil seem closely allied to *Hyla x-signata*. The first, *Hyla craspedospila* Lutz shows the following combination of characters: insular dark spots with a still darker margin distributed on the dorsal surface, sometimes assuming a certain bilateral symmetry reminiscent of the inverted parentheses of *Hyla x-*

*signata;* very marked glandular ridges on the tarsus and slightly lesser ones on the forearm; extensively webbed feet. Known distribution insular: Paraiba River Valley and Teresópolis in the state of Rio, respectively 400 and 800 m above sea level and Pombas in Minas Gerais, at 400 m altitude. Average males 29 mm from snout to vent.

The other, *Hyla pachycrus* Miranda Ribeiro (average 30 mm), is characterized by the stout hindlimbs with disproportionately long tibiae and by the presence of a dark subcanthal line widening into a brilliant clove-colored or black stripe behind the tympanum, ending at or near the sacrum; dorsal pattern generally absent or more or less vestigial. Bromelicolous. Northeastern subprovince of the Continental province.

## *Hyla craspedospila* Lutz, 1925

Lutz, A. 1925. Batraciens du Brésil. *C. R. Soc. Biol. Paris* 93(22):211–224. *H. craspedospila*: 211.

————. 1926. Nota prévia sobre Especies novas de batrachios brasileiros. New Species of Brazilian Batrachians Preliminary Note. *Publ. Inst. O. Cruz* 10(3):3–9 Portuguese, 10–16 English. *H. craspedospila* 6 & 13.

Cochran, D. M. 1955. Frogs of Southeastern Brazil. U.S.N.M. Bull. 206. *H. crospedospila*: 130, fig. 15, pl. 11, figs. E–F.

I begin by re-establishing the correct name, *craspedospila,* derived from the Greek *kraspedon,* i. e. an edge or border, and *spilos,* a spot, in this case the dark border of the insular spots found on the trunk and dorsal aspect of the limbs from which Lutz derived the trivial name. It was misprinted *crospedospila* in the original publication and was thus reproduced by Cochran (1955).

*H. craspedospila* is a small form of the *H. x-signata–H. rubra* group. It shows a certain similarity to *Hyla cuspidata* and to the specimens of *H. r. altera* from the coastal lowlands near Rio, formerly put to *Hyla fuscomarginata* from the highlands. The real *H. fuscomarginata* from the highlands is very much smaller and has a different range. *H. r. altera* has a rough skin, the dorsal pattern of the *H. rubra* sector of the group and a lowland distribution, along the coast. *Hyla cuspidata* is a very well characterized species, with smooth skin, copper-colored eyes and green bones. None of these species shows affinity with the *x-signata* pattern as *Hyla craspedospila* does.

DIAGNOSTIC CHARACTERS. The small size; the insular spots with a darker edge on the dorsal aspect; the glandular ridges on the tarsus and to a lesser degree on the forearm; the long webs on the feet.

TYPES AND TYPE LOCALITY. Syntypes nos. 655 and 654 A. Lutz Collection at MNR and USNM 96926-32, 96934, leg. Zikan, Jan. 20, 1924, at Campo Bello. N. 655 is the same as USNM 96933, re-exchanged to the Lutz Collection; n. 654 served as model for the watercolor sketch by Sandig.

Lutz mentions Rio de Janeiro and São Paulo in his diagnosis. Campo Bello is in the state of Rio de Janeiro, not far from the border of the state of São Paulo, in the valley of the Rio Paraiba, at approximately 400 m altitude. It is now called Itatiaia because it is at the foot of the Itatiaia Mountains.

DESCRIPTION. Size small. Syntypes 29 mm, other specimens 25–32 mm snout to vent. Build robust for the size. Body moderately elongate, postaxillary region almost as wide as the head. Hindlimb fairly long, the tibiotarsal articulation reaching in front of the eye to its anterior corner, or between it and the nostril when the leg is adpressed. Head slightly longer than wide. Snout seen from above elongate, ogival in outline, acuminate at the tip, triangular between the canthi, declivous beyond the nostril and projecting greatly over the mouth in profile. Canthus rostralis thick near the eye, concave behind the nostril. Loreal region slightly concave between nostril and eye. Nostril at about two-thirds the distance from the eye to the tip of the snout, superolateral, canthal, tumefied. Eye large, prominent, its horizontal diameter two-thirds as long as the distance to the tip of the snout. Tympanum very distinct, half the diameter of the eye. Interorbital space much wider than the internarial space. Tongue large, oval, rounded in front, notched and slightly free behind. Vomerine teeth in two short, robust, very approximate patches between the choanae.

Hand webbed only at the base. Fingers very long. Disks, short, wide, very large. A callosity at the base of the first finger; a large palmar tubercle. Foot about three-fourths webbed; a fringe on the inner side of the first toe; web narrow between the first and second, oblique between the first and third toes, reduced to a fringe beyond the first tubercle on the inner side of the second, wide to the second tubercle on the inner side of the third to just below the disk on the outer side of the second, third, fifth, and to the penultimate tubercle on both sides of the fourth toe. A large inner and a small but very distinct outer metatarsal tubercle. A serrated row of glandules on the tarsus from below the knee to the inner metatarsal tubercle; a parallel, outer row, continuing onto the foot and the fifth toe; a similar though less distinct row on the forearm. Disseminated glandules on the dorsal surface, especially the upper eyelids, occiput, sacrum, and leg, also at the knee. A supratympanic ridge. A fold of skin across the chest.

VARIATION. The length of the hindlimb relative to the snout to vent length offers the main variation. In most specimens the adpressed tibiotarsal articulation reaches the eye, often its anterior half, or its anterior corner. In some it reaches in front of the eye and in a few between it and the nostril (syntypes ALC 655 and USNM 96926). The shape of the tongue and the size and degree of approximation of the patches of vomerine teeth are also somewhat variable. In some specimens the snout seems slightly shorter or less acuminate. Some individuals are short legged. Development of glandules and glandular ridges is variable. Other minor differences also occur.

SECONDARY SEX CHARACTERS. Vocal sac sometimes very large. Forearms of breeding males robust; glandular ridges and glandules marked.

SIZE. The three male syntypes are 29 mm from snout to vent. Our smallest adult males, 25 and 26 mm snout to vent, are from the Paraiba River Valley at Itatiaia, the largest, 32 mm, from the National Park above it. One was taken at 800 m in an artificial pond, the two others are from Mauá, in the Minas Gerais sector of the park, at over 1,000 m altitude. No females with ripe eggs were available for measurement. Specimens without secondary sex characters are from 24–30 mm, the larger probably nonbreeding females.

COLOR. According to Lutz, "Ground color of dorsum 'beige' with brown spots scattered over the trunk and forming crossbands on the limbs, all of them with a distinct darker margin. Venter light."

PATTERN (dorsum.) The insular brown spots with a margin of darker dots on a light ground mentioned by Lutz form the pattern of the dorsal surface. On the body they comprise the interocular spot and a series of elongate dorsal spots on each side of the trunk, with or without an additional spot or two

between them and generally with additional spots or dots behind them. A few specimens have small dots and dashes all over the back. The lateral spots are generally large and elongate. In shape they are often reminiscent of the double pair of inverted parentheses-like spots of the *x-signata* sector of the group. One or both elements, or pairs, may be fragmented, but they are mostly recognizable. They are generally wide but in some specimens they are narrow. In such specimens, one or two, entire or fragmented longitudinal stripes are present, sometimes followed by dots. In some specimens all the spots are very small, and in a few only the subcanthal stripe is evident.

The interocular spot, which is also part of the *x-signata* pattern, may be entire or fragmented. When entire, it either forms a narrow angular band between the eyes or is prolonged backward into a rough, often excentric triangle; it may also be shield-shaped. In some specimens it is substituted by two small, discrete, generally unequal spots.

A certain number of specimens show a light halo or area around the dark margin of the spots.

A dark subcanthal stripe widens into a dorsolateral band behind the tympanum and continues to the postaxillary region or beyond. It may remain entire or it may be fragmented and accompanied or followed by a number of dots. A similar dark longitudinal band occupies the anterior part of the upper arm, with a less distinct one on the anterior upper part of the femur; the bands lie along the body in repose. They go over into indistinct pigmentation, dotting, or mottling on the ventral edges of the body and limbs. Posterior dorsal aspect of femur concealed in repose is similar to the edges of the concealed anterior strip. On the permanently visible dorsal aspect of limbs, femur, tibia, tarsus, foot, forearm, and hand, the dark brown spots incline to become rectilinear and thus form disruptive crossbands. Webs mottled.

This pattern varies individually but specimens caught together are often rather similar.

VOICE. A croak, often double and always sounding rather nasal and plaintive.

HABITS AND ECOLOGY. This species has been collected in bromeliads and on the vegetation at the edges of standing water, as mentioned by Lutz (1925). It is very much infested by larvae of mites. This is a common occurrence in small bromeliad-dwelling frogs.

DISTRIBUTION. First known from the Paraiba

River Valley in the states of Rio de Janeiro and São Paulo, beginning at approximately 400 m altitude. It is found at 800 m at the edges of artificial ponds, in the Itatiaia National Park, near the type locality, and at much higher altitudes at Mauá in the Minas Gerais part of the National Park. It also occurs on the northern block of the Serra do Mar, for instance at Teresópolis, where it calls from the vegetation of open marshy ground, or above pools. The specimens from Teresópolis are very typical and agree perfectly with Lutz's diagnosis and Cochran's description. *Hyla craspedospila* has also been obtained on vegetation near still reaches of the river at the agricultural station of Pomba in Minas Gerais. I have seen no specimens from the coastal plains in the collections examined.

## *Hyla pachycrus* Miranda Ribeiro, 1937

(*Hyla pickeli* Lutz & B. Lutz, 1938)

> MIRANDA RIBEIRO, A. 1937. Sobre uma coleção de vertebrados do nordeste Brasileiro. Primeira parte: Peixes e batraquios. O Campo, Jan., 1937: 54–56. *H. pachychrus*: 55.
>
> LUTZ, A., and LUTZ, B. 1938. I. On *Hyla aurantiaca* Daudin and *Sphoenorhynchus* Tschudi and on two allied Hylae from southeastern Brazil. II. Two new Hylae: *Hyla albosignata* n. sp. & *Hyla pickeli*. An. Acad. Bras. Sc. 10(2):175–194. *H. pickeli*: 189–191, 193.

This northeastern species has been collected only a few times: in the state of Pernambuco by A. L. de Carvalho and by Dom Bento Pickel; in Natal, state of Rio Grande do Norte by A. Lutz and J. Venancio; at Cachoeira, state of Bahia, by B. Lutz, and in Salvador, the capital of the same state, by Dr. Davies.

DIAGNOSTIC CHARACTERS. The combination of relatively small size, robust hindlimbs, and disproportionately long tibiae; the simple pattern; the bromelicolous habitat and the range in the northeastern subarea of the Continental province.

TYPES AND TYPE LOCALITY. *Hyla pachycrus* was described on the basis of seven specimens collected by Antenor Leitão de Carvalho, 1936, at Poção, Pernambuco, on the Serra do Acahi, which reaches 1,200 m elevation. Four of them, MNR nos. 237, were seen by the author.

The type and a long series of paratypes described by A. Lutz and B. Lutz as *H. pickeli* are from Tapera, Pernambuco, leg. D. Bento Pickel O.S.B., No-vember 1927 and November 1928, A. Lutz Collection nos. 1702–1722 and n. 1452 at MNR, A. Lutz Collection, no. 1715 can be considered as the type.

DESCRIPTION. Size relatively small. Largest specimen seen 33 mm, average 29–31 mm snout to vent. Build delicate, slightly elongate. Greatest width at ocular and postocular region, narrowed beyond the sacrum. Forelimb short, thin. Hindlimb long, robust. Tibia disproportionately long, the tibiotarsal articulation reaching almost to nostril when the leg is adpressed. Head slightly longer than wide. Snout somewhat elongate, elliptic in outline from above, obliquely rounded and sloping backward, projecting well over the opening of the mouth in profile. Canthus rostralis distinct to nostril, slightly curved. Loreal region high, very slightly concave. Nostril at about two-thirds the distance from the eye to the tip of the snout, superolateral, very delicate, slightly tumefied. Eye prominent, its diameter about two-thirds of the eye-snout distance. Tympanum distinct, approximately one-half the diameter of the eye. Interorbital space much wider than the internarial space. Vomerine teeth in two short, transverse patches between the choanae. Tongue wide, rounded, notched, posterior border free. Fingers with hardly a trace of web at the base; disks very wide, slightly flattened in front, narrowed at the base. A flat tubercle under the first finger, a bifid one under the third and fourth fingers. Toes three-fourths webbed; wide part of web reaching the first subarticular tubercle on the inner side of second toe, the second on the inner side of the third, the third on both sides of the fourth; web inserted below the disk on outer side of second, third, and fifth toes, just above the tubercle on the outer side of the first toe. An average inner and a very small outer metatarsal tubercle. Scattered glandules on the dorsal surface. Belly and midventral aspect of the thigh coarsely granular. A dorsolateral fold, a short supratympanic ridge, a slight inner ridge on the tarsus, a fold across the chest; in male gular folds above it. Specimens seen range from 21–30 mm snout to vent. Four-legged juveniles, 12 or 13 mm long, are quite recognizable.

VARIATION. The adpressed hindlimb reaches beyond the snout in many specimens, in a few to the tip of the snout, in others to the nostril or between the nostril and the tip of the snout. The tongue may be rounded or slightly longer and oval, well-notched or only slightly emarginate.

COLOR. Dorsal aspect drab or clay colored, fairly

light. One of Miranda Ribeiro's preserved cotypes brown, not very dark.

PATTERN. The most evident and constant element of the pattern is a dark, shiny, clove-brown, almost black, subcanthal line, beginning behind the nostril, widening into a dorsolateral stripe behind the tympanum and ending at or before the sacral region. In many specimens no other pattern is present. The perpendicular dark bars on the permanently visible dorsal aspect of the limbs, mentioned in both descriptions, are generally rather indistinct, slightly more visible in the brown cotype and in the Lutz watercolor, which shows lighter intervals between the bars.

VARIATION (preserved specimens). Miranda Ribeiro's brown cotype shows an interocular spot prolonged into a narrow triangle behind the eyes and one pair of elongate, inverted parentheses-like spots on the back with a few dark dots between them. In another, paler, syntype they are shorter and less distinct and in a third vestigial. The recently dead specimen from Tapera used in the watercolor painted for A. Lutz shows a rather shadowy, longitudinal, symmetrical dark area behind the eyes and down the middle of the back, with a longitudinal light area to each side of it. One male from Cachoeira, Bahia, has dark spots and large dots of the same color as the dorsolateral stripe, disposed longitudinally to the inside of it and a short postocular stripe or shadow down the midback. The white interocular crescent-shaped halo in the A. Lutz watercolor appears to be individual.

VOICE. Like the sound produced by winding a watch (A. Lutz).

HABITS AND ECOLOGY. The specimens collected by A. Lutz and J. Venancio were moving about at the edge of the Manoel Felippe Lagoon at Natal. Most of the other specimens in the Lutz Collection, including the relatively large number of juveniles, were collected in bromeliads. My adult pair from Cachoeira was found in epiphytic bromeliads on the grounds of a fazenda with much standing water in the vicinity.

KNOWN DISTRIBUTION. Salvador, the capital of Bahia on the coast, and Cachoeira, slightly inland on the Paraguassú River, Tapera and Poção in Pernambuco and Natal in Rio Grande do Norte. Poção is on the highlands.

AFFINITIES. *Hyla pachycrus* shows affinities with the *Hyla rubra–Hyla x-signata* group through the robust hindlimbs and the short patches of vomerine teeth between fairly small choanae. The pattern seen in a few specimens is also similar to that of the *H. rubra* sector of the group.

# 12. The *Hyla rubra* Group

## RACES OF *HYLA RUBRA* DAUDIN

The *Hyla rubra* Daudin pattern of longitudinal stripes is relatively rare in Brazil. Three races of this species are recognized here. The nominate form, *Hyla rubra rubra* Daudin, was described from the Guianas and hardly seems to enter Brazil. It is characterized by the moderate size, the pattern of a dorsal and a dorsolateral longitudinal dark stripe on each side separated by a light interval, and by the yellow ocelli on the concealed limb surfaces, especially the posterior part of the thigh and the knee. The only typical Brazilian examples of this form seen by me come from Cape Orange near the frontier of French Guiana.

*Hyla rubra huebneri* Melin is larger and more robust in build; females may be well over 40 mm long and males as large as average *H. rubra rubra* females. Pattern on the concealed surfaces, including flanks and limbs, mostly very ornate with a strong black reticulation and large yellow ocelli or areas in between. It seems to occupy most of the valley of the Amazonas River.

*Hyla rubra altera* B. Lutz is characterized by the stout build, despite the moderate size, and by the rough skin. It is also characterized by the absence of flash colors and ornamentation on the surfaces concealed in repose. It lives on the coastal lowlands of the Atlantic province, perhaps continuously from Santa Catarina to Pernambuco, or at least to Bahia. It is very common on the coastal lowlands known as Baixada Fluminense, in the states of Rio de Janeiro and Guanabara.

## *Hyla rubra rubra* Daudin, 1802

> DAUDIN, F. M. 1802. *Histoire naturelle des rainettes, grenouilles et crapauds. H. rubra*: 19, pl. 28, figs. 1–2.

Daudin's diagnosis and short description are quite accurate and usable. As L. Müller (1912) remarks, his figures, though not very good, permit recognition. Consequently, I transcribe the original diagnosis and translate the description:

"Hyla fuscorubra, cum maculis rotundatis albidis femoribus insuper."

"PHYSICAL CHARACTERS. Length 14 lines. Iris golden. Head small and slightly pointed. Color red-brown above, with two longitudinal lines of a pale ash-color, starting from the eyes and prolonged on each flank to near the anus; some small round and whitish dots on the thighs; underside of body whitish, slightly tinted here and there with pale reddish; abdomen granular as also underside of the thighs. Digits of hands free, of feet half-webbed." In life the round dots (ocelli) are yellow.

TYPES AND TERRA TYPICA. Daudin goes on to say that the specimen figured by him is in the Muséum d'Histoire Naturelle in Paris and belongs to Seba's Cabinet, and that he received several individuals from Surinam (ded. Marin de Baize, fide Sonini, Hist. Nat. des Reptiles). The specimens from the Guianas, which I saw, agree with the original description.

The largest sample belongs to the DZSP and comprises four hundred specimens collected at Langamann (?) Kondré, Marowijne District Surinam, by B. Malkin, May 1966. A number of them were lent and ten given to me for study and measurement. Three other specimens from Surinam were collected by Geyskes at the Botanical Garden in Paramaribo (ALC 5182 ♂, 5183 ♂, 5184 juv.) and one male at Lelydorp (ALC 5181) and presented to Dr. Lutz by Dr. Stahel.

Some specimens from British Guiana, collected by Rodway, were obtained by exchange with the AMNH, also one specimen from the USNM n. 118056 labeled Kartabo and collected by Beebe. There also two from Cayenne which show no marked sex characters and are somewhat atypical. These were given to me in 1947 by Dr. Hervé Floch, director of the Institut Pasteur de la Guyane Française et du Territoire de l'Inini.

The original description does not apply to our specimens from the Brazilian Hylaea, which seem to be a separate subspecies. I except only two, without marked sex characters, collected by Dr. Ernani Martins in an Indian Village near Cape Orange on the Brazilian frontier with French Guiana; they are small and very like those from Cayenne.

DESCRIPTION (based on the Surinam specimens). Size small, adults 28–35 mm snout to vent. Build mostly slender, elongate. Hindlimb variable in length, the tibiotarsal articulation reaching the eye or slightly in front of the eye when adpressed. Head small, slightly longer than wide. Snout triangular, blunt from above, slightly pointed and sloping obliquely to the mouth opening in profile. Canthus rostralis blunt, loreal region nearly vertical, slightly concave. Nostril slightly tumefied, halfway between the tip of the snout and the eye. Eye prominent, as long as the distance to the nostril. Tympanum small, about one-half the diameter of eye. Interorbital space 1.5 times the internarial space. Tongue wide, rounded, notched or slightly emarginate. Groups of vomerine teeth small, rounded. Disks very wide. Fingers free, toes half

webbed or more. A tubercle under the first finger, a bifid one under the third and fourth fingers. A small inner, a minute outer, metatarsal tubercle. Skin slightly pustular above, granular on abdomen and midventral aspect of thigh. A slight supratympanic ridge. A fold at the base of the throat, a distinct fold below it across the chest (female).

SECONDARY SEX CHARACTERS. Our females with eggs range from 29–34 mm snout to vent. The larger ones are robust and short legged, the tibiotarsal articulation not reaching beyond the eye when adpressed. The males range from 28–33, with only one 35 mm from snout to vent. Eight of the males have vestiges of pigment on the chest, the size and shape of the deciduous plaques seen in breeding males of several forms of the *H. rubra–H. x-signata* complex. A number of specimens up to 31 mm long show no sex characters, a fact observed in other members of the complex. The larger ones of these specimens with short legs may be subadult or not breeding females.

COLOR. Unfortunately not seen alive. Some preserved specimens are reddish brown, as stated by Daudin, whereas others are gray, drab or brown, from light to dark. Light ocelli, yellow in life and in recently preserved specimens, occur on the upper posterior aspect of the thigh near the knee and, in many specimens, also on the inner ventral aspect of the tibia near the knee and on the anterior edge of the thigh at the flank. Ventral aspect pale, immaculate.

PATTERN. Daudin stresses the light interval between the dark dorsal and dorsolateral stripes on each side. In fact it is often more evident than the stripes. Altogether the pattern stands out best in not very dark specimens. It comprises the usual elements of the *H. rubra* sector of the complex with longitudinal stripes, not inverted parentheses-like, as in the *x-signata* sector. The interocular spot is mostly shallow but in many specimens it has a median prolongation behind. The dark dorsal and dorsolateral stripes are either quite straight or slightly sinuous; they vary somewhat in width and shape from specimen to specimen. The dorsolateral stripe is generally shorter than the dorsal, the hind part of which is sometimes fragmented. The light longitudinal interval between the stripes is very conspicuous in small specimens and in those whose background contrasts with the stripes. The whole pattern is surrounded by a halo in some specimens; it has the appearance of stippling in others, especially juveniles. A dark subcanthal stripe is often present. It generally widens beyond the tympanum, which is light brown. The oblique bars or lines on the permanently visible dorsal aspects of the limbs are often indistinct, fragmented, or reduced to a dark powdering. The ocelli are often not very marked. In light specimens there are sometimes no ocelli at all. Ventral aspect light, immaculate, save a few dark dots on the throat (females) or vestiges of dark pigment the shape of the nuptial plaques on the chest of some males.

VARIATION. The three Geyskes Surinam specimens also have the dorsal stripe longer than the dorsolateral and slightly darker at the edges. In the male from Paramaribo there is a light halo around it and also in front of the interocular spot. It is irregular and fragmented in the female, elongately triangular in the other two. A dark subcanthal stripe completes the pattern on the surfaces visible in repose.

Those collected by Rodway in British Guiana are mostly very faded with the pattern obsolete. Some of them seem doubtful to me. One robust female, 13041, with a rather rough skin shows very distinct ocelli on the edges, covered by the permanently visible parts of the limbs. The Beebe specimen is rather surprising; though faded, the dorsal pattern is very evident, with the light interval between the stripes quite brilliant; there are distinct bars on the permanently visible dorsal aspect of the limbs and small ocelli on the concealed surfaces. This female looks as if, the dark color having been bleached out, the pattern stands revealed. Several juveniles of *H. rubra huebneri* and of *H. r. altera* are somewhat like this specimen.

The specimens from French Guiana are rather dark with obscure dorsal pattern and more accentuated pattern on the thighs and flanks. Those from Cape Orange caught in an Indian hut in Brazil are rather like them.

## *Hyla rubra huebneri* Melin, 1941

(sive *H. affinis* Spix ?)

MELIN, D. 1941. Contributions to the knowledge of the amphibia of South America. *Medd. f. Goeteborgs Musei Zool. Avd.* 88. 71 pp., 38 text figs. *H. rubra huebneri*: 32–34, figs. 16, 17.
SPIX, J. B. VON. 1824. *Animalia nova sive species novae testudinum et ranarum quas in itinere per Brasiliam annis 1817–20, collegit et descripsit. Hyla affinis*: 33, table VII, fig. 3.

DIAGNOSTIC CHARACTERS. The robust build and large size, especially of full-grown females (males smaller but as large as females of typical *rubra rubra* as described by Daudin); the striking pattern of the concealed surfaces, with black reticulation enclosing large, light ocelli on thigh, flank, and inner side of tibia, often extensive to dorsal aspect of tarsus. Dorsal pattern variable, inclined to reticulation but apparently derived from the straight longitudinal stripes often present. Range wide along the basin of the Amazonas River system.

TYPES AND TYPE LOCALITIES. Melin indicates "2 males, 1 female Taracuá, Rio Uaupés, 11.5 and S. Gabriel, Rio Negro, August 1924 and vicinity of Manaus, 15.11, 1923, Brazil. The female is from near Manaus."

DESCRIPTION. Size medium for the complex. Build robust, especially in full-grown females. Hindlimb short, plump, the tibiotarsal articulation reaching the eye or slightly beyond it when adpressed. Head plane, slightly longer than wide. Body as wide in postaxillary region as the head. Snout fairly short, oval from above, rounded, slanting slightly over the mouth opening in profile. Canthus rostralis blunt. Loreal region high, slightly oblique. Nostrils at approximately two-thirds the distance from eye to tip of snout, slightly tumefied. Eye large, prominent, as long as or slightly longer than its distance from nostril. Interorbital space wider than the internarial space. Tympanum approximately two-fifths the diameter of the eye. Tongue large, rounded, slightly emarginate and free behind. Vomerine teeth in two short groups between the choanae. Disks short, very wide. Hands with a rudiment of web at the base. Feet from two-thirds to four-fifths webbed. A tubercle at the base of the first finger, a minute one under the third or fourth. An oval inner and a very small outer metatarsal tubercle. Skin with disseminated pustules above. Chest, abdomen, and midventral aspect of the thigh granular. A supratympanic ridge, a mass of glandules at its base and at the upper corner of the mouth. A fold below the throat, a distinct fold across the chest, sometimes forming a slight bib to the root of the arms.

MEASUREMENTS. Females: average 38–42 mm, extremes 32 (1) and 45 (1) snout to vent. Males 29–33 mm, seldom more.

SECONDARY SEX CHARACTERS. Females attain a large size compared to males; abdomen hard when distended by eggs. One unusually small female, from Serra do Navio, Amapá, is only 32 mm long.

Males are generally slender and small, especially those from the western part of the range. The vocal sac forms folds at the base. Forearms enlarged in some breeding males. A few males, some of them small, from the western part of the Brazilian range show vestiges of pigment in the shape of nuptial pads on the breast.

COLOR. Unfortunately not seen alive. Preserved specimens mostly dark, fuscous gray to black, occasionally reddish brown. Some specimens melanistic, others pale, including isolated individuals, from several larger samples and a number of juveniles.

PATTERN. The light flash color and dark marks on the surfaces concealed in repose are more characteristic and striking than the dorsal pattern. They occupy the hind part of the flank, posterior and anterior parts of the dorsal aspect of the thigh, inner ventral aspect of the tibia, and, in well-marked specimens, the inner dorsal part of the tarsus and the edge of the upper arm.

The fundamental pattern of the dorsal surface seems derived from the longitudinal pattern of *Hyla rubra rubra*, composed of a long dorsal and a shorter dorsolateral stripe on each side with a light interval between them. In many specimens, including those from Amapá and northern Pará, the dorsal stripes are quite straight, rather thick and grow less distinct caudad.

VARIATION. The stripes are often plain, sometimes slightly wavy or surrounded by a lighter halo. They also tend to form a reticulum on the back, though some specimens show only the white alveoli that are recurrent in diverse other forms of the complex, for instance in *Hyla x-signata similis*. In larger samples there generally occur one or more individuals in which the dorsal stripe is broken in two longitudinally and, more rarely, into isolated fragments that recall the double inverted parentheses of the *Hyla x-signata* sector of the complex. The latter are more common in unusually light individuals. A few aberrant specimens, either from a sample or caught alone, recall *Hyla hayii* from the southeastern mountains of Brazil. Their dorsal aspect is more or less olivaceous and either uniform, without any marks at all, or with faint vestiges of dorsal, entire or fragmented, stripes. Conversely, in very rare individuals (only one in all the eastern samples, more in the western ones) the dorsal stripes become confluent into a large dark median figure which may be entire, fenestrated, or reticu-

late. Bars on the permanently visible aspect of limbs generally not distinct. In juveniles and one or two adults the dorsal surface is light; a gay pattern of fragmented stripes on the back and bars plus additional ornamentation on the limbs stand out. This applies to a certain number of very small young collected at Eirunepé, Conceição do Raimundo and on the Itacoai River, near the Peruvian frontier of Brazil, by Miss Kloss and Dr. J. C. M. de Carvalho. However, two large females from the eastern territory of Amapá are similar to them.

The pattern on the concealed surfaces, though conspicuous in all but very melanistic specimens, is also not quite uniform. Mostly there are either round or elongate ocelli on the limbs and similar light areas on the flanks with a network of black, more or less dendritic lines around them. In melanistic individuals the ocelli are small. In those that are devoid of dark pigment and *hayii*-like in appearance, the ocelli are disposed in a series on the background. In two from Amapá (Puxacá, Serra do Navio) and Pará (Serra do Ererê), the marks on the flanks are substituted by large dots and small blotches. This pattern is common in the specimens from the Peruvian part of the Amazonian Hylaea.

VOICE. Unknown.

HABITS. Melin states that the two male types were caught on the ground, one of them in his camp, the other under bark in a clearing in the forest. The female came from an *igarapé* or rivulet. Miss Kloss also obtained a number of small specimens on the forest floor and others at small heights on vegetation. Mr. Rauschert noted that his nineteen fine specimens from the Erepecurú were found at a small pond, and that in the evening they also sat on the bushes above it.

DISTRIBUTION. This form seems to have a very wide distribution. We have specimens from the territory of Amapá and from the Erepecurú or Cuminá River, which is an affluent of the Trombetas, a northern tributary of the Amazonas in the state of Pará. Melin's types are from the state of Amazonas, and were obtained at Manaus on the Solimões and on tributaries of the northern rivers of Uaupés and Rio Negro. Our specimens from Manaus and Itacoatiara are juvenile, relatively small males. We have, however, some large, fine adults from the western frontier of Brazil, which were taken at Benjamin Constant together with juveniles. One specimen from Colombia, dedit Dunn, is labeled Morelia,

Caquetá. This river is called Japurá in Brazil and also flows into the Solimões. We have also seen Brazilian specimens from Borba on the Madeira River near the confluence with the Amazonas. The Peruvian specimens seen belong to the FMNH and are from the province of Loreto (Pebas, Ucayali) Cuzco and, what is more surprising, from Madre de Dios, which is farther south. Many of the former were taken near the Ucayali, one of the headwaters of the Amazonas, the latter from the terrain around the Madre de Dios, one of the headwaters of the Madeira. These specimens have mostly large dark dots and small blotches on the flanks. This distribution seems to justify considering the whole Hylaea, or basin of the Amazonas River system, as the range of *H. r. huebneri*. The Peruvian specimens are slightly smaller like some of the western Brazilian ones. They may belong to another race, but the descriptions of *H. funerea* Cope, *H. rubra inconspicua* Melin and *H. coerulea* Spix do not fit them.

## *Hyla rubra altera* nom. nov.

(nomen novum for *Hyla rubra orientalis* B. Lutz, 1968)

> LUTZ, B. 1968. New Brazilian Forms of Hyla. Texas Memorial Museum. The Pearce-Sellards Series 10:15–18, fig. 8.

This is an eastern form of *Hyla rubra* from the Atlantic area of Brazil. It is known to us from Pernambuco to Santa Catarina. The subspecific name, published in 1968, was derived from the range along the seaboard of Brazil. For a long time the specimens of this *Hyla* collected near Rio de Janeiro were loosely put into *Hyla fuscomarginata* Lutz, 1925, but that is a dwarf form first found in Minas Gerais. The subspecific name had to be changed from *orientalis*, as it was preoccupied.

DIAGNOSTIC CHARACTERS. Similar to *Hyla rubra rubra* and *Hyla duartei* in size, but differing from both by the more robust build, rougher skin, and the absence of ocelli or bright flash colors on the parts of the flanks and limbs concealed in repose. Smaller than *H. r. huebneri*. Range different from that of the other forms.

TYPES AND TYPE LOCALITY. Out of a series of fifteen specimens from Crubixá, county of Sta. Leopoldina, state of Espirito Santo, collected by Elio Gouvea, March 16, 1960, MNR n. 4030 was se-

lected as the male holotype and MNR n. 4031 as the female allotype; the others are paratypes.

DESCRIPTION. Size small but not minute, up to 32 mm snout to vent. Build robust. Body almost uniform in width from eye to sacrum. Hindlimb short, tibiotarsal articulation reaching the eye when adpressed. Snout triangular, wide at the base, narrow in front, sometimes appearing pointed beyond and below the nostrils. Canthus rostralis straight to the nostril, moderately distinct. Loreal region slightly concave. Nostrils subcanthal, small, slightly tumefied. Eye prominent, slightly longer than the distance to nostril. Tympanum small, not more than one-third the horizontal diameter of eye, very distinct. Tongue subcircular, slightly emarginate and free behind. Vomerine teeth in two short, subcontiguous groups between the small choanae. Disks short but well-developed, especially on the hand, rounded in front. Fingers free. Webs on toes more or less straight, reaching to below the disk on the outer side of the second and third and on the fifth, to the penultimate tubercle on both sides of the fourth toe. A tubercle below the first finger; palm well padded, especially below the third and fourth fingers. An elongate inner, a very small, outer, metatarsal tubercle. Skin pustular on the back and sides; belly and midventral aspect of thigh granular. A glandular supratympanic ridge; distinct folds of skin below the gula and across the chest.

MEASUREMENTS. Females 25–32 mm snout to vent. Males 23–30; average 29 mm. The specimens from Espirito Santo and those from Santa Catarina are mostly large and very robust. The latter may be differentiating into a separate race.

SECONDARY SEX CHARACTERS. Not marked except for the yellow gula of the male and the distension of the body by the egg mass in the female just before spawning. Size not necessarily greater in nuptial females than in males, though the former grow somewhat larger.

COLOR. (Rio de Janeiro population). Dorsal coloring dull, olivaceous brown, or drab, variable at different times as to depth and intensity, even in the same individual. Pattern darker than background. Tympanum light brown and conspicuous. Iris the color of the sides of the head, upper half slightly iridescent, pinkish and greenish in incident light, but much paler than in *H. cuspidata*; a pseudocolobom and dark reticulation on the iris.

Sometimes the whole body has a slightly metallic glint. Ventral aspect whitish on abdomen, gray on limbs; gula grayish in female; yellow in male.

PATTERN. The full pattern consists of two pairs of longitudinal dark stripes or bands separated by a lighter interval, an interocular spot and sometimes a longitudinal vertebral line, all darker than the background. Inner, dorsal stripe more constant and more evident, wider and longer than the outer, dorsolateral one. The latter sometimes very dark, almost linear and/or short; in some individuals the outer stripe is followed by a few dark blotches or spots. Interval between the stripes either the same color as the dorsal background or lighter; very conspicuous in small specimens and in juveniles. Interocular spot often absent or barely distinct; variable in shape but often somewhat reminiscent of an irregular Phrygean cap with the base between the eyes. Vertebral dark line very often absent, at best vestigial. Details and intensity of pattern variable. One juvenile with a very ornate livery of spots between the stripes is reminiscent of some specimens of other, northern, races of *Hyla rubra*.

GEOGRAPHIC VARIATION. Occasionally, one or more specimens of a sample from the Baixada Fluminense have the inner dorsal stripe divided into a fore and a hind part and very slightly curved inwards, tending toward the pattern of the forms belonging to the *H. x-signata* sector of the group. In most specimens from Rio de Janeiro, the pattern is, however, inclined to simplification, with a conspicuous inner dorsal band, a very dark but short, narrow outer band, and the rest of the pattern indistinct. The samples from Espirito Santo have a marked pattern on the back, often with a light halo round the dark bands, which are variable in shape; there is also a white area along the upper jaw. The samples from Santa Catarina mostly have a very marked dorsolateral pattern. A number of them show a light area at the edge of the flank and thigh, obscure mottling on the concealed posterior part of the latter, and oblique spots or bands on the permanently visible dorsal aspect of the limbs.

VOICE. The call of *Hyla r. altera* heard in Rio and in southern Bahia agrees with the usual croak of the *rubra x-signata* complex. It sounds something like *creê, ccreê, ccreê.*

HABITS AND ECOLOGY. This form, like others of the complex observed alive, calls on vegetation above ponds and other sheets of standing water in which it breeds. At Sernambetiba (Recreio dos Bandeirantes) outside Rio, it often sits on small banana trees at the edge of a canal. In southern Bahia it was found by us in daytime sheltering in epiphytic bromeliads, some of which were growing on trees in swampy ground while others were clinging to dead trees or telephone poles in full sunlight. The microclimate inside the bromeliads probably remains moist and cool except during long periods of drought.

RANGE. There is a hiatus in the known distribution of *Hyla rubra* "sensu lato" along the coast, between Cape Orange and Pernambuco in Brazil. Our large samples of *H. r. altera* are from the states of Bahia, Espirito Santo, Rio de Janeiro, Guanabara, and Santa Catarina, plus a few from São Paulo and one from Tapera in Pernambuco. It is possible that some very small specimens from Rio Grande do Sul, collected by Milstead at Porto Alegre, belong to it, though they have no vestige of livery left. They are already within the range of *Hyla eringiophila*, but this belongs to the *Hyla x-signata* sector of the complex.

NOTE. Two samples, one from Cabo Frio in the state of Rio de Janeiro, one from Canavieiras, in southern Bahia, are much smaller in size but include breeding females with eggs. However, one of the Guanabara samples also includes juveniles very like them besides adults with the usual robust build. Perhaps some populations are stunted in growth.

## ALLIED FORMS

Three other Brazilian forms belonging to this complex display the longitudinal entire stripes associated with *Hyla rubra*. Two of them are very close to each other but occur at different points of the Serra da Mantiqueira. The third is a dwarf form.

*Hyla duartei duartei* ranges in size from 28–37 mm. It is rather like *H. r. rubra*, but the dorsal stripes are much better developed than the lateral ones, and they converge or coalesce in front, forming a bridge between the eyes. Yellow ocelli are present on the posterior, upper concealed part of the thigh, often also on the anterior one and on the hind part of the flanks; a few specimens show them on the inside of the leg. This form lives on the Itatiaia Mountains, mostly above 2,000 m altitude.

*Hyla duartei caldarum* is smaller; males often 25, females 28–32 mm long, rarely more. Build slender, with elongate snout and robust hindlimbs. Dorsal pattern very similar but more variable than in *H. d. duartei;* the dorsal stripes meet or coalesce in front only in a few individuals. Ocelli small, pale yellow or cadmium yellow in life. This race, or at least very divergent population, has elected a very specialized biotope; the thorny rosette of leaves of an *Eryngium* growing at Poços de Caldas in the mountains of Minas Gerais.

*Hyla fuscomarginata* Lutz is a dwarf form not over 23 or, at most, 24 mm long. It is characterized by the small size, slender build, abrupt backward slope of the snout, short legs, and free digits. Dorsal surface pustular with two wide, fuscous, dorsal, and dorsolateral pairs of stripes separated by a very narrow interval, a similar vertebral stripe generally bisected by an interocular line. *Hyla fuscomarginata* lives in the mountainous area of Minas Gerais and Goiás, and perhaps eastern Bolivia (*H. parkeri*). Quite similar specimens have, however, also been found on the plateau near São Paulo and seem to descend into the valley of the Rio Paraiba.

## *Hyla duartei duartei* B. Lutz, 1952

> Lutz, B. 1951. Nota previa sobre alguns anfíbios anuros do Alto Itatiaia. *O Hospital*, May 1951. Rio de Janeiro.
> ———. 1952. New frogs from Itatiaia Mountain, Brazil. *Copeia* 1(1952):27–28.

*Hyla duartei*, from montane southeastern Brazil, was described as subspecies of *Hyla rubra*, of which the typical form hails from the Guianas. They, and *Hyla r. altera* from the coast of Brazil, are very similar, but there are some differences between them.

DIAGNOSTIC CHARACTERS. *Hyla d. duartei* is characterized by the size, pattern, and distribution. The size varies from 28 to 37 mm. The dorsal pattern consists of a pair of dark longitudinal stripes, one on each side of the back, which converge and often coalesce in front, between, or just behind the eyes. There are light ocelli on a dark ground on the posterior dorsal portion of the thigh

and sometimes on the hind part of the flank concealed in repose; in some specimens the ocelli also appear on the anterior part of the thigh and, more rarely, on the inner side of the leg. *H. r. altera* is smaller; it has double dorsolateral stripes, no pattern on the concealed surfaces, and is a lowland form. *H. r. rubra* has ocelli on the upper concealed aspect of the thigh and on the inside of the leg near the knee. In neither of them do the dorsal stripes converge or coalesce.

TYPES AND TYPE LOCALITY. Male holotype from Macieiras in the Itatiaia Mountains collected by Elio Gouveia, March 29, 1945, at 1,900 m altitude; MNR n. 3257; three paratypes, same data, MNR no. 4091–93 from Brejo da Lapa, at 2,200 m, same collector, same location. Female allotype, n. 4094, collected January 1952 by B. Lutz and E. Gouveia.

DESCRIPTION. Male type 35 mm, female allotype 33 mm, snout to vent. Build fairly robust. Body narrower at the postaxillary region than the head, tapering slightly beyond the sacrum. Tibiotarsal articulation reaching the anterior part of the eye when the leg is adpressed. Head large, elongate, very slightly longer than wide. Snout oval, slightly acuminate at the tip; from above, rounded, declivous, projecting beyond the mouth in profile. Canthus rostralis well defined to the nostrils, loreal region very slightly concave. Nostrils small, slightly tumefied, marking the end of the canthus, placed at approximately two-thirds of the distance from the eye to the tip of the snout. Eye large, prominent, as long as its distance from the nostril and two-thirds to four-fifths its distance from the tip of the snout. Tympanum distinct, very small, less than one-half the diameter of the eye. Vomerine teeth in two small, round groups between the choanae, which are small. Tongue subcircular, slightly emarginate and free behind. Disks short, wide. A small tubercle under the first finger, a similar double one under the third and fourth fingers. A rudiment of web between the two outer fingers. Feet one-half webbed or less. A narrow strip of web from the inner metatarsal tubercle to the first subarticular tubercle on the inner side of the first toe; web wide to the first tubercle on the outer side of the second and third, to the second tubercle on both sides of the fourth, reaching somewhat below the disk on the inner side of the second, third, and on the fifth toes. Inner metatarsal tubercle small, outer minute. Palmar, plantar, and subarticular tubercles small. Scattered glandules on the dorsal surface, more noticeable on the head and upper eyelids. Gula minutely granular, belly and midventral strip of thigh coarser.

VARIATION. Individual variation moderate in our series of over seventy specimens from the Itatiaia. Leg slightly longer in juveniles and in some small individuals, the tibiotarsal articulation reaching in front of the eye when the hindlimb is adpressed. Leg short, the tibiotarsal articulation reaching only to the hind part of the eye in just one adult. Tongue wide but oval, entire and hardly free behind in some specimens, narrower and more elongate in a few others. Vomerine teeth variable in size and degree of approximation. The only adult from the Serra da Bocaina is a quite typical female.

MEASUREMENTS (mm). Females 30–37; extremes, especially upper one, exceptional. Males 28–35, large ones rarer. Head length to width mostly 12:11. Tibia 13–18 mm long, in males mostly 14–15, in females more often 16 mm. Smallest specimens seen 26 mm snout to vent.

SECONDARY SEX CHARACTERS. Except for the male vocal sac, which may be quite large, forming folds or a balloon, sex characters not very marked. Females slightly larger, the abdomen distended when filled with ripe eggs.

COLOR. Dorsal coloring olivaceous greens and browns, the pattern darker; limbs similar, somewhat lighter, especially the parts concealed in repose. Ocelli lemon yellow or chrome yellow on a dark brown ground. Ventral aspect pale, immaculate.

PATTERN. Two dark, longitudinal stripes, one on each side of the back, more or less straight but not quite uniform in width and often slightly divergent posteriorly; anteriorly they converge between or just behind the eye, either forming two club-shaped heads or coalescing into a horizontal interocular bridge. A narrow subcanthal dark line widens into a stripe behind the eye and tympanum and dies out in the postscapular or presacral region. Light ocelli on dark ground, disposed in one or two rows on the posterior dorsal aspect of the thigh, yellow in life; in female allotype and a certain number of other specimens the ocelli also appear on the hind part of the flank; a lesser number of individuals have ocelli on the anterior concealed upper aspect of the thigh and a few on the inner edge of the tibiae as well. Permanently visible dorsal aspect of limbs either plain or with more or less distinct,

oblique bars or marks. A stippling of dark dots on the edges of the lower surfaces, gula, sides, and limbs; hands and feet darker.

VOICE. The call is a rasping croak, like that of the other lesser members of the group: *craa, craa, craa, craa.* It is repeated continuously. When many males are calling it sounds very loud.

HABITS. *H. d. duartei* gathers at the ponds and pools available in the upper reaches of the serras. Some of the pools are formed by water flowing from the numerous sources and brooks into natural hollows, others are caused by artificial dams built across rivulets. *H. d. duartei* is very abundant at a pond caused by a dam at Brejo da Lapa (2,200 m altitude) on the same Itatiaia Mountains as the strict type locality, Macieiras (1,900 m). It sits either on the ground or on low vegetation near the pond when it is calling. It has also been collected in bromeliads. Many specimens have larvae of mites under the skin, which are common in bromeliad-sheltering or dwelling montane frogs.

RANGE. One of our specimens was taken at 880 m altitude at another artificial pond, near the headquarters of the Itatiaia National Park. The other specimens from the Itatiaia were all obtained above 1,900 m. The two specimens, one adult and one juvenile from Lageado on the Serra da Bocaina were taken at 1,650 m altitude. We do not have it from other localities as yet: Itatiaia is part of the Mantiqueira Range and the Serra da Bocaina part of the Maritime Range. The climate of Itatiaia and the Bocaina is *Cfb* Köppen, i. e. subtropical with cool summers. The mean yearly temperatures should be around 16°, 18°, or 20°C, with considerable fluctuations and low winter temperatures. Precipitation is not less than 2,000 mm, probably nearer 3,000 or 3,500 mm per year.

NAME. This little frog is named for Dr. Wanderbilt Duarte de Barros, former director of the Itatiaia National Park, who gave naturalists every facility for studying the fauna of one of the most interesting spots in Brazil.

## *Hyla duartei caldarum* B. Lutz, 1968

LUTZ, B. 1968. New Brazilian Forms of Hyla. Texas Memorial Museum. The Pearce-Sellards Series 10:1–19. *H. d. caldarum:* 11–13, fig. 8.

The frogs collected by Dr. Johann Becker and his assistants during a survey of naturally radioactive areas carried out at Poços de Caldas, Minas

Gerais, include a small, apparently new form of *Hyla* belonging to the *Hyla rubra–Hyla x-signata* complex. I called it *Hyla d. caldarum* after the type locality, whose name is derived from the thermal springs found there.

DIAGNOSTIC CHARACTERS. The small size, elongate, fairly slender build, long snout, and robust hindlimbs allied to a variant of the *H. rubra* pattern. This comprises an interocular spot, a pair of longitudinal stripes on the back, and light ocelli, which are lemon chrome or pale cadmium in life, located on the concealed areas of thighs and flanks. It is very close to but diverges from *H. d. duartei* by its smaller size, slight differences of pattern, and its biotope.

TYPES AND TYPE LOCALITY. Poços de Caldas, Minas Gerais, 21° 50′ 20″ S, 46° 33′ 53″ W Gr, alt. 1,100 m s/m. Male holotype, MNR n. 4002 (one of six males), from a marsh north of Morro do Ferro, leg O. Roppa and O. Leoncini, Jan. 28, 1965. Female allotype, MNR n. 4001, from marsh to the right of the road between Poços de Caldas and Andradas, leg J. Becker and O. Roppa, March 20, 1964; 18 male paratypes: 3988–4000, 4003–4007. Now many additional specimens.

DESCRIPTION. Size small; male type 25 mm snout to vent; female larger, 28–32, one 35 mm long. Build elongate, postscapular region almost as wide as the head, narrowing beyond it. Hindlimb robust, fairly long, the tibiotarsal articulation reaching between nostril and eye when the leg is adpressed. Head slightly longer than wide. Snout long, triangular, depressed beyond the nostrils, projecting obliquely over the mouth opening in profile. Canthus rostralis not marked; loreal region rather high, slightly concave between nostril and eye. Nostril superolateral, not terminal, very slightly tumefied. Eye average, approximately as long as its distance from the nostril, considerably shorter than its distance from the tip of the snout. Tympanum very distinct, one-third to one-half the diameter of the eye. Interorbital space wider than the internarial space. Tongue wide, oval, slightly notched and free behind. Vomerine teeth in two short transverse, almost contiguous groups between the choanae. Fingers long; in some specimens the lateral ones have a trace of web at the base. Disks short. An elongate callosity on the edge of the first, an indistinct tubercle below the third and fourth fingers, a number of minute palmar tubercles. Foot narrow. Toes half-webbed; wide

part of webs rather straight. An inner and a small outer metatarsal tubercle. A very slight ridge of glandules on the inner edge and a still slighter one on the outer edge of the tarsus; similar, less distinct ones on the edges of the forearm, the outer one continued onto the hand. Skin slightly rough, with disseminated glandules on the dorsal surface and limbs, especially on the upper eyelid and vertex. Beneath granular, with minute dots on the vocal sac. A fold across the chest, concealed in males by the vocal sac; a peritympanic ridge and a series of glandules below the tympanum.

FEMALE ALLOTYPE. Build more robust. Hindlimb shorter, snout more acuminate. Folds across the chest and axillae more evident.

MEASUREMENTS (mm): Male holotype: snout to vent 25. Hindlimb 48: femur 14, tibia 14, tarsus 9, foot 11. Other males 23–27, mostly 24 or 25 snout to vent.

Female allotype: snout to vent 28. Hindlimb 53: femur 14, tibia 16, tarsus 10, foot 13. Other females measured: three 28 snout to vent, one 29, four 30, two 32, and an unusually large one 35 snout to vent. Body distended by eggs.

VARIATION. Fifteen of the male paratypes and most of the additional specimens are very like the type. There is not more than one millimeter difference among most of them as to snout to vent length. The tip of the snout is sometimes pointed. The hindlimb is variable as usual in Brazilian species of *Hyla*, the adpressed tibiotarsal articulation attaining some point or other between the eye and the nostril, nearer to the latter in some, nearer to the former in a few. The other differences are minute and regard the width of the tongue, the degree of approximation of the groups of vomerine teeth, and the distinctness of the glandular ridges and pustules. Two male paratypes from Rio das Antas differ more: they are very slightly larger (27 and 26 mm snout to vent); these males are more robust and more elongate in build, with very long and pointed snout and shorter hindlimb; the tibiotarsal articulation reaching in front of the eye in one, to its anterior part in the other. They are also very dark. A third one is average in size and aspect.

COLOR IN LIFE. In daytime, the dorsal aspect is pale bronze, slightly olivaceous or pale wood brown, occasionally drab, generally with a metallic glint. Spots of flash color often very small, variable in shape and from lemon yellow to a pale cadmium tone. Lower aspect pale, grayish, slightly violaceous, especially on the limbs. Belly whitish over the opaque peritoneum, gula white or slightly pigmented. Iris the color of the background, slightly darker in the lower half, which coincides with a darker area around the tympanum. Pattern of dorsolateral stripes and interocular spot and their halos generally less evident than in preserved specimens.

The two large paratypes from Rio das Antas mentioned above and about one-fifth or one-sixth of the additional specimens are very dark. They remain dark after preservation, whereas the usual light specimens tend to become gray after death.

PATTERN (preserved specimens). The pattern is that of the *Hyla rubra* sector of the complex; a discrete dark subcanthal line or area, lighter brown tympanum, interocular spot, and a pair of longitudinal dorsal stripes. The interocular spot is often trapezoid with the longer part in front; it is generally not prolonged backward but may have small median, anterior, and posterior notches plus minute anterior and posterior lateral prongs. The pair of dark dorsal stripes is almost always entire; one or both may touch the interocular spot or be united to it. The stripes are slightly sinuous. They curve inward toward each other between shoulder and forearm, diverge again, become more or less straight on the sacrum, and fade out. Both interocular spot and dorsal stripes are often surrounded by a light halo or, in dark specimens, by light spots.

In some specimens one or both the longitudinal stripes show a strangulation at some point. Stripes divided right across into an anterior and a posterior portion are very rare. The pattern is then slightly reminiscent of that of the *x-signata* sector of the complex. Only one specimen seen, a large female, has the stripes fragmented into several irregular portions, some of them small and disposed on the middle of the back. This pattern recalls that of *Hyla craspedospila*. In dark individuals the pattern is often rather indistinct, though not so in those that have a distinct halo or brilliant white spots around the stripes, even when the back is quite dark. The halo around the spots is, however, also variable, very distinct in some, less so in others, and absent in a few.

Bar-like oblique spots on the permanently visible aspect of the limbs, especially the tibia and forearm, are present but not always very distinct.

The pattern is completed by a few rather irregular light ocelli on the hind part of the flank and on the dorsal aspects of the thigh concealed in repose. Some specimens have showy ocelli; in others they are very small and indistinct. Vestiges of yellow are visible in recently preserved individuals. Gula pigmented in dark specimens. Ventral aspect immaculate.

HABITS AND ECOLOGY. Dr. Becker informs me that *H. d. caldarum* is quite common at Poços de Caldas and lives in the rosette of leaves of an Umbellifera, *Eryngium*, and of some large Eriocaulaceae of similar habit. As *Eryngium* is very thorny, the little frogs are well protected by their choice of a biotope.

DISTRIBUTION. Known only from the type locality.

AFFINITIES. *Hyla d. caldarum* shows a quite superficial resemblance in build to *Hyla squalirostris*, a species from the marshes of the Brazilian Serra do Mar and from the Plana Bonariense in Argentina. The shark-line snout of the latter is, however, much more produced, the skin smooth translucid, the pattern different, and the build still more slender and more elongate. Moreover, the affinities of *squalirostris* are with the *Hyla polytaenia* group, whereas *H. d. caldarum* is very evidently a member of the *Hyla rubra* complex. The pointed snout, the halo around the spots, and the ridges of glandules on tarsus and forearm are somewhat reminiscent of *Hyla craspedospila*, but only one female of *caldarum* has a fragmented pattern like that of this other member of the *rubra-x-signata* complex, whose spots are usually surrounded by a dark border and which lives at lower altitudes. The dark individuals resemble *Hyla cuspidata* somewhat, but the latter has a smooth skin, copper-colored eyes, green bones, and is devoid of flash colors. The distribution is also different.

After seeing the more abundant material now available it seems best to consider *H. d. caldarum* as a subspecies or perhaps even as an aberrant population of *Hyla d. duartei*, smaller in size, with longer legs and a slightly divergent pattern, adapted to a specialized biotope.

## *Hyla fuscomarginata* Lutz, 1925

LUTZ, A. 1925. Batraciens du Brésil. *C. R. Soc.*

*Biol. Paris* 93(21):137–139. *Hyla fuscomarginata*: 138.

———. 1926. Nota previa sobre especies novas de batrachios do Brasil. New species of Brazilian batrachians. Preliminary note. *Publ. Inst. O. Cruz*, March 10, 1926. *Hyla fuscomarginata*: 6, 13.

GAIGE, HELEN T. 1929. Three new tree-frogs from Panama and Bolivia. *Occ. Pap. MZUM*, n. 207, p. 6. *Hyla parkeri*: 1–13.

MÜLLER, L., and HELLMICH, W. 1936. *Wissenschaftliche Ergebnisse der Deutschen Gran Chaco Expeditionen*. I Teil: Amphibia, Chelonia, Loricata. 120 pp., 35 figs., 8 pls., map. *H. lindneri*: 63–64, fig. 22.

BOKERMANN, W. C. A. 1964. Duas nuevas especies de *Hyla* de Rondônia, Brasil. *Neotropica* 10(31):1–6.

*Hyla fuscomarginata* was described forty years ago by A. Lutz on early specimens from Belo Horizonte, Minas Gerais. The specimens from São Paulo mentioned in the description were no longer extant in the Lutz Collection when it was sent to the National Museum. However, the MNR has a few examples from New Manchester inside the city of São Paulo and Suzano near it. Those from Rio de Janeiro are different; they are much larger and more robust, have a shorter head and a slightly diverse pattern; they belong to an eastern geographical race of *H. rubra* Daudin.

DIAGNOSTIC CHARACTERS. The very small size allied to the narrow elongate build, short legs, free fingers; the very characteristic slope of the snout in profile; the pustular dorsal surface and the pattern, composed of dark, wide, double, fuscous dorsal and dorsolateral margins; a dark vertebral stripe mostly bisected by an interocular one and dark-edged canthi, all on a lighter brown background.

TYPES AND TYPE LOCALITY. In his preliminary notes (1925, 1926) Lutz mentioned Belo Horizonte, São Paulo and Rio de Janeiro as finding places but did not designate either types or type locality. Belo Horizonte can, however, be inferred from dates of collecting, the maximum size of 23 mm mentioned by Lutz in his notes and his choice of a Belo Horizonte example for the watercolor of *H. fuscomarginata* painted for him by Sandig. Cochran (1955) based her description on a cotype from the same place.

SYNTYPES. A. Lutz Collection, nos. 845, 846 (and USNM 96964) collected by A. Lutz at Belo Hori-

zonte November 30, 1924. The two former at the MNR.

DESCRIPTION. Size very small; maximum indicated by Lutz 23 mm, mostly less. Build narrow, elongate. Head longer than wide. Snout forming an elongate triangle with obtuse apex when seen from above, sloping back sharply and overhanging the mouth in profile. Body narrow, postaxillary region as wide as the head, postsacral narrower. Hindlimb short, the adpressed tibiotarsal articulation reaching the eye. Canthus rostralis straight, blunt; loreal region plane. Interorbital space not wider or only slightly wider than the internarial space. Tympanum distinct, between one-third and one-half the horizontal diameter of the eye, which is about equal to the distance from its anterior corner to the nostril. Tongue large, wide, oval, slightly free behind and emarginate. Vomerine teeth in small groups, close together, between and near the posterior border of the choanae. Fingers free. A callosity under the first, a bifid tubercle under the third and fourth fingers; palm padded with tubercles. Lateral toes between one-half and two-thirds webbed. An elongate, inner, and a very small, round, outer metatarsal tubercle. Soles also padded with tubercles. Skin pustular above, especially the vertex between the eyes, the upper eyelids, the dorsolateral margins, and the sides of body. Belly and midventral portion of thigh granular. A fold of skin across the chest; a narrow supratympanic fold.

SIZE. 18–23 mm snout to vent, average: 19–20, tibia 9, head width 5 or 6.

VARIATION. Some specimens have the tongue entire. In a very few the tibiotarsal articulation reaches beyond the eye or fails to reach it. The specimens from Minas Gerais are slightly larger than the others.

SECONDARY SEX CHARACTERS. The few females seen are 20 mm long and hail from Bahia, Goiás, and Itatiaia. Most of our preserved males have a very large vocal sac.

COLOR AND PATTERN. Lutz describes the dorsal background of *Hyla fuscomarginata* as light brown, "like coffee with much milk"; he indicates a vertebral stripe and an interocular stripe across it forming a brown cross, a double brown band from eye to the inguinal region, and a dark line under the canthus. Some of the preserved specimens incline to fade even more than usual in *Hyla*. In others the pattern is well preserved. The dorsolateral margins are generally more distinct than the vertebral stripe, especially the interocular one; they may be separated longitudinally by a very narrow light interval, but the light interval is often indistinct. The vertical stripe is irregular in width, widening at one or more places, especially between the eyes, forming an irregular cross, swollen at the intersection, with the median part of the interocular stripe. Gula of male citrine or lemon yellow. Rest of ventral aspect cream or light gray, with dots of black pigment on the limbs and at the edge of the gula, also on the female. Some specimens have additional indistinct longitudinal lines between the vertebral stripe and the margins and/or obscure oblique bands or spots on the visible parts of the limbs.

ECOLOGY. The specimens seen alive by me were collected near standing water, under the usual conditions for small species breeding in it.

These metamorphic specimens, from 13–15 mm snout to vent length, have tails ranging from 18 mm to mere stumps.

SYNONYMS AND RELATIONSHIPS. This form belongs to the *Hyla rubra x-signata* complex, and is probably the smallest member of the group. It so closely resembles *Hyla parkeri* Gaige, 1929, that the latter must be either synonymous with it or a subspecies of it. Dr. Gaige's description applies perfectly to *fuscomarginata*, except for the slightly larger size: 24 instead of 23 mm, according to the description, 26 mm fide D. Cochran (1955), the less pustular dorsal skin and the perhaps slightly larger tympanum. *Hyla lindneri* Müller & Hellmich (1936) from Formosa, Argentina, seems to have slightly longer limbs, shorter webs, and a slightly different pattern, but it is probably also conspecific. The types of *lindneri* were destroyed in the Second World War, and no specimens are available for comparison.

DISTRIBUTION. The Lutz Collection and that of the MNR comprise sixteen good specimens from Belo Horizonte and places near it (Vespasiano and Lagoa Santa). Dr. Cochran's cotype is a poor and a slightly doubtful specimen of the original lot from Belo Horizonte. Her description of *H. fuscomarginata* and of *Hyla parkeri* both agree with our good specimens from Minas Gerais. She has some from Lassance, further north on the Rio das Velhas, and juveniles from Pirapora on the São Francisco River. The Lutz Collection also includes five small specimens from Salvador, the capital of Bahia. Dr. Vanzolini collected *H. fuscomarginata* at Lagoa Formosa in Goiás. There are also some specimens from New Manchester, MNR 1674, in the suburbs of São Paulo and Suzano. Both the author and the DZSP have very good specimens from the valley of the Paraiba River at Itatiaia. The type locality of *H. parkeri* is Buena Vista in the department of Santa Cruz, Bolivia, where a hundred specimens were obtained by Steinbach; a few others were obtained at Ixiamas. *H. lindneri* belongs to the German Gran Chaco collections.

This distribution is very surprising at first. However, Minas Gerais, Bahia, and Goiás lie within one of the three large natural provinces of South America, east of the Andes, which I call the Continental province. It comprises not only the lowlands of the Gran Chaco and the semiarid northwestern part of Brazil, but also the highlands of Minas Gerais and Goiás and apparently the lowest eastern slopes of the Andes in Argentina and Bolivia. Some other species of Anurans, like *Bufo paracnemis*, occupy most of this area. The Brazilian plateau, also in this province, reaches the city of São Paulo, just beyond the maritime montane rain forest. *Hyla fuscomarginata* seems to be traveling down the Paraiba River valley.

*Hyla madeirae* Bokermann (1964) from Rondonia Territory is probably also synonymous with *Hyla fuscomarginata*. Bokermann compares it to *Hyla parkeri* Gaige, which I have put to the synonymy of *Hyla fuscomarginata*. Bokermann states that the head is wider and the snout more prominent. His paratype, WCAB 10.771, MNR A 3963, sent to the museum under the terms of his grant from the National Research Counsel, does not have a wide snout. It differs from *H. fuscomarginata* only in the following details: the light interval between the double fuscous dorsolateral stripes is wider and the outer, lateral interval is shorter and less distinct. Bokermann does not mention the yellow gula of the male. *Hyla fuscomarginata* is very widespread, and the characters cover those of *madeirae* quite well.

# 13. Smooth-Skinned Forms with Pointed Snout

*Hyla aurata* and *Hyla cuspidata* are put at the fringe of the *Hyla rubra–Hyla x-signata* complex because, though somewhat akin to it, they show less affinity than the species dealt with before. They are, however, closely allied to each other. The distinguishing characters are mentioned in the descriptions.

## *Hyla aurata* Wied, 1825

> WIED-NEUWIED, PRINCE MAXIMILIAN ZU, 1821. *Reise nach Brasilien* 2:249.
> ———. 1824. *Recueil de planches colorées d'animaux du Brésil.* VIIème livraison.
> ———. 1825. *Beitraege zur Naturgeschichte von Brasilien* 1:531–533.

For a hundred and forty years after its description, this handsome little tree frog seems to have been entirely overlooked. It is not mentioned by Boulenger, Nieden, or Cochran. In 1941, I had the good fortune to collect it in the outskirts of Salvador, the capital of the state of Bahia, and slightly further inland, at Cachoeira, near São Felix, on the Paraguassú River.

DIAGNOSTIC CHARACTERS. The discoverer sets forth the very distinctive pattern in the text to the figure of the frog, translated here from the French edition: "Upper parts dark brown-olive, with three longitudinal interrupted lines the color of gold, and a similar one in front of the eyes; lower parts pale grayish-yellow; chin and throat deep yellow." The following characters also accrue: relatively small size, triangular head, pointed snout, robust patches of vomerine teeth, glandules concentrated on the upper eyelids and disseminated over the back, and dark brown iris.

TYPES AND TYPE LOCALITY. In Prince Maximilian's time, neither types nor type localities were as strictly designated as now. The whereabouts of his specimens of this species seems unknown. Santa Agnes Bahia, more correctly Santa Inés, on the Rio de Contas, may be accepted as the type locality.

DESCRIPTION. Size small, average 22–23 mm snout to vent length. Build robust. Hindlimb stout, not very long; the tibiotarsal articulation reaches between the eye and the nostril when adpressed. Tibia 2 or 3 mm longer than the femur. Head triangular, wide at the base. Postaxillary region of the body as wide as the head. Snout pointed in front, from above and beneath. Canthus rostralis fairly well defined; loreal region slightly concave, sloping to the edge of the mouth. Nostrils superolateral, much farther from the eye than from the tip of the snout, not terminal, but marking the end of the canthus and the beginning of the declivity of the upper jaw. Eye prominent, its horizontal diameter greater than the distance from its anterior corner to the nostril. Tympanum small, approximately one-third the diameter of the eye. Interorbital space more than 1.5 times the internarial space, almost double the width of the upper eyelid. Vomerine teeth in two short, robust, transverse, slightly separated patches between the choanae. Tongue rounded, slightly emarginate and free behind. Fingers webbed at the base. An elongate callosity under the first finger, a flat, rather indistinct, palmar tubercle under the third and fourth fingers. Disks short, thick, rounded in front. Toes rather short, more than one-half webbed. The web is inserted below the disk on the inner side of the second, third, and fifth toes, reduced to a fringe at or near the level of the last articular tubercle on the outer side of the first and of the penultimate tubercle on the second, third and on both sides of the fourth toe. An elongate, inner, a small, rather indistinct, round, outer metatarsal tubercle. Skin smooth and shiny above but with some glandules on the upper eyelids and disseminated over the back. Belly and midventral portion of thigh granular. A narrow fold over the tympanum. A fold across the chest.

AVERAGE DIMENSIONS: Wied indicates 1 inch, 1 line for his largest specimen. Ours are smaller, between 18 and 23 mm, one only 24 mm snout to vent; tibia 10–13 mm, head width 7 or 8 mm.

SECONDARY SEX CHARACTERS. Not marked. Neither females with eggs in our small samples nor dead males with large vocal sacs, though some have longitudinal folds on the gula.

VARIATION. The samples are small and the morphological variation is moderate, affecting the degree of separation between the patches of vomerine teeth, the entire or slightly emarginate posterior border of the tongue, and the point reached by the tibiotarsal articulation when the hindlimb is adpressed; it inclines to be nearer to the eye than to the nostril, although in one of our specimens it reaches the nostril.

COLOR AND PATTERN. In *Beitraege zur Naturgeschichte von Brasilien* Wied gives a more detailed description of both color and pattern: "Coloring: Upper parts dark brownish-olive-green; a yellow, really golden line, across the forehead from one eye to the other; at the neck begins an interrupted midline divided in two parts; on each side of the back a similar more entire line. Lower aspect of body a dirty grayish yellow color; chin and throat deep yellow, like the stripes on the back. Iris of eye dark." Our best specimens agree with this description, though they present some variation. The lines are really stripes or narrow bands, bordered in dark, the borders generally not uniform but composed of rather large dots or small blotches forming a more or less sinuous outline, which contrasts with the lighter band between them. In two melanistic specimens the pattern is rather obscure but perceptible, and two very light ones show very little contrast; there is also one in which the dorsal surface is a more or less uniform, the intermediate color relieved only by the large dots that should constitute the outer border of the absent light bands. The interocular stripe is very characteristic; it is either convex or almost angular in front. As already pointed out by Prince Maximilian, the outer stripes are more continuous than the median one. There are similar light spots or patches and dark edges composed of dots on the permanently visible dorsal surfaces of the limbs, especially of the leg. Gula of male deep citron yellow. The dark brown iris pointed out by Wied serves to distinguish *aurata* from the more southern *H. cuspidata* described by Lutz a hundred years later, since the latter has a copper-colored iris.

VOICE. The call has the sound produced by winding a watch. It is similar but shorter than the call of *Hyla rubra altera* of the *Hyla rubra–Hyla x-signata* complex.

HABITS. Wied points out that *H. aurata* lives in bromeliads and on shrubs in the interior of the province of Bahia. He adds that he found it in the swamps at Santa Agnes, together with the "smith," i. e. *Hyla faber*, and that it was caught by the light of torches made of ignited sawdust.

I collected it in a trench, with deep water holes in the low ground of the Baixão de Brotas and in the reservoir known as Tanque dos Cabritos at Salvador. It sat on the stone wall above the water, perhaps to get away, as it was being pursued by water snakes swimming around rapidly. At Cachoeira near São Felix we got *H. aurata* out of bromeliads.

KNOWN DISTRIBUTION. At present, only the coastal area of the state of Bahia, from Salvador and São Felix to the Rio de Contas.

AFFINITIES. Wied mentions the similar pattern

of the species described and figured as *Hyla trivittata* by Spix (p. 35 and pl. IX), which he rightly considers different. *H. trivittata* Spix is really *Dendrobates trivittatus* (Spix).

*Hyla aurata* is very closely related to *Hyla cuspidata* and their affinities are with the *Hyla rubra* group, but their dorsal surface is unusually smooth, thin, and shiny.

## *Hyla cuspidata* Lutz, 1925

LUTZ, A. 1925. Batraciens du Brésil (II) *C. R. Soc. de Biol. Paris* 93(22):211–214. *H. cuspidata*: 211.
———. 1926. Nota previa sobre especies novas de batrachios brasileiros. New species of Brazilian Batrachians. Preliminary note. *Publ. Inst. O. Cruz.* March 10. *H. cuspidata*: 6, 13.

This is one of several small species of *Hyla* from the vicinity of Rio de Janeiro that remained undescribed until A. Lutz began to study Brazilian frogs. It is very common on the coastal lowlands of the state of Guanabara, especially in the bromeliads growing on the great boulders near the sea.

DIAGNOSTIC CHARACTERS. The broad-based, triangular head with cuspidate snout, projecting above the ogival outline of the mouth; the smooth skin, with metallic sheen; in life, the copper-colored iris and long, green bones of most specimens. Very closely allied to *Hyla aurata* Wied from Bahia, but with a different pattern and different-colored eyes; perhaps slightly larger.

TYPES AND TYPE LOCALITY. Coastal lowlands on the outskirts of Rio de Janeiro; ALC: 299–302, xii, 1922.

DESCRIPTION. Size rather small. Adults rarely more than 22–29 mm snout to vent. Build robust. Body rather flat, postaxillary region almost as wide as the head, somewhat narrowed toward the groin. Hindlimb stout; tibiotarsal articulation reaching a point between the eye and the nostril when the leg is adpressed. Tibia generally 2–3 mm longer than the femur. Head wide at the base, triangular. Snout pointed in front, projecting greatly over the mouth, sharply declivous beyond the nostrils, ending in a point. Nostrils superolateral, one half nearer the tip of the snout than the eye. Canthus rostralis not marked; loreal region sloping, slightly concave. Interorbital space very wide, more than 1.3 times the internarial space, not quite double

the width of the upper eyelid. Eye prominent, as long or slightly longer than the distance from its anterior corner to the nostril. Tympanum very small, approximately two-fifths the horizontal diameter of the eye, very distinct. Tongue wide, rounded, entire or slightly emarginate, slightly free behind. Vomerine teeth in two short, robust, slightly separated patches between the choanae. Fingers webbed at the base. A callosity below the first finger, a plane, bilobate, palmar tubercle under the third and fourth; palms padded. Disks round and short, but wide and thick. Toes very extensively webbed, the web reaching the disk or slightly below it on the inner side of the second, third, and fifth toes. The web is reduced to a fringe on the last articulation below the disk on the outer side of the first, second, third, and on both sides of the fourth toe. An elongate inner and a small outer metatarsal tubercle. Skin of dorsal surface quite smooth and shiny. A moderate glandular ridge above the tympanum; a fold of skin across the chest. Belly and midventral portion of the thigh granular. A few glandules under the tympanum of one or two of the specimens.

AVERAGE DIMENSIONS (mm). Snout to vent 24 or 25; head width 8 or 9; femur 11 or 12; tibia 13 or 14, rarely 15; tarsus 7, occasionally 8; foot 9–11.

VARIATION. Habit and proportions less variable than in many other Brazilian species of *Hyla*, except perhaps the length of the hindlimb. Vomerine teeth from slightly separate to contiguous. Tongue either entire or slightly emarginate. Size variable. The specimens introduced into the edge of the Tijuca Mountains at slightly below 400 m altitude are larger and more ornate than those from the plain.

SECONDARY SEX CHARACTERS. The male has a citrine vocal sac, indicated in most preserved specimens only by a few longitudinal folds. Females not necessarily larger; better differentiated when distended by masses of eggs.

COLOR IN LIFE. Olivaceous, inclined to a dull dark greenish tone; skin smooth and rather shiny, in contrast with that of the components of the *Hyla rubra–H. x-signata* complex. Permanently visible aspects of limbs more yellowish in tone; sides of body and gula of male olive yellow. Iris copper or copper bronze; the reddish color very striking, even at a distance, when light falls on it; pupil transversely elliptic, lower half deeper than the upper. Dorsal surface of limbs concealed in repose brownish gray with a somewhat purplish tinge. Ventral aspect of limbs gray, including the disks and webs; the hands and feet slightly darker; belly lighter or whitish, with a faint pinkish or violaceous tinge in some light.

PATTERN. The basic dorsal pattern diverges from that of *Hyla aurata* because the lemon or olive yellow color serves merely as a border to the dark dorsolateral stripes or bands. These may be entire, more or less straight, or inclined to form a peak toward the back, like angular parentheses inverted left to right, a very common pattern in the *H. rubra* and in the *Hyla catharinae* groups. The stripes may also be fragmented in two sections recalling the pattern of *Hyla x-signata*. Occasionally the stripes or their fragments anastomose on the back. The main forms seen are longitudinal, entire stripes; fragmented, *x-signata*-like ones; and stripes anastomosed or forming irregular ornamental figures on the back. The borders of small lemon yellow, yellow olive or dull gold spots also vary from very distinct to intermediate or quite indistinct.

A sample of thirty-seven specimens from the Açude da Solidão (380 m altitude) examined for variations in patterns showed the following, rather even, results:

Stripes entire, 13 specimens
Stripes fragmented, 13
Additional ornamentation, 7
Pattern almost absent, 4
Outlines brilliant, 12
Outlines dull, 11
Outlines intermediate, 10
Outlines absent, 4

A dark canthal and a similar subtympanic line are joined together by a dark equatorial line across the iris forming a pseudocolobom. The interocular spot is generally very indistinct, though there are a few exceptions. When it is distinct, this is mostly due to the presence of light marginal dots like those of the stripes on the body, but which are still more often absent. It is never striking like the interocular spot of *Hyla aurata*, which is golden, narrow, and sometimes slightly pointed in front; that of *H. cuspidata* is dark and more or less irreg-

ular, rather shield-like. Marks similar to those of the body occur on the permanently visible dorsal surfaces of the limbs, especially the leg (tibia). They are oblique and inclined to be rounded, with edges similar to those of the body but mostly quite dull. Some specimens show a few lemon yellow dots on the limbs.

Preserved specimens are olivaceous or brownish, sometimes pale. The pattern is present in many, but in others only the canthal and supratympanic lines are visible. The yellow edges become white. The skin of the gula is very translucent so that the outline of the tongue is visible from the outside. The shape of the sternum is barely perceptible.

VOICE. The call is similar to the sound of winding a watch or a small clock: *ccrrr, ccrrr, ccrrr* (A. Lutz) and rather similar to the calls of the smaller members of the *Hyla rubra* group. The males call individually on the vegetation above water.

HABITS. *Hyla cuspidata* likes to shelter in bromeliads and is very abundant in those growing on rocks near the coast. It has been imported to the Açude da Solidão, an artificial pond at the edge of the montane Tijuca woods, where the bromeliads are epiphytic. It maintains itself and seems larger than on the lowlands but does not penetrate into the forest.

EGGS. Eggs with dark animal and light vegetal pole, as usual in *Hyla*. Metamorphosis occurs at approximately 10.5 mm snout to vent length.

AFFINITIES. *Hyla cuspidata* has a superficial resemblance to the small regional coelonotous Hylids, especially to *Flectonotus fissilis* that has a smooth, moist skin and cuspidate snout. The *Hyla* closest to it seems to be the more northern *Hyla aurata* Wied, from which it diverges by the characters indicated above. Very ornate specimens approach *Hyla craspedospila* Lutz, but that is bigger, has a different distribution, and has a less translucent skin. *Hyla rubra altera* is also similar, but like *craspedospila* it has a rough skin. It also has a very clear-cut and constant pattern. They are both members of the *Hyla rubra–H. x-signata* group.

KNOWN DISTRIBUTION. So far collected only in the state of Guanabara and the adjacent state of Rio de Janeiro.

# IV. The *Hyla catharinae* Complex

# 14. Species with Yellow-Orange Flash Colors

*Hyla flavoguttata* Lutz & B. Lutz, 1939

> Lutz, A., and Lutz, B. 1939. New Hylidae from Brazil. Hylideos Novos do Brasil. *An. Ac. Bras. Sc.* 11(1). *Hyla flavoguttata*: 75–78, 86–88, pl. II, figs. 4, 4a, 4b.

The first specimen was sent to Dr. Lutz by a professional collector from the Mantiqueira Range, near Passa Quatro in the state of Minas Gerais. The species was, however, described from a better specimen collected later in the Serra da Bocaina on the Maritime Range. It also occurs on the Serra de Cubatão outside São Paulo, and in the northern block of the Serra do Mar; it is quite abundant in the forested part of Teresópolis turned toward the sea. Dr. Cochran based her description on a cotype from Petrópolis.

DIAGNOSTIC CHARACTERS. The orange or cadmium yellow drops on the concealed aspects of the hind-limbs that separate it from sympatric forms of *Hyla catharinae*; the relatively dark color of the lower surface, intensely vermiculated in brown on a lighter ground. Head long, oval, with lacertilian or croco-dilian aspect. Disks short, spatulate, very wide in front, narrowed at the base. Montane rain-forest form found in the vicinity of running water.

TYPES AND TYPE LOCALITY. The type, a grown female, n. 2090 of the ALC in the MNR, was col-lected by A. Lutz, B. Lutz, and J. Venancio, Janu-ary 2, 1930, at the Fazenda do Bonito in the Serra da Bocaina, on the borders of the states of São Paulo and Rio de Janeiro; with it a small paratype, n. 2091. Other paratypes: 2166–73 from Teresó-polis, n. 1360 of the ALC, and USNM 121.636, the latter two from Petrópolis.

DESCRIPTION. Size fairly large for the group. Type ♀, 42 mm, other females 40–43.1; one small, only 36 mm snout to vent. Males considerably smaller. Build robust, rather elongate. Hindlimb average, the tibiotarsal articulation reaching be-tween the eye and the tip of the snout when ad-pressed. Head oval, as long as wide, constricted into a neck. Canthus rostralis curved, thick, and moderately distinct; loreal region concave below the canthus, flaring greatly to the upper jaw. Snout truncate in front between the raised nostrils, slop-ing sharply backward to the mouth opening in pro-file. Interorbital space only slightly wider than the internarial space. Nostrils set wide apart, tumefied on the outside and in front. Eye large, very promi-nent. Tympanum small but very distinct, its di-ameter generally equal to two-fifths or one-third the horizontal diameter of the eye. Vomerine teeth in two short, heavy, transverse, semicircular patches between the choanae. Tongue large, rounded or oval, with a shallow notch behind, irregularly grooved longitudinally, posterior border slightly free. Lateral fingers with a rudimentary web or free. Toes unequally webbed, the web rudimentary between the first and second; others more than half webbed, but the web narrows to a fringe on the inner side and on the last two joints of the fourth toe, or leaves them free. Disks spatulate, wide, almost straight in front, narrowed at the back, sometimes with longitudinal folds beneath. Palmar and plantar tubercles. No projecting rudiment of the pollex. An oval, inner metatarsal tubercle; outer minute and round or absent. Skin very warty above, with tubercles of different sizes, disseminated in more or less longitudinal rows on the head and body, densely so on the upper eyelids, occiput, tympanic region, and sometimes on the dorsolateral and anal regions; also short glandular folds. In some specimens a tubercle on the canthus and/or a few tubercles on the limbs. A short supratympanic ridge. Skin of chest, belly, and lower aspect of the thigh granular; gula less so, with shiny white glandules.

VARIATION. The usual variation of the Brazilian species of *Hyla*, plus some individual variation as to the number of tubercles.

SECONDARY SEX CHARACTERS. Secondary sex characters of the male very little marked, so that one may be left in doubt as to their adult status if they are not calling when caught. The voice of the whole *catharinae* group is feeble, and a large vocal sac is not evident. There is also no sharp pollex rudiment.

VOICE. The call is relatively sharper and louder than in *Hyla catharinae* "sensu stricto."

COLOR AND PATTERN. The specific name is derived from the vivid, rounded, orange, sometimes cadmium yellow, drop-like spots on the concealed parts of the thigh, the adjacent part of the flanks, and the leg. They vary in number and size but are quite constant and typical. After death they fade to white. The iris has a coppery or golden glint and a bold, dark reticulation on a brown background, which is visible even in some well-preserved specimens, and a dark pseudocolobom. The free rim of the transparent part of the lower lid is dark-edged, and there is some reticulation at its base. Dorsal background generally dark brown, sometimes olivaceous. Pattern obscure in many specimens, but better defined in others. Several tones of brown present, with or without light glandular margins outlining certain areas of the back and the sides.

Interocular and sacral areas often dark; when distinct spots are present the interocular spot is often roughly W-shaped and the sacral spot chevron-shaped. When the interocular spot is triangular with the point directed toward the back and the sacral spot is also triangular or chevron-shaped and both are outlined in light, an almost hourglass-like design is produced. In other specimens a similar figure is produced by the different tones of brown on the back. The dorsolateral spots are often reduced to dark areas from the eyes to the elbow. Short, oblique, light bars radiate from the eye to the mouth. The head may also have a light outline. The edges of the limbs and body that outline the frog in repose are glandular with a few larger tubercles. The dark crossbars on the permanently visible dorsal surface of the limbs are generally more distinct than the dorsal pattern; the light intervals between them are variable in width and shape but generally narrower than the dark bars and sometimes very much reduced. They are often coincident with the lighter outlines on the back and the drops of flash color on the concealed surfaces. The glandules are generally dark on the dark areas and light on the light outlines. Ventral aspect densely vermiculated in brown on a lighter surface. Webs pigmented.

ECOLOGY. *Hyla flavoguttata* is a montane rainforest species, generally found near running water. The type and several other specimens were collected on Hymenophyllaceae, on mosses growing on permanently wet cliffs, or on trees in very humid stations. One of the Petrópolis specimens was taken inside a house at Independencia, and another was taken from under a fallen tree trunk. The juvenile paratypes were in the reservoir of the Goeldi Fazenda, Colonia Alpina, outside Teresópolis. Small specimens are also common in the stands of *Hedychium coronarium* and *H. gardnerianum* growing on the edges of the road from the Organ Mountains National Park to Soberbo, near the falls of the Paquequer River. We have not collected *H. flavoguttata* below 790 m (2,400 feet) altitude.

LARVA. It seems probable that some very specialized tadpoles found by us in January 1930 and March 1934 belong to this species. They were living in a swift-flowing mountain brook at Ponte Alta on the Serra da Bocaina, and are characterized by the sucker-like mouth by which they attach themselves to the rocky bottom, stones, or pieces of wood found in the water, thus avoiding being carried downstream. When pried loose they promptly attached themselves again, sometimes even to the collectors' hands or gum boots. The sucker is formed by the very much dilated lips, which show several rows of robust papillae. Chitinous teeth on the beak in $\frac{2}{3}$ rows. Body elliptic, anterior part very much produced, edges of sucker prominent, central part hollowed. When found they were 22 mm long; head and body were 7–8 mm. We managed to keep them alive for some time but not until full metamorphosis. One developed hindlimbs with good disks, webs, and dark crossbands to the toes, not unlike those of *Hyla flavoguttata*, the only species found in the vicinity, which was carefully searched.

AFFINITIES. *Hyla flavoguttata* undoubtedly belongs to the group of *Hyla catharinae* Boulenger. However, in the past this name has been indifferently applied to a number of tree frogs which in life can be told apart by size, texture of skin, flash color, reproductive behavior, and ecology. In the true *catharinae* and a cluster of other small forms the flash colors are blue, gray, green-blue, opaline, or violaceous. This character is important and denotes a greater systematic differentiation between *H. flavoguttata*, which has orange flash colors, than obtains between similar forms with blue, greenish, or violaceous concealed surfaces. *Hyla flavoguttata* was considered by Cochran (1955) as a race of *H. strigilata* Spix, but this is quite unlikely. The fauna of Bahia is generally different from that of the coastal serras, and Peters (1872) mentions vestiges of blue color in the type of *H. strigilata* examined by him. Moreover, Spix mentions ranid-like disks quite different from the spatulate disks of *H. flavoguttata*.

DISTRIBUTION. The forested coastal serras of southeastern Brazil. Known from the type locality, Serra da Bocaina, from the Serra da Estrela, and the Serra dos Orgãos, all of them branches of the Serra do Mar, the two latter located in the northern block. It also occurs farther south. *Hyla flavoguttata* does not occur in the mountains near the city of Rio de Janeiro, which are lower, so that only naked rocks rise to what seems to be the usual altitude of its habitat. The species has also been found in the Serra da Mantiqueira.

## *Hyla perpusilla* Lutz & B. Lutz, 1939

LUTZ, A., and LUTZ, B. 1939. New Hylidae from Brazil. *An. Ac. Bras. Sc.* 11:67–89, 3 pls. *Hyla perpusilla* n. sp., 78–81, 88–90, pl. III, fig. 5.

*Hyla perpusilla* is one of the smallest Brazilian species of *Hyla*. It was discovered in the scrub vegetation on the coast of the former Federal District, Rio de Janeiro, which is now the state of Guanabara. Its very small size and special habitat probably helped it to escape notice until the last half century. It is the smallest form of the group of *Hyla catharinae*.

DIAGNOSTIC CHARACTERS. *Hyla perpusilla* is characterized by its small size, yellow flash color on the concealed surfaces, and strictly bromelicolous habitat. All stages of its life history are spent in the leaf cups. Its general appearance is that of the group of *Hyla catharinae* "sensu latissimo" to which it belongs.

DISTRIBUTION. *Hyla p. perpusilla* has quite a long known range on the coastal lowlands, from Santa Catarina (Joinville and Guaramirim) to (Tapera), Pernambuco. In the states of Guanabara, Rio de Janeiro, and São Paulo the species has been collected not only near the sea but also on the mountains, always within its biotope, at altitudes of 1,000 m or more above sea level.

The lowland form is regarded as the nominate race and is described in the next section.

## *Hyla perpusilla perpusilla* Lutz & B. Lutz, 1939

LUTZ, A., and LUTZ, B. 1939. New Hylidae from Brazil. *An. Ac. Bras. Sc.* 11:67–89, 3 pls. *Hyla perpusilla* n. sp., 78–81, 88–90, pl. III, fig. 5.

TYPE AND TYPE LOCALITY. Type and paratypes collected by Bertha Lutz, October 7, 1935, at Recreio dos Bandeirantes, Sernambetiba, GB. The type, a ♀, is now no. 2622 and the paratypes are nos. 2623–39 of the ALC at the MNR.

DESCRIPTION. Size very small. ♀ type 22 mm; other females from 18–25 mm, average 18–20 mm snout to vent; ♂ smaller, 15–18 mm, one specimen, USNM, 22 mm snout to vent (Cochran 1955). Build elongate; postaxillary region slightly narrower than the head. Body and hindlimbs plump in full-grown, living specimens. Tibiotarsal articulation reaching the nostril or the tip of the snout when adpressed. Head flat, very slightly longer than wide, constricted to a neck. Snout acutely rounded from above, more bluntly so in profile, with raised subterminal nostrils. Canthus rostralis not well defined, curved; loreal region concave, sloping. Upper jaw projecting considerably beyond the lower one. Outline of the head, seen from below, oval. Interorbital space wider than the internarial space. Eye prominent, shorter than the distance from its anterior corner to the tip of the snout. Tympanum small, less than one-half the diameter of the eye, very distinct. Vomerine teeth in two short groups between the choanae. Tongue oval, slightly emarginate, and free behind. Fingers free; three outer toes about one-third webbed. Inner toes inserted one above the other in a very characteristic manner. An inner and an outer metatarsal tubercle; palmar and plantar tubercles; a row of tubercles on the dermal ridge on the outer side of the tarsus. Dorsal skin finely granular, with pustules on the upper eyelids, head, and body, in more or less parallel, longitudinal, widely-spaced rows; a wide, glandular, peritympanic ridge. Belly and thighs slightly granular; a fold of skin across the chest. In life, lower aspect translucent, the tongue and some of the internal organs discernible.

VARIATION. The main variation seems to affect the extent of the webs on the feet, which are longer in some specimens than in others, noticeably so in montane specimens, which, on an average, are also slightly larger in size. They are considered a separate race and are described below.

COLOR AND PATTERN. *Hyla perpusilla* is rather like lichenous tree bark in color, affecting tones from sage green to olive buff, in life with a rather metallic sheen.

The dorsal pattern is fundamentally the pattern of the group of *Hyla catharinae* "sensu latissimo," but it diverges more than usual. Only a relatively small percentage of specimens shows independent and well-defined spots, especially the sacral spot and the dorsolateral stripes. The interocular spot, generally present, is narrow and shallow, straight or slightly divided in front, horizontal, or like a very shallow W behind; it does not cover the whole of the eyelids nor does it extend much beyond the eyes; it generally has a light halo, especially in front. The usual dark sacral spot is often absent; when present it is frequently open, reduced and/or anastomosed to the dorsolateral dark stripes or areas if these are present. A pale sacral area is very constant, conveying a subtle suggestion of an imaginary marsupium. The dorsolateral dark stripes, like inverted parentheses, may be short or long, entire or fragmented, wide or narrow, straight or converging toward the middle of the back.

The variations in form, extent, independence, or confluence of the dark spots and areas produce many varieties of dorsal pattern. The most striking one occurs when the interocular and sacral spots are entirely absent and the dorsolateral stripes are straight, wide, and continuous, beginning on the sides of the head and continuing to the end of the body, leaving only room enough for a narrow, longitudinal, median area or for a wide vertebral light stripe. This pattern is less common in the type locality than elsewhere, even in populations living not far from it.

The dorsal pattern is completed by a dark subcanthal stripe, light and dark bars between the eye and the mouth, and dark bars on the permanently visible dorsal parts of the limbs to the outer digits. The light areas on the parts concealed in repose and on the adjacent surface on the sides of the body are flavescent. Sides of the body sometimes mottled. Sometimes a few dark spots on the gula or throat. Belly immaculate. Margins of the dorsal pattern visible from beneath in some specimens. Under magnification (X6) the whole dorsal surface of the live specimen has a metallic sheen, which is more intense on the iris, tympanum, pustules, and lower surfaces. Young specimens appear so dusted with golden dots that only the interocular spot and the proximal longitudinal part of the pattern are discernible.

Iris golden with dark veins; periphery tawny; slight notches in the middle of the free rim, the lower one more distinct. Pupil rhomboid. A pseudocolobom of pigment apparently prolonging the rhomboid pupil sideways.

VOICE. A thin *trrrc trrrc trrrc*, heard both at night and in daytime. The males call sitting on the broad outer leaves of thorny-edged species of bromeliads but plunge into the lower, cylinder-shaped part of the rosette when danger threatens. Our first specimens were obtained by uprooting the bromeliads in which frogs had been seen, pouring out the water, and detaching leaf by leaf. On the coastal lowlands and rocks, bromeliads growing on the ground (species of *Bromelia, Neoregelia,* and other genera) are used, whereas in the mountains both epiphytic and earth-growing species serve.

ECOLOGY. *Hyla perpusilla* is a strict bromeliad dweller at all stages. The eggs are laid in the leaf cups, and the tadpoles develop in the water contained in them. The tadpoles have been found a number of times, generally only a few at a time and by no means in all specimens containing rain water. They may float on top, but they also go to the bottom where they probably find bubbles of oxygen. On the coastal lowlands the only other relatively small hylid that lays in bromeliads is *Amphodus,* but it is considerably larger and does not cover the whole range of *Hyla perpusilla perpusilla.*

LARVA. Body oval, outline of snout rounded. Tail long, double-bladed, like a very elongate, oval symmetric leaf; upper crest narrow, reaching onto the back; lower crest slightly wider, converging into a point. Spiraculum not far from the middle, slightly nearer the tip of the snout than the anus. Rows of teeth $\frac{2}{3}$, otherwise $\frac{1}{\frac{1-1}{\frac{1}{1}}}$; only the inner, upper one is bipartite. Skin dark above, with punctiform pigment dusted with gold, extensive to the tail; beneath also dark, very translucent, especially on the belly, the organs and pulsating blood vessels perfectly visible. Near metamorphosis the upper crest of the tail becomes slightly more pigmented, and a sinuous, vermiculated band of pigment develops on the lower crest. Eye round, iris narrow and golden. Length at metamorphosis 10–13 mm. Alternate black and light crossbars on the developing hindlimbs. In a few days the dark interocular band becomes visible, and the dark bars on the legs deepen in tone. The montane form is considered a separate race and is described in the following section.

## *Hyla perpusilla v-signata* B. Lutz, 1968

LUTZ, B. 1968. Geographic variation in Brazilian Species of *Hyla.* Texas Memorial Museum. The Pearce-Sellards Series 12:7–8, fig. 3.

Some time after discovering *Hyla perpusilla* in the ground-dwelling bromeliads of the coastal plain, we began to find specimens in the bromeliads, both ground-growing and epiphytic, of the adjacent coastal serras. These specimens, while conforming to the general coloring, morphology, voice, habitat, and ecology of the nominate form, differ from it by attaining a slightly larger size and more intense pigmentation, especially on the gula. The proportion of the different patterns is also not quite the same. I consider this form as an altitudinal race, which I call *H. p. v-signata.*

DIAGNOSTIC CHARACTERS. The accumulation of pig-

ment on the gula, which forms a thick, V-shaped figure, either entire, fragmented into the two arms, or slightly out of shape; sometimes it is broken up into dark flecks; the slightly larger size, the deeper and more abundant flash color; the montane distribution.

TYPES AND TYPE LOCALITY. Over one hundred specimens were examined. The types were chosen from the Organ Mountains population, whose sample is more numerous than the others and also the most characteristic. Holotype MNR n. 3607, ♀ paratypes MNR nos. 3608, 3609, from the Organ Mountains National Park at Teresópolis, collected by the author, the type in November 1956, the paratypes in December 1956.

DESCRIPTION. Size slightly larger than that of the nominate form: ♀ 27 mm, others 24, 26, and 24 mm snout to vent. Build rather elongate and robust for the size. Hindlimb variable, the tibiotarsal articulation reaching between the eye and the nostril in three, only to the front of the eye in the other. Feet slightly more webbed. Otherwise morphological characters in agreement with *H. p. perpusilla.* Dorsal aspect rather moss-like or lichenous. Pattern of the *H. catharinae* group of species more complete than usual in the nominate form. Interocular spot a very shallow W with a light halo in front. Sacral spot roughly crescent-shaped, somewhat longer and slightly excentric in the largest paratype. Dorsolateral spots very distinct, like inverted (left to right), pointed parentheses, the convexity turned upward onto the back. Bars on limbs distinct; light intervals wide; flash color extensive; a light area on the flanks between the dorsolateral dark areas and the sacral spots; concealed pattern perceptible from beneath. Warts rather numerous, especially on the head and edges of the body.

SECONDARY SEX CHARACTERS. Very little marked; unopened specimens can only be securely sexed if a vocal sac is present or eggs are visible in the abdomen. Vocal sac slightly larger than on the plains, especially in two smallish specimens from the Serra da Bocaina.

COLOR. Dorsal color olive brown and gray. Flash color orange to cadmium orange. Iris slightly tawny, rather like the nominate form. Background of gula grayish. Chest pale gray, belly with white glandules, the viscera showing through dark blue; ventral aspect of the thighs paler, slightly violaceous.

DIAGNOSTIC V. The montane race was first separated from the lowland form because of the pigmented gula. At its best the V is rather wide, entire, composed of two thick not very oblique branches; it occupies the upper part of the throat. In some specimens the branches are thicker at the top; in others they are almost horizontal; they may also be broken up into separate parts. Occasionally the V-shaped spot is prolonged downward by a double or a single streak of pigment coming near to a Y. In others the V is substituted by a single squarish blotch. Occasionally, though not often, there is another pair of blotches below the first pair or again the pigment is dissolved into a number of flecks and dots. Whereas the V is very striking in living specimens, it is unfortunately liable to fade after death. By varying the incidence of light it can frequently be sufficiently illuminated to stand out.

PATTERN. The most common pattern is that just described. It is more distinct than in the nominate form, especially as to the dorsolateral parentheses that invade the back with their apices. The interocular spot is shallow, W-shaped in both races, and its anterior halo very distinct in *H. p. v-signata*. Sacral spot generally crescent-shaped though sometimes slightly prolonged excentrically forward. The longitudinal pattern of two wide dark streaks on the sides leaving either a narrow or wide, light, median area is much more rare than in the lowland race. It was seen in only three out of ninety-nine specimens examined as to pattern; all three came from the Serra da Bocaina.

Sometimes the dorsal pattern is obliterated by a general metallic greenish glint over the whole dorsal surface. This is more common in large specimens, whereas in the lowland race it is the small ones that tend to be metallic and covered by golden flecks. In the montane race the juveniles are rather plain, and when preserved they become grayish with longitudinal dark, rectilinear, dorsolateral stripes, sometimes anastomosed with the sacral spot. Wide light intervals between the very distinct dark bars on the limbs and a large light area on the flanks are common.

VOICE. Similar to that of *H. p. perpusilla*, but slightly stronger.

HABITAT. Bromeliads constitute a habitat with an independent microclimate that emancipates their inhabitants from the general environment. The cooler climate of the serras seems to favor size and an intense flash color.

POPULATIONS. As mentioned above, the subspe-

cific characters are especially marked both as to size and pattern in the large sample (fifty-two specimens) from the Organ Mountains. They were mostly taken in the National Park, where a great many bromeliads have been planted on the ground. It is less impressive in the smaller specimens from the Tijuca Mountains near Rio, but in these also some form of V is present. The sample from the Serra da Bocaina (twenty-eight specimens) in the northern part of the state of São Paulo is extremely variable as to dorsal pattern; on the whole the little frogs are smaller in size and shorter-legged than those from the Organ Mountains. The bars on the limbs are very narrow and the flash colors extensive. The six specimens from Itatiaia are melanistic.

DISTRIBUTION. At present we have specimens from the mountains round and south of Rio (Serra Carioca) and from the Serras da Estrela, Barro Branco, and Serra dos Orgãos in the northern block of Serra do Mar; in the south from Paraty, state of Rio de Janeiro, Serra da Bocaina and Serra de Cubatão in São Paulo, all in the Maritime Range. Itatiaia is on the Serra da Mantiqueira. It probably occurs all over the southeastern and southern coastal mountains.

ISLAND POPULATION. A little tree frog of this species was collected on the island of Queimada Grande on the coast of the state of São Paulo by the preparator Braulio Prazeres of the National Museum in Rio. The specimen is brown and rather granular above, and has a very marked dorsal pattern and deep flash color. It is much closer to *Hyla p. v-signata* than to the nominate form. Should it prove to be distinct, it might be called *Hyla p. queimadensis* after its island home.

## *Hyla berthae* Barrio, 1962

> BARRIO, A. 1962. Los Hylidae de Punta Lara, Provincia de Buenos Aires. *Physis* 23 (65): 129–142. *Hyla berthae*: 137–138, fig. 3.
> ———. 1964. Characteristics of *Hyla berthae*. *Copeia* 3:583–585, fig. 1.

Barrio described *Hyla berthae* from the Argentinian province of Buenos Aires. It is included here because the platine and cisplatine frog fauna of Argentina is generally found in southern Brazil, and Barrio seems to have taken it also in Brazil. *Hyla berthae* is quite evidently a member of the group *Hyla catharinae* and comes closest to the members of the group with a yellow flash color, especially *Hyla perpusilla*.

DIAGNOSTIC CHARACTERS. The small size, elongate build and snout, the longitudinal dorsal pattern, and the orange-yellow flash color.

Differs from *Hyla perpusilla* by the longer and more declivous snout, which is not tilted up, the different pattern, and the habitat.

TYPES AND TYPE LOCALITY. Holotype an adult male, Laboratorio de Investigaciones Herpetologicas, Facultad de Ciencias Exactas y Naturales of the University of Buenos Aires, n. 1080, collected at Punta Lara, province of Buenos Aires, November 3, 1961, by Dr. Avelino Barrio. Allotype adult ♀, LIH 1081, also from Punta Lara. Eight paratypes: LIH 1082–1083 from Ingeniero Maschwitz, Buenos Aires province; LIH 1084–1087 from the type locality, taken together with the holotype; LIH 1088–1089 from São Bernardo do Campo, state of São Paulo, Brazil.

DESCRIPTION (based on female paratype, LIH 1084 from Punta Lara, and two specimens, female and male from San Isidro, Buenos Aires, leg. et ded. A. Barrio). Size small, females 22 mm, male 21 mm long. Build elongate. Hindlimb rather short, the adpressed tibiotarsal articulation reaching the anterior corner of the eye. Head slightly longer than wide; postaxillary region narrower than the head except in the female with eggs. Snout elongate, bluntly pointed at the tip, declivous and projecting over the mouth opening in profile. Outline of mouth oval, elongate. Canthus rostralis marked. Loreal region concave below the canthus. Nostrils subcanthal, lateral, slightly tumefied. Eye prominent, its horizontal diameter slightly shorter than the distance from its anterior corner to the tip of the snout. Tympanum round, very distinct, about half the diameter of the eye. Interorbital space slightly wider than the internarial space. Tongue wide, oval, slightly emarginate and partly free behind. Vomerine teeth in two short, posteriorly converging groups between the large choanae. Disks short, wide, spatulate. Fingers free. Palmar and subarticular tubercles well developed. Toes webbed. A fringe of web on both sides of the first toe, web narrow and oblique on the inner side of the second and third, wide to below the disk, or to above the penultimate tubercle, on their outer side and on the fifth, narrowing to a fringe on the two last phalanges of the fourth toe. An elongate inner and a minute outer metatarsal tubercle. Dorsal aspect granular in life. Preserved specimens with a few scattered glandules; the latter more noticeable on the sides of the body of paratype 1084. Gula almost smooth; chest, belly, and midventral aspect of thigh granular. A supratympanic ridge.

VARIATION. The extent of webbing seems slightly variable. The specimens from San Isidro seen by me have shorter webs than the female from the type locality.

MEASUREMENTS. The male holotype is 18.1 mm long. Barrio mentions 19 mm for males in general. The female holotype is 20.6; those seen by me are both 22 mm long. Barrio indicates 25 mm as average for females.

SECONDARY SEX CHARACTERS. The male is small and the vocal sac not very marked. The females are larger and may be distended by eggs.

COLOR AND PATTERN. The living frog is brownish. The preserved specimens are also brown above with a darker pattern. The interocular spot is shallow, W-shaped, or composed of two triangles. The sacral spot is absent or indistinct. The dorsolateral longitudinal stripes begin behind the eyes, are slightly drawn up toward each other in front, then run down the back, diverging and fading out beyond the sacrum. A shorter lateral pair passes below the canthus, above the tympanum, and down the sides, fading out on the flanks. Dark bars are present on the permanently visible upper parts of the limbs, forearm, thigh, tibia, and tarsus; smaller spots on the hands, feet, and outer digits. The two specimens from San Isidro show distinct light areas corresponding to the faded orange-yellow flash color on the anterior aspect of the thighs and adjacent hind part of the flanks. In the paratype they are rather indistinct. Ventral aspect speckled in brown, especially the gula. Some specimens lighter. Ventral aspect of limbs darker than the body. The male seen was paler than the two females.

VOICE. Barrio recorded the call and published a sonagram of it. He compares it to the sound produced by green grasshoppers of the family Tettigonidae. The males call sitting on emergent stalks, especially of *Scirpus giganteus*, which seems to serve as a soundbox. In September they were heard early in the evening, but mostly they begin to call later at night and the chorus continues until dawn. A recording played to them induced calling and was used to ascertain their presence.

BREEDING HABITS. Spawning was observed by Barrio in late November and early December. The eggs were deposited on submerged stalks.

ECOLOGY. *Hyla berthae* differs from *Hyla perpusilla* in its habitat and spawning site. *Hyla perpusilla* is a bromeliad dweller in all the phases of its life history. It spawns in the leaf cups of the bromeliads in which the adults live.

DISTRIBUTION. *Hyla berthae* was found in the coastal area of the Platine province of Buenos Aires and probably extends to Uruguay and Rio Grande do Sul. The specimens from São Paulo ought to be reexamined. They may be the *H. rizibilis* of Bokermann.

A few little specimens were found on two occasions, once in the Brazilian and once in Argentinian national parks at Iguassú Falls. These specimens have a dark vertical bar on the iris, making a cross with the pseudocolobom. The flash color is diverse. The interocular spot is wider; the dorsolateral stripes are fragmented; the sacral spot is absent. The gula is lemon colored; the yellow spots on the concealed surfaces are larger, more numerous and horizontally disposed. One of the specimens has a distinct light area on the sides of the head. It was collected in the roots of a grass growing in wet ground where it was calling, very effectively concealed. It seems akin to *Hyla berthae*.

## ADDITIONAL FORMS

### *Hyla rizibilis* Bokermann, 1964

> BOKERMANN, W. C. A. 1964. Uma nova especie de *Hyla* da Serra do Mar em São Paulo. *Rev. Bras. Biol.* 24(4):429–434, 14 text figs.

*Hyla rizibilis* was fully described by Bokermann, who obtained fourteen adults during two visits to the type locality. The eggs and tadpoles were also described and the latter reared to metamorphosis. The original description includes a sonagram.

DIAGNOSTIC CHARACTERS. The call, which is compared to bursts of laughter with shorter calls in between. Also characteristic are the white border to the upper jaw and the very characteristic pattern produced on it by the triangular looplike prolongation of the subcanthal stripes, forming a bow above the tip of the snout, plus the oblique stripes from the eyes to the edge of the upper jaw.

TYPES AND TYPE LOCALITY. Holotype male, WCAB 13947; allotype female, WCAB 13948; ten para-types, 13837–46, collected by Bokermann, October 5, 1963, at the type locality, Campo Grande, Santo André, state of São Paulo, plus two male paratypes, WCAB 14021–22, which he collected in the same place on October 20, 1963.

DESCRIPTION. Males 25–27 mm, female allotype 34 mm from snout to vent. Build average. Head large, body elongate, slightly narrower than the head. Snout triangular, wide at the base, very slightly pointed at the tip from above and projecting well over the mouth opening in profile. Canthus rostralis evident. Loreal region concave. Nostrils lateral, directed slightly backward. Eye prominent, its horizontal diameter slightly shorter than its distance from the nostril. Tympanum small, less than one-half the diameter of the eye in the specimens sent to the MNR by Bokermann and examined by me. Interorbital space slightly wider than the internarial space. Tongue rounded, free behind, slightly emarginate. Vomerine teeth in two small groups between the choanae. Disks short, wide, spatulate. A trace of web between the outer fingers. Outer toes about half-webbed. A small tubercle on the first finger and a bifid one below the third and fourth fingers. A small inner and a minute outer metatarsal tubercle. Skin of dorsal aspect smooth, but a few glandules disseminated on the head and back. A distinct supratympanic fold. Skin of the ventral aspect of the body and the midventral part of the thigh granular.

SECONDARY SEX CHARACTERS. Male with a moderate subgular vocal sac and a slight thickening at the base of the first finger. Female much larger than the male, as usual in this group.

COLOR. The dorsal coloring of living or recently preserved specimens is described as yellowish brown with a bronze tone except on the thighs. Iris silvery yellow in life; apparently with dark reticulation and a narrow black pseudocolobom. Tympanum light brown.

PATTERN (WCAB 36243, MNR 4046). Edge of upper jaw white; pattern composed of an oblique bar between the jaw and each eye and a pair of similar subcanthal stripes widening into an elongate triangular loop below it in front; the upper corners of their curved bases meet to form a very characteristic figure like a bow above the tip of the snout; additional dark smudges to the sides. A dark interocular spot with an almost black outline. A pair of dorsolateral stripes with similar outlines, which converge behind the eyes, then diverge and narrow, fading away on the sacrum; a similar, shorter stripe on each side of the body, beginning behind the eye and passing over the tympanum. An indistinct, tapestry-like background on the back and on the sides; a series of obscure elongate spots down the middorsal area. Dark bars on the permanently visible upper aspects of the limbs but not on the inner digits, which are concealed in repose. Dark blotches, confluent behind, on the anterior part of the thigh; marks on the flanks smaller. According to the original description the light intervals are devoid of bright flash color. Ventral aspect lightly stippled or pale.

Voice. The call is compared to bursts of laughter by Bokermann, an unusual feature for this group. The sonagram shows a longer series of notes grouped together at uniform intervals and two short introductory groups of four and three notes respectively. The latter are not unlike the sonagrams of *Hyla perpusilla v-signata* and *Hyla berthae*.

This species may correspond to the specimens of *H. berthae* listed for São Paulo by Barrio.

Habits. The specimens were obtained in a clearing inside a small stretch of wood. The clearing occupied a hollow only a few meters square. About one meter of water had gathered in it, and tall grasses were growing there. The males were sitting on the stalks and calling about 50 cm above the water.

Larvae. The tadpoles, which were raised from eggs, show no very distinctive features. The tooth formula is the usual ⅔. The upper crest reaches the back and rises a little higher just behind it. The tail is not so trapezoid as that of the group of *Hyla rubra*. The larvae metamorphosed at 11 mm of head and body length. The livery of the juveniles is the same, but the pattern is much more distinct than in the adults.

Affinities. In the Museu Nacional, Rio de Janeiro, there is a large sample of much smaller frogs with the same pattern on the upper jaw from northern Santa Catarina. They will be dealt with next.

## *Hyla mirim* B. Lutz, 1972

Lutz, B. 1972. New forms of the group of *Hyla catharinae*. *Bol. Mus. Nac. Rio Zoology*, no. 288.

Examination of a series of sixty-nine small tree frogs from Rio Vermelho, outside São Bento in the mountains of northern Santa Catarina, showed the pattern found in *Hyla rizibilis* but in a population that is very much smaller in size. Eight of them are females very much distended by eggs. The largest, in a very poor condition, is 28 mm long. Four of the others are 27, one is 26, and the smallest only 24 mm long. The males with an evident vocal sac range from 19 to 23 mm; the other specimens fall within the two extremes. Size alone seems to preclude them from being typical *Hyla rizibilis*. They are here described as a southern form under the name of *Hyla mirim*. The name is an Indian word denoting reduced size. Morphologically near *H. berthae*.

Diagnostic characters. Some characters of both species allied to the very small size, with the female only as large as the males of *H. rizibilis*. A diagnostic, white, elongate, horizontal area under each eye, prolonged to the tip of the snout and sometimes to the tympanum and transversed by three oblique bars or blotches directed forward from the eye to the edge of the mouth plus the prolongation of the subcanthal stripes that form a bow-shaped figure at the slightly pointed tip of the snout.

Type and types locality. Six ♀ syntypes, MNR nos. 3626–3631; three ♂ allotypes, MNR nos. 3632, 3633, 3634, collected by F. Rank and his children in January 1950 at Rio Vermelho, outside São Bento do Sul, state of Santa Catarina, (26° 14′ 55″ S. 40° 22′ 50″ W. Gr., approximately 800 m altitude) and sold to the Museu Nacional in Rio de Janeiro.

Description. Size small, female syntypes 27 (4), 26 (1), and 24 (1) mm snout to vent; male allotypes 23, 22, and 21 mm long. Build average. Hindlimb variable, the adpressed tibiotarsal articulation reaching only to the eye in the gravid female types, somewhat in front of it in the other smaller specimens. Head large, slightly longer than wide. Snout oval in outline, appearing truncate between the nostrils but declivous and slightly pointed in front, sloping well over the opening of the mouth in profile. Canthus rostralis evident, loreal region slightly concave. Nostrils below the canthus, slightly tumefied, open above. Diameter of the eye about equal to its distance from the nostril. Tympanum less than one-half the diameter of the eye. Interorbital space slightly wider than the internarial space. Tongue rounded, free behind, entire or very slightly emarginate. Vomerine teeth in two small groups between the choanae, which are relatively large. Fingers with a rudiment of web at the base. Disks wide, spatulate, proportionately narrower on the first finger. Outer toes about one-half webbed. A small but distinct inner metatarsal tubercle. Dorsal aspect punctuated by glandules on the head and the edge of the spots and stripes or on the areas corresponding to them. Beneath minutely granular. A narrow fold over the tympanum. A few glandules at the edge of the tarsus.

COLOR AND PATTERN. The most useful element for recognition of specimens with a well-preserved pattern is the white horizontal area under the eye prolonged forward and the design on it. This is composed of three oblique bars or blotches from the eye to the edge of the mouth and of the prolongation of the subcanthal stripes. In a very well-preserved condition these are seen to end in a loop, often enclosing the nostril and to form a bow-shaped figure over the pointed tip of the snout. The series exhibits a good deal of variation: pattern and color, from dark brown to pale gray, from all the elements of the *Hyla catharinae* group present to complete absence of any pattern. The groups merge into each other but can be roughly subdivided as follows:

Dark brown specimens, 19, including two female syntypes

Medium brown specimens, 19, including one female syntype

A light brown median apron over the dorsal surface, 5 females distended with eggs

Gray with the interocular spot perceptible, 20, including 1 male paratype

Gray with slightly more pattern, 1

Pale gray without any vestiges of pattern, 4, including 1 male paratype

The interocular spot is generally only slightly prolonged onto the eyelids, forming a shallow, W-shaped figure, often with a very short median prong in front and two prongs or blunt branches behind the eyes, sometimes unequal in length. In some specimens the spot is longer, more blunt, and not W-shaped. The sacral spot, when present, is crescent shaped, entire or interrupted in the middle, or, less often, irregular and chevron shaped. Very often it is absent. The dorsolateral stripes, when at their best, are like inverted parentheses (left to right), forming a sharp, rather anterior apex on the back; sometimes the stripes are narrow and rectilinear; in a few specimens they are more or less anastomosed with the sacral spot.

The dark bars on the limbs of the whole *Hyla catharinae* group are present but much more distinct in the dark specimens than in the light ones. There are lighter intervals between them, but there is no indication of a flash color except for some light areas beneath the dark prolongations of the spots on the flanks of syntype 3626 and a few other specimens. In a small proportion, the gula and, in a still smaller proportion, the chest are brown flecked. Midventral part of the thighs generally darker than the rest of the ventral aspect.

VOICE, HABITS, AND ECOLOGY. Unfortunately, nothing is known about the living animal. The collector works for the Water Reservoir and lives near it. To judge from the other species sent, he collected in the vicinity, including the edges of the open water trenches.

AFFINITIES. Several small Brazilian species of *Hyla* have a white spot under the eye, but it generally is small and rounded. None of the others show affinities to the group of *Hyla catharinae* to which this one belongs. Further study is needed to clarify the taxonomic relationship of *H. berthae*, *H. rizibilis*, and *H. mirim*.

# 15. Species with Blue to Violet Flash Colors

## MONTANE FORMS

### *Hyla catharinae* Boulenger

BOULENGER, G. A. 1888. A list of batrachians from the province of Santa Catharina, Brazil. *An. Mag. Nat. Hist.*, ser. b, 2:417.

In 1888 Boulenger described *Hyla catharinae* in a list of frogs from the province of Santa Catarina. The description is excellent, but, as is sometimes the case with older descriptions, it fits a number of closely related forms, especially as to morphology. For a long time, all the specimens from Brazil that the description fitted more or less, like a ready-made garment, were lumped together under the name of *H. catharinae*. Of late years, more intense field work in the coastal serras and a few stretches of adjacent lowlands has brought to light a number of differences which are conducive to a necessary but somewhat difficult subdivision of the group.

DIAGNOSTIC GROUP CHARACTERS. Dorsal aspect rather like tree-bark, skin often warty. Flash colors on the parts of the flanks, thighs and some of the other limb surfaces concealed in repose. Build elongate in large forms and specimens. Head crocodilian, flaring at the sides, constricted behind and with raised nostrils. Tongue rounded; groups of vomerine teeth short, between the choanae. Disks short, spatulate, wide in front, narrowed behind. Sexual differences not marked except for the much larger size and more robust habit of the females. Voice feeble, call generally resembling *tch, tch, tch* or similar sounds.

COMPOSITE DESCRIPTION. Size variable, females 32–50 mm snout to vent; build robust and elongate in large specimens, in gravid females the body often distended by the masses of eggs; male smaller and frailer. Body rather flat. Hindlimb not very long, the tibiotarsal articulation reaching between eye and nostril when the leg is adpressed, generally less far in females full of eggs. Head somewhat depressed, crocodilian in aspect, with a nuchal constriction and raised nostrils; length and width of head equal or subequal. Snout as long as or slightly longer than the diameter of eye, truncate between the nostrils; canthus rostralis curved, moderately distinct; loreal region concave, flaring to the edge of the mouth. Outline of head from beneath ogival. Interorbital space slightly wider than internarial space. Eye prominent when raised. Tympanum small, one-third, two-fifths, or even less of the diameter of the eye. Tongue rounded or oval, very slightly free, entire or slightly notched. Groups of vomerine teeth short, transverse, sometimes slightly arched or oblique, situated between the nostrils. Hand unwebbed or with a rudiment of web between the lateral fingers. Feet one-half to two-thirds webbed. Disks short, spatulate, wide in front, constricted behind. Disseminated warts on the dorsal surface, especially on the head and along the edges of the pattern, often very conspicuous on the upper eyelids. Belly and ventral aspect of thigh granular. No tarsal fold, generally no fold across the chest.

COLOR AND PATTERN. Dorsal surface brown, gray or olive, often like tree bark, with or without a light mantle, network, or additional ornamentation; spots darker. Basic pattern composed of an interocular spot, a sacral spot and a pair of dorsolateral stripes, all variable. A dark stripe under the canthus rostralis; often light and dark bars between the eye and the edge of the upper jaw. Interocular spot triangular, obtriangular, slightly pentagonal, W- or crescent-shaped, variable in length and width but present in most forms. Sacral spot sometimes forming a wide crescent, more frequently a long, irregular and excentric chevron, entire or open, often divided longitudinally. Sacral spot often absent or vestigial. Dorsolateral stripes paired; straight or angular and forming an inward-directed apex, similar to a pair of inverted parentheses (left to right). Disruptive dark bars separated by flash colors in life, on the permanently visible dorsal surface of the limbs, to the outer digits, variable in shape and width. Black or very dark blotches on the flanks and thighs of most forms, generally on a blue, violet or grayish flash color. Pattern of concealed surfaces more or less visible when viewed from beneath. Ventral aspect light or stippled with dark dots, the thighs often more pigmented than the body; hind edge of thigh and margins of the other limb-segments similar to the dorsal surface.

Dead specimens often gray or with a metallic sheen; the spots, stripes, and blotches persistent but the flash color faded to white intervals.

SECONDARY SEX CHARACTERS. Not marked except for the large size and robust habit of the females. Males small and inconspicuous, vocal sac hardly noticeable, forearms slightly thickened in the nuptial period. Females and female types more numerous in collections than usual.

VOICE. The voice of the whole group is feeble, the call resembling a low *tch, tch, tch,* quite diagnostic for those used to differentiate frogs by their call.

DISTRIBUTION. Atlantic area of Brazil. Montane rain-forest forms in the southeastern coastal serras. An allied separate species on the coastal lowlands. Others were in northern parts of the Atlantic area.

## *Hyla catharinae catharinae* Boulenger, 1888

BOULENGER, G. A. A list of batrachians from the province of Santa Catharina, Brazil. *An. Mag. Nat. Hist.,* ser. 6, 1:415–417.

This is the nominal form described by Boulenger. It is also the most southern of the known races of the species. I have seen some specimens, mostly preserved, from the mountains of northern Rio Grande do Sul and of northern Santa Catarina and have also examined the types in the British Museum of Natural History.

DIAGNOSTIC CHARACTERS. The diagnostic characters of the species are mentioned above. Those of this race are difficult to evaluate. The females are large, the livery is variable, and the flash color of living specimens from Rio Grande do Sul is coeruleous with large black blotches.

TYPES AND TERRA TYPICA. There are two females syntypes in the British Museum, 12.65 and 12.66. The type locality is imprecise: "Sierra de Catarino," leg. Michaelis. They are probably from the northern mountains where the German immigrants settled.

DESCRIPTION (based on Boulenger and specimens seen). Females large, robust. Types 42 and 41 mm long; largest specimen seen 45 mm from snout to vent. Males smaller, around 33 mm, less robust. Hindlimb variable in length, the adpressed tibiotarsal articulation often reaching between the eye and the nostril, less far in females distended by masses of eggs. Head large, plane, as long as wide, with crocodilian aspect. Snout as long as the diameter of the orbit or slightly longer, rounded from above. Outline of mouth ogival. Canthus rostralis rather indistinct; loreal region concave. Nostrils slightly tumefied. Eye large and prominent. Tympanum very distinct, about half the diameter of the eye. Interorbital space slightly wider than the internarial space. Tongue large, rounded, emarginate, or slightly notched. Groups of vomerine teeth short, close together, between the choanae. Disks wide, short, spatulate, smaller than the tympanum. A rudiment of web between the outer fingers. Outer toes about two-thirds webbed. Upper aspect slightly warty or with disseminated glandules. Belly and midventral portion of the thigh granular.

COLOR AND PATTERN. Brown or grayish above, sometimes reminiscent of tree bark or lichens. Pattern variable; composed of the usual interocular spot, dorsolateral, inverted parentheses (left to right), and sacral spot; not always distinct. The dorsal aspect may be plain, mantled, or intermediate.

(a) *Plain Specimens:* Different tones of brown, like tree bark; interocular spot roughly triangular, large; sacral spot crescent- or (more often) chevron-shaped, long, irregular, sometimes divided longitudinally; dorsolateral parentheses present.

(b) *Mantled:* Snout light; two brilliant, light, scalloped bands involving the interocular spot, confluent behind it, interrupted by the dark sacral area; dorsolateral parentheses not distinct. This was called the *leucophaea* livery by Lutz and is similar but not as elaborate as the dorsal pattern of *Hyla catharinae bocainensis.*

(c) *Intermediate:* Mantle present, but broken up by the spots and their fragments.

The flash color of the upper surfaces concealed in repose is coeruleous blue with bold black blotches; it is also conspicuous when viewed from beneath (Rio Grande do Sul specimens).

A series of examples in the Lutz Collection (ALC, MNR) are either plain or mantled. The types show an intermediate livery; the larger one is slightly more ornate than the other two specimens from Rio Grande do Sul; two are plain; one, a male, is intermediate and inclined to be melanistic.

LIVING SPECIMENS. No notes are available except the fact that the three frogs from Rio Grande do Sul were living in a covered well on the property of Professor Rudolph Gliesch at São Francisco de Paula, where the forest has been preserved.

DISTRIBUTION. Santa Catarina: Serra do Mar, near São Bento do Sul (26° 14′ 55″ S. 49° 22′ 50″ W. Gr.; approximately 800 m altitude).

Rio Grande do Sul: Serra Geral at São Francisco de Paula (29° 20′ 00″ S. 50° 31′ 21″ W. Gr.; approximately 900 m altitude).

## *Hyla catharinae bocainensis* B. Lutz, 1968

LUTZ, B. 1968. Geographic variation in Brazilian species of *Hyla.* Texas Memorial Museum. The Pearce-Sellards Series 12:3–5, fig. 1.

This form was first seen by A. Lutz in 1925 at his brother's Fazenda do Bonito, located in the Serra da Bocaina at approximately 1,100 m altitude. All but two of the specimens obtained there agree with this form. One of them is aberrant. The other, a small specimen, was taken above timber line and agrees with the form I call *Hyla obtriangulata*, which is dominant on the Itatiaia Range across the Paraiba Valley, also above the timber line.

DIAGNOSTIC CHARACTERS. *H. c. bocainensis* is best characterized by the light, scalloped, and festooned network, surrounding and enclosing or limiting the dark dorsal spots and dorsolateral areas. The females are large and robust, not less than 40 mm from snout to vent.

TYPE AND TYPE LOCALITY. There are eleven specimens, including three large females in the A. Lutz Collection and one in that of the DZSP. The description that follows is based on the latter, as it is more recent and in perfect condition. It was collected at Fazenda do Bonito by Mrs. Maria Aparecida Volcano of the DZSP in January 1960, field no. 56. The female paratypes are ALC nos. 2517, 2518, and 2335 in the MNR. The name was selected long ago by A. Lutz.

DESCRIPTION. Size: type 44 mm snout to vent. Other females from 41.5 to 46.5. Build robust. Males much smaller, less robust, 33–36.5 mm snout to vent. Leg average, the tibiotarsal articulation reaching between the eye and the nostril when the hindlimb is adpressed. Head oval, as wide as long. Snout truncate between the nostrils, rounded in front with moderately distinct canthus rostralis and concave loreal region flaring to the mouth. Eye large, very prominent, its horizontal diameter longer than the distance from its anterior corner to the nostril, equal to its distance from the tip of the snout. Tympanum moderate, one-third the diameter of the eye. Internarial space one-fourth less than the interorbital space. Tongue large, round, emarginate. Vomerine teeth in two small groups between the choanae, contiguous in the type. Disks short, wide, the largest slightly rounded in front, all constricted behind. A rudiment of web between the lateral fingers. Web on foot oblique and narrow between the first and second toes, slightly wider between the second and third, wide and quite symmetrical between the third, fourth, and fifth, inserted below the disk on the outer side of the second, third, and on the fifth, wide to the second subarticular tubercle on the inner side of the third and on both sides of the fourth toe. A callus under the first finger and another, wider one under the third and fourth; an elongate inner and a minute outer metatarsal tubercle. Palmar and plantar tubercles as in typical *Hyla catharinae*. Skin very slightly warty on the head, granular on the ventral aspect.

VARIATION. The series shows some slight variation as to the shape of the tongue, which may be entire, and the position of the vomerine teeth, which are sometimes slightly separate.

SECONDARY SEX CHARACTERS. Not marked. Males smaller and frailer than the females, which are robust as usual in the large forms of *Hyla catharinae* "sensu lato." At times they are much distended by the masses of eggs.

COLOR. The colors of the living frog are unknown, including that of the flash color or background of the aspects concealed in repose.

PATTERN. In *H. c. bocainensis* the light mantle of the mantled morph of *H. c. catharinae* from Santa Catarina is substituted by a very conspicuous light network with scalloped and festooned edges, surrounding and invading the dark brown dorsal spots and areas. The interocular spot retains its form best; it has a slight dent in front between the eyes, and is prolonged backward, narrowing gradually to a blunt point that is bipartite in some specimens. The sacral spot is broken up into a number of fragments. In the type, the largest fragment is narrow, roughly chevron shaped, and very much prolonged in front; it is followed by two slightly excentric ocelli and a quite irregular and excentric portion. In some specimens the sacral spot is broken up into insular spots. In others there are only vestiges of the chevron left. The network is prolonged onto the top of the head and the nostrils as a light cap and may contain one or two large dark spots. The sides of the head below the canthi are dark, with four (type) or even five light, oblique bars from below the eye to the edge of the upper jaw. Light areas, similar to the network, are also present on the limbs, enclosing broad, dark, sometimes spool-shaped spots. Ventral aspect similar to that of the typical form. Pattern on concealed part of the limbs not marked nor visible from beneath. Edges of limbs dark.

ABERRANT SPECIMEN. One female from the Serra da Bocaina, 37 mm snout to vent. It was found at the Rio Segredo Fazenda do Bonito at approximately 1,100 m altitude, together with a typical *bocainensis*. Build slightly shorter but even more robust. Middorsal pattern more like that of the smaller form, *brieni*, found further south in the same state of São Paulo. Much more glandular than either, very melanistic. Concealed pattern drop-like, extremely conspicuous from the ventral aspect.

## *Hyla catharinae brieni* De Witte, 1930

WITTE, G. F. DE. 1930. Liste des reptiles et batraciens récoltés au Brésil par la Mission Massart (1922–23) et description de sept nouvelles espèces. In "Une Mission Biologique Belge au Brésil" 2:214–230, pls. 1–8 *Hyla brieni*: 227, pl. 8, figs. 3–4.

The notes that follow apply to the form of *Hyla catharinae* that has been collected on the Serra de Cubatão near the capital of the state of São Paulo, which is part of the Serra do Mar.

DIAGNOSTIC CHARACTERS. This race is characterized by the very ornate pattern on the back and on the sides, the pale bluish color of the concealed areas, and the rather abundant marks or stippling on the light ventral aspect.

TYPE AND TYPE LOCALITY. The holotype was collected by the Belgian Mission at the Biological Station of Alto da Serra on April 27, 1922. It was described as a full species and is now at the Musée Royal de Belgique in Brussels.

DESCRIPTION. Size: type 35 mm; females seen 34–40 mm long; males much smaller. Build of large females robust, rather like that of the nominate form and of good specimens of *Hyla c. bocainensis*. Hindlimb not long, the adpressed tibiotarsal articulation reaching the anterior part of the eye or slightly in front of it. Head large, length and width subequal. Snout oval, rounded in front, pointed at the tip. Canthus rostralis blunt and curved. Loreal region concave below the canthi, sloping down to the edge of the mouth. Interorbital space not much wider than the internarial space. Nostrils lateral, canthal, open above. Horizontal diameter of the eye shorter than its distance from the tip of the snout. Tympanum small in our specimens. Tongue wide, rounded, notched, and free behind. Vomerine teeth in two small groups, close together, between the choanae. Disks short, wide, spatulate. A rudiment of web at the base of the outer fingers. Disks of toes slightly smaller. Web narrow, forming fringes on the proximal side of the inner toes, wide to above the penultimate tubercle on the outer side of the second, third, and fifth, to the penultimate tubercle on the fourth toe. A distinct inner metatarsal tubercle. Skin smooth above except for disseminated glandules. Ventral aspect granular, especially on the belly and midventral part of the thighs.

COLOR AND PATTERN. Silvery grays and/or drab slightly vinaceous browns. Interocular spot generally very distinct, often bluntly triangular. Dorsolateral parentheses rather short, drawing together behind the interocular spot then drawing apart. Sacral spot, when evident, very roughly chevron shaped, often fragmented. Additional stripes on the sides of the body, parallel to the dorsolateral ones, sometimes confluent or anastomosed, and large blotches on the flanks. A dark subcanthal stripe and two or three oblique bars from the eyes to the edge of the upper jaw are also present. The dorsal pattern is often surrounded by a silvery gray mantle over the head and back, similar to that of the mantled specimens of the nominate form from Santa Catarina and Rio Grande do Sul. In some individuals the mantle is scalloped and the meeting points between it and the different elements of the pattern are beset with glandules. In others it follows the contours of the stripes and spots as if the whole dorsal surface had been bisected longitudinally into lighter and darker fields. The mantle itself may be very ornate.

There are dark bars with lighter intervals between them on all the permanently visible upper aspects of the limbs to the digits. The light, rectilinear, intervals on the upper aspect of the thigh and the inner one of the tibia concealed in repose may appear drop-like in certain positions when the legs are partly folded. The flash color is, however, pale blue and not deep yellow like the drops of *Hyla flavoguttata*, which at Alto da Serra is sympatric with *H. c. brieni*. Ventral aspect pale, slightly bluish, with dark flecks and stippling. Inner ventral parts of the thighs and other limb segments immaculate, pale blue like the upper concealed areas. Iris grayish, blending with the background.

Some individuals with a much plainer dorsal livery are present in the samples, especially juveniles. Four of these, 23–25 mm long, have a pattern like that of *Hyla obtriangulata* and are thus similar to the three small specimens from Nova Friburgo put to that species. They may be conspecific with it. However, it is also possible that the initial pattern is more simple than that of full-grown individuals.

DISTRIBUTION. Most of the examples seen come from the biological stations at Boracea and Alto da Serra Cubatão, outside the city of São Paulo. However, the *H. c. brieni* has also been collected on the grounds of the Butantan Institute by young Alfonse Richard Hoge, a gifted boy naturalist.

## *Hyla catharinae trapicheiroi* B. Lutz, 1954

LUTZ, B. 1954. Anfíbios anuros do Distrito Federal. The Frogs of the Federal District of Brazil. *Mem. Inst. O. Cruz* 52(1):155–238, 1 map, 19 pls. *Hyla trapicheiroi*: 159–160, 222, pl. XVI, figs. 2, 5.

This form is so closely akin to the nominate form *Hyla c. catharinae* that unless seen alive it might be considered identical with it. Nevertheless, I have not seen any specimens of it in collections from outside Rio de Janeiro, which is its terra typica. It was first found in the grounds of the water reservoir of the Rio Trapicheiro at the edge of the Tijuca Mountains, but it occurs all over the montane rain forest of the state of Guanabara. A few specimens from other places, including the Serra da Estrela outside Petrópolis, a chain relatively near the isolated mountains of the state of Guanabara, are rather similar. On the next chain belonging to the Maritime Range, the Serra dos Orgãos at Teresópolis, other forms of the *H. catharinae* complex occur.

DIAGNOSTIC CHARACTERS. A well-defined race of *H. catharinae*, its morphological characters and the components of the dorsal pattern present on a rather olivaceous, slightly metallic or bark-like background. Flash color deep blue on the thighs, enclosed in a thick black reticulation that leaves only small spots visible; more diffuse on the sides of the body. Interocular spot very large, prolonged well onto the back, almost rectangular, bilobate, or bipronged posteriorly; the prongs sometimes anteverted and curved, fenestrated in some specimens. Sacral spot wide, crescent shaped, roughly pentagonal, pyramidal, or quite irregular in shape. Dorsolateral stripes not always very distinct, generally short, sometimes split longitudinally or coincident with the darker tones of the sides of the body. Bars on the limbs very regular and distinct. Flash color very extensive on the sides. Lower aspect gray with dark dots; edges of limbs bark-like and similar to the upper aspect. Female fairly large, 35–40 mm snout to vent; larger specimens rare. Male much smaller, 25–30 mm snout to vent.

TYPE AND TERRA TYPICA. Three females: holotype

MNR n. 3615; paratypes 3616 and 3617; five male allotypes MNR 3618–3622; and three paratypes MNR nos. 3623–3625, all collected at the Açude da Solidão, Tijuca Mountains, Rio de Janeiro, by Bertha Lutz and J. Venancio.

DESCRIPTION. Size fairly large, though smaller than some of the other subspecies of *H. catharinae*. Type: female 40 mm. Build robust, elongate only in large specimens. Leg not long, the tibiotarsal articulation reaching in front of the eye when the hindlimb is adpressed. Head slightly longer than wide; nostrils raised, canthus rostralis first curved then straight; loreal region concave beneath the eye, flaring to the mouth. Profile crocodilian. Eye large, very prominent, only slightly shorter than the distance from its anterior corner to the tip of the snout. Tympanum small, about two-fifths the diameter of the eye. Interorbital space a little wider than the internarial space. Tongue rounded, free, and slightly notched behind. Groups of vomerine teeth short, slightly separated, between the choanae. Fingers free, with large, spatulate disks, rounded in front, constricted at the base. A narrow strip of web between the first and second toes; lateral toes two-thirds or more webbed, but the web is narrow on the inner side of the third and fifth and on both sides of the fourth toe. Two rather indistinct, large tubercles at the base of the hand; a small, oval inner and a very minute, round, outer metatarsal. Subarticular and palmar tubercles moderate. Skin smooth above except for some disseminated pustules, especially on the head; a small, tight fold above the tympanum, often followed by a row of pustules. Beneath minutely granular on the gula, body, and midventral strip of the thigh; otherwise smooth.

VARIATION. Some variation is apparent as to the extent of the webbing and the position of the vomerine teeth, which in some specimens are slightly oblique and in a few practically contiguous. In some examples from the Corcovado, the dorsolateral spots are straight.

SECONDARY SEX CHARACTERS. As little marked as in the other components of the group of *Hyla catharinae* except for the much smaller size of the males (25–30 mm). Vocal sac small. Call feeble: *tchê, tchê, tchê.* Throat yellowish. An elongate narrow pad outside the first finger. Leg generally longer, the tibiotarsal articulation reaching between the eye and the nostril when adpressed.

COLOR. Dorsal aspect somewhat like tree bark but rather olivaceous, the spots considerably darker. Flash color a deeper blue than in the other races, very extensive on the sides of the body and on the concealed aspect of the limbs. Sides of the body, between the blue flanks and shoulder region, gray; ventral surface also gray. Lower aspect of leg and tarsus more pigmented than the body; edges like the dorsal surface in color and texture.

PATTERN. Interocular spot large, extending well onto the back, squarish, but variable in outline. In the holotype, MNR n. 3615, the interocular spot forms a small crescent on each eyelid, with a minute point in front where the spot has a light halo; behind two prongs bent forward. Sacral spot wide, crescent shaped, excentrically interrupted in front. Dorsolateral spots short, split longitudinally. Bars on limbs more distinct on the proximal parts but reaching the outer digits as usual. Spots on thighs very small, caught in a heavy black reticulation. Oblique bars on the sides of the head fairly distinct. In paratype n. 3616 the peak in front of the interocular spot is more pronounced, and the spot is slightly fenestrated behind; the bars on the upper jaw are more distinct. In the small paratype n. 3617 the anterior peak still more pronounced and the curved prongs behind bent forward, forming a figure like the heraldic fleur-de-lis. In still others the interocular spot almost quadrangular but with a slightly ondulated outline. Sacral spot not always very distinct, more or less pyramidal, pentagonal, or quite irregular. On these and many other specimens, shadowy and blurred bars occur between the bars on the permanently visible parts of the limbs. Size of the spots of flash color on the thigh variable, in some larger than usual. On the flanks more or less vermiculated dark spots on blue ground. Pigmentation of underside also variable. In large females, dark color mostly concentrated on the limbs. In smaller specimens diffuse flecks of brownish pigment on the gula and the chest between the shoulders.

BEHAVIOR. *H. c. trapicheiroi* likes to hide in crevices of rock and occasionally seeks bromeliads. Young specimens are often found asleep in large, young, rolled-up leaves of *Maranta, Heliconia,* and other similar plants. In the evening the adults are apt to sit on stones, vegetation, on walls, or inside reservoirs and small pools found in the forest. They will even use small tanks meant for watering gardens or for washing clothes. Late at night they can be found climbing out of the water. As many as thirty pairs have been observed at a time in the Açude da Solidão (a large artificial pond). They have also been observed swarming by A. Lutz and J. Venancio; the males were forming a long cluster hanging over the water of the Trapicheiro Reservoir.

SPAWN. *H. c. trapicheiroi* may spawn in slow reaches of small brooks but seems to prefer the standing waters mentioned in the preceding paragraph. As usual in *Hyla*, the eggs are small and have a dark animal and a light vegetal pole. The spawn forms a veil that floats on the water.

METAMORPHOSIS. Occurs between 8 and 12 mm of head and body length. We have seen several young climbing out at 9 to 10.5 mm, the tails then still varying between 2 and 16 mm in length. At 12 to 14 mm snout to vent, there may be just a knob visible at the end of the body. At first the spots are shadowy or just outlined by pustules. The pattern and the blue flash color develop during the first fortnight. At the end of that time the crocodilian shape of the head, which is characteristic of the whole *H. catharinae* group, is already quite marked.

DISTRIBUTION. The terra typica of this form is the rain forest on the mountains of the state of Guanabara, which are isolated from the rest of the Serra do Mar and less high. Some specimens from the Serra da Estrela, 65 km away, resemble it somewhat. Two specimens from the Ilha Grande, a large island at the latitude of Angra dos Reis (approximately 23° 00′ 33″ S. 44° 18′ 57″ W. Gr.), also resemble it but seem to have a violaceous flash color.

## *Hyla catharinae opalina* B. Lutz, 1968

> LUTZ, B. 1968. Geographic variation in Brazilian species of *Hyla*. Texas Memorial Museum. The Pearce-Sellards Series 12:6–7, fig. 2.

This is a handsome race of *Hyla catharinae* from the northern block of the Serra do Mar.

DIAGNOSTIC CHARACTERS. *Hyla catharinae opalina* differs from the nominate form by the generally very light color of the dorsal aspect with a rather indistinct pattern and especially by the opaline flash color on the flanks and the upper and inner aspect of the hindlimbs concealed in repose.

TYPES AND TYPE LOCALITY. Type female MNR 4037, leg. B. Lutz and G. Rita Kloss, September 8, 1950, at the Granja Comari, Teresópolis, female paratypes MNR 4058, leg. B. Lutz, March 1945, and MNR 4059 and 4059a, leg. Gualter A. Lutz and Elio Gouvea, January 10th, 1948, in the Organ Mountains National Park. Male allotype MNR 4038, leg. B. Lutz, September 1948, also in the National Park. Type locality, Teresópolis, state of Rio de Janeiro (22° 26′ 12″ S. 42° 52′ 42″ W. at 800–1000 m altitude). A large series of paratypes in the MNR.

DESCRIPTION. Female: type 40, paratypes 43 and 44 mm from snout to vent, much larger than the male. Build robust, slightly elongate. Head large, slightly longer than wide and slightly narrowed at the back. Tibiotarsal articulation reaching the eye or slightly beyond it when adpressed. Canthus rostralis thick, curved, truncate between the nostrils; loreal region concave below the canthus; snout sloping to the opening of the mouth. Eye large, very prominent. Tympanum small, about two-fifths the diameter of the eye. Interorbital space only slightly wider than the internarial space. Tongue large, oval, slightly free and emarginate behind. Vomerine teeth in two small, slightly oblique groups, close together, between the choanae. Disks of fingers very wide, spatulate. A trace of web between the outer fingers. Palm well padded. Disks of toes slightly smaller. Web short between the first and second toes, very oblique from the second to the third, reaching below the disk on the outer side of the third and on the fifth, close to the penultimate tubercle on the fourth toe, continuing as fringes to the disks. A distinct inner metatarsal tubercle. Skin of dorsal aspect with many glandules, a conspicuous one at the heel and two at the edges of the anus. Ventral aspect of body and thigh granular.

ALLOTYPE. Male considerably smaller than the female. Allotype 30 mm, average 28 to 30 mm from snout to vent. Build less elongate. Hindlimb longer. Vocal sac small. Voice rather weak.

JUVENILES. Without sex characters, up to 27 mm long; the larger ones are probably immature females. The legs are generally longer, the adpressed tibiotarsal articulation almost reaching the nostril. The pattern is more distinct in some.

COLOR AND PATTERN. Pale brown above, sometimes grayish. Pattern darker, often indistinct or more distinct anteriorly. Dark subcanthal stripe generally quite evident. Interocular spot shallow, mostly W-shaped, sometimes fragmented or reduced to the eyelids and adjacent interocular area, more seldom crescent shaped. Dorsolateral parentheses more marked anteriorly or much reduced. Sacral spot often absent; when present, shallow, crescent shaped, or irregular; concave behind. Bars on the permanently visible aspect of the legs often more evident than the pattern on the body. Iris similar to the background, slightly more gray with a fine pattern of veins; a pseudocolobom and a shallow notch in the middle of the lower part of the inner rim. In some lights, the eyes have a pale blue or a slightly pinkish sheen. Flash color opaline, slightly greenish; bold black bars on the upper aspects of the thigh and the inner one of the leg concealed in repose; smaller blotches on the flanks and dark marks on the inner upper aspect of the tarsus and foot. Ventral aspect pale, slightly flecked on the body; a more distinct vermiculation on the ventral aspect of the thighs.

VARIATION. Some individuals are more pigmented, and their pattern stands out better. In a few the spots are fragmented and form an irregular, obscure network on the back. One male from Nova Friburgo has a slightly more distinct tapestry-like pattern; all the elements are present and have multiple outlines.

Morphological variation generally affects the length of the hindlimbs. Two of our specimens have only one set of vomerine teeth.

VOICE. Rather weak. Call something like *tche, tche, tche*. It has been recorded on Uher Report L 4000. The males generally call individually, perched on shrubs near running water.

ECOLOGY. Adults and juveniles are often found sitting on *Hedychium coronarium* at the entrance of the Organ Mountains National Park. They are common there and in the Granja Comari, and are generally found on vegetation near the small streams and brooks where they breed. The tadpoles have a white spot between the nostrils.

DISTRIBUTION. Similar specimens have been collected at Nova Friburgo in the northern block of the Serra do Mar (22° 16′ 42″ S. and 42° 21′ 34″ W. Gr.) at similar altitudes.

## *Hyla obtriangulata* nom. nov.

(nomen novum for *Hyla simplex* B. Lutz, 1968)

> LUTZ, B. 1968. Geographic variation in Brazilian species of *Hyla*. Texas Memorial Museum. The Pearce-Sellards Series 12:5–6.

*Hyla obtriangulata* seems rather close to *Hyla catharinae*, but it occurs together with one or another of its races in several of the places where it has been collected in the Serra da Mantiqueira and in the Serra do Mar. Consequently it has to be given specific rank.

DIAGNOSTIC CHARACTERS. *Hyla obtriangulata* is characterized by the elongate and narrow build, the relatively simple longitudinal pattern of the dorsal aspect, and the dull color of the surfaces concealed in repose.

TYPES AND TYPE LOCALITY. Male holotype, MNR 4035, collected by B. Lutz, November 1954; female allotype, MNR 4036, collected by A. Leitão de Carvalho and H. Berla, December 1962; type locality Brejo da Lapa, Alto Itatiaia, Serra da Mantiqueira, at 2,200 m altitude (22° 31′ 15″ S., 44° 39′ 00″ W. Gr.).

DESCRIPTION. Female syntype 37 mm; females 35–39 mm from snout to vent. Males considerably smaller, 25–28 mm, rarely more. Build elongate, narrow except in females distended by masses of eggs. Body long. Hindlimb short, the adpressed tibiotarsal articulation reaching the eye in females with eggs or slightly beyond it (smaller specimens). Head large, length and width subequal. Snout flat above, slightly pointed beyond the nostrils, sloping down slightly to the mouth opening in profile. Canthus rostralis curved, loreal region grooved below the canthus. Nostrils small, opening upward. Eye prominent, slightly longer than its distance from the nostril. Interorbital space slightly wider than the internarial space. Tongue wide, rounded, slightly notched and free behind. Vomerine teeth in two small, slightly oblique groups, close together, between the choanae. Disks wide, short, spatulate. Fingers free. Toes about one-half webbed; a narrow fringe of web on the inner side of the first, second, and third toes; web wide to above the penultimate subarticular tubercle on the outer side of the second and third, slightly longer on fifth, not reaching the penultimate tubercle on fourth toe, thence fringed. A small tubercle under the first finger; a slightly larger bifid one under the third and fourth; a small inner and a minute outer metatarsal tubercle. Skin of the dorsal aspect and the sides smooth; minute glandules disseminated on the head, especially on the upper eyelids, the supratympanic ridge, and the interocular spot, forming a row down the stripes. Ventral aspect of the body and midventral portion of the thigh granular.

MEASUREMENTS. Males average 25-28 mm; females 34–39 mm. One unusually large female from Teresópolis is 47 mm from snout to vent.

COLOR AND PATTERN. Dorsal aspect medium brown, much lighter than the pattern. This is longitudinal and composed of a dark subcanthal stripe, an oblique bar from the eye to the edge of the mouth, a large, triangular interocular spot, a pair of dorsolateral stripes, and additional stripes on the sides. Sacral spot generally indistinct; often a faint longitudinal pattern on the middorsal area.

VARIATION. In most specimens the interocular spot is obtriangular, generally blunt; in some individuals it is pointed; sometimes it is asymmetrical or bifid at the tip. The dorsolateral stripes may converge anteriorly or run straight to the sacral region where they are deflected onto the flanks; there they and the lateral stripes may become somewhat anastomosed; dark spots are also present on the flanks. Some specimens show a smallish irregular excentric spot or shadow on the sacral area or one or two dots on the midline of the back. The dorsolateral stripes are sometimes fragmented; in one specimen the fragments are oblique. Two individuals show a light halo around the interocular spot and the stripes. Wide, perpendicular, or oblique coincident bars are present on all the permanently visible upper parts of the limbs, with light, slightly ornate intervals between them. The dark bars are variable in width; in a few individuals they coalesce at the back. The edges of the pattern may be very marked when viewed from beneath. Flash color of the hidden surfaces a dull grayish violet. A sprinkling of dark pigment or dark vermiculation present on the ventral aspect.

Iris a light brownish pink at the periphery, pale yellow at the center, with thin zig-zag black veins, a narrow black pseudocolobom, and a small median notch in the lower part of the free inner rim.

VARIATION. Some of the specimens from the type locality show a more ornate background, a greater contrast between it and the pattern, or more marked spots and stripes. The ones from Mauá and the lower parts of the Itatiaia are similar but paler and more ornate. Also more ornate are those from Cidade Azul, on the same Serra da Mantiqueira, state of São Paulo, in the collection of the DZSP. In one sample of eight, seven show the longitudinal pattern, four with additional ornamentation on the back, two with very marked dorsolateral and lateral stripes, one of these with additional dark marks on the head; one has the outline of the interocular spot and the stripes punctuated by glandules. In the other, the back-

ground forms a roughly X-shaped figure that surrounds the hind part of the interocular spot and continues down the back. Similar but more attenuated dorsal backgrounds also occur in the type locality. Specimens from Poços de Caldas, Minas Gerais, are also very ornate.

The specimens from the Serra do Mar are plain. They exhibit the usual livery of spots and stripes on a relatively uniform background. A very small female with eggs (34.5 mm long) was obtained by F. Segadas Vianna above the timber line at Lageado on the Serra da Bocaina, across the Paraiba Valley from the Itatiaia. It has a long, triangular, interocular spot, a few marks on the back, and the usual stripes. A slightly larger one was taken at Parati slightly further south. It has a long interocular spot, a thin narrow sacral chevron, and the stripes. Isolated individuals have been found at Teresópolis, including the giant female mentioned above. Their livery is similar to that of the others from the Maritime Range.

Many years ago three small frogs (ALC 2597-99) were collected by us in Nova Friburgo, also in the northern block of the Serra do Mar. A. Lutz labeled then *Hyla obtriangulata* but did not describe them. The interocular spot is blunt, the longitudinal dorsolateral stripes are present but short and unequal. One has a narrow, pointed, chevron-shaped sacral spot, and another two have rectilinear dark fragments on the sacral area. Four juveniles found together with adult *Hyla catharinae brieni* on the Serra de Paranapiacaba near São Paulo are similar to these specimens from Nova Friburgo. They may, however, be juveniles of *Hyla catharinae brieni*, since a few, mostly small, individuals of this very ornate race are plainer than the others.

ECOLOGY. *Hyla obtriangulata* is abundant at the type locality. It congregates on the marginal vegetation of a large artificial pond produced by damming a stream. The water is almost still and very cold. In other places only isolated individuals have been obtained.

KNOWN RANGE. Serra da Mantiqueira from Itatiaia to Campos do Jordão; also in Poços de Caldas in the neighboring state of Minas Gerais. Serra do Mar from the northern block in the state of Rio de Janeiro to the southern limit of that state with the state of São Paulo; it also occurrs further south.

NEW NAME. The name has been changed since Duellman points out that *simplex* is preoccupied.

A. Lutz's mss. name, *H. obtriangulata*, is used in its place.

ABERRANT SPECIMENS. Two specimens, probably females, from Araraquara, Serra do Mar, in southern Paraná (25° 52′ S. 48° 34′ W. Gr.), 37.5 and 39 mm snout to vent. Dorsal background a rather dull reddish brown on the head, middorsal mantle, and bars on the limbs. Interocular spot roughly triangular, slightly invaded by the outline of the mantle. Sacral spot somewhat vestigial, nearer to a chevron in the larger, fragmented in the smaller; in both continuous with one of the dark blotches on the flanks. Anterior part of the dorsolateral stripes in the larger reduced to a line that is punctuated by dark glandules in the smaller specimen. Concealed pattern very distinct from beneath; the light flash color, not seen in life, becomes rather drop-like, but forms a double row in the larger specimen. Webs very narrow between the two inner toes, wide and symmetrical between the outer three.

## INSULAR AND COASTAL FORMS

Certain preserved specimens belonging to the group of *Hyla catharinae* from isolated points near the coast or from continental islands close to it in the states of São Paulo and Rio de Janeiro are present in the collections examined. Some of them belong to the species described above. Others are difficult to allocate despite the fact that these islands are emergent portions of partly drowned mountainous terrain. It is evidently necessary to collect *Hyla catharinae* and related forms much more intensely in this area, to examine such specimens alive, and to compare them with living examples of the better-known forms.

The most southern of these islands from which there are frogs available, the Ilha da Queimada Grande, yielded only *Eleutherodactylus binotatus* and *Hyla perpusilla,* either a population of large and well-patterned *Hyla perpusilla v-signata* or a form very similar to it (see above).

### Hyla catharinae alcatraz B. Lutz, 1972

LUTZ, B. 1972. New forms of the group of *Hyla catharinae. Bol. Mus. Nac. Rio Zoology,* no. 288.

On the Ilha dos Alcatrazes, very slightly farther north and out, Aristoteris T. Leão collected three specimens (MNR 4084, 4085, 4086) that show the following characters: size small, 32, 26, and 20 mm from snout to vent. Build robust for the size. Hindlimb average, the adpressed tibiotarsal articulation reaching the eye in the larger specimen, between it and the nostril in the two smaller ones. Head large, oval, wide before and behind the eye. Snout appearing truncate beyond the nostrils from above, sloping slightly to the mouth opening in profile. Canthus rostralis straight, not very marked; loreal region not very concave. Nostrils subterminal, slightly tumefied. Eye prominent, shorter than its distance from the tip of the snout. Tympanum very distinct, about three-eighths of the diameter of the eye. Tongue round, emarginate, hardly free behind. Vomerine teeth in two short contiguous convex patches, between the choanae. Disks short, spatulate. Hand unwebbed. A callosity below the first finger, a larger one under the third and fourth fingers. Palmar and subarticular tubercles well developed. Outer toes webbed, to the penultimate articulation on the third and fifth, to the antepenultimate one on the fourth toe. Dorsal aspect of the body rough and glandular. Chest, belly, and midventral portion of thigh granular; gula less so. A distinct supratympanic fold. Color a pale buff. Pattern rather indistinct. Interocular spot shallow; a shadowy area behind it in the two smaller specimens. Dorsolateral parentheses darker almost linear. Sacral spot not evident. Bars on the limbs also indistinct.

As this form seems to be new, I propose the name of the island for it: *Hyla c. alcatraz.*

### Hyla catharinae angrensis B. Lutz, 1972

LUTZ, B. 1972. New forms of the group of *Hyla catharinae. Bol. Mus. Nac. Rio Zoology,* no. 288.

Two specimens from Angra dos Reis, in the southern part of the state of Rio de Janeiro (23° 00′ 33″ S. 44° 18′ 57″ W. Gr.; altitude 0–1,200 m): MNR 2018 leg. A. L. Carvalho and H. Berla, May 1948, and MNR 2512, G. Myers and H. Travassos, August 15, 1942, at Fazenda Japuíba.

These specimens may constitute a separate, small, slender, warty, rather long-headed race, *H. c. angrensis.* Middorsal pattern somewhat reminiscent of the typical plain form from Santa Catarina, but the interocular spot is quite shallow.

DESCRIPTION. Larger specimen (2512): Interocular spot W-shaped, narrow, slightly pointed in front; sacral spot complex, composed of an oval area preceded by an elongate irregular chevron, flanked and followed by figures like the anastomosed branches of another chevron. Dorsolateral stripes double, deflected onto the sides, anastomosed to parts of the dorsal design. Bars on limbs narrower than the light intervals but reaching the outer digits. Innermost bar on thigh continued as a dark blotch surrounding the light area on the concealed part of the flank; bars on thighs partly confluent behind; an indistinct, light, longitudinal area on the ventral aspect of the thigh and light intervals on the inside of the tibia. One group of vomerine teeth absent in this individual.

Smaller specimen (2018): Build similar. Canthus rostralis sharp. Interocular spot very narrow, widely interrupted between the eyes. Sacral and middorsal pattern similar to that of the other, but even more intricate. Dorsolateral parentheses very short, fragmented. Concealed pattern similar; pigment and light intervals disposed longitudinally on the ventral aspect of the thigh; ventral aspect of body slightly more stippled.

MEASUREMENTS. MNR 2512, 32 mm. snout to vent; hindlimb 55 mm. MNR 2018, 25 mm snout to vent; hindlimb 46 mm.

## ABERRANT SPECIMENS

From the larger island of São Sebastião, also in the state of São Paulo, I have seen only two specimens. One (DZSP 9780) is a very fine *Hyla flavoguttata*. The other, female from the Rio Una, 39 mm long, is very similar in build to the females of *Hyla catharinae catharinae* from Santa Catarina and Rio Grande do Sul, but very dark and glandular. Interocular spot shallow and W-shaped, the prongs short and wide apart. Dorsolateral parentheses black, thick, short, glandular. Sacral spot concealed by the middorsal ornamentation, which is more similar to that seen in the smaller, more slender and very ornate *Hyla catharinae brieni* from the vicinity of the capital of São Paulo. Dark spots are present on the light intervals between the bars on the permanently visible dorsal aspect of the limbs, but there is hardly any room for a light flash color between the dark blotches on the parts of the thighs and flanks concealed in repose. Con-

cealed pattern only slightly visible from the ventral surface, which is somewhat darker than usual.

MNR 2196. Two specimens collected by Dr. Helmut Sick on the Ilha Grande, an island on the coast of the state of Rio de Janeiro, March 4, 1944, (latitude and longitude of Angra dos Reis). Both are very dark brown, perhaps due to the perservative, with very indistinct pattern and a dark violaceous tint on the lighter areas concealed in repose.

Smaller one: interocular spot large, squarish, sacral spot between crescent and pyramid shaped; both rather indistinct on a slightly lighter background; anterior part of dorsolateral stripes visible.

Larger one: interocular spot very indistinct, outlined by dark glandules, long, wide, bipronged posteriorly; sacral spot and dorsolateral stripes quite indistinct; sides of the body dark. In both specimens the bars on the limbs are moderately visible, a black network divides the concealed area in very minute spots reaching rather far forward on the flanks. Visible parts of the concealed pattern somewhat reminiscent of *H. c. trapicheiroi*, but the specimens are small and dark.

MEASUREMENTS. 33 and 26 mm snout to vent; hindlimbs 62 and 45 mm.

MNR 2433: one large and three very small specimens, leg. A. L. Carvalho, August 11, 1939, in the Fazenda do Rubião at Mangaratiba, state of Rio de Janeiro (22° 57′ 45″ S. 44° 2′ 4″ W. Gr.; sea level to 1,000 m altitude).

Large female specimen, 39 mm snout to vent. Head large; legs rather long, the tibiotarsal articulation reaching almost to the nostril when the hindlimb is adpressed. Faded; pattern obliterated; body distended by masses of eggs. Interocular spot crescent shaped, concave forward, narrow, not exceeding the upper eyelids. Sacral spot and dorsolateral stripes indistinct. Light areas on flanks very extensive; the blotches occupy less space; light spots on the upper anterior aspect of the thigh and inside of tibia; on the flanks there seem to be vestiges of blue. Concealed pattern visible from beneath. A light spot on the gula. One group of vomerine teeth smaller than the other.

MEASUREMENTS. 39 mm snout to vent; hindlimb 72 mm. Three other small specimens: 13, 15, and 16 mm long; the former is similar to the adult. The others are like *H. perpusilla v-signata* and probably belong to it.

# 16. Allied Lowland Species

## Hyla humilis Lutz & B. Lutz, 1954 (in B. Lutz, 1954)

> LUTZ, B. 1954. Anfíbios Anuros do Distrito Federal. The Frogs of the Federal District of Brazil. *Mem. Inst. O. Cruz* 52(1):155–197 (Portuguese) 219–238 English. *Hyla humilis*: 160 (P.) 185 (Chave): 222–223 (English) 231 (Key), pl. 16, figs. 9–10, pl. 17, fig. 9.

In the late 1930s *H. humilis* began to be found in the coastal lowlands of the former Federal District and those of the adjacent state of Rio de Janeiro, by Joaquim Venancio, me, and Maria Amelia Teixeira, a Portuguese cook with a good interest in natural history. It was described succinctly, at a much later date, by me from joint notes of A. Lutz's and mine. The name was given because of the small size and very unobtrusive habits of this member of the *H. catharinae* group.

DIAGNOSTIC CHARACTERS. The relatively small size, long, robust hindlimbs, truncate, slightly raised snout, turquoise to Nile blue concealed surfaces, handsome pattern, and lowland distribution.

TYPES AND TYPE LOCALITY. Type locality: Rio Baby, Baixada Fluminense, State of Rio de Janeiro. Female type, MNR 2248, leg. Passarelli, no date; female paratypes, MNR 1478, same collector, and A. Lutz Collection n. 2826; male allotype A. Lutz

Collection n. 2827, the two latter leg. J. Venancio, October 1937.

DESCRIPTION. Size relatively small. Females 30–34 mm, snout to vent. Males 23–28 mm, juveniles 10–11. Build slender. Head slightly longer than wide, snout distinctly truncate. Leg long though variable; the adpressed tibiotarsal articulation reaches the tip of the snout or the nostril, in large females (types) between the nostril and the eye but nearer to the former. Outline of head crocodilian with raised nostrils, slightly angular canthus rostralis and concave loreal region, flaring to the edge of the jaw. Eye prominent, its horizontal diameter slightly longer or equal to the distance from its anterior corner to the nostril, slightly shorter than the distance to the tip of the snout. Tympanum small, about one-fourth the diameter of the eye. Interorbital space about one and a half times the internarial space. Tongue oval, large, slightly notched behind. Vomerine teeth in two very small groups, close together, between the choanae. Hand unwebbed, two large pads on the palm; disks wide, short, rounded in front. Disks of the toes smaller; foot not much more than half-webbed; a prominent inner and a small, rounded outer metatarsal tubercle. Many glandules on the dorsal surface, especially on the head and upper eyelids; disposed more or less longitudinally on the body; a few on the tibiae. Ventral aspect of the body and midventral strip of the thigh minutely but very distinctly granular. A fold across the base of the throat and the chest; a distinct supratympanic ridge. Dead specimens inclined to be curved.

SECONDARY SEX CHARACTERS. Male smaller, vocal sac present.

VARIATION. Except for the slightly greater or shorter length of the very robust hindlimb, there is not much variability present in our relatively short series of specimens from a rather restricted area.

COLOR. Dorsal background tones of either brown or gray. Ventral aspect relatively well pigmented, with dots of brown on the gula and body passing into elongate horizontal dashes on the ventral aspect of the limbs, especially the thighs. Iris golden, with marginal black veins forming very characteristic loops that do not reach the inner zone; a black horizontal pseudocolobom across the middle. Free rim of the lower palpebral membrane dark-edged. Flash color pale Nile blue to very pallid turquoise, occupying the inguinal region, flanks, armpits, and concealed upper and lower surfaces of the limbs; dark marks or blotches on the flanks and thighs.

PATTERN. Interocular spot W-shaped, but shallow and somewhat irregular, punctuated by glandules (type), with or without a median point in front and two behind. Sacral spot mostly indistinct. A very handsome tapestry or scroll-like pattern occupying the whole back in the male allotype. In one specimen the sacral spot is present and has a slightly excentric point in front and three unequal little prongs behind (Caxias); in another it is almost divided into two halves along the middle. Dorsolateral stripes very distinct, divided longitudinally, the inner arms like an inverted pair of parentheses (left to right) somewhat approximated in the middle anteriorly; posteriorly, the stripes are generally digitiform and deflected onto the sides of the body; they are often light-edged. Bars on the limbs oblique, more distinct than the lighter intervals; alternate dark and light bars on the sides of the head; a dark subcanthal stripe.

VOICE. Low and similar to that of the whole group of *Hyla catharinae*.

ECOLOGY. Found on the vegetation of the marshy ground of the coastal lowlands of the states mentioned above, comprehensively called the Baixada Fluminense. A few specimens have been found in similar stations on the adjacent parts of the mountains at Estrela and Barro Branco in the state of Rio de Janeiro.

KNOWN DISTRIBUTION. So far known only from the states of Rio de Janeiro and Guanabara.

SPECIFIC STATUS. The blue-green flash color of this southeastern lowland form brings it nearer to *Hyla catharinae* than to the species of the group with orange or yellow concealed surfaces. The distribution, allied to the small size, truncate snout, and robust hindlimbs seems to warrant according it full specific status.

## *Hyla strigilata*? Spix, 1824

SPIX, J. B. VON. 1824. *Species novae testudinum et ranarum quas in itinere per Brasiliam, annis 1817–20, collegit et descripsit*; p. 14, pl. 10, fig. 3. Species 26: *Hyla strigilata*.

PETERS, W. 1872. Ueber die von Spix in Brasilien gesammelten Batrachier des Koengl. *Naturalien-Kabinets zu Muenchen*. H. strigilata: 214–216.

———. 1872. Ueber eine Sammlung von Batrachiern aus Neu-Freiburg in Brasilien, ibid: 680–684.

A series of four very small specimens collected by Miss G. Rita Kloss, in Afonso Claudio, Espírito Santo, on June 10, 1950, in "marsh overgrown with bamboos," may perhaps belong to *Hyla strigilata* Spix, whose exact status is difficult to judge as the type has been destroyed. Peters seems to confound two forms under this name, one with blue and the other with yellow flash colors, the latter from a montane station where the fauna of Bahia generally does not occur.

ORIGINAL DIAGNOSIS AND DESCRIPTION. "Mediocris, supra brunnea fusca; striis dorsi lateralis obliquis, albis, femoribus albo fasciatis, abdomine albicante, nigro-variegate.

"Corpus mediocre, laeve, supra brunneo-fuscum, subtus cinereo-albicans, lituris fuscis variegatum; caput planum, infra-oculos albo-bistriatum, ore rotundato, naribus subapproximatis; dorsi latera utrinque oblique albostriata; hypochondria fusca, antice albo-bimaculata, pone albo-oculata; femora nigra, albo fasciata; digiti longiores, ranaeformis, posteriores sub-palmati, apice subfrimbriati. Longitudo corporis 1 ¾ l.

"Habitat in Provincia Bahiae."

DIAGNOSTIC CHARACTERS (four specimens). Very granular skin; very distinct oblique white bars on the sides of the head from the eye to the edge of the mouth, in one specimen also under the tympanum. General effect of the dorsal pattern more or less lichenous or bark-like, interpretable as strigilae, especially in one specimen; dorsolateral stripes present in three, similar to those of other forms of the group of *Hyla catharinae* but rather indistinct.

MORPHOLOGICAL CHARACTERS. Those of the group of *Hyla catharinae*, i. e., crocodilian profile, raised nostrils, rounded, slightly emarginate tongue, and very small, transverse, groups of vomerine teeth, between the choanae. Length of leg unequal but fairly long for the group, the adpressed tibiotarsal articulation reaching between the eye and the nostril in one, to the nostril in another. Fingers free, toes about half-webbed.

MEASUREMENTS. 21, 21, 20, and 19 mm snout to vent.

COLOR AND PATTERN. Not seen alive. Dead specimens olivaceous brown and green above. Dorsal pattern very intricate: interocular spot present, roughly W-shaped, varying in shape from one to the other, quite excentric in one. Sacral spot more or less chevron-shaped but caught up in series of alternately lighter and darker parallel stripes; in one, more tapestry-like, deflected onto the flanks to form alternate light and dark areas; indistinct in the other specimens; dorsolateral stripes present in three, similar to those of other forms of the group of *Hyla catharinae* but rather indistinct; alternative light and dark oblique bars on the limbs. Ventral aspect whitish with some dots of pigment.

SPECIFIC STATUS. These specimens are too small for adult males of the species, to judge by the size indicated for the male type. They may, however, be juveniles.

Peters discussed *H. strigilata* at great length. He pointed out some errors in the figure of the type published with the description by Spix. The figure may, however, not have been examined by Spix, as his book was a posthumous publication. Peters also stressed that the first finger is not longer than the second, as shown, but shorter. This difference suggests that the picture may be that of an *Eleutherodactylus ramagii*. The regular light strigilae almost united into V-shape are also not present in the Spix specimen, according to him.

In the same volume of the Monatsberichte, and apropos of a collection of frogs from Nova Friburgo in the state of Rio de Janeiro. Peters listed a second specimen of *Hyla strigilata*. Of this one he said that the large light spots on the concealed surfaces are yellow. This is good instance of an error due to lack of opportunity to compare living specimens. The Nova Friburgo specimen is evidently *Hyla flavoguttata*. Theoretically, the form nearest to *Hyla strigilata* would seem to be *Hyla flavoguttata*, but the terra typica of Spix's *strigilata* should preclude this southeastern montane forest species. Flash colors are constant and diagnostic specific characters.

## *Hyla egleri* B. Lutz, 1968

> LUTZ, B. 1968. New Brazilian Forms of *Hyla*. Texas Memorial Museum. The Pearce-Sellards Series 10:8–10, figs. 4, 5.

In the coastal lowlands of northern Brazil there occurs a *Hyla* that is similar to the *Hyla catharinae* group as to the fundamental dorsal pattern, but that has a more elongate snout. The skin is rather glandular, but this applies to the whole *Hyla catharinae* group. We have a number of specimens of this *Hyla* from Belém do Pará. Five others from the northeastern states of Paraiba and Alagoas seem conspecific with it, but were not seen alive. They are described separately below.

DIAGNOSTIC CHARACTERS. Long snout, with raised, not quite terminal nostrils, giving it a crocodilian profile; small choanae; dull green-gray to slate color of the concealed surfaces (Belém specimens); pattern of the iris, with a dark horizontal pseudocolobom and two median, vertical, bar-like spots producing an incomplete dark cross. Hindlimb apparently longer than usual in the group of *Hyla catharinae*, though this character is variable in Brazilian species of *Hyla*.

TYPES AND TYPE LOCALITIES. The specimens on which this description is based were collected in Belém, the holotype ( ♂ ) and the allotype ( ♀ ) by A. L. Carvalho; the paratypes were got in the *pirarucú* pond of the Museu Goeldi by the author and Misses Alba Maranhão and Dinah Silveira. Additional paratypes were sent by Dr. Walter Egler, the late director of the museum. Male holotype MNR no. 4055, female allotype MNR no. 4056.

DESCRIPTION. Males with vocal sac 23–29 mm snout to vent; female allotype 40 mm; 1 female 35 mm long; specimens without marked sex characters 22–23 mm snout to vent. Build robust; body elongate, narrowed between the sacrum and the groin. Hindlimb variable in length, the tibiotarsal articulation reaching the nostril ( ♀ and some others), the tip of the snout (juveniles) or between the nostril and the eye. Head slightly longer than wide. Snout elongate, slightly acuminate in front, truncate in profile; nostrils tumefied, not quite terminal; canthus rostralis moderate, loreal region slightly concave under the eye. Outline of mouth ogival. Eye moderately large, its horizontal diameter about equal to the distance from its anterior corner to the nostril. Tympanum distinct, vertical, small, its horizontal diameter between one-fourth and two-fifths the diameter of the eye. Interorbital space slightly wider than the internarial space. Tongue oval, distinctly notched, slightly free behind. Vomerine teeth in two small, transverse, curved groups, close together, between the choanae, which are not large. Disks short and wide on the fingers, slightly smaller on the toes. Outer fingers free or with a rudimentary web. Toes more than half webbed; a narrow fringe of web between the first and second toe, in some specimens an even narrower fringe outside the first. Web oblique between the second, third, fourth, and fifth toes, wide to the penultimate subarticular tubercle on the fourth, reaching below the disk on the outer side of the second, third, and on the fifth toe. Skin of the dorsal surface with many scattered glandules, especially on the head, upper eyelids, margins of the limbs, and sometimes on the edges of the spots. Glandules on the eyelids and the heel very distinct; one of these glandules sometimes larger than the others and pointed, but not forming a conical appendage. Sometimes the dorsal pattern outlined and the dorsolateral spots covered by glandules. A supratympanic ridge, a slight fold across the chest. Skin of the ventral aspect of the thigh, of the belly, or of the whole ventral surface of the body granular.

SECONDARY SEX CHARACTERS. The males have a relatively large median vocal sac for their size. The female is much larger than the males, more robust, and might be referred to a different species were it not for the common finding place. Hindlimb long. Tympanum almost half the diameter of the eye. Very glandular and dark specimen.

VARIATION. The usual variation as to the relative length of the hindlimb; in the female it almost attains the nostril; the very small specimens are almost all very long-legged, the tibiotarsal articulation reaching the snout or even beyond it.

COLOR IN LIFE (based on several Belém specimens without much dorsal pattern, sent by Egler and photographed on Ektachrome by G. A. Lutz). Dorsal ground color very slightly roseate tones of brown; pattern very indistinct, especially in the light specimens. Alternate light and dark bars on the limbs more distinct than the pattern on the body and reaching the outer digits. Lower aspect light, belly white, gula with indistinct dotting; ventral aspect of the limbs grayish; the thighs and legs have a greenish tint.

The dorsal color of dead specimens varies somewhat. The males from Belém do Pará are relatively light, either buff, brown, or olivaceous brown, mostly with distinct pattern, a few lacking such a pattern.

PATTERN. The basic components of the dorsal pattern are those usual in the group of *Hyla catharinae*: interocular and sacral spots and dark dorsolateral areas like inverted parentheses. Interocular spot elongate, somewhat narrowed posteriorly, forming a blunt, truncate triangle devoid of its apex, except in one that has two blunt points behind. Sacral spot more or less rectilinear; in the Belém specimens either elongately quadrilateral or prolonged backward and sometimes downward at the hind edges. Outline of dorsal spots often more distinct and darker than the contents. There may be a prolongation from the interocular spot backward or from the sacral spot forward, a spot between them, or a few small spots behind the sacral one. Two of the specimens have an additional light margin around the interocular spot; in one it is reddish. The dorsolateral dark areas begin at the eyes and are narrow over the tympana, becoming wider and deflected onto the sides of the body, stopping at the elbows or just beyond them. They are indistinct in some specimens but these have a complex of large black peritympanic glandules. Oblique bars on the permanently visible dorsal aspect of the limbs are present in all the specimens, generally reaching the outer digits. Concealed pattern on the thighs consisting of black spots on a light ground, its edges visible from beneath in many but not in all specimens.

The pattern of the dead female allotype is difficult to distinguish. She has two unusually light anterior areas on the back to the inside of the dark parentheses. Interocular spot not long but rather wide and glandular. Sacral spot very much obscured by the background but apparently with two points in front. Dorsolateral, parentheses-like, areas very dark, glandular, and distinct as in a number of other specimens. Dark bars on the limbs very distinct; between them narrower and fainter brown ornaments on a lighter ground. The bars cover the three outer digits of both hands and feet. Very marked, alternate light and dark, oblique bars from the canthus, the eye, and the tympanum to the mouth. In most of the males they are not very distinct. On the hindpart of the flanks smallish black mottling on a faintly bluish ground. Concealed pattern on the thighs composed of large black blotches somewhat constricted by the brown color of the permanently visible portion of the thighs.

Iris of some of the males with vestiges of dark gold or light copper color, an incomplete horizontal pseudocolobom and two large vertical spots of dark pigment in the middle of the upper and lower margin, thus forming an incomplete cross. This pattern is less distinct than in the northeastern specimens, which are discussed below. Free rim of the transparent part of the lower palpebral membrane dark with a metallic glint.

RANGE. *H. egleri* has also been collected at Livramento, in the state of Pará, not far from the capital and type locality, Belém. Similar northeastern specimens are described separately below.

AFFINITIES. *Hyla egleri* is a northern species akin to the southeastern Brazilian forms of *Hyla catharinae*, but the latter have a less elongate snout and are mostly montane.

Attempts will probably be made to lump *Hyla egleri* together with other species, such as *H. boulengeri* from Central America, or the frogs from Venezuela called *Hyla palpebrogranulata* by Lutz (1925) and named *Hyla lutzi* by Melin.

Before this is done it will be necessary to check carefully the color of the surfaces of the limbs concealed in repose. This is a very important point in these various forms. The frogs with yellow or orange flash colors cannot be considered conspecific with others whose occult colors are glaucous green or blue, or with those whose colors are dull gray or violaceous, as in *Hyla egleri*.

This species is named for Dr. Walter Egler, who perished on a botanical expedition, and who generously sent me a number of frogs while he was director of the Museu Paraense Emilo Goeldi in Belém.

NORTHEASTERN FORM. I have seen two samples of very similar frogs from northeastern Brazil. One is from Mamanguape, in the state of Paraiba, and belongs to the DZSP. The three specimens examined are uniform in size, 26 mm from snout to vent. The other sample seen comprised one frog from Rio Largo, DZSP no. 9270, 25 mm snout to vent, and a smaller one 23 mm long, WCAB no. 2602, from Engenho Riachão.

Unfortunately they were not seen alive. Four of them are dark gray; one of those from Mamanguape is pale. It shows very marked black spots on a light background on the upper parts of the thighs concealed in repose. They all have dark flecks on the gula and one of them on the belly as well. The pattern on the iris is very distinct; the crossbar is bolder, and there are additional dark dots.

## *Hyla ehrhardti* L. Müller, 1924

MÜLLER, L. 1924. Neue Laubfroesche aus dem Staate Santa Catharina, S. Brasilien. *Zool Anz.* 59:233–234.

In 1924 Lorenz Müller described a new species of tree frog from Santa Catarina under the name *Hyla ehrhardti*, after its collector, I have not been able to identify this species, though I may have seen specimens of it abroad. I presume that it belongs to the group of *Hyla catharinae*. The types were destroyed during the Second World War.

TYPE AND TYPE LOCALITY. An adult male, no. 80/1921 of the Zoological Collection of the State of Bavaria. Type locality: Humboldt (basin of the Rio Novo) in the state of Santa Catarina, leg. W. Ehrhardt, September 1918.

ORIGINAL DESCRIPTION (translated). Head medium, only slightly broader than long, widest at the hind edge of the tympanum, narrowing only slightly from there to the eye. Eye medium, relatively prominent. Head separated from the body; the latter flat, as wide as the head in front, narrowing posteriorly. Tongue a wide oval, slightly nicked behind, only the posterior border free. Vomerine teeth in two long, very slightly curved patches, converging to a blunt point in front but separated in the middle. The apex of the angle formed by them lies between the elongate choanae, which are larger than usual and also converge in front; the hind end of each patch of teeth reaches slightly beyond the hind edge of the choana on the same side. Snout forming a sharp angle but slightly rounded in front, 1.5 times as long as the diameter of the eye, not overhanging the opening of the mouth. Nostrils double as far from the eye as from the tip of the snout. Canthus rostralis rounded; loreal region concave, sloping down obliquely. Interorbital space 1.5 times as wide as the upper eyelid. Tympanum distinct, its longitudinal diameter equal to the diameter of the eye. Fingers plane. First finger shorter than the second, with a strongly marked pollex rudiment forming a semicircular border. Disks large, their diameter equal to that of the eye. Web rudimentary between the first and second, more than one-third the length of the fingers between the second and third and the third and fourth fingers, but continuing as a small fringe almost to the disk, especially on the third. Toes also plane. Web about a third between the first and second toes, about one-half between the others. Disks only slightly smaller than those of the fingers. Subarticular tubercles flat, very well developed. Inner metatarsal tubercle medium and very distinct; outer absent. No tarsal fold; a hint of a spur on the heel.

The adpressed tibiotarsal articulation of the hindlimb reaches the tip of the snout. Femur and tibia approximately equal in length; the latter about 1.5 times the length of the head. Skin of the upper aspect with quite minute wrinkles and adpressions, therefore appearing almost smooth. A distinct fold from the hind edge of the eye, over the tympanum to the axilla. Anterior part of the gula smooth; hind part, belly, chest, and underside of the thighs granular. Gula and chest separated by a sharp fold, the middle part of which is somewhat covered by the skin of the throat, but no evident vocal sac present.

Dorsal and ventral aspects ocher yellow. The upper aspect slightly darker than the lower and covered with small, pale brown spots, which are sparse on the upper arm and the thigh and very dense on the hindpart of the back. A dark point is in the middle of many of these small spots. Forearm and tibia densely spotted. Ventral aspect immaculate.

Head and body length 30 mm; tip of the snout to the hind edge of the tympanum 13 mm; hindlimb 56 mm; tibia 18 mm; tibiotarsal articulation to the tip of the longest toe 24 mm.

# V. Very Small Species

# 17. Small to Minute Forms

## HYLA BIPUNCTATA AND ITS ALLIES

### Hyla bipunctata Spix, 1824

SPIX, J. B. VON. 1824. *Animalia nova, sive species novae testudinum et ranarum quas in itinere per Brasiliam, annis 1817–20, collegit et descripsit.* H. bipunctata: 12, pl. 9, fig. 3.

REUSS, A. 1834. *Zoologische Miscell. Mus. Senck.* 1(1833) H. capistrata: 58, pl. 3, fig. 4.

DUMÉRIL, A. M. C., and BIBRON, G. 1841. *Erpétologie générale, ou histoire naturelle complète des reptiles 8.* H. pumila: 656.

GÜNTHER, A. C. L. G. 1858. *Catalogue of the batrachia salientia in the British Museum.* 160 pp., 12 pls. H. capistrata: 106.

*H. bipunctata* is one of the prettiest and certainly the most characteristic of the small species of *Hyla* found in Brazil. It has been described several times. The oldest description is that of Spix, whose name, figure, and diagnosis do not mention the most distinctive characters. Duméril and Bibron's description is in agreement with their usual high standard of observation. Günther uses the name *capistrata* given by Reuss (1834), whose publication I have not seen but who certainly seized the most distinctive feature, that is the pattern on the sides of the head, which remains visible after death.

DIAGNOSTIC CHARACTERS. The unique pattern of light alveolar spots caught in a dark network, which occupies the sides of the head; in life, the lemon-colored ventral surface of the body and flame-scarlet to orange concealed surfaces of the hindlimbs; the somewhat roseate tinge of the dorsal surface, also present in well-preserved specimens; the short truncate snout, with vertical, not concave, loreal region and poorly defined canthus rostralis.

ORIGINAL DESCRIPTION. "Species 22. *Hyla bipunctata* Tab. IX, fig. 3. Minor, rosea, dorso medio nigro-bipunctato; ano infra albo-bipunctato; linea inter oculos transversa, fusca; tarso breviter calcareo.

"Corpus minus, supra roseum, infra flavo-albicans, granulosum. Caput rotundatum, breve, inter oculos transverse fusco-lineatum; stria versus nares approximata V-formi; lingua rotunda, connata, pone vix excisa; dorsum medium nigro bipunctatum. Longitudo corporis 1.1.

"Habitat in Provincia Bahiae, foemina mare parum maior."

TYPES AND TERRA TYPICA. Spix indicates the state of Bahia as the terra typica. The type specimens, belonging to the Zoological Collection of the state of Bavaria, were destroyed during the Second World War.

DESCRIPTION. Size small, females 24 to 27, rarely 28 mm, mostly smaller; males 19–25, mostly 23 or 24 mm from snout to vent. Build plump in healthy or well-preserved specimens. Leg fairly long but variable, the tibiotarsal articulation reaching either the tip of the snout, the nostril, or a point between the eye and the nostril, occasionally only to the front of the eye. Head short, length and width equal or very slightly wider than long. Snout very short, rounded in front from above, truncate and hardly projecting in profile. Canthus rostralis blunt, loreal region vertical. Nostrils superolateral, not quite at the tip of the snout. Tympanum distinct, about one-half the diameter of the eye, whose horizontal diameter is about equal to the distance from its anterior corner to the nostril. Tongue rounded, wide, very slightly emarginate and free behind. Vomerine teeth in small transverse groups between the choanae. Hands one-third webbed, feet two-thirds to three-fourths webbed. A small inner metatarsal tubercle. Skin above opaque on the body and permanently visible aspects of the limbs, translucent on those concealed in repose, the color of the muscles perceptible. Beneath granular on the belly and midventral aspect of the thigh. A fold of skin over the chest.

COLOR IN LIFE. Dorsal color somewhat variable in life, but displaying hues that contain much orange. Underside more constant, lemon-colored on the gula and body; folds of the vocal sac and hands less bright; concealed surfaces of the legs, including the dorsal surfaces of the thigh not visible in repose, inside of the legs and tarsi, dorsal and ventral aspect of the inner toes scarlet to orange. Capistrate pattern on the sides of the head composed of a dark network, inclosing light cream or buff spots. Background of iris similar to the dorsal surface with an angular reticulation of darker veins not reaching the periphery. Alveolar pattern on the sides of the head extensive to the lower eyelid.

PATTERN. The most diagnostic and constant element of the pattern is the design of light spots surrounded by a dark network producing circles of different sizes on the sides of the head. It may be limited to the loreal region or extend further down the sides toward the elbows, narrowing posteriorly and dying out. The dorsal pattern is variable. A few specimens have no pattern at all, and a few others only the two points mentioned by Spix. The most common patterns are an irregular figure like a badly drawn, inverted Y or like the furcula of a bird on the back, and large distinct spots on the dorsal surfaces.

There may be a distinct interocular spot and an equally distinct sacral one, but in many specimens they become anastomosed and occupy most of the dorsal surface, assuming a number of different shapes that can only be properly conveyed by drawings or photographs. In a few individuals the dorsal spots are areolated with minute white dots, the color of the background, reminiscent of the pattern on the sides of the head. A dark patch over the anus and a dark stripe along the tarsus are constant. Generally dark crossbands on the legs and forearms. All concealed surfaces are immaculate.

The proportion of the different liveries is variable in different lots of specimens.

SECONDARY SEX CHARACTERS. As mentioned by Spix, the female is slightly larger than the male, which has a very large median vocal sac.

VOICE. The call is a chirp: *crr, crr, crr* or *tsss, tsss*, like that of a cricket but very loud. The males at one station all seem to call together and often until quite late at night. The chorus can be heard a long way off. At one time, while living in an apartment house, I found that they could be heard several floors below the terrace on which they occupied a vivarium so that they had to be moved elsewhere.

In the daytime *Hyla bipunctata* can be found in trees above the pools of standing water in which it breeds.

DISTRIBUTION. The species is common on the coastal lowlands of the states of Guanabara and Rio de Janeiro, but we do not have typical specimens from beyond Espírito Santo and Bahia, which is the terra typica. In Rio de Janeiro they have been introduced into an artificial pool, the Açude da Solidão, at the edge of Tijuca forest at about 380 m altitude. They are surviving but have not spread into the forest. A specimen labeled Belém, Pará, has been found in the MNR.

AFFINITIES. *Hyla bipunctata* does not show any marked affinities except with *H. minuta*. The short head and rounded vertical snout are reminiscent of this species and to a lesser degree of some small species belonging to the group of *Hyla senicula* and *H. microps*, which have a patagium and do not belong to this group.

## Hyla minuta Peters, 1872

PETERS, W. C. B. 1872. Ueber eine Sammlung von Batrachiern aus Neu-Freiburg in Brasilien. *Monatsh. Akad. Wiss. Berlin*: 680–684. *H. minuta*: 680.

COPE, E. D. 1887. Synopsis of the batrachia and reptilia obtained by H. H. Smith in the province of Matto Grosso, Brazil. *Proc. Amer. Phil. Soc.* 24:44–60. *H. velata*: 46.

BOULENGER, G. A. 1888. A list of batrachians from the province of Santa Catarina, Brazil. *An. Mag. Nat. Hist.* 1:187–188, and 2:415–417. *H. bivittata*: 188, 417.

BOULENGER, E. G. 1911. On a new tree-frog from Trinidad. *Proc. Zool. Soc. London*, pp. 1082–1083, pl. 64.

LUTZ, A. 1925. Batraciens du Brésil (II). *C. R. Soc. Biol. Paris* 93(22):211–224. *H. pallens*: 212.

MIRANDA RIBEIRO, A. 1926. Notas para servirem ao estudo dos gymnobatrachios (anura) brasileiros. *Arch. Mus. Nac. Rio* 27. *H. suturata*: 93, pl. 10, figs. 5–5b.

MERTENS, R. 1927. Neue Froschlurche aus Rio Grande do Sul, Brasilien. *Blaetter Aquar. Terrariumk.* 38(2):1–4, figs. 1–3. *H. emrichi*: 1, fig. 1–2.

SCHMIDT, K. P. 1944. New frogs from Misiones and Uruguay. *Zool. Ser. Field Mus. Nat. Hist.* 29(9): 153.

*Hyla minuta* is one of the most widespread of the small Neotropical species of *Hyla*. It ranges from Trinidad B.W.I. to southern Brazil, into Argentina, and from the Atlantic coast to Bolivia. Owing perhaps to its multiple livery, it has been described a number of times by good herpetologists. For such a small species it has a formidable array of synonyms: *H. velata* Cope, *H. bivittata* Blgr., *H. goughi* E. Blgr., in part, as shown by his colored plate, *H. pallens* Lutz, *H. suturata* Mir. Rib., *H. emrichi* Mertens, and *H. uruguaya* K. Schmidt, the latter fide Barrio. The names given by Boulenger and the two Brazilian authors apply to diverse dorsal patterns exhibited by the species.

DIAGNOSTIC CHARACTERS. The negative characters of this species are almost more distinctive than the positive ones. It is smaller and paler than *Hyla bipunctata*, which seems nearest to it but is sympatric with it in Rio de Janeiro and probably elsewhere. *Hyla minuta* lacks the capistrate pattern on the sides of the head and the brilliant ventral coloring of *H. bipunctata*. Dorsal color variable, ranging from pale buff or yellow to darkish or olivaceous brown; underside also pale. Two main dorsal patterns, both variable in details: a large more or less hourglass-shaped spot, sometimes followed by a crescent-shaped one, or two opposite triangles on the back; or a pair of dorsolateral stripes, separate or anastomosed in front, simple or elaborate. Both patterns occur with or without a white outline. In some specimens the pattern is aberrant or obscure. Size small. Head short, snout rounded, eye large.

TYPES AND TYPE LOCALITIES. *H. minuta* Peters: Nova Friburgo, Serra do Mar, state of Rio de Janeiro, types in the ZMB; *Hyla velata* Cope: Mato Grosso, leg. H. H. Smith; *Hyla bivittata* Blgr.: Lages, Santa Catarina, Serra Geral, types BM. 88.2.7.26–31, leg. Michaelis. *H. goughi* E. Blgr.: Trinidad, BWI, leg. Gough. *Hyla pallens* Lutz: Rio de Janeiro, syntypes in Lutz Collection. *Hyla suturata* Mir. Rib.: Teresópolis, in the same northern block of the Serra do Mar as Nova Friburgo, leg. C. Miranda Ribeiro. *Hyla emrichi*: Montserrat, Porto Alegre, Rio Grande do Sul, leg. K. Emrich 1926. Natur Museum Senckenberg, NMS no. 21758, and *Hyla uruguaya* Schmidt (1944).

DESCRIPTION. Size small, 19–24 mm, seldom 25 or 26 mm snout to vent. Build plump in life and in well-preserved specimens. Hindlimb variable in length, the tibiotarsal articulation generally reaching somewhere between the eye and the tip of the snout, occasionally beyond it, or only to the eye. Leg generally thick. Arm short. Head as wide as long; a slight constriction behind it in some specimens. Snout short, rounded, blunt from above, sloping slightly but hardly projecting in profile, with obtuse canthus rostralis and rather flat loreal region. Eye large, as long as or approximately as long as the snout. Nostrils superolateral, not terminal, much nearer to the tip of the snout than to the eye. Tympanum small, two-fifths to one-half the diameter of the eye, often indistinct or just perceptible beneath the skin. Interorbital space wider than the internarial space. Vomerine teeth in two relatively heavy groups, transverse or slightly oblique, between or partly beyond the choanae, Tongue rounded, slightly notched and free behind. Fingers webbed at the base or, at most, one-third webbed. Toes two-thirds to four-fifths webbed. A distinct callosity under the first finger, a lesser one under the third. A distinct inner metatarsal tubercle. Skin smooth above or with a few scattered pustules. Beneath, large, flat granulations on the belly and midventral aspect of the thigh; rest of skin smooth, translucent, the organs visible on the sides of the belly. A short, weak supratympanic ridge.

SECONDARY SEX CHARACTERS. Remarkably little difference in size between the sexes. Vocal sac of male very large, sometimes ballooning out to the shoulders; callosity under the first finger more marked than in the females. Eggs visible at the sides of the body of the female all the way to the shoulders.

As pointed out by Cochran, the number of males collected is quite disproportionate to the small number of females obtained. This is probably due to the cryptic habits of this small tree frog. Rivero (1961) mentions an assembly of several hundred males in an inundated area between Puerto Ayacucho and Sanarapo, Venezuela. No eggs were laid and he believes that no females were present.

VOICE AND BEHAVIOR. The call is very insistent and rather similar to the call of *Hyla bipunctata*: *tsi, tsi, tsi* or *ti, ti, ti*, often with a tonic accent on the third staccato note. A number of males are generally present, and even the individual call sounds very loud. They like to sing on emergent plants growing in ponds where they are probably better protected than on shore. In Venezuela, Rivero heard them calling from very shallow water.

COLOR. Less colorful and paler than *Hyla bipunctata*, as expressed by the name *pallens* given to one of the forms by A. Lutz. According to him, dorsal background the color of coffee with very much milk; ventral aspect yellowish white. Miranda Ribeiro calls the dorsal surface of *suturata* isabella colored and the lower whitish. Peters, whose specimens of *H. minuta* were dead, indicates olive-brown or greenish for the dorsal surface, whereas Cope calls his specimens from Mato Grosso (*H. velata*) golden brown. The hues vary

greatly from very pale to quite dark. As Emrich puts it (*H. emrichi* Mertens), "they may be light brown-gray in daytime and become mahogany or shellac-brown at dusk." The tones seen contain much orange. I have seen dark specimens in several populations both on the plains and at the edge of the Tijuca Mountains where the species has been accidentally introduced together with other small species like *H. bipunctata* and *H. leucophyllata* probably in water hyacinths or other aquatic vegetation brought in from the coastal plains.

Iris brown, coppery to bronze with a lighter brilliant rim. Ventral aspect yellow over the opaque peritoneum, a dull brownish yellow on the gula, midventral aspect of the thighs, hands, and feet.

According to A. Lutz the iris is a dull, very brownish bronze, not standing out from the side of the head. Cochran calls it silvery with pink and other iridescent colors and many fine brown lines. My notes indicate a very light cinnamon background, at times with a golden sheen; inner rim more metallic, outer darker; between them, either many dark dots the color of lacquer or dried blood, an irregular venation, or just a series of irregular dark lines.

PATTERN. The dorsal pattern is so variable that it has induced a number of descriptions as separate species. There are two main patterns, one that covers *minuta* and *suturata* and another that applies to *velata, bivittata, pallens,* and *emrichi*. There are also a number of variations that suggest intermediate stages between the two main patterns. A few specimens have no dorsal pattern at all or only a number of irregularly disposed, very large black dots, but no name has been coined for these specimens.

The *minuta* pattern, described by Peters, is composed of a large, more or less hourglass-shaped spot, with the anterior wide edge between the upper eyelids and the posterior one on the midback, often followed by a crescent-shaped, or band-like, spot across the sacral region. The hourglass may be quite irregular and its posterior edge curved like a sickle. It may also be broken up into two triangles with the apices facing each other and the bases at opposite ends. The sacral spot may be missing, chevron-shaped, divided, or simplified. Oblique bands, similar to the spots on the back, on the permanently visible upper aspects of the limbs and on the legs, where they coincide with the ends of the sacral spot. When the dorsal pattern has a white outline, which looks like a seam, it corresponds to Miranda's *Hyla suturata*. The *minuta-suturata* pattern predominates in states of Rio de Janeiro and Guanabara, both on the lowlands and on the mountains of the northern block of the Serra do Mar, where the type localities of both forms are located. In our samples from the mountains, the pattern is more variable than on the plains, though there are also exceptions in the lowlands.

The other pattern and its variants are longitudinal and dorsolateral rather than middorsal. The simplest form is that described as *H. bivittata* by Boulenger, with two parallel darker bands along the back, widening out and sometimes uniting in the interorbital region. When these become widely anastomosed in front and the forepart enlarged, the pattern becomes reminiscent of that described by Cope for *velata*, forming a large patch that may be finely dusted with dark brown and have a narrow dark brown border extending from between the eyes to the middle of the back, and sending a branch down each side. In the *pallens* pattern, as described by Lutz, and *emrichi*, described later by Mertens, the bands also may or may not anastomose in front, but the pattern is more elaborate due to the presence of supplementary curves or blotches on the middorsal region. In the *pallens* type, the dorsal color is relatively pale and the bands are outlined in light, like the spots in *suturata*. Mertens shows two figures of *emrichi*, one with and one without the light outline. The longitudinal pattern predominates in the southern part of the known Brazilian range of this frog and extends northward along a broad western zone in the states of Paraná, São Paulo, and Minas Gerais. *H. pallens* was, however, described from Rio de Janeiro and its range given as the adjacent states. This is an example of the occurrence in one region of a pattern predominant in another part of the range. The pattern described by Cope for *velata* is also seen outside of Mato Grosso, which I interpret as a trend toward the *H. minuta* pattern. Some specimens have a rather rectilinear spot, whose posterior edge is variable, in the place of the hourglass described by Peters. The crescent-shaped sacral mark mentioned by both Peters and Cope also belongs to the *H. minuta-suturata* pattern rather than to the *bivittata-pallens-emrichi* pattern.

GEOGRAPHIC VARIATION. The most southern specimens described from Brazil are the relatively ornate types of *H. emrichi* Mertens from Porto Alegre. Ours, from the northeastern coastal mountains of Rio Grande do Sul, Lages, the type locality of *H. bivittata* (1,200 m altitude), in southern Santa Catarina and from the mountains of northern Santa Catarina are simple and more like *bivittata* than *emrichi*, with a predominantly absent light outline and of bands joined in front. The anastomosed forepart tends to become larger in the coastal mountains of the states of São Paulo and Rio de Janeiro and tends toward the middorsal *minuta-suturata* pattern, though with very aberrant shapes. There may also appear fenestrations in the fore part tending toward the pattern of the *Hyla pallens* type. Aberrant hourglass patterns of *H. minuta* recur in the northern block of the Serra do Mar, especially in one sample of four from Petrópolis collected by us in February 1941. One specimen from Teresópolis is a distinct *bivittata*, and a few have no pattern at all. Others from this locality have the pattern described by Peters or variants of it.

Our inland specimens range from Paraná through São Paulo, into Minas Gerais and Bahia. The specimens from Iguassú might be expected to be near *H. velata* Cope in pattern, but only one seems to conform to his description. They have yellowish legs long after preservation.

Most of the specimens from the state of São Paulo, both in the west and near the capital, also conform to the longitudinal pattern, except for those mentioned above from the Serra do Mar. One out of 160 specimens from New Manchester, near São Paulo, has a *minuta* pattern; one more is intermediate. A few are aberrant.

Our Minas examples are all longitudinal, not only those from Belo Horizonte and environs but three from Juiz de Fora, near the coastal mountains, and Passa Quatro on the Mantiqueira Range. One out of two specimens from the inland Serra do Cipó north of Belo Horizonte has the pattern reduced to a slightly X-shaped outline made up of large dots. The pattern of all these populations can also be summed up as longitudinal, with few exceptions and with a predominance of specimens without a light outline and slightly more ornate middle than the typical *bivittata* and thus nearer to the *emrichi* pattern. The Minas Gerais frogs are mostly light in color.

The sample from the state of Bahia is rather surprising. One small specimen from the southern coast of Bahia at Caravelas has a slightly aberrant *minuta* pattern, which evidently extends northward along the coast. Four specimens from the road between São Gonçalo and Cachoeira, not far inland or from the capital, have the longitudinal pattern, two without a light outline and two with it, albeit one of these shows a trend toward an hourglass-shaped spot. The MNR has seven fine specimens collected far inland, at Barreiras, in the basin of the Rio São Francisco, where one would expect to find longitudinal patterns. They are, however, also nearer to the *H. minuta* pattern. The hourglass is aberrant in shape, especially in one, and five out of seven have a light outline, which is an inversion of the usual rule.

The *minuta-suturata* coastal pattern recurs in Belém, Pará, on the Serra do Navio in the Brazilian territory of Amapá, and in Trinidad, B.W.I.

These findings suggest the predominance of certain genetic patterns in certain regions, without total exclusion of the regionally less common ones.

ECOLOGY. *Hyla minuta* breeds in standing water. It must be very tolerant and adaptable to judge by its range not only in longitude and latitude (some 40° N–S and some 30° E–W), but also in altitude (sea level to 1,000 m). It may have formed geographical races, but phenotypically they are obscured by the different patterns, their variation in detail and their recurrence in distant places where other patterns predominate.

RANGE. From Trinidad, BWI, to Rio Grande do Sul in Brazil into Uruguay and Misiones in Argentina. From the Atlantic coast to the eastern part of Bolivia.

## *Hyla limai* Bokermann, 1962

> BOKERMANN, W. C. A. 1962. Cuatro Nuevos Hylidos del Brasil. *Neotropica* 8(27):81–92. *Hyla limai*: 81–83 text figs. 1–5.

The name *Hyla limai* is applied by Bokermann to a single, early specimen of his private collection, WCAB 4. It was collected by J. Lima, January 1956, at São Vicente on the coast of the state of São Paulo and does not seem to have been met with again. The author mentions a similarity to *Hyla m. werneri* and to *H. minuta,* which belong to different groups.

He points out the short snout, large eyes, and the absence of a well-defined pattern and of the vomerine teeth as diagnostic characters.

*Hyla limai* may be a good species, but in that case it ought to have been found again during the intervening years. The head is shorter, higher and wider than in the species used by Bokermann for comparison. The type seems too pale for *H. bipunctata.* The absence of vomerine teeth occurs in a number of small species of *Hyla* from southeastern Brazil and is common in *Hyla decipiens* and *H. sanborni.*

It seems better to await the discovery of more specimens of *H. limai* before acknowledging a separate specific status for the lone holotype.

## FORMS OF *HYLA DECIPIENS*

### *Hyla decipiens* Lutz, 1925

> LUTZ, A. 1925. Batraciens du Brésil. *C. R. Soc. Biol. Paris.* 93(2):211–224. *H. decipiens*: 211.
> ———. 1926. Nota previa sobre especies novas de batrachios brasileiros. New Species of Brazilian Batrachians. Preliminary note. *Publ. Inst. O. Cruz.*

Unlike some other small species of *Hyla* from accessible places in Brazil and though rather abundant on the outskirts of the city of Rio de Janeiro, *Hyla decipiens* was discovered only in 1925. Consequently it is not burdened by a number of synonyms. In 1948 Cochran described *H. bipunctata branneri,* which is either identical with *H. decipiens* or a geographic race of it; it will be discussed below.

### *Hyla decipiens decipiens* Lutz, 1925

DIAGNOSTIC CHARACTERS. The ornate dorsal pattern of characteristic specimens, similar to that of juvenile *H. leucophyllata,* which induced Lutz to call it *decipiens*; the absence of vomerine teeth in many specimens; the presence of nuptial excrescences on the outside of the first finger of tiny breeding males from the type locality; the habit of depositing the spawn on leaves pendant over water, into which the hatching embryos fall.

TYPES AND TYPE LOCALITY. Grounds of the Instituto Oswaldo Cruz, at Manguinhos and adjacent Bom Sucesso in the former Federal District, now the state of Guanabara. Syntype USNM no. 96194, leg. A. Lutz and J. Venancio, April 3, 1925, Bom Sucesso.

DESCRIPTION. Size small, females with eggs 18–21 mm snout to vent, males with vocal sac generally 15–18 mm, rarely 13–14 or 19–20 mm long. Build plump. Body slightly elongate. Hindlimb short, the tibiotarsal articulation generally reaching the eye when the leg is adpressed. Head slightly wider than long. Snout short, rounded, obtusely truncate in front, sloping back to the mouth opening in profile. Canthus rostralis blunt, loreal region vertical, slightly concave. Nostrils superolateral, at approximately one-third the distance from the tip of the snout to the eye. Horizontal diameter of the eye equal to or slightly shorter than the distance from its anterior corner to the tip of the snout. Interorbital space much wider than the internarial one, approximately twice the width of the narrow upper eyelid. Tympanum small, one-half, or even less of the diameter of the eye. Tongue rounded, free behind, generally entire, occasionally emarginate. Vomerine teeth, when present, between the choanae, slightly convergent posteriorly. Fingers up to one-third webbed. Toes about three-fourths webbed. An elongate callosity outside the first finger, a smaller one under the fourth finger. A projecting inner metatarsal tubercle. Skin smooth except on the belly and midventral aspect of the thigh. A fold of skin across the chest. A slight ridge above the tympanum.

SECONDARY SEX CHARACTERS. Horny nuptial excrescences were observed on the callosity outside the first finger of minute breeding males in the vicinity of Rio. They have not been seen in those from other localities, but may be deciduous. Vocal sac very large, pleated, or balloon-like. Other sex differences not very marked. One male from Teresópolis as large as our largest females, two as large as smaller females.

MORPHOLOGICAL VARIATION. The vomerine teeth are the most variable feature of *Hyla d. decipiens*.

The specimens from the type locality, on which Lutz's diagnosis was based, are mostly small and devoid of vomerine teeth. In one sample of twenty-one topotypes they are absent in all. According to Dr. Cochran, this is also the case of syntype USNM no. 96194, from Bom Sucesso, and of USNM no. 96150 from Manguinhos, although the bone that usually holds the teeth is barely perceptible. Three topotypes, USNM nos. 96151–3, have rather weakly developed teeth. This ridge without definite teeth is quite apparent in the mouth of USNM no. 97642, from Saco de São Francisco. Cochran mentions as a remarkable fact that "in a series of 9 frogs, USNM nos. 97578–86, from Sernambetiba (Recreio dos Bandeirantes) some miles away from the type locality, all taken on clumps of bulrushes not 50 feet apart, six individuals have very strongly apparent sets of posteriorly converging, well separated teeth between the choanae, two examples (nos. 97579 and 97582) have a set of teeth on one side of the mouth and none on the other, while one (no. 97581) is entirely toothless."

The population from Sernambetiba is on the whole slightly larger and more robust than that from the type locality. Consequently one might think that in *Hyla* the presence of vomerine teeth depends on a certain threshold of size, much lower than that which prevails in other hylid genera such as *Phyllomedusa* and *Pithecopus*. However, a sample from Teresópolis, in the Organ Mountains, composed of relatively large and robust individuals, is also toothless. It is thus possible that the frequency of the toothless condition varies in populations rather than individuals. The absence, or partial absence, of vomerine teeth also occurs, though in a far lesser degree, in *H. d. branneri*, treated below as a subspecies of *H. decipiens*, in *H. m. meridiana*, and in *H. elongata*, which are also very small. The variability of this character in several small species or races underlines the artificial nature of the distinction between the genus *Hyla* and the toothless genus *Hyllela* and supports the authors who consider the latter as one more synonym of the former.

The other morphological variations observed in *H. d. decipiens*, such as the occasionally emarginate tongue, the differences in proportion between the diameter of the eye and the distance from its anterior corner to the tip of the snout, the slight variation in webbing, and the greater variation in relative head-body and hindlimb lengths are common to all the Brazilian species of *Hyla* examined so far.

COLOR AND PATTERN. The most characteristic specimens, that is the "deceptive" ones from which the trivial name was derived, have a light triangular area on the head between the eyes and the canthi, prolonged down the sides of the back, tapering off near the sacrum and enclosing a brown area occupying the median part of the back. The light parts are pale gold, lemon-yellow, or very pale buff, almost cream; the dark area is a slightly ruddy brown in most specimens, but somewhat olivaceous in those with lemon-colored light parts. Sometimes a darker vertical stripe is present on it. The sides of the head and body often show a similar dark band.

Many specimens are devoid of a clear-cut pattern and have only the light cap and dorsolateral margins. Others, again, are a more or less uniform brown above, with a few small and ill-defined marks on the back and a dark line along the dorsolateral margin. The permanently visible parts of the limbs are similar to the back, with a few indistinct marks. Living specimens often have a metallic glint above. Iris pale golden with coppery or dark brown granulations of pigment toward the periphery, paler, sometimes almost orange toward the inner free rim; a pseudocolobom that appears to be a continuation of the brown band on the sides of the head. Dorsal aspects of the limbs hidden in repose and ventral surfaces immaculate. Beneath pale carneous or pale yellow, devoid of the blue-green tones seen in *H. d. branneri*. Anterior part of the belly opaque white (peritoneum), rest of lower surfaces translucent, dull yellowish; sac and digits less pale than the rest.

A very interesting feature is the presence in several specimens from Teresópolis in the Organ Mountains of a light area under the eyes along the upper jaw. It is short in some, longer in others, but does not quite form the round subocular spot characteristic of a proportion of specimens of *H. decipiens branneri*; a more rudimentary and ill-defined light opaque area occurs in a few specimens from the coastal lowlands. Its presence confirms the relationship between *H. d. decipiens* and *H. d. branneri*.

VOICE. An insistent chirping, twittering sound. Calling males apparently more isolated than in the extremely gregarious coastal populations of the more northern form, *H. decipiens branneri*. *H. d. decipiens* is sometimes heard calling in marshes during the day. The call has been recorded recently at Teresópolis on an Uher 4000 RL.

When handled *H. d. decipiens* gives out a smell of crushed leaves.

REPRODUCTIVE BEHAVIOR AND LIFE HISTORY NOTES. This very small tree frog spawns above water like *Centrolenella* and *Pithecopus*, but it does not wrap the spawn up into a funnel inside the leaf, like the latter, nor does it deposit the spawn on the underside of the leaf like the former. The masses of eggs seen by us were just pendant over water from the lower part of leaves with drip points. On February 14, 1935, A. Lutz, D. Cochran, and J. Venancio had the opportunity of seeing a large number of such egg masses at Saco de São Francisco, Niteroi, across the bay from Rio. Cochran relates collecting between thirty and forty in a few minutes. Some were fixed. One was accommodated inside a glass funnel by A. Lutz so that the stem provided a wet runway down which the hatching embryos could slide into the water. They were photographed doing it. Part of the tadpoles were reared by J. Venancio and me; they eventually transformed into miniature *H. d. decipiens*.

In March 1941, J. Venancio and I found seven egg masses on leaves of an arboreal *Ficus*, a *Peperomia*, and *Hedychium coronarium* above the runoff ditch of a reservoir at Covanca, state of Guanabara. We took four, one of which hatched in transit.

Some of the nuptial males and one or two females in the collection in the Museu Nacional are clutching eggs in their hands or holding them between the arms and the body. Two specimens had an egg or two inside the mouth.

EMBRYOS. The embryos hatch with a head and body length of 1.5–2.5 mm and 4.5 mm of tail. In some of our preserved embryos, the tail is curved as if still inside the egg. They are born with external gills, two large cement glands, one at each side, below the stomodaeum, a pineal gland and small dorsolateral eyes. From beneath, the vitellus is visible but not the intestine, though a slight deflection to the right indicates the proctodaeum.

The embryos are black with golden patches on the tail.

Next day the external gills are still present, and the portion anterior to them still narrower than the body, producing the usual pear-shape of very young larvae.

LARVA. The perfect tadpoles have a very characteristic livery, especially on the underside and tail. The latter is crossed by a number of wide, vertical, disruptive, dark bars that separate hyaline parts and break up the visual image of the organ. The most proximal bar comes right up to the body and is continued on the abdomen. The tip is hyaline. At an early stage there are fewer and narrower bars, but they gradually increase in number and size, and the last one sometimes takes the shape of an arrowhead continued by the dark end of the tail muscle. The bars are somewhat irregular but they are generally widest at the periphery of the crests, concave and narrower toward the muscle on which they have a more rounded posteriorly convex shape. They are extremely characteristic and, once seen, permit instant recognition of *H. decipiens* tadpoles. The body remains dark for a long time with a pair of golden dorsolateral lines above and a lighter horizontal area over the middle of the abdomen.

DESCRIPTION. Head and body oval in outline. Tail elongate, oval, leaf-like, the crests almost equal, the lower very slightly narrower than the upper, which does not continue onto the back. Both widest about the middle, narrowed forward and especially backward, the terminal part forming a minute flail. Mouth ventro-terminal, very small, its diameter very inferior to the internarial space. Nostrils anterolateral. Eyes much farther back and much wider apart than the nostrils. Spiraculum sinistral, about halfway between the anus and the eye, more or less straight. Width of body slightly superior to half the length. Height of tail about half its length at the stage with short hind-limbs and formed toes.

These tadpoles cannot be confounded with *Hyla leucophyllata* larvae, which have a different pattern and are much larger. There is however a certain resemblance in the form of the body and in the elongate, leaf-like shape of the tail ending in a flail, and between the larvae of these species, those of *Hyla anceps* and small *Pithecopus* larvae, which

use the tail as a flail. The tadpoles of *Hyla decipiens* generally swim around very fast and have the same habit of floating upright as those just mentioned, but the other species prefer deeper water.

METAMORPHOSIS. The captive larvae mentioned by Cochran took about three months to metamorphose as from hatching; this seems rather a long time for so small a species, but conditions may not have been entirely favorable. Metamorphosis occurred at 7, 8, 8.5, or 9 mm of length. The tail was more than double the length of the head and body at the incipient stage but dwindled fast. Once the forearms were out the metamorphosing young climbed out of the water. At first they were still dark, but in those with the typical pattern the light cap and sides became visible soon after metamorphosis so that they were quite like the adults from above while the abdomen still showed the larval livery.

BEHAVIOR. Some juveniles are very alert. One of ours did not hesitate to climb into a vivarium of large *Hyla mesophaea* in pursuit of young cockroaches too big for it to swallow.

KNOWN RANGE. The known range of *H. d. decipiens* is very small, especially if *H. d. branneri* is treated as a subspecies. The distribution is rather peculiar in both races. Most of our specimens of *H. d. decipiens* are from the coastal lowlands of the state of Guanabara and adjacent parts of Rio de Janeiro (Baixada Fluminense), and a few from Espírito Santo. They are almost at the seashore in Manguinhos and in Bom Sucesso, inside Guanabara Bay; at Sernambetiba (Recreio dos Bandeirantes) they occur just behind the dunes. *Hyla d. branneri* occupies a similar biotype in northeastern Brazil. *H. d. decipiens* also travels along the Baixada Fluminense, up the Maritime Range, and extends to 800 m at Teresópolis.

TRANSITION FORMS. Two specimens were collected further inland, in wet rice fields at Juiz de Fora, unfortunately without a record of the colors in life. They have the white subocular spot much better defined than the Teresópolis specimens. They may be forms of transition to *H. d. branneri.* Ornate specimens of *H. decipiens* "sensu lato" have been collected at and near the mouth of the Paraiba River in the state of Rio de Janeiro.

A description of *H. d. branneri*, based on a large

number of specimens, follows. It is possible that some day, when the large gaps in distribution are filled, a different taxonomic arrangement of the populations of this species may have to be adopted.

## *Hyla decipiens branneri* Cochran, 1948

COCHRAN, D. M. 1948. A new subspecies of tree-frog from Pernambuco, Brazil. *J. Wash. Acad. Sc.* 38(9):316–318 (*H. b. branneri*).

BOKERMANN, W. C. A. 1963. Nova especie de *Hyla* da Bahia, Brasil. *Acta Soc. Biol. Rio* 7(2):6–8, 3 text-figs. (*H. oliveirai*).

This very small tree frog was described by Cochran from Bonito, Pernambuco, as a subspecies of *H. bipunctata*. She dedicated it to Branner, the collector and one of the most distinguished pioneers in the study of the geology of Brazil. In 1963 it was redescribed from Bahia by Bokermann as a full species, *H. oliveirai*. A. Lutz had already seen it in 1925 and had two watercolor sketches made of specimens from Natal by Sandig, on which he jotted down a tentative name, *H. scrobiculata*. He omitted to describe it, probably for lack of more abundant material that would permit a clearer definition of its taxonomic status. Between 1940 and 1960, I collected a number of specimens and received many others. It is very abundant on the northeastern coast of Brazil and extremely variable. It is too small and too distant from *Hyla bipunctata* in habit and call to be a subspecies of that very distinctive frog. The main point of similarity is the rosy tinge of many preserved specimens of both. It is nearer to *decipiens,* as realized by Bokermann, and may perhaps have to be completely synonymized with it when the gaps in distribution are closed.

DIAGNOSTIC CHARACTERS. The very small size allied to the short head, with much-curved, concave canthus rostralis; the plump build; the brilliant white spot under the eye of a certain proportion of specimens; the rosy tinge of the dorsal surface of part of the preserved individuals; the call and the distribution. It diverges from *H. bipunctata* by the much smaller size, the lack of the areolate pattern on the sides of the head and of the brilliant ventral coloring and the patagium, and also by the call. It differs from the more southern *H. d. decipiens* by the better developed vomerine teeth, the narrower vertex of the head, the plumper leg, the blue-green color of parts of the ventral aspect, the much more variable dorsal livery. It seems vicariant to it, apparently with a much greater range than the nominate race.

TYPES AND TYPE LOCALITY. The series from which Cochran's type and paratypes were taken was collected for the MCZ by A. C. Branner, probably in the last century, at Bonito in the state of Pernambuco. Type an adult female, USNM 28861, donated by Barbour in 1912; paratypes USNM 48862–4 and MCZ 2827 A–P, altogether twenty specimens.

DESCRIPTION. Size very small, females with eggs 17–21 mm, males 15–19 mm mostly 16 or 17 mm from snout to vent. Build plump for the size. Body slightly elongate. Hindlimb short but variable, the adpressed tibiotarsal articulation generally reaching some point of the eye. Head very slightly shorter than wide, with very abbreviated snout, rounded from above, truncate and projecting slightly in profile; canthus rostralis curved, runing into a point; loreal region steep. Eye large, generally longer than or equal to the distance from its anterior corner to the nostril or to the tip of the snout. Nostrils subcanthal, at one-third the distance from the tip of the snout to the eye. Tympanum small, at most one-third of the diameter of the eye. Interorbital region very much wider than the internarial space. Tongue wide, rounded, slightly emarginate. Groups of vomerine teeth between the choanae, sometimes slightly oblique, mostly separated, sometimes contiguous; in a few specimens, mostly small, teeth palpable but not visible. A slight web between the lateral fingers, sometimes slightly longer between the third and fourth fingers. In life, first finger held horizontally, away from the others. Toes three-fourths to four-fifths webbed, the webs climbing steeply to the disks, except on the fourth, which is fringed to a longer but variable extent. A tubercle under the first finger, a smaller one under the third and fourth toe. An elongate inner metatarsal tubercle. Skin smooth above or with a few pustules, minutely granular on the abdomen and midventral aspect of the thigh. A fold of skin across the chest.

SECONDARY SEX CHARACTERS Vocal sac very large, much pleated in nuptial males, which are much more numerous than the females in our samples. Differences of size rather deceptive as several males with a vocal sac are as large as some of the females.

VARIATION. The usual variations of Brazilian species of *Hyla* as to the relative length of the hindlimb and the snout to vent length are very evident. There are also minor variations as to the degree of notching and the width of the tongue, the extent of the webbing, etc. Growth allometric, the young with relatively longer legs. In twenty-six juvenile specimens from Bahia, Salvador, the tibiotarsal articulation reaches to the nostril in six, between the nostril and eye in eleven, in front of the eye in two, and to the anterior corner of the eye in seven. The smallest is 11 mm snout to vent.

The most impressive difference in our specimens is the size of the only sample from an inland population, collected by A. L. Carvalho at the bar of the Rio Tapirapés, a tributary of the Araguaya in northern Mato Grosso, near the border of the state of Pará. The males are as large as some of the females from the coastal lowlands, and the females one-fifth longer than the coastal females and correspondingly robust. Strangely, some of these specimens have weak vomerine teeth, not visible but only perceptible to the touch.

COLOR AND PATTERN. The silvery white spot under the eye, mentioned by Cochran and Bokermann, is not present in all the specimens. The proportion of individuals with it and without it varies from sample to sample but if one has enough specimens some will certainly show it. In life it may be slightly pinkish and luminous. It also varies in size and shape and can be round or oblong, large, small, or absent from under one eye. In very light individuals it melts into the lighter edge of the upper jaw. Iris pale gold to light copper with a concentration of dark dots of pigment near the inner rim.

Otherwise the color and pattern are variable and even more deceptive than in *H. d. decipiens*. Part of the dead specimens incline to a rosy dorsal coloring, especially those that did not have a distinctive dorsal pattern in life.

Living specimens are either pale olivaceous or brownish, more or less orange or tawny above; beneath either grayish or, more often, especially the males, glaucous, with a lemon-colored vocal sac over a greenish to bluish background. Articulations deep blue-green, belly a very pale light yellowish green over the opaque peritoneum, grayish or bluish, slightly yellowish green at the sides of the body and the extremities, and more or less translucent. Thighs and inside of legs yellow or pale orange, except at the joints. This coloring separates *branneri* effectively from *H. d. decipiens*.

The main dorsal pattern can be divided into three forms:

A. The majority of specimens. This pattern is reminiscent of plain specimens of *H. d. decipiens*, *H. m. meridiana*, and *H. m. werneri*, but the two latter are more elongate and paler. The back is more or less uniform tawny or light brownish orange; the dorsolateral edges may be light or dark, or the dark pigment may occur only on the sides of the head and body. Generally there are a few indistinct marks on the back, either forming a very irregular and elongate figure like a series of circumflex accents or an inverted V or W; more rarely, two long interrupted lines like those seen in *H. misera* and *H. elongata*.

B. This pattern, which is rare, approaches the pattern of the ornate form of *H. d. decipiens*. Head, between the canthus rostralis and sides of the back, light yellow or pale gold; the rest of the dorsal surface, limited by them, either chestnut or a similar slightly reddish brown. The light part may be less brilliant and conspicuous and the inner dark part subdivided in two, generally with a longer portion in front and a shorter one behind it.

C. The third pattern is very beautiful. The dorsal surface is uniformly olivaceous including the permanently visible part of the limbs. It is, however, bordered to a lesser or greater extent by drop-like spots of pale gold or pinkish cream color, which are adspersed over the sides of the head, the edges of the body, and those of the permanently visible dorsal portions of the limbs. The spots are often large and generally not all of the same size. When they are smaller and the background is brown, they produce the pattern of the specimens from Natal that Lutz tentatively labeled *H. scrobiculata*. Cochran, whose specimens had been preserved for a long time, mentions that some of them showed spots.

A very few specimens have a pattern intermediate between B and C.

The permanently visible dorsal surfaces of the limbs are not quite uniform. They may show small indistinct marks of the same kind as those on the back (A) or golden spots (C). Dorsal aspect of the thigh concealed in repose immaculate, either pale yellow or a pale tint of orange. Other concealed surfaces, including the sides and the digits, inclined to olivaceous tones and to a slight translucency.

Preserved specimens become pink or brownish when devoid of ornate pattern. They show the pattern for some time after preservation; the large dark spots on the back seem permanent.

VOICE. This form is gregarious and sings mostly in a very loud chorus that sounds like the jingling of coins or even the beating together of the edges of the palms of folded hands. After collecting it in a number of lagoons, some of them close by the sea in the state of Bahia, I have been able to identify the call in airports and towns of the northeastern subprovince of the Continental Province.

ECOLOGY. Both at Caravelas in southern Bahia, and at Salvador, the capital, we collected this species in different kinds of places. Some of them were in lagoons quite close to the sea, not only within sound of the waves, but even liable to flooding by breakers during storms. Others were got in large artificial ponds or in the water collected at the bottom of marshland. In Maceió I heard it again (1962) at the edge of the lagoons from which the state of Alagoas derives its name; a solitary individual was obtained. At Caravelas, a large aquatic Hemipteron was seen piercing the chest of a small *H. d. branneri* and draining its blood.

RANGE. Lutz obtained his specimens at Natal in Rio Grande do Norte, and others were sent him by D. Bento Pickel from Tapera, Pernambuco, the state where the Cochran types were collected. Mine are from Alagoas, Bahia, and Belém do Pará, from where other specimens were sent. Besides these, the Museu Nacional in Rio has the large individuals from Tapirapés, northern Mato Grosso, a few from Espírito Santo (Linhares, Afonso Claudio) and even from the northern part of the state of Rio de Janeiro, Campos, on the Rio Paraiba and São João da Barra at its mouth. This would seem to indicate a very long coastal distribution, from 21° 38′ S. in the state of Rio de Janeiro to 1° 28′ at Belém do Pará, and from slightly over 35° W. on the northeastern coast to nearly 49° W. on the Araguaya. Some specimens from Agua Limpa, Juiz de Fora, Minas Gerais, very near to *H. d. decipiens* probably also belong to this form.

## THE *HYLA MISERA–HYLA MICROCEPHALA* GROUP

The study of a very small, short-headed *Hyla*, very abundant in the lowlands in the vicinity of Rio de Janeiro, led to comparison with *Hyla misera* (*Hyla goughi* in part) from Venezuela and Trinidad. As a result, I described it in 1954 as a subspecies, *H. m. meridiana*. Later, material obtained from the Amazonian Hylaea showed that a similar form occurs there. Another slightly divergent form was taken in Santa Catarina. Finally, examination of the tree frogs from Costa Rica, which were placed at my disposal by Mr. Antenor Leitão de Carvalho, brought to light a further similarity to *Hyla phlebodes* and to *H. underwoodi*. Specimens of *Hyla microcephala* seen in the United States also favored the conclusion that all these forms belong to a natural group of small, very short-headed forms of *Hyla* with a much reduced dorsal pattern that centers around Cope's *Hyla microcephala*. They, or some of them, may be full species, or they may all be geographical races. At the present moment it is not possible to come to a definite decision because of the enormous gaps between the relatively few places where these diverse forms have been collected. There are at least three of these forms in Brazil. They are treated here as races of *Hyla misera*, but it is possible that further investigation may put them in *Hyla microcephala* Cope, as suggested for the northern one by Fouquette in 1968.

## *Hyla misera meridiana* B. Lutz, 1954

LUTZ, B. 1954. Anfíbios Anuros do Distrito Federal. The Frogs of the Federal District of Brazil. *Mem. Inst. O. Cruz*, 52(1):155–238, pls. I–XIX. *H. m. meridiana*: 160, 187, 223, 252. Pls. XVII, fig. 1.

*H. m. meridiana* is undoubtedly very close to *H. misera* Werner from Venezuela and the partly synonymous *H. goughi* Boulenger from Trinidad, BWI. It differs, however, by the short hindlimb, the indistinct vomerine teeth, and the smaller size of even the largest southern specimens. For these reasons, I described it as a separate subspecies in 1954.

DIAGNOSTIC CHARACTERS. The small size; the short hindlimb; the feeble, not always visible, vomerine teeth; the southeastern Brazilian distribution. Dorsal color from tawny to pale cream with a pair of longitudinal, more or less curved or broken lines along the back, often crossed between the eyes by one or two similar lines; sometimes additional short longitudinal lines to the inside of the main ones.

TYPES AND TYPE LOCALITY. Female holotype, four female paratypes, male allotype, six male paratypes and two juveniles, from Largo dos Abrolhos, Moça Bonita, state of Guanabara, formerly the Federal District, collected March 1947 by me and Joaquim Venancio, now nos. MNR 3671, 3672, 3673–3684.

DESCRIPTION. Size small, holotype: female with eggs 23 mm, female paratypes 20–23 mm snout to vent; male allotype and paratypes 17–19 mm snout to vent. Build somewhat elongate. Hindlimb short, the adpressed tibiotarsal articulation reaching the eye. Head short, barely wider than long. Snout very short, vertical, projecting slightly in profile; canthi rostrales meeting in a deflected point; loreal region high with a small concavity between the nostril and the eye. Horizontal diameter of the eye slightly longer than or equal to the distance from its anterior corner to the tip of the snout. Tympanum small, one-third or two-fifths the diameter of the eye, moderately distinct. Tongue rounded, generally wide, slightly notched and free behind. Vomerine teeth forming two slightly oblique groups, converging posteriorly in the type; in most paratypes covered by skin, palpable but not visible. Lateral fingers about one-third webbed, the webs very oblique. Toes about four-fifths webbed, the webs also oblique, inserted below the disk on second, third, and fifth, forming a slight fringe on the last phalanx or from slightly below it on the fourth toe. A tubercle outside the first finger, an elongate inner metatarsal tubercle. Skin smooth above and beneath except for the granular belly and midventral portion of the thighs. Dorsolateral edge forming a slight fold above the tympanum. A slight fold from the armpits to the chest.

VARIATION. The female paratypes are 23 mm (no. 3672) 21 mm (nos. 3673–3674) and 20 mm (no. 3675) from snout to vent. The vomerine teeth of two male paratypes (nos. 3673, 3675) are palpable but not visible. Two (nos. 3672, 3674) have the tongue narrower and more oval. The leg is slightly longer in the smallest one (no. 3675) than in the others.

The teeth of the males, which are smaller, are more indistinct. They are readily perceptible in one. In another one patch is better developed than the other. The teeth are only palpable in the rest. Two

(nos. 3676, 3678) have the tongue entire and thick. Length of leg also variable but always short, the tibiotarsal articulation reaching from the posterior corner of the eye to just in front of it.

Nearly one hundred other specimens measured show the same variations.

SECONDARY SEX CHARACTERS. The males have a very large, much folded vocal sac. The callosity on the outside of the first finger seems better developed than in the female. The holotype and paratype 3673 contain ovarian eggs.

COLOR. The color of the permanently visible dorsal aspect varies from a light tawny orange to a pale very slightly pinkish cream. The skin is opaque. Iris ochraceous orange flecked with brown pigment except near the free inner rim. Concealed upper parts of the thigh pale orange, translucent like the lower aspect and the inner and ventral aspects of the other segments of the limbs. Veins in the thigh visible by translucency. Gula of male yellow, of female pale. Chest and belly opaque, white or with a very pale wash of orange or pink.

PATTERN. Two slightly irregular, angular, or broken longitudinal lines on the back, from the interocular region to the sacral one, generally drawing apart or curved outward and fading out; in the interocular region the longitudinal lines are sometimes crossed by a horizontal, irregular, and generally broken line, occasionally by two such lines. In many individuals two or three shorter, longitudinal lines, from the end of the body toward the sacrum, to the inside of the long lines. Often dark dots scattered on the whole dorsal surface. A series of narrow oblique bars on the permanently visible dorsal surfaces of the limbs (tibia, tarsus, and forearm). In very light individuals pattern sometimes absent. Beneath the canthus and the dorsolateral edge a pigmented longitudinal brown area. Thighs and whole ventral aspect immaculate. Only two males out of a series of over two hundred specimens have a white spot under each eye, like that seen in most specimens of the closely allied Hyla m. werneri.

VOICE. Tsik, tsik, tsik (Cochran).

HABITS. H. m. meridiana is quite crepuscular and nocturnal; it begins to call early in summer and continues to do so for a long time. Early in the season it generally calls from shrubs or trees but later descends to ponds and other still waters. In the daytime we have found it in wet marshland asleep inside upright pieces of bamboo, hollow leaf sheaths, and reeds, including *Typha* growing in ponds. The watery surrounding must afford it a certain amount of protection against predators.

LARVA. The tadpole is tawny and very stream-lined. A white edge, with a very definite contour, limits the dorsal surface, dying out at the hind part of the body but forming a broad white area on the sides including over the eyes. A pattern of dark lines is present on the lower aspect. Tail tawny, with a very long point.

KNOWN RANGE. We have this form from a number of points on or near the coast in the states of Guanabara, Rio de Janeiro, and Espírito Santo, including the outskirts of Rio de Janeiro, Campos, São João da Barra, and Santa Teresa. One specimen from Angra dos Reis, south of Rio, seems somewhat intermediate with *H. m. werneri*.

This is a lowland form and probably the most abundant of the small species of *Hyla* found in the Baixada Fluminense, the coastal plain of the states of Guanabara and Rio de Janeiro.

### *Hyla misera misera* Werner, 1903

WERNER, F. 1903. *Zool. Anz.* 26:252 (*H. misera*).
BOULENGER, E. G. 1911. *Pr. Zool. Soc.*, p. 1082, pl. 64 (*H. goughi*).
LUTZ, A. 1925. Estudios de zoologia y parasit-ologia venezolanas 1925. Notas sobre batrachios da Venezuela e da Ilha de Trinidad. Notes on Batrachians from Venezuela and Trinidad. *Mem. Inst. O. Cruz*, 20(1):39, 43, 49, pl. 11, fig. 16, pl. 15, fig. 37.
RIVERO, J. A. 1961. Batrachia of Venezuela. *Bull. Mus. C. Zool.* 126(1):135 pp.

The specimens of *Hyla misera* Werner (1903) from Venezuela in the Lutz Collection and the collection of the MNR agree with Werner's description on most points. They are slightly variable as to the relative length of the eye and the eye-snout distance and as to the difference between the width of the interorbital space and that of the upper eyelid, but these details do not seem very relevant. The specimens from the Lutz Collection, now at the MNR, are small; the larger ones were apparently lost at the Instituto Oswaldo Cruz. A specimen obtained by the author near Caracas (1954) and two given her by Roze are larger and nearer the size indicated for the type of *H. misera*. *Hyla goughi* Boulenger (1911), as pointed out by A. Lutz

(1925, 1927), seems to be the same. Some of the E. G. Boulenger cotypes are, however, *H. minuta*, as shown in the colored plate accompanying his description. This makes no difference, since Werner's name has priority over that of Boulenger and is consequently the valid one. Lutz found this form common near Caracas and Maracay. He points out that it may vary in pattern and color, but that the size and voice are characteristic. He compares the voice with the sound produced by winding a watch. He adds that the frogs are gregarious and generally found on the taller plants growing in swamps.

MEASUREMENTS. A. Lutz specimens from Aragua: Maracay extant in the ALC at the MNR, 19–19.5 mm; specimens given by Roze from Aragua, 21–22 mm; specimens collected in 1954 by B. Lutz at Alta Gracia del Orituco: 23 mm; B. Lutz specimen from near Caracas: 22 mm snout to vent.

Two of the larger specimens seen by me have the dorsal lines broken up into fragments and one end of the segments slightly thickened, like the head of a musical note. They seem not only larger but more robust and less elongate than *H. m. meridiana*.

### *Hyla misera werneri* Cochran, 1952

WERNER, F. 1894. Herpetologische Nova. *Zool. Anz.* 17:410–415. *Hyla pygmaea*: 411.
COCHRAN, D. M. 1952. Two Brazilian frogs: *Hyla werneri*, n. nom. and *Hyla similis* n. sp. *J. Wash. Acad. Sc.* 42(2). *Hyla werneri* n. nom.: 50.
———. 1953. Three new Brazilian frogs. *Herpetologica* 8(4):114–115.
———. 1955. Frogs of southeastern Brazil. *U.S. N.M. Bull.* 206: *H. werneri*: 127–128, pl. 11, figs. A-D. *Hyla goughi baileyi*: 113–115, fig. 13.

In 1894 Werner described a new and very small *Hyla* from Blumenau, Santa Catarina, as *Hyla pygmaea*. In 1952 Cochran proposed a new name for it, since Loveridge had placed *Hyperolius pygmaeus* Meyer, an older species from Dutch New Guinea, in the genus *Hyla*. In her monograph of the southeastern Brazilian frogs (1955) she described the new form. In 1953 and again in the 1955 monograph she described as a new form *Hyla goughi baileyi* from Juquiá, near the coast of the state of São Paulo. Except for the slightly larger size of the type of the latter, I do not find any significant differences between *H. werneri* and *H. g. baileyi*. In fact, careful examination of our series of specimens from Santa Catarina leads me to believe that *werneri* and *g. baileyi* are the same and that, like *H. m. meridiana*, they are a subspecies of *H. misera*.

DIAGNOSTIC CHARACTERS. *H. m. werneri* differs from *H. m. meridiana* mainly by the different pattern, the better defined groups of vomerine teeth, and the presence in about two-thirds of the specimens of a brilliant white spot under each eye, more seldom under only one of them. The voice and call seem the same or very similar to those of *H. m. meridiana*.

TYPE AND TYPE LOCALITY. The type of *H. pygmaea* Werner is from Blumenau, Santa Catarina, and was exceptionally large: 23 mm, probably a female. Cochran's allotype, USNM no. 66564, an adult male, was collected in November 1918 by Fritsche at Humboldt, northern Santa Catarina; paratypes of same date, USNM 66562–3, 66565–6, 118242. The type of *H. g. baileyi*, MZUM 106737, is an adult male from Fazenda Poço Grande, 8 km north of Juquiá, São Paulo, collected by J. R. Bailey, February 25–28, 1941; paratypes MZUM 104119, 104127, 10431, USNM 132913–6, same collector, date, and locality.

The series of specimens on which the description below is based are from Brusque (3), Joinville (16), and Santa Luzia (3–12) in the coastal plain of Santa Catarina; like Blumenau, Joinville and Santa Luzia are nearer to the foothills of the Serra do Mar.

DESCRIPTION. Size small. Female 22–23 mm, male 18–20 mm snout to vent. Build elongate, similar to that of *H. m. meridiana*. Hindlimb rather short, the adpressed tibiotarsal articulation reaching from the posterior corner of the eye to in front of it. Head short, snout rounded, projecting slightly above the mouth; canthus rostralis distinct, loreal region almost vertical. Nostrils superolateral, not terminal, somewhat nearer the tip of the snout than the eye. Eye prominent, its horizontal diameter slightly longer or equal to the distance from its anterior corner to the tip of the snout. Tympanum about two-fifths the diameter of the eye. Interorbital space slightly wider than the internarial space. Tongue rounded, slightly emarginate or entire, somewhat free behind. Vomerine teeth in two small groups close to each other, between the choanae. Fingers one-third webbed, toes almost entirely webbed, the

webs oblique on hand and foot. Skin smooth above, with a few scattered pustules. Belly and lower median area of thigh granular. A large median vocal sac in the male.

VARIATION. A slight variation in the length of the hindlimb was observed in the sample from Joinville, the adpressed tibiotarsal articulation reaching the posterior corner of the eye in one specimen, mideye in five, the anterior corner in two, and in front of it in five. The specimens from Brusque are plumper than the others. The vomerine teeth are indistinct in only one specimen. Some have a slightly narrower tongue.

SECONDARY SEX CHARACTERS. Only one female is present in our samples from Joinville. Werner's type was evidently also a female, to judge from the size, 23 mm. Our female contains eggs, is slightly larger than the males, and has shorter hindlimbs. Our males are 19 and 20 mm from snout to vent; they show a slight ridge outside the first finger and a very large median vocal sac.

VOICE AND HABITS. The call, heard by me and J. Venancio in Brusque, Santa Catarina, seemed the same as the typical call of *H. m. meridiana*. We collected three males there on January 2, 1956, in wet pasture land. They were perched on herbaceous vegetation like that used by *H. m. meridiana*.

COLOR AND PATTERN. The coloring is very similar, cream to tawny above with immaculate concealed aspect of the thighs. The dark area on the sides of the head and the short oblique bars on the permanently visible dorsal surface of the hindlimbs are also the same. The main difference resides in the presence in many preserved specimens of a very distinct round, snow-white spot under each eye. They are present in 25 percent of our thirty-four adult specimens; a few have the spot under only one eye, and in a few the spots are small and irregular. The edge of the outline is generally also snow-white. The dorsal pattern is different from that of *H. m. meridiana*. Some specimens have an irregular elongate X-shaped outline of darker pigment on the midback from the eyes toward the sacrum, whereas in others the dark part on the back is filled out. Most specimens show some dots of pigment spaced along the edges, generally a dark patch on the knee and a similar one on the elbow. Some specimens have dark dots over the whole dorsal surface. In a few specimens the dorsal pattern approximates that of *H. m. meridiana* from Rio. A few others are almost devoid of pattern, especially the pale ones. Werner indicates a grayish red dorsal surface and a rosy ventral one with the belly yellow.

DISTRIBUTION. This form is typical for the eastern plains of Santa Catarina, between the sea and the Maritime Range. It seems to extend to the state of São Paulo, to judge by the specimens from Juquiá described as *H. g. baileyi* by Cochran. This form does not occur in the state of Guanabara, though a very few specimens of *H. m. meridiana* may approximate the pattern somewhat. I have seen the white spot under the eyes in only three specimens of *H. m. meridiana* out of over two hundred from the Baixada Fluminense closely examined for it. A single specimen from the River Japuhyba, north of Angra dos Reis, collected by G. Myers and H. Travassos many years ago seems slightly intermediate between the two forms but does not have the white spot under the eye. Some specimens seen from Piassaguera, near the coast between Santos and São Paulo, are very similar to those from Angra dos Reis.

AFFINITIES. This is the most southern known member of the group of *Hyla misera–H. microcephala.*

VALID NAME. Cochran did not furnish a description of this frog when she offered the new name for it. The description of her *H. g. baileyi*, which is synonymous with it, came first. However, the original description by Werner is quite adequate. Consequently only a new name was needed when the name *pygmaea* proved to be preoccupied. Hence the use of the name *werneri* instead of *baileyi*.

## *Hyla berthalutzae* Bokermann, 1962

> BOKERMANN, W. C. A. 1962. Cuatro Nuevos Hylidos del Brasil. *Neotropica* 8(27):81–92. *H. berthalutzae*: 84–86, text figs. 6–10.

This species is recognized here on account of its call and its breeding habits rather than because of the small differences in morphology and pattern between it, *Hyla misera meridiana*, and *H. m. werneri*. There have been a few specimens of it in the Lutz Collection for some years, including a watercolor sketch. However, it was only a short time ago that I heard its call on an excursion with Drs. W. F. Blair and L. D. Vizotto to the Açude da

Solidão in the Tijuca woods. Meanwhile, Dr. Izecksohn offered me a few specimens from the coastal lowlands and informed me of its reproductive behavior.

DIAGNOSTIC CHARACTERS. The call, which is loud, drawn out and hardly inflected, and more reminiscent of *Hyla minuta* than of the regional forms of *Hyla misera*; the habit of hanging its large clutch of eggs on vegetation above water, like *Hyla decipiens*, which is quite different from it. Build robust for the size, head wide, pattern differing in details from that of the other forms of the same size.

TYPES AND TYPE LOCALITY. Holotype male collected by W. C. A. Bokermann, September 9, 1962, at Paranapiacaba; male paratypes from Campo Grande, Santo André, both places in the area between the city of São Paulo and the edge of the Maritime Escarpment. Holotype now WCAB no. 6597; paratypes also male now WCAB nos. 9096–9101 in Bokermann's private collection; a paratype at the MNR.

DESCRIPTION. Size small. Males 18–21 mm, mostly 20, female 24 mm long. Build robust for the size, head rather wide, body narrower but not tapering greatly. Hindlimbs not very long, the adpressed tibiotarsal articulation reaching from the anterior corner of the eye toward the nostril. Snout rather blunt from above, slightly longer than the horizontal diameter of the eye. Canthus rostralis evident, nostrils small. Eye very prominent. Tympanum small, about one-third the diameter of the eye, rather indistinct. Interorbital space much wider than the internarial space. Tongue rounded, slightly notched, extensively free behind. Vomerine teeth in two small, separate groups between the choanae. Fingers wide with relatively large disks; three outer fingers webbed at the base; a slight enlargement at the base of the first finger. Toes appearing three-fourths webbed, the web wide to below the disk on the outer side of the first, second, third, and on the fifth toe, forming a long fringe on the inner side of the first, second, and third and on both sides of the last joint of the fourth toe. Inner metatarsal tubercle present, outer minute. Dorsal aspect smooth, belly and midventral portion of the thigh granular, otherwise smooth.

MEASUREMENTS. Our female, 24 mm snout to vent.

SECONDARY SEX CHARACTERS. The female is larger

and masses of eggs may be visible by translucency. The vocal sac of the male may balloon out to the level of the arms, but some preserved specimens show only the translucent openings on the floor of the mouth.

COLOR. The dorsal color ranges from pale almost straw color to tawny, with or without a sprinkling of dark chromatophores like those seen in Bokermann's figure of the type; when numerous they may obscure the pattern. Some individuals show a few white spots (guanine?), which are not usual in this group.

PATTERN. The original description mentions an interocular bar and X-shaped pattern on the back. The latter is not unlike that of a certain proportion of specimens of *H. m. werneri* in which the X thickens into a dark median portion. In some specimens of *H. berthalutzae* seen by me, the oblique bars of the anterior part of the X leave a central portion of the lighter background free of pigment; some are fenestrated once more before dying out in quite irregular hind branches. Oblique bars present on the permanently visible upper aspect of the limbs. No white spot under the eye in the specimens examined.

VOICE. The call, heard at night under pouring rain at the Açude da Solidão, Tijuca, Rio, in the company of Drs. W. F. Blair and L. D. Vizotto, consisted of a long, drawn-out note without much inflection and surprisingly loud for the size of the frog.

REPRODUCTIVE HABITS. Izecksohn, who has had the opportunity to observe the fauna of the lowlands of the state of Rio de Janeiro very closely, informs that this species hangs its clutches from the vegetation above the still water in which it breeds. *Hyla decipiens* has similar habits but the clutch is smaller. The two species cannot be confounded. It seems likely that in *Hyla berthalutzae* reproductive isolation has been achieved.

KNOWN RANGE. The known range of this species is small. The Bokermann types come from the escarpment outside the capital of the state of São Paulo; the places mentioned are somewhat above 700 m altitude. The Açude da Solidão, state of Guanabara, is 380 m above sea level. The coastal lowlands of the state of Rio de Janeiro, where it also occurs, are very near sea level. For the time being, the species is thus known from the south-eastern part of the Atlantic Province between 22° and 24° of southern latitude.

## HYLA RUBICUNDULA, HYLA NANA, AND ALLIED FORMS

*Hyla rubicundula, Hyla nana, Hyla elongata,* and *Hyla sanborni* have a number of characters in common, and their variations follow similar trends. The relationship is closer between *Hyla rubicundula* and *Hyla elongata* on the one hand, and between *Hyla nana* and *Hyla sanborni* on the other, as the following descriptions and observations will endeavor to show.

*Hyla rubicundula* was described over a hundred years ago by the Danish authors Reinhardt and Lütken. Nevertheless, it is poorly known. This may be due to the publication of the original description in a Scandinavian language unknown to most herpetologists. It is a very well-characterized species, small, elongate, with short head, long body, and short hindlimbs. It is green in life, but the opaque permanently visible dorsal aspect becomes pink to violaceous purple after preservation.

*Hyla elongata* Lutz is very similar and may be conspecific, perhaps a geographic race. It is much smaller and shows a trend toward rudimentation of the vomerine teeth much less evident in the larger *Hyla rubicundula. Hyla elongata* was discovered in the outskirts of São Paulo, near the edge of the plateau.

*Hyla nana* was described by Boulenger from Resistencia, the capital of the Chaco province of Argentina. It is quite common all over the Continental Depression and well known to Argentinian and Brazilian herpetologists. It ranges from pale to reddish, but Boulenger's indication of a pinkish or pale vinaceous brown color above is somewhat misleading on account of the color of *Hyla rubicundula. Hyla nana,* though morphologically not unlike *Hyla rubicundula,* is not identical with it. It does not remain in the low, central marshlands, but occurs in the higher *cerrado* country. Both species have been collected along the valley of the São Francisco River.

*Hyla sanborni* K. Schmidt was described from Uruguay and is a Platine form rather than Brazilian, though it does occur in the south. Its general aspect is that of an attenuated *Hyla nana.*

*Hyla walfordi* Bokermann is evidently synonymous with dark specimens of *Hyla nana*.

*Hyla tritaeniata* Bokermann is admitted as a separate species of this group.

## *Hyla rubicundula* Reinhardt & Lütken, 1862

REINHARDT, J., and LÜTKEN, C. F. 1862. Bidrag til Kundskab om Brasiliens Padder og Krybdyr. *Vid. Medd. Naturh. Foren. Kjobenhavn* 3 (10–15):143–242, 4 pls. *H. rubicundula*: 197.

The earliest description of a small tree frog of this group is that of *Hyla rubicundula* by Reinhardt and Lütken. The Danish authors anteceded Boulenger's description of *Hyla nana* by more than a quarter of a century. Nevertheless, the description is poorly known. The specimens of this species can, however, be readily identified in life and especially after preservation.

DIAGNOSTIC CHARACTERS. The opaque skin and the color of the dorsal surface of well-preserved specimens, ranging from pink or grayish-pink to a purplish color; the generally slightly larger size, longer head and freer tongue, and the greater constancy of the morphological characters than in the other forms of the group. In life, pale green above, cream below, with orange-yellow gula and concealed surfaces on the limbs.

TYPES AND TYPE LOCALITY. Two syntypes from Lagôa Santa, at the edge of a lagoon of the same name outside Belo Horizonte, the capital of the state of Minas Gerais and the headquarters of the great Danish paleontologist Lund. They now belong to the collection of the Museum of Natural History in Copenhagen. Types seen by the author, one there, the other at the British Museum (Natural History) in 1952.

DESCRIPTION. Size small, types 24.5 and 20 mm long. Males 17–24, mostly 19–21 mm snout to vent. Build robust for the size but elongate. Hindlimb not long, the tibiotarsal articulation reaching the eye or quite near to it when the leg is adpressed. Snout narrowed and blunt from above, declivous and projecting slightly over the mouth in profile, with distinct canthus rostralis and high, almost vertical, loreal region. Nostrils small, subcanthal, not terminal, but much nearer to the tip of the snout than to the eye. Horizontal diameter of the eye nearly the same as the eye-snout length. Tympanum small, often indistinct. Tongue rounded, entire or slightly emarginate, extensively free behind. Vomerine teeth in two transverse patches between the choanae. Lateral fingers webbed at the base. An elongate callosity below the first finger. Toes rather fully webbed but the web narrow on the inner side of the second, third, and on both sides of the fourth, reduced to a fringe on the phalanx below the disk. Disks well rounded. An elongate inner, sometimes an indistinct, small, outer metatarsal tubercle. Skin of the permanently visible dorsal surfaces quite smooth and opaque. Belly and midventral portion of the thigh granular.

VARIATION. Our seventy-one male specimens show the following variations: tongue entire in twenty-seven, slightly emarginate in twenty-three, more extensively emarginate in twenty, wider and more irregular in one, furrowed only in a few, attached in one, in a few less free than usual and than stated in the original description. Vomerine teeth less variable than usual. One specimen lacks one patch, the teeth are indistinct in another; the patches are oblique and reach the posterior edge of the choanae in a few. Length of hindlimb variable, as usual in Brazilian species of *Hyla*. Out of sixty-three males measured the tibiotarsal articulation failed to reach the eye in ten, reached the posterior corner in thirteen, the hind half in twenty-four, mideye in eleven, almost to the anterior corner in one, in front of the eye in four.

SECONDARY SEX CHARACTERS. The male has a very large vocal sac, the lower part much pleated longitudinally. Our only female has relatively short legs, the tibiotarsal articulation failing to reach the eye; no eggs were seen.

MEASUREMENTS. Our female specimen, from Pirapora, Minas Gerais, is 22 mm from snout to vent; tibia 10 mm; head-width 7 mm. The authors of the name mention that their smaller specimen has a vocal sac. The other is probably a female, 24.5 mm long. Few males are less than 19 mm or more than 21 mm long; we found eleven out of seventy. The other fifty-nine are between 19 and 21 mm long.

COLOR. In life the dorsal surface of the body and the permanently visible dorsal surfaces of limbs are pale green. Gula and surfaces of limbs concealed in repose, orange-yellow; belly green.

Dead specimens acquire a rose to purple tint, which explains the name *H. rubicundula*. The tones seen by the author vary from pale pink (rare; Vespasiano specimens) to dark, almost purple (specimens from Pirassununga, in the state of São Paulo). Mostly they are intermediate and have either a distinctly pink or a grayish-pink tint. The original description mentions a fine rosy color and a dark border standing out from the lighter color of the back. The dark area on the sides is variable.

The color is extensive to the permanently visible dorsal aspect of the limbs. The dark area on the sides of the head and body and the light upper parts of the limbs concealed when at rest are sharply separated from the rosy color, which forms a mantle of vivid opaque skin.

PATTERN. The examples seen alive by us did not show any pattern. Two-thirds of those examined after death were also devoid of pattern. The others showed vestiges of two longitudinal lines or series of dots, between the dorsolateral edges and the midline, apparently associated with samples from certain localities. This pattern is similar to that described for *H. nana* but very attenuated. The exact percentages were 3:1, i. e.; no pattern visible after death in fifty-four specimens, vestigial pattern in eighteen specimens.

ECOLOGY. The type locality Lagôa Santa is on the margin of the lagoon that lies in a hollow at the edge of the *cerrado* formation outside Belo Horizonte. *H. rubicundula* was collected by me in a large artificial pond at Fazenda da Baleia, on other outskirts of Belo Horizonte, and I have three specimens from Vespasiano not far from Lagôa Santa, also obtained on the shores of a very large pond or lagoon by A. Machado. The little frogs were calling on the emergent or marginal herbaceous vegetation in both places. No females were taken.

DISTRIBUTION. Most of the specimens seen belong to the Museu Nacional in Rio de Janeiro and the Lutz Collection. Besides these from the vicinity of Belo Horizonte, there is a number from different places in the valley of the São Francisco River, namely Pirapora and Januaria (Minas Gerais), Barreiras, Barreirinhas, Manga, and Jupaguá (Bahia), collected by A. L. Carvalho and Bailey while traveling down the São Francisco River. There are also some specimens from Pirassununga and farther west in the *cerrado* formation of the state of São Paulo, some of them belonging to Vizotto's collection.

AFFINITIES. This form is very similar to *Hyla elongata*, and Lutz left a note to the effect that his *H. elongata* also occurs in Belo Horizonte. *H. elon-gata* from eastern São Paulo is, however, much smaller, has a shorter and relatively wider snout, the tongue is less free and more variable, and the vomerine teeth are also more variable, generally oblique and sometimes vestigial or absent. Living *Hyla elongata* may become green, as observed by Lutz, but often they are yellow above with orange-tipped disks.

Two specimens from Lagôa Santa, the type locality of *H. rubicundula*, might almost suggest the possibility of *Hyla rubicundula* being the same as *H. nana*. These specimens are dark brown with a slight reddish-purple tint; the *nana* pattern is, however, perfectly distinct and morphologically they belong to it. *Hyla nana* also occurs in the basin of the São Francisco River.

Reinhardt and Lütken compare their species with *Hyla rhodopepla* Gthr. from the Andes of Ecuador. The latter has additional purple dots on the dorsal aspect, a larger tympanum, and one-third webbed fingers. This may well be the juvenile livery of a large frog; it must be considered as a quite distinct species, as stated by Reinhardt and Lütken.

## *Hyla elongata* Lutz, 1925

LUTZ, A. 1925. Batraciens du Brésil. *C. R. Soc. Biol. Paris* 93(21):137–139. *H. elongata*: 139.
———. 1926. Nota previa sobre especies novas de batrachios brasileiros. New species of Brazilian batrachians. Preliminary note. *Publ. Inst. O. Cruz*, March 10, 1926. Portuguese: 3–9, English: 10–16. *H. elongata*: 13.
COCHRAN, D. M. 1955. Frogs of southeastern Brazil. *U.S.N.M. Bull.* 206:107–109.

*Hyla elongata* is a very small form, very close to *Hyla rubicundula* Reinhardt and Lütken. It was first found by the author in 1923, in a partly flooded aviation field outside the city of São Paulo. Since then it has been found in other places near the capital.

DIAGNOSTIC CHARACTERS. The very small size plus the very short snout, forming a triangle with a rather wide base and not more than one-seventh of the snout to vent length. Vomerine teeth variable, from distinct, relatively heavy patches, converging between and slightly beyond the posterior border of the choanae, to small patches, barely visible or only palpable, sometimes altogether absent. In life, yellow above with orange tinted disks, occasionally light green. After death gray, with or without a dorsal pattern of two longitudinal lines of dashes or dots. Differs from *Hyla rubicundula* by the smaller size, shorter and relatively wider snout, less free tongue, and by the less-perfect development of the vomerine teeth. Preserved specimens seen by us not pink. Differs from *Hyla nana* and *H. sanborni* by the size, build, shape of the snout and by the color of the living specimens.

TYPES AND TYPE LOCALITY. Types collected by B. Lutz, January 7, 1923, at Campo de Marte, now Aerodromo Marte, a military aviation field not far from the Tietê River and about 4 km outside the city of São Paulo. Male type no. 335 in the A. Lutz Collection. At the MNR, female allotype USNM no. 96861, in Washington, D. C.

DESCRIPTION. Size very small. Male holotype (ALC no. 335) 16 mm, female allotype (USNM 96861) 20 mm from snout to vent. Build slender. Body elongate, contrasting with the very short snout; greatest width of the body at the eyes. Hindlimb rather short, the tibiotarsal articulation reaching the eye when the leg is adpressed. Snout very short, rounded from above, slightly compressed beyond the nostrils, bluntly truncate, declivous and projecting somewhat above the mouth opening in profile. Canthus rostralis indistinct, loreal region vertical. Nostrils superolateral, about one-third of the distance from the eye to the tip of the snout. Interorbital space not quite one and a half times the width of the upper eyelid. Eye large, prominent, its horizontal diameter about equal to the distance from it to the tip of the snout. Tympanum partly visible, less than one-third the diameter of the eye. Tongue rounded, flat, practically entire (types), its posterior border almost attached. Vomerine teeth (types) in two posteriorly convergent, not very distinct groups, between the choanae reaching slightly beyond their posterior border. Fingers webbed at the base. An elongate callosity at the base of the first ( ♂ ). Toes about three-fourths webbed. A distinct inner metatarsal tubercle. Disks rounded, very neat. Skin smooth, except the belly and the midventral portion of the thigh. A slight fold of skin below the gula, a more distinct one across the chest ( ♀ ).

VARIATION. The patches of vomerine teeth and the tongue are variable in our samples. They vary from visible and oblique to palpable or absent. Both types have the tongue practically entire and almost completely attached behind and the vomerine teeth visible and oblique.

SECONDARY SEX CHARACTERS. A very large vocal sac in the male with large folds on the sides and minute median pleats beneath.

COLOR. On the watercolor painting of the living type A. Lutz wrote: "Dorsum the color of egg-yolk or light green, changing from one day to another. Dark dots also seen. Disks orange-tinted (*alaranjados*). Lower aspect whitish, gula and extremities lemon colored." Iris light yellow.

PATTERN. Dead specimens are drab or gray. A pattern of two longitudinal lines may be present but seems to appear only after death. As Lutz puts it: "Dorsal side green in life, dotted with somewhat purple red after death. No cross-bars on the limbs, but sometimes one or two dark longitudinal stripes on legs and tarsus." Elsewhere he says that though similar in pattern to what we now call *Hyla misera meridiana*, it differs from it because the latter is never green.

Among 150 well-preserved specimens we found fragmented lines in eighty-two, lines of dots in forty-eight, and no pattern in twenty.

VOICE. The syntypes were collected by me forty years ago, at the very beginning of Lutz's work on frogs, and I do not remember the call accurately.

ECOLOGY. Found in flooded fields or open marshy ground at altitudes of approximately 800 m above sea level.

KNOWN DISTRIBUTION. This small form has been collected near the city of São Paulo at several points: Campo de Marte (type locality), Ipiranga and Vila New Manchester respectively some 4, 6, and 10 km away. One set of ten individuals from the vicinity of the Tietê River collected by Aristoteris Leão does not seem adult. A large series from New Manchester are tentatively put in here, also a short series from Passa Quatro in Minas Gerais. A series of sixteen minute juveniles of this group from Porto União in Santa Catarina leg. Braulio Prazeres, MNR, may or may not belong in here.

AFFINITIES. *Hyla elongata, Hyla nana, Hyla rubicundula,* and *Hyla sanborni* are so closely related structurally that one remains in doubt as to their distinct status. *Hyla elongata* seems smaller than either *nana* or *rubicundula*. From *Hyla nana* it differs mainly by the absence of a clear-cut pattern and by the bright dorsal color of living specimens, from *Hyla rubicundula* by the smaller size, variable teeth, less free tongue and the lack of a rosy color in our preserved specimens. Vizotto mentions such colored specimens from the northwestern part of the state of São Paulo, but it is not quite certain to which form of the group they belong.

STATUS. So far the main differences between *Hyla elongata* and *Hyla rubicundula* boil down to smaller size, less well-developed vomerine teeth, larger number of individuals with a perceptible rudimentary dorsal pattern, besides more often yellow than light green dorsal color in life and the lack of rose to violaceous pigmented skin in preserved specimens. The differences that can be observed in dead specimens were rechecked in a series of nine pink to violaceous specimens caught in the *cerrado* section of São Paulo by Vizotto and kindly lent to me. In some the teeth were palpable without being very distinct; two showed a few faint dots on the back; these two and three others had a few dark dots on the legs. In size, color, and other morphological details they were nearer to *Hyla rubicundula*. This raises the point as to the systematic status of *elongata*: is it a marginal population, geographic race, or full species?

## *Hyla nana* Boulenger, 1889

BOULENGER, G. A. 1889. On a collection of batrachians made by Prof. Charles Spegazzini at Colonia Resistencia, South Chaco, Argentine Republic. *An. Mus. Nat. Hist. Genova* 7(27): 246–249, 2 pls. *H. nana*: 249, pl. 2, figs. 2–2a.

BOKERMANN, W. C. A. 1962. (*Hyla walfordi* sp. n.) *Atas Soc. Bras. Biol.* 8(5):53–55, figs. 1–8.

This form was described by Boulenger from the Chaco, i. e., the Continental Depression east of the Andes. It seems, however, to occur also in other parts of the Continental province, including the valley of the São Francisco River; a few specimens have been taken in the semiarid northeastern subprovince.

DIAGNOSTIC CHARACTERS. The inland distribution allied to the small size, relatively short leg and the other characters of the group. Tongue less free than in the larger *Hyla rubicundula*, vomerine teeth more constant and less oblique than in the smaller *Hyla elongata*. Differs in color from both; dorsal surface clay-colored in life, with the two longitudinal lines described by Boulenger; our specimens drab or buff to brown after preservation, the pattern generally distinct.

TYPES AND TYPE LOCALITY. The syntypes were collected by Prof. C. Spegazzini at Colonia Resistencia, South Chaco, Argentina. Now nos. 89, 19,

21–22 in the British Museum Collection. They were seen by the author in 1952. According to Boulenger the types were rosy when he saw them.

DESCRIPTION. Size small: males 19–22 mm, mostly 18–19 mm, females mostly 20–21 mm, only exceptionally more in the Chaquean subprovince from which this form was described. Build robust; this is especially so in the specimens from the São Francisco River valley in Minas Gerais and Bahia put into this species, which are generally slightly larger. Hindlimb short, the tibiotarsal articulation reaching from tympanum to eye when the leg is adpressed. Snout elongate, bluntly triangular from above, very slightly declivous to the mouth in profile, with marked canthus rostralis and almost vertical loreal region. Nostrils very small, just below the canthus, very much nearer the tip of the snout than the eye. Eye fairly large and prominent, its horizontal diameter the same, or almost the same, as the distance from its anterior corner to the tip of the snout. Tympanum very small, often rather indistinct. Tongue rounded, entire or slightly emarginate, posterior border slightly free. Vomerine teeth in two short, generally transverse patches between the choanae, rarely oblique and reaching slightly beyond their posterior margin. Fingers webbed at the base. A large callosity under the first, another under the third and fourth fingers. Toes not quite fully webbed, the web oblique on the inner side of the second and third, reaching the base of the disk on the third and fifth and the last subarticular tubercle on both sides of the fourth toe. An elongate, inner, metatarsal tubercle. Disks rounded, well-developed. Skin smooth except the belly and midventral portion of the thigh, which are granular or paved. A fold of skin across the chest, more evident in females as it is not covered by a vocal sac.

SECONDARY SEX CHARACTERS. Vocal sac from moderate to very large. Callosity under the first finger apparently more marked in nuptial males; occasionally their forearms more robust. Some females are so much dilated by the eggs that the pattern is obliterated by the darker hue. There are remarkably few females in our samples, though more than in those of *Hyla rubicundula*.

VARIATION. Some specimens have the tongue slightly emarginate and a very few have it wider and irregular in outline behind. The proportions are variable. All our specimens have the vomerine teeth present. They are short, transverse, and between the choanae in most. We have found oblique groups of teeth in one specimen from Primavera, upper Paraguay, and in two from Miranda, southern Mato Grosso.

GEOGRAPHIC VARIATION. Our specimens considered as *H. nana* from the valley of the São Francisco River in Minas Gerais and Bahia are more numerous than those from the Chaco. They are slightly larger, with 1 or 2 mm more of head-body length. The snout also seems proportionately slightly longer and the build more robust. The Chaquean specimens are larger than *Hyla elongata,* but morphologically more like it than those from the Minas-Bahia subarea.

SIZE. Male specimens from the Continental Depression seen by us range from 17 to 22 mm snout to vent length, but out of twenty specimens there is only one each 17, 21, and 22 mm long. Our eighty-five males from the valley of the São Francisco River range from 17–23 mm, but also with few specimens at the periphery and a predominance of those from 19–21 mm in total length. Miss Cochran had one male from Bolivia measuring 26 mm from snout to vent, a most unusual length. Our twelve females from the Chaquean subarea range from 19–21 mm. Seven females from the valley of the São Francisco River range from 21–23 mm snout to vent length.

COLOR. The specimens collected in southern Mato Grosso at Miranda and Porto Esperança by J. Venancio and the author were clay-colored on the dorsal aspect with a very dark brown band on the sides of the body. Throat and thighs of males cadmium yellow to light lemon yellow.

PATTERN. A few specimens are pale and show no pattern at all. In a few others the pattern is obscure; however, in most specimens there are two straight or slightly sinuous, longitudinal, lines down the whole dorsal surface, not far from the midline. They may be entire, but as a rule they are broken up into a series of fragments or composed of large dots. Sometimes they are intermediate, being partly composed of dashes and partly of dots. Besides these, there is often a uniform sprinkling of smaller dots on the back. A few specimens have additional lines, and in a very few the pattern is more confused and composed of multiple fragments or dots. Some specimens also have a light vertebral line, and in some the dorsal surface grows lighter toward the edges. Longitudinally disposed marks, similar to those on the back, are often present on the perma-nently visible parts of the limbs (mainly the tibiae), but there are no crossbars in any of them.

Dr. Cochran has a specimen from Bolivia with additional lines and we have one from Primavera, upper Paraguay. In our other Bolivian and Paraguayan specimens the lines are rather sinuous and almost entire; the fragments are more widely spaced in one from Paraguay. A light vertebral line is present in several. Our largest sample, from southern Mato Grosso (Miranda) shows entire lines in four, fragments in four, and dots in one; the pattern is obscure in three, multiple and confused in one, and two are pale. The vertebral line is present in two, and the dorsolateral edges are well defined in two. The few other southern Mato Grosso specimens fit into these different patterns indicated above. The sprinkling of lines is sometimes present in *Hyla elongata.* The longitudinal lines are seen in some preserved specimens of *H. elongata* and of *H. rubicundula,* but are generally less distinct than in *Hyla nana* and sometimes limited to the fore part of the dorsal surface. The confused pattern composed of multiple fragments and larger dots more disseminated on the back is reminiscent of the pattern of *Hyla sanborni* K. Schmidt. The presence of two longitudinal lines down the back and of similar fragments on the limbs is also somewhat reminiscent of the pattern of the *Hyla misera–microcephala* group. There may be some affinity between the two groups.

The specimens from the valley of the São Francisco River also conform to one or the other of these patterns. One set from Pirapora (MNR 906) inclines to be intermediate between fragments and dots, but the sprinkling of small dots is present. Another sample (MNR 914) inclines to light dorsolateral edges and shows the different patterns indicated above; the light vertebral line appears in some of them. In twelve out of nineteen specimens from Jupaguá, Bahia, the light dorsolateral edges and the light vertebral line are present in eight. The regular lines are either formed of fragments (eight) or intermediate between fragments and dots (eleven), rather obscure in one. These samples can be summed up as showing a tendency toward an intermediate pattern of fragments and dots, with light dorsolateral edges and sometimes a light vertebral line. The specimens from other localities are less numerous and also fit into one of the forms mentioned above.

VOICE. Unrecorded.

ECOLOGICAL NOTES. This is one more small form; like most of the unspecialized small kinds of *Hyla* it calls on herbaceous vegetation, in or at the edge of standing water. Phillips collected specimens in a bromeliad as well as in a pond, on the outskirts of the village of Primavera in upper Paraguay. Our specimens from Miranda in southern Mato Grosso were obtained immediately after the onset of the rains. They were got in a relatively small pond so crowded with calling frogs that some of the lesser species of *Hyla,* including some of these, were sitting on the heads or backs of larger ones, such as *Hyla nasica.* Like *H. rubicundula* and *H. elongata,* this form seems to belong to the *cerrado* formation (scrub vegetation). I collected a few on the window panes in the Brazilian National Park at Iguassú Falls.

DISTRIBUTION. Cochran (1955) mentions specimens from Bolivia. We have a few small ones from Buena Vista in that country, out of a series belonging to the MZUM. *Hyla nana* is probably found all over Paraguay, since besides those from Primavera we have some from Isla Bela and from Asunción. The types hail from Resistencia, Argentina. In Brazil it has been obtained in southern Mato Grosso, at Salobra, Miranda, Porto Esperança, and São Luiz de Caceres. All these samples are composed of few individuals the largest being the one from Miranda (seventeen individuals). It seems to reach Rondonia at the edge of the Hylaea (*H. walfordi* Bok.)

A. L. Carvalho and J. R. Bailey took apparently typical specimens in several localities in the valley of São Francisco River. These specimens tend to be slightly larger in average size than those in the Continental Depression. They were obtained together with others, apparently quite typical *H. rubicundula,* in several of these places, namely Pirapora, Januaria, Barreiras, Barreirinhas, Manga, and Jupaguá. A few small specimens from the northeastern subarea have also been seen. One must conclude that this form is peculiar to what I call the Continental province, between the Brazilian Coastal Mountains and the Andes, but reaching the coast in northeastern Brazil.

SYNONYMS. Examination of Bokermann's description of *H. walfordi* and of specimens 38036–38038 of the WCAB Collection, apparently topotypes, leads the author to the conclusion that *Hyla walfordi* is synonymous with *Hyla nana* Boulenger. The length of the hindlimb of the three specimens is variable and the extra width of the head mentioned in the description is not evident. Individuals with a light vertebral line seem to predominate in Bokermann's type locality, but this also occurs elsewhere; the additional dorsal lines are no clearer in two of the topotypes than in specimens from other regions and only one of them has the marked dots on forearm and tibia given as a constant character.

The main interest of these specimens and description lies in the further extension of the already known very great range of *Hyla nana,* from Paraná in Brazil to Argentina and Bolivia. Forte Príncipe da Beira, a long-established military post, is in Rondonia, a region where the Gran Chaco and the Amazonian Hylaea practically meet.

AFFINITIES. *Hyla nana* is so like *Hyla rubicundula* that Dr. Cochran used one of the latter, taken from Lassance in Minas Gerais, in her description of *H. nana.* Her specimens from there were compared to the types of *H. nana* by Parker and considered identical. Both forms seem present in Lassance. The main difference lies in the freer tongue and the opaque rosy or vinaceous color of preserved specimens of *Hyla rubicundula* and perhaps in its slightly longer snout. This puts us in a dilemma. Either *H. nana* and *H. rubicundula* are conspecific, but only part of the specimens becomes rosy or vinaceous after death, whereas others do not; or, we have two different sympatric species before us. The two liveries occur together in Minas Gerais and Bahia. According to Boulenger's statement as to the rosy color of his preserved specimens of *H. nana,* the same situation occurs in the Continental Depression as well as in the highlands. The specimen from the Chaco figured as *H. nana* by Müller and Hellmich is a *Hyla minuta* with the *bivittata* or *velata* livery.

## *Hyla sanborni* K. Schmidt, 1944

SCHMIDT, K. P. 1944. New Frogs from Misiones and Uruguay. *Zool. Ser. Field Mus. Nat. Hist.* 29(9):153–160, figs. 20–22. *H. sanborni:* 155–156, fig. 20.

BARRIO, A. 1962. Los Hylidae de Punta Lara, Provincia de Buenos Aires. *Physis* 23(65): 129–142. Photos. *H. sanborni:* 134–137, fig. 2.

*Hyla sanborni,* described in 1944 by K. Schmidt, from Uruguay, is somewhat like *Hyla elongata* Lutz, 1925, but still more like *Hyla nana,* of which it is probably a geographic race.

DIAGNOSTIC CHARACTERS. Schmidt considers the small size and the absent vomerine teeth as very important characters. However, Cochran (1955) found that in three of the paratypes, USNM nos. 101457–9, the protuberances on which the vomerine teeth are disposed were palpable and visible. The rudimentation is thus not absolute but more marked than in the other forms of the group; this is not surprising considering the small size. *Hyla sanborni* differs from *Hyla nana* in these points but is very similar to it in color and pattern, though the pattern is apt to be more intricate. From *Hyla elongata*, which is yellow or more seldom pale green in life and has bright orange disks, it differs by the color and the presence of a well-defined pattern.

TYPES AND TYPE LOCALITY. Hacienda Alvarez, 15 km northeast of San Carlos, Uruguay. Collected October 21, 1926, by Karl P. Schmidt. Type no. 9581, FMNH; paratypes nos. 9568–79, 9582–84, 9586–89, some in the USNM; also obtained in other places in Uruguay by Sanborn, for whom it is named.

DESCRIPTION. Size very small, males 15–17 mm, females 17–20 mm from snout to vent. Build robust for the size. Head short, blunt. Body elongate. Hindlimb short, the tibiotarsal articulation reaching the posterior half or the hind corner of the eye when adpressed. Snout rounded from above, projecting slightly in profile. Canthus rostralis blunt. Nostrils almost at the tip of the snout, slightly tumefied. Eye prominent. Tympanum small, about one-third of the horizontal diameter of the eye. Interorbital space slightly wider than the internarial space. Tongue entire or slightly emarginate. Digits with small rounded disks. Fingers with a trace of web at the base. Toes about three-fourths webbed. A small inner metatarsal tubercle. Skin smooth above, granular beneath.

SECONDARY SEX CHARACTERS. The female is slightly larger and more robust than the male, which has a very large vocal sac.

COLOR. Varying from pale tan to brown above and on the sides, pale beneath. Barrio (1962) once saw an individual acquire a green procryptic dorsal tint. Vocal sac canary yellow.

PATTERN. Very similar to that of *Hyla nana* but sometimes more intricate. Two longitudinal, generally interrupted lines on the back occur in 40 percent of the specimens; dark dots are disseminated on the dorsal aspect and the sides. There may be an additional dorsolateral dark line. In dark phases the dots are sometimes very profuse. Five percent of the specimens have a narrow, whitish, vertebral line.

VOICE. According to Barrio the call is a monotonous repetition of a syllable containing an *i* (*e* in English). The song goes on from dusk to about midnight. The chorus is monotonous. Barrio publishes a sonagram.

HABITS. In daytime Barrio found them asleep in the leaf sheaths of Gramineae and Cyperaceae. At night they call sitting on the marsh vegetation 5–15 cm above water.

KNOWN DISTRIBUTION. This form pertains to the Platine and Cisplatine province. It was described from Uruguay. It is quite common in the La Plata Basin in Argentina. Barrio considers it co-dominant. It occurs also in southern Brazil. A number of specimens were collected by Milstead in Rio Grande do Sul and some juveniles from Santa Catarina are very like it. The smallest of these is 13 mm long.

AFFINITIES. Karl Schmidt considers *H. sanborni* as allied to *H. parvula* Boulenger and *Hyla uranscopa* L. Müller on account of the lack of vomerine teeth. This is a grievous mistake, as both these species belong to the genus *Centrolenella*.

## *Hyla tritaeniata* Bokermann, 1965

BOKERMANN, W. C. A. 1965. Tres novos batraquios da região Central de Mato Grosso, Brasil. *Rev. Bras. Biol.* 25(3):257–264. *H. tritaeniata*: 260–262, fig. 2.

This is one more member of the *Hyla rubicundula, nana, elongata,* and *H. sanborni* complex. Bokermann compares it to *Hyla elongata* but not to *Hyla rubicundula*, which is the oldest member of the group and which it resembles most.

TYPES AND TYPE LOCALITY. Holotype male WCAB 16211; female allotype 16210, male paratypes 16212–69 plus 15217–24, the last eight from another locality. The type locality is São Vicente, Cuiabá, Central Mato Grosso, approximately 800 m altitude, collected by the author and others.

DESCRIPTIVE NOTES. Comparison of *H. tritaeniata* with *H. rubicundula* brings out even fewer differences than comparison with *Hyla elongata*. Both are at the periphery of the range of *H. rubicundula*, but *elongata* is in the south and *tritaeniata* in the northwest. The type localities of all three lie at about 800 m elevation, differing in this from *Hyla nana* described from the Chaco, i. e. the Continental

Depression and the Atlantic province, and from *H. sanborni*, which ranges into higher latitudes.

In size *H. tritaeniata* is near to *H. rubicundula*. Males of *tritaeniata* range from 18 to 20 mm, with a mean at 19 mm; the holotype is 20 mm long, the average for *rubicundula*. Female 22 mm in *H. tritaeniata*, up to 24 in *H. rubicundula*. *H. elongata* is smaller.

The morphological features do not differ greatly either. Bokermann's large series shows a trend toward rudimentation of the vomerine teeth almost absent in *H. nana*, rare in *H. rubicundula*, present in *H. elongata* and most marked in *H. sanborni*, the smallest form of the complex. The paratypes of *tritaeniata* at the MNR, no. 4086, have the teeth present and obliquely disposed. The main structural difference thus lies in the shorter web of the foot, perhaps slightly more than the one-third given by Bokermann, and continued by long fringes.

SECONDARY SEX CHARACTERS. The vocal sacs of the males sent to the MNR are large, much pleated, and folded back parallel to the mouth opening.

COLOR. The color in life also seems closer to *H. rubicundula*, though Bokermann's color notes are rather inadequate. He says that the permanently visible surfaces of body and limbs are pale green. This is also the case of *Hyla rubicundula*. *H. elongata* is sometimes pale green, but at other times it is light yellow in life. The gula of *H. rubicundula* males is orange; the belly cream-colored, which is not very different from the yellowish white color mentioned for the ventral aspect of his form by Bokermann. Most specimens of *H. nana* have two distinct longitudinal lines near the middle of the back. *Hyla rubicundula* generally does not show lines on the dorsal aspect in life and only in a proportion of dead specimens. In *H. elongata* they may be present but are evanescent. *H. sanborni* has more pattern. The main character of *H. tritaeniata*, at least in the type locality, is the constant appearance of two lateral chestnut to reddish brown lines, one from each eye to the sacrum and a median one from the sacrum to the anal region. The similar dorsolateral edges also seem very distinct.

The whole group, including *H. sanborni*, are found in marshy ground. *Hyla tritaeniata* frequents the humid groves of *Mauritia flexuosa*, a palm not found at the higher latitudes, except perhaps toward the northeastern periphery of *H. rubicundula* and *Hyla nana*.

## INSUFFICIENTLY KNOWN FORMS

### *Hyla tintinnabulum* Melin, 1941

> MELIN, D. 1941. Contributions to the knowledge of the amphibia of South America. *Medd. f. Goeteborgs Musei Zool. Avd.* 88, 71 pp., 38 text figs. *Hyla tintinnabulum*: 29–30, fig. 13.

*Hyla tintinnabulum* is one of the species described from Brazil by Melin. It is a small species belonging to the Hylaean fauna whose small forms are less well known than those from the other cisandean provinces.

DIAGNOSTIC CHARACTERS. The small size, bell-like voice, coloring, and details of morphology, differing in one way or another from each of the southern small species of *Hyla*.

TYPES AND TYPE LOCALITY. Three males from the Rio Uaupés, some days journey north of Ipanoré, northern Amazonas, collected by Melin, May 17, 1924. Now at the Museum of Natural History at Goeteborg where I saw them in 1952.

DESCRIPTION. Size very small, 19–20 mm long. Build sturdy for the size. Head short, wide, body slightly attenuated at both ends, not elongate; hindlimb fairly long, the adpressed tibiotarsal articulation reaching beyond the eye. Snout bluntly triangular, short, rounded, not longer than the diameter of the eye. Canthus rostralis blunt, somewhat angular; loreal region almost vertical. Nostril near the tip of the snout. Eye large, prominent. Tympanum about one-third of the diameter of the eye and rather indistinct. Interorbital space much wider than the internarial space. Tongue subcircular, flat, hind edge truncate, free. Vomerine teeth in small, round, almost rudimentary well-separated patches near the hind edge of the choanae. Lateral fingers nearly one-fourth webbed; toes two-thirds webbed. Disks small. A callosity at the edge of the first finger, which is thickened at the base. A narrow, elliptical, inner metatarsal tubercle. Skin above fine, smooth. Belly and midventral aspect of the thigh granular. A slight supratympanic fold. Pectoral fold distinct to the sides of the vocal sac.

SECONDARY SEX CHARACTERS. Only males were caught by Melin. The vocal sac was puckered longitudinally. As mentioned above, the pollex is thickened at the base.

COLOR AND PATTERN (fide Melin). "Above grayish-green with a brown tint, beneath bluish-green; toes orange-colored; in alcohol above a little white-

# 228

**228**

Very Small Species

powdered; fine brownish dots on the back and limbs (excluding part of the forearms and thighs) often forming diffused bands between the eyes and along the vertebral line; upper eyelids partly dark; iris with metallic luster on a black ground; a diffuse brownish band along the sides of the head and anterior part of the body, partly edged with white above and fading away behind the forelimbs."

VOICE. The species name is evidently derived from the call, which according to Melin has a brittle, bell-like sound.

BEHAVIOR. Melin mentions the abundance of individuals present, sitting and calling on high grasses and Melastomaceous bushes along an *igarapê* ("rivulet") on the eastern side of the main river. He also recalls their indifference to the light flashed on them and their sluggish condition with the vocal sac distended. It seems possible that they were blinded by the light.

AFFINITIES. The coloring above and beneath and the pattern of this species are somewhat reminiscent of *Hyla decipiens branneri*. The orange disks recall those of *Hyla elongata*. The general impression conveyed to me by the types was of closer affinity to the group of *H. nana* to which *elongata* belongs.

## *Hyla goinorum* Bokermann, 1962

> BOKERMANN, W. C. A. Cuatro nuevos Hylidos del Brasil. *Neotropica* 8(27):81–91. *H. goinorum*: 86–88, figs. 11–15.

DIAGNOSTIC CHARACTERS. The small size allied to the slender elongate build and the *Phyllobates*-like habit. Hand rather large.

TYPE AND TYPE LOCALITY. Holotype female (WCAB 1401) from Tarauacá, Acre, Brazil. Leg. Bokermann, no date given; now in the private collection maintained by him in São Paulo.

The species is named for Drs. Coleman and Olive Goin of Florida University. The homage is just, but the name is rather cumbersome for such a tiny frog.

DESCRIPTION. Size small, female holotype and only known specimen 20 mm long. Build slender, elongate. Head longer than wide. Body also elongate, straight until the sacrum. Hindlimb fairly long, the adpressed tibiotarsal articulation reaching between the eye and the nostril. Snout long, triangular from above, sloping obliquely to the mouth opening in profile. Canthus rostralis distinct; loreal region slightly concave between nostril and eye,

flaring below. Eye not very prominent in the preserved specimen but standing out slightly at the side. Tympanum one-third the diameter of the eye. Interorbital space slightly wider than the internarial space. Tongue rounded, slightly wavy and free behind. Vomerine teeth in two well-separated, somewhat elongate patches between and mostly behind the choanae. Hand rather long, unwebbed. First finger short with relatively small disk; third very long. Disks rounded. Carpal and subarticular tubercles poorly developed. Toes short, almost fully webbed; web inserted below the disk on outer side of all toes except the fourth, forming a fringe on both sides of its penultimate articulation and on the inner side of the second and third toes. Metatarsal tubercles rather minute. Skin granular on the belly.

MEASUREMENTS (fide Bokermann). Snout to vent 20 mm; head width 6 mm, diameter of eye 2.5 mm; of tympanum 0.9 mm; eye to nostril 2.2 mm. Forelimb 12 mm, hindlimb 32 mm.

COLOR. Now brown; deepest on the sides of the head and body, forming a dark band from the tip of the snout almost to the groin, where it fades out; very much like the sides of some *Phyllobates* or *Colostethus*. Back lighter, more yellowish; according to Bokermann dirty yellow in life.

PATTERN. Now rather obscure; according to Bokermann it has faded gradually; tapestry-like, composed of indistinct, longitudinal, partly anastomosed elements. Incomplete and irregular bars on the dorsal aspect of the limbs, including the forearm, most of the dorsal surface of the thigh, the tibia, tarsus, and the outer edge of foot. Beneath immaculate.

Collected at night on an Araceous plant growing on the ground in a marsh not far from the forest; taken together with *H. granosa* and a northern form of *H. leucophyllata*.

AFFINITIES. Though somewhat similar in size and build to *Hyla fuscomarginata* and allied forms, *H. goinorum* does not convey the impression of close relationship.

Known only from the type locality in the former territory of Acre, whose anuran fauna is very much in need of closer study.

## *Hyla haraldschultzi* Bokermann, 1962

> BOKERMANN, W. C. A. 1962. Cuatro nuevos Hylidos del Brasil. *Neotropica* 8(27):81–91. *H. haraldschultzi*: 88–91, figs. 16–20.

This is a small thin frog, without evident affinities, from the northwestern frontier of Brazil, a part of the Hylaea that probably has further surprises in store for herpetologists.

DIAGNOSTIC CHARACTERS. The pustular glandules on the dorsal surface, especially dense on the head, allied to the small size and obscure pattern of longitudinal darker lines on a brown background.

TYPE AND TYPE LOCALITY. Holotype and two paratypes, all females, from Santa Rita do Weil on the Solimões, slightly above São Paulo de Olivença, state of Amazonas, collected in October 1956 by the ethnologist Harald Schultz. Now nos. WCAB 2896 (holotype) and WCAB 2897–2898 (paratypes) in Bokermann's private collection.

DESCRIPTION (based on paratype 2898, the only one seen). Size small, female 22 mm snout to vent. Build thin, narrow. Head widest at the corner of the mouth, slightly more massive than the body, which is gradually attenuated from the suprascapular region to the sacrum and groin. Hindlimb slender, the adpressed tibiotarsal articulation reaching between nostril and eye. Snout bluntly triangular, rounded, not projecting greatly in profile. Canthus rostralis evident but not sharp. Nostril slightly tumefied. Eye not prominent in the dead specimen, its horizontal diameter about equal to the distance from its anterior corner to the nostril. Tympanum less than one-third the diameter of the eye. Interorbital space wider than the internarial space. Tongue small, rounded, fleshy, slightly free behind and with a slightly wavy posterior outline. Vomerine teeth in small, robust, practically contiguous groups between and mostly behind the choanae. A short web between the outer fingers. Disks small, slightly pointed in this specimen. A very modest elongate callosity below the first finger ( ♀ ). Web on the foot short between the inner digits, very cut out between the three outer ones, wide to above the last subarticular tubercle, except on the fourth, where it reaches beyond the first subarticular tubercle; metatarsal tubercles minute. Skin of ventral aspect slightly granular on the body, not on the limbs. Dorsal skin beset with small and very characteristic pustules, agglomerated on the head.

COLOR AND PATTERN (preserved paratype). Dorsum brown with darker longitudinal stripes from the interocular region to the groin. Black dots on the limbs. Ventral aspect pale in preserved specimens, immaculate. Dorsal pattern more distinct on the smallest paratype than in the others, according to Bokermann's figure and description and with light halos at the edges of the main stripes. Pattern of paratype 2898 very obscure; vertebral stripe slightly more distinct.

This *Hyla* has no affinities with the longitudinally striped larger forms of the southeastern *H. polytaenia* group mentioned in the original description. It may approach some of the forms described by Fowler from Ecuador but there are no elements available for careful comparison, and the altitude of the finding places is very different.

## *Hyla leali* Bokermann, 1964

BOKERMANN, W. C. A. 1964. Dos nuevas especies de *Hyla* de Rondonia, Brasil. *Neotropica* 10(31):2–6. *Hyla leali*: 3–5, text figs. 1–3.

Under this name, which is that of the then governor of the federal territory of Rondonia, Coronel P. N. Leal, Bokermann describes one more small *Hyla*. He compares it to *Hyla minuta* and points out small morphological differences besides a diverse call.

DIAGNOSTIC CHARACTERS. The short head and snout, and the comparatively large eyes; the call.

TYPES AND TYPE LOCALITY. Holotype male, allotype female and twenty-five male paratypes collected by Bokermann in November 1962 at Forte Principe da Beira in Rondonia Territory. Nos. WCAB 10397 holotype. 10398 allotype. 10372–96 paratypes. One, paratype at the MNR.

DESCRIPTION. Size 20–23 mm from snout to vent. Build robust for the size. Head and snout very short, relatively wide. Body elongate. Hindlimb average for the size, the adpressed tibiotarsal articulation reaching the eye. Snout quite short, rounded, canthus rostralis blunt, loreal region concave. Nostrils almost terminal, small. Eye large, its horizontal diameter longer than the distance to the nostril. Tympanum distinct, about one-half the diameter of the eye. Interorbital space wider than the internarial space. Tongue average, slightly emarginate. Vomerine teeth in small patches (?) behind the choanae. Hands and fingers short, disks round. Outer fingers with a short web. A callosity below the first finger. Toes also small with small rounded disks; very extensively webbed. Skin smooth except for the abdomen and midventral part of the thigh.

MEASUREMENTS. The male holotype is 22 mm long; the others vary from 20–23 mm. Female allotype 23 mm.

SECONDARY SEX CHARACTERS. Vocal sac of the male large. Female allotype 1 mm longer than the holotype, the abdomen distended with eggs.

COLOR. Pale brown to straw-colored above, the pattern darker. Iris vivid brown with a rosy tint. Beneath pale, immaculate.

PATTERN. The pattern of the holotype is composed of an interocular bar produced behind, continued as a longitudinal pattern down the middle of the back and ending beyond the shoulder in two branches producing a half-moon or sickle shape. The sacral spot is horizontal with a rounded peak in front and a sinuous outline behind. A small supra-anal spot is also present. This pattern varies somewhat; the interocular bar may be partly or entirely separated from the median longitudinal design and the sacral and supra-anal spots absent. There are similar oblique bars on the forearm and leg. Otherwise immaculate.

VOICE. Bokermann compares the call to that of *Hyla nana*, which is rather surprising.

ECOLOGY. His series, the only one known, was calling on shrubs about one meter from the ground in a flooded place.

AFFINITIES. The pattern is possibly allied to one of the many variants of pattern seen both in *Hyla minuta* and in *Hyla bipunctata*. The color of the iris seems nearer to the first, and it lacks the capistrate pattern and bright colors of the second. Similar patterns also occur in some other little frogs of the *Hyla decipiens* group.

The characters of *Hyla leali* are too mixed, the series too short, and the gaps between Rondonia and the known range of the other species too wide to permit closer approximation.

## Hyla schubarti Bokermann, 1963

> BOKERMANN, W. C. A. 1963. Duas novas especies de *Hyla* de Rondonia, Brasil. *Rev. Bras. Biol.* 23(3):247–250, text figs. 4–6.

Bokermann described a new species from Rondonia Territory in the Brazilian Hylaea under the name of *Hyla schubarti*. The new species is compared to *Hyla leucophyllata* and is based on alleged small differences between the two; perhaps also on the presumption that, the frog fauna of Rondonia being poorly known, the species is probably new.

I cannot see any structural affinity between *Hyla leucophyllata* and the new form, which is very much smaller and seems closer to the group of *Hyla decipiens* in size, build, and in the trend toward rudimentation of the vomerine teeth. White spots under the eye are present in *Hyla decipiens branneri*, although they also occur in *Hyla misera werneri*. *H. sanborni* of the *H. nana* group, which is as small as *Hyla schubarti*, also often lacks vomerine teeth.

TYPES AND TYPE LOCALITY. Holotype WCAB 7845, paratypes 7846 and 7847 collected at Rondonia, Rondonia Territory, in January 1962 by A. Machado. The smallest now at the MNR.

MORPHOLOGICAL CHARACTERS. Size very small. Three males, one 18 and two 19 mm long. Build robust; head wide, body not elongate; hindlimb short, the tibiotarsal articulation reaching between the eye and the nostril. Canthus rostralis well defined. Eye large, prominent, longer than the distance to the nostril. Tympanum small, one-third the diameter of the eye. Interorbital space very wide. Vomerine teeth small in small separate groups, absent in one paratype. Tongue circular, slightly emarginate and free behind. Web of hand rudimentary; web of foot long but not reaching the disks. Skin smooth above, granular beneath.

COLOR AND PATTERN. No notes are available on the color of the living frogs. The pattern of a darker interocular bar and dorsolateral stripes converging behind and short lateral dark stripes figured for the type is completely absent from the paratype presented to the MNR, which is colorless and devoid of any marked characters. There are also no ethological or ecological data available.

AFFINITIES AND STATUS. *Hyla schubarti* is presumably one of the very minute Brazilian tree frogs that are only well known in the Atlantic and southeastern areas. Only time and the collecting of more specimens with more abundant data will clarify its affinities and taxonomic status.

# VI. Borderline Species

# 18. Two Unrelated Species

## Hyla truncata Izecksohn, 1959

IZECKSOHN, E. 1959. Uma nova especie de "Hylidae" da Baixada Fluminense, Estado do Rio de Janeiro, Brasil. *Rev. Bras. Biol.* 19(3):259–263, 6 text figs. English summary: 263.

As mentioned by Izecksohn in the original description, this species is somewhat aberrant from the type genus of the family. However, it does not fit into any of the other genera either. Consequently, pending the anatomical study promised by him, it is left here.

DIAGNOSTIC CHARACTERS. The truncate head and snout, like a decapitated triangle with a wide base; the flat habitus; elongate build; short hindlimb; the shagreened, uniform brown skin of the dorsal aspect, and the absence of flash colors.

TYPE AND TYPE LOCALITY. Holotype female and twenty-three paratypes were collected on November 26, 1958, by Izecksohn and S. Nunes, in an epiphytic bromeliad, at km 37 of the Presidente Dutra Road, Itaguai, state of Rio de Janeiro. Now holotype no. 107, paratypes nos. 106, 108, 109 of the Izecksohn Collection at the Federal Rural University, state of Rio de Janeiro. Additional paratypes nos. 101–105 from the same area of the coastal lowlands known as Baixada Fluminense.

DESCRIPTION. Size medium; female holotype 42 mm snout to vent. Habitus depressed. Head wide, triangular in front, rectilinear behind the eyes. Body elongate. Hindlimb short, the adpressed tibiotarsal articulation reaching the axilla. Snout truncate in front, trapezoid in shape; canthus rostralis oblique, quite straight; loreal region slightly concave. Nostrils subcanthal near the tip of the snout. Eyes directed somewhat forward, pupil rhomboid. Tympanum inconspicuous, very small. Interorbital space wider than the internarial space. Tongue elliptic, posterior border free. Patches of vomerine teeth separated, placed at the level of the hind edge of the choanae. Maxillary teeth numerous. Lateral fingers about one-third webbed, fringed. Disks rounded, larger than the tympanum. Toes more than one-half webbed, fringed. A small inner metatarsal tubercle. Skin finely shagreened above, appearing thick; minutely granular beneath. Skin of head not concrescent with the skull.

MEASUREMENTS. The author indicates snout to vent lengths from 34 to 42 mm, with the male smaller than the female; type 42 mm long.

SECONDARY SEX CHARACTERS. Apparently not marked except for the difference in size.

COLOR. The color is unusually simple and uniform without any pattern. The dorsal aspect is brown, slightly inclined to mahogany, uniform but somewhat variable from lighter to darker in the same individual. The concealed aspects of the thigh are also brown and devoid of pattern or flash colors. The inner digits are slightly lighter in tone. The sides of the body tend to be darker. The ventral aspect of the body and the midventral portion of the thigh are quite light with a slightly greenish-cream tint more pronounced on the abdomen. The other segments of the limbs are dark, including the hands and feet. Webs also dark. Tympanum the color of the skin not standing out from it. Iris dark like the rest of the color scheme but with a coppery glint, especially on the outer rim.

The juveniles have a less uniform, brighter, livery (fide Izecksohn).

VOICE. The call is a croak described by the author as *craa* or *craap*.

HABITS AND ECOLOGY. This frog is evidently not very abundant, but has been collected a number of times by the author in the same and adjacent terrain. It is a bromeliad dweller like several other hylids. The masses of small eggs seen in the type and other females suggest ordinary larval development. Izecksohn states that *H. truncata* is a good climber, which is in accord with the disks. The individual kindly given me by him spends most of its time concealed in a hollow leaf stalk similar to a bromeliad, but sometimes comes out and lies flat for a while in the water beneath. It has not been observed hunting, but it must feed since it has survived several months of captivity.

TAXONOMIC STATUS AND AFFINITIES. Until *H. truncata* has been more thoroughly investigated its generic status will remain uncertain, like that of a few other species put to *Hyla* but showing trends away from it. The conjunction of its habitus and coloring, rhomboid pupil, numerous maxillary teeth and loose skin on the head do not agree with the combination of characters of any of the well-defined specialized genera. It is perhaps nearer to *Sphoenorhynchus*, but the habitus, color, and ecology do not agree. A special genus may be needed to accommodate it.

## Hyla albolineata Lutz & B. Lutz, 1938

LUTZ, A., and LUTZ, B. 1938. New Hylidae from Brazil. *An. Ac. Bras. Sc.* 9(1):69–71, pl. I, figs. 2, 2a, 2b.

This is an extremely rare species, very unlike any other of the light-green frogs of the southeastern coastal mountains of Brazil. So far only two large specimens have been collected within an interval of thirty-six years.

DIAGNOSTIC CHARACTERS. The short second finger, covered by the first, held in front of it as if opposable. Disks of the inner digits very narrow. A unique pattern of white lines, disposed in pairs on the limbs, forming circles or other closed figures, surrounding fields of the back and the sides, either plain or containing a dark dot. Color green, very deep on the dorsal surface, lighter on the sides of the body and on the concealed surfaces of the limbs. Iris yellow, with light, narrow inner zone, wide outer one and a crown of burnt-orange pigment between them.

TYPE LOCALITY AND HOLOTYPE. A male, collected by Prof. Heymons at Teresópolis, in the mountains of the state of Rio de Janeiro, March 1929, and presented by him to Dr. Adolpho Lutz; now ALC no. 1778 at the MNR. Only other specimen, collected February 1955, by J. Moraes Pacheco, in the Serra dos Orgãos National Park, at Teresópolis, in the collection of the MNR no. 3223. Altitude over 900 m above sea level, 22° 26′ 12″ lat. S. 42° 54′ 42″ W. Gr. Climate *Cfb* (Koeppen), subtropical with cool summers. Rain forest vegetation.

DESCRIPTION. Size: Type male, 35 mm, additional specimen 40 mm long. Build robust, body heavy, ovoid, slightly narrowed near the groin. Head large, wider than long. Leg fairly short, the adpressed tibiotarsal articulation reaching just in front of the eye. Snout rounded, truncate, one and a half times the length of the eye; nostril subterminal, subcanthal. Canthus rostralis distinct, slightly curved; loreal region concave. Interorbital space much wider than the internarial space. Eye oblique, fairly large, two-thirds below the canthus rostralis. Tympanum about one-half of the diameter of the eye. Vomerine teeth in well separated, slightly oblique groups between and behind the choanae. Tongue large, heart-shaped, very extensively free behind. Lateral fingers webbed at the base, the web slightly longer between the third and fourth; second finger short; first finger one-half disk longer than the second; in our preserved specimens held so as to cover it. Subarticular tubercles well developed. Web short between the first and second toes, about halfway between the second and third, longer on the outer ones. A prominent inner metatarsal tubercle. Disks of first finger and of first and second toes distinctly smaller than the others. Skin smooth above save for the minutely granular upper eyelids; granular beneath, on sides and throat minutely, on belly and lower surface of the thigh more coarsely so; abdominal granulation disposed in parallel, horizontal rows; chest almost smooth. A series of narrow folds under the armpits, a narrow fold over the eye and tympanum, a dorsolateral fold. A short ridge above the anus. A narrow ridge on the tarsus, continuing onto the knee.

MEASUREMENTS. Type: male 35 mm snout to vent; hindlimb 51 mm, femur 15, tibia 15, tarsus and foot 21. Head length to width 12:14. Interorbital space to upper eyelid 6:3. Tympanum 2, eye 4, eye-nostril 4.

Additional specimen (MNR no. 3223), snout to vent 40 mm, hindlimb 63, femur 19, tibia 19, tarsus 10, foot 15. Head length to width 12:15. Interorbital space to upper eyelid 7:3. Tympanum 3, eye 5, eye-nostril 4.

COLOR AND PATTERN. In life (as recorded in a watercolor of the type) dorsal surfaces are deep green, on occasion lighter; a contrasting red-brown color on the fourth and fifth toes, including the web between them. Sides of the body and concealed surfaces of the limbs less vivid. Iris yellow, with a narrow, light, inner rim and a similar, wide, outer zone; a crown of reddish brown or burnt orange pigment in between. Upper eyelid bronzed. Tympanum whitish in the center, green at the periphery. Outline of upper jaw white, widening into an irregular, dorsolateral band in the axillary region, continuing backward; tarsal, tibial, and anal ridges also white, all of them underlined in dark; when the frog is quiescent they form a continuous outline. A number of narrow white circles and lines on the dorsal aspect, i. e. three, irregular linear white circles on the distal third of the back, enclosing fields of the same color as the rest of the background; two of them small, side by side and close together, with a chestnut dot in the center of each, the third larger, behind the others and without the central dot; three similar chestnut dots, one median, in the postocular, two slightly more external, in the axillary region. A few irregular white splashes on the dorsal surface (guanine?); a few minute white dots on the sides of the body; one circle each over the fourth and fifth toes; three pairs, concave in front, over the tibiae; one to each side of the anus, directed forward onto the back.

In the newer specimen, the white band was very conspicuous on the upper jaw and beyond it, ending at the elbow, above a large dot; the white edges of the foot, tarsus, and heel were also very marked. The three pairs of concave white lines on the leg were matched by similar pairs of lines or circles on the thigh; the pattern was completed by five chestnut dots on the back, a small single one between the eyes, plus two larger and more distinct pairs, one pair over the shoulders, the other before the sacrum, the latter slightly wider apart; dark chestnut marks on the tarsus; outer toes also chestnut, as in the type.

The preserved specimens have faded to ivory, as it generally happens with light-green tree frogs. In the type, the white margins on the jaw and on the dorsolateral region, above the anus and on the tarsus remained visible for a long time; vestiges of the ground color and the deeper pigment on the iris lasted over thirty years. In the additional specimen the white edges and their chestnut borders are still distinct as also the chestnut dots and the white spots of guanine. The continuation of the white edges to the upper jaw forms a very conspicuous dorsolateral band ending between the elbow and the sacrum and justifying the choice of the trivial name.

VOICE, BEHAVIOR, AND ECOLOGY. Unknown.

JUVENILE. A metamorphic (?) juvenile with identical coloring was seen in the same locality, but we refrained from collecting it since the species seems so rare.

RELATIONSHIPS. *Hyla albolineata* does not show any affinity with the other green species of *Hyla*. It is even possible that it may be a *Gastrotheca*. Two species at least occur in the same mountains and are also rare.

# 19. An Entirely Glandular Species

*Hyla adenoderma* B. Lutz, 1968

LUTZ, B. 1968. New Brazilian Forms of *Hyla*. Texas Memorial Museum. The Pearce-Sellards Series 10:1–19. *H. adenoderma*: 3–5, figs. 1–2.

A very unusual and interesting large-sized Hylid is described here. I received it from the Swiss ethnographic explorer F. Casper, who collected it while on a trek along the Rio Branco in the former territory of Guaporé, on a visit to an Indian chief. This territory, now named Rondonia, lies in the southwestern corner of the Brazilian sector of the Amazonian Hylaea; mesetas occur in its southern part.

DIAGNOSTIC CHARACTERS. The extremely coriaceous, entirely glandular and mammillate skin of the dorsal surface and sides of the body, adorned by a net composed of wide meshes surrounding rather large patches of the back; the short rounded head; the large size, the extensive webs.

TYPE AND TYPE LOCALITY. The holotype and unique, perhaps slightly immature, specimen was received September 1, 1959, and is now n. 4054 of the amphibian collection of the MNR. It was collected by F. Casper somewhere on the banks of the Rio Branco, a subtributary of the Rio Madeira in Rondonia, Brazil. The Rio Branco flows more or less toward the north from the meseta called Chapada dos Parecis. Rondonia lies approximately between 8°–14° S. and from below 60° to slightly above 66° W. Gr. The finding place is somewhere between 10°–12° S. and 62° to 63° 30′ W.; climate *Am.* Köppen, i. e. hot and humid, with ill-defined dry season and large-leafed rain forest in the lowlands.

DESCRIPTION. Size large; holotype approximately 64 mm snout to vent; difficult to measure accurately on account of the bent head and slightly curved body. Build very robust. Head massive, wider than long. Body also robust, as wide as the head at the shoulders, tapering somewhat beyond the sacrum. Hindlimb impossible to adpress; the tibiotarsal articulation probably not reaching beyond the eye. Snout very short, rounded, not projecting above the mouth. Canthus rostralis very short, blunt, truncate at the nostrils, which are lateral, subcanthal, and slightly tumefied; loreal region high, slightly concave. Eye of preserved specimen oblique, longer than the distance from its anterior corner to the nostril. Tympanum distinct, partly covered by a thick ridge, about half the diameter of the eye. Interorbital space slightly wider than internarial space. Tongue rounded, short, wide, entire, somewhat free behind. Vomerine teeth in two short, well-separated, transverse groups between and to the posterior border of the choanae. Forelimb not thin; hand large, with robust fingers and large, rounded disks, the first slightly smaller than the others, the third almost as large as the tympanum. An oblique narrow web between the first and second fingers; web to below the disk on the outer side of the second and on the fourth, to the penultimate tubercle on both sides of the third, hence fringed. Tibia slightly shorter than the femur, both moderately stout; foot long. Web oblique between the first and third toes, wide to below the disk on the outer side of the first, second, third, and on the fifth, to the penultimate joint on both sides of the fourth toe. Disks very slightly smaller than on fingers. Subarticular tubercles average. An elongate callosity under the first finger and the first toe, a rather flat one below the outer fingers. Skin unusually coriaceous, mammillate over the whole dorsal surface and the sides; with regular raised rows of glandules; a glandular ridge and larger glandules in the peritympanic region. Beneath granular especially the gula, belly, and midventral portion of thigh. Limbs smooth above and beneath. A fold of skin forming a tiny bib at the base of the throat and folds on the sides below the mouth. Skin of the head not concrescent with the bone.

MEASUREMENTS (mm). Head and body, measured separately on account of the bent head: 20+44=64. Head length to width 20:24. Eye 8, tympanum 4, eye-nostril 6, interorbital space 7, internarial space 5. Hindlimb: 114, femur 35, tibia 34, tarsus 19, foot 26. Hand 22.

COLOR AND PATTERN. The preserved specimen is tan, the pattern deeper brown in color, very irregular, with broad meshes, some of them open, delimiting large intervals; quite regular bars on the permanently visible dorsal aspects of the limbs, very distinct on thigh, leg, and outer edge of tarsus and foot; otherwise immaculate; pustules lighter than the network. Snout in front of the eye devoid of network, lighter than the rest. Concealed upper aspects of the limbs and ventral aspect of the body immaculate.

Unfortunately no data were provided with the specimen. It differs from all other species of *Hyla* known to me by the texture of the skin. It may come near to the evidently rare *Hyla coriacea* Peters from Surinam. It keys out near it both by the Boulenger and the Nieden keys. However, the skin is mammillate, not pitted, as described by Peters, and the pattern is quite different; some of the morphological characters also disagree. The finding places are both in the Hylaean region, but practically at its most divergent extremes. The shape of the head and especially its bent position suggest a certain degree of phragmosis; the build is very reminiscent of *Trachycephalus,* but the skin of the head is not concrescent with the bone nor is there a perceptible occipital ridge. In the absence of adult male characters, one cannot be certain of paired vocal sacs. Though near *P. venulosa,* the two are not identical.

# VII. Species with Double Vocal Sacs and Irritating Secretion

# 20. Phrynohyas

*Phrynohyas venulosa* (Laurenti), 1768

> LAURENTI, J. N. 1768. *Specimen medicum, exhibens synopsin reptilium emendatum cum experimentis circa venena et antidota reptilium austriacorum.* 214 pp., 5 pls. *Rana venulosa*: 31.
>
> SEBA, A. 1734. *Locupletissimi rerum naturalium thesauri accurata descriptio, et iconibus artificiosissimis expressio, per universam physices historiam* 1:113, table 72, fig. 4.

The names *Hyla, Acrodytes,* or *Phrynohyas venulosa* designate a species and a group of large and very well differentiated species of Neotropical tree frogs. It has been in use for a very long time and comprises a number of forms that cover a very large territory, from Mexico and Central America to Brazil and Argentina. Several classic authors have described some form of *H. venulosa,* the earlier ones sometimes in a rather inadequate manner; the later ones generally from one or another part of the range, sometimes apparently mistaking two color phases for separate species.

SYNONYMS. *Hyla venulosa* has been given an unusually large number of generic and trivial names. For South America they include: *Rana americana, R. surinamensis* and *R. virginiana altera* Seba, 1734; *R. venulosa* and *R. tibiatrix* Laurenti, 1768; *R. reticulata, aurantiaca,* and *tibiatrix* Lacepède, 1788; *R. zebra, R. venulosa, R. meriana* G. Shaw; *H. venulosa, H. tibiatrix* Daudin, 1802–1803, *H. zonata* and *H. bufonia* Spix, 1824; *H. vermiculata* Duméril and Bibron, 1841, perhaps *H. quadrangulum* Boulenger, 1882, and evidently *H. ingens* Duellman, 1956. *H. resinifictrix* may also be synonymous, although the types I saw in Europe had an almost *Trachycephalus*-like head. Outside South America other names have been used, such as *H. spilomma* Cope, 1877; *H. paenulata* Brocchi, 1879; *H. nigropunctata* Boulenger, 1882; *H. inflata* Taylor, 1944; *Hyla modesta* Taylor & Smith, 1945 and *H. latifasciata* Duellman, 1956. The Mexican forms and the figures given by Duellman (1956) can be matched to a very large extent by South American specimens. The latter will be discussed below.

Besides its wealth of specific appelations, *H. venulosa* as a group has been placed in several genera, beginning with *Rana* and *Hyla*. The main Hylid ones are *Acrodytes* and *Phrynohyas* Fitzinger, 1843, and *Scytopis* Cope, 1862. *H. venulosa* is indicated by Fitzinger as the type species for his genus *Acrodytes, H. zonata* for *Phrynohyas,* and *H. hebes* for *Scytopis* by Cope. The shifting of the tree frogs of this group from the type genus *Hyla* is due to some of their rather aberrant diagnostic characters.

Similar attempts to divide the unwieldy type genus *Hyla* into a number of other genera, made several times during the last two centuries, have mostly met with a very indifferent degree of success. The facts show that the Neotropical forms of *Hyla* tend to form a certain number of groups of correlated taxa and that each group shows a slight degree of differentiation from the other groups. However, these differences mostly seem too slight to warrant putting them into different genera until the exact limits of each group become clear. Under the circumstances it would seem prudent to attempt to revive some of the older names, not at the generic but at the subgeneric level. Another alternative would be to consider *H. venulosa* as a super species.

One or two recent American authors have again attempted to revive some of the older generic names and have put groups of *Hyla* into them. Thus Duellman (1956), in regard to *Hyla venulosa*, uses the name *Phrynohyas* Fitzinger, 1843. *H. zonata* Spix, 1824, is the type species, though it is generally looked upon as a synonym of *Hyla venulosa* (Laurenti), 1768, type species of another Fitzinger genus, *Acrodytes*. This generic appelation was used by Cope until he himself proposed a third generic name, *Scytopis*, for *H. hebes*, also a member of the *H. venulosa* group. *Acrodytes* has also been used by more modern authors such as Taylor and Smith. Duellman pleads that the figure of Seba (1734) of *Rana virginiana altera*, which is universally conceded to be the same as Laurenti's *venulosa*, cannot by any exercise of the imagination be accepted as a hylid frog. And yet that is precisely what everyone has done until now, apparently without any undue exertion. Refusing to consider this form a hylid, he indicts it and the genus *Acrodytes*, of which it is the type, as *nomina dubia*. He also stresses the fact that Laurenti put his species *venulosa* into *Rana*. I do not altogether agree with Duellman. The name *venulosa* has stood for a very long time. Seba's figure may not be good, but it is not much worse than many other contemporary figures: even newer ones like those of *H. zonata* and *H. bufonia* in the Spix book are rather defective. Excess ornamentation of drawings was not uncommon at the time; the disks are not quite as bad as Duellman says, and inaccuracies as to webbing are very common in amateurish drawings, even now. Moreover, in the days of Laurenti, the European authors, including Linnaeus, mostly put the

new exotic frogs into the genus *Rana*. The tenth edition lists *Bufo marinus, Leptodactylus ocellatus,* and *Pseudis paradoxa* under *Rana*. The frog depicted on the same plate of Seba under the name of *Rana virginiana exquisitissima* is also generally accepted as a figure of another Laurenti species, *H. maxima*. If one accepts *H. venulosa,* as corrected by Daudin 1803, both it and *Acrodytes* cease to be *nomina dubia,* and there is no valid reason for not following the classic authors who granted valid hylid status to *H. venulosa*.

I reluctantly accept the decision of the Committee on Zoological Nomenclature in adopting the name proposed by Duellman, i. e. *Phrynohyas,* which places it in another genus. I leave it here as a transition form to the next subfamily.

DIAGNOSTIC CHARACTERS. The main characters are the double vocal sacs, the thick glandular skin, almost forming parotoids, and its abundance of granular glands with sometimes poisonous secretion; the absence of the sharp, curved pollex rudiment present in the males of many other large species, which in *Phrynohyas* are substituted by corneous nuptial pads on the first and sometimes on the second finger; also the absence of a frontoparietal fontanelle.

*Trachycephalus* also has two vocal sacs, and its skin is lubricated by a more fluid secretion that makes it slippery, but the skin is concrescent with the skull. Deciduous nuptial pads occur in several species, including the minute *H. decipiens* Lutz.

However, the cutaneous secretion of the *H. venulosa* group is rather unique in Neotropical hylids. It has a latex-like consistency and dries into a sort of rubber that clings. It is more or less abundant and probably provides a means of defense instead of the curved pollex rudiment, which the males of other large species use as a weapon, but the secretion occurs in both sexes. The effects of the secretion have been variously described from diverse parts of the range by different persons. The variation may be regional, but more likely it is due to different physiological states of the secreting tissue at the time of the encounter. The vocal sacs are irretractible. They swell to a very large size when inflated and when limp hang down behind the corners of the mouth, sometimes almost to the shoulders.

IRIS. The pattern and color of the iris are very characteristic and are good differential characters.

They vary in the Brazilian forms from different parts of the range in which the iris has been examined, a routine process with me in late years.

These forms will be discussed successively, together with the differences observed in them. The types, type localities, voice, secretion, size, pattern, and other peculiarities will be included in the description. The forms with known iris are first separated in accordance with the key given below.

Neither size nor dorsal pattern seem to provide adequate criteria for separation of the diverse forms of *Phrynohyas*.

SIZE. Nuptial males with large vocal sacs and corneous excrecences on the first finger vary greatly in size. The same applies to females distended by masses of eggs.

The dorsal coloring fluctuates between olive-brown and greenish olive tones. More precise indications will be given for the different forms discussed below. In all of them the long bones and disks are green.

DORSAL PATTERN. The dorsal pattern is not very helpful in separating geographical races of *P. venulosa*. It varies in the same area and recurs elsewhere. The patterns of diverse forms of the group, which are generally regarded as good species, are often very similar and seem to constitute variations on the same theme.

The forms of *Phrynohyas venulosa* that occur in South America show two main types of dorsal pattern corresponding *grosso modo* to the names given by Spix to the Brazilian forms described by him from the Hylaea, i. e., *H. zonata* and *H. bufonia*. The excellent pictures by Baumann (1912), A. Lutz (1927), and several by Duellman (1956), as well as some of our Brazilian specimens, also show patterns of large blotches on the back between lighter areas, or of light fields with dark spots. They may be considered as allied to but aberrant from the *zonata* pattern.

ZONATA PATTERN. The *zonata* pattern is characterized by a dorsolateral band on each side of the body, generally beginning behind the upper eyelids, and a darker central area. The snout is light from the interocular region forward. The details of the light band vary and are discussed below under the cisandean-cisplatine forms. The central dark portion of the *zonata* pattern also varies. In its simplest form it is quadrangular, as seen in one of the

Lutz figures from Venezuela (1927, Pl. 14, fig. 33). It is also in evidence in *H. quadrangulum* Boulenger from western Ecuador and in some specimens of Miranda Ribeiro's *H. imitatrix* from southeastern Brazil. The light bands of the *zonata* pattern are similar to those of *P. mesophaea* from the Atlantic province of Brazil, but in the latter the bands are long and straight, and the middle portion of the back is uniformly dark.

A highly ornate form of the *zonata* pattern occurs rather rarely. It is figured by Duellman (Pl. I, fig. 1) as *P. hebes,* and by Cochran (1955, text figure 8) as *H. venulosa.* Both specimens are from the same place within the range of *P. hebes* from Piraporinha, Minas Gerais, not from Mato Grosso as stated by Duellman. A similar ornate pattern is exhibited in his pictures of *P. spilomma* (Pl. IV, fig. 1), a specimen from Veracruz, Mexico, and especially in figure 2, a specimen from Guatemala.

The dorsal aspect may be ornamented with large median dark blotches, either symmetrical or not, and sometimes quite irregular in shape. (See Baumann's figures of *H. venulosa* and Pl. V, figs. 1 and 2 of Duellman, both called *P. zonata* by him; the first is from British Guiana, the second from Costa Rica; the latter is more aberrant.)

A large light field covering the head and the anterior part of the back also occurs occasionally. Variants of this are shown by Duellman's Pl. II, fig. 1 of *P. inflata* from Michoacán, Mexico, Pl. III, fig. 1 of *P. latifasciata* from Sinaloa, also in Mexico, and Pl. VI, fig. 2 of *P. zonata* from Venezuela. The picture of *P. inflata* shows a dark quadrangle and white spots beyond the sacrum; the other two have a few slightly darker spots on the white field; all three exhibit light spots on the dorsal aspect of the limbs.

A number of the patterns mentioned above are not clear-cut but tend to merge into the other patterns in one or more respects.

BUFONIA PATTERN. The *bufonia* pattern is quite different. It is plain and much less variable and consists of a uniform, or almost uniform, dark, dorsal color with more or less numerous flat glandules scattered over it. It is rather like the figure of the type of *H. bufonia* Spix found on the same river as his *H. zonata*, but at Ega, now called Teffé, at the mouth of the river. This pattern seems to be the most common one in the western parts of the

Hylaea but also occurs in the east. It covers most of our western Hylaean specimens, including one from Pebas in Peru and one from Montalvo, eastern Ecuador in the Pastaza basin. We have, however, a specimen from Benjamin Constant on the Brazilian frontier that does not conform to it.

The *bufonia* pattern also occurs in the western parts of Mato Grosso, which lie north of the Pantanal and south of the Chapada dos Parecis, that is an area where the limits between the Hylaea and the Continental province are imprecise and probably subject to some seasonal fluctuation. The specimen figured in Pl. VI, fig. 1 by Duellman as *H. zonata* also seems near to the *bufonia* pattern.

This pattern is common in the Chaquean form. Cope's choice of the name *hebes* and description of the type denote that he had one of these dull specimens before him. The *bufonia* pattern does not seem to occur in the frogs from Atlantic area, even in the darkest specimens of *P. mesophaea,* which show quite dull dorsolateral bands.

The figure of *Phrynohyas ingens* Duellman from Maracaibo, Venezuela, published by him (Pl. II, fig. 2) together with his remarks above about its size, make it possible that this specimen belongs to the *bufonia* livery. The same may apply to the Mexican *H. nigropunctata,* as described by Boulenger and placed into the synonymy of *P. spilomma* by Duellman, to *modesta* Taylor and Smith (Pl. III, fig. 2) and to part of the specimens of *H. lichenosa* Guenther, considered in part as *zonata,* in part as *spilomma,* by Duellman.

Most of the forms have dark bands on the limbs, or alternatively light and dark areas across their permanently visible portions. These are very variable. They are very striking in large specimens of the Chaquean frogs *(H. hebes),* especially those with much pattern. They are absent from *P. mesophaea* except for a sample of unusually large specimens obtained in the Biological Reserves of the state of Espirito Santo and one or two others from the lowlands of the state of Rio de Janeiro.

The names *H. vermiculata* Duméril & Bibron (Mexico) and *la Rainette réticulaire* Daudin (Hylaea) are explained by the presence of stippling on the dorsal, permanently visible surfaces of some of the frogs seen and/or by the reticulation in the upper hind area of the thigh concealed in repose. This reticulation is very evident in many of the frogs from the area of *H. hebes* Cope. *H. vermiculata* is considered as *P. zonata* by Duellman.

*Phrynohyas venulosa* has no frontoparietal fontanel. In some old and large specimens, the skin of the head seems very rugose, without being concrescent with the bone or having the characteristic raised occipital outline of the frogs belonging to the genus *Trachycephalus.*

As already seen, the iris has become further differentiated than the dorsal pattern; size and habit do not afford clear-cut distinctions. The impression gained from the study of the literature and the summing up in Duellman's paper is that there are too many names for the Mexican and Central American representatives of *Phrynohyas venulosa* as well as for the South American frogs. This can, however, be decided only by those who have access to the living forms from the northern part of the Neotropical region. I would advise them to put them to the test of the color and pattern of the iris. I shall confine my own observations to the cisandean-cisplatine forms.

I have seen alive all but one of the forms that occur in Brazil. However, we lack living specimens of the group from the northeast, between Bahia and Pará. There seems to be very little difference between the *P. v. venulosa* from the Hylaea and *P. v. hebes* from the Continental province, except for the light parts of the iris. This is not surprising considering that the limit between the two areas is ill-defined. For the time being they are treated as subspecies of the *Phrynohyas venulosa* group.

*Hyla mesophaea* Hensel from the lowlands and *H. imitatrix* from the southeastern mountains of the Atlantic province seem further differentiated and *mesophaea* is treated as a full species.

*Phrynohyas venulosa* "sensu latissimo"
Key to the Iris

1. Iris gold or tawny, the color forming four oblique, petal-like spots, based on the free inner rim and separated from each other by black intervals, which comprise the pupil, a horizontal pseudocolobom and a vertical bar or area

*P. venulosa*
Amazonian Hylaea (specimens from Belém, Pará)
*P. resinifictrix Göldi*
(types; eastern Pará)

2. Iris golden, divided by a horizontal and a vertical black bar but showing additional black veins

*P. venulosa*
described by Boulenger (specimen from Presidio, Mexico)

3. Iris with dark background, the golden color broken up into a number of more or less centripetal flecks

*P.v. hebes* (Cope)
Chaquean subarea of the Continental province (specimen from Iguaçu at the frontier of Brazil, Argentina, and Paraguay)

4. Iris forming four light petals like those of 1, but light bluish green and surrounded by small horizontal peripheral spots of the same color

*P.v. imitatrix* Miranda Ribeiro
southeastern coastal serras of Brazil (specimen from Paraná)

5. Iris golden, slightly greenish toward the middle and orange toward the upper periphery, with a few large irregular black zig-zag veins and a horizontal pseudocolobom, but without the vertical bar and the petal-like spots

*P. mesophaea* Hensel
lowlands of the Atlantic province, Brazil (specimens from the state of Rio de Janeiro)

6. Iris not known

*P. quadrangulum* Boulenger
Ecuador

7. Iris not known

Specimens from other parts of the Neotropical region: Central America, Mexico

## *Phrynohyas venulosa (zonata, bufonia)* Spix, 1824

LAURENTI, J. N. 1768. *Specimen medicum, exhibens synopsin reptilium emendatum cum experimentis circa venena et antidota reptilium austriacorum.* 214 pp., 5 pls. *Rana venulosa*: 31.
DAUDIN, F. M. 1802. *Histoire naturelle des rainettes, grenouilles et crapauds.* 71 pp., 28 pls.
————. 1802. *Histoire naturelle générale et particulière des reptiles* 8:439 pp., 8 pls.
SPIX, J. B. VON. 1824. *Animalia nova sive species novae testudinarum et ranarum.* 53 pp., 22 pls. *Hyla zonata*: 41, pl. 12, fig. 1. *H. bufonia*: 42, pl. 12, fig. 2.

The forms of *Phrynohyas (Hyla) venulosa* found in the Hylaea should correspond to the original *Hyla* or rather *Rana venulosa* Laurenti, 1768. They have been taken as such by both classic and modern authors until Duellman (1956) contested the hylid nature of Seba's figure and tried to reject the name *venulosa* in favor of the name *H. zonata* Spix. Brazil was opened to scientific research much later than the Guianas, and most of the frogs from the Hylaea described before the nineteenth century hailed from the Guianas.

SYNONYMS. If Laurenti's name continues in use,

not only *P. zonata* but almost certainly also *P. bufonia* Spix fall into synonymy. It seems unlikely that they should be different species of the same group; the type localities of both are on the same southern affluent of the upper Amazon, the Rio Teffé. The main difference lies in Spix's words regarding the finding place of *H. zonata* and *H. bufonia*, respectively: "in arbustis et arboribus ad flumen Teffé" and "prope Ecga in sylvis." Ega, which is now also called Teffé, is near the mouth of the river. Spix also states that *Hyla bufonia* is "subtus fulva," which is rather unexpected in *Phrynohyas*. I have not seen *bufonia* alive. This ventral coloring may be a specific difference but it may also be only a color phase or a periodic phenomenon. Perhaps *P. ingens* Duellman, 1956, is a separate species, but in view of the finding of giant individuals in the form from the Chaquean subarea (*S. hebes* Cope) and in the species from the Atlantic lowlands, *H. mesophaea* Hensel, and of the allometric growth of *Phrynohyas* it seems more likely that his specimens come from a population of unusually large individuals of *P. venulosa* in the *bufonia* livery. The iris of *ingens* needs to be examined.

DIAGNOSTIC CHARACTERS. The tawny or slightly

reddish golden color of the iris, disposed in four petal-like spots, based on the inner rim and separated from each other by black intervals composed of the pupil, the horizontal pseudocolobom, and a median vertical black stripe or area. Two main color phases: *P. v.* (*zonata*), with broad, light, dorsolateral bands, deflected onto the sides of the body and *P. v.* (*bufonia*), uniformly dark with disseminated black flat glandules generally disposed longitudinally; an intermediate form with dark median area, either quadrangular or blotched longitudinally on a lighter background. Besides these, the group characters: latex-like secretion, lateral, irretractible vocal sacs, absence of the frontoparietal fontanel.

Types and type localities. The original diagnosis of Laurenti states briefly, "Habitat in Indiis." Dr. Cochran did not find the Spix types in Munich before the Second World War. If they were there they must have been destroyed. Peters evidently had them for his revision of the Spix species in 1872. It is to be hoped that they remained in Berlin. The type of *P. ingens,* UMMZ 55570, is an adult female and the type locality La Fria, Pueblo Nuevo, Depto. Zulia, Venezuela; it was collected April 20, 1920, by H. B. Baker.

Description (based on Brazilian specimens). Size average, not very large for *Phrynohyas venulosa.* Build robust. Head short, flat, rather rectilinear from the level of the tympana to the shoulders. Hindlimb also short, the tibiotarsal articulation reaching the eye. Body elongate. (These characters are more evident in well-grown specimens.) Snout very short, rounded in front, with blunt canthus rostralis, concave loreal region and well-defined jaws, the lower one standing out at the sides. Interorbital space equal to or slightly wider than the upper eyelid, which is equal to or slightly wider than the internarial space. Tympanum large, one-half or slightly more than one-half the diameter of the eye. Eye large, prominent, often one-third longer than the distance from the anterior corner to the nostril. Tongue large, wider than long, circular, entire or slightly emarginate, very little free behind. Vomerine teeth in two short groups between the choanae, generally straight, very slightly arched in some specimens. Digits flat, with very large disks, those of the fingers often equal to the diameter of the tympanum; well-developed subarticular tubercles. Web of hand short, from one-fourth to one-half, often one-third between the lateral fingers. No projecting rudiment of pollex. Web of foot about three-fourths, generally inserted at the base of the disks but mostly narrower on the inside of the inner toes and not reaching much beyond the penultimate articulation of the fourth toe, thence forming a fringe. A prominent, elongate, inner, and a very small, round outer metatarsal tubercle (sometimes absent). Skin of dorsal surface very glandular, shagreened, often with scattered pustules. A series of parallel horizontal pleats or ridges at the level of the tympanum. Skin aureolated on the ventral surface, very granular on the sides. In old specimens skin of the head sometimes rough, almost concrescent. A marked peritympanic ridge; tissue of this region parotoid-like. A fold beneath the gula. A strong pectoral fold. Dorsal surface sometimes covered by rests of secretion.

Secondary sex characters. The sex characters of the adult male are paired vocal sacs, nonretractile, one at each corner of the mouth; a pad of deciduous, corneous excrescences on the first finger and a smaller one on the second finger, while breeding. Pollex not protruded as in the subgenera *Boana* and *Plectrohyla*. Females with egg masses wider, sometimes considerably so, over the abdomen than across the head. Eggs of the *Hyla* type: small, very numerous, with one dark and one light-colored pole.

Variation. The main variation is in color and livery and will be discussed below. The usual variation of hylids in size, proximity, angle of the groups of vomerine teeth, outline of tongue, relative length of leg. As already mentioned by Duellman, the dark-colored (*bufonia*) phase gives the impression of a slightly longer and narrower snout and head. This does not, however, apply to very large specimens. The western populations may have a relatively longer leg, but too few individuals have been collected for positive assertion on this point.

Color. Male from Belém, Pará; *zonata* pattern; tones of olive brown and green, with lighter interocular area in front of the snout and white dorsolateral bands, deflected onto the sides between the shoulder and the sacrum, somewhat lighter midsacral and postsacral areas. Limbs barred, light and dark, often with dark spots on the light areas and light dots on the dark bands. Vocal sacs dark olive green. Webs and subarticular tubercles gray. Ventral aspect light glaucous green. Iris with four tawny or slightly reddish gold, petal-shaped spots resting on the inner rim and separated by the dark pupil, black horizontal pseudocolobom and vertical dark bars. Belly olive or buff; disks green; bones green; inside of mouth not green.

PATTERN. If our interpretation of the forms described by Spix is correct, there are two main patterns in the *Phrynohyas venulosa* of the Hylaean area of South America. As stated above, they correspond roughly to *Hyla zonata* and *Hyla bufonia,* plus some intermediate forms with large blotches somewhat similar to the pattern of *Hyla spilomma* from Mexico and to Baumann's (1912) excellent figures of *P. venulosa.* These forms may occur close together, to judge by their type localities, but *zonata* is common in the eastern part of the Hylaea and *bufonia* in the western one. The blotched pattern is more often seen away from the coast.

The frogs seen from the state of Pará near Belém, Livramento, and Cafezal (Instituto Agronomico do Norte), and one juvenile from the territory of Amapá are characterized by two light dorsolateral bands, not unlike those of *P. mesophaea,* but deflected onto the sides of the body before the sacrum; there is a darker area in between over most of the back. The sides are covered by the sac-like terminal part of the light bands plus dark areas. The permanently visible surfaces of the limbs show wide dark bands, often three, and narrower light intervals. These bands seem more uniform and regular than in the Chaquean form. Their edges are still darker and there may be a dark dot on the light field between them. In our juveniles, the light bands are brilliant white, almost silvery; thus in the two juveniles from Cafezal (Instituto Agronomico do Norte) the deflected *zonata* pattern is very brilliant, in one of them like the foot of a stocking, in the other truncated.

In the *bufonia* livery, the color is dark in a more or less uniform tone. Spix calls them black or a steely sooty color above. There are generally flat pustules scattered more or less longitudinally on the back. The bands on the limbs are visible in some but often obscure in the darker specimens.

Unfortunately, I have not seen them alive. The MNR has three such specimens from near Obidos in the state of Pará. The fourth one has obscure spots.

Most of the specimens from the western part of the *Hylaea* seem to conform to this pattern, but two of ours from Benjamin Constant show vestiges of double longitudinal blotches down the middle of the back, which approach the *spilomma* pattern or the more obscure blotches seen in the continental area of Brazil. Another small one has a large quite irregular spot on the middle of the back. This pattern is so variable that it is best shown in a series of photographs.

One of the specimens from Venezuela figured by Lutz (1925), has the simple *bufonia* pattern; the other is intermediate with a dark blotch behind the eyes and the interocular region and the rest of the back to the sacrum rather light. They and two of the Baumann figures show very distinct bands on the permanently visible parts of the limbs.

SECRETION. Three living individuals kindly sent from Belém, Pará, by Dr. Walter Egler, late director of the Museu Goeldi, produced a certain amount of secretion when handled for photographic purposes. This secretion did not cause any unpleasant effects. The secretion of the specimens from Benjamin Constant not far from the Peruvian frontier collected by Miss Kloss and Dr. J. M. C. Carvalho were quite different in this respect. Miss Kloss tells that she tried to brush aside *Culicoides* that were bothering her eyes while some of the dried brown secretion of *P. venulosa* was clinging to her hand. Ten minutes later her eyes became inflamed, and she had difficulty seeing during the whole night. The aftermath next day was a terrific headache. These two observations and those about specimens from other areas that follow below confirm my opinion that the physiological condition of the secreting tissue is variable.

VOICE. The author has not heard the call of the *P. (H.) venulosa* males from the northern part of South America. A. Lutz and J. Venancio, who heard it near Port of Spain, Trinidad, B.W.I., and at Maracay, Venezuela, describe it as a very rough croak. Miss Rita Kloss, who also heard the call at Benjamin Constant, near the Peruvian frontier, says that locally *P. venulosa* is called the "boatman" frog because the croak resembles the sound produced by the rhythmic hit of the oars against the canoes used by the Indians. Both parties mention that *P. venulosa* generally call sitting aloft, which makes catching them very difficult.

BEHAVIOR. The specimens from Maracay, Venezuela, caught by A. Lutz and J. Venancio bear a note to the effect that these frogs like to sit in hollow posts or metal tubes containing water that are used as supports for fences. This behavior needs to be juxtaposed with similar habits of *P. v. resinifictrix* and *P. v. hebes* and is in good accord with the depressed position of the head of most preserved specimens; it probably denotes an incipient degree of phragmosis, which again may be correlated with the absence of a frontoparietal fontanel. It also is in agreement with the observations of André Goeldi, told to Lorenz Müller (1912), that *P. resinifictrix* E. Goeldi does not really line with resin the cavities within which it is found, but uses cavities already so lined by wild bees. It remains to be shown whether such cavities are really used for spawning.

A. Lutz and Venancio also found *P. venulosa* sitting in the metal troughs used for catching rain water at the edges of roofs, where the latter could see their eyes shining.

Cott mentions the vol-planing ability of *P. (H.) venulosa*, which he tried out by letting this frog fall from increasing heights, finding that it always managed to reach the ground unhurt. This is probably not peculiar to *P. venulosa*, but a function of good webbing. We once recovered an only very slightly hurt *H. langsdorffii* in the garage of an apartment house after it leaped from a sixth-story terrace.

KNOWN RANGE. As mentioned above, this form seems to differ from the other forms I have seen alive chiefly by the combined color and pattern of the iris. Unfortunately, this character has been looked for only in a very few living frogs and is not easy to see in preserved specimens. Consequently it cannot help to separate ranges as yet. It seems probable that the nominal form occupies the whole or at least the forested part of the Hylaea, with a preponderance of the *zonata* pattern in the eastern part, of the *bufonia* livery in the western one and scattered blotched individuals.

The specimens in the A. Lutz Collection from Trinidad and Venezuela are rather faded and do not show many vestiges of pattern, except one of them has a pattern on the head. They conform with the illustrations published by Lutz (1927, Pl. 14). Duellman (1956) lists a larger size and somewhat longer legs for his form *Hyla ingens* from the northwestern area of Venezuela. We have one *venulosa* from Pebas, Peru, and another from Montalvo, Ecuador, which have longer legs than usual. All of them are of the *P. v. bufonia* type.

Boulenger described *P. quadrangulum* from Ecuador, whose characters are given below. The leg may be slightly longer, but the adpressed tibiotarsal articulation reaches only the front of the eye. There is great need to see the iris of the northern and northwestern South American frogs, especially those with plain or blotched dorsal livery.

TRANSITIONS. The *zonata* pattern is not essentially different from that of *P. mesophaea*, but the iris does differ. One specimen from Caxias, in the state of Maranhão, adjacent to the state of Pará, has the *zonata* livery; the other, from Carolina, also in Maranhão is of the *bufonia* type. Three from Fortaleza, in the state of Ceará, were given by Prof. Rocha, founder of the former Museu Rocha. Two of them are faded to ivory white; the third is quite dark except for two very narrow dorsolateral light stripes like those seen in one specimen of *P. mesophaea* from Sooretama in the state of Espirito Santo. The only one from Pernambuco has a large, handsome, and completely irregular blotch on the middle of the dorsal field, which is of a uniform lighter color. Those from Tapirapés in northern Mato Grosso, almost in the state of Pará, and more or less at the edge of savanna, are divided between *bufonia* and blotched.

Our western specimens are of the *bufonia* type and rather like those from western Mato Grosso further south, but there is a young individual of the continental blotched type from Tarauacá, Acre territory, and two from Benjamin Constant, state of Amazonas, with an obscure blotched pattern.

## *Phrynohyas resinifictrix* Goeldi, 1907

(= *P. venulosa?*)

GOELDI, E. A. 1907. Description of *Hyla resinifictrix* Goeldi, a new Amazonian tree-frog peculiar for its breeding habits. *Pr. Zool. Soc. London*, 1907, pp. 135–140, text figs. 56–59.

BAUMANN, F. 1912. Brasilianische Batrachier des Berner Naturhistorischen Museums Zool. *Jhb.*

Abt. f. Syst. Geogr. u. Biol. 33(2):87–172, Taf. 4–6; *H. resinifictrix*: 105–107, pl. 4, fig. 4.

Müller, Lorenz. 1912. Zoologische Ergebnisse einer Reise in das Muendungsgebiet des Amazonas. *Abhdl. d. Koenig. Bay. Ak. Wiss* 26(1) 42 pp., 3 Taf. *H. resinifictrix*: 15.

*Hyla resinifictrix* was described by Emil Goeldi while he was director of the Museum at Belém do Pará, which is now named after him. Both the name and the description emphasize the habit, attributed by Goeldi to this frog, of lining cavities in hollow trees with aromatic resin for the purpose of spawning in water uncontaminated by rotting wood. Later, André Goeldi (a cousin of Emil Goeldi), who was in charge of an agricultural station at Peixe Boi in the same state, informed Lorenz Müller that this was a mistake, since what the frogs frequently did, though not invariably, was to use cavities that had been lined with wax by wild bees known to live in hollow trees. Goeldi did not follow the larval stage to metamorphosis, and his observations need to be taken up once more. Very little is known of the life history either of *P. resinifictrix* or of *P. (H.) venulosa*, which resemble each other to the point of making it likely that they are conspecific. The habit of hiding in hollows can be observed both in the Hylaean and the Continental *venulosa*. As the head of dead specimens is often inclined and there is no frontoparietal fontanel, an incipient degree of phragmosis may also occur. The only specimens of *P. resinifictrix* known are the types and those that Lorenz Müller obtained at Peixe Boi, but the latter have become casualties of war; consequently it is very necessary to collect again in both localities.

DIAGNOSTIC CHARACTERS. Two of the types seen by me have a very short flat head with rugose skin that is somewhat reminiscent of *Trachycephalus*. Whether there is adherence to the bone also needs to be tested. Some old individuals of *P. venulosa* have very rugose heads and there is a small series of *Trachycephalus* from the São Francisco basin, in the Museu Nacional, whose morphological characters and pattern are rather like those of *P. venulosa*. The iris described by Goeldi seems very like that of *P. venulosa* from Belém. The bold and warty pattern is somewhat akin to that seen in some large, unusually well-developed individuals of *Phrynohyas venulosa*.

TYPES AND TYPE LOCALITIES. In his description, Goeldi mentions four specimens. I saw one at the British Museum of Natural History and another at the Natural History Museum in Bern.

The type at the British Museum is labeled 1907.-2.23.1. The type locality is Santo Antonio do Prata, Rio Maracanã, Pará; leg. E. Goeldi.

DESCRIPTION. The resemblance to *P. venulosa* and the lack of specimens makes it seem preferable to limit myself to a few remarks.

Baumann (1912) published a colored figure of *P. resinifictrix* from an illustration furnished by Goeldi, and gives, among others, the following details: tongue heart-shaped; head circular from above. Lateral fingers one-half webbed, a rudiment of web between the first and second. Toes two-thirds webbed, fringed to the disks. Tibiotarsal articulation reaching between the eye and the tip of the snout when the hindlimb is adpressed. Dorsal surface greenish yellow with dark brown spots. A trapezoid-shaped, dark spot from the eyes to the tip of the snout; a light interocular bar; from its hind edge on a dark spot reaching somewhat beyond the shoulder, then a light interval, and another dark spot on the sacral region. In this particular, the specimen diverges from the united dark dorsal spot of the colored figure (Pl. 4, fig. 4) as already pointed out by Baumann. Ventral aspect green-yellow, warty (i. e. granular); two large vocal sacs. Disks green. Both the cotype at the British Museum and the cotype in Bern have a rough, rugose, short, and flat head. The tongue is emarginate. They are too dry for juxtaposing the hindlimb and to see the full extent of the fresh webs.

The Bern cotype is very warty. The cotype at the British Museum has an excentrically-shaped, notched tongue with one lobe larger than the other.

MEASUREMENTS (mm). The measurements taken there in 1952 (45 years after the description) were as follows:

BM. 1907.2.23.1. SV/HL 80:122. Femur 38. Tibia 37. Tarsus 22. Foot 25. HL to HW 24:25. T 5. E 8. E–N 6. E–S 8. IS 8. Ue 6.

COLOR AND PATTERN. Goeldi calls the dorsal color "greenish-yellow with blackish brown markings." In the type, which corresponds to Baumann's figure 4, Pl. 4), the dark spot covers most of the back. The light, dorsolateral areas correspond somewhat to the *zonata* pattern, but the middorsal, dark area is of the more or less aberrant quadrangular or blotched intermediate type. In the specimens figured by Goeldi (1907, text figs. 56–57) described by Baumann, the central dark area is fragmented into a more or less scapular and a sacral part. Goeldi's figure 57, letter A, is the only specimen of the *Phrynohyas* group besides *P. imitatrix* in which I have seen an ocellus as part of the dorsal pattern.

The dark dorsal blotches are described by Goeldi as being thickly studded with thorn-like elevations (pointed warts) with light colored apex. This is reminiscent of the spinose condition of the males of *P. v. imitatrix*. The ventral surface is light greenish yellow according to Goeldi, and thus again similar to *P. v. venulosa*.

SECRETION. No mention of the secretion is made by Goeldi or Lorenz Müller.

VOICE. Again according to Goeldi, "the voice is surprisingly strong and sounds like *queng-queng* three or four times repeated."

LIFE HISTORY. E. Goeldi indicates that development is rapid and takes place inside the lined hole in the tree hollow. This is not entirely contested by A. Goeldi, but as mentioned above there is need to collect and observe the life history of this frog once more.

TAXONOMIC POSITION. Only further study will bring to light whether *P. resinifictrix* is a good species or belongs to an unusually robust, slightly divergent population of *H. venulosa*.

KNOWN DISTRIBUTION. So far, *P. resinifictrix* has only been collected in two places, the type locality, Santo Antonio do Prata, and Peixe Boi, neither of which is far from Belém do Pará.

## *Phrynohyas v. hebes* (Cope), 1862

> COPE, E. D. 1862. Catalogue of the reptiles obtained during the explorations of the Paraná, Paraguay, Vermejo and Uruguay Rivers by Captain Thos. L. Page, U.S.N. *Pr. Ac. Nat. Sc. Phila.* 14:346–359. S. *hebes*: 354–355.

This is one of the frogs collected during the exploration of the rivers of the Paraná basin mentioned in the title of Cope's paper. It was described by him and provided with a new generic name as well as a specific one: *Scytopis hebes*. Cope must have been struck by the structure of

the skin, which he detached at one point of the skull of the type, and by the dull color of most of the specimens. Formerly he had used Fitzinger's name *Acrodytes* for *Hyla venulosa*. The fact that the type of *P. v. hebes* is a female without vocal sacs may have led Cope to separate the continental frogs from the more northern specimens.

DIAGNOSTIC CHARACTERS. The iris probably provides the main diagnostic character. One preserved specimen and the watercolor made from it alive show golden flecks on a dark ground, which suggest a fragmentation of the petal-like spots of the northern South American form. Dorsal coloring inclined to dark olivaceous tones, dull and uniform in a large proportion of the specimens seen and thus in agreement with Cope's name. Dorsal pattern variable, either dull all over, with some dark scattered glandules, or showy with large dark spots or blotches, mostly longitudinal and more or less bilaterally symmetric on the back, or, again, head and dorsolateral areas light, brilliant, the rest of the dorsal surface dark. Group characters present, i. e. latex-like secretion, double vocal sac, absence of sharp pollex rudiment and fontanel.

TYPE AND TYPE LOCALITY. Cope's type, female, USNM n. 98537 is listed from Paraguay and unfortunately somewhat faded, but both the vestiges and the description indicates that it belonged to the dull *hebes* pattern. Duellman's proposal that Asunción be fixed as type locality does not seem justified, since the form occurs all over Paraguay and also in the adjacent parts of Bolivia, Argentina, and Brazil, and the expedition covered a good deal of territory.

DESCRIPTION. Size medium to large for *Phrynohyas venulosa*. Nuptial males seen: 63–92 mm snout to vent, females 80–89 mm. Build robust. Head very wide; snout short, flat. Body long in large specimens. Hindlimb as usual in *P. venulosa;* the tibiotarsal articulation reaching the eye when the leg is adpressed. Eye large, prominent, its horizontal diameter greater than the distance between it and the nostril. Tympanum two-fifths to one-half the diameter of the eye, the part left uncovered by the glandular ridge overhanging it variable. Interorbital space as wide as the upper eyelid or slightly wider. Internarial space slightly less. Tongue wider than long, very slightly free and scarcely emarginate. Patches of vomerine teeth straight or very slightly arched, contiguous or separate. Jaws prominent. Canthus rostralis rounded but distinct. Loreal region concave. A short web between the three outer fingers. Web on feet perhaps slightly shorter than in the northern specimens; the wide part reaching the penultimate articulation on fourth toe and continuing as a fringe to the disk. Skin of dorsal surface coriaceous, shagreened, fairly smooth in some specimens, in others with low, scattered pustules. Ventral aspect areolate, as usual in *Phrynohyas*.

MEASUREMENTS (mm). Type, fide Cope: snout to vent 3 inches 3 lines. Hindlimb 5 inches 6 lines. Head length (symphisis to postgular fold 6 lines wide: angle to angle of mouth, beneath, 1 inch 3 lines).

Growth seems allometric, the hindlimb of the juveniles generally reaching between eye and nostril.

SECONDARY SEX CHARACTERS. Male characterized by the lateral vocal sacs. Deciduous corneous plaques on the first finger and smaller ones on the second during the nuptial period. End of pollex rudiment not protruded as in large species of *Hyla* (subgenera *Boana* and *Plectrohyla*). Voice very loud and rough. Females not strikingly larger than males. Specimens less than 63 mm long are devoid of sex characters.

COLOR. The coloring inclines to olivaceous, somewhat greenish tones; occasionally the lighter parts are nearer to ochraceous yellow, tawny olive, or clay color. Webs greenish; disks green.

PATTERN. Three main types of dorsal pattern:

A. The plain *hebes* pattern consists of a fairly uniform dorsal coloring without darker areas or very shadowy ones and a scattering of low, black pustules on the back. This pattern comes close to that described under the name of *Hyla bufonia* by Spix and probably also to that given for *P. (H.) nigropunctata* by Boulenger and *Phrynohyas modesta* Taylor, from Mexico.

B. Pattern composed of a fairly dark dorsal background ornamented with large dark areas or blotches in the middorsal region. Sometimes the dark area almost square; at others irregular or wider on the sacrum; often composed of two longitudinal, more or less separated or anastomosed, contiguous large blotches, occasionally fragmented or fenestrated, which occupy much of the back. The dark area or blotches may be deflected or prolonged onto the sides of the body,

which are then marbled or reticulated and very ornate. This pattern is similar to that shown in the figures of *H. venulosa* Baumann (1912) and to a less-perfect figure of Müller and Hellmich (1926). It is also seen in specimens from other parts of Brazil, nor is it unlike the pattern of *P. spilomma* Cope from Mexico.

C. An extremely ornamental but apparently rare pattern consists of a brilliant light- or cream-colored snout from the interocular region forward and similar broad bands on the dorsolateral edges of the back, which may produce a marbled or reticulate aspect on the sides when deflected. This pattern is figured by Duellman (Pl. I, fig. 2) and by Cochran (1955), fig. 8); both specimens from Piraporinha in Minas Gerais and in the Rio São Francisco basin. I have seen this pattern in one fine female specimen from Paraguay and also in a juvenile of *P. venulosa* from Amapá territory adjacent to the Guianas. It certainly does not correspond to the description or the name chosen by Cope on the basis of the more usual dull specimens of the Paraguay basin.

All these phases are accompanied by distinct bars on the limbs, though they are more accentuated in the more ornate specimens. Duellman uses the respective width of the dark bars and the lighter areas as a diagnostic character for Cope's form, but our specimens show a very great range of variability as to width, shape and conspicuousness. There is frequently a reticulation in the upper posterior area of the thigh concealed in repose, or a more bold alternation of light and dark tones in ornate individuals. The dark bars often enclose light dots, dashes, or even small spots and, vice versa, the light ones may include dark spots or dashes. However, the most characteristic element of the bars on the limbs is their extension to the outer digits, which are also visible in repose.

SECRETION. The secretion of the specimens obtained alive by us in southern Mato Grosso failed to irritate even when experimentally applied by me to the mucous membrane of the lower lip. Nevertheless, it can be very abundant. Mulford and Racine Foster, the bromeliad growers and collectors, who also got me some of these frogs in southern Mato Grosso, called them the "india-rubber frog" because the latex-like secretion was plentiful enough to shape into small pellets.

BEHAVIOR AND HABITS. The first part of my 1945

trip to Mato Grosso was made during very dry weather, because the incipient rains ceased soon after we started. J. Venancio, who had great intuitive knowledge of the ways of wild creatures, therefore began to look for them in the simple bathrooms in the houses of the guards along the Northwestern Railway on which we were traveling. A number of specimens were found in the reservoirs above the water closets. A few dived and had to be recovered from the bowl or escaped down the drain. At Bodoquena, one small juvenile was found asleep among the leaves of a climbing *Vanilla*. The Foster specimens were collected from bromeliads at Camisão and elsewhere in the same part of the state.

One of their specimens had the maggots of a Sarcophagid fly in one eye socket when brought to me. This may have been a postmortem invasion, though Mertens and Klingelhoeffer (1955) have obtained parasitic dipteran larvae from the eyes of frogs.

VOICE. The voice of the Paraguayan form was heard during the collecting trip to southern Mato Grosso (1945) and later on a short visit to Iguaçu Falls (1953). It is very loud and rough, somewhat reminiscent of a loud, short-circuited automobile horn. At Miranda, some of the males calling were sitting on the hollow posts of a fence surrounding the local pond, a few of them with smaller tree frogs sitting on their backs and/or heads, also vocalizing. Others were floating on the water of the pond. Sitting and singing on hollow posts is well in accord with the observations of A. Lutz and J. Venancio on *P. venulosa* in Venezuela, and with the customs of Goeldi's *Hyla resinifictrix*. In the Brazilian National Park at Iguaçu Falls, on the Argentine border, three enormous males were caught at Poço Preto, calling loudly afloat on the water of forest inundated to almost a meter. These three males are extremely large and have very ornate limbs.

KNOWN RANGE. The better known part of the range of this form is what I call the Chaquean subarea of the Continental province of the cisandine-cisplatine subregion of South America. This covers not only the western part of the Brazilian states of Paraná, São Paulo, and Mato Grosso, but also Paraguay and adjacent parts of Argentina and Bolivia, below the Cordillera. L. Müller and Hellmich described specimens taken by the German Gran Chaco Expeditions, which extended to these countries. The specimens from the São Francisco River drainage also belong here; this basin is part of the Continental province and leads to the semi-arid northeastern subarea.

AFFINITIES. This form is probably a regional variant, of the large assembly of Neotropical tree frogs belonging to *Phrynohyas (Hyla) venulosa* Laurenti.

## Phrynohyas v. imitatrix Miranda Ribeiro, 1926

> MIRANDA RIBEIRO, A. 1926. Notas para servirem ao estudo dos gymnobatrachios (anura) brasileiros. *Arch. Mus. Nac. Rio* 27:77, pl. X, figs. 2, 2a, 2b.

This form was discovered by Miranda Ribeiro in Teresópolis, where he lived for some time. His son, P. Miranda Ribeiro, informed me that a large number of specimens were obtained there at Araras, which lies between the valley of the Paquequer River and the forested slopes. There are twenty-four of them in the Museu Nacional.

DIAGNOSTIC CHARACTERS. Very closely allied to *P. v. venulosa*, of which it may be an eastern montane race. Iris very characteristic, with a distinctive pattern composed of four petal-like, light sea-green spots, two above, two below, disposed in a rosette, based on the free inner rim and encircled by a few other small, similar spots. Dorsum generally ornamented with a large dark, quadrangular spot between the eyes and the sacrum, sometimes followed by a smaller ocellus; occasionally different. Permanently visible dorsal aspect of limbs crossbarred. Coloring: olive greens and browns above; below, immaculate, light bluish and yellowish green. Differs from the Ecuadorian *P. v. quadrangulum* (Boulenger), to which it is compared in the original description, by the distribution of the more contiguous vomerine teeth and perhaps by the additional ocellus. From *P. v. venulosa* by the details in the pattern of the iris and the more slender and elongate build. According to Dr. D. M. Cochran, the skin is less thick and the head not quite so wide as in *P. v. venulosa*. Skin spinescent in nuptial males.

TYPES AND TYPE LOCALITY. The types are among the specimens in the collection of the MNR (nos. 154, 155, 156), but none of them were labeled as such nor do they agree with Miranda Ribeiro's figures. His son designated nos. 154, male and female, as lectotypes. Type locality: Teresópolis, in the Organ Mountains of the Serra do Mar, 20° 26′ 12″ S. 42° 58′ 55″ W. Gr.; altitude 800 m up. Vegetation: montane rain forest and open valley. Climate *Cfb* Köppen.

DESCRIPTION. Size fairly large; males: 51.6–57.1 mm, females 69.1–70.1 mm snout to vent. Build robust but not very stout and rather elongate. Hindlimb short, the tibiotarsal articulation generally reaching the eye when adpressed. Body rectilinear from the eye to beyond the elbow, narrowing slightly beyond the sacrum. Head as wide as, or only slightly wider than long. Snout short, oval, truncate between the nostrils, sloping very slightly down to the mouth. Canthus rostralis rounded but distinct; loreal region grooved between the eye and nostril, the thick upper jaw flaring slightly. Eye longer than the distance from its anterior corner to the nostril. Tympanum one-half to four-sevenths the diameter of eye. Vomerine teeth in two short, barely separated groups behind the choanae. Tongue heart-shaped. Hand about one-third webbed; fingers fringed, a fringe of web on the inner side of the first. Web on foot reaching the disks but reduced to a fringe on the inner side of the first three toes and beyond the penultimate subarticular tubercle of the fourth toe. Pollex rudiment in the shape of a blunt callosity on the lower part of the first finger. A distinct inner and a minute outer metatarsal tubercle. Skin of the dorsal surface slightly thick, spinescent in the male. Granular beneath, especially on the abdomen and ventral aspect of thigh, less so on the gula; chest fairly smooth. An agglomeration of glandules round and below the tympanum. A very distinct fold of skin across the chest, another fold at the base of the throat.

SECONDARY SEX CHARACTERS. The sexes seem to vary as to the texture of the skin. In the male the whole dorsal surface may become very spinose, including the edge of the upper jaw, as pointed out by Dr. Cochran (1955). Unlike most species of *Hyla*, but as in the *Phrynohyas venulosa* group, there are two large dark lateral vocal sacs instead of a median one. Also, unlike large species of *Hyla*, the pollex rudiment does not seem to end in a sharp point but forms a callosity on the outer side of the first finger, which becomes covered by a corneous pad at the nuptial period when the male characters are very much in evidence.

The large females are much distended by eggs, which stretch the skin and distort the pattern somewhat. No eggs were seen in our females that were less than 60 mm from snout to vent. The fold across the chest and the smaller one at the base of the throat are more apparent in the female, as is the pattern on the sides of the head behind the tympanum, as it is masked by the vocal sacs in the male. The differences in pattern considered as sex characters by Miranda Ribeiro are not sex linked, though secondary ocelli occur in five out of nine females and only in four out of twenty males examined.

COLOR AND PATTERN. According to Miranda Ribeiro (translated by Cochran, translation revised by B. Lutz): "The color imitates that of *Hyla quadrangulum*, having in life an olive-green or sepia ground, more yellowish on the abdominal surface. A large quadrilateral goes from eyes to sacrum; its corners are rounded and it is delineated by a black line, externally bordered by another white one; in the middle of the space thus limited, the color of which is sepia, there are larger black dots and smaller white ones; a transverse sepia bar on the forearm, margined with black and white; another on the thigh, not always present, and one or two on the leg. This is the coloration of the male; the female has one or two ocelli after the quadrangle, and various spots and another dark longitudinal line on the sides; the transverse bars of the legs are more frequently two or three."

I have not seen any white spots. In the first two specimens, both from the Serra da Bocaina, the dark brown quadrangle stood out from a pale brown slightly pinkish background.

IRIS. The most diagnostic feature is the pattern and color of the iris, which has four large, petal-like, light sea-green spots, two above, two below, based on the free inner rim, encircled by other small similar light spots. In *v. zonata* and *hebes* the iris is not green. The fundamental dorsal pattern consists of a large quadrangular spot, from the interocular region to the sacrum, sometimes followed by one or more small ocelli. An elongate spot on the sides of head and body, from the back, behind the tympanum to beyond the elbow, and bars on the limbs complete the livery.

All these elements are somewhat variable. The quadrangle varies somewhat in size, is rather irregular in outline, and has rounded corners. It is darker than the dorsal background and often encloses large dark dots. These vary from a few scattered dots to several longitudinal regular rows or to a large number occupying most of the surface, some of them being elongate as if two of the spots had partly merged. The inner border of the quadrangle is very dark, from clove color to black and quite regular. The quadrangle may be entirely closed by this dark border, open in front, or only partly closed by a few large dots. The outer light border varies from a mere light halo to a band wide enough to alter the appearance of the pattern as a whole. In some specimens from Itatiaia it is very brilliant. In one or two others, slightly less so (lectotypes).

The ocellus behind the quadrangle is present in five females, absent from three female topotypes in the Lutz Collection, and one juvenile female from the Serra da Bocaina. Three male topotypes from Teresópolis have it and one male from the Itatiaia. The proportion in females is 5/9 and in males 1/5 of the specimens seen. It may be large and oval, smaller and accompanied by other ocellar spots, squarish and narrowed behind or even double, like two parallel drops; other specimens have faint spots.

In males, the dark spot on the side of the head is rather effectively masked by the vocal sacs. At its best it is elongated and curved like a stocking or a sac. It may be square cut at the back, or fragmented in two. In several specimens it is reduced to a curved dark border like a parenthesis. It is often followed or accompanied and sometimes substituted by large dots on the sides of the body.

The perpendicular bars on the dorsal aspect of the limbs are similar to the quadrangle. They comprise a wide inner part, darker than the background, generally wide and straight but occasionally narrower. There is generally one bar on the forearm. Some specimens also show a smudge on the upper arm, and there may be an additional one on the wrist. The bars on the legs, of which there are often two, but not invariably so, are often bluntly triangular. In some specimens, there are two bars on each tarsus, one of which may overlap onto the feet. There may be just one or none.

GEOGRAPHIC VARIATION. Three specimens from the Serra da Bocaina, in the same Maritime Range as the Organ Mountains but farther south, conform perfectly to the pattern. One of them, a small female is very like the plain male figured by Dr. Cochran (1955), though the quadrangle is concave at the back and there is a smudge on the upper arms and a bar on the wrists. The male specimen from Itatiaia, on the Mantiqueira Range, is the most ornate one seen but it still falls within the *imitatrix* pattern. There is an additional bar on each upper arm and wrist and a spot above each knee, besides two on the tarsi and an incomplete one on the feet. Another specimen from Campos do Jordão, in the same range, is aberrant as to the dorsal pattern. There is no quadrangle on the back, which displays only a few dark dots and streaks plus a dark border, from the tympanum to the elbow, followed by two series of dots on the sides of the body. One bar on each forearm, a dark stripe on the right wrist, three similar, short stripes on the thighs, two oblique bars on the tibia and incomplete ones on the tarsi and feet.

All these specimens conform to the diagnostic pattern of the iris of *P. v. imitatrix*.

SOUTHERN FORM. Two specimens from the more southern states of Paraná, collected at Marumbi between Curitiba and the sea, at 800 m altitude, have the same pattern in the iris. One from São Bento do Sul, Santa Catarina, is very dark and the pattern of the iris is not visible in this specimen. Otherwise it is like the other two. All three are males, much larger in size and more elongate in build than the others, i. e. 62.1, 61.2 (Marumbi), and 61.1 mm snout to vent (São Bento do Sul). Vocal sacs very large and very dark. A corneous pad on the first finger and a small pad on the inner side of the second finger. Forearms thick. Skin rough, spinose.

COLOR (from 6x6 Kodachrome of smaller Marumbi specimen). Dorsal aspect greenish, buff, and grayish tones of olive. A reddish brown suffusion, especially on the head and on the lighter stripes between the bars on the limbs; at articulations and on inner surfaces of limbs more green. Ventral aspect light immaculate; glaucous green on the ventral aspect of thighs and upper arms, slightly paler, more grayish, on the disks.

PATTERN. There is no quadrangle in any of the southern specimens. It is substituted by a dark border, enclosing a field of the same color as the rest of the back. In the larger specimen from Marumbi this field lies between the tympanum and the elbow. It has the outline of a roughly heart-shaped leaf. Behind it there come two small ocelli, one on each side, next a slightly larger one in the middle, and finally two other small ones at the level of the first two, all of them on the back. The sides of the body display a few large dark dots. The other specimen is somewhat lighter in color. The enclosed area is shorter, slightly more pointed in front and more hollowed out behind, and it lies farther back. It is preceded by a quite regular, oval ocellus, between the eyes and the tympana; there are also two dark dots and a short dorso-lateral dark stripe from each tympanum to the end of the vocal sac. Behind the large spot there are four quite excentric small ocelli on the back, plus a few more ocelli and some large dots on the sides. Both specimens have a short bar on the upper arms, a good one on the forearms, one on the wrists and a short ring-shaped stripe across the base of the third finger, continued as an indistinct smudge on the fourth finger of the larger specimen. There are two spots to the sides of the anus, two bars on the thighs, one on the knees, two on the legs, two on the tarsi, and one across the outer part of the feet; plus a ring-like stripe across the fourth toe of the larger one. The lighter specimens show short lighter stripes between the bars on the hindlimb.

In the specimen from Estrada Saraiva, São Bento do Sul, the spot is roughly oval, quite open in front and contains a few dark dots; it is followed by one slightly excentric median ocellus and a few smaller ocelli and large dots on the sides. Bars on the limbs similar to those of the other two.

Voice. Unknown.

Behavior and ecology. Miranda Ribeiro's specimens were obtained at Araras, which is a fairly open section of the Teresópolis between the Paquequer River and the forested slopes. One of ours was found sitting on the bridge above the river at the entrance of the Organ Mountains National Park. The other two were collected by a boy in a garden at Agriões, a similar place to Araras. All these sites are practically ecotones.

Secretion. The first of our Serra da Bocaina specimens was dropped by a bird after a scuffle in a grove of Araucaria pines with epiphytic bromeliads. This was probably due to the irritating secretion of the skin of P. v. imitatrix. The frog was very sticky when I picked it up and was conveyed to the house close by in a handkerchief tied into a sac with two other frogs; these were stuck together and dead on arrival. Shortly after, a rash broke out on my hand and forearm, very similar to a nettle rash in appearance and in the sensation it caused. It subsided after a while. Next day the second specimen was obtained asleep in a tree fern near a brook by Joaquim Venancio. When warned of the effects he laughed and brushed them aside, arguing the difference between the delicate hand of a white woman and his own rough black hand. This did not, however, prevent the rash from appearing. The third specimen, a young female, obtained many years later, laid a leg across the back of my hand while being caught. The weal produced lasted several days, although the irritation soon passed.

Affinities. The closest affinity is with the other members of the Phrynohyas (Hyla) venulosa group.

Distribution. So far P. v. imitatrix is known from the Serra do Mar at different points, and from two places on the parallel Serra da Mantiqueira. The specimens from the northern block of the Serra do Mar (type locality) and the branch called Serra da Bocaina in northern São Paulo, have the livery of the original description. It is slightly modified and somewhat variable on the Mantiqueira Range; the two points where it was found, Itatiaia and Campos do Jordão are roughly parallel to the Serra da Bocaina. The southern specimens have the livery described above for the southern form. This gives a probable range from northern Santa Catarina to the northern part of the state of Rio de Janeiro, between 26°–22° S. and 45°–50° W. Gr. and at altitudes of 800–1,200 m above sea level.

## Phrynohyas quadrangulum (Boulenger), 1882

Boulenger, G. A. 1882. Catalogue of the batrachia salientia in the collection of the British Museum, p. 367, pl. XXV, fig. 2.

The type of P. quadrangulum Boulenger from western Ecuador is rather small, only 58 mm long, although it is considered a female. It may not be adult unless eggs were seen or felt. One of the dorsolateral bands in Boulenger's figure, inverted in the photograph kindly sent me by Dr. H. W. Parker, puts out a horizontal prong that stretches partly across the rear part of the quadrangle, which does not seem differentiated from the rest of the dorsal color. The alternate light and dark banding on the limbs is very ornamental and reaches the outer digits. The color of the dead specimen is stated as grayish olive. The webs seem slightly longer than in the cisandean-cisplatine forms. The head is wide, the body robust and the leg seems slightly longer than usual, but this may be correlated with the lesser size. The tongue is described as circular, and the teeth conform to the *P. venulosa* character.

Duellman states that he saw a living specimen of what he calls *P. zonata* from Hacienda San Miguel, Milagro, Guayas province, Ecuador. "The specimen, a large adult male, had a dorsal ground color of golden brown; the dorsal dark patch was light chocolate brown tending toward a dark chocolate brown on the edges. The ground color of the limbs was somewhat darker than that of the dorsum; the transverse limb bands were dark chocolate brown. Iris flecked with golden." This livery seems nearest to that of the Continental Chaquean form.

## *Phrynohyas mesophaea* Hensel, 1867

HENSEL, R. 1867. Beiträge zur Kentniss der Wirbelthiere Südbrasiliens. *Archiv für Naturg.* 1: 120–163. *H. mesophaea*: 154–156.

*P. mesophaea* was described by Hensel from Rio Grande do Sul, where he lived for some years. This is the southern limit of the known distribution. *P. mesophaea* does not seem to have been described again but may sometimes have been confounded with *P. venulosa*.

DIAGNOSTIC CHARACTERS. The color and pattern of the iris, which is golden to light bronze, with a few quite irregular, zig-zag veins at the periphery and toward the center and a dark pseudocolobom; the very regular pattern of the back, composed of two light dorsolateral bands delimiting a dark area between the eyes and the sacral region. Bars on limbs generally absent. Skin shagreened but less thick than in *P. venulosa*. Build more elongate. Lowlands in the Atlantic province of Brazil.

TYPE AND TYPE LOCALITY. Dr. Cochran lists specimen n. 33-6810 of the ZMB in Berlin, which is probably the type, and another specimen from Rio Grande do Sul, ZMB n. 33-6256, caught by Michaealis. Hensel mentions a third specimen, ZMB n. 33-3133, collected by the botanist Sellow, but does not indicate any type locality. I have not seen any of these specimens.

DESCRIPTION. Size large, very variable, perhaps geographically so; male ranging from 52 mm (Santa Catarina) to 85 mm (Espírito Santo); female from 61 mm (Santa Catarina) to 100 mm (Espírito Santo). Build elongate, less stout than *P. venulosa*. Body straight until the sacral region, slightly wider between the shoulders than across the head. Leg relatively short, the tibiotarsal articulation generally reaching the eye when the hindlimb is adpressed. Head also relatively short, very slightly wider than long. Snout very short, bluntly truncate between the nostrils, rounded below them. Canthus rostralis blunt, loreal region very concave, the upper jaw flaring below it. Nostrils superolateral. Eye fairly large and prominent, its horizontal diameter slightly greater than the distance to the nostril. Tympanum very distinct, approximately one-half the diameter of the eye (often three-sevenths, four-sevenths, or five-elevenths), sometimes partly concealed by the glandular tissue surrounding it. Tongue large, round to heart-shaped, slightly emarginate and free behind. Vomerine teeth in two short groups behind the choanae, either contiguous or slightly separate. Disks large. A narrow fringe of web outside the first finger and first toe. Lateral fingers slightly less than half-webbed. Toes webbed to the disks, but the web is narrow on the inner side, reduced to a fringe on the apical part of both sides of the third finger and fourth toe. A large pad outside the first finger, but no sharp pollex rudiment. Inner metatarsal tubercle elongate, outer minute or absent. Skin of dorsal surface shagreened, of ventral aspect granular, including the gula, body and midventral aspect of the thigh, in both sexes. A thick glandular peritympanic ridge. A distinct fold of skin under the gula and a larger one across the chest, its edges visible from above.

SECONDARY SEX CHARACTERS. Male with a pair of large lateral vocal sacs, appearing continuous with the outer part of the fold across the gula; a dark deciduous, corneous, nuptial pad on the first finger and a smaller one on the corresponding part of the second finger. Forearms thick.

Female wider over the abdomen than the head or shoulders when distended by masses of eggs. Larger than male. Folds over the gula and chest very evident.

VARIATION. Variation seems to affect size, pattern, relative position of the groups of vomerine teeth and amount of webbing. There may be a geographic cline of increasing size south-north. Hensel does not give any measurements. The specimens seen by us from Santa Catarina are relatively small; those from the state of Rio de Janeiro are somewhat larger, and those from two biological stations in the state of Espírito Santo over 30 mm longer than the southern ones. On the other hand, one couple from Uruçuca near Ilheus, southern Bahia, is not larger than the specimens from the lowlands of the state of Rio de Janeiro. There is also an increase of dorsal pattern in the large specimens from Espírito Santo, especially the females.

Twenty preserved specimens are housed in the Museu Nacional (MNR 1684), sixteen of which are from Sooretama in Espírito Santo; the other four are males from Barra Seca, Espírito Santo, and are much larger than the others. Both these finding places are biological reserves, but we do not know if this has permitted them to live longer and grow larger.

PATTERN. The fundamental dorsal pattern consists of a pair of light, dorsolateral bands, variable in width, tint, brilliancy, and in the sharpness of their dark inner and outer borders. They limit a large central area from the interocular region toward the sacral one or beyond it in many specimens; in others the bands become less distinct caudad, and the color of the middle of the back merges with that of the hind part of the body and the permanently visible dorsal aspect of the limbs. Top of the head often lighter than the body from the dark line between the eyes to the tip of the snout. In most specimens no other dorsal pattern. Some of the specimens from the biological reserves in Espírito Santo have large black dots on the sides of the body; they are very profuse in part of them and reach the light dorsolateral margins, which in these two series are also variable in shape. Such spots are rare in other specimens but may also be located on the back. Three of the Espírito Santo females have rather large quite irregular elongate light spots on the middle of the back. Such spots have been seen by us only in a female bred from the egg and her mother both from the lowlands of Rio de Janeiro, both of them very large examples (both 72 mm long). Less conspicuous similar spots have been seen in male specimens from both areas. Some Espírito Santo specimens show variable, more or less distinct bars on the dorsal aspect of the limbs and some spotting on the thighs. The ventral aspect is flecked with gray in some of them.

COLOR. The coloring of the iris is very distinctive. It has a golden to light bronze tint, slightly greenish in glint near the middle of the upper part, darker, more orange to rufous towards the periphery, with a few irregular zig-zag black veins; a pseudocolobom either covers the whole median part of the iris, making it appear continuous with the pupil, or is composed of larger, very irregularly shaped spots. Two small median notches, an upper and a lower one, in the free inner rim.

Dorsal coloring dull and rather simple, olivaceous in the dark parts as if resulting from mixing orange, yellow, and neutral gray. Dark area between the bands chocolate, according to the notes of A. Lutz, reddish brown (Hensel) or clove brown (D. M. Cochran), which may all be correct; various olivaceous tones in my living specimens. Light bands a dirty cream color (A. Lutz), the outer edges chestnut or clove brown (B. Lutz). Ventral aspect a dirty ochraceous color (A. Lutz). Throat citron. Axillae and inguinal region a glaucous green. Skeleton green. Tongue flesh-colored, not green as in some other large Brazilian species of hylids.

SECRETION. *P. mesophaea* has a sticky secretion that Mr. Leitão de Carvalho found very abundant in the large Sooretama (Espírito Santo) specimens. It was not irritating to the skin in a series of them collected by me and some assistants on a stormy night (November 10, 1939) in the coastal lowlands of Rio de Janeiro. The secretion of a half-grown female raised from an egg was tasted later and found slightly caustic and bitter.

NUPTIAL BEHAVIOR. Eight males were caught by us on the Baixada that night; they had robust forearms, large vocal sacs, and well-developed nuptial pads. One of them serenaded the only female during the whole journey home for about two hours, although he was confined alone in a wet stocking, the bags being used up. One of the others had already seized her in the bag. After being put into the terrarium the songster tried to dislodge the other suitor, one of our poorest specimens. He butted him with the head and pushed him with his arms and legs, but the other clung on effectively.

VOICE. The call of *P. mesophaea* is more like that of a *Paludicola* than of a *Hyla*, though much louder and gruffer. It sounds like a mixture of muttering and whining. According to A. Lutz there is a preliminary *quáa, quáa, quáa,* followed by sounds like *woo-ah woo-ah.* When heard by us for the first time on that November night, we first looked for the songsters on the ground but soon found them sitting on the trunks and branches of trees over a yard high. On other occasions they have been caught in bromeliads and in standing water at Angra dos Reis and Sooretama. They seem abundant in both places.

LIFE HISTORY. The frogs were put into a terrarium at midnight. By six o'clock next morning (November 11) the female had laid a large clutch, which looked like a piece of floating veil and must have comprised several hundred eggs. Some of them still showed a light blastopore, but it was covered in most of them. Many of the embryos hatched already next day (November 12). The embryos that hatched and survived spent from sixty-eight to seventy-seven days in the water before metamorphosis between January 20 and February 11, 1940. One of the metamorphosed young was kept alive for slightly over two years, being raised to an adult female by Mr. J. Venancio.

LARVAE. The newly hatched embryos are very dark gray, almost black. One short pair of external gills is visible; the others are indistinct. Since magnification was not available, they were not examined until the next day.

The one-day-old larvae (November 13) have three pairs of pectinate gills; the first is longer than the others and pectinate to the tip. Operculum partly open. Body straight in front and at the sides until the gills, widest at the eyes, then narrowing into a goblet shape, the tail forming the stem. Head and body 3 mm, tail 5 mm, ratio 3:5. Body gray above, lighter beneath. Tail also gray but lighter than the back; muscular part very narrow, crests oval to the tip. The small larvae occasionally take a brisk swim around but spend most of the time hanging down vertically from the surface, forming a veritable fringe of tadpoles.

Three days later, the external gills have involved. The body is oval from then on. A conspicuous spot forms in front of the eyes. Mouth ventral with papillae; upper beak rounded, lower sharply V-shaped. Tooth formula $\frac{2}{3}$, or $\frac{1-1}{3}$, the inner upper row slightly interrupted, the lower one longer, the three lower ones slightly curved outward. A few lateral glands have developed.

In ten-day-old larvae the sinistral spiraculum and dextral anus of the genus are very evident. The brown pigment of the spots in front of the eyes has increased. Iris black with golden flecks and greenish gold free inner rim. Tail muscle black, crests gray, with dark pigment disposed in dashes interrupted by light intervals.

DESCRIPTION (twelve-day-old larva). Spiraculum sinistral, rather ventral, nearer the anus than the mouth but nearest the eye. Anus dextral. Body oval, straight in front. Eyes lateral, at the greatest width of the body. Mouth ventral, black, including the papillae, which are well-developed on the sides. Lungs visible by translucency. Crests of tail narrowing toward the tip; upper reaching the back, gray; the lower sparsely pigmented. Legs beginning to burgeon.

These tadpoles feed on the ground, swim about below, collide with each other, and come up to the surface periodically. As they grow older, great differences in size become established. A regular pattern of dots develops on the tail crests. The glandular lateral lines become very distinct.

Late phase: Body still oval and widest at the eyes, tapering very slightly forward, somewhat more caudad, at first gradually then sharply to the insertion of the hindlimbs. In profile, body slightly attenuated downward and caudad, tail more so. Mouth ventroterminal. Interocular space wider than the mouth, which is wider than the internarial space. Tail long, not very high, muscular part wide anteriorly, narrowing toward the middle, tapering greatly near tip; crests not very wide nor expanded at any point, their edges constantly parallel to the edge of the muscular part and narrowing with it. Background of dorsal surface olive or a rather light brown, darker on the sides of the head; dorsum flecked all over with dark, regularly disposed spots, which extend to the dorsal edge of the tail muscle. A pair of lateral lines of yellow to pale golden glandules forms a bilaterally symmetrical pattern composed of a short horizontal branch behind each nostril and a longer longitudinal one from the postnasal to the postocular area, which is straight only in the most anterior part; after that it forms two successive curves then narrows and fades out over the lungs. Well to the inside of this pair, there is the beginning of another short pair that outlines the median part of the posterior half of the back to the insertion of the upper tail crest, Iris yellow to golden. These large tadpoles may show extra labial teeth; innermost row on lower lip robust, composed of two short curved groups, median ones longer, also robust; outer, extra ones, shorter and less robust; on the upper lip the extra teeth form just a few isolated groups. Lower lip trilobed, inner lobe larger, marginal ones shorter but deeper, sometimes folded in preserved specimens.

METAMORPHOSIS. On January 20 the first and on February 11 the last specimens left the water. Those that remained in it during the last fortnight were mostly pathological specimens with widely distended spiraculum; they all died.

SIZE. At metamorphosis they seemed rather small for such a large species, but they may have been adversely affected by the artificial conditions of capitivity.

During the early phases of change, the metamorphic young occasionally returned to the water for a while, a usual occurrence in hylids. When they climbed out, they sat closely applied to the glass walls of the terrarium adhering by the whole ventral surface.

COLORING. Light, somewhat golden, above, grayish blue-green beneath, the flesh appearing greenish near the long bones. The green color of the skeleton is already evident during the development of the pelvis and hindlimbs. Except for the light dorsal surface and the bluish tinge and translucency of the lower aspect, they are very similar to the adults. The truncate snout is quite characteristic and so are the very evident light dorsolateral bands. In large tadpoles there are similar bands on the upper part of the tail muscle. The pseudocolobom begins to form on the second day and, together with the minute notches in the median upper and lower part of the iris, helps to identify them. The maxillary teeth are already present.

JUVENILES. At this stage the young are very lively. They already begin to jump while the tail is still long. The more advanced ones sit up very straight. On the second day of terrestrial life they sought the dark upper parts of the terrarium and got into a small bromeliad provided for them. At night they became active and were quite agile at catching the small fare offered them. Nevertheless, they proved less hardy than the larvae and gradually all died except one. The reason is not very clear. They were good hunters and feeders, very quick to detect and follow the flight of flies.

By March 7 there were only six left; then two ran away from the terrarium and by April 16 there was only one left. This one, however, lived for two years and developed into a large female under the expert care of Mr. Venancio.

DEVELOPMENT. At less than three months from metamorphosis this specimen was already half its full size. By April 24 it had begun to lose its juvenile coloring and had become olive gray-brown. In the middle of August it was pea green and grayish brown. The secretion of its skin, though less abundant than that of the adults, tasted bitter and was slightly caustic to the tongue.

It was easy to feed. For instance, the first time it was offered small cockroaches, it immediately climbed right into the glass containing them. On August 26, when the first termites began to fly, they were caught and introduced into its terrarium through a small hole in the wire mesh. It immediately sat under the hole and caught them smartly, one by one, either in midair or as they alighted on a piece of tree bark. It liked to get under small pieces of wood in the terrarium and to hide in its bromeliad.

By January 1941 it had grown to slightly over five-sevenths of its full size. During the summer of 1941–1942 it was plentifully fed with grasshoppers and other insects caught by the Venancio boys. It took to sitting on the glass wall waiting for food, in daytime, and it came in response to tapping on the glass. It lived until January 1942 and became a rather corpulent female that was full of eggs when she died unexpectedly

PREDATION BY ARBOREAL SNAKES. On November 12, 1939, *P. mesophaea* gave us the opportunity to watch predation by arboreal snakes in the same place where the large series had been caught the night before. A tree frog was heard crying loudly and insistently on a tree in daytime. Investigation showed that a *Phylodryas schottii* (?) had taken hold of a *P. mesophaea* by the side of the body. The frog was struggling and screaming. Suddenly it deflated its lungs causing the snake to loosen its hold. However, it immediately recaptured the frog by a leg. I then poked the snake with a long stick, and it dropped the frog once more. The frog lost no time in diving into a small pool nearby. While J. Venancio attended to the snake, I fished the *P. mesophaea* out. It had two sets of fang marks, but it survived.

KNOWN DISTRIBUTION. *P. mesophaea* belongs to the fauna of the coastal lowlands of the Atlantic Province of Brazil. It is known from Rio Grande do Sul to Bahia. The specimens studied by us range from Brusque, Santa Catarina (approximately 27° S. and 49° W. Gr.), to Uruçuca, county of Ilheos, southern Bahia (14° 47′ 55″ S. 39° 2′ 0″ W. Gr.). The largest set of Lutz specimens was collected on the lowlands of Rio de Janeiro, but we have a few from Guapy, which is very slightly higher on the road to Teresópolis. It seems common at Angra dos Reis in the southern part of the same state (23° 0′ 33″ S. 44° 18′ 57″ W. Gr.). The giant-sized specimens from Espírito Santo hail from Sooretama and Barra Seca, in the county of Linhares, where they were caught by my colleague Mr. A. L. de Carvalho.

AFFINITIES. *P. mesophaea* is evidently a member of the *Phrynohyas venulosa* group.

# APPENDIX A: Doubtful Species

I have been unable to obtain specimens or data permitting the identification of the following species, presumably from Brazil, listed by Bokermann (1966) in his *Annotated List of Type-Localities of Brazilian Frogs*.

*Hyla affinis* Spix, 1824, *Hyla coerulea* Spix, 1824, *Hyla cinerascens* Spix, 1824, and *Hyla stercoracea* Spix, 1824. The descriptions do not tally with Peters's (1872) interpretation of the Spix species, and the types have perished.

*Hyla albovittata* Lichtenstein & Martens, 1856, "Brasilien."

*Hyla dolloi* Werner, 1903, "Brazil."

*Hyla fiebrigi* Ahl, 1927(?) Brazil; *Hyla minima* and *Hyla wettsteini* Ahl, 1933, type locality Santarem, Pará.

*Hyla occipitalis* Fitzinger, 1826, "ex America, Brasilia."

*Hyla sceleton* Laurentius, 1768, "Brasilia."

Neither have I seen *Hyla marginata* Boulenger, 1887, and *Hyla ehrhardti* Lorenz Müller, 1924, the former from Rio Grande do Sul, the latter from Santa Catarina.

# APPENDIX B: Synonyms

The species listed in the left-hand column are considered synonyms of those on the right.

*Hyla appendiculata* Blgr., 1856 . . . . . . *Hyla geographica* Spix, 1824
*Hyla astartea* Bokermann, 1965 . . . . . . *Hyla circumdata* Cope, 1867
*Hyla bracteator* Hensel, 1867 . *Hyla pulchella pulchella* Dum. & Bibr., 1841
*Hyla capistrata* Reuss, 1834 . . . . . . . . *Hyla bipunctata* Spix, 1824
*Hyla corticalis* Burmeister, 1856 . . . . . . . *Hyla pardalis* Spix, 1824
*Hyla emrichi* Mertens, 1927 . . . . . . . . *Hyla minuta* Peters, 1872
*Hyla eurydice* Bokermann, 1966 . . . . . . *Hyla fuscovaria* Lutz, 1925
*Hyla evelynae* K. Schmidt, 1944 . . . . . *Hyla squalirostris* Lutz, 1925
*Hyla giesleri* Mertens, 1950 . . . . . . . . *Hyla microps* Peters, 1872
*Hyla goughi* E. G. Boulenger, 1911 . . . . . *Hyla misera* Werner, 1903
*Hyla goughi baileyi* Cochran, 1952 . . *Hyla misera werneri* Cochran, 1952
*Hyla granulata* Peters, 1871 . . *Hyla pulchella pulchella* Dum. & Bibr., 1841
*Hyla hillii* Boulenger, 1920 . . . . . . . . *Hyla microps* Peters, 1872
*Hyla hypocellata* Mir. Ribeiro, 1926 . . . *Hyla lanciformis* (Cope), 1870
*Hyla infulata* Wied, 1824 . . . . . . . *Hyla albomarginata* Spix, 1824
*Hyla leucotaenia* Günther, 1868 . . . . *Hyla guentheri* Boulenger, 1882
*Hyla lichenosa* Günther, 1858 . . . . . . *Hyla venulosa* Laurenti, 1768
*Hyla lundii* Burmeister, 1856 . . . . . . . . *Hyla pardalis* Spix, 1824
*Hyla madeirae* Bokermann, 1964 . . . . *Hyla fuscomarginata* Lutz, 1925
*Hyla massarti* de Witte, 1930 . . . . . . *Hyla albomarginata* Spix, 1824
*Hyla megapodia* Mir. Ribeiro, 1937 . . . . . *Hyla fuscovaria* Lutz, 1925
*Hyla multifasciata* Günther, 1858 . . . . . . . *Hyla raniceps* Cope, 1862
*Hyla nebulosa* Spix, 1824 . . . . . . . *Hyla albopunctata* Spix, 1824
*Hyla nigra* Cope, 1887 . . . . . . . . . *Hyla geographica* Spix, 1824
*Hyla oliveirai* Bokermann, 1956 . . *Hyla decipiens branneri* Cochran, 1948
*Hyla oxyrhina* Reinhardt & Lütken . . . . *Hyla albopunctata* Spix, 1824
*Hyla pallens* Lutz, 1925 . . . . . . . . . *Hyla minuta* Peters, 1872
*Hyla palmata* Dum. & Bibr., 1841 . . . . . . . *Hyla faber* Wied, 1821
*Hyla parkeri* Gaige, 1929 . . . . . . . *Hyla fuscomarginata* Lutz, 1925
*Hyla pickeli* Lutz & B. Lutz, 1938 . . . *Hyla pachycrus* Mir. Ribeiro, 1937
*Hyla pumila* Dum. & Bibr., 1841 . . . . . *Hyla bipunctata* Spix, 1824
*Hyla pustulosa* Reinhardt & Lütken, 1862 . . . . *Hyla pardalis* Spix, 1824
*Hyla pygmaea* Werner, 1894 . . . . . . *Hyla m. werneri* Cochran, 1952
*Hyla spectrum* Reinhardt & Lütken, 1862 . . . *Hyla geographica* Spix, 1824
*Hyla spegazzinii* Boulenger, 1889 . . . . . . *Hyla raniceps* Cope, 1862
*Hyla striata* Peters, 1878 . . . . . . . . *Hyla polytaenia* Cope, 1870
*Hyla suturata* Mir. Ribeiro, 1936 . . . . . . *Hyla minuta* Peters, 1872
*Hyla trachythorax* L. Mueller & Hellmich, 1936 . *Hyla fuscovaria* Lutz, 1925
*Hyla triangulum* Günther, 1868 . . . . . *Hyla leucophyllata* Beireis, 1783
*Hyla variolosa* Spix, 1824 . . . . . . . *Hyla punctata* Schneider, 1799
*Hyla velata* Cope, 1887 . . . . . . . . . *Hyla minuta* Peters, 1872
*Hyla vittigera* Werner, 1894 . . . *Hyla bischoffi bischoffi* Boulenger, 1887
*Hyla walfordi* Bokermann, 1962 . . . . . . *Hyla nana* Boulenger, 1885

# APPENDIX C: Species Belonging to Other Genera

*Hyla abbreviata* Spix, 1824, is probably a *Thoropa*.

*Hyla angustifrons* Werner, 1893, is a *Trachycephalus*.

*Hyla aurantiaca* Daudin, 1803, *Hyla aurantiaca surda* Cochran, 1953, *Hyla lactea* Daudin, *Hyla (Sphoenohyla) orophila,* and *H. (S.) planicola* Lutz & B. Lutz, 1939, belong to Tschudi's genus *Sphoenorhynchus,* which has had many names.

*Hyla bicolor* (Boddaert) is *Phyllomedusa bicolor* (Boddaert), the largest Amazonian species of its genus.

*Hyla cochranae* Mertens, 1952, is synonymous with *Aplastodiscus perviridis* Lutz, in B. Lutz, 1950.

*Hyla luteola* Wied, 1824, belongs to Peters's genus *Amphodus.*

*Hyla nigerrima* and *Hyla trivittata* Spix, 1824, belong to *Dendrobates trivittatus* Spix, 1824.

*Hyla goeldii* Boulenger, 1894, and *Hyla ohausi* Wandolleck, 1907, are now called *Fritziana.*

*Hyla parkeri* de Witte, 1930, is *Gastrotheca parkeri* (de Witte, 1930).

*Hyla (Hyllela) eurygnatha* Lutz, 1925, is *Cochranella eurygnatha* (Lutz, 1925).

*Hyla uranoscopa* L. Müller, 1924, is *Cochranella uranoscopa* (L. Müller, 1924).

*Hyla stercoracea* Spix, 1824, is not a *Hyla.* Since the type has been destroyed, it cannot be identified.

*Hyla trachycephalus villarsi* Melin is *Osteocephalus villarsi* (Melin, 1941).

# SUPPLEMENTARY REFERENCES

Reference is made under each species to the original description or earliest publications dealing with it. This list comprises only general works that include the Brazilian or Neotropical anuran fauna. A few books are added for those who are not herpetologists but who wish to learn more about frogs.

ANGEL, F. 1947. *Vie et Moeurs des Amphibiens.* 317 pp. 232 drawings by the author. Paris: Payot.

BOULENGER, G. A. 1882. *Catalogue of the Batrachia Salientia in the Collection of the British Museum.* 2nd ed. 503 pp. 30 pls.

BURMEISTER, C. H. C. 1856. *Erläuterungen zur Fauna Brasiliens.* 115 pp. 32 pl. Berlin: Georg Reimer Verlag.

COCHRAN, D. M. 1955. *Frogs of Southeastern Brazil.* 423 pp. 28 figs. 34 pls. [Contains a good bibliography.]

COTT, H. B. 1941. *Adaptive Coloration in Animals.* 508 pp. 49 pls. New York: Oxford University Press.

———. 1956. *Zoological Photography in Practice.* 370 pp. 68 pls. London: Fountain Press.

DUMÉRIL, A. M. C., and BIBRON, G. 1841. *Erpétologie générale ou histoire naturelle complète des reptiles.* Vol. 8. 784 pp. [Atlas with a few figures of frogs.]

ESPADA, M. J. DE LA. 1875. *Vertebrados del viaje al Pacífico verificado de 1862 a 1865 por una Comisión de naturalistas.* Batracios. 208 pp. 6 pls. Madrid: Impr. A. Miguel Ginesta.

GADOW, H. 1901. *Cambridge Natural History.* Vol. 8, *Amphibians and Reptiles.* 668 pp. 181 figs.

GOIN, C. J., and GOIN, O. B. 1962. *Introduction to Herpetology.* 340 pp. 17 figs. San Francisco and London: W. H. Freeman.

GÜNTHER, A. C. L. G. 1858. *Catalogue of the Batrachia Salientia in the Collection of the British Museum.* 160 pp. 12 pls.

HENSEL, R. F. 1867. "Beiträge zur Kentniss der Wirbelthiere Südbrasiliens." *Arch. Naturg.* 33:120–162.

LUTZ, B. 1972. Geographical and Ecological Notes on Cisandine to Platine Frogs. *J. of Herp.* 6(2): 83–100, 3 maps, 1 text fig.

MERTENS, R. 1959. *La vie des Amphibiens et Reptiles.* 207 pp. 96 pls. Paris: Horizons de France.

MIRANDA RIBEIRO, A. DE. 1926. "Notas para servirem ao estudo dos Gymnobatrachios (Anura) brasileiros." *Arch. Mus. Nac. Rio de Janeiro* 27. 277 pp. 110 figs. 22 pls.

NIEDEN, F. 1923. *Das Tierreich.* Vol. 1, *Anura.* 584 pp. 380 figs.

NOBLE, G. K. 1931. *The Biology of the Amphibia.* 577 pp. 174 figs. New York and London: McGraw-Hill.

SPIX, J. B. VON. 1824. *Animalia nova, sive species novae Testudinum et Ranarum, quas in itinere per Brasiliam, annis 1817–1820 . . . collegit et descripsit.* Atlas. 22 pls.

TSCHUDI, J. J. *Classification der Batrachier mit Berücksichtigung der fossilen Thiere.* Mém. Soc. Sci. Nat. Neuchatel. 99 pp. 9 pls.